W9-CNX-124

STAR WARS

HAN SOLO

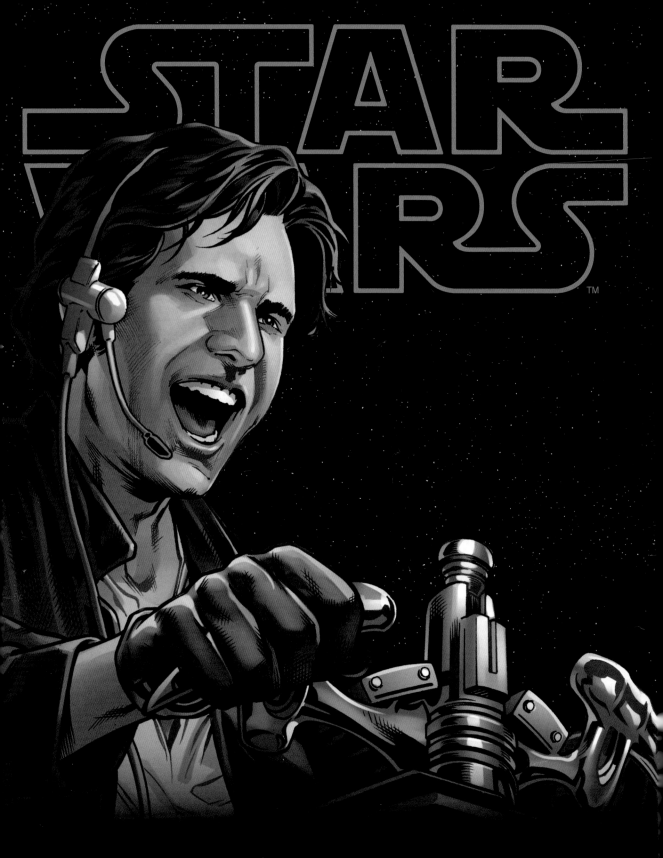

Collection Editor	**JENNIFER GRÜNWALD**
Assistant Editor	**CAITLIN O'CONNELL**
Associate Managing Editor	**KATERI WOODY**
Editor, Special Projects	**MARK D. BEAZLEY**
Senior Editor, Special Projects	**JEFF YOUNGQUIST**
SVP Print, Sales & Marketing	**DAVID GABRIEL**
Book Designer	**ADAM DEL RE**

STAR WARS: HAN SOLO. Contains material originally published in magazine form as HAN SOLO #1-5 and STAR WARS #8-12. First printing 2018. ISBN 978-1-302-91210-9. Published by MARVEL WORLDWIDE, INC., a subsidiary of MARVEL ENTERTAINMENT, LLC. OFFICE OF PUBLICATION: 135 West 50th Street, New York, NY 10020. STAR WARS and related text and illustrations are trademarks and/or copyrights, in the United States and other countries, of Lucasfilm Ltd. and/or its affiliates. © & ™ Lucasfilm Ltd. No similarity between any of the names, characters, persons, and/or institutions in this magazine with those of any living or dead person or institution is intended, and any such similarity which may exist is purely coincidental. Marvel and its logos are ™ Marvel Characters, Inc. **Printed in China.** DAN BUCKLEY, President, Marvel Entertainment; JOE QUESADA, Chief Creative Officer; TOM BREVOORT, SVP of Publishing; DAVID BOGART, SVP of Business Affairs & Operations, Publishing & Partnership; DAVID GABRIEL, SVP of Sales & Marketing, Publishing; JEFF YOUNGQUIST, VP of Production & Special Projects; DAN CARR, Executive Director of Publishing Technology; ALEX MORALES, Director of Publishing Operations; SUSAN CRESPI, Production Manager; STAN LEE, Chairman Emeritus. For information regarding advertising in Marvel Comics or on Marvel.com, please contact Vit DeBellis, Custom Solutions & Integrated Advertising Manager, at vdebellis@marvel.com. For Marvel subscription inquiries, please call 888-511-5480. **Manufactured between 12/29/2017 and 3/12/2018 by R.R. DONNELLEY ASIA PRINTING SOLUTIONS, CHINA.**

10 9 8 7 6 5 4 3 2 1

HAN SOLO

HAN SOLO #1-5

Writer	MARJORIE LIU
Penciler	MARK BROOKS
Inkers	MARK BROOKS (#1, #4-5) & DEXTER VINES (#2-3)
Colorists	SONIA OBACK WITH MATT MILLA (#4)
Letterer	VC's JOE CARAMAGNA
Cover Art	LEE BERMEJO (#1, #3), TULA LOTAY (#2), OLIVIER COIPEL (#4) & KAMOME SHIRAHAMA (#5)

STAR WARS #8-12

Writer	JASON AARON
Penciler	STUART IMMONEN
Inker	WADE VON GRAWBADGER
Colorist	JUSTIN PONSOR
Letterer	CHRIS ELIOPOULOS
Cover Art	STUART IMMONEN, WADE VON GRAWBADGER & JUSTIN PONSOR

Assistant Editor	HEATHER ANTOS
Editor	JORDAN D. WHITE
Executive Editor	C.B. CEBULSKI

Editor in Chief	C.B. CEBULSKI
Chief Creative Officer	JOE QUESADA
President	DAN BUCKLEY

For Lucasfilm:

Senior Editor	FRANK PARISI
Creative Director	MICHAEL SIGLAIN
Lucasfilm Story Group	JAMES WAUGH, LELAND CHEE, MATT MARTIN

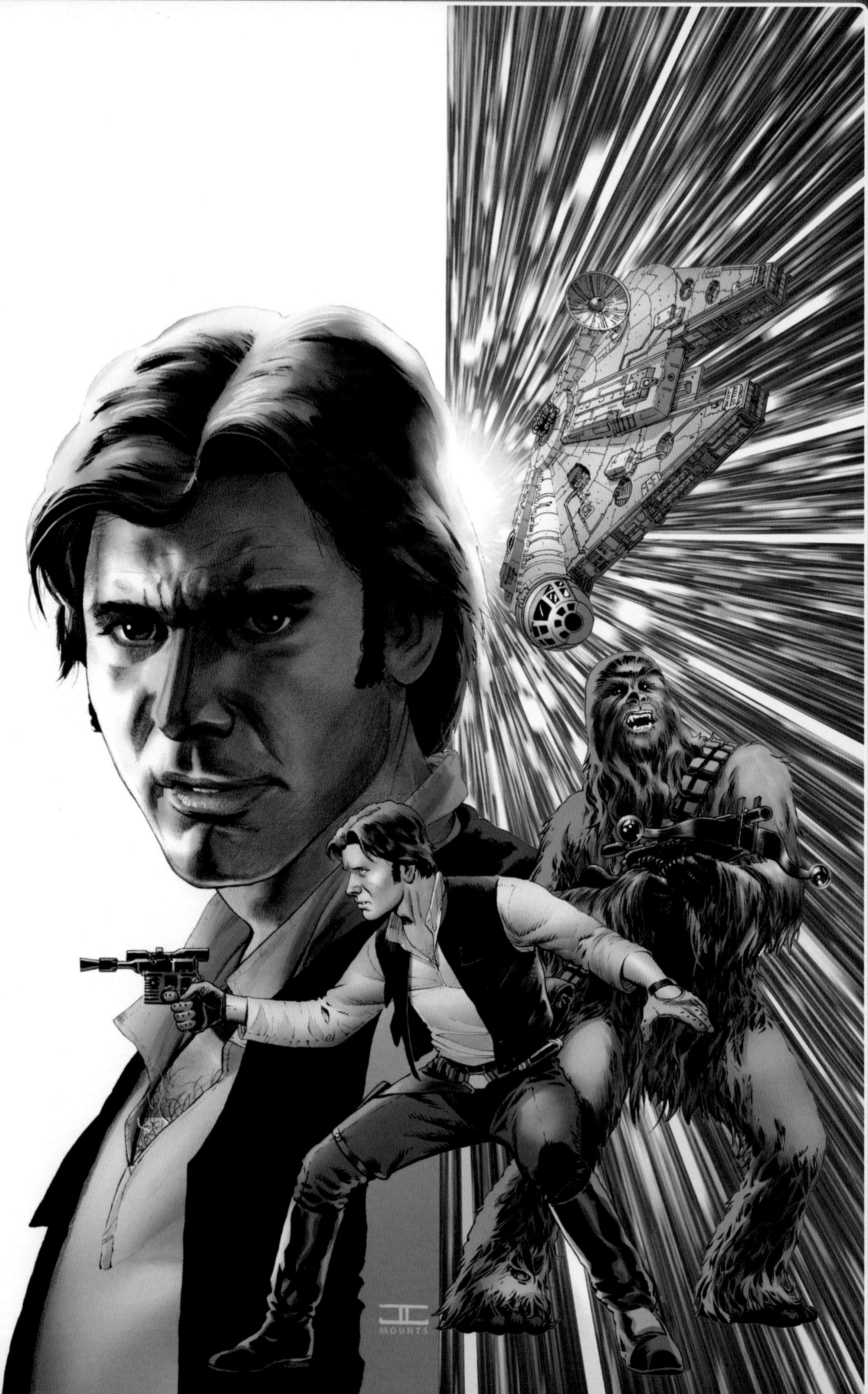
MOUNTS

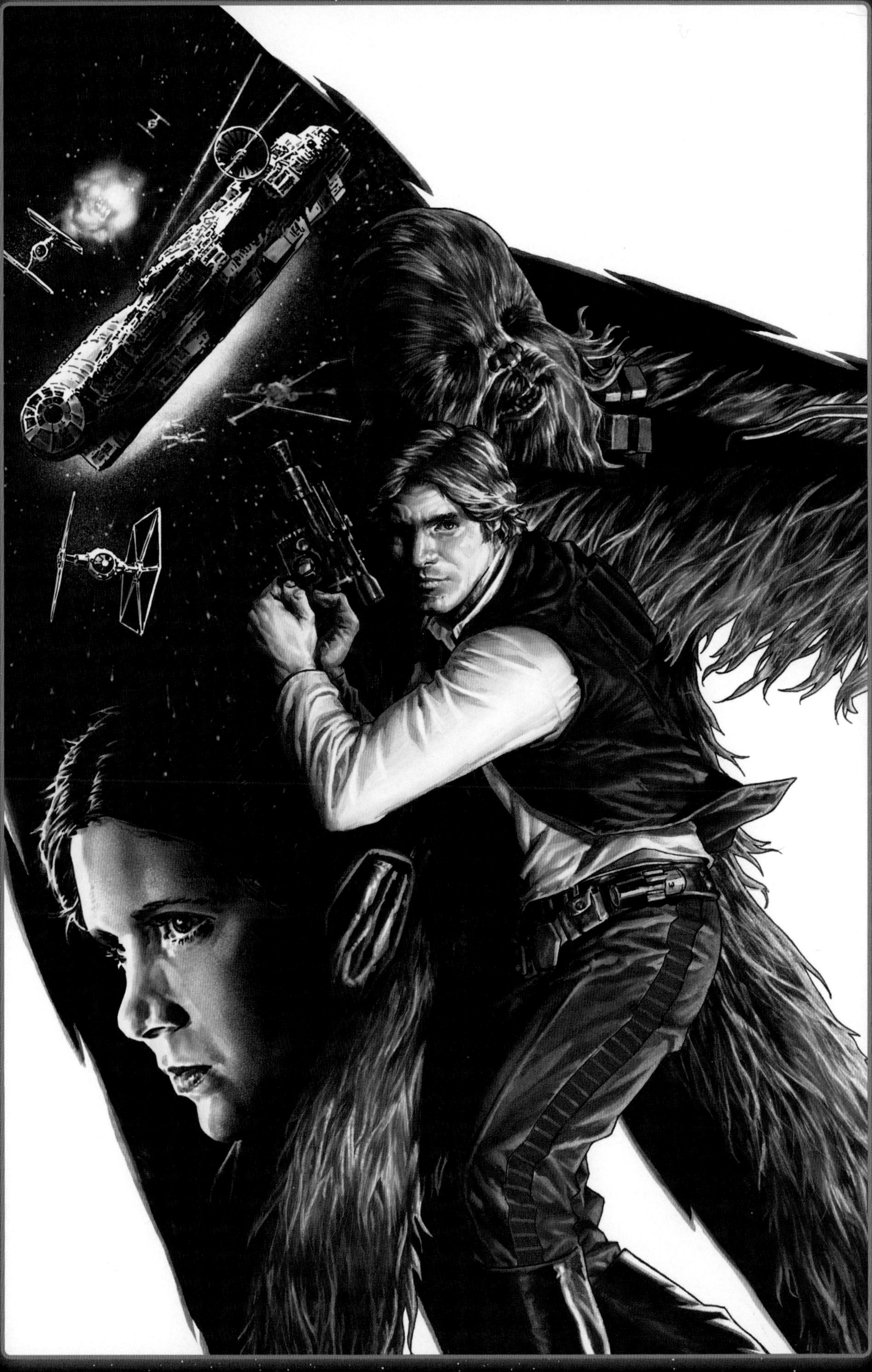

HAN SOLO 1

HAN SOLO

It is a period of unrest. In a galaxy oppressed by the Empire's unrelenting brutality, there is little hope for change. Nonetheless, rebels have banded together to fight back against such corruption.

While the Rebellion grows in power, Imperials fight to crush any hope for an overthrow. With the Empire's hands full, the opportunities for crime are endless.

HAN SOLO has taken a step back from the rebel cause, returning his focus to what he does best - smuggling. Untrusting by nature, he's skeptical of any who cross his path. Unfortunately for him, he cannot stay under the radar forever....

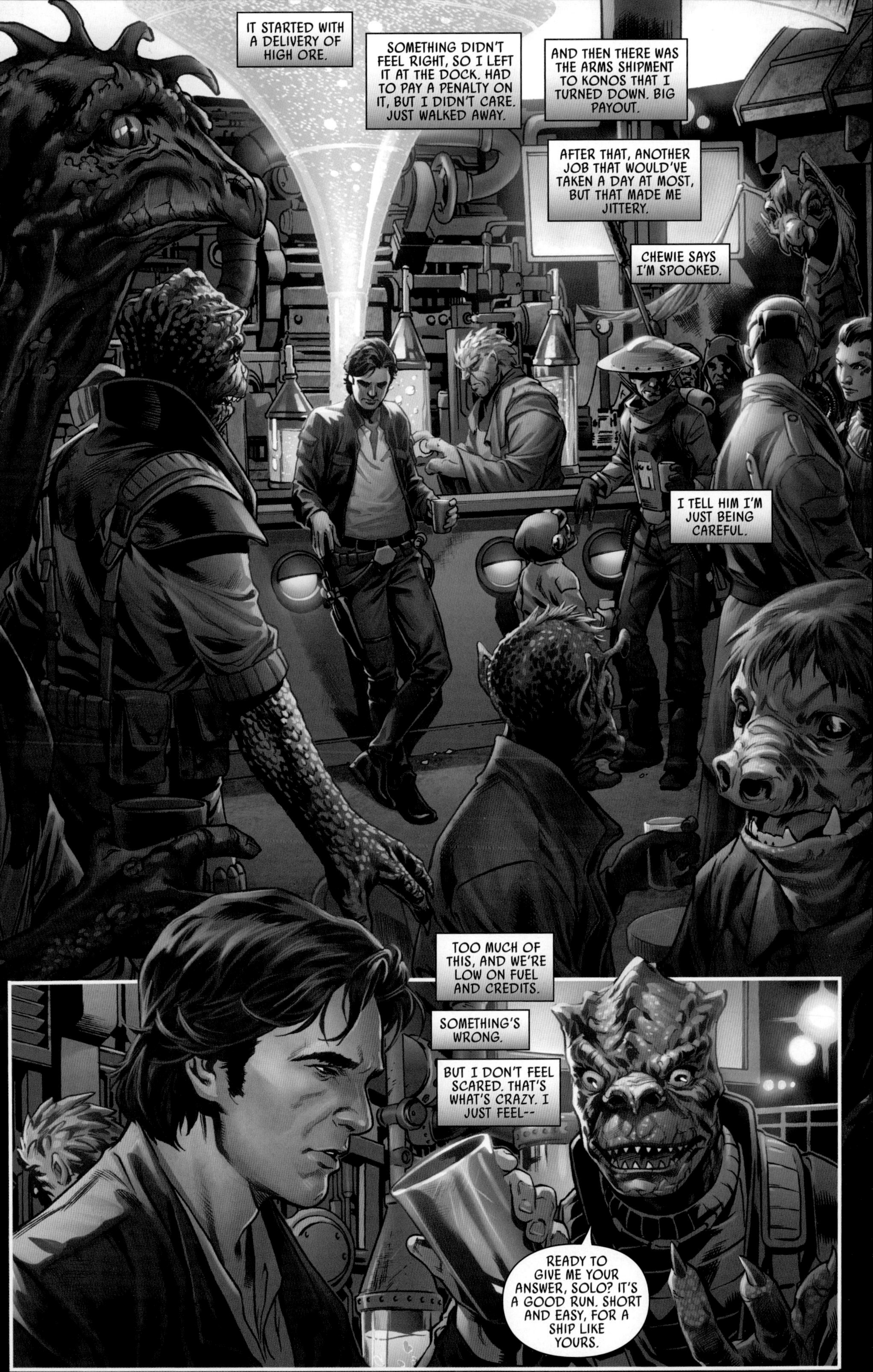
IT STARTED WITH A DELIVERY OF HIGH ORE.
SOMETHING DIDN'T FEEL RIGHT, SO I LEFT IT AT THE DOCK. HAD TO PAY A PENALTY ON IT, BUT I DIDN'T CARE. JUST WALKED AWAY.
AND THEN THERE WAS THE ARMS SHIPMENT TO KONOS THAT I TURNED DOWN. BIG PAYOUT.
AFTER THAT, ANOTHER JOB THAT WOULD'VE TAKEN A DAY AT MOST, BUT THAT MADE ME JITTERY.
CHEWIE SAYS I'M SPOOKED.
I TELL HIM I'M JUST BEING CAREFUL.
TOO MUCH OF THIS, AND WE'RE LOW ON FUEL AND CREDITS.
SOMETHING'S WRONG.
BUT I DON'T FEEL SCARED. THAT'S WHAT'S CRAZY. I JUST FEEL--
READY TO GIVE ME YOUR ANSWER, SOLO? IT'S A GOOD RUN. SHORT AND EASY, FOR A SHIP LIKE YOURS.

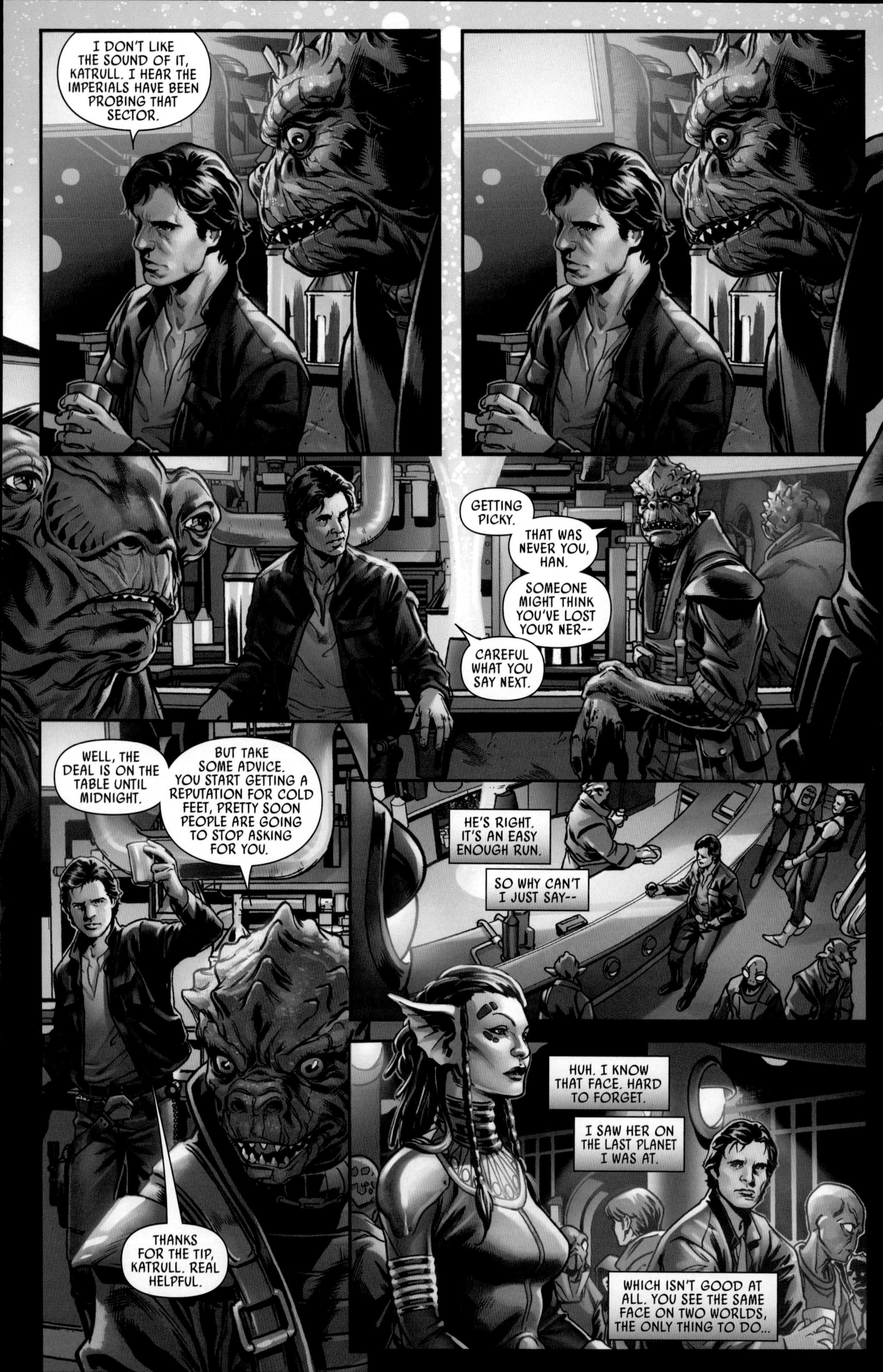
I DON'T LIKE THE SOUND OF IT, KATRULL. I HEAR THE IMPERIALS HAVE BEEN PROBING THAT SECTOR.
GETTING PICKY.
THAT WAS NEVER YOU, HAN.
SOMEONE MIGHT THINK YOU'VE LOST YOUR NER--
CAREFUL WHAT YOU SAY NEXT.
WELL, THE DEAL IS ON THE TABLE UNTIL MIDNIGHT.
BUT TAKE SOME ADVICE. YOU START GETTING A REPUTATION FOR COLD FEET, PRETTY SOON PEOPLE ARE GOING TO STOP ASKING FOR YOU.
THANKS FOR THE TIP, KATRULL. REAL HELPFUL.
HE'S RIGHT. IT'S AN EASY ENOUGH RUN.
SO WHY CAN'T I JUST SAY--
HUH. I KNOW THAT FACE. HARD TO FORGET.
I SAW HER ON THE LAST PLANET I WAS AT.
WHICH ISN'T GOOD AT ALL. YOU SEE THE SAME FACE ON TWO WORLDS, THE ONLY THING TO DO...

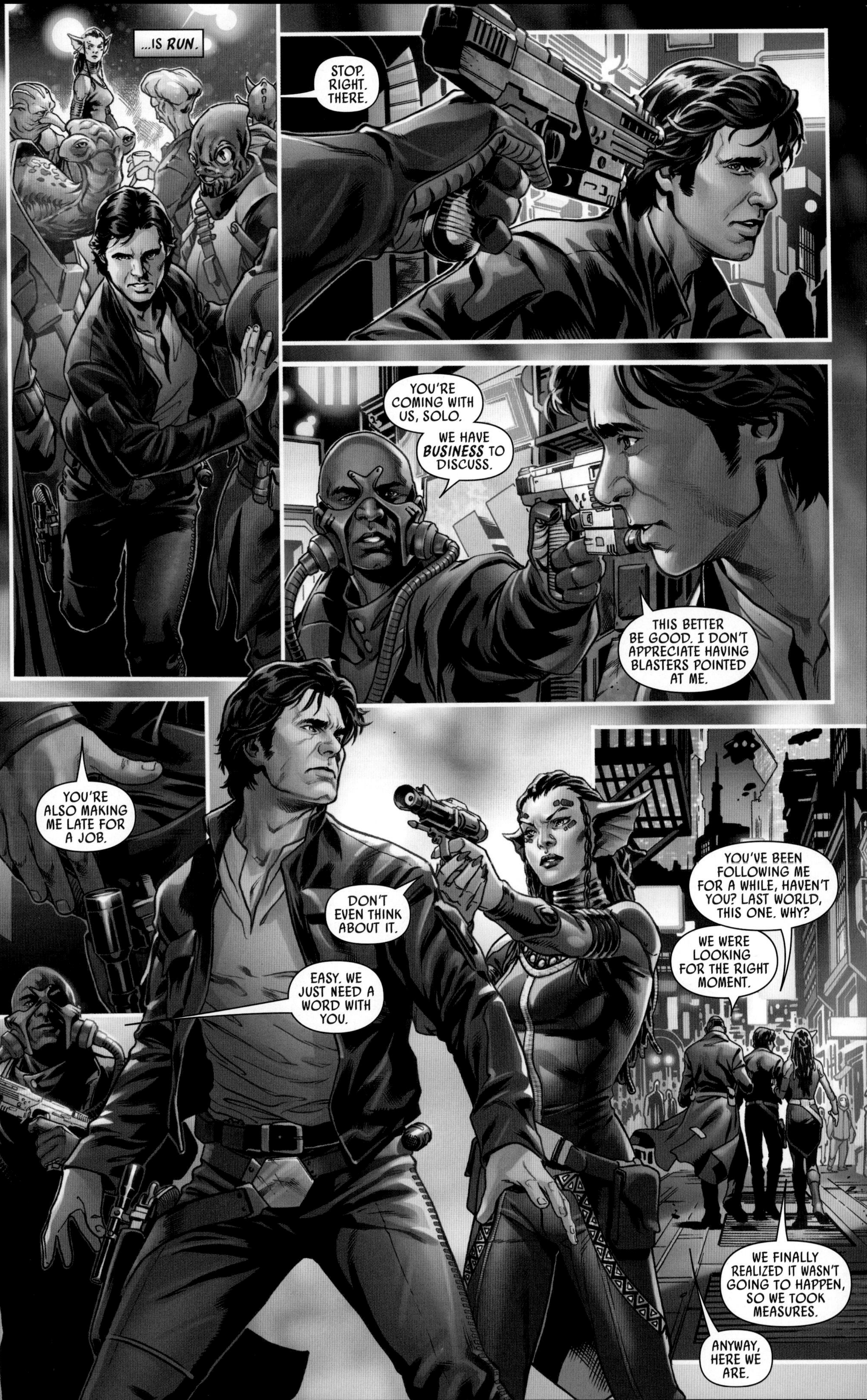
...IS RUN.
STOP. RIGHT. THERE.
YOU'RE COMING WITH US, SOLO.
WE HAVE BUSINESS TO DISCUSS.
THIS BETTER BE GOOD. I DON'T APPRECIATE HAVING BLASTERS POINTED AT ME.
YOU'RE ALSO MAKING ME LATE FOR A JOB.
DON'T EVEN THINK ABOUT IT.
EASY. WE JUST NEED A WORD WITH YOU.
YOU'VE BEEN FOLLOWING ME FOR A WHILE, HAVEN'T YOU? LAST WORLD, THIS ONE. WHY?
WE WERE LOOKING FOR THE RIGHT MOMENT.
WE FINALLY REALIZED IT WASN'T GOING TO HAPPEN, SO WE TOOK MEASURES.
ANYWAY, HERE WE ARE.

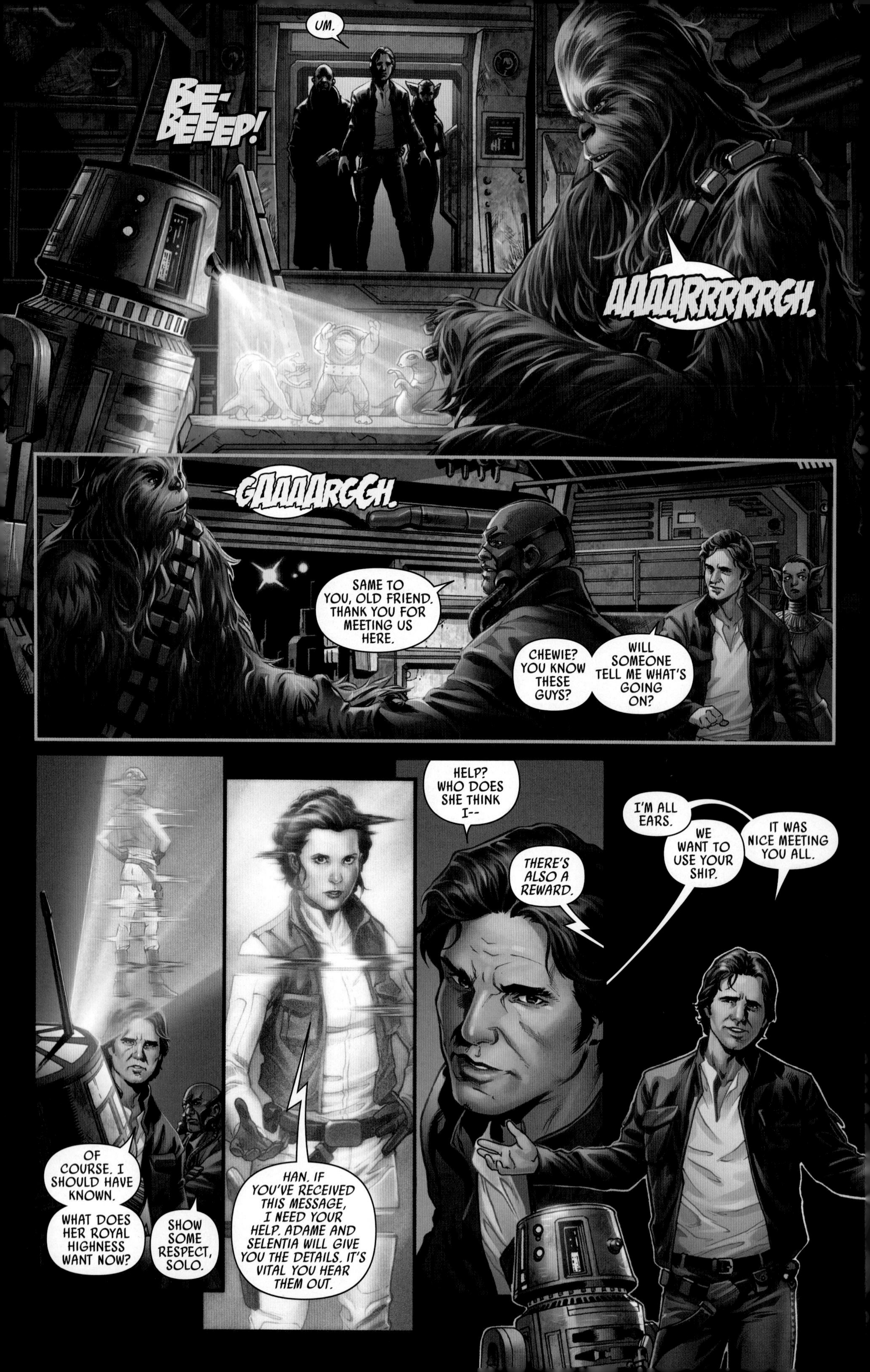

UM.
BE-BEEEP!
AAAARRRRRGH.
GAAAARGGH.
SAME TO YOU, OLD FRIEND. THANK YOU FOR MEETING US HERE.
CHEWIE? YOU KNOW THESE GUYS?
WILL SOMEONE TELL ME WHAT'S GOING ON?
OF COURSE. I SHOULD HAVE KNOWN.
WHAT DOES HER ROYAL HIGHNESS WANT NOW?
SHOW SOME RESPECT, SOLO.
HAN, IF YOU'VE RECEIVED THIS MESSAGE, I NEED YOUR HELP. ADAME AND SELENTIA WILL GIVE YOU THE DETAILS. IT'S VITAL YOU HEAR THEM OUT.
HELP? WHO DOES SHE THINK I--
THERE'S ALSO A REWARD.
I'M ALL EARS.
WE WANT TO USE YOUR SHIP.
IT WAS NICE MEETING YOU ALL.

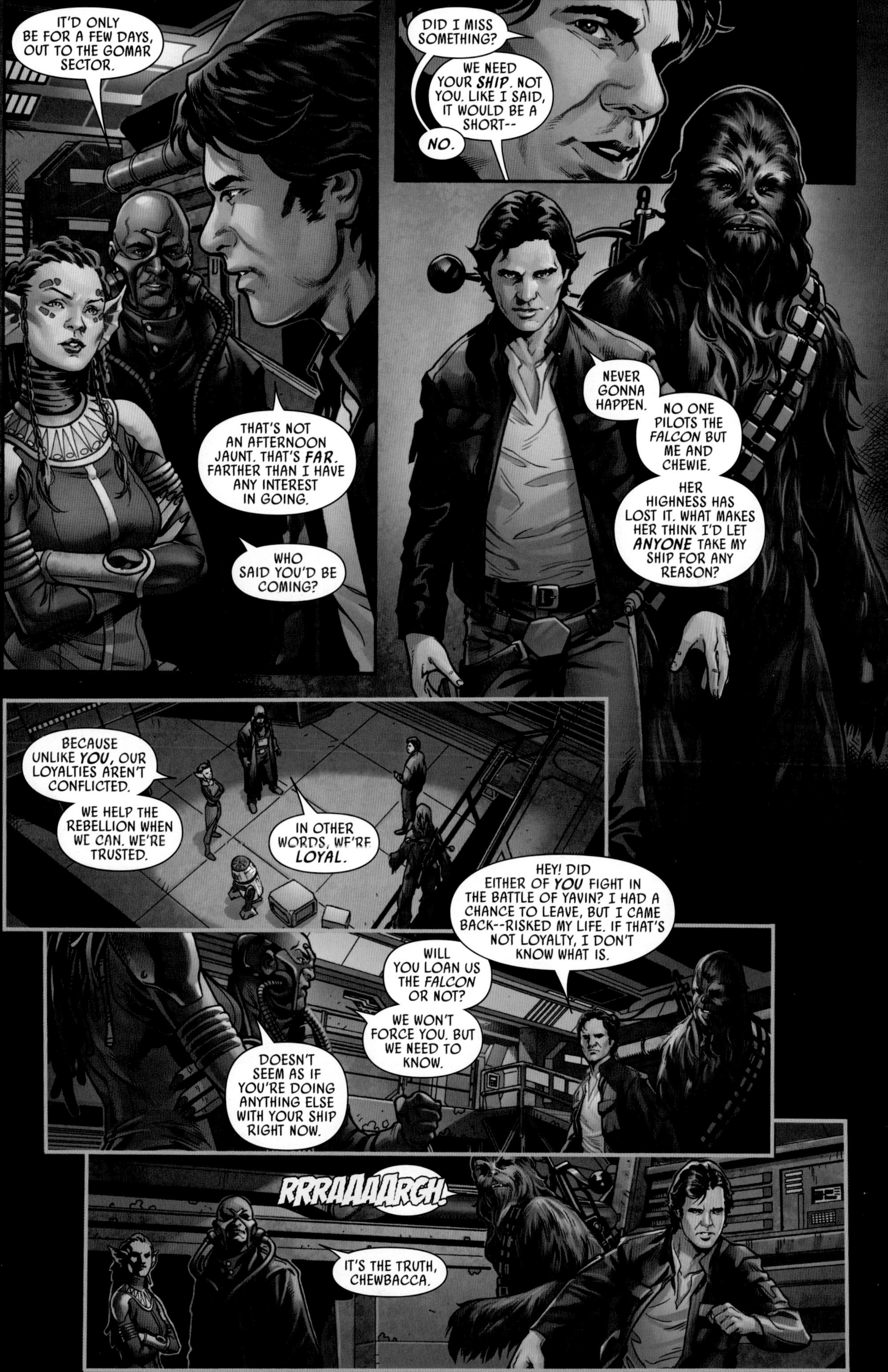

IT'D ONLY BE FOR A FEW DAYS, OUT TO THE GOMAR SECTOR.
THAT'S NOT AN AFTERNOON JAUNT. THAT'S FAR. FARTHER THAN I HAVE ANY INTEREST IN GOING.
WHO SAID YOU'D BE COMING?
DID I MISS SOMETHING?
WE NEED YOUR SHIP. NOT YOU. LIKE I SAID, IT WOULD BE A SHORT--
NO.
NEVER GONNA HAPPEN.
NO ONE PILOTS THE FALCON BUT ME AND CHEWIE.
HER HIGHNESS HAS LOST IT. WHAT MAKES HER THINK I'D LET ANYONE TAKE MY SHIP FOR ANY REASON?
BECAUSE UNLIKE YOU, OUR LOYALTIES AREN'T CONFLICTED.
WE HELP THE REBELLION WHEN WE CAN. WE'RE TRUSTED.
IN OTHER WORDS, WE'RE LOYAL.
HEY! DID EITHER OF YOU FIGHT IN THE BATTLE OF YAVIN? I HAD A CHANCE TO LEAVE, BUT I CAME BACK--RISKED MY LIFE. IF THAT'S NOT LOYALTY, I DON'T KNOW WHAT IS.
WILL YOU LOAN US THE FALCON OR NOT?
WE WON'T FORCE YOU. BUT WE NEED TO KNOW.
DOESN'T SEEM AS IF YOU'RE DOING ANYTHING ELSE WITH YOUR SHIP RIGHT NOW.
RRRAAAARGH!
IT'S THE TRUTH, CHEWBACCA.

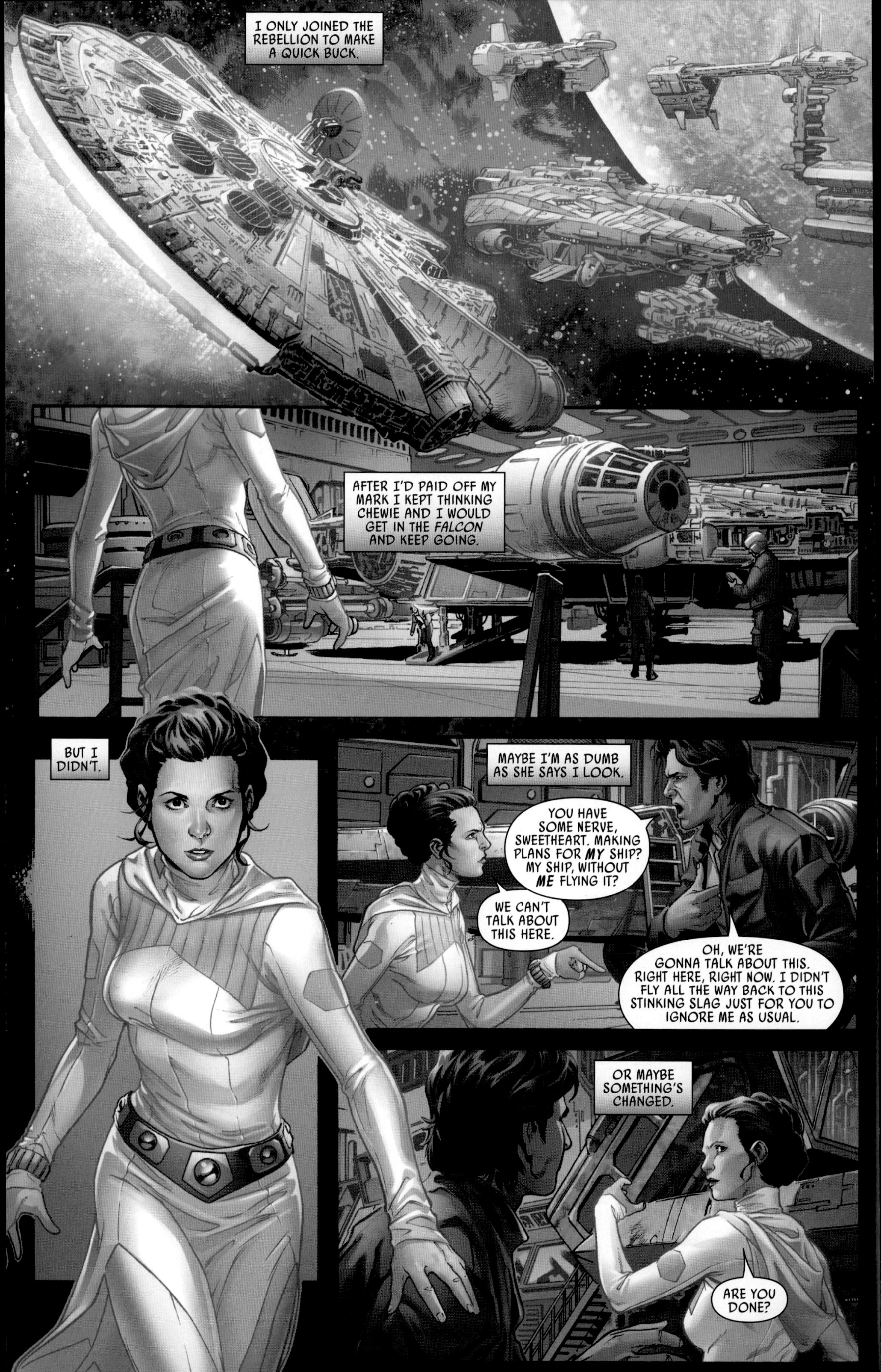
I ONLY JOINED THE REBELLION TO MAKE A QUICK BUCK.
AFTER I'D PAID OFF MY MARK I KEPT THINKING CHEWIE AND I WOULD GET IN THE FALCON AND KEEP GOING.
BUT I DIDN'T.
MAYBE I'M AS DUMB AS SHE SAYS I LOOK.
YOU HAVE SOME NERVE, SWEETHEART. MAKING PLANS FOR MY SHIP? MY SHIP, WITHOUT ME FLYING IT?
WE CAN'T TALK ABOUT THIS HERE.
OH, WE'RE GONNA TALK ABOUT THIS. RIGHT HERE, RIGHT NOW. I DIDN'T FLY ALL THE WAY BACK TO THIS STINKING SLAG JUST FOR YOU TO IGNORE ME AS USUAL.
OR MAYBE SOMETHING'S CHANGED.
ARE YOU DONE?

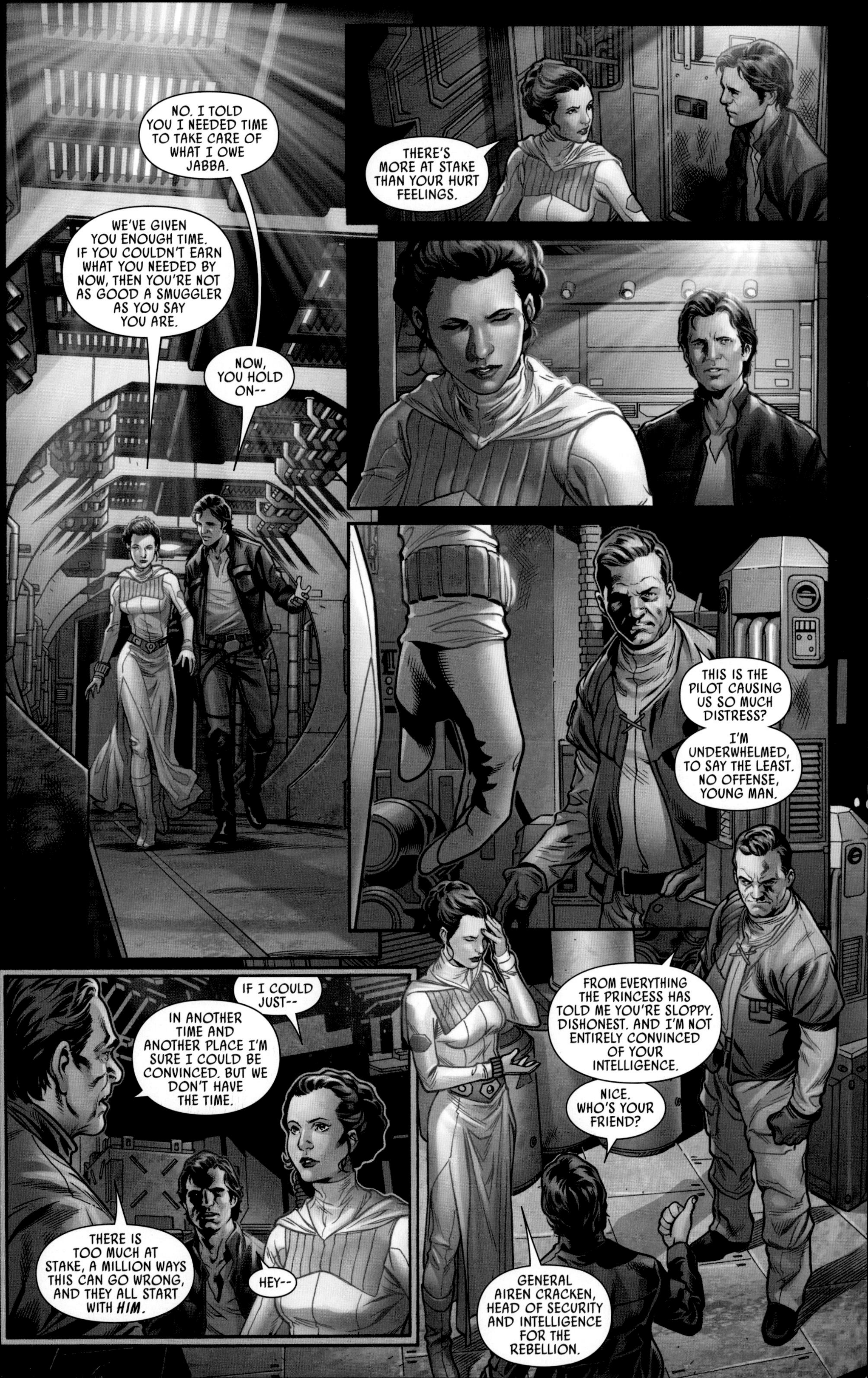
NO. I TOLD YOU I NEEDED TIME TO TAKE CARE OF WHAT I OWE JABBA.
WE'VE GIVEN YOU ENOUGH TIME. IF YOU COULDN'T EARN WHAT YOU NEEDED BY NOW, THEN YOU'RE NOT AS GOOD A SMUGGLER AS YOU SAY YOU ARE.
NOW, YOU HOLD ON--
THERE'S MORE AT STAKE THAN YOUR HURT FEELINGS.
THIS IS THE PILOT CAUSING US SO MUCH DISTRESS?
I'M UNDERWHELMED, TO SAY THE LEAST. NO OFFENSE, YOUNG MAN.
FROM EVERYTHING THE PRINCESS HAS TOLD ME YOU'RE SLOPPY. DISHONEST. AND I'M NOT ENTIRELY CONVINCED OF YOUR INTELLIGENCE.
NICE. WHO'S YOUR FRIEND?
GENERAL AIREN CRACKEN, HEAD OF SECURITY AND INTELLIGENCE FOR THE REBELLION.
IF I COULD JUST--
IN ANOTHER TIME AND ANOTHER PLACE I'M SURE I COULD BE CONVINCED. BUT WE DON'T HAVE THE TIME.
THERE IS TOO MUCH AT STAKE, A MILLION WAYS THIS CAN GO WRONG, AND THEY ALL START WITH HIM.
HEY--

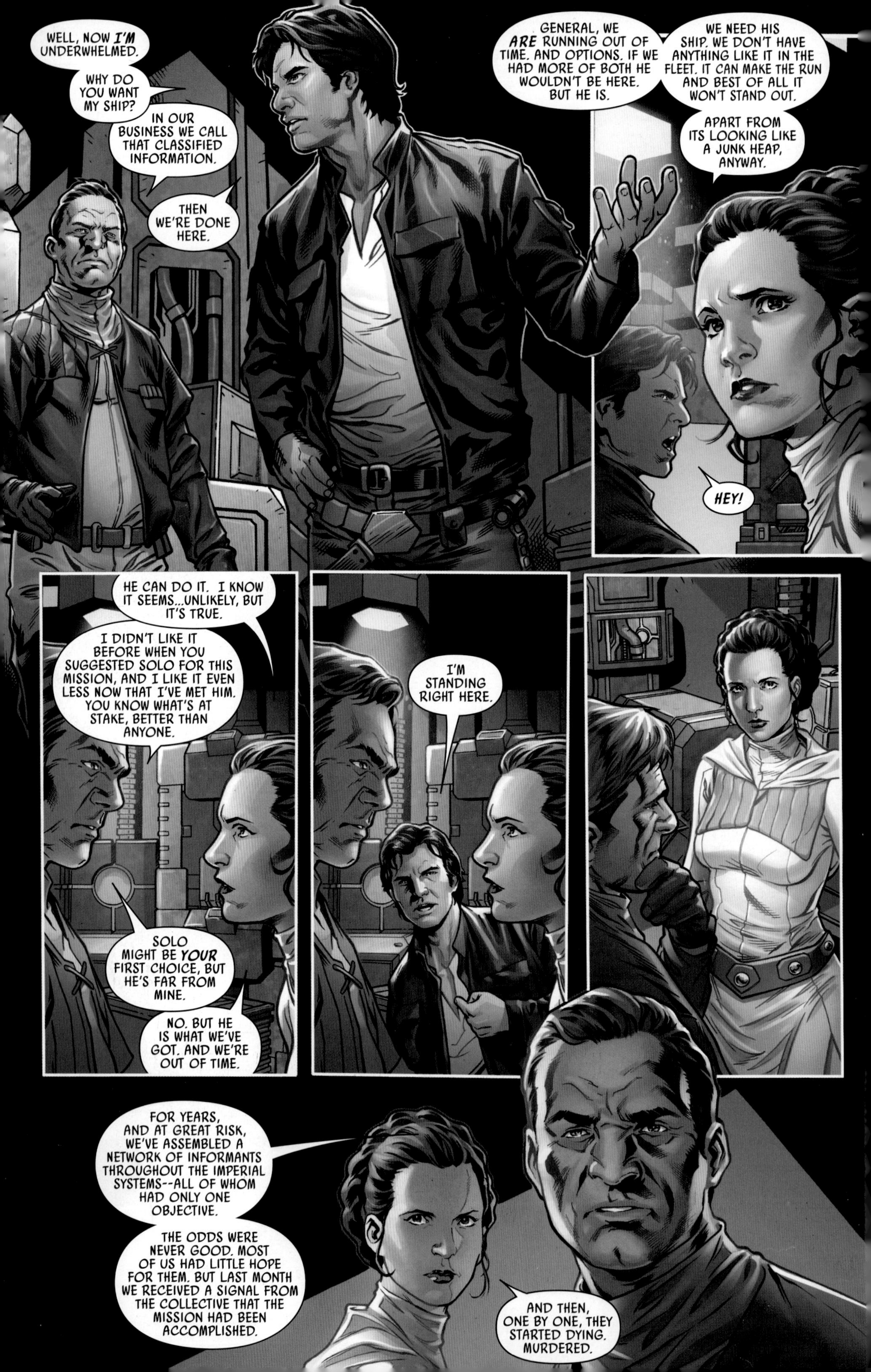
WELL, NOW I'M UNDERWHELMED.
WHY DO YOU WANT MY SHIP?
IN OUR BUSINESS WE CALL THAT CLASSIFIED INFORMATION.
THEN WE'RE DONE HERE.
GENERAL, WE ARE RUNNING OUT OF TIME. AND OPTIONS. IF WE HAD MORE OF BOTH HE WOULDN'T BE HERE. BUT HE IS.
WE NEED HIS SHIP. WE DON'T HAVE ANYTHING LIKE IT IN THE FLEET. IT CAN MAKE THE RUN AND BEST OF ALL IT WON'T STAND OUT.
APART FROM ITS LOOKING LIKE A JUNK HEAP, ANYWAY.
HEY!
HE CAN DO IT. I KNOW IT SEEMS...UNLIKELY, BUT IT'S TRUE.
I DIDN'T LIKE IT BEFORE WHEN YOU SUGGESTED SOLO FOR THIS MISSION, AND I LIKE IT EVEN LESS NOW THAT I'VE MET HIM. YOU KNOW WHAT'S AT STAKE, BETTER THAN ANYONE.
SOLO MIGHT BE YOUR FIRST CHOICE, BUT HE'S FAR FROM MINE.
NO. BUT HE IS WHAT WE'VE GOT. AND WE'RE OUT OF TIME.
I'M STANDING RIGHT HERE.
FOR YEARS, AND AT GREAT RISK, WE'VE ASSEMBLED A NETWORK OF INFORMANTS THROUGHOUT THE IMPERIAL SYSTEMS--ALL OF WHOM HAD ONLY ONE OBJECTIVE.
THE ODDS WERE NEVER GOOD. MOST OF US HAD LITTLE HOPE FOR THEM. BUT LAST MONTH WE RECEIVED A SIGNAL FROM THE COLLECTIVE THAT THE MISSION HAD BEEN ACCOMPLISHED.
AND THEN, ONE BY ONE, THEY STARTED DYING. MURDERED.

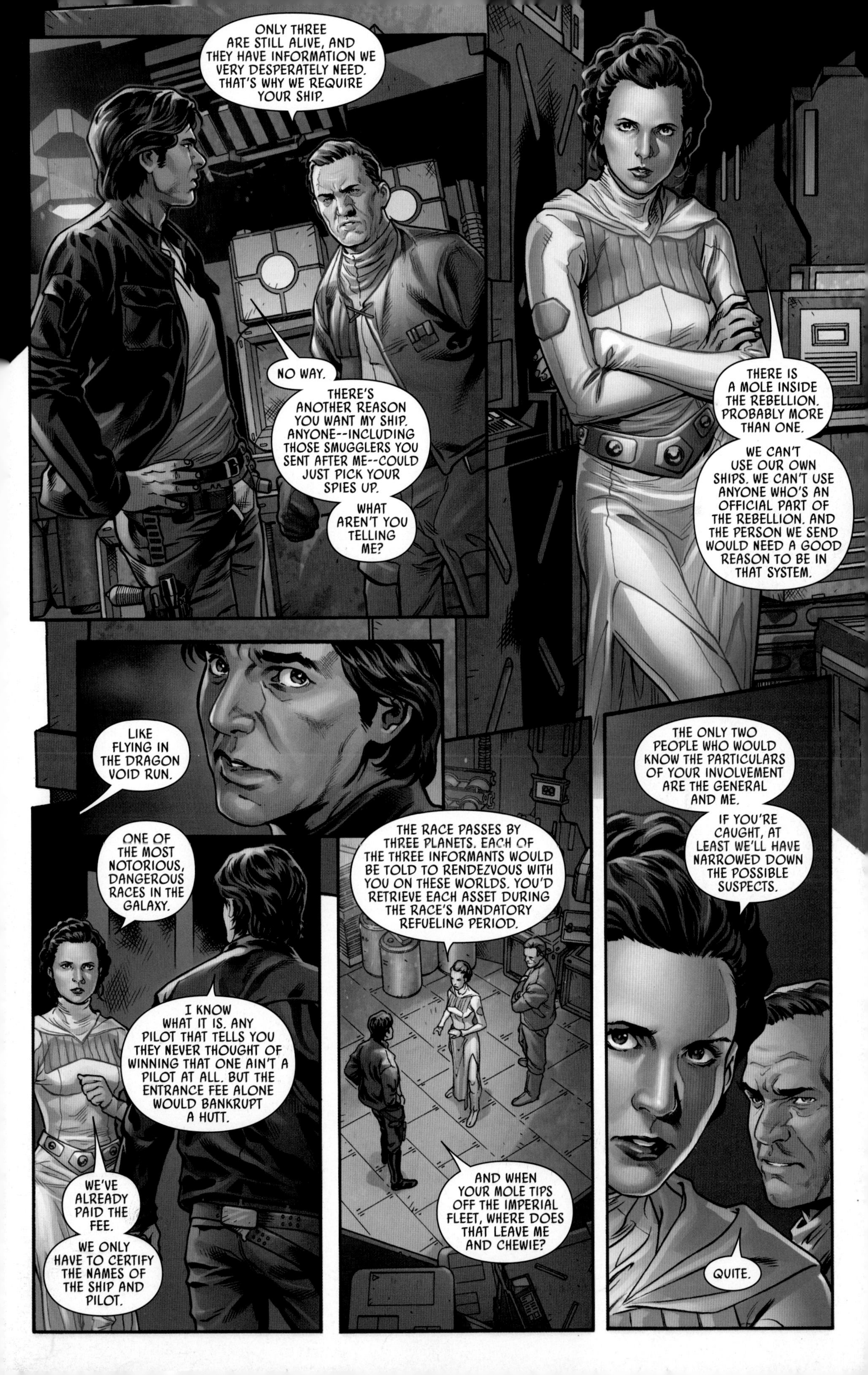
ONLY THREE ARE STILL ALIVE, AND THEY HAVE INFORMATION WE VERY DESPERATELY NEED. THAT'S WHY WE REQUIRE YOUR SHIP.
NO WAY.
THERE'S ANOTHER REASON YOU WANT MY SHIP. ANYONE--INCLUDING THOSE SMUGGLERS YOU SENT AFTER ME--COULD JUST PICK YOUR SPIES UP.
WHAT AREN'T YOU TELLING ME?
THERE IS A MOLE INSIDE THE REBELLION. PROBABLY MORE THAN ONE.
WE CAN'T USE OUR OWN SHIPS. WE CAN'T USE ANYONE WHO'S AN OFFICIAL PART OF THE REBELLION. AND THE PERSON WE SEND WOULD NEED A GOOD REASON TO BE IN THAT SYSTEM.
LIKE FLYING IN THE DRAGON VOID RUN.
ONE OF THE MOST NOTORIOUS, DANGEROUS RACES IN THE GALAXY.
I KNOW WHAT IT IS. ANY PILOT THAT TELLS YOU THEY NEVER THOUGHT OF WINNING THAT ONE AIN'T A PILOT AT ALL. BUT THE ENTRANCE FEE ALONE WOULD BANKRUPT A HUTT.
WE'VE ALREADY PAID THE FEE.
WE ONLY HAVE TO CERTIFY THE NAMES OF THE SHIP AND PILOT.
THE RACE PASSES BY THREE PLANETS. EACH OF THE THREE INFORMANTS WOULD BE TOLD TO RENDEZVOUS WITH YOU ON THESE WORLDS. YOU'D RETRIEVE EACH ASSET DURING THE RACE'S MANDATORY REFUELING PERIOD.
AND WHEN YOUR MOLE TIPS OFF THE IMPERIAL FLEET, WHERE DOES THAT LEAVE ME AND CHEWIE?
THE ONLY TWO PEOPLE WHO WOULD KNOW THE PARTICULARS OF YOUR INVOLVEMENT ARE THE GENERAL AND ME.
IF YOU'RE CAUGHT, AT LEAST WE'LL HAVE NARROWED DOWN THE POSSIBLE SUSPECTS.
QUITE.

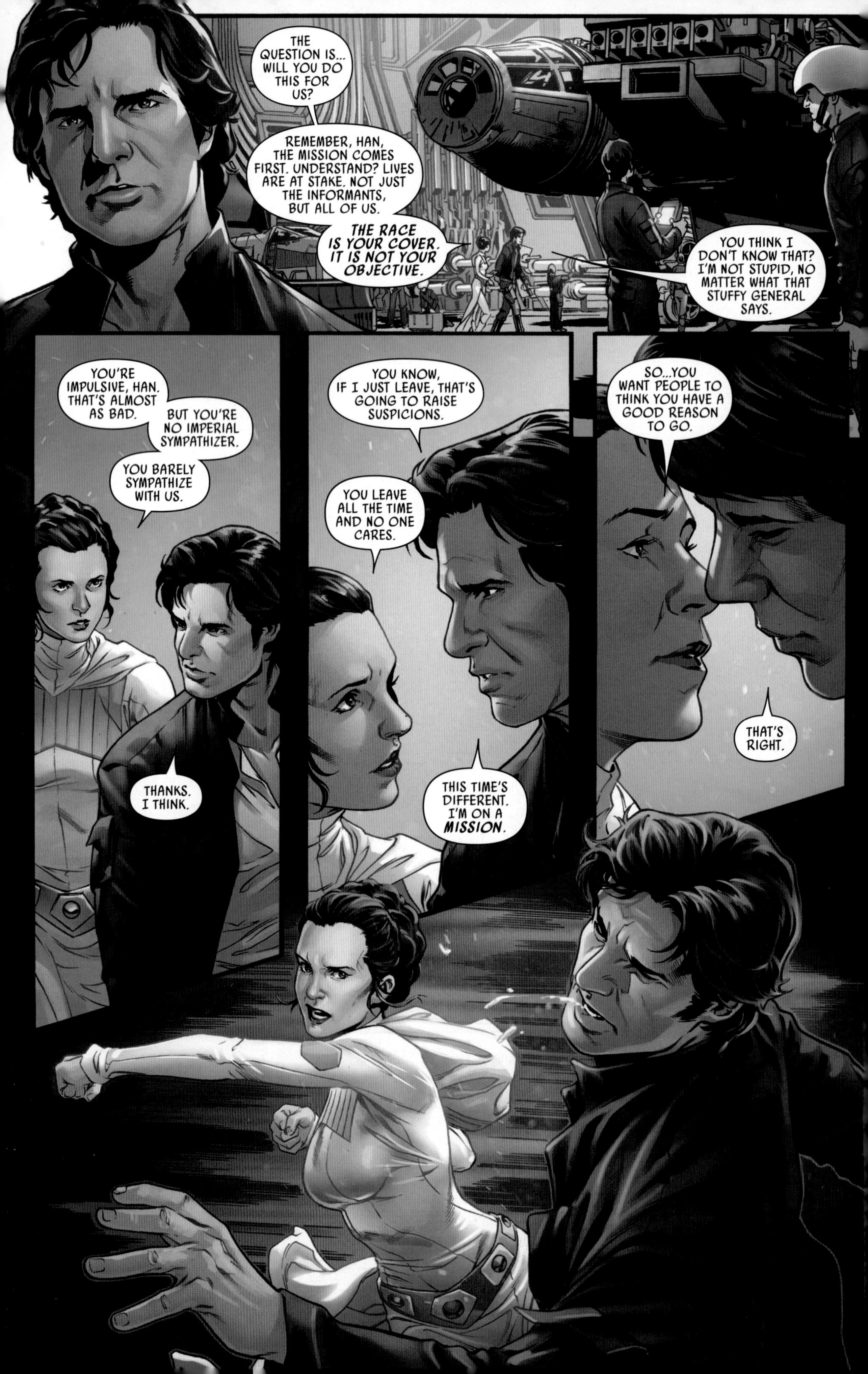
THE QUESTION IS... WILL YOU DO THIS FOR US?
REMEMBER, HAN, THE MISSION COMES FIRST. UNDERSTAND? LIVES ARE AT STAKE. NOT JUST THE INFORMANTS, BUT ALL OF US.
THE RACE IS YOUR COVER. IT IS NOT YOUR OBJECTIVE.
YOU THINK I DON'T KNOW THAT? I'M NOT STUPID, NO MATTER WHAT THAT STUFFY GENERAL SAYS.
YOU'RE IMPULSIVE, HAN. THAT'S ALMOST AS BAD.
BUT YOU'RE NO IMPERIAL SYMPATHIZER.
YOU BARELY SYMPATHIZE WITH US.
THANKS. I THINK.
YOU KNOW, IF I JUST LEAVE, THAT'S GOING TO RAISE SUSPICIONS.
YOU LEAVE ALL THE TIME AND NO ONE CARES.
THIS TIME'S DIFFERENT. I'M ON A MISSION.
SO...YOU WANT PEOPLE TO THINK YOU HAVE A GOOD REASON TO GO.
THAT'S RIGHT.

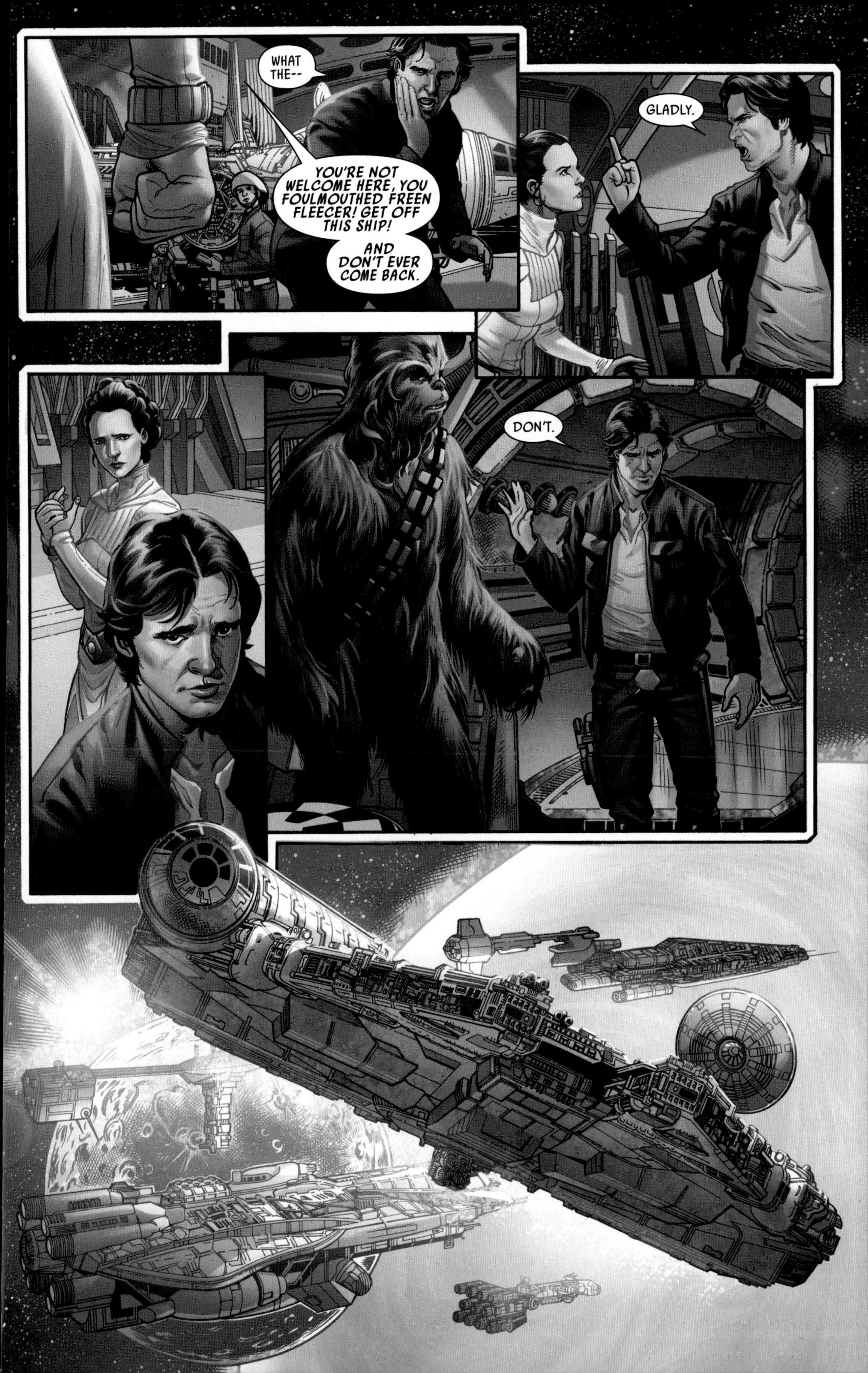
WHAT THE--
YOU'RE NOT WELCOME HERE, YOU FOULMOUTHED FREEN FLEECER! GET OFF THIS SHIP!
AND DON'T EVER COME BACK.
GLADLY.
DON'T.

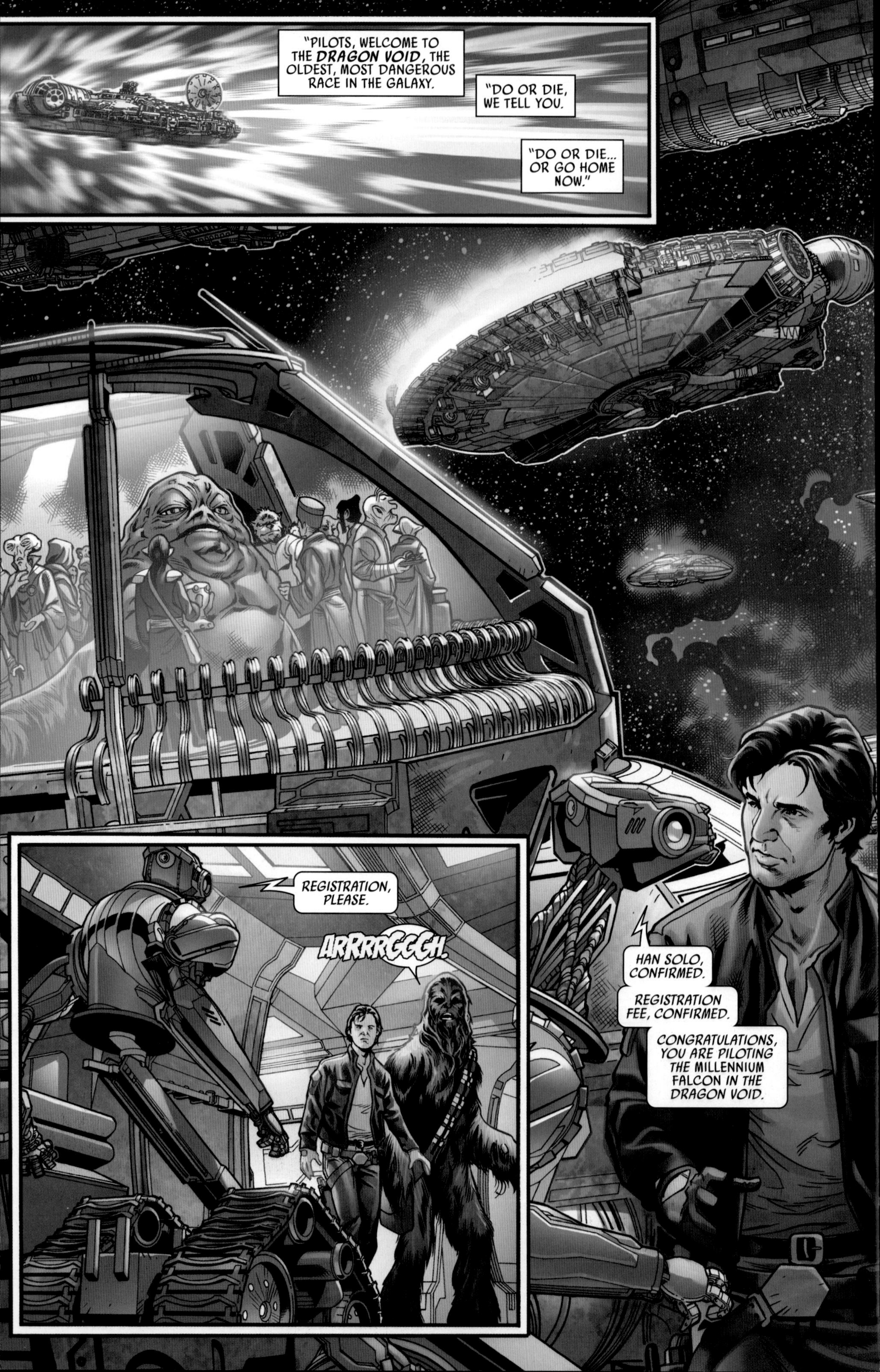
"PILOTS, WELCOME TO THE DRAGON VOID, THE OLDEST, MOST DANGEROUS RACE IN THE GALAXY.
"DO OR DIE, WE TELL YOU.
"DO OR DIE... OR GO HOME NOW."
REGISTRATION, PLEASE.
ARRRRGGGH.
HAN SOLO, CONFIRMED.
REGISTRATION FEE, CONFIRMED.
CONGRATULATIONS, YOU ARE PILOTING THE MILLENNIUM FALCON IN THE DRAGON VOID.

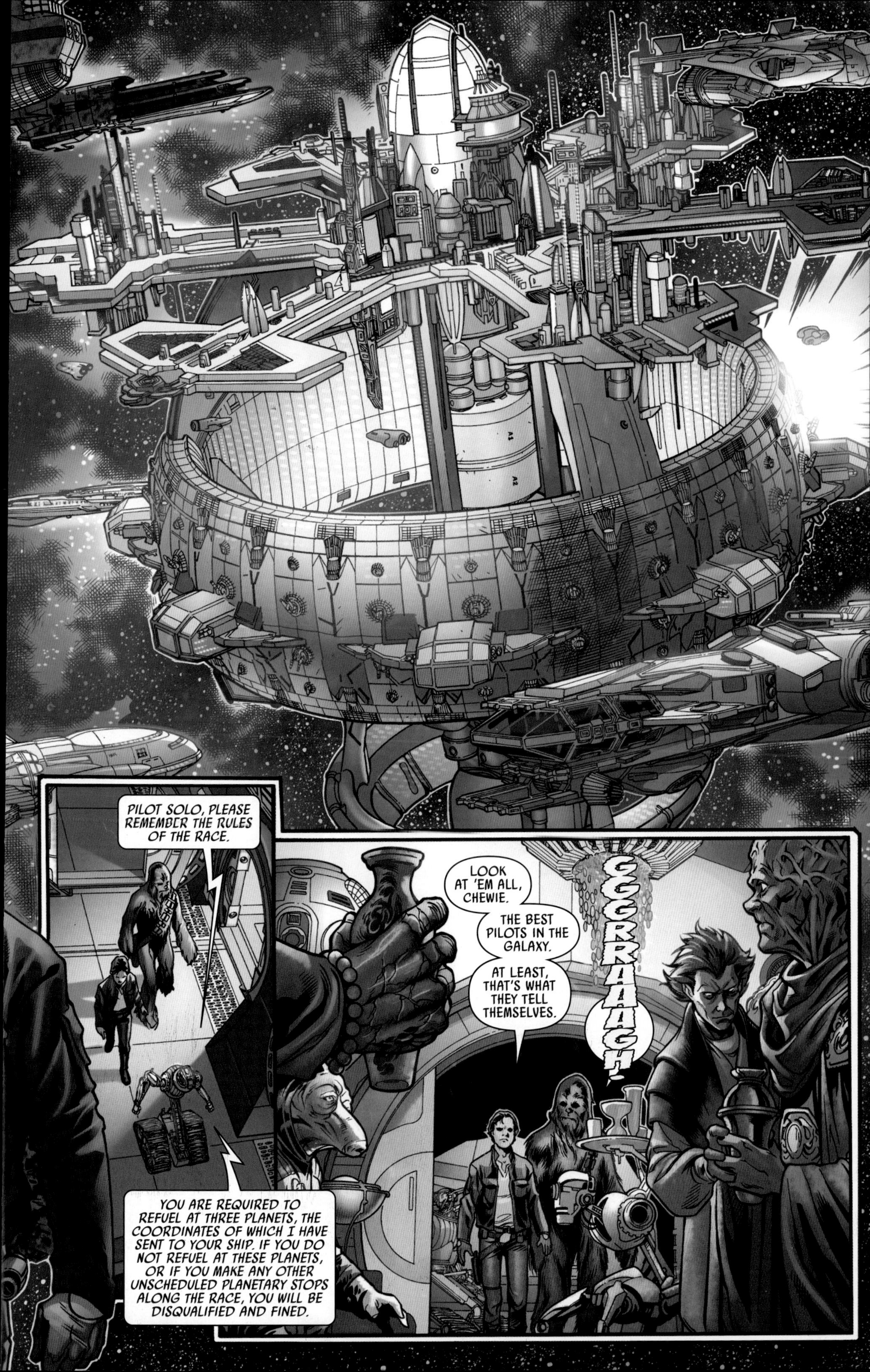
PILOT SOLO, PLEASE REMEMBER THE RULES OF THE RACE.
YOU ARE REQUIRED TO REFUEL AT THREE PLANETS, THE COORDINATES OF WHICH I HAVE SENT TO YOUR SHIP. IF YOU DO NOT REFUEL AT THESE PLANETS, OR IF YOU MAKE ANY OTHER UNSCHEDULED PLANETARY STOPS ALONG THE RACE, YOU WILL BE DISQUALIFIED AND FINED.
LOOK AT 'EM ALL, CHEWIE.
THE BEST PILOTS IN THE GALAXY.
AT LEAST, THAT'S WHAT THEY TELL THEMSELVES.
GGGRRAAAAGH!

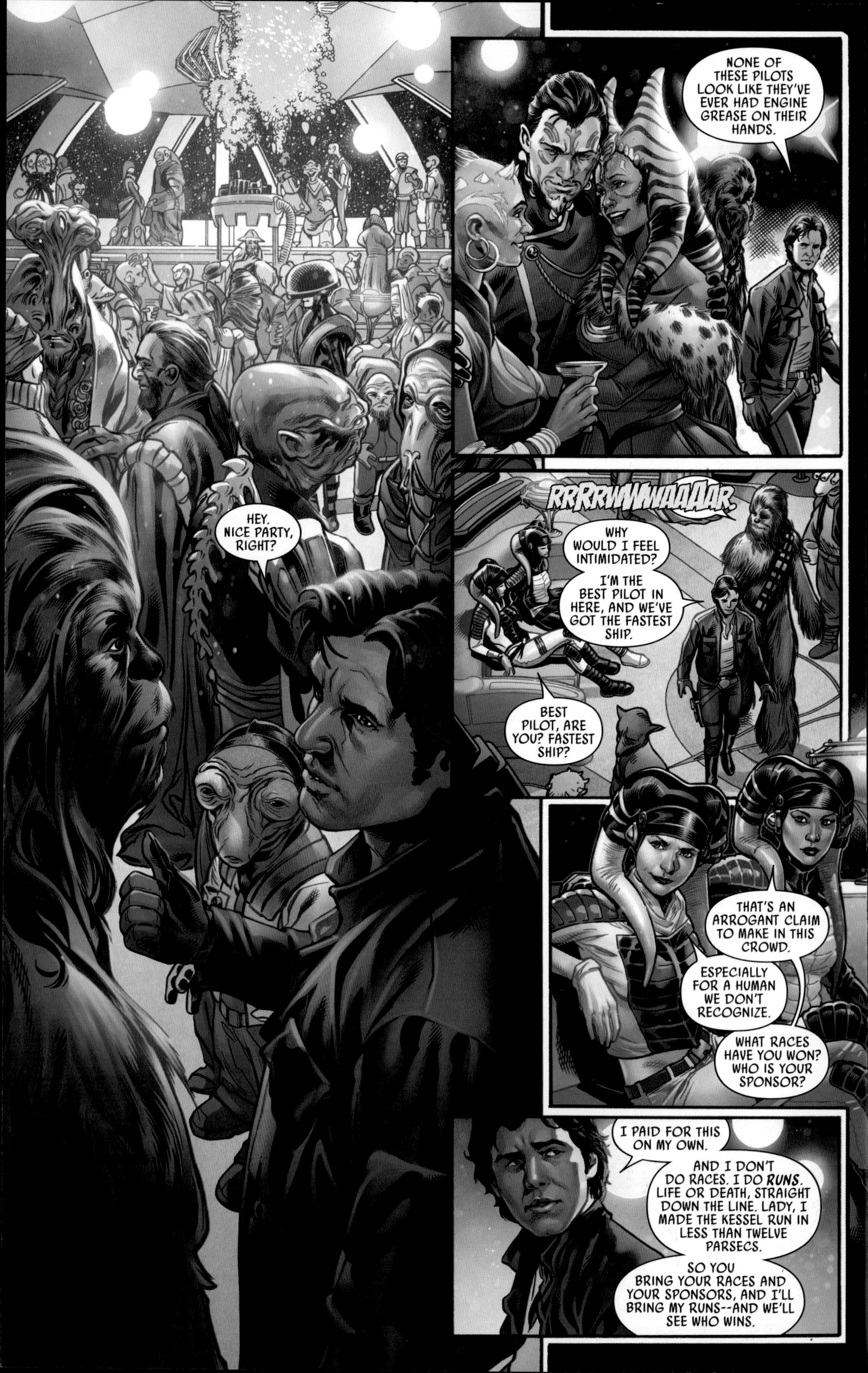
HEY. NICE PARTY, RIGHT?
NONE OF THESE PILOTS LOOK LIKE THEY'VE EVER HAD ENGINE GREASE ON THEIR HANDS.
RRRRWWWAAAAR.
WHY WOULD I FEEL INTIMIDATED?
I'M THE BEST PILOT IN HERE, AND WE'VE GOT THE FASTEST SHIP.
BEST PILOT, ARE YOU? FASTEST SHIP?
THAT'S AN ARROGANT CLAIM TO MAKE IN THIS CROWD.
ESPECIALLY FOR A HUMAN WE DON'T RECOGNIZE.
WHAT RACES HAVE YOU WON? WHO IS YOUR SPONSOR?
I PAID FOR THIS ON MY OWN.
AND I DON'T DO RACES. I DO RUNS. LIFE OR DEATH, STRAIGHT DOWN THE LINE. LADY, I MADE THE KESSEL RUN IN LESS THAN TWELVE PARSECS.
SO YOU BRING YOUR RACES AND YOUR SPONSORS, AND I'LL BRING MY RUNS--AND WE'LL SEE WHO WINS.

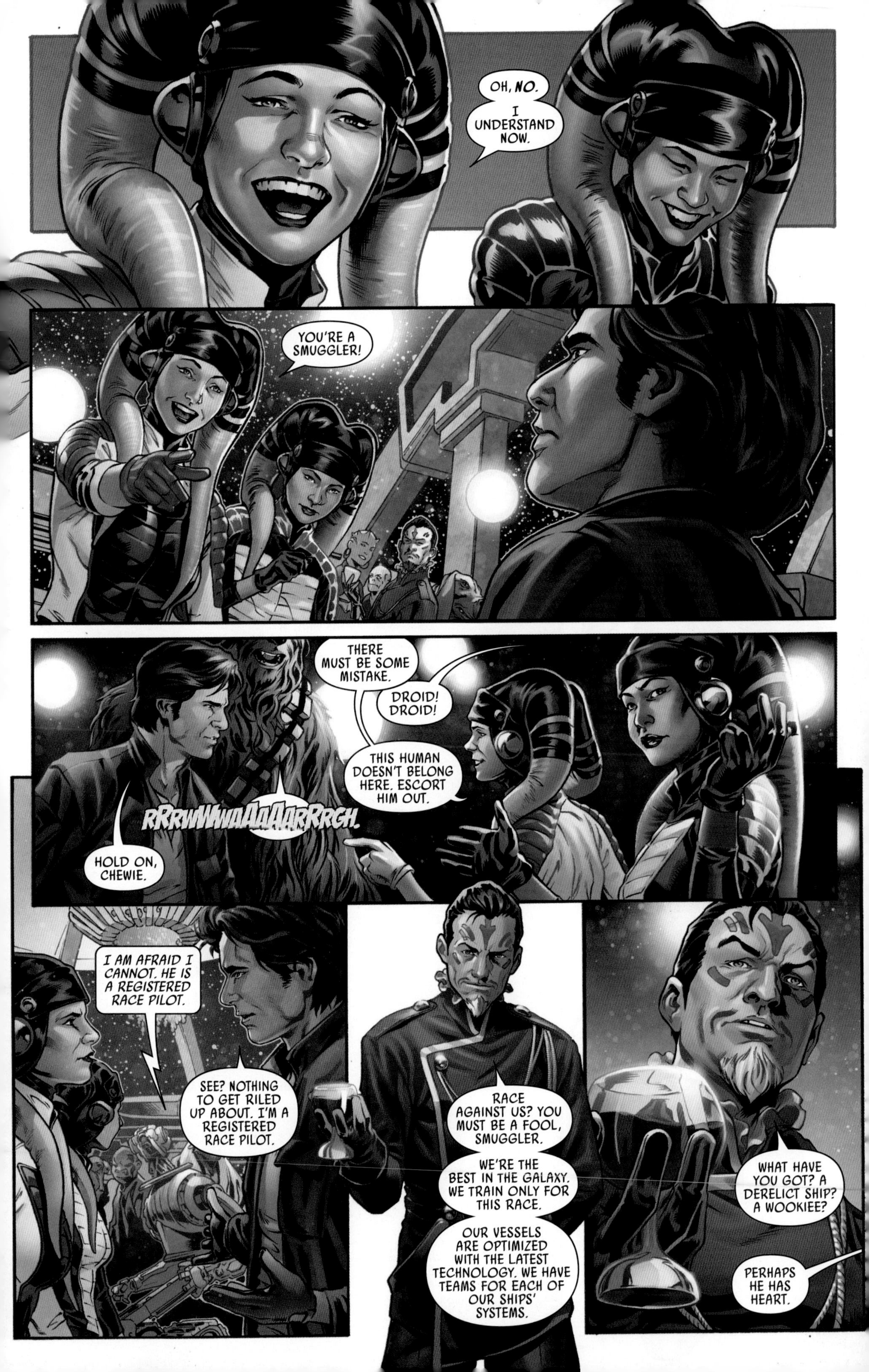
OH, NO.
I UNDERSTAND NOW.
YOU'RE A SMUGGLER!
THERE MUST BE SOME MISTAKE.
DROID! DROID!
THIS HUMAN DOESN'T BELONG HERE. ESCORT HIM OUT.
RRRWWWWAAAAARRRGH.
HOLD ON, CHEWIE.
I AM AFRAID I CANNOT. HE IS A REGISTERED RACE PILOT.
SEE? NOTHING TO GET RILED UP ABOUT. I'M A REGISTERED RACE PILOT.
RACE AGAINST US? YOU MUST BE A FOOL, SMUGGLER.
WE'RE THE BEST IN THE GALAXY. WE TRAIN ONLY FOR THIS RACE.
OUR VESSELS ARE OPTIMIZED WITH THE LATEST TECHNOLOGY. WE HAVE TEAMS FOR EACH OF OUR SHIPS' SYSTEMS.
WHAT HAVE YOU GOT? A DERELICT SHIP? A WOOKIEE?
PERHAPS HE HAS HEART.

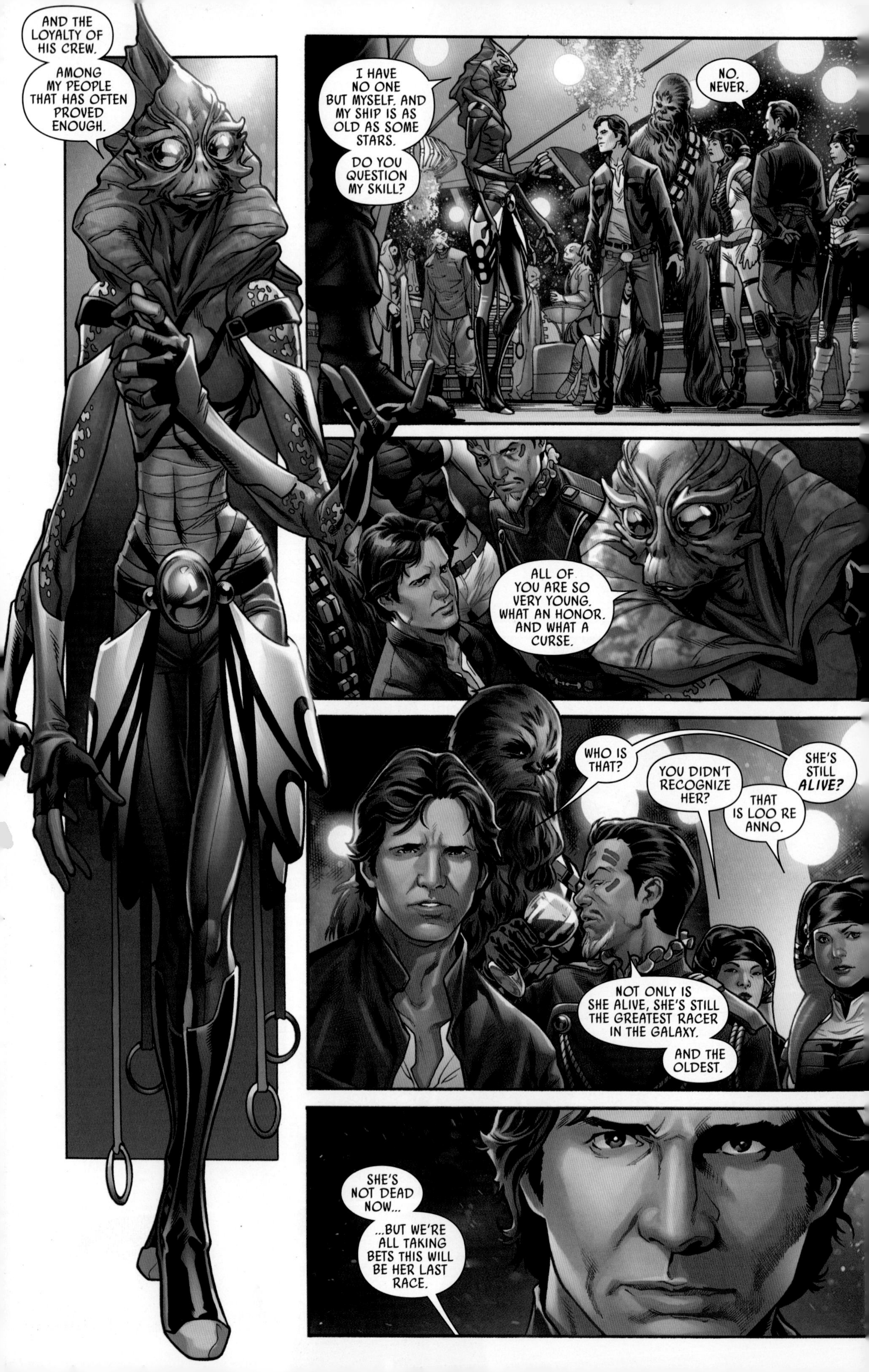
AND THE LOYALTY OF HIS CREW.
AMONG MY PEOPLE THAT HAS OFTEN PROVED ENOUGH.
I HAVE NO ONE BUT MYSELF, AND MY SHIP IS AS OLD AS SOME STARS.
DO YOU QUESTION MY SKILL?
NO. NEVER.
ALL OF YOU ARE SO VERY YOUNG. WHAT AN HONOR. AND WHAT A CURSE.
WHO IS THAT?
YOU DIDN'T RECOGNIZE HER?
SHE'S STILL ALIVE?
THAT IS LOO RE ANNO.
NOT ONLY IS SHE ALIVE, SHE'S STILL THE GREATEST RACER IN THE GALAXY.
AND THE OLDEST.
SHE'S NOT DEAD NOW...
...BUT WE'RE ALL TAKING BETS THIS WILL BE HER LAST RACE.

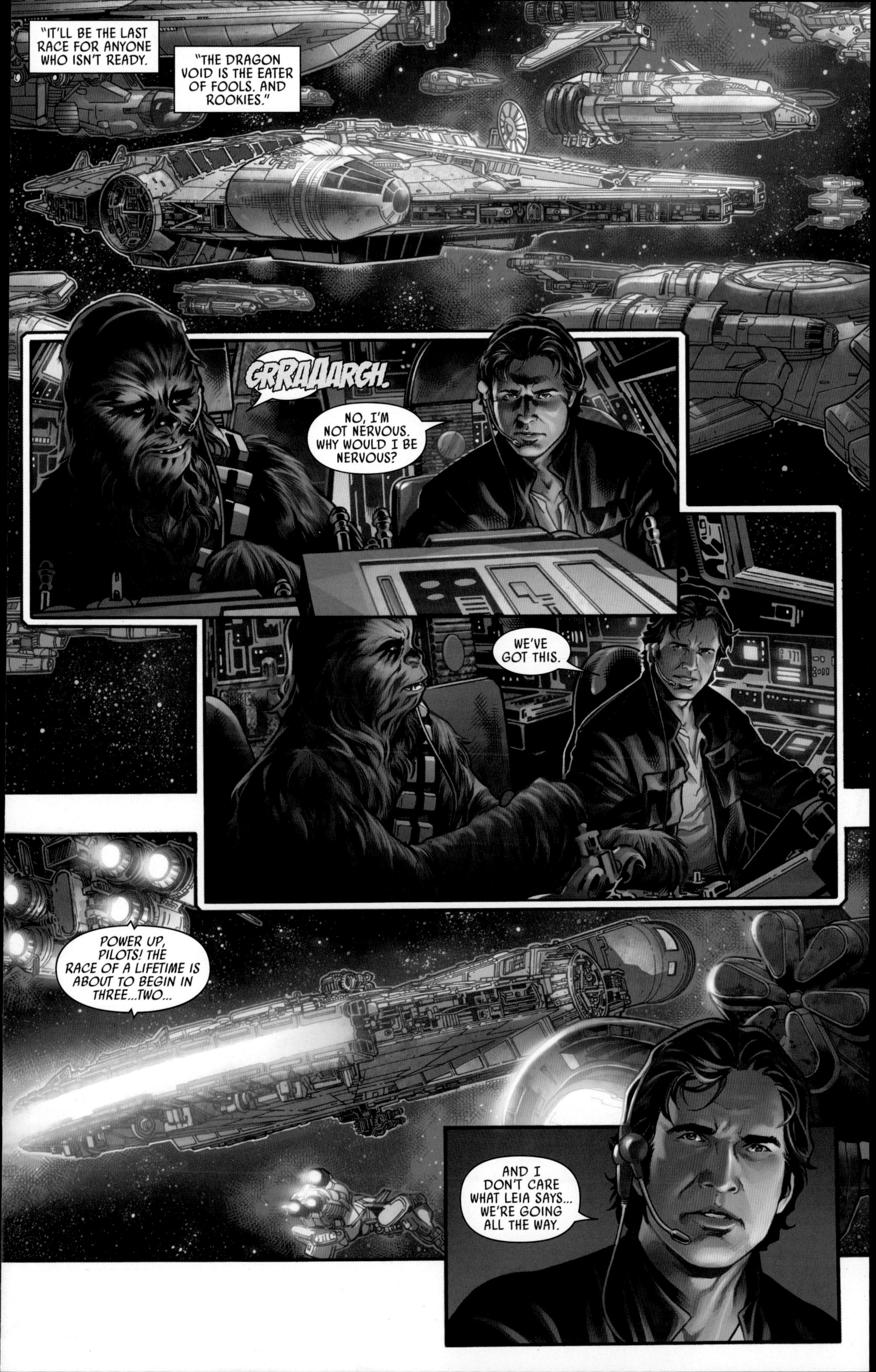
"IT'LL BE THE LAST RACE FOR ANYONE WHO ISN'T READY.
"THE DRAGON VOID IS THE EATER OF FOOLS. AND ROOKIES."
GRRAAARGH.
NO, I'M NOT NERVOUS. WHY WOULD I BE NERVOUS?
WE'VE GOT THIS.
POWER UP, PILOTS! THE RACE OF A LIFETIME IS ABOUT TO BEGIN IN THREE...TWO...
AND I DON'T CARE WHAT LEIA SAYS... WE'RE GOING ALL THE WAY.

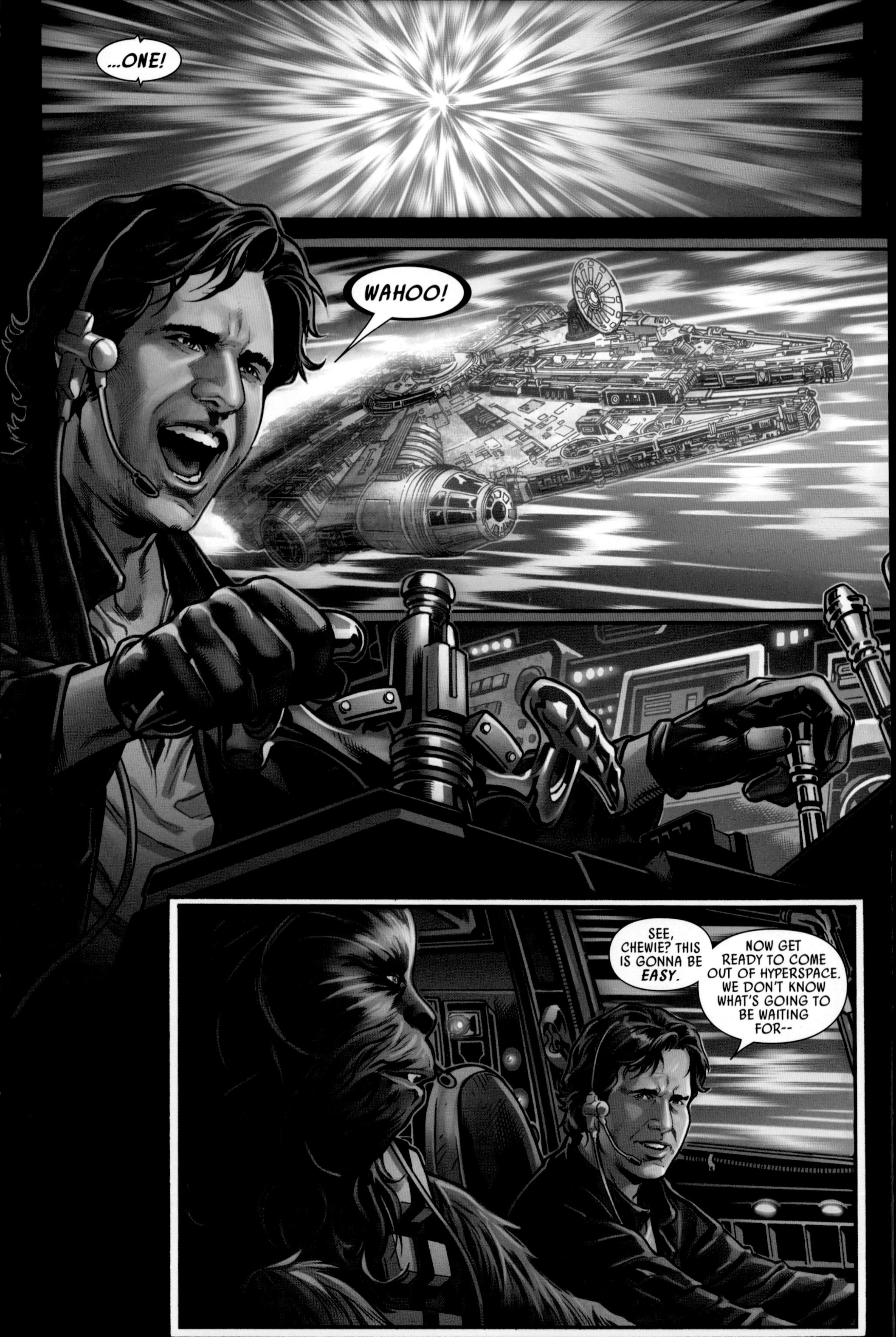
...ONE!
WAHOO!
SEE, CHEWIE? THIS IS GONNA BE EASY.
NOW GET READY TO COME OUT OF HYPERSPACE. WE DON'T KNOW WHAT'S GOING TO BE WAITING FOR--

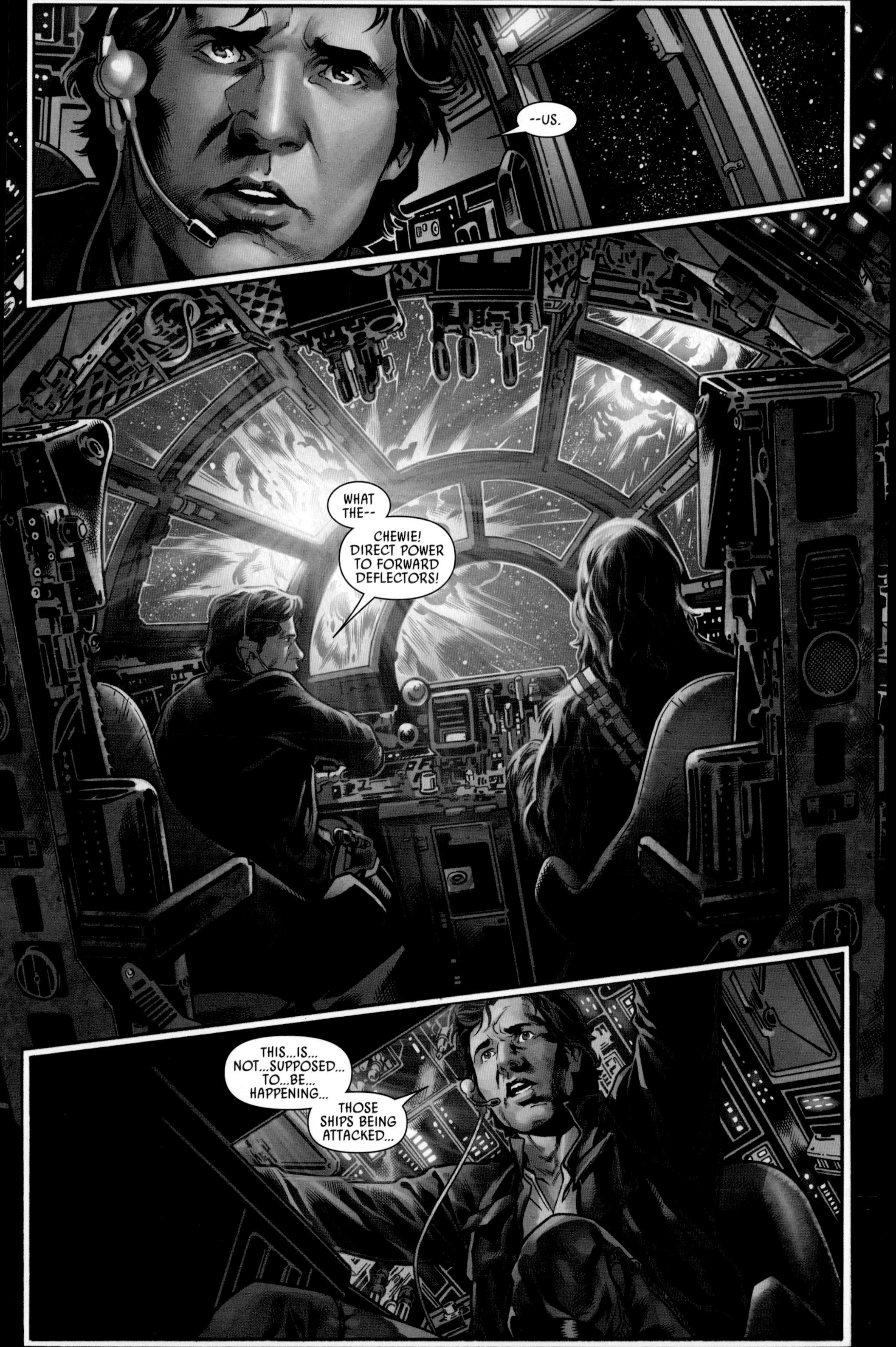
--US.
WHAT THE--
CHEWIE! DIRECT POWER TO FORWARD DEFLECTORS!
THIS...IS... NOT...SUPPOSED... TO...BE... HAPPENING...
THOSE SHIPS BEING ATTACKED...

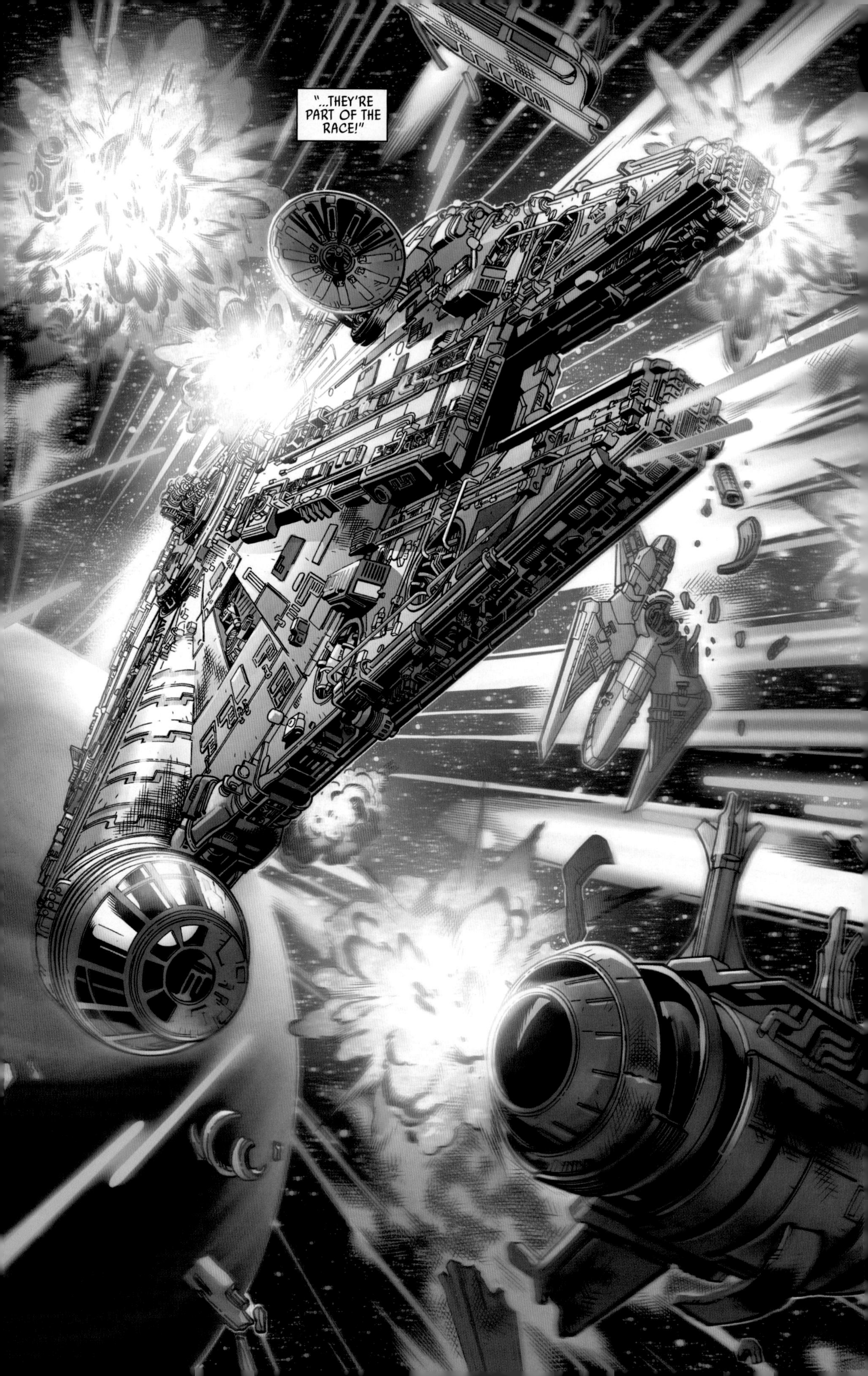
"...THEY'RE PART OF THE RACE!"

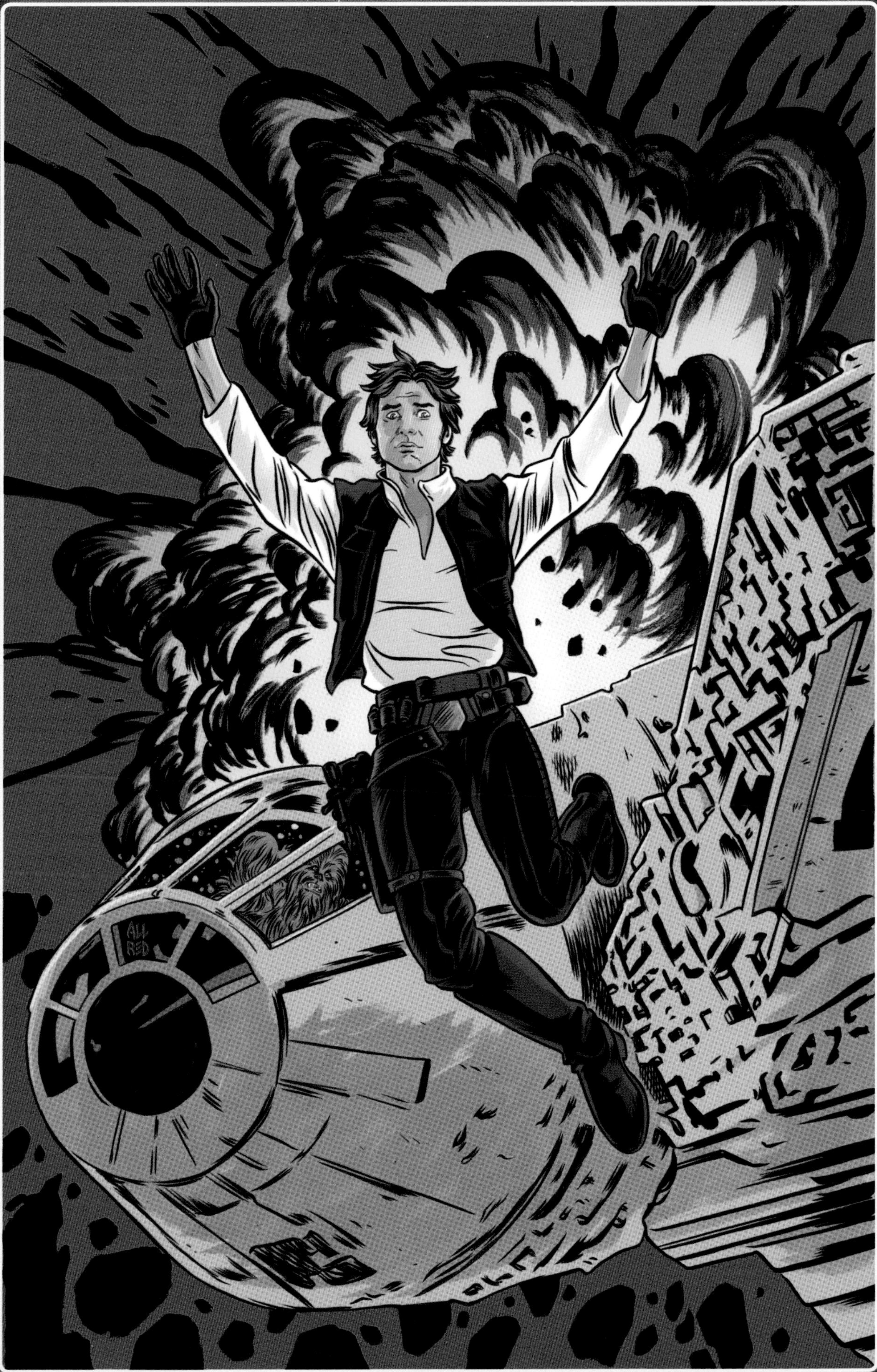

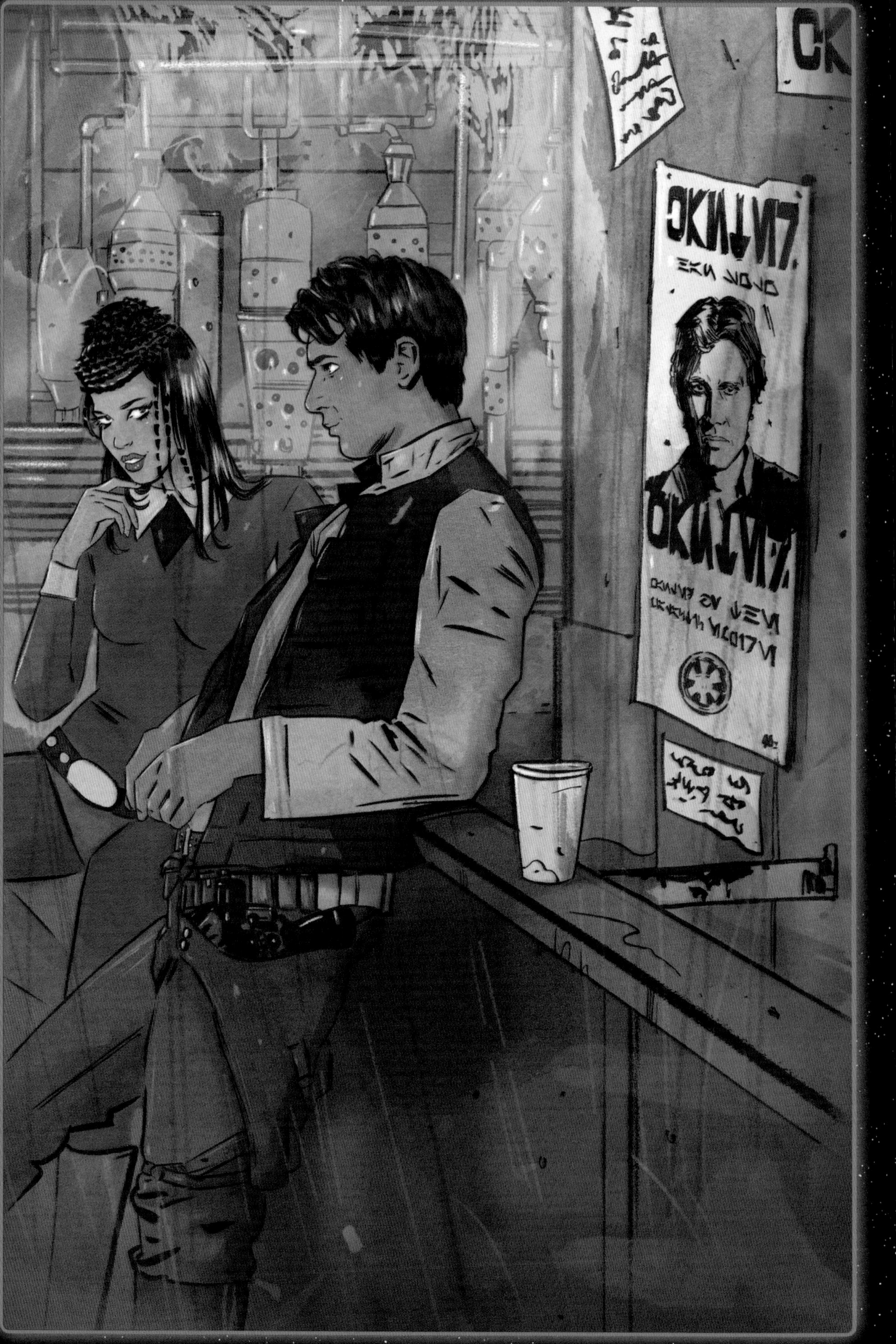

HAN SOLO 2

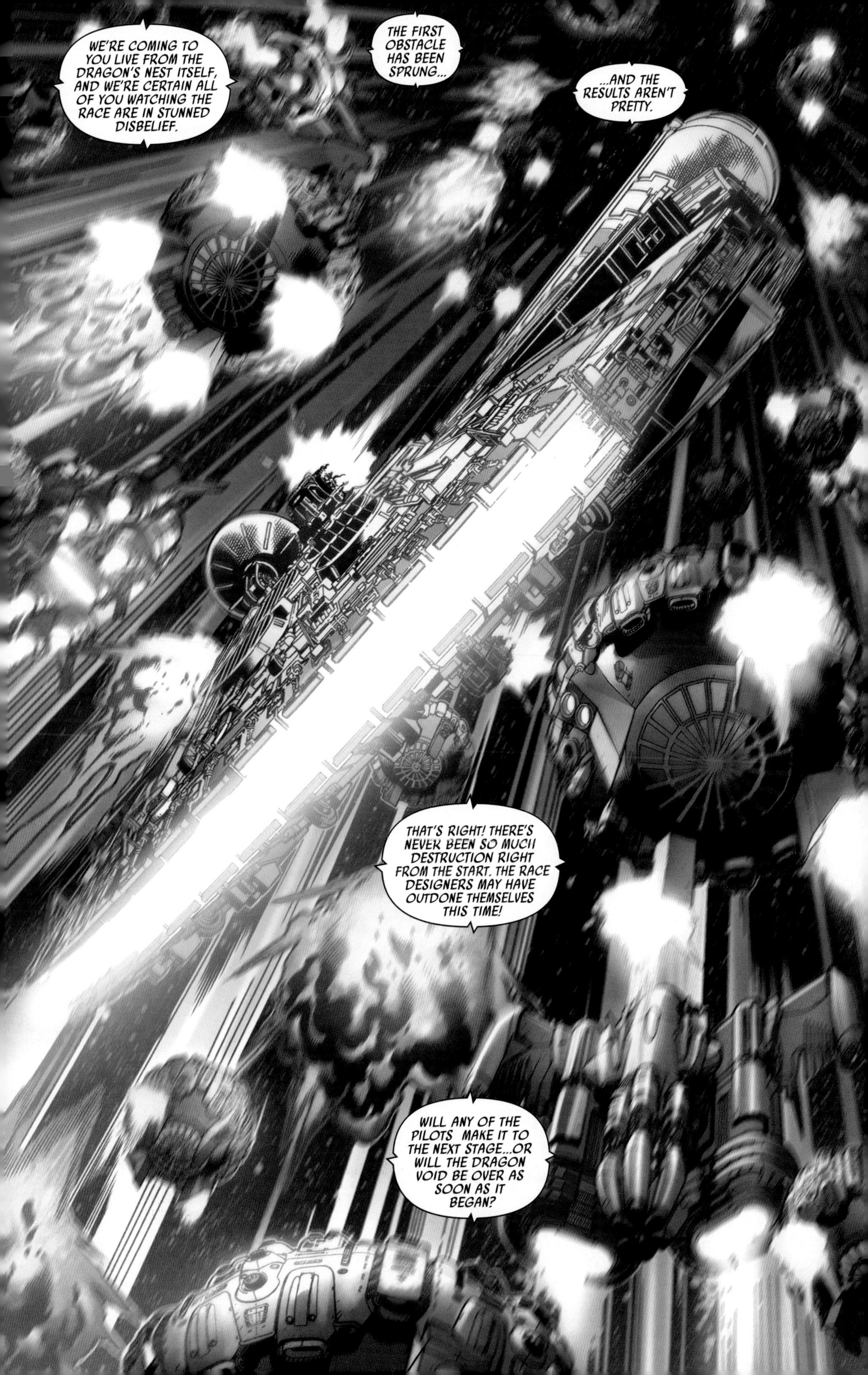
WE'RE COMING TO YOU LIVE FROM THE DRAGON'S NEST ITSELF, AND WE'RE CERTAIN ALL OF YOU WATCHING THE RACE ARE IN STUNNED DISBELIEF.
THE FIRST OBSTACLE HAS BEEN SPRUNG...
...AND THE RESULTS AREN'T PRETTY.
THAT'S RIGHT! THERE'S NEVER BEEN SO MUCH DESTRUCTION RIGHT FROM THE START. THE RACE DESIGNERS MAY HAVE OUTDONE THEMSELVES THIS TIME!
WILL ANY OF THE PILOTS MAKE IT TO THE NEXT STAGE...OR WILL THE DRAGON VOID BE OVER AS SOON AS IT BEGAN?

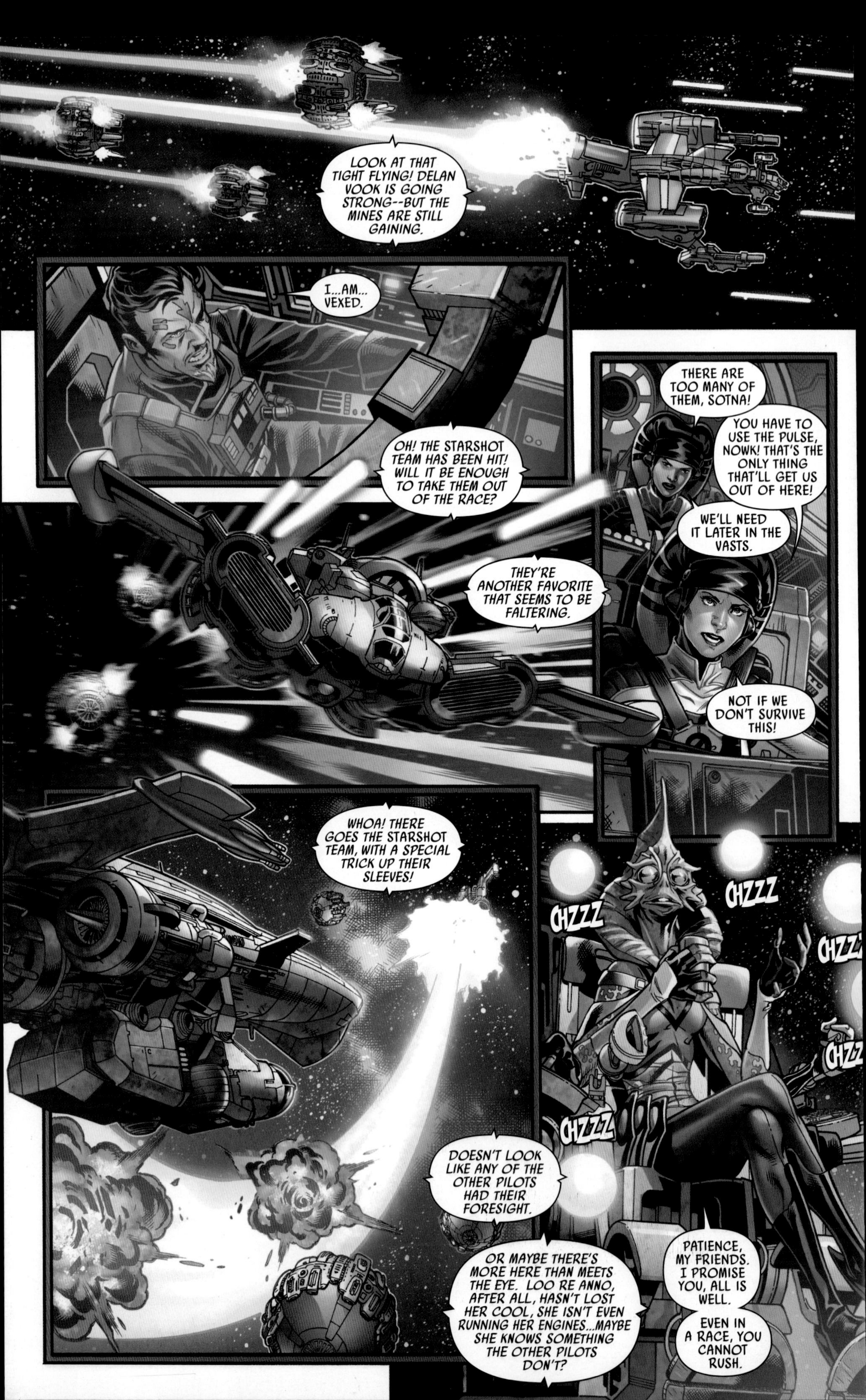
LOOK AT THAT TIGHT FLYING! DELAN VOOK IS GOING STRONG--BUT THE MINES ARE STILL GAINING.
I...AM... VEXED.
OH! THE STARSHOT TEAM HAS BEEN HIT! WILL IT BE ENOUGH TO TAKE THEM OUT OF THE RACE?
THEY'RE ANOTHER FAVORITE THAT SEEMS TO BE FALTERING.
THERE ARE TOO MANY OF THEM, SOTNA!
YOU HAVE TO USE THE PULSE, NOWK! THAT'S THE ONLY THING THAT'LL GET US OUT OF HERE!
WE'LL NEED IT LATER IN THE VASTS.
NOT IF WE DON'T SURVIVE THIS!
WHOA! THERE GOES THE STARSHOT TEAM, WITH A SPECIAL TRICK UP THEIR SLEEVES!
DOESN'T LOOK LIKE ANY OF THE OTHER PILOTS HAD THEIR FORESIGHT.
OR MAYBE THERE'S MORE HERE THAN MEETS THE EYE. LOO RE ANNO, AFTER ALL, HASN'T LOST HER COOL, SHE ISN'T EVEN RUNNING HER ENGINES...MAYBE SHE KNOWS SOMETHING THE OTHER PILOTS DON'T?
CHZZZ
CHZZZ
CHZZZ
CHZZZ
CHZZZ
PATIENCE, MY FRIENDS. I PROMISE YOU, ALL IS WELL.
EVEN IN A RACE, YOU CANNOT RUSH.

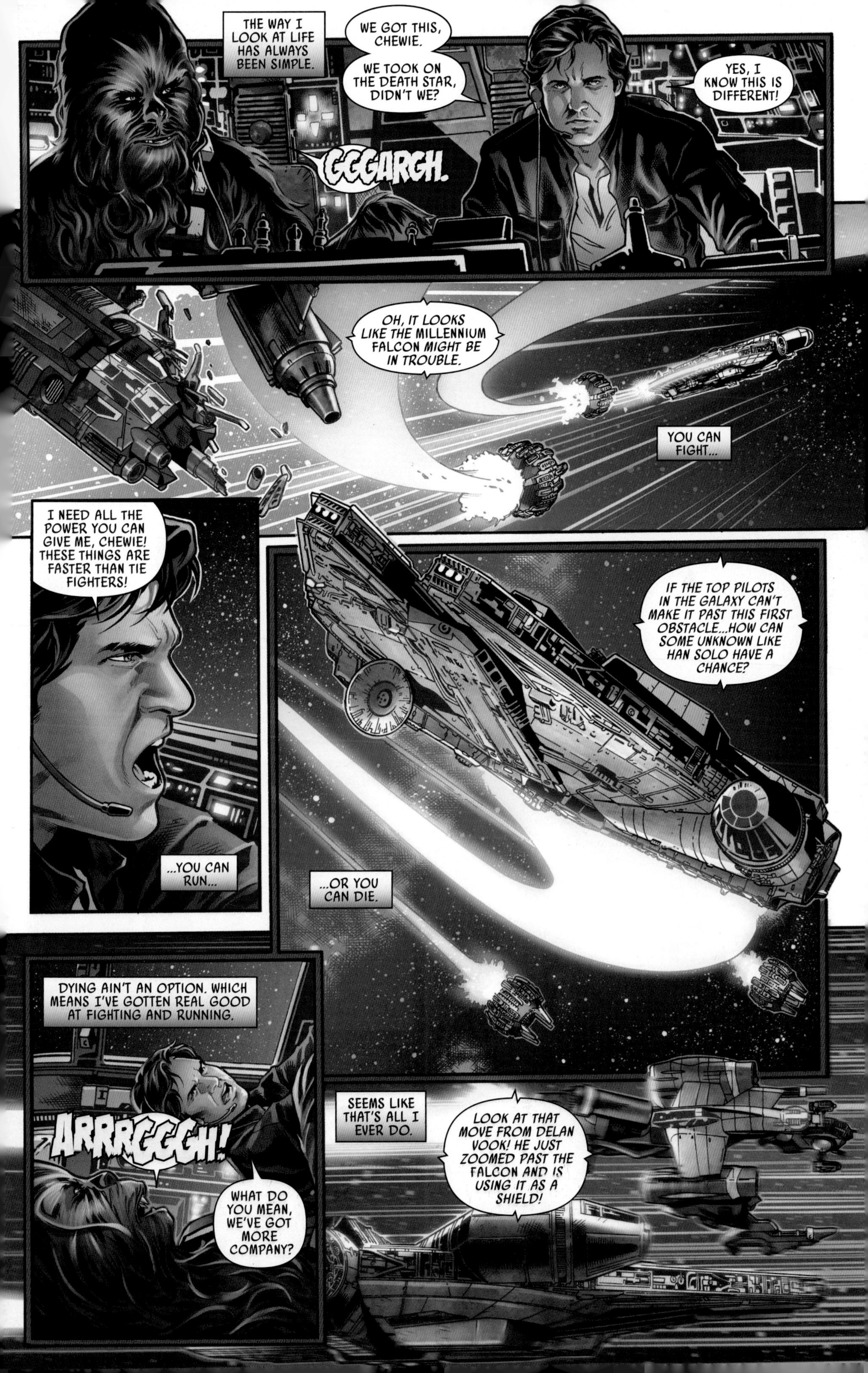

THE WAY I LOOK AT LIFE HAS ALWAYS BEEN SIMPLE.
WE GOT THIS, CHEWIE.
WE TOOK ON THE DEATH STAR, DIDN'T WE?
GGGARGH.
YES, I KNOW THIS IS DIFFERENT!
OH, IT LOOKS LIKE THE MILLENNIUM FALCON MIGHT BE IN TROUBLE.
YOU CAN FIGHT...
I NEED ALL THE POWER YOU CAN GIVE ME, CHEWIE! THESE THINGS ARE FASTER THAN TIE FIGHTERS!
...YOU CAN RUN...
IF THE TOP PILOTS IN THE GALAXY CAN'T MAKE IT PAST THIS FIRST OBSTACLE...HOW CAN SOME UNKNOWN LIKE HAN SOLO HAVE A CHANCE?
...OR YOU CAN DIE.
DYING AIN'T AN OPTION. WHICH MEANS I'VE GOTTEN REAL GOOD AT FIGHTING AND RUNNING.
ARRRGGGH!
WHAT DO YOU MEAN, WE'VE GOT MORE COMPANY?
SEEMS LIKE THAT'S ALL I EVER DO.
LOOK AT THAT MOVE FROM DELAN VOOK! HE JUST ZOOMED PAST THE FALCON AND IS USING IT AS A SHIELD!

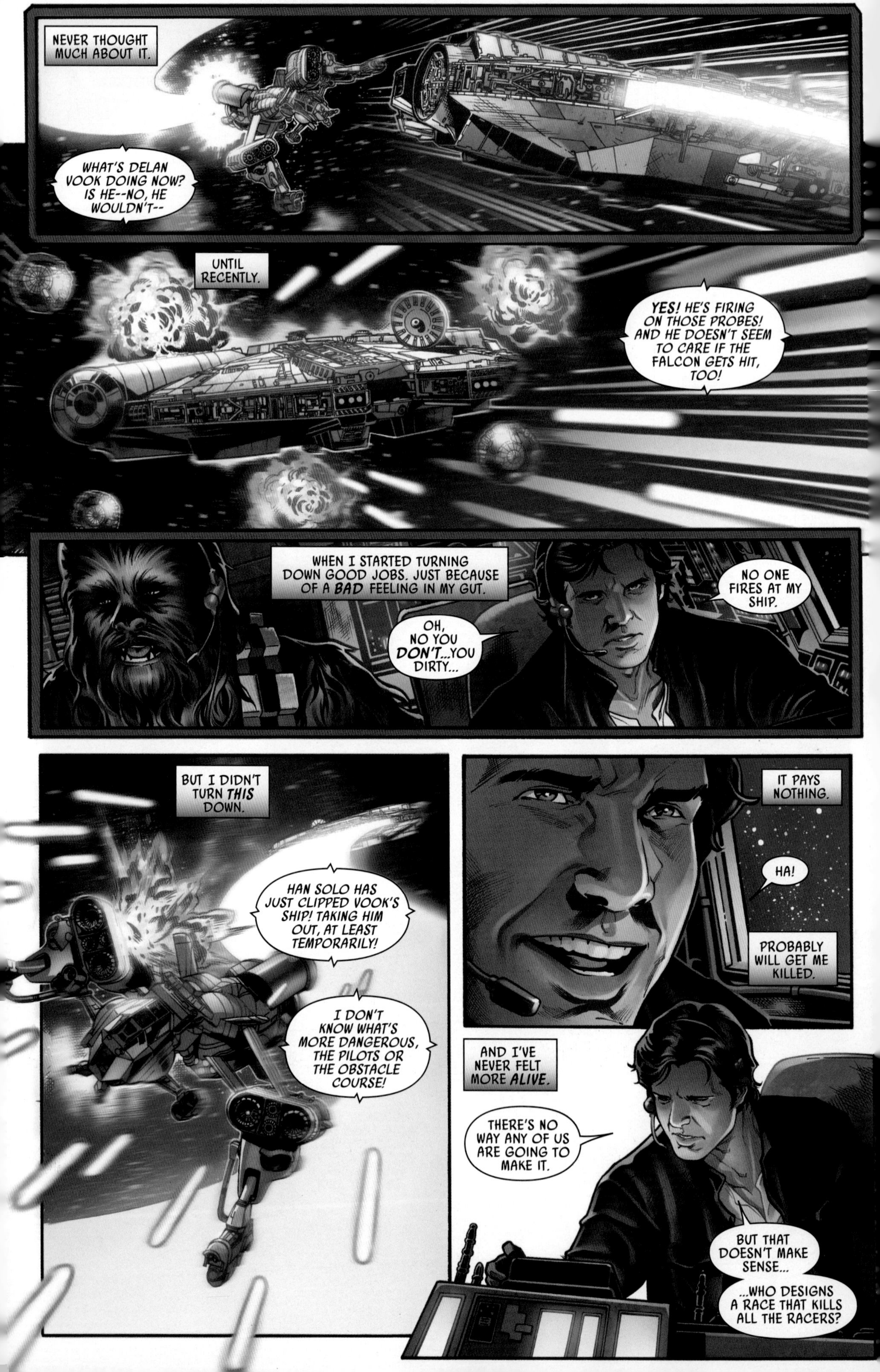

NEVER THOUGHT MUCH ABOUT IT.
WHAT'S DELAN VOOK DOING NOW? IS HE--NO, HE WOULDN'T--
UNTIL RECENTLY.
YES! HE'S FIRING ON THOSE PROBES! AND HE DOESN'T SEEM TO CARE IF THE FALCON GETS HIT, TOO!
WHEN I STARTED TURNING DOWN GOOD JOBS. JUST BECAUSE OF A BAD FEELING IN MY GUT.
NO ONE FIRES AT MY SHIP.
OH, NO YOU DON'T...YOU DIRTY...
BUT I DIDN'T TURN THIS DOWN.
HAN SOLO HAS JUST CLIPPED VOOK'S SHIP! TAKING HIM OUT, AT LEAST TEMPORARILY!
I DON'T KNOW WHAT'S MORE DANGEROUS, THE PILOTS OR THE OBSTACLE COURSE!
IT PAYS NOTHING.
HA!
PROBABLY WILL GET ME KILLED.
AND I'VE NEVER FELT MORE ALIVE.
THERE'S NO WAY ANY OF US ARE GOING TO MAKE IT.
BUT THAT DOESN'T MAKE SENSE...
...WHO DESIGNS A RACE THAT KILLS ALL THE RACERS?

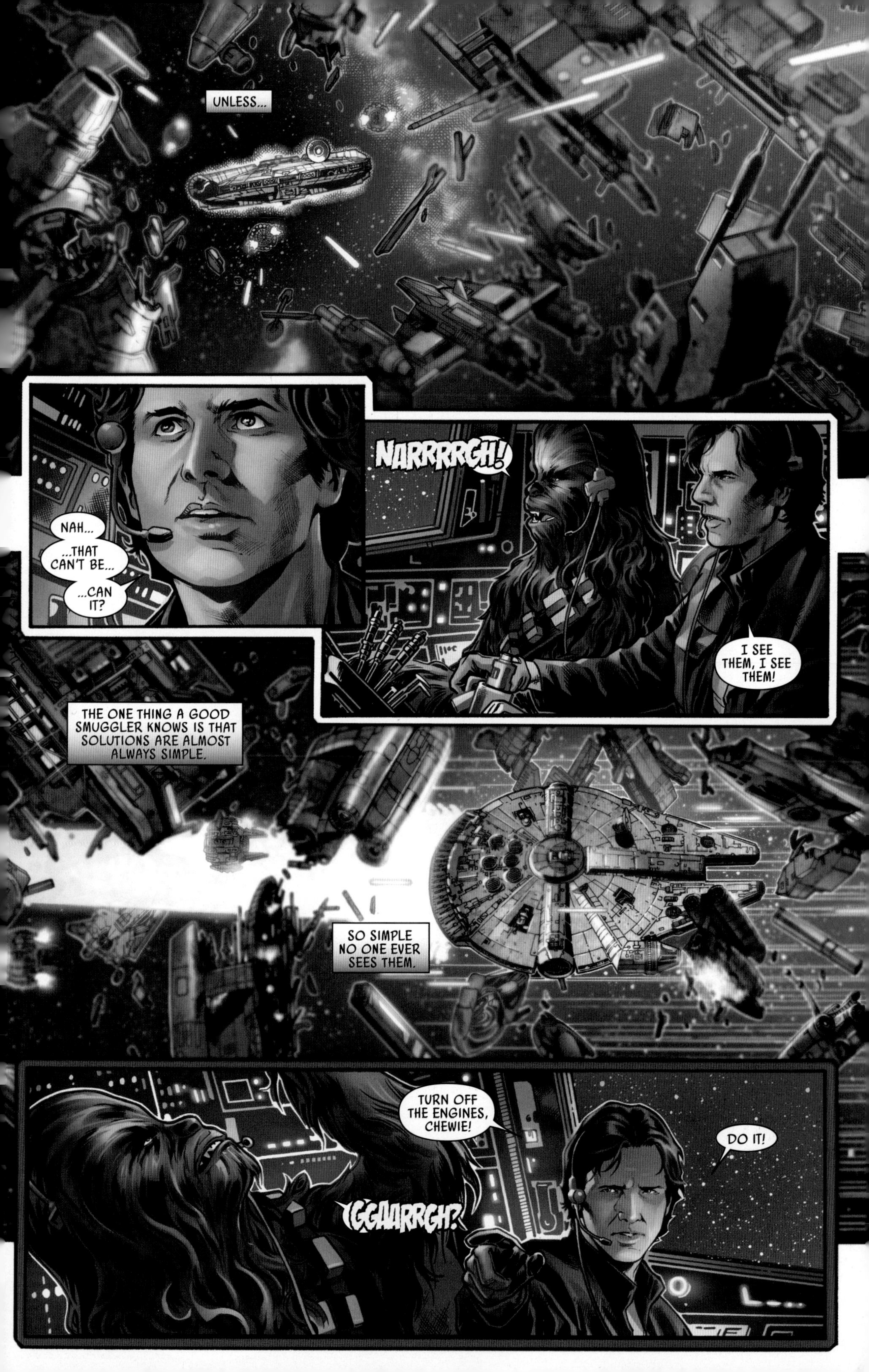
UNLESS...
NAH...
...THAT CAN'T BE...
...CAN IT?
NARRRRGH!
I SEE THEM, I SEE THEM!
THE ONE THING A GOOD SMUGGLER KNOWS IS THAT SOLUTIONS ARE ALMOST ALWAYS SIMPLE.
SO SIMPLE NO ONE EVER SEES THEM.
TURN OFF THE ENGINES, CHEWIE!
DO IT!
IGGAARRGH?

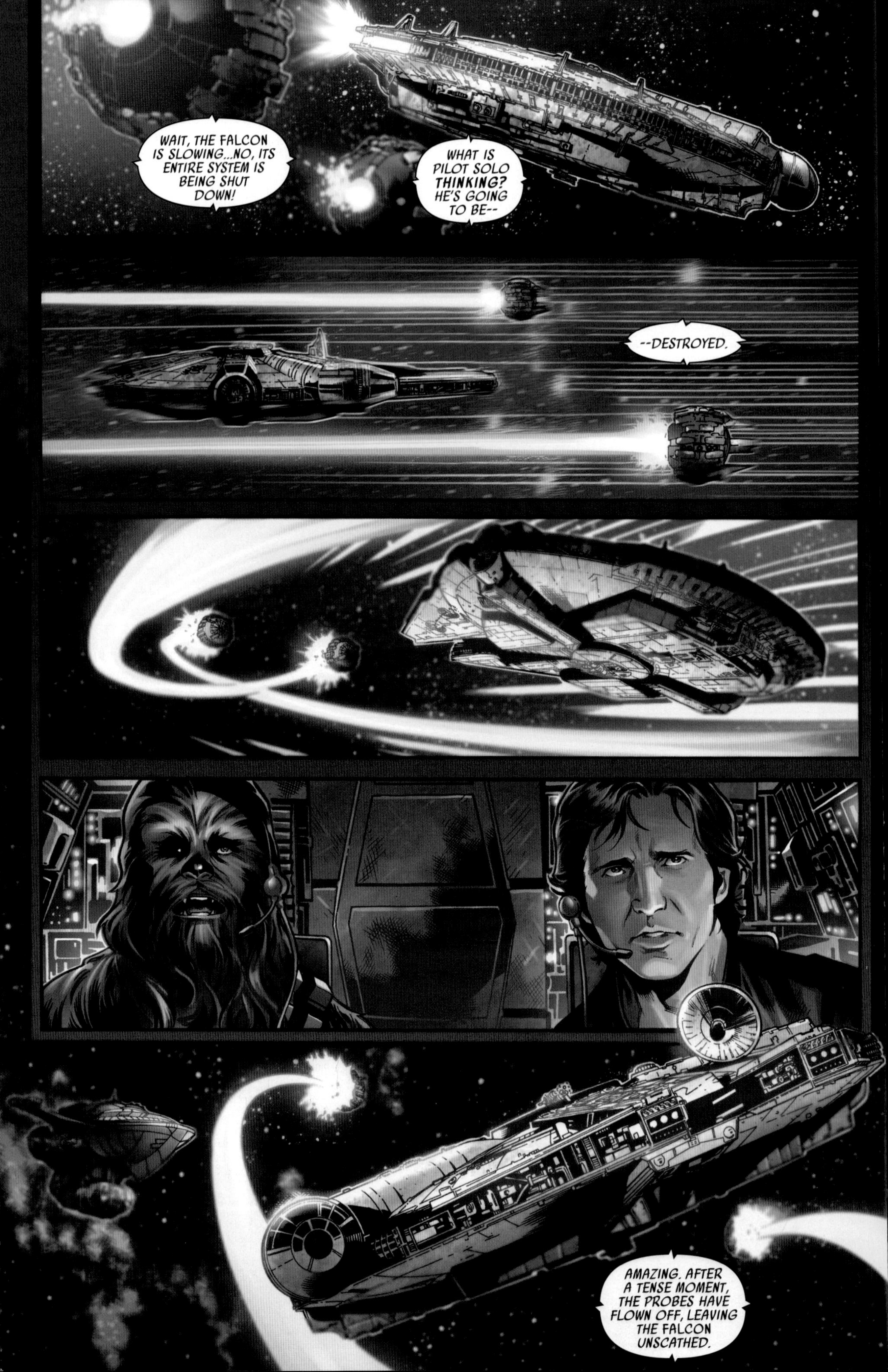
WAIT, THE FALCON IS SLOWING...NO, ITS ENTIRE SYSTEM IS BEING SHUT DOWN!
WHAT IS PILOT SOLO THINKING? HE'S GOING TO BE--
--DESTROYED.
AMAZING. AFTER A TENSE MOMENT, THE PROBES HAVE FLOWN OFF, LEAVING THE FALCON UNSCATHED.

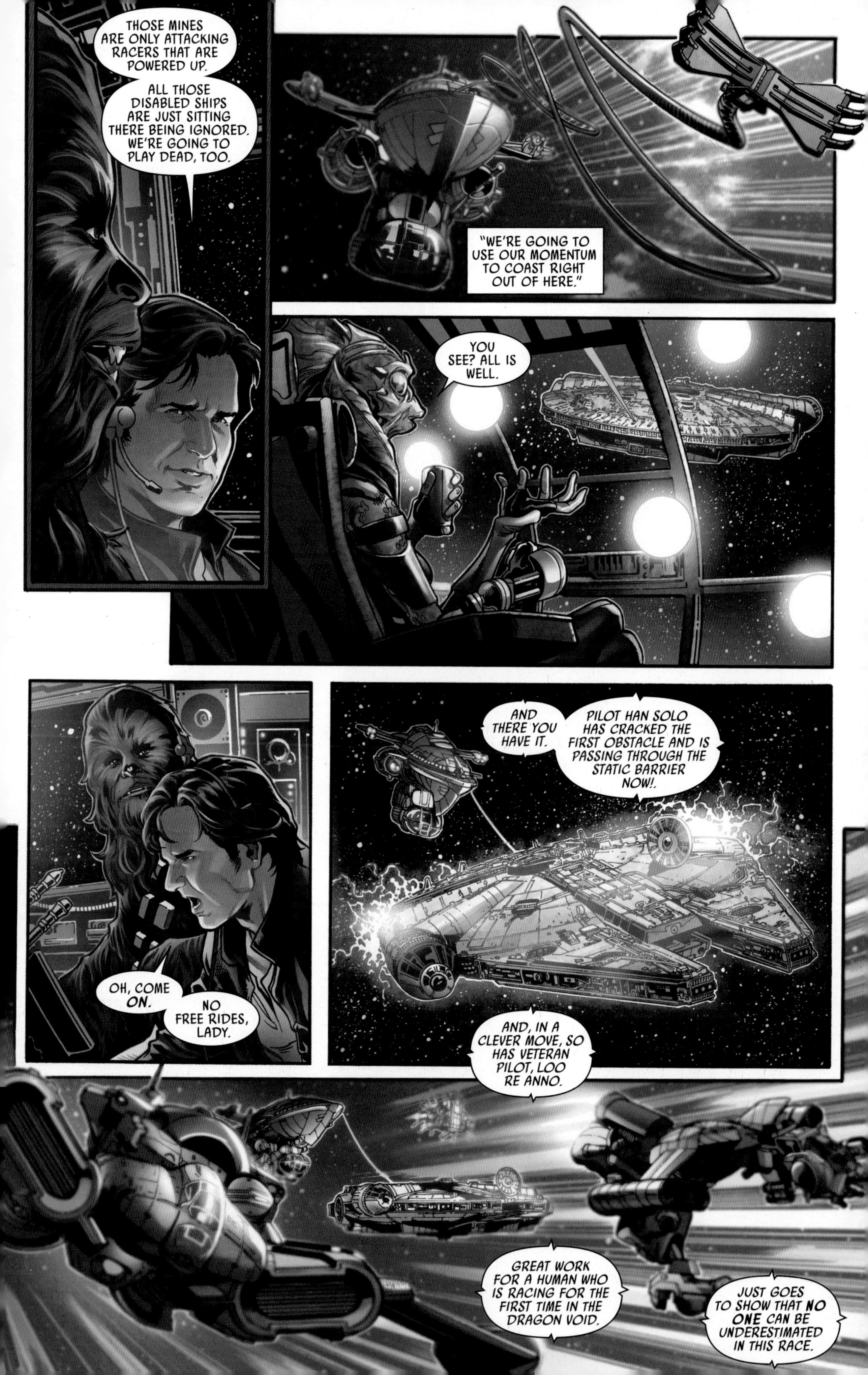
THOSE MINES ARE ONLY ATTACKING RACERS THAT ARE POWERED UP.
ALL THOSE DISABLED SHIPS ARE JUST SITTING THERE BEING IGNORED. WE'RE GOING TO PLAY DEAD, TOO.
"WE'RE GOING TO USE OUR MOMENTUM TO COAST RIGHT OUT OF HERE."
YOU SEE? ALL IS WELL.
OH, COME ON.
NO FREE RIDES, LADY.
AND THERE YOU HAVE IT.
PILOT HAN SOLO HAS CRACKED THE FIRST OBSTACLE AND IS PASSING THROUGH THE STATIC BARRIER NOW!.
AND, IN A CLEVER MOVE, SO HAS VETERAN PILOT, LOO RE ANNO.
GREAT WORK FOR A HUMAN WHO IS RACING FOR THE FIRST TIME IN THE DRAGON VOID.
JUST GOES TO SHOW THAT NO ONE CAN BE UNDERESTIMATED IN THIS RACE.

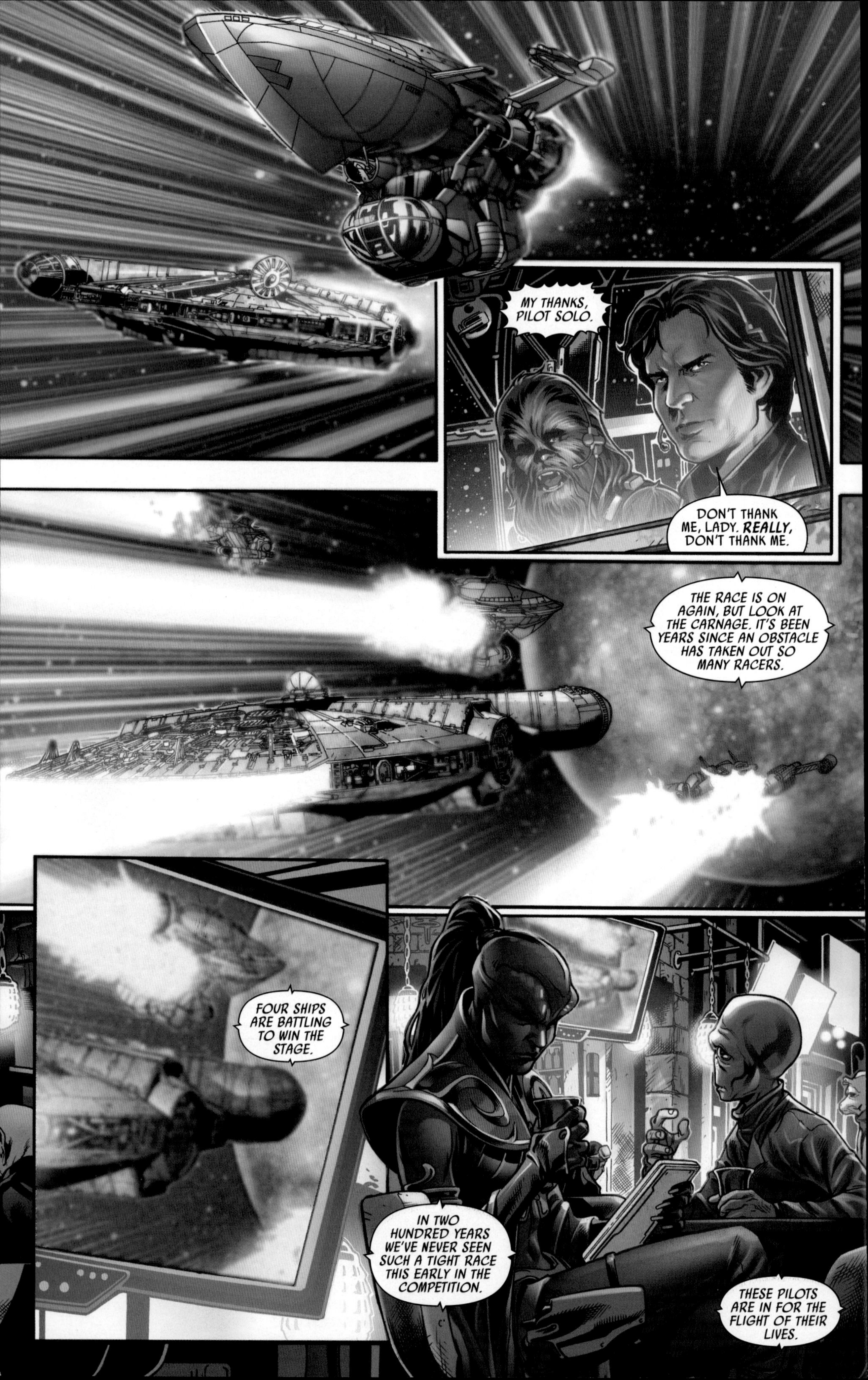
MY THANKS, PILOT SOLO.
DON'T THANK ME, LADY. REALLY, DON'T THANK ME.
THE RACE IS ON AGAIN, BUT LOOK AT THE CARNAGE. IT'S BEEN YEARS SINCE AN OBSTACLE HAS TAKEN OUT SO MANY RACERS.
FOUR SHIPS ARE BATTLING TO WIN THE STAGE.
IN TWO HUNDRED YEARS WE'VE NEVER SEEN SUCH A TIGHT RACE THIS EARLY IN THE COMPETITION.
THESE PILOTS ARE IN FOR THE FLIGHT OF THEIR LIVES.

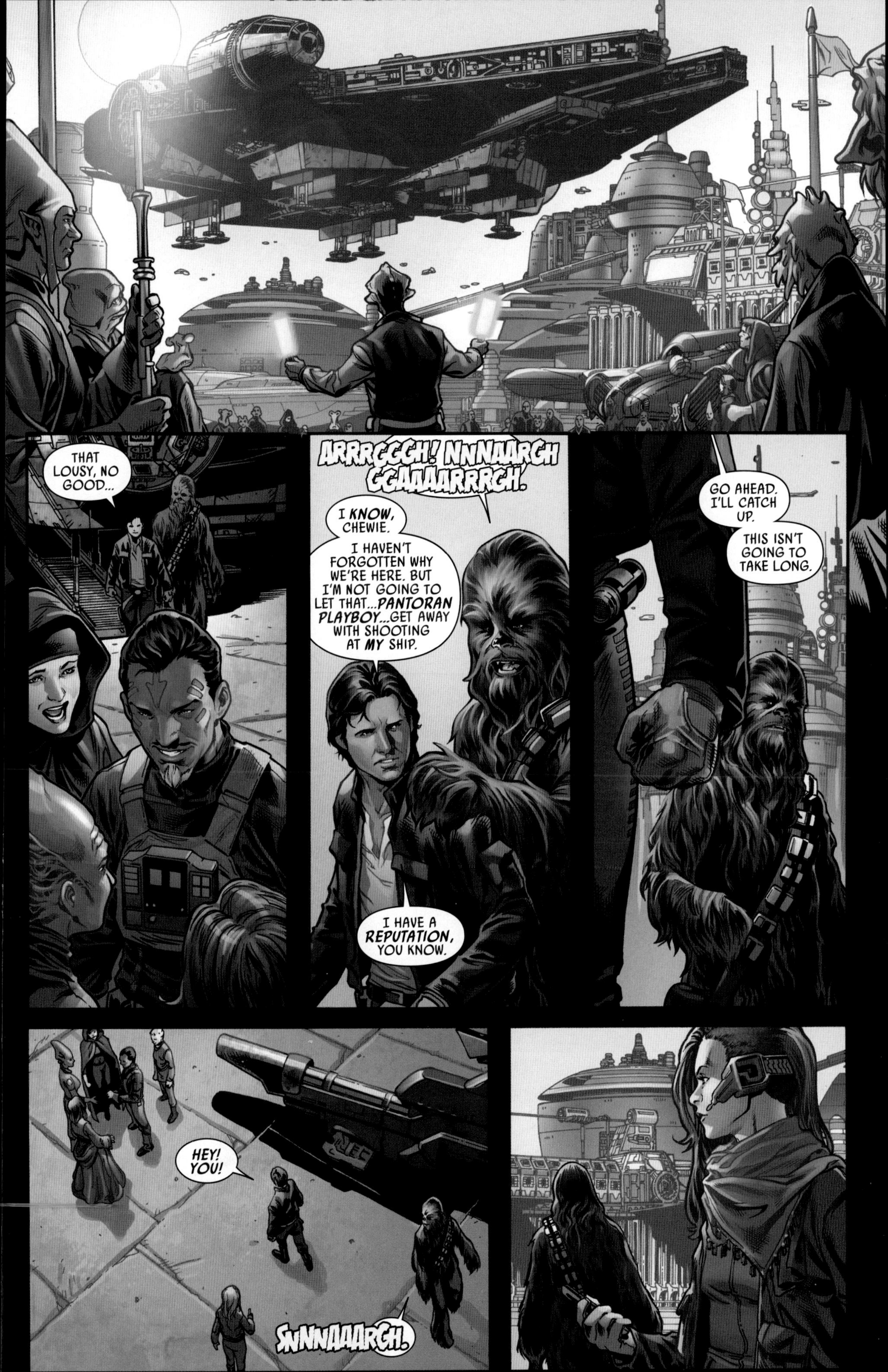
THAT LOUSY, NO GOOD...
ARRRGGGH! NNNAARGH GGAAAARRRGH.
I KNOW, CHEWIE.
I HAVEN'T FORGOTTEN WHY WE'RE HERE. BUT I'M NOT GOING TO LET THAT...PANTORAN PLAYBOY...GET AWAY WITH SHOOTING AT MY SHIP.
I HAVE A REPUTATION, YOU KNOW.
GO AHEAD. I'LL CATCH UP.
THIS ISN'T GOING TO TAKE LONG.
HEY! YOU!
SWNNAAARGH.

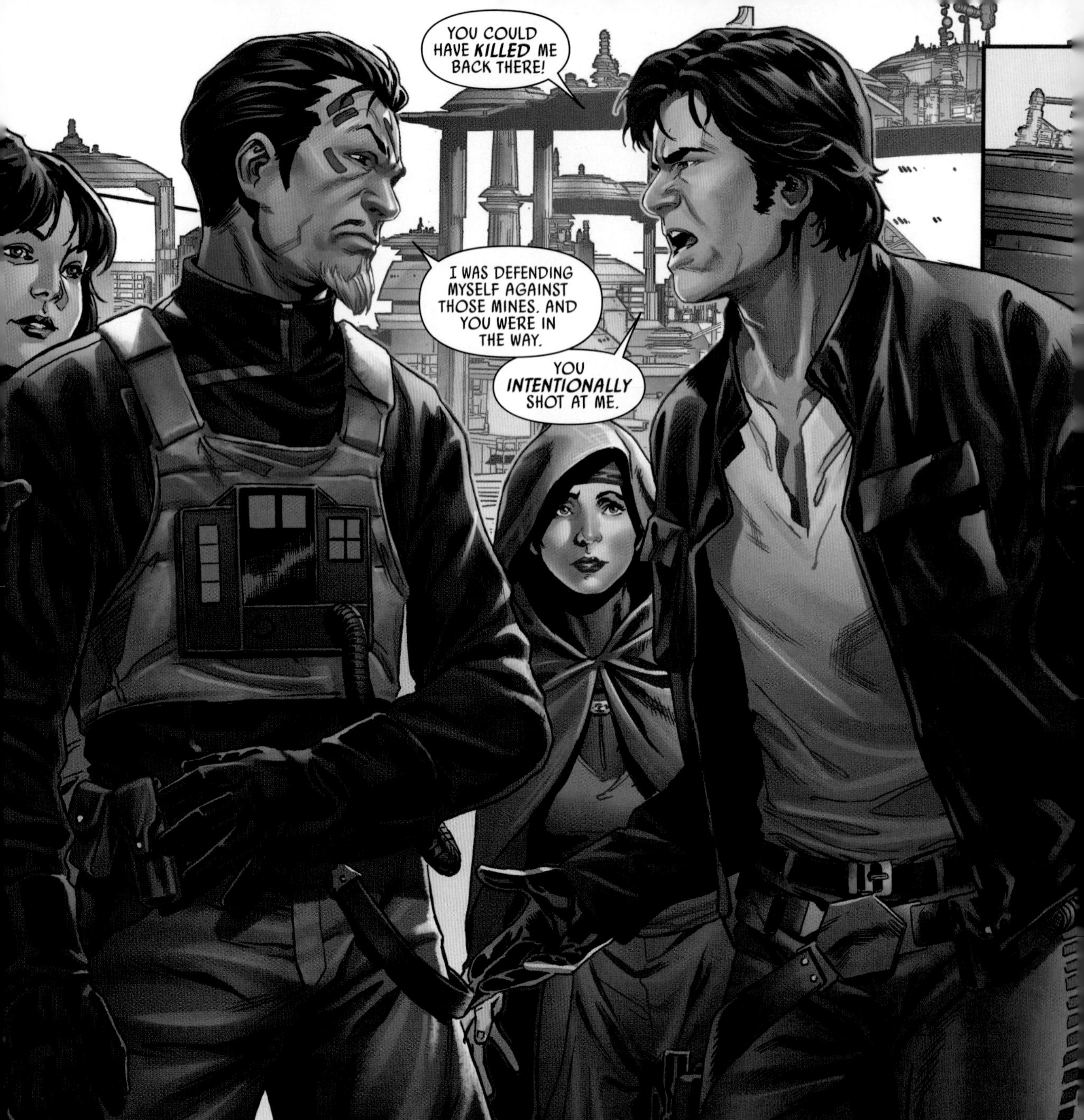
YOU COULD HAVE KILLED ME BACK THERE!
I WAS DEFENDING MYSELF AGAINST THOSE MINES. AND YOU WERE IN THE WAY.
YOU INTENTIONALLY SHOT AT ME.
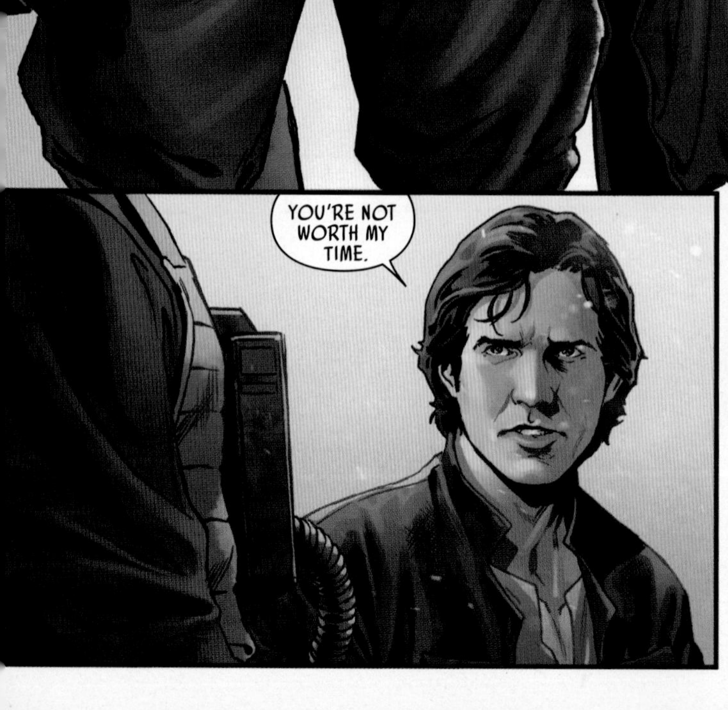
YOU'RE NOT WORTH MY TIME.
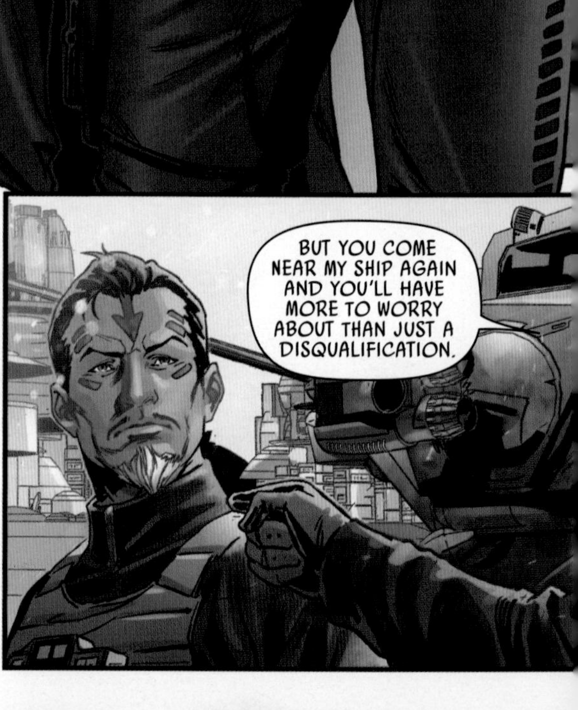
BUT YOU COME NEAR MY SHIP AGAIN AND YOU'LL HAVE MORE TO WORRY ABOUT THAN JUST A DISQUALIFICATION.

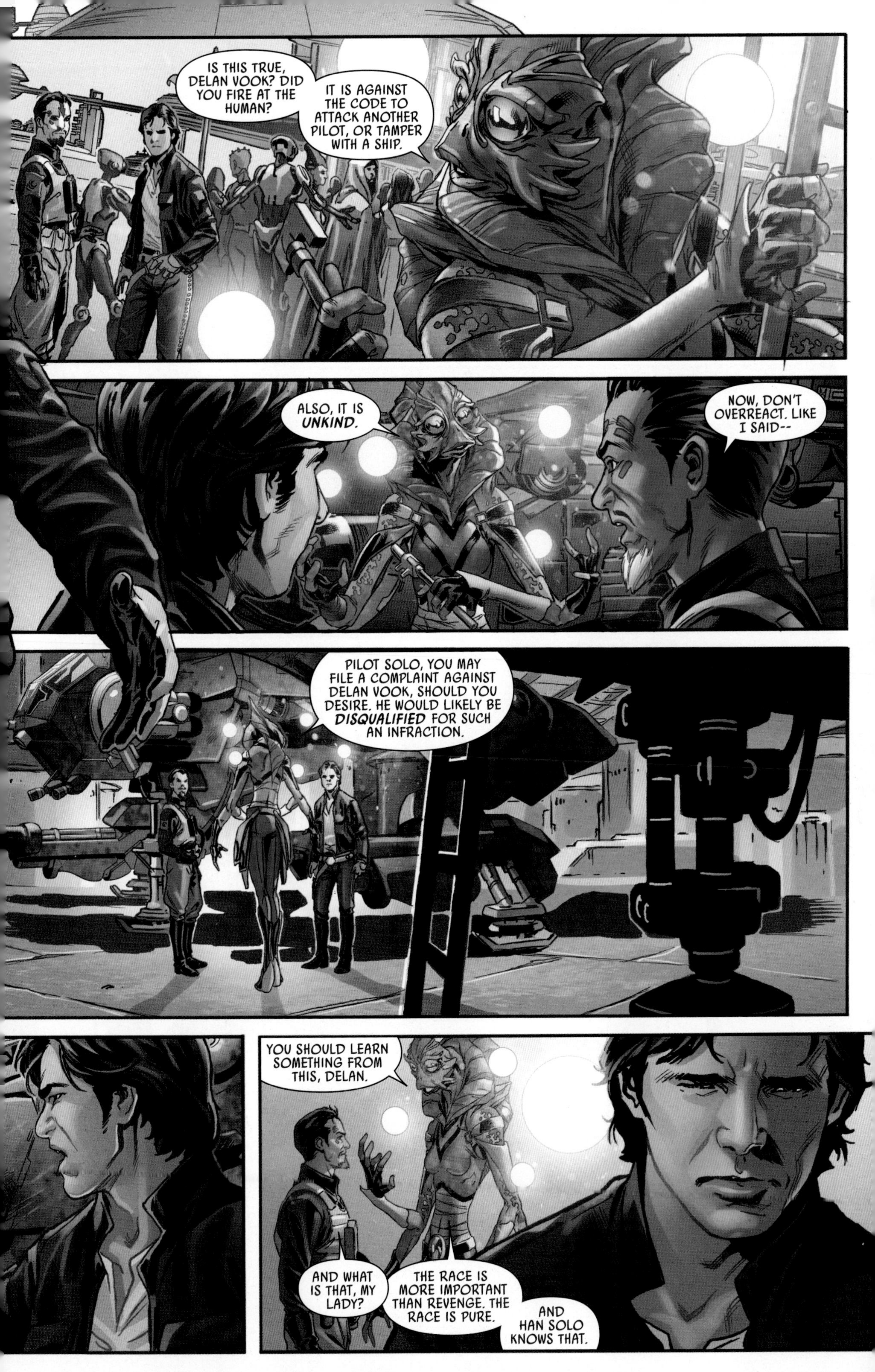
IS THIS TRUE, DELAN VOOK? DID YOU FIRE AT THE HUMAN?
IT IS AGAINST THE CODE TO ATTACK ANOTHER PILOT, OR TAMPER WITH A SHIP.
ALSO, IT IS *UNKIND.*
NOW, DON'T OVERREACT. LIKE I SAID--
PILOT SOLO, YOU MAY FILE A COMPLAINT AGAINST DELAN VOOK, SHOULD YOU DESIRE. HE WOULD LIKELY BE ***DISQUALIFIED*** FOR SUCH AN INFRACTION.
YOU SHOULD LEARN SOMETHING FROM THIS, DELAN.
AND WHAT IS THAT, MY LADY?
THE RACE IS MORE IMPORTANT THAN REVENGE. THE RACE IS PURE.
AND HAN SOLO KNOWS THAT.

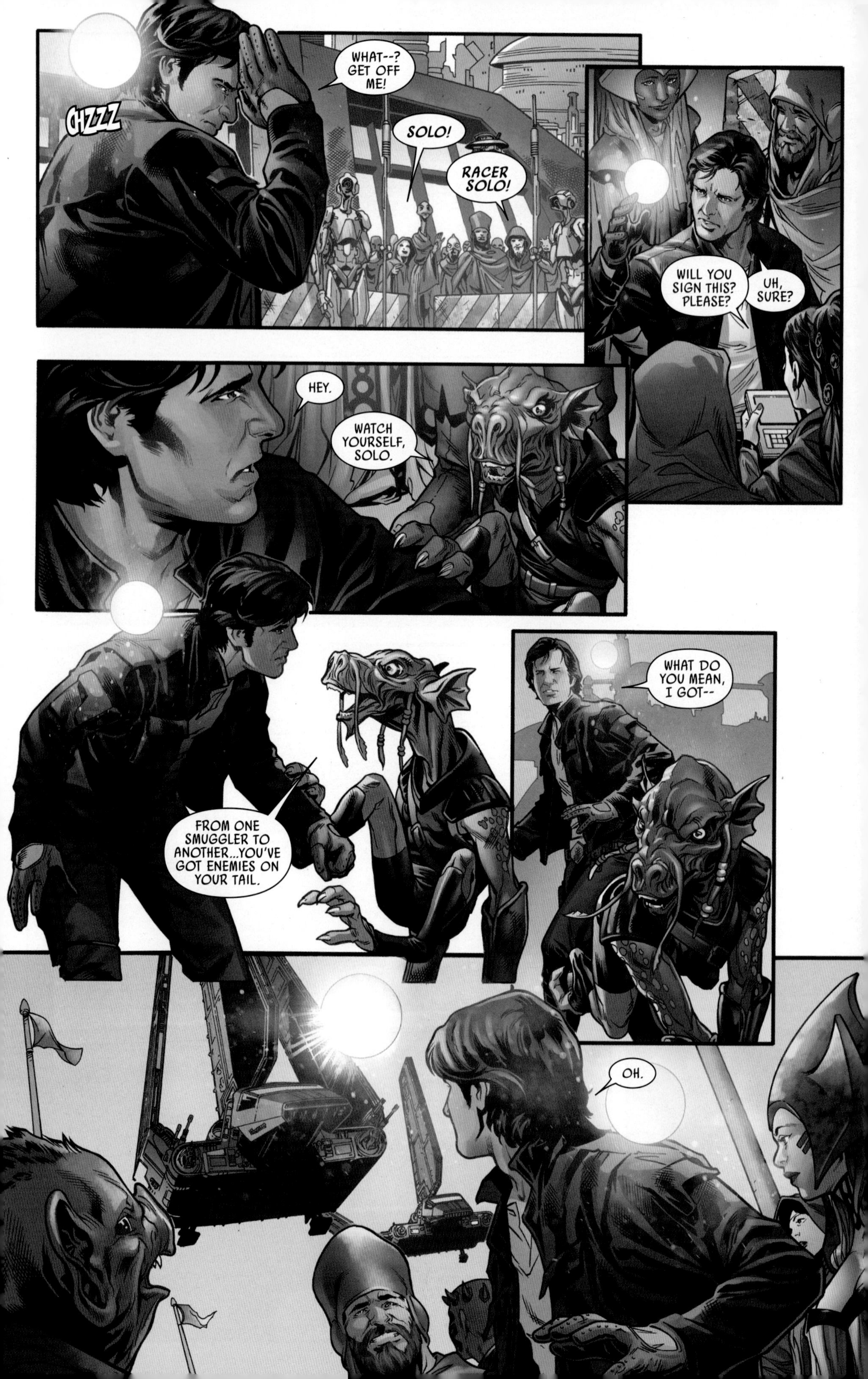
CHZZZ
WHAT--? GET OFF ME!
SOLO!
RACER SOLO!
WILL YOU SIGN THIS? PLEASE?
UH, SURE?
HEY.
WATCH YOURSELF, SOLO.
FROM ONE SMUGGLER TO ANOTHER...YOU'VE GOT ENEMIES ON YOUR TAIL.
WHAT DO YOU MEAN, I GOT--
OH.

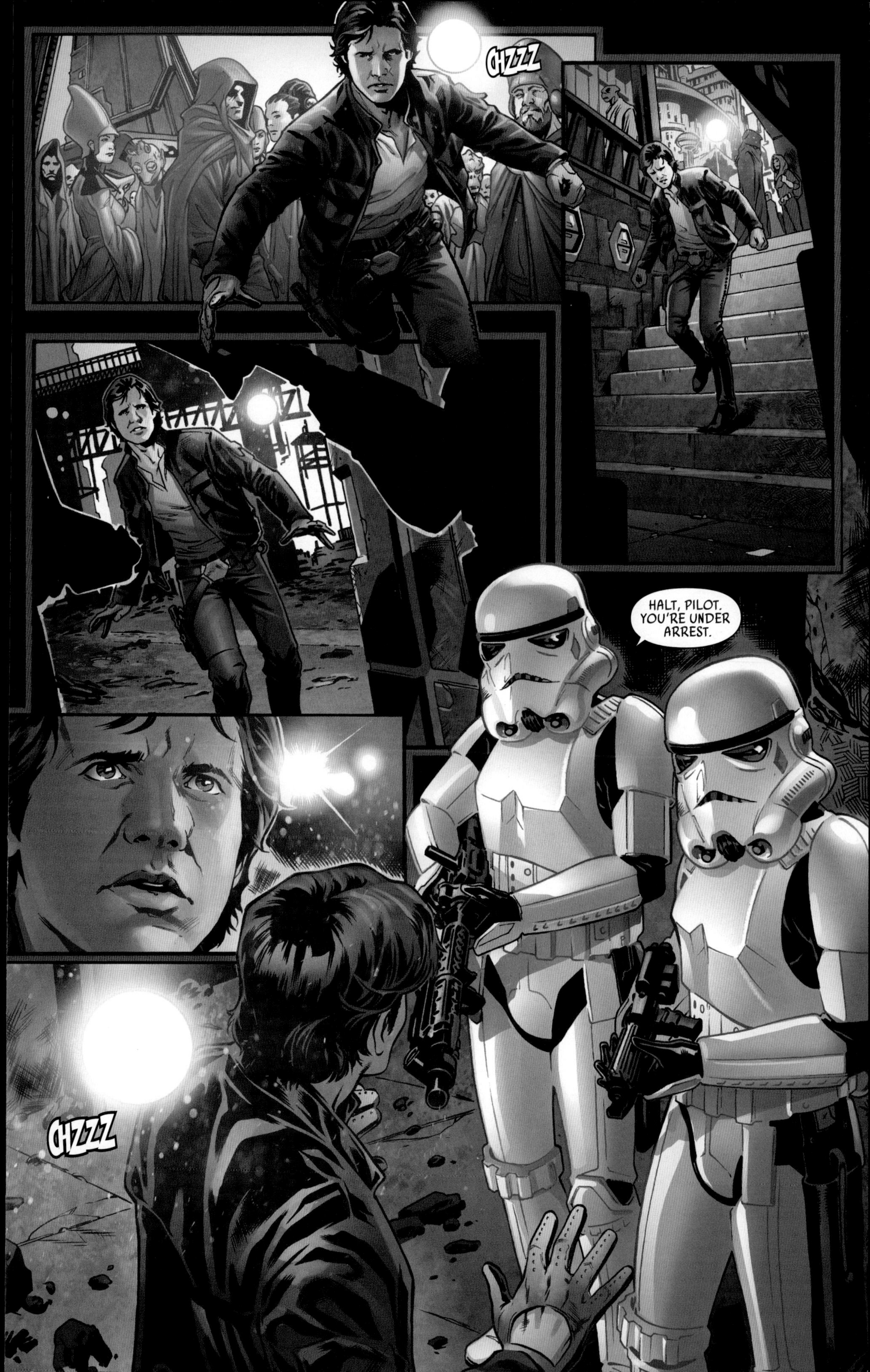
CHZZZ
HALT, PILOT. YOU'RE UNDER ARREST.
CHZZZ

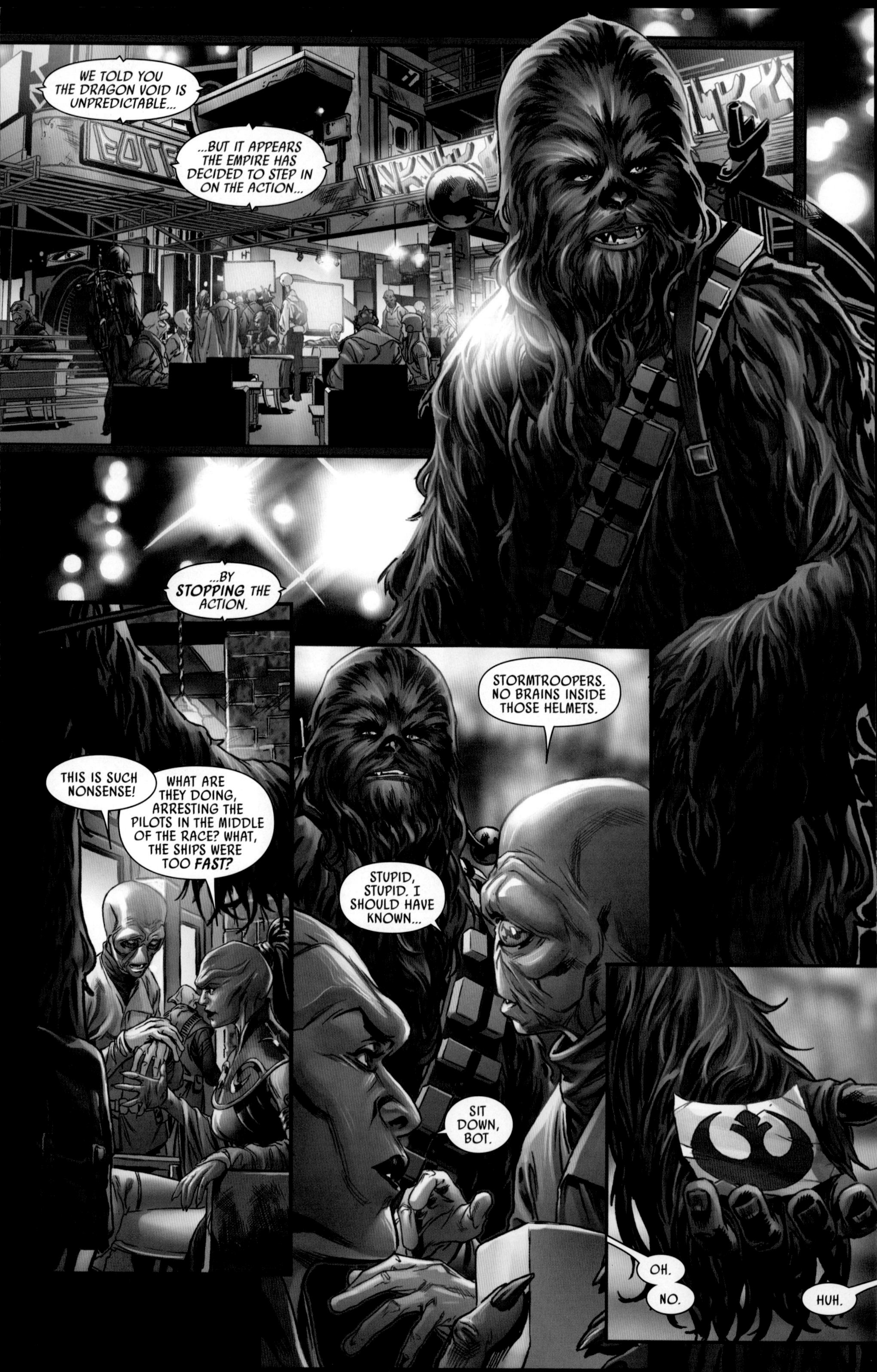
WE TOLD YOU THE DRAGON VOID IS UNPREDICTABLE...
...BUT IT APPEARS THE EMPIRE HAS DECIDED TO STEP IN ON THE ACTION...
...BY STOPPING THE ACTION.
THIS IS SUCH NONSENSE!
WHAT ARE THEY DOING, ARRESTING THE PILOTS IN THE MIDDLE OF THE RACE? WHAT, THE SHIPS WERE TOO FAST?
STORMTROOPERS. NO BRAINS INSIDE THOSE HELMETS.
STUPID, STUPID. I SHOULD HAVE KNOWN...
SIT DOWN, BOT.
OH.
NO.
HUH.

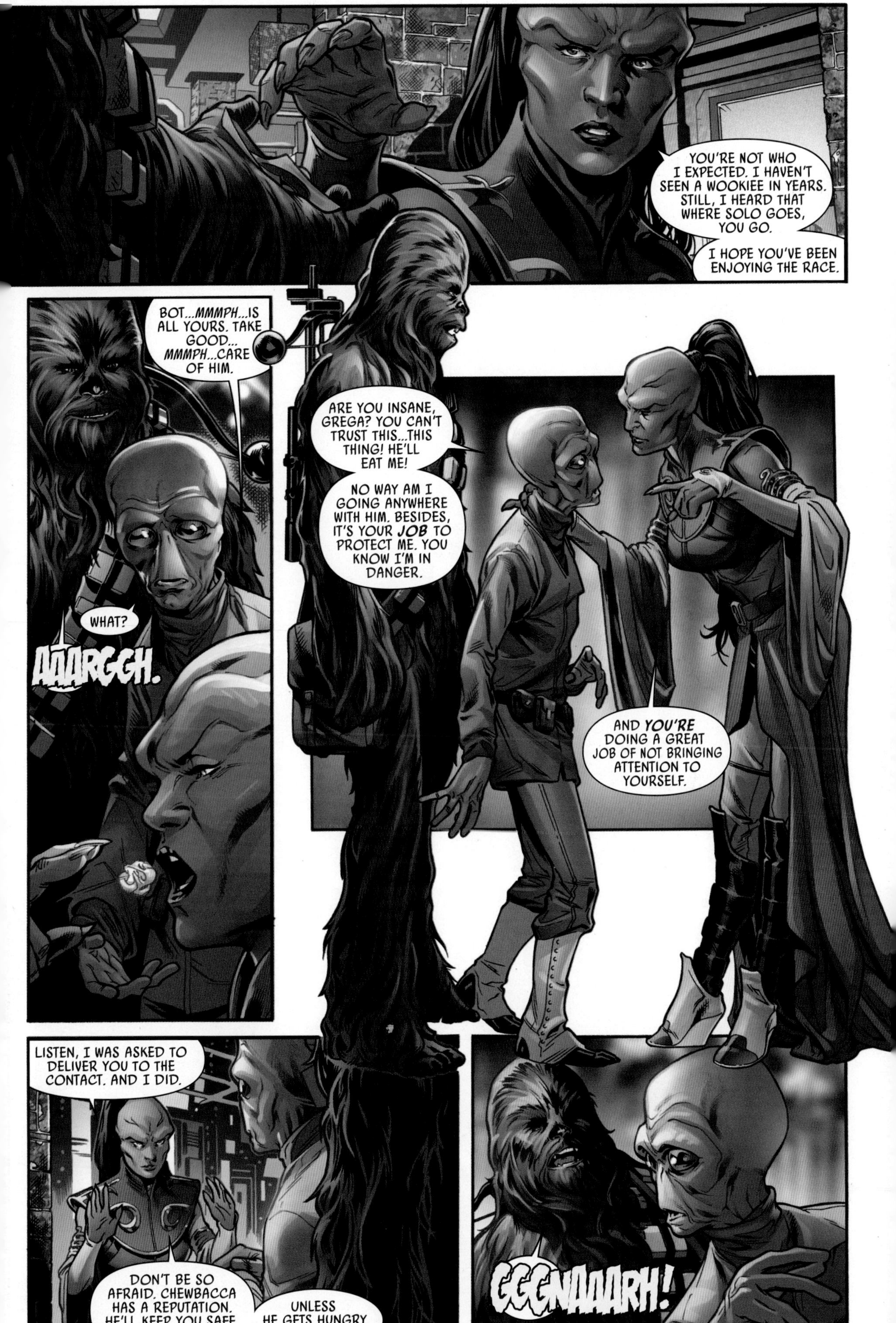
YOU'RE NOT WHO I EXPECTED. I HAVEN'T SEEN A WOOKIEE IN YEARS. STILL, I HEARD THAT WHERE SOLO GOES, YOU GO.
I HOPE YOU'VE BEEN ENJOYING THE RACE.
BOT...MMMPH...IS ALL YOURS. TAKE GOOD... MMMPH...CARE OF HIM.
WHAT?
AAARGGH.
ARE YOU INSANE, GREGA? YOU CAN'T TRUST THIS...THIS THING! HE'LL EAT ME!
NO WAY AM I GOING ANYWHERE WITH HIM. BESIDES, IT'S YOUR JOB TO PROTECT ME. YOU KNOW I'M IN DANGER.
AND YOU'RE DOING A GREAT JOB OF NOT BRINGING ATTENTION TO YOURSELF.
LISTEN, I WAS ASKED TO DELIVER YOU TO THE CONTACT. AND I DID.
DON'T BE SO AFRAID. CHEWBACCA HAS A REPUTATION. HE'LL KEEP YOU SAFE.
UNLESS HE GETS HUNGRY.
GGGNAAARH!

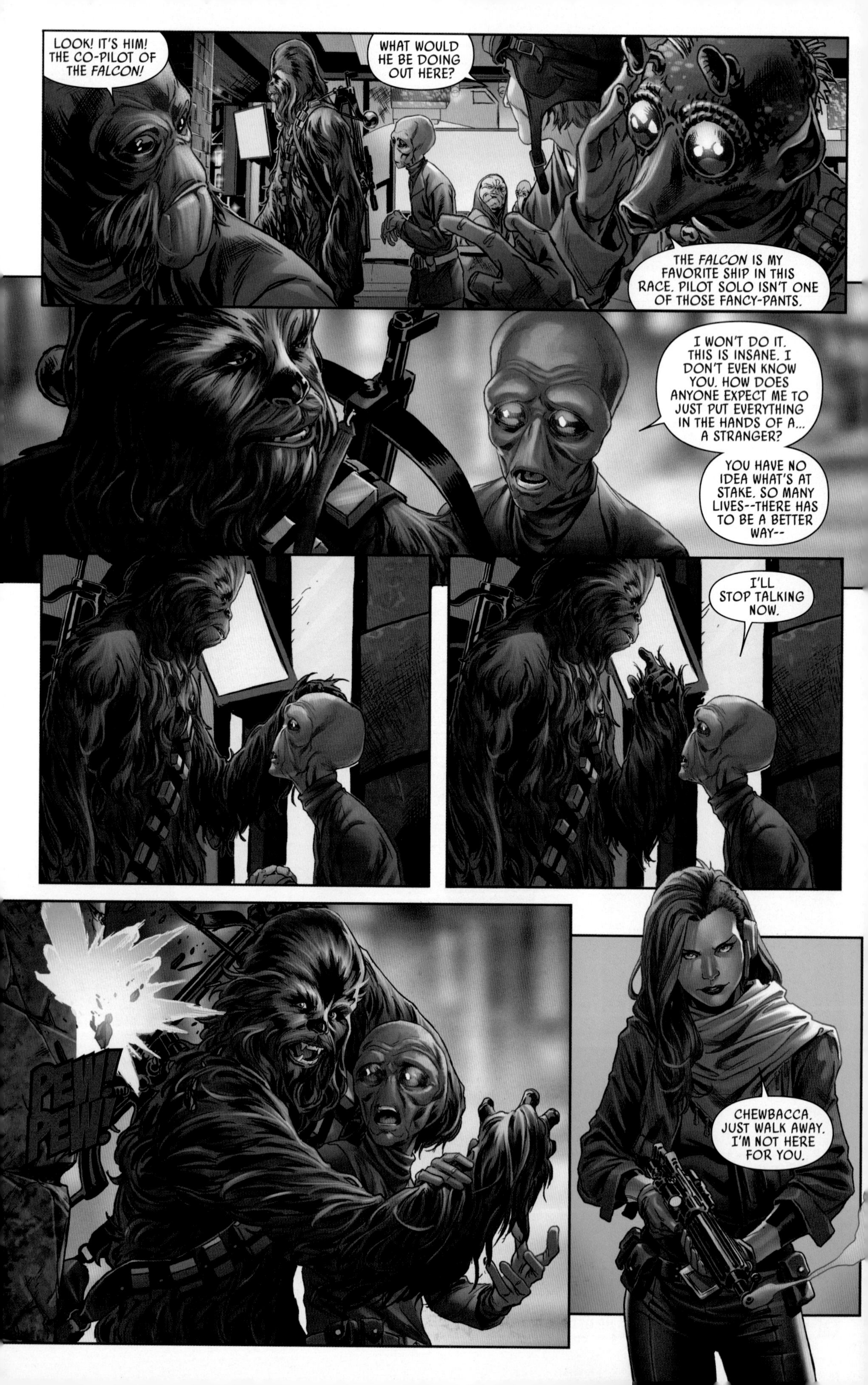
LOOK! IT'S HIM! THE CO-PILOT OF THE *FALCON!*
WHAT WOULD HE BE DOING OUT HERE?
THE *FALCON* IS MY FAVORITE SHIP IN THIS RACE. PILOT SOLO ISN'T ONE OF THOSE FANCY-PANTS.
I WON'T DO IT. THIS IS INSANE. I DON'T EVEN KNOW YOU. HOW DOES ANYONE EXPECT ME TO JUST PUT EVERYTHING IN THE HANDS OF A... A STRANGER?
YOU HAVE NO IDEA WHAT'S AT STAKE. SO MANY LIVES--THERE HAS TO BE A BETTER WAY--
I'LL STOP TALKING NOW.
PEW! PEW!
CHEWBACCA. JUST WALK AWAY. I'M NOT HERE FOR YOU.

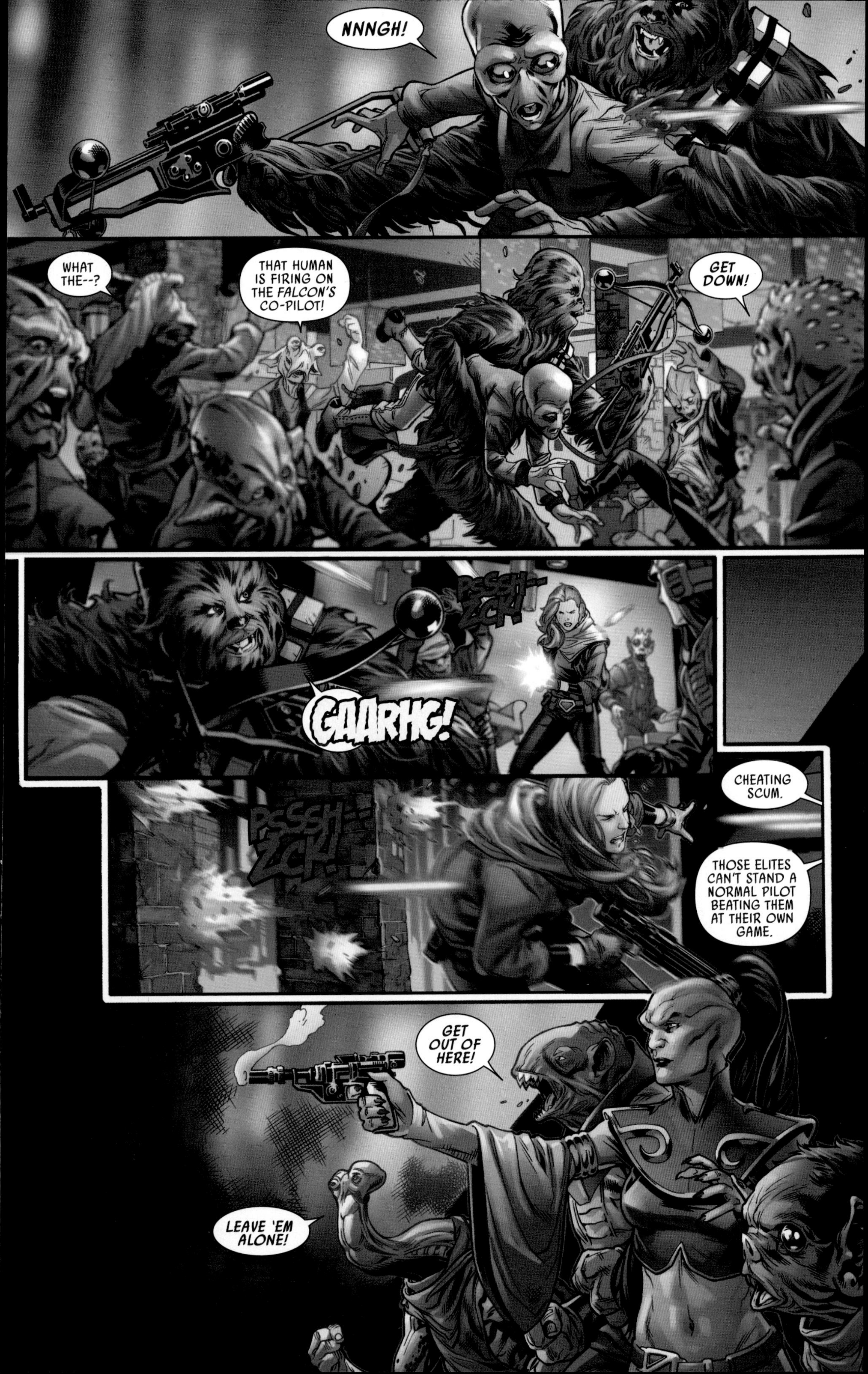
NNNGH!
WHAT THE--?
THAT HUMAN IS FIRING ON THE *FALCON'S* CO-PILOT!
GET DOWN!
PSSSH-ZCK!
GAARHG!
PSSSH-ZCK!
CHEATING SCUM.
THOSE ELITES CAN'T STAND A NORMAL PILOT BEATING THEM AT THEIR OWN GAME.
GET OUT OF HERE!
LEAVE 'EM ALONE!

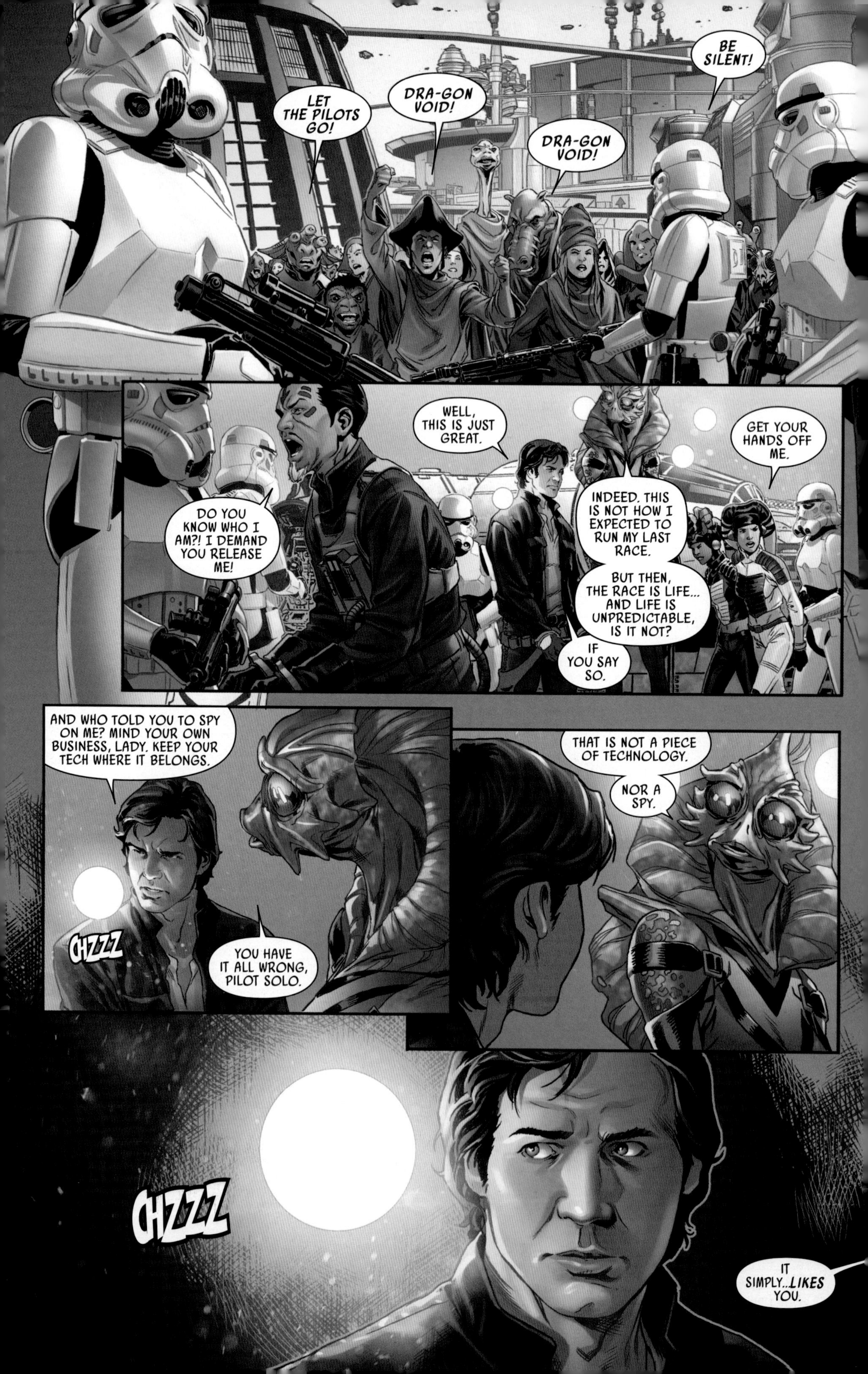
LET THE PILOTS GO!
DRA-GON VOID!
DRA-GON VOID!
BE SILENT!
DO YOU KNOW WHO I AM?! I DEMAND YOU RELEASE ME!
WELL, THIS IS JUST GREAT.
INDEED. THIS IS NOT HOW I EXPECTED TO RUN MY LAST RACE.
BUT THEN, THE RACE IS LIFE... AND LIFE IS UNPREDICTABLE, IS IT NOT?
IF YOU SAY SO.
GET YOUR HANDS OFF ME.
AND WHO TOLD YOU TO SPY ON ME? MIND YOUR OWN BUSINESS, LADY. KEEP YOUR TECH WHERE IT BELONGS.
CHZZZ
YOU HAVE IT ALL WRONG, PILOT SOLO.
THAT IS NOT A PIECE OF TECHNOLOGY.
NOR A SPY.
CHZZZ
IT SIMPLY...LIKES YOU.

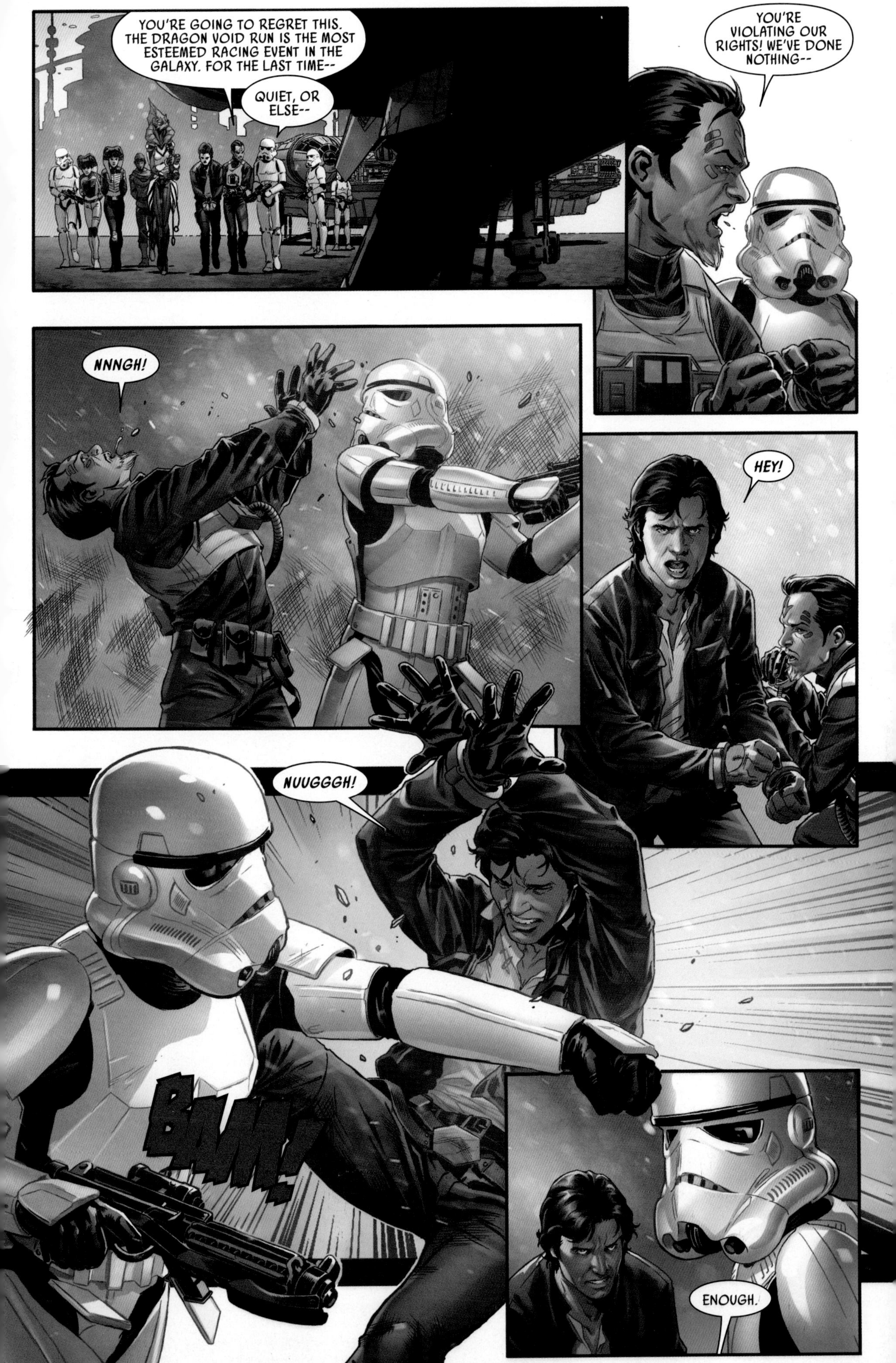
YOU'RE GOING TO REGRET THIS. THE DRAGON VOID RUN IS THE MOST ESTEEMED RACING EVENT IN THE GALAXY. FOR THE LAST TIME--
QUIET, OR ELSE--
YOU'RE VIOLATING OUR RIGHTS! WE'VE DONE NOTHING--
NNNGH!
HEY!
NUUGGGH!
ENOUGH.

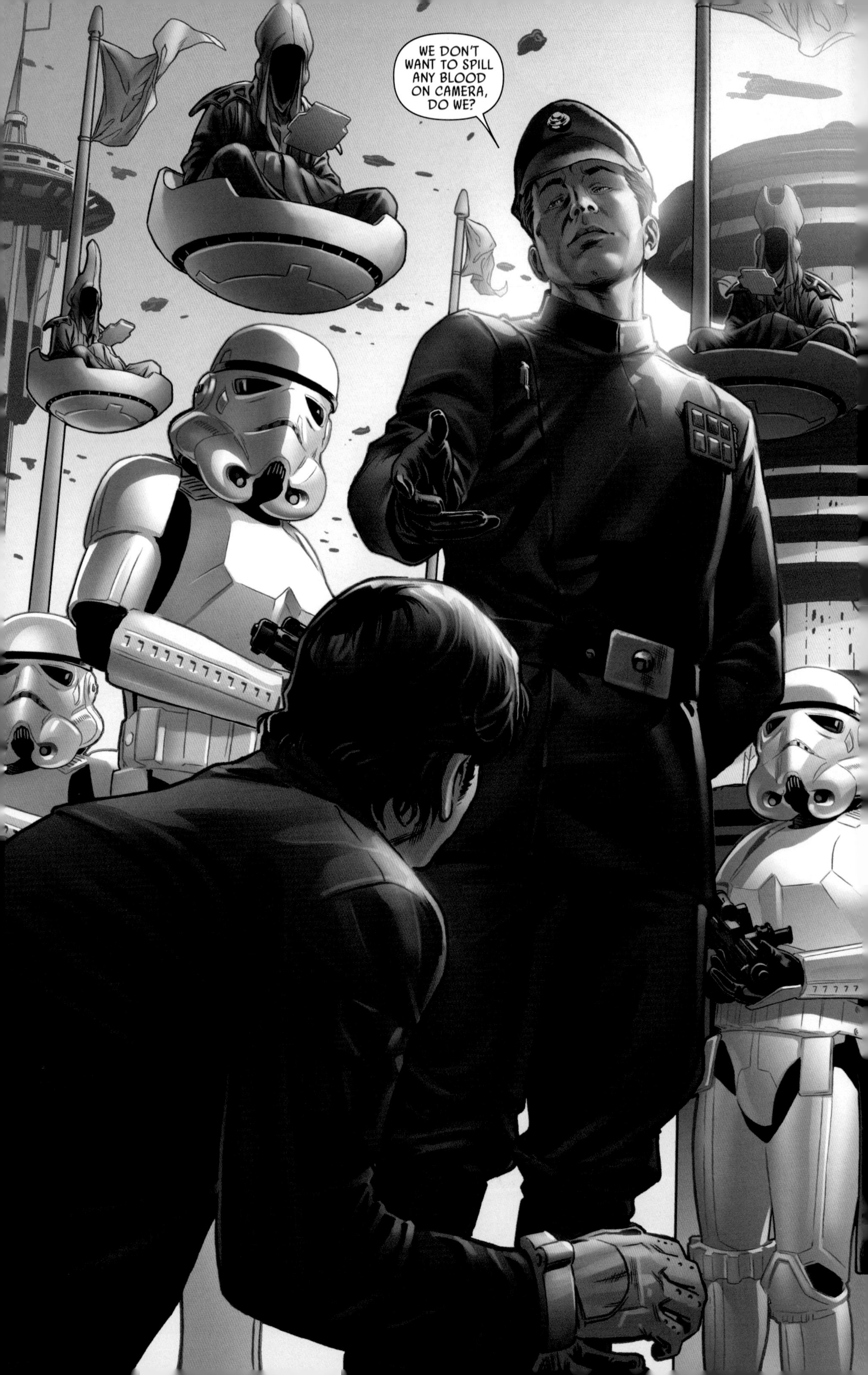
WE DON'T WANT TO SPILL ANY BLOOD ON CAMERA, DO WE?

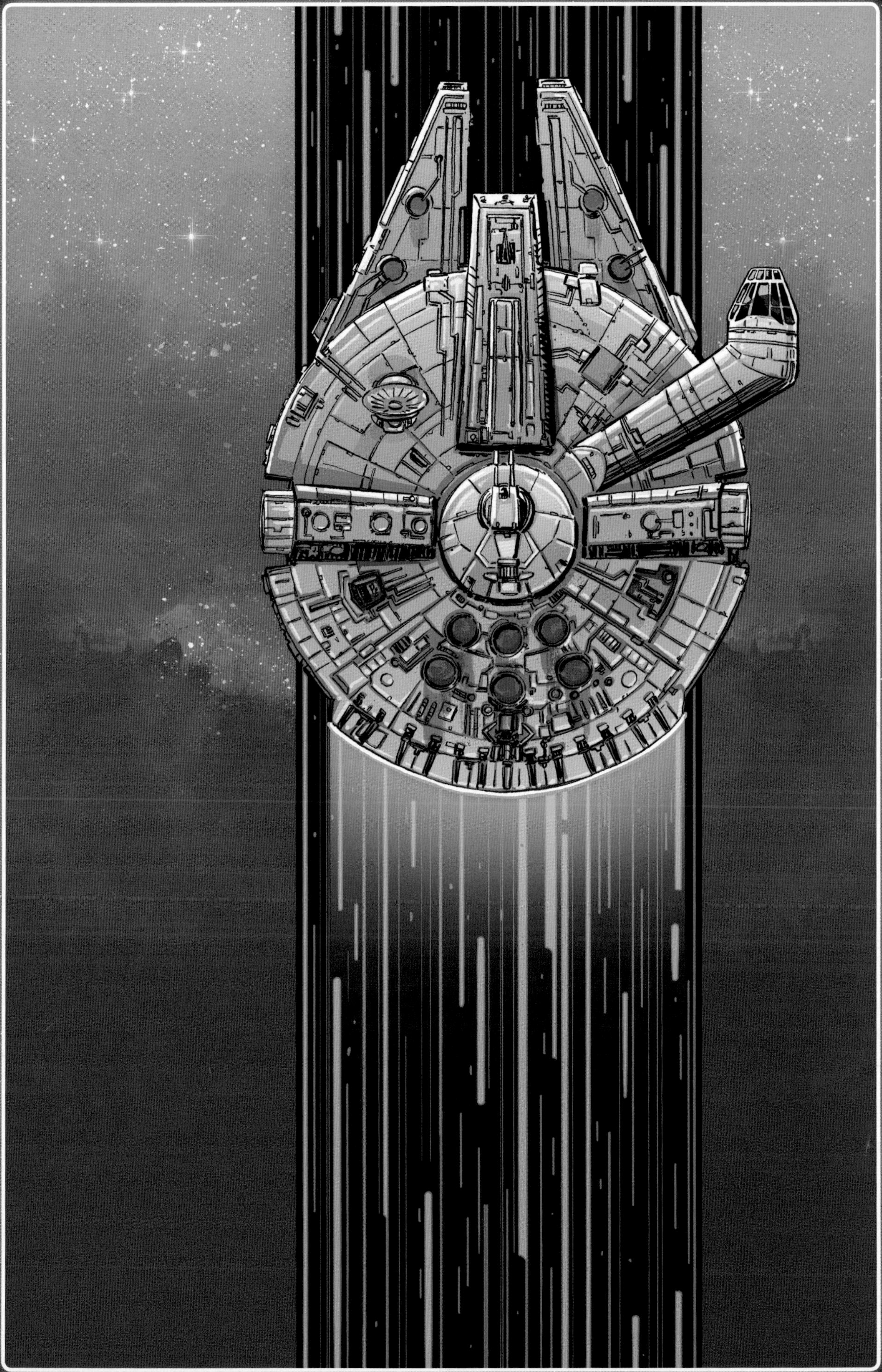

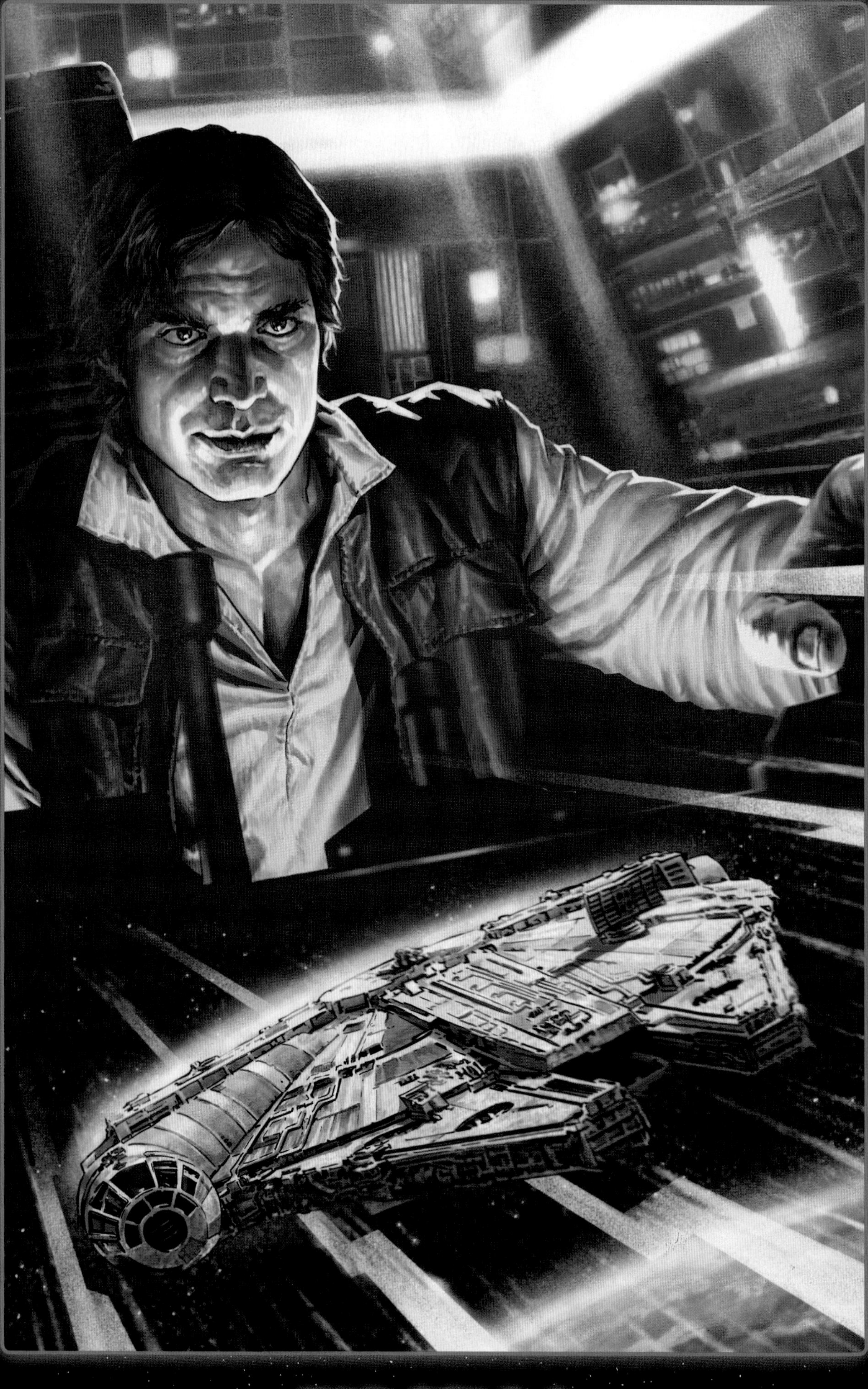

HAN SOLO 3

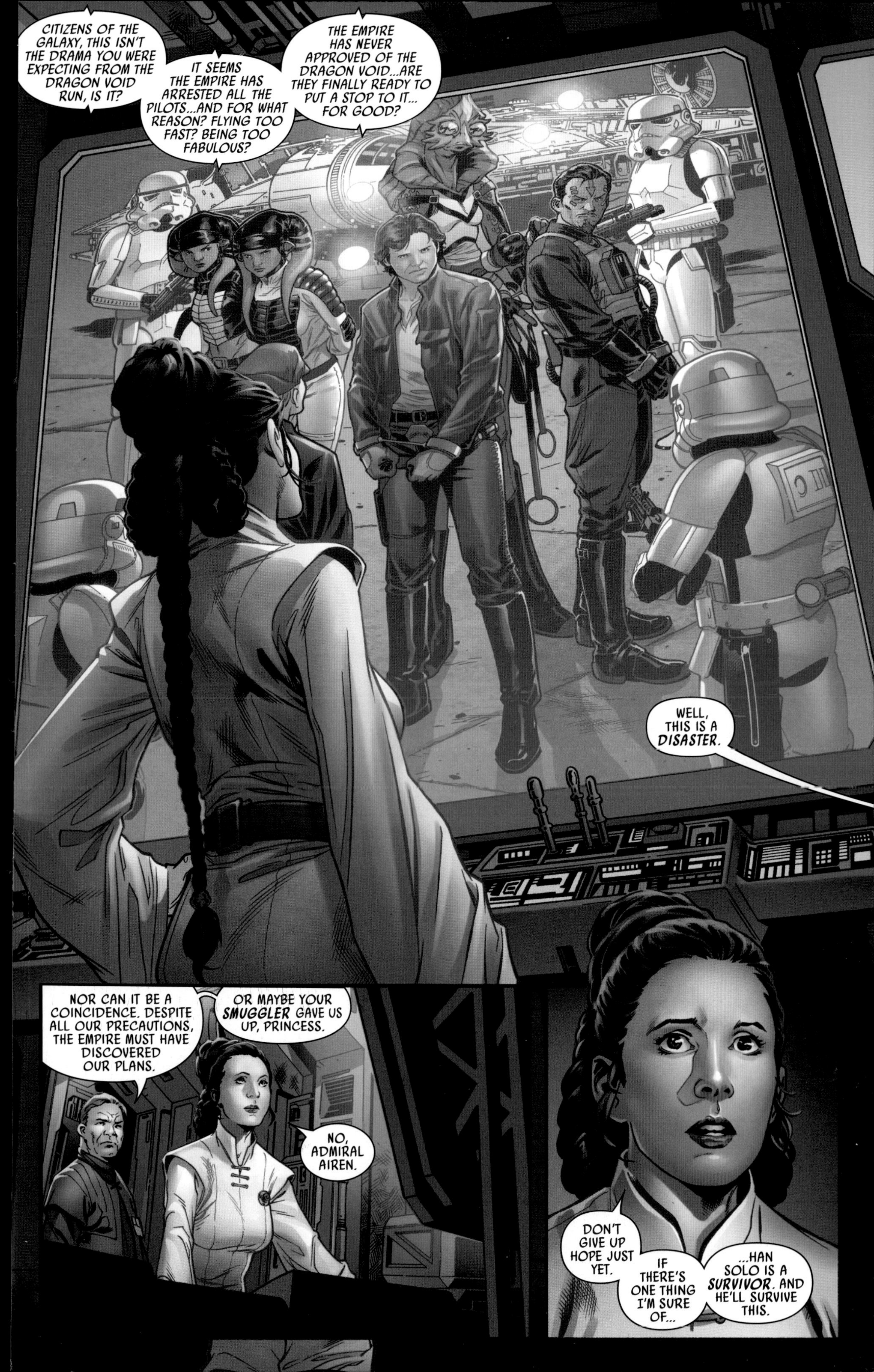
CITIZENS OF THE GALAXY, THIS ISN'T THE DRAMA YOU WERE EXPECTING FROM THE DRAGON VOID RUN, IS IT?
IT SEEMS THE EMPIRE HAS ARRESTED ALL THE PILOTS...AND FOR WHAT REASON? FLYING TOO FAST? BEING TOO FABULOUS?
THE EMPIRE HAS NEVER APPROVED OF THE DRAGON VOID...ARE THEY FINALLY READY TO PUT A STOP TO IT... FOR GOOD?
WELL, THIS IS A DISASTER.
NOR CAN IT BE A COINCIDENCE. DESPITE ALL OUR PRECAUTIONS, THE EMPIRE MUST HAVE DISCOVERED OUR PLANS.
OR MAYBE YOUR SMUGGLER GAVE US UP, PRINCESS.
NO, ADMIRAL AIREN.
DON'T GIVE UP HOPE JUST YET.
IF THERE'S ONE THING I'M SURE OF...
...HAN SOLO IS A SURVIVOR. AND HE'LL SURVIVE THIS.

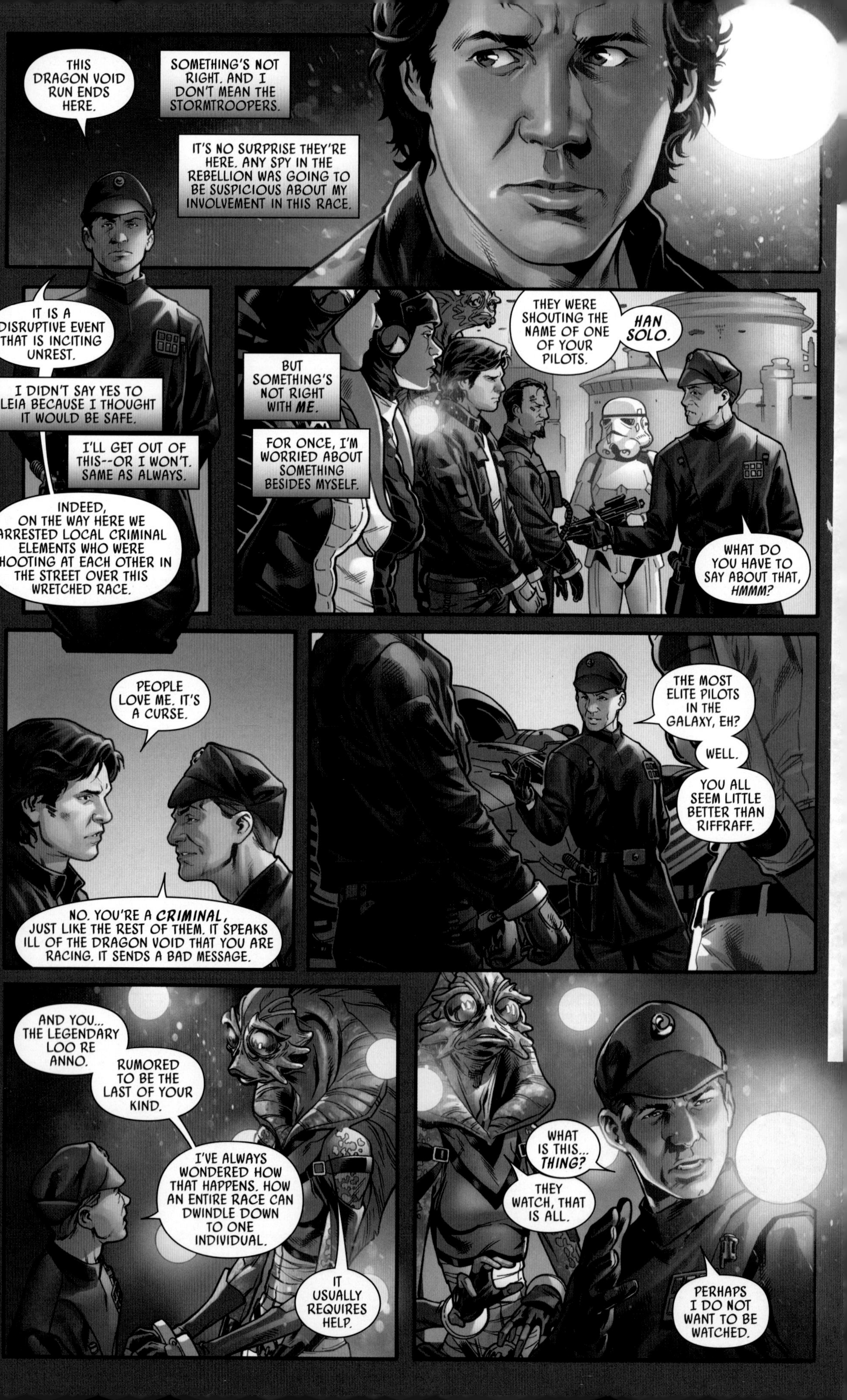
THIS DRAGON VOID RUN ENDS HERE.
SOMETHING'S NOT RIGHT. AND I DON'T MEAN THE STORMTROOPERS.
IT'S NO SURPRISE THEY'RE HERE. ANY SPY IN THE REBELLION WAS GOING TO BE SUSPICIOUS ABOUT MY INVOLVEMENT IN THIS RACE.
IT IS A DISRUPTIVE EVENT THAT IS INCITING UNREST.
I DIDN'T SAY YES TO LEIA BECAUSE I THOUGHT IT WOULD BE SAFE.
I'LL GET OUT OF THIS--OR I WON'T. SAME AS ALWAYS.
INDEED, ON THE WAY HERE WE ARRESTED LOCAL CRIMINAL ELEMENTS WHO WERE SHOOTING AT EACH OTHER IN THE STREET OVER THIS WRETCHED RACE.
THEY WERE SHOUTING THE NAME OF ONE OF YOUR PILOTS.
HAN SOLO.
BUT SOMETHING'S NOT RIGHT WITH ME.
FOR ONCE, I'M WORRIED ABOUT SOMETHING BESIDES MYSELF.
WHAT DO YOU HAVE TO SAY ABOUT THAT, HMMM?
PEOPLE LOVE ME. IT'S A CURSE.
NO. YOU'RE A CRIMINAL, JUST LIKE THE REST OF THEM. IT SPEAKS ILL OF THE DRAGON VOID THAT YOU ARE RACING. IT SENDS A BAD MESSAGE.
THE MOST ELITE PILOTS IN THE GALAXY, EH?
WELL.
YOU ALL SEEM LITTLE BETTER THAN RIFFRAFF.
AND YOU... THE LEGENDARY LOO RE ANNO.
RUMORED TO BE THE LAST OF YOUR KIND.
I'VE ALWAYS WONDERED HOW THAT HAPPENS. HOW AN ENTIRE RACE CAN DWINDLE DOWN TO ONE INDIVIDUAL.
IT USUALLY REQUIRES HELP.
WHAT IS THIS... THING?
THEY WATCH, THAT IS ALL.
PERHAPS I DO NOT WANT TO BE WATCHED.

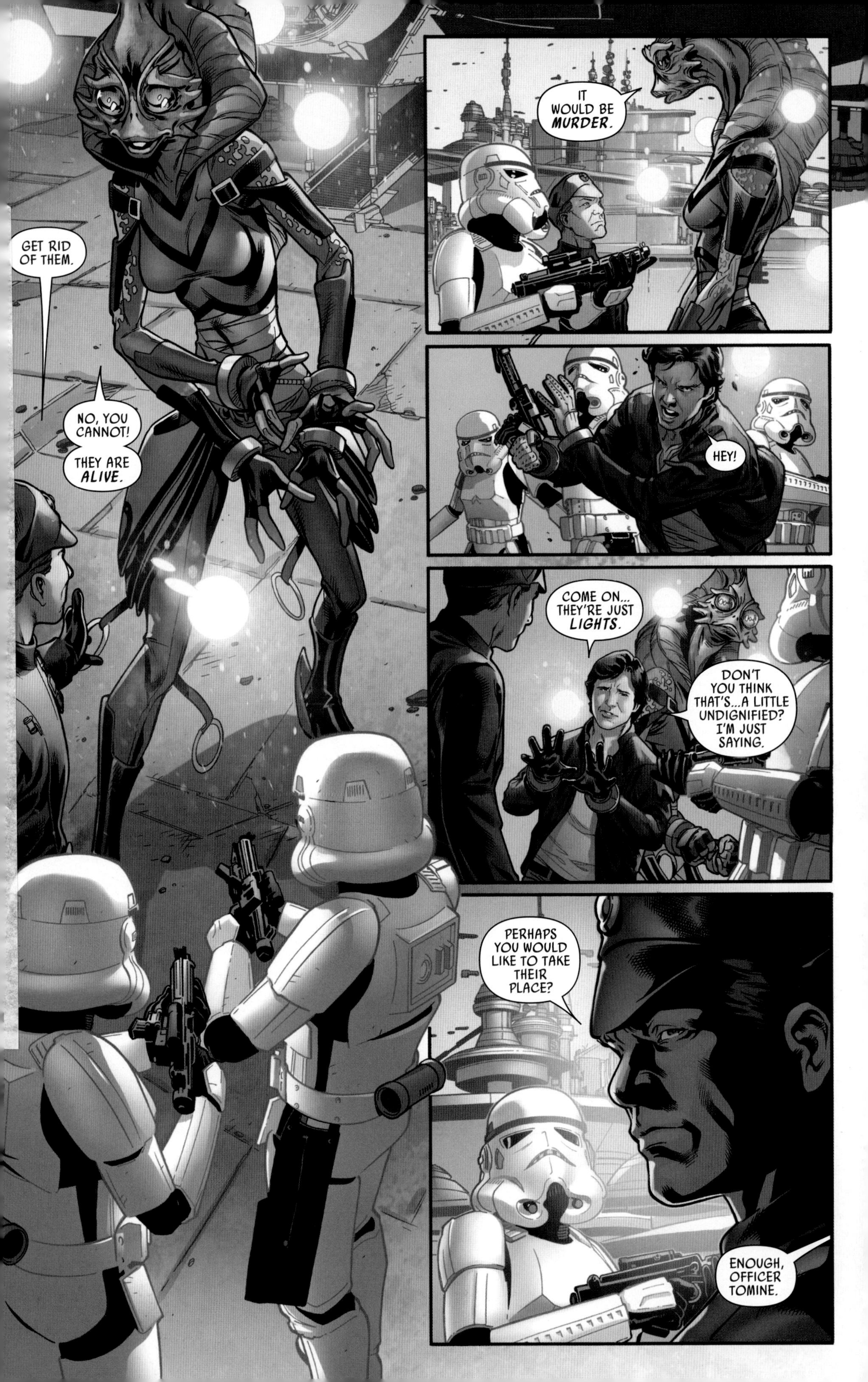
GET RID OF THEM.
NO, YOU CANNOT!
THEY ARE ALIVE.
IT WOULD BE MURDER.
HEY!
COME ON... THEY'RE JUST LIGHTS.
DON'T YOU THINK THAT'S...A LITTLE UNDIGNIFIED? I'M JUST SAYING.
PERHAPS YOU WOULD LIKE TO TAKE THEIR PLACE?
ENOUGH, OFFICER TOMINE.

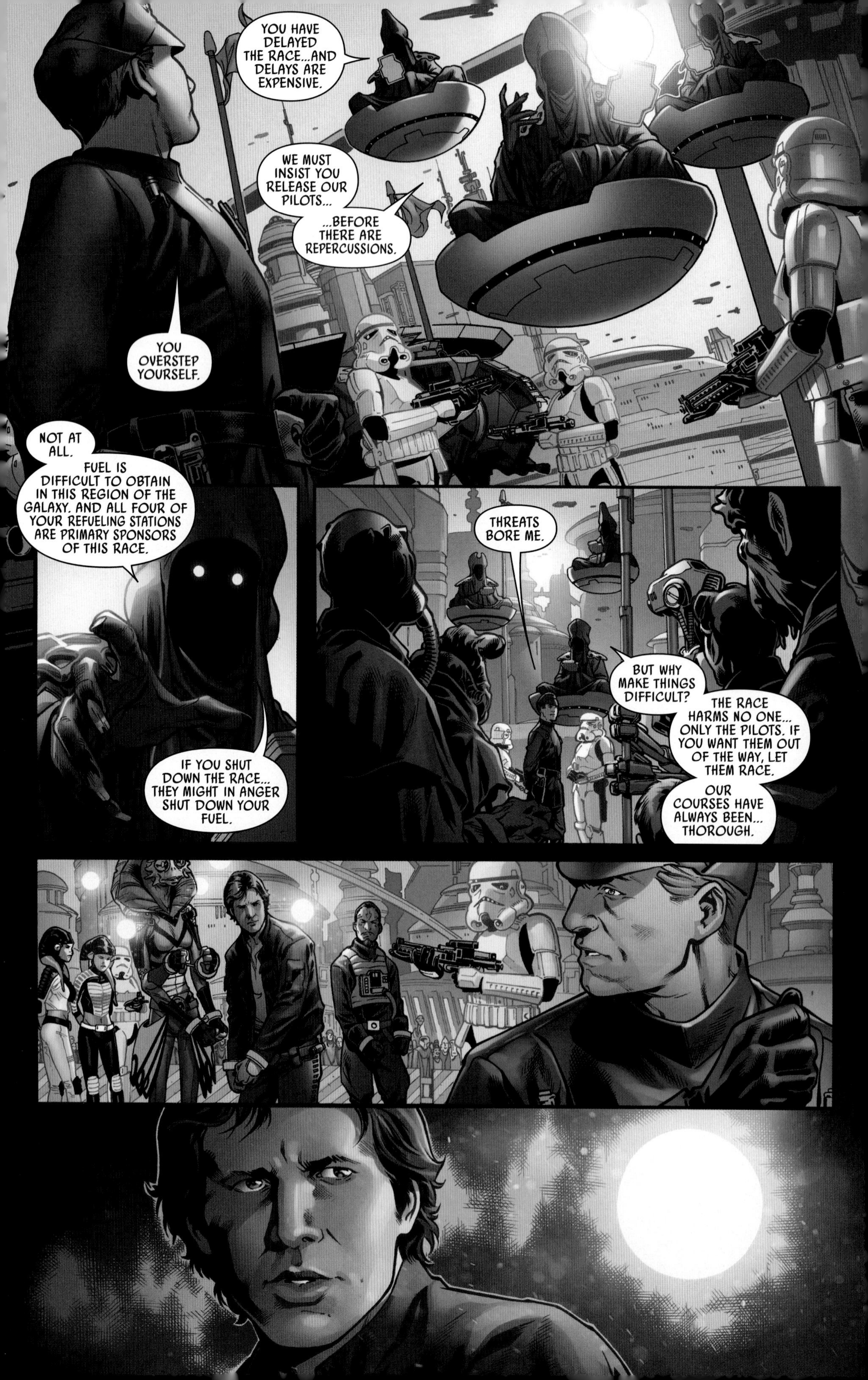
YOU HAVE DELAYED THE RACE...AND DELAYS ARE EXPENSIVE.
WE MUST INSIST YOU RELEASE OUR PILOTS...
...BEFORE THERE ARE REPERCUSSIONS.
YOU OVERSTEP YOURSELF.
NOT AT ALL.
FUEL IS DIFFICULT TO OBTAIN IN THIS REGION OF THE GALAXY. AND ALL FOUR OF YOUR REFUELING STATIONS ARE PRIMARY SPONSORS OF THIS RACE.
IF YOU SHUT DOWN THE RACE... THEY MIGHT IN ANGER SHUT DOWN YOUR FUEL.
THREATS BORE ME.
BUT WHY MAKE THINGS DIFFICULT?
THE RACE HARMS NO ONE... ONLY THE PILOTS. IF YOU WANT THEM OUT OF THE WAY, LET THEM RACE.
OUR COURSES HAVE ALWAYS BEEN... THOROUGH.

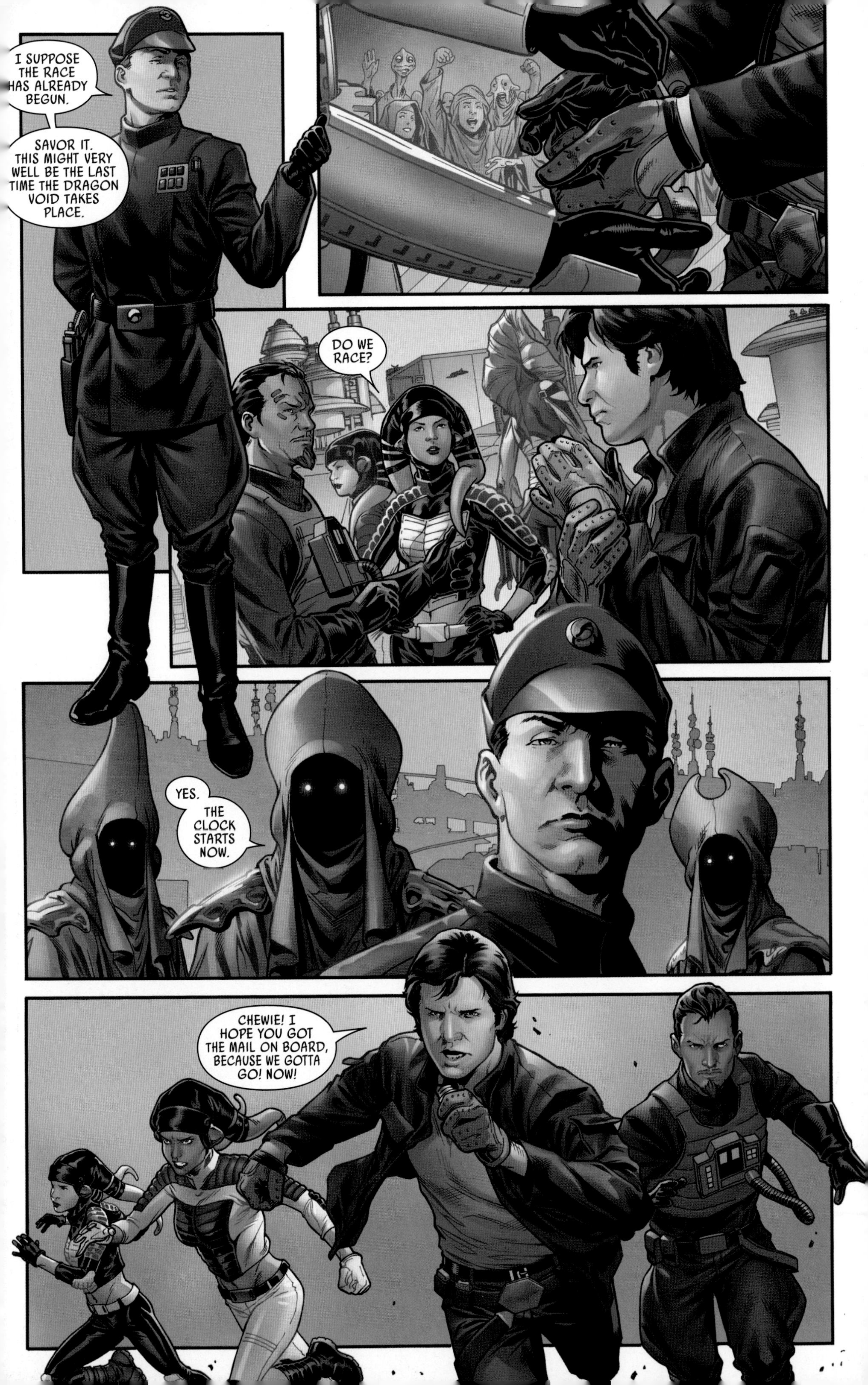
I SUPPOSE THE RACE HAS ALREADY BEGUN.
SAVOR IT. THIS MIGHT VERY WELL BE THE LAST TIME THE DRAGON VOID TAKES PLACE.
DO WE RACE?
YES.
THE CLOCK STARTS NOW.
CHEWIE! I HOPE YOU GOT THE MAIL ON BOARD, BECAUSE WE GOTTA GO! NOW!

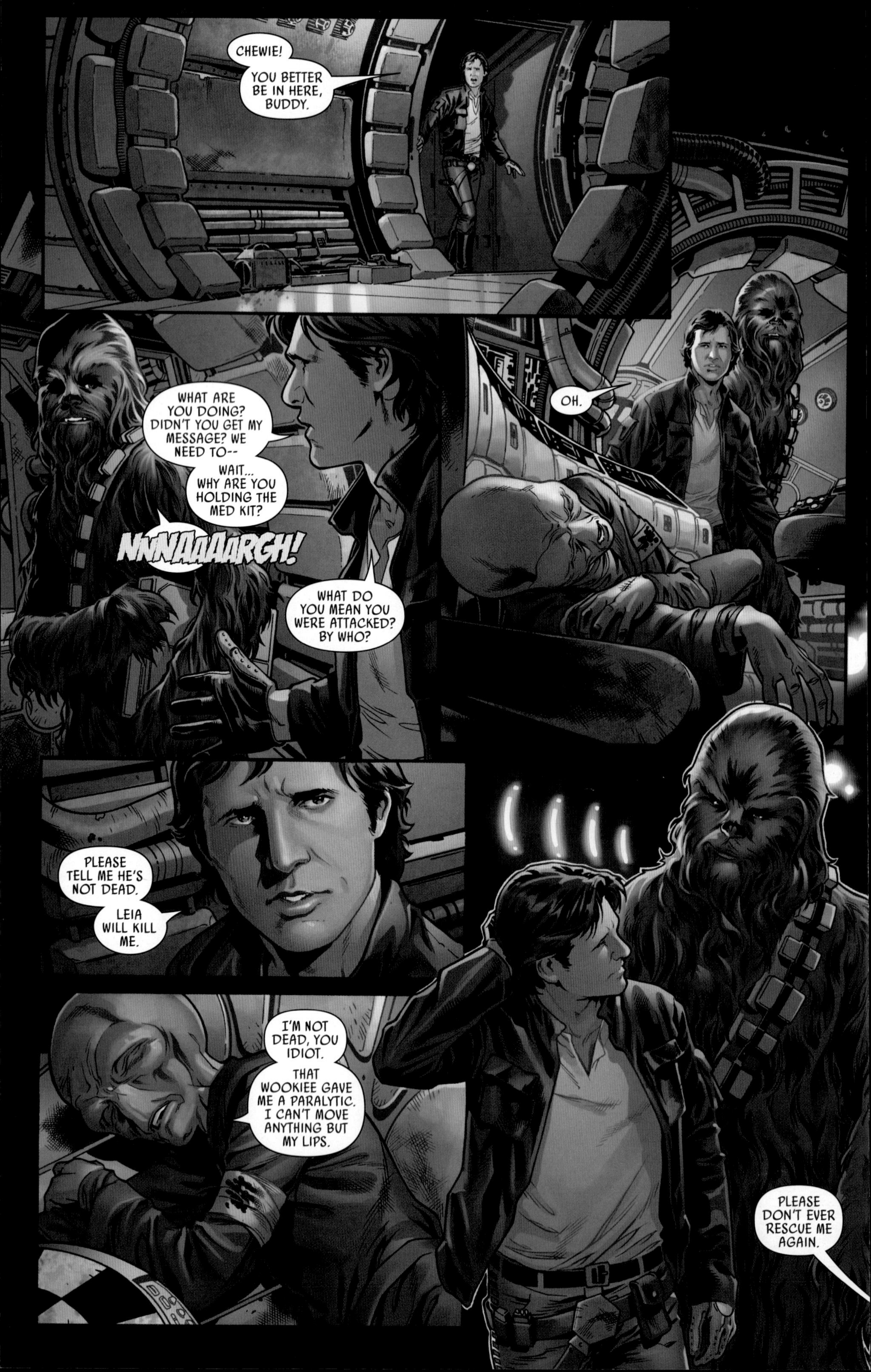
CHEWIE!
YOU BETTER BE IN HERE, BUDDY.
WHAT ARE YOU DOING? DIDN'T YOU GET MY MESSAGE? WE NEED TO--
WAIT... WHY ARE YOU HOLDING THE MED KIT?
NNNAAAARGH!
WHAT DO YOU MEAN YOU WERE ATTACKED? BY WHO?
OH.
PLEASE TELL ME HE'S NOT DEAD.
LEIA WILL KILL ME.
I'M NOT DEAD, YOU IDIOT.
THAT WOOKIEE GAVE ME A PARALYTIC. I CAN'T MOVE ANYTHING BUT MY LIPS.
PLEASE DON'T EVER RESCUE ME AGAIN.

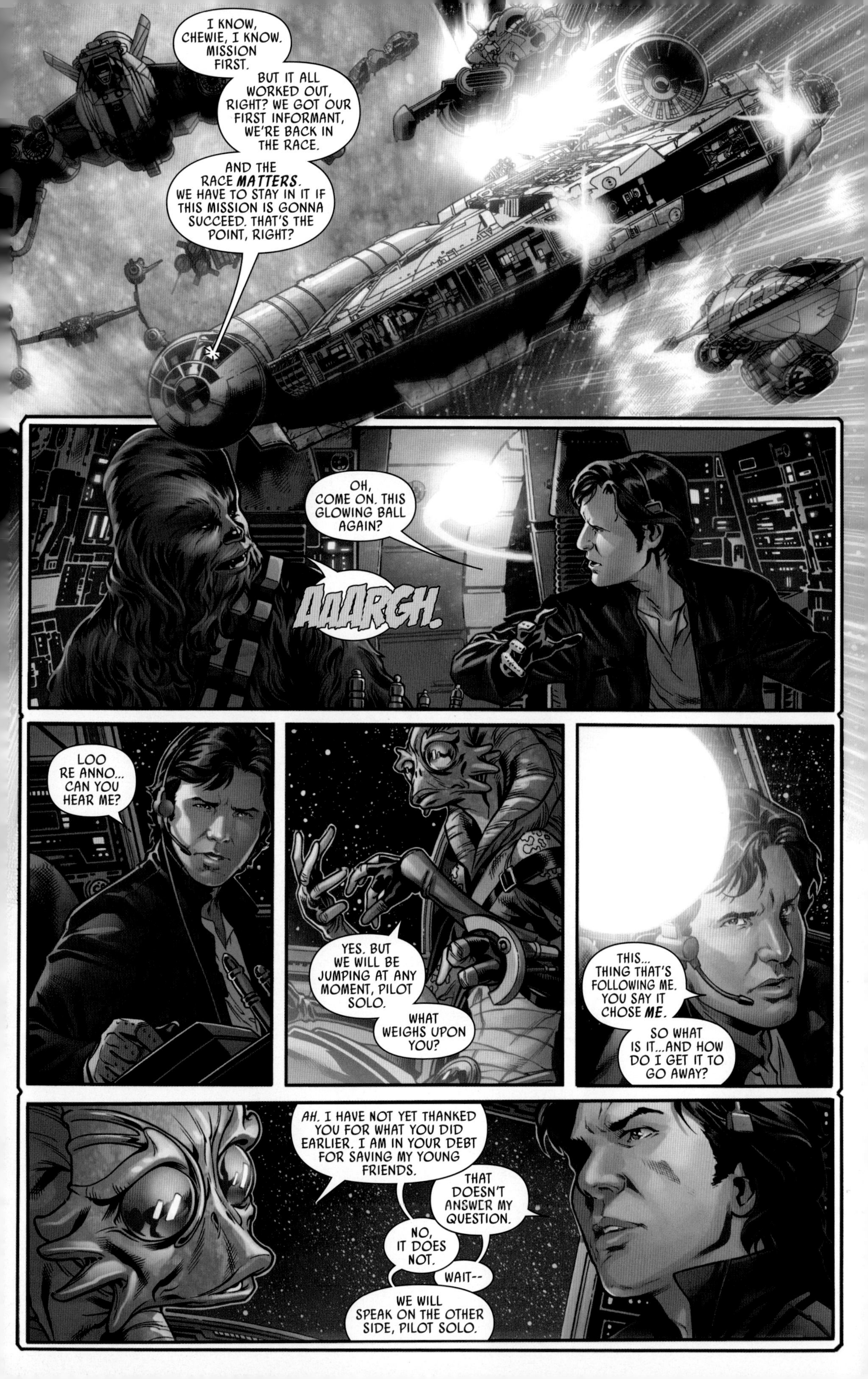
I KNOW, CHEWIE, I KNOW. MISSION FIRST.
BUT IT ALL WORKED OUT, RIGHT? WE GOT OUR FIRST INFORMANT, WE'RE BACK IN THE RACE.
AND THE RACE MATTERS. WE HAVE TO STAY IN IT IF THIS MISSION IS GONNA SUCCEED. THAT'S THE POINT, RIGHT?
OH, COME ON. THIS GLOWING BALL AGAIN?
AAARGH.
LOO RE ANNO... CAN YOU HEAR ME?
YES. BUT WE WILL BE JUMPING AT ANY MOMENT, PILOT SOLO.
WHAT WEIGHS UPON YOU?
THIS... THING THAT'S FOLLOWING ME. YOU SAY IT CHOSE ME.
SO WHAT IS IT...AND HOW DO I GET IT TO GO AWAY?
AH. I HAVE NOT YET THANKED YOU FOR WHAT YOU DID EARLIER. I AM IN YOUR DEBT FOR SAVING MY YOUNG FRIENDS.
THAT DOESN'T ANSWER MY QUESTION.
NO, IT DOES NOT.
WAIT--
WE WILL SPEAK ON THE OTHER SIDE, PILOT SOLO.

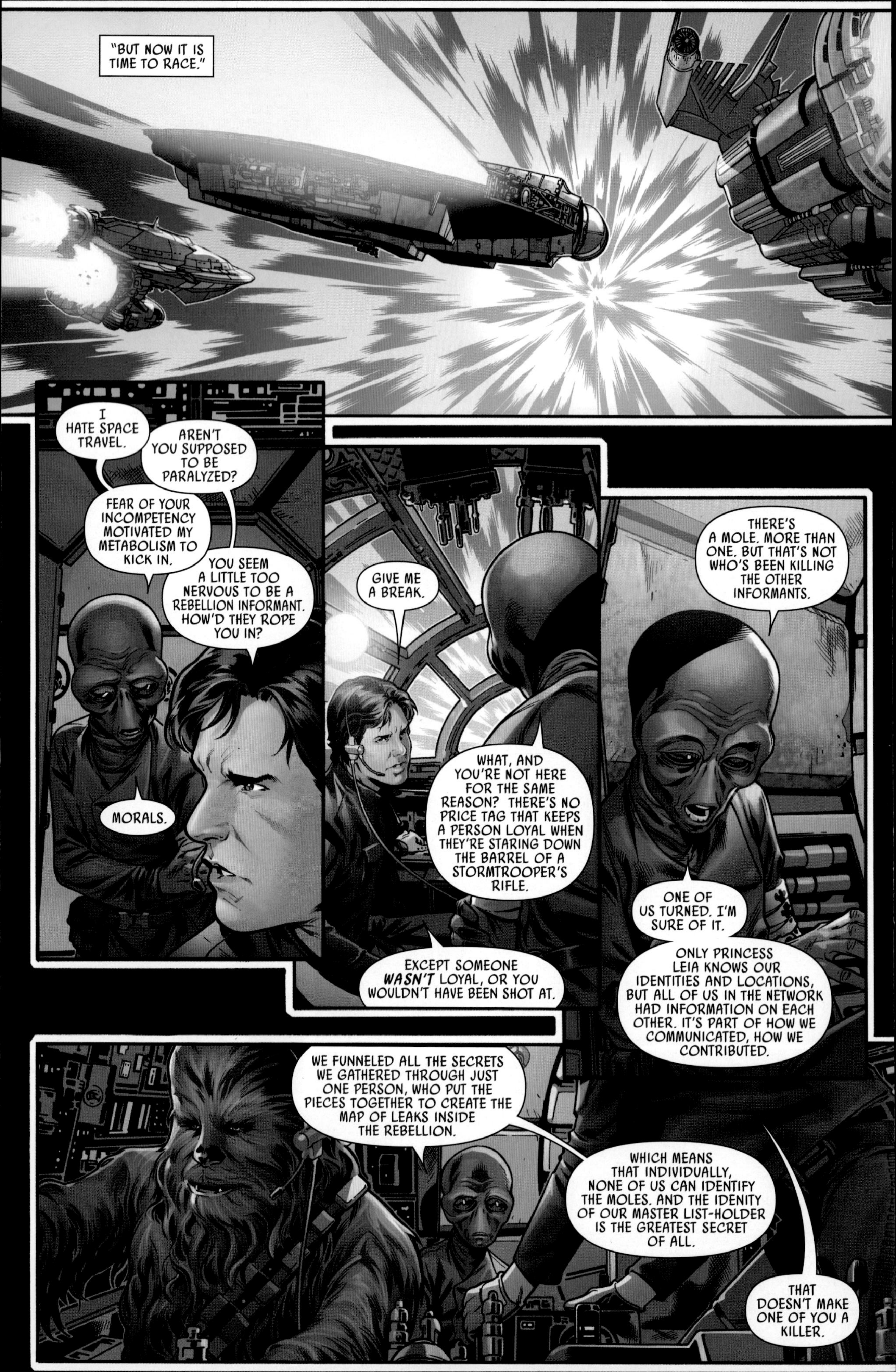
"BUT NOW IT IS TIME TO RACE."
I HATE SPACE TRAVEL.
AREN'T YOU SUPPOSED TO BE PARALYZED?
FEAR OF YOUR INCOMPETENCY MOTIVATED MY METABOLISM TO KICK IN.
YOU SEEM A LITTLE TOO NERVOUS TO BE A REBELLION INFORMANT. HOW'D THEY ROPE YOU IN?
MORALS.
GIVE ME A BREAK.
WHAT, AND YOU'RE NOT HERE FOR THE SAME REASON? THERE'S NO PRICE TAG THAT KEEPS A PERSON LOYAL WHEN THEY'RE STARING DOWN THE BARREL OF A STORMTROOPER'S RIFLE.
EXCEPT SOMEONE *WASN'T* LOYAL, OR YOU WOULDN'T HAVE BEEN SHOT AT.
THERE'S A MOLE. MORE THAN ONE. BUT THAT'S NOT WHO'S BEEN KILLING THE OTHER INFORMANTS.
ONE OF US TURNED. I'M SURE OF IT.
ONLY PRINCESS LEIA KNOWS OUR IDENTITIES AND LOCATIONS, BUT ALL OF US IN THE NETWORK HAD INFORMATION ON EACH OTHER. IT'S PART OF HOW WE COMMUNICATED, HOW WE CONTRIBUTED.
WE FUNNELED ALL THE SECRETS WE GATHERED THROUGH JUST ONE PERSON, WHO PUT THE PIECES TOGETHER TO CREATE THE MAP OF LEAKS INSIDE THE REBELLION.
WHICH MEANS THAT INDIVIDUALLY, NONE OF US CAN IDENTIFY THE MOLES. AND THE IDENITY OF OUR MASTER LIST-HOLDER IS THE GREATEST SECRET OF ALL.
THAT DOESN'T MAKE ONE OF YOU A KILLER.

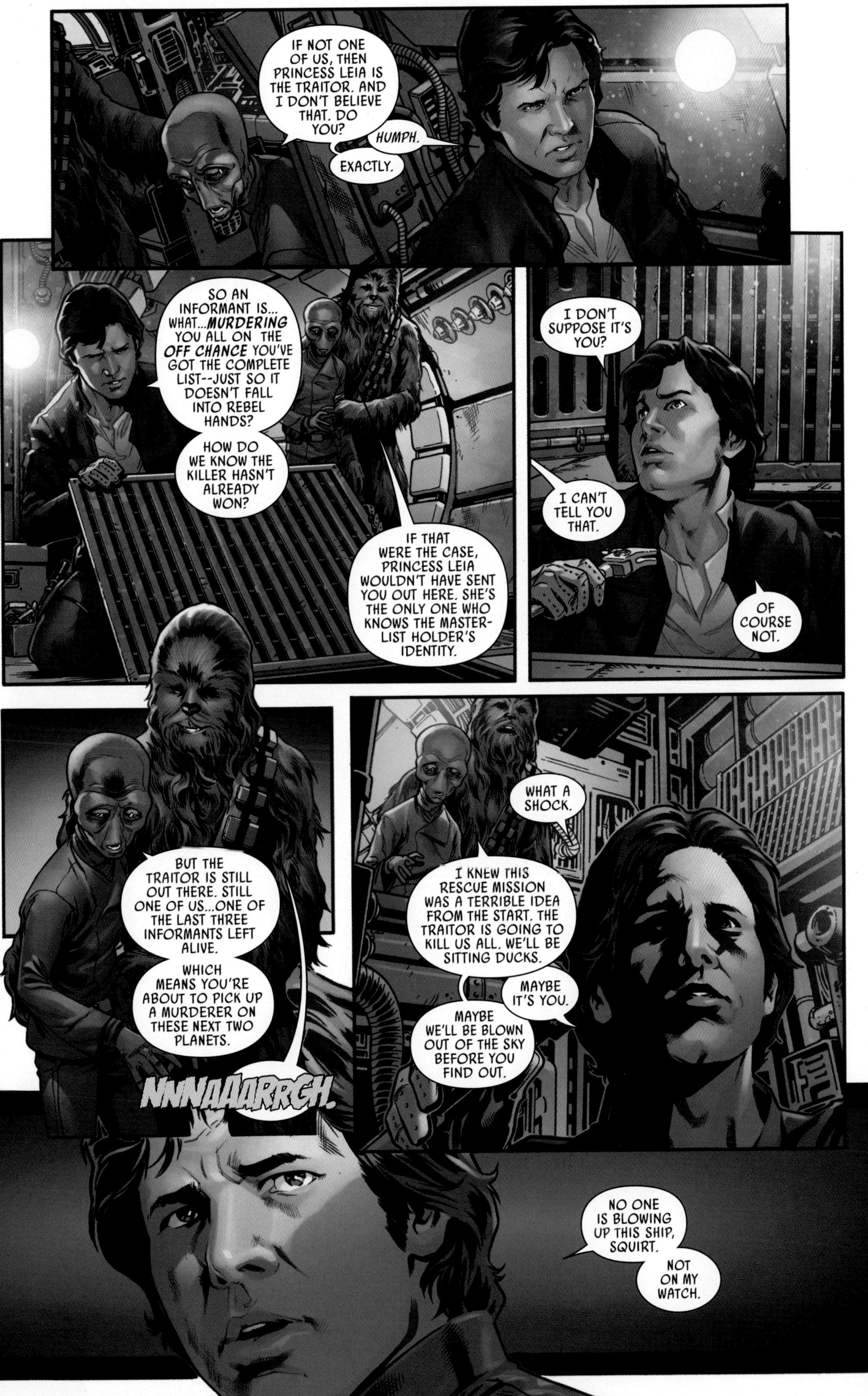

IF NOT ONE OF US, THEN PRINCESS LEIA IS THE TRAITOR. AND I DON'T BELIEVE THAT. DO YOU?
HUMPH.
EXACTLY.
SO AN INFORMANT IS... WHAT...MURDERING YOU ALL ON THE OFF CHANCE YOU'VE GOT THE COMPLETE LIST--JUST SO IT DOESN'T FALL INTO REBEL HANDS?
HOW DO WE KNOW THE KILLER HASN'T ALREADY WON?
IF THAT WERE THE CASE, PRINCESS LEIA WOULDN'T HAVE SENT YOU OUT HERE. SHE'S THE ONLY ONE WHO KNOWS THE MASTER-LIST HOLDER'S IDENTITY.
I DON'T SUPPOSE IT'S YOU?
I CAN'T TELL YOU THAT.
OF COURSE NOT.
BUT THE TRAITOR IS STILL OUT THERE. STILL ONE OF US...ONE OF THE LAST THREE INFORMANTS LEFT ALIVE.
WHICH MEANS YOU'RE ABOUT TO PICK UP A MURDERER ON THESE NEXT TWO PLANETS.
NNNAAARRRGH.
WHAT A SHOCK.
I KNEW THIS RESCUE MISSION WAS A TERRIBLE IDEA FROM THE START. THE TRAITOR IS GOING TO KILL US ALL. WE'LL BE SITTING DUCKS.
MAYBE IT'S YOU.
MAYBE WE'LL BE BLOWN OUT OF THE SKY BEFORE YOU FIND OUT.
NO ONE IS BLOWING UP THIS SHIP, SQUIRT.
NOT ON MY WATCH.

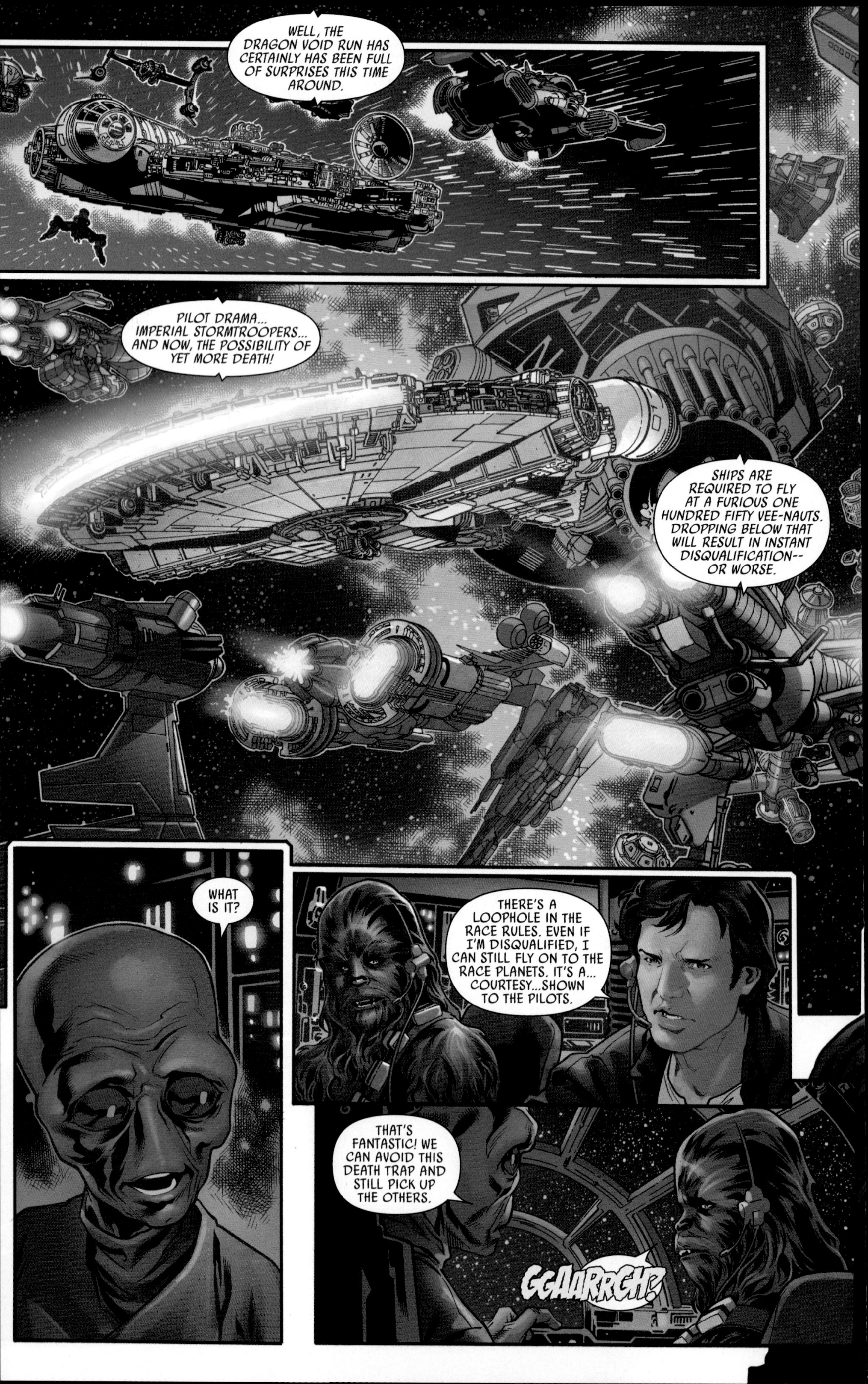
WELL, THE DRAGON VOID RUN HAS CERTAINLY HAS BEEN FULL OF SURPRISES THIS TIME AROUND.
PILOT DRAMA... IMPERIAL STORMTROOPERS... AND NOW, THE POSSIBILITY OF YET MORE DEATH!
SHIPS ARE REQUIRED TO FLY AT A FURIOUS ONE HUNDRED FIFTY VEE-NAUTS. DROPPING BELOW THAT WILL RESULT IN INSTANT DISQUALIFICATION-- OR WORSE.
WHAT IS IT?
THERE'S A LOOPHOLE IN THE RACE RULES. EVEN IF I'M DISQUALIFIED, I CAN STILL FLY ON TO THE RACE PLANETS. IT'S A... COURTESY...SHOWN TO THE PILOTS.
THAT'S FANTASTIC! WE CAN AVOID THIS DEATH TRAP AND STILL PICK UP THE OTHERS.
GGAARRGH!

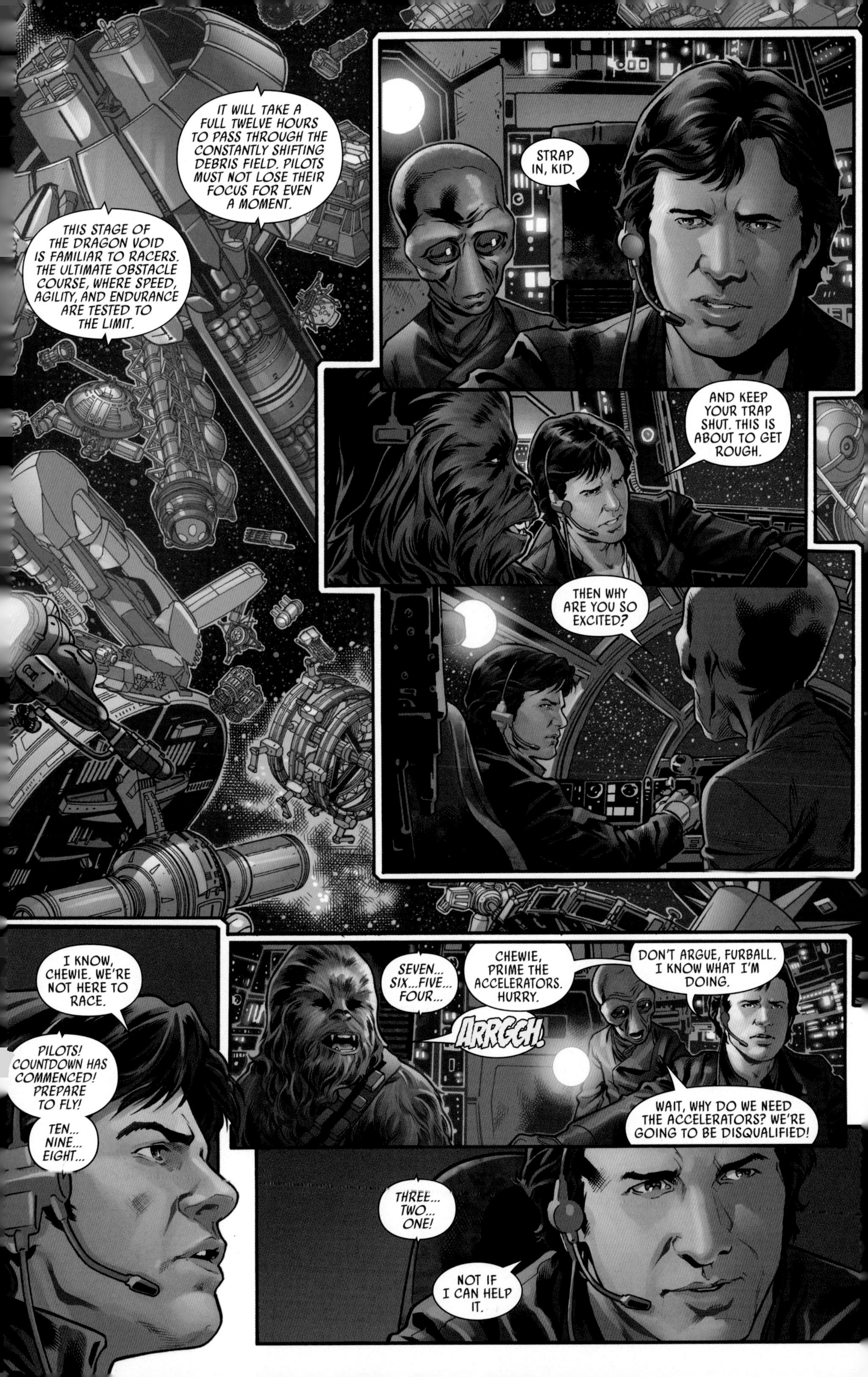

THIS STAGE OF THE DRAGON VOID IS FAMILIAR TO RACERS. THE ULTIMATE OBSTACLE COURSE, WHERE SPEED, AGILITY, AND ENDURANCE ARE TESTED TO THE LIMIT.
IT WILL TAKE A FULL TWELVE HOURS TO PASS THROUGH THE CONSTANTLY SHIFTING DEBRIS FIELD. PILOTS MUST NOT LOSE THEIR FOCUS FOR EVEN A MOMENT.
STRAP IN, KID.
AND KEEP YOUR TRAP SHUT. THIS IS ABOUT TO GET ROUGH.
THEN WHY ARE YOU SO EXCITED?
I KNOW, CHEWIE. WE'RE NOT HERE TO RACE.
PILOTS! COUNTDOWN HAS COMMENCED! PREPARE TO FLY!
TEN... NINE... EIGHT...
SEVEN... SIX...FIVE... FOUR...
ARRGGH!
CHEWIE, PRIME THE ACCELERATORS. HURRY.
DON'T ARGUE, FURBALL. I KNOW WHAT I'M DOING.
WAIT, WHY DO WE NEED THE ACCELERATORS? WE'RE GOING TO BE DISQUALIFIED!
THREE... TWO... ONE!
NOT IF I CAN HELP IT.

AND THEY'RE OFF!

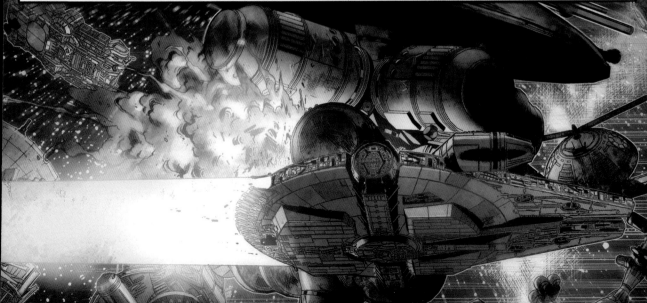

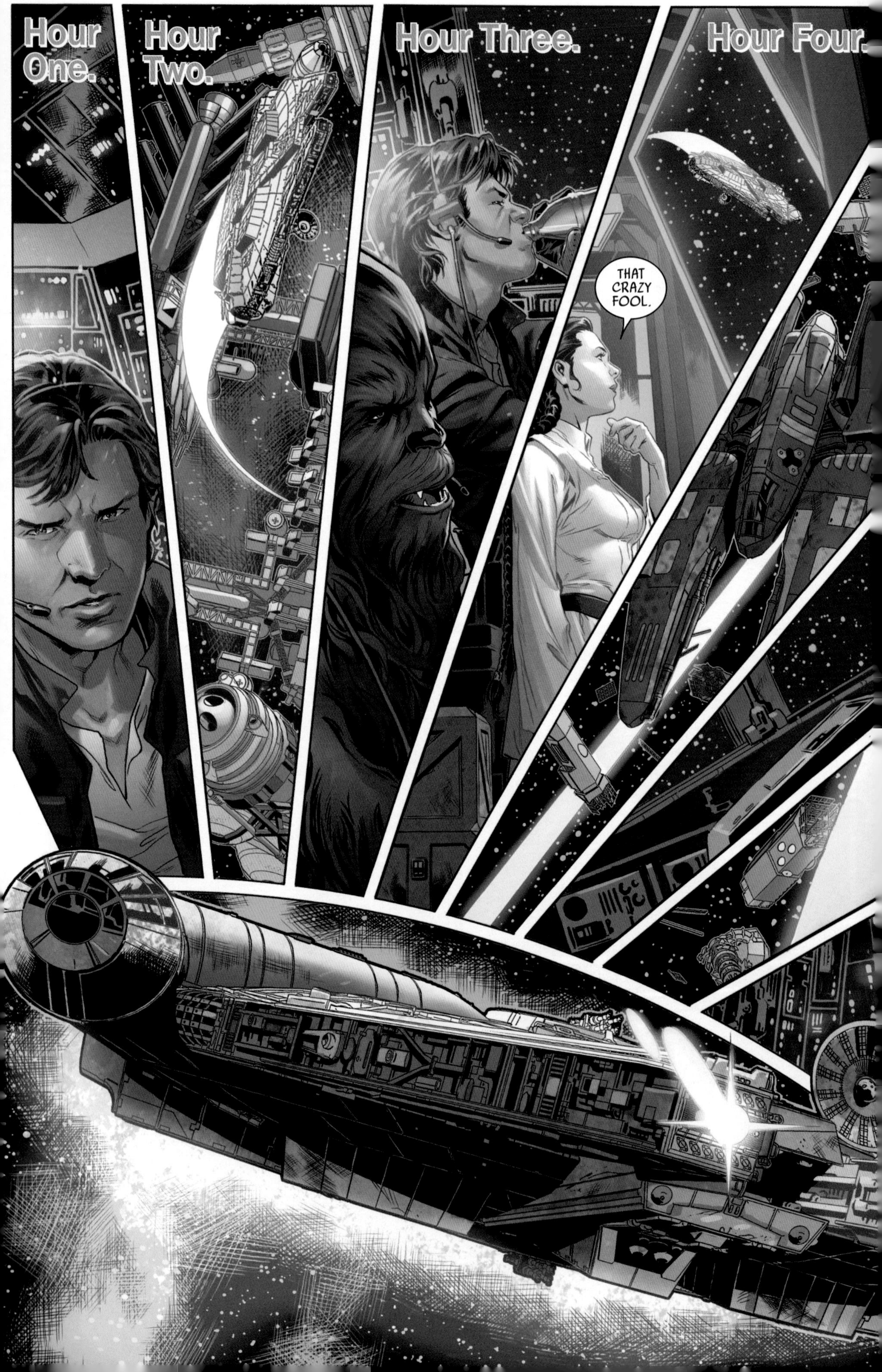
Hour One.
Hour Two.
Hour Three.
Hour Four.
THAT CRAZY FOOL.

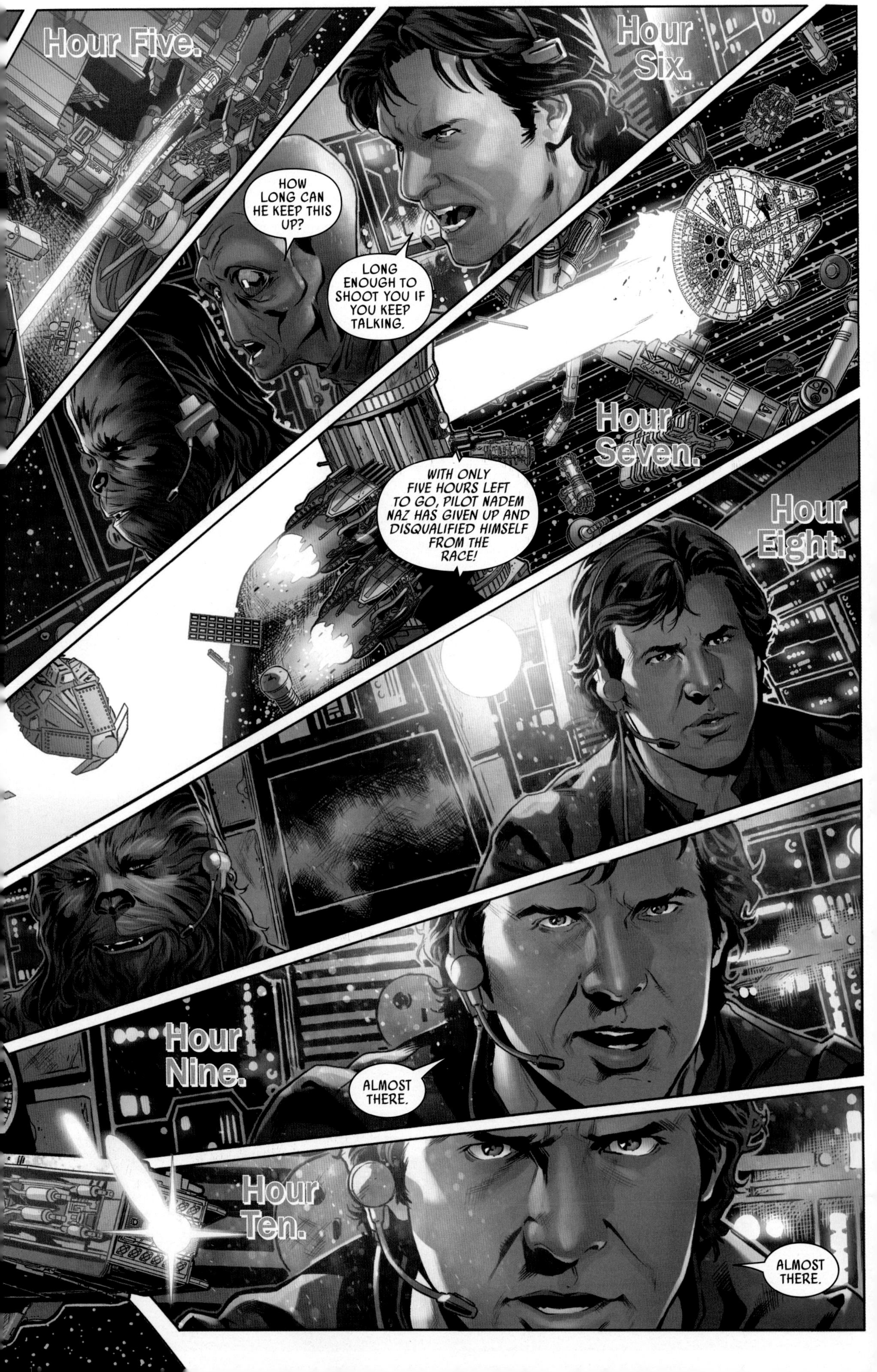
Hour Five.
Hour Six.
HOW LONG CAN HE KEEP THIS UP?
LONG ENOUGH TO SHOOT YOU IF YOU KEEP TALKING.
Hour Seven.
WITH ONLY FIVE HOURS LEFT TO GO, PILOT NADEM NAZ HAS GIVEN UP AND DISQUALIFIED HIMSELF FROM THE RACE!
Hour Eight.
Hour Nine.
ALMOST THERE.
Hour Ten.
ALMOST THERE.

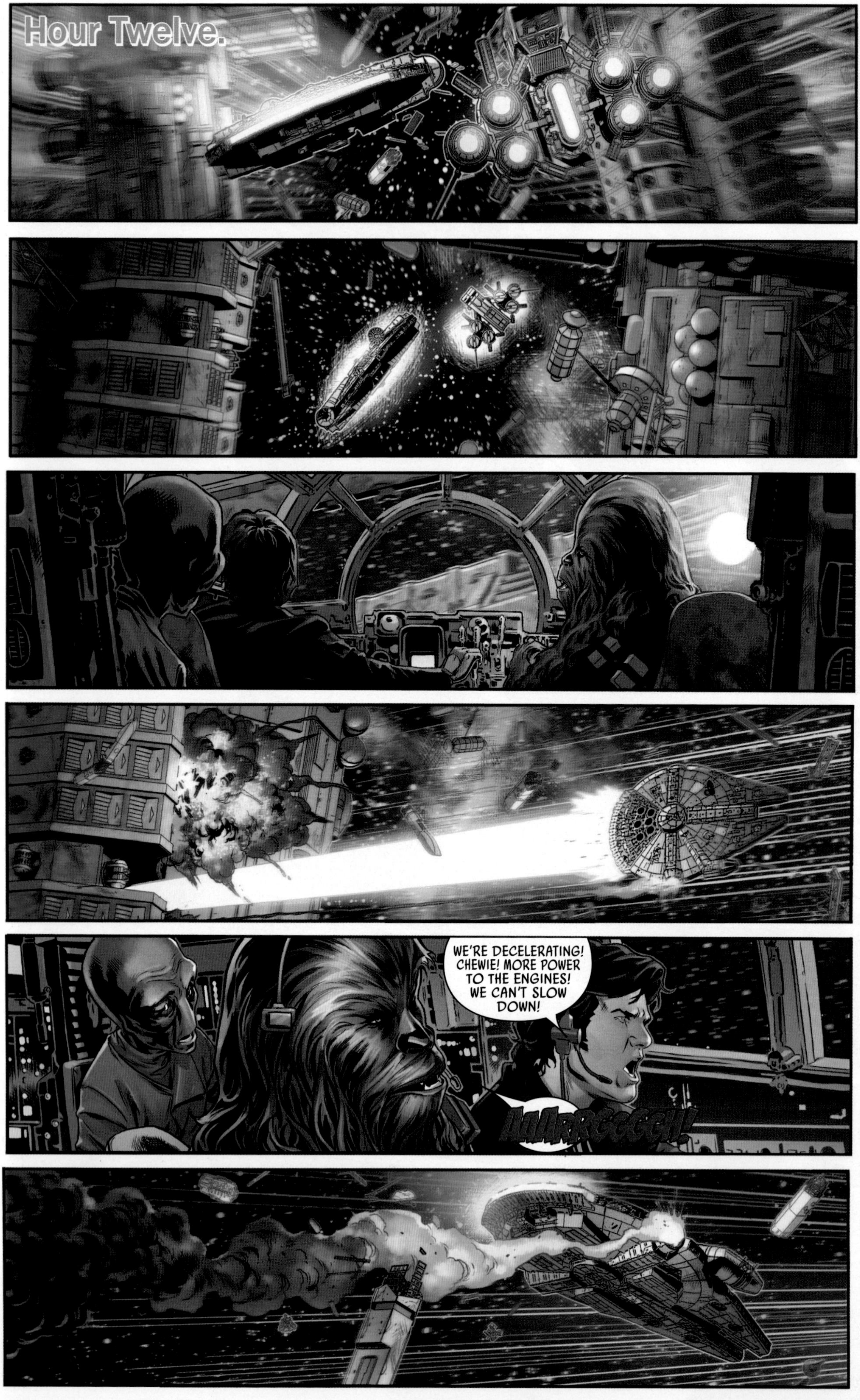
Hour Twelve.
WE'RE DECELERATING! CHEWIE! MORE POWER TO THE ENGINES! WE CAN'T SLOW DOWN!
AAARRRGGGGH!

WE'RE *EVEN*, SMUGGLER.

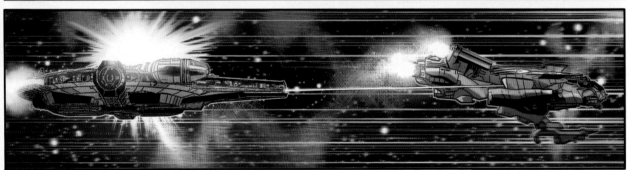

I GUESS WE ARE, ACE. THANKS FOR THE LIFT.

THE DRAGON VOID PILOTS HAVE BEEN WHITTLED DOWN TO BUT A HANDFUL, AND THEY'LL BE ALLOWED ONLY AN HOUR ON THE NEXT PLANET'S SURFACE TO MAKE REPAIRS AND REFUEL.

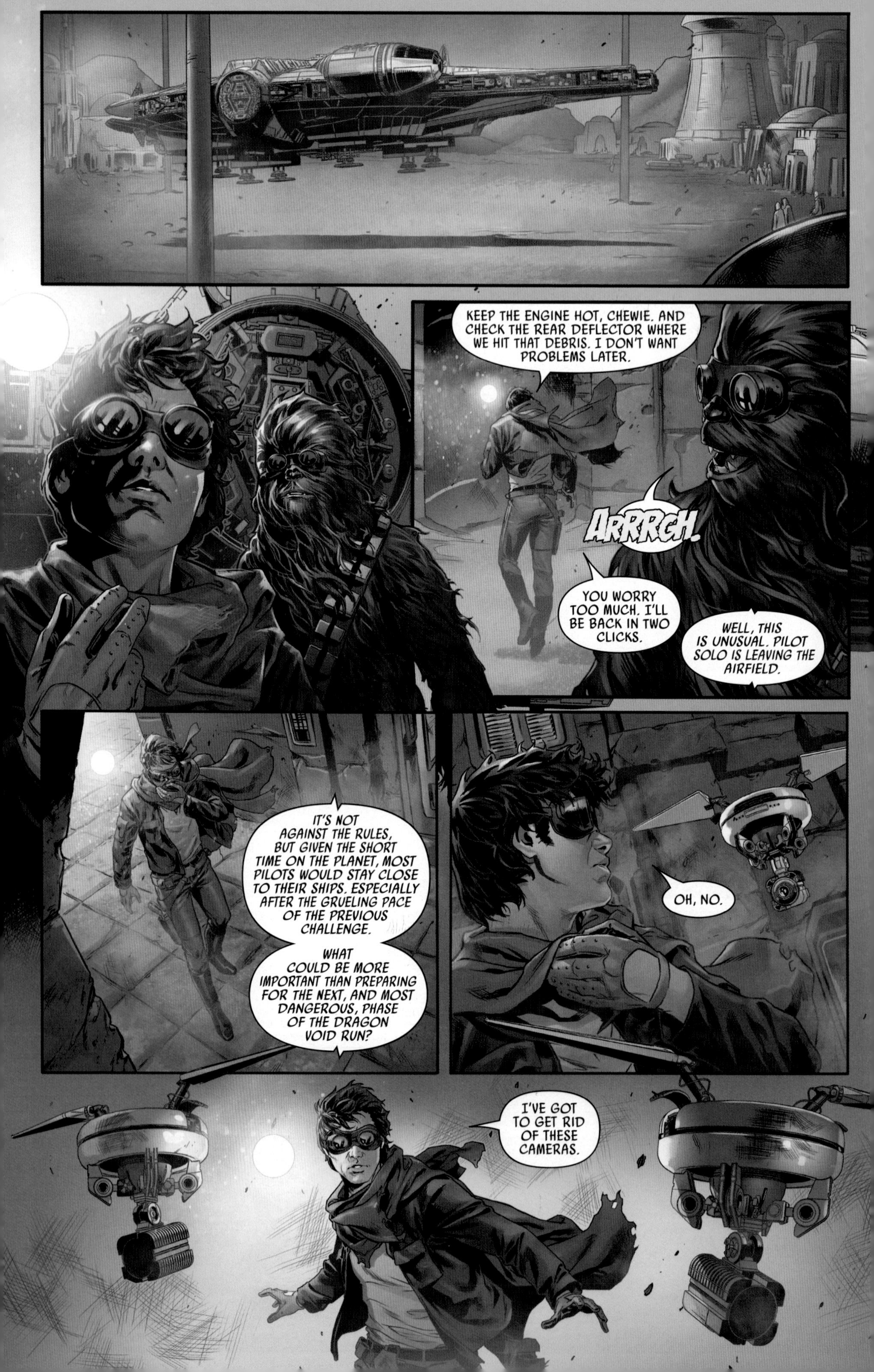
KEEP THE ENGINE HOT, CHEWIE. AND CHECK THE REAR DEFLECTOR WHERE WE HIT THAT DEBRIS. I DON'T WANT PROBLEMS LATER.
ARRRGH.
YOU WORRY TOO MUCH. I'LL BE BACK IN TWO CLICKS.
WELL, THIS IS UNUSUAL. PILOT SOLO IS LEAVING THE AIRFIELD.
IT'S NOT AGAINST THE RULES, BUT GIVEN THE SHORT TIME ON THE PLANET, MOST PILOTS WOULD STAY CLOSE TO THEIR SHIPS. ESPECIALLY AFTER THE GRUELING PACE OF THE PREVIOUS CHALLENGE.
WHAT COULD BE MORE IMPORTANT THAN PREPARING FOR THE NEXT, AND MOST DANGEROUS, PHASE OF THE DRAGON VOID RUN?
OH, NO.
I'VE GOT TO GET RID OF THESE CAMERAS.

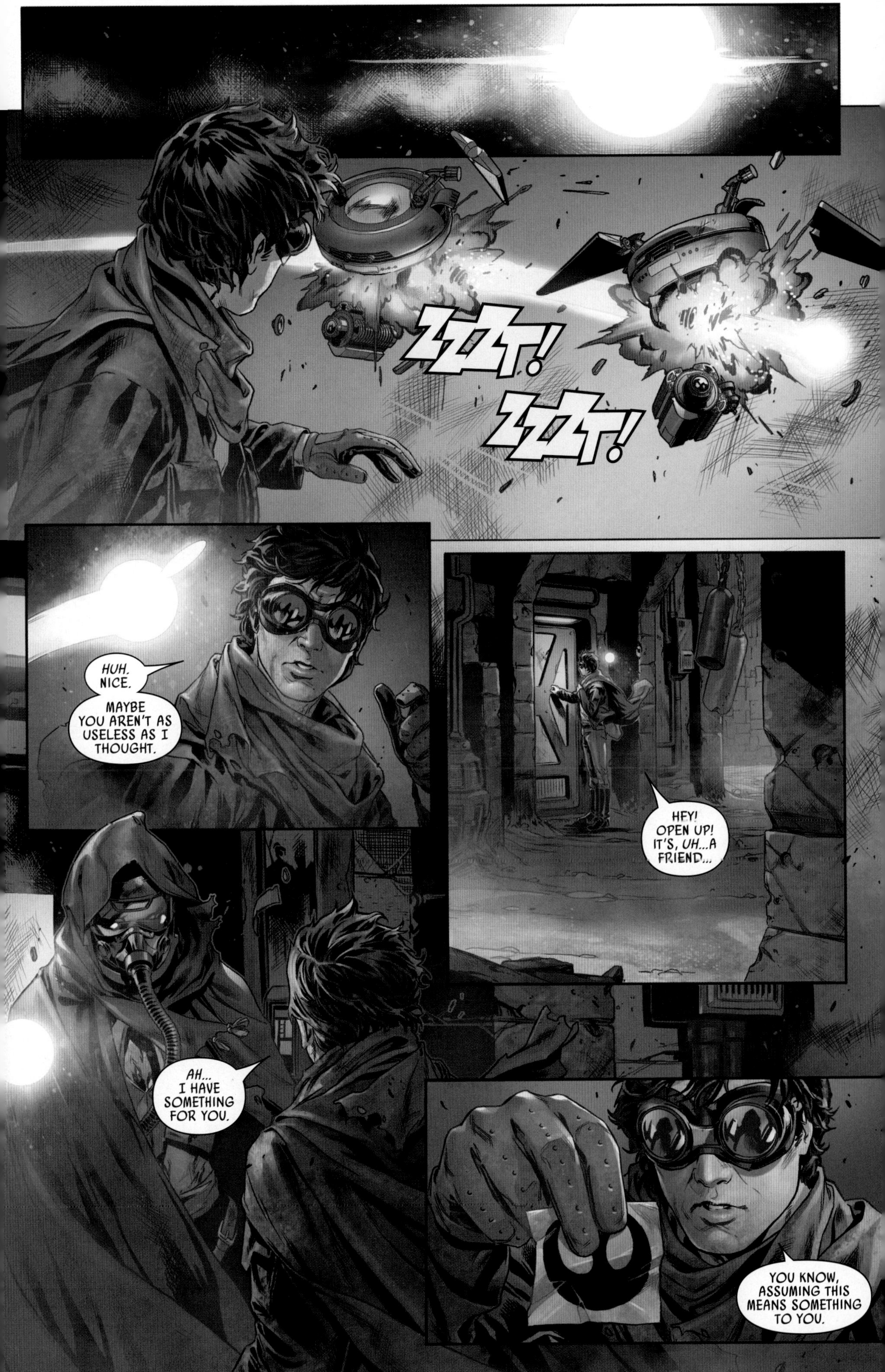
ZZZT!
ZZZT!
HUH. NICE.
MAYBE YOU AREN'T AS USELESS AS I THOUGHT.
HEY! OPEN UP! IT'S, UH...A FRIEND...
AH... I HAVE SOMETHING FOR YOU.
YOU KNOW, ASSUMING THIS MEANS SOMETHING TO YOU.

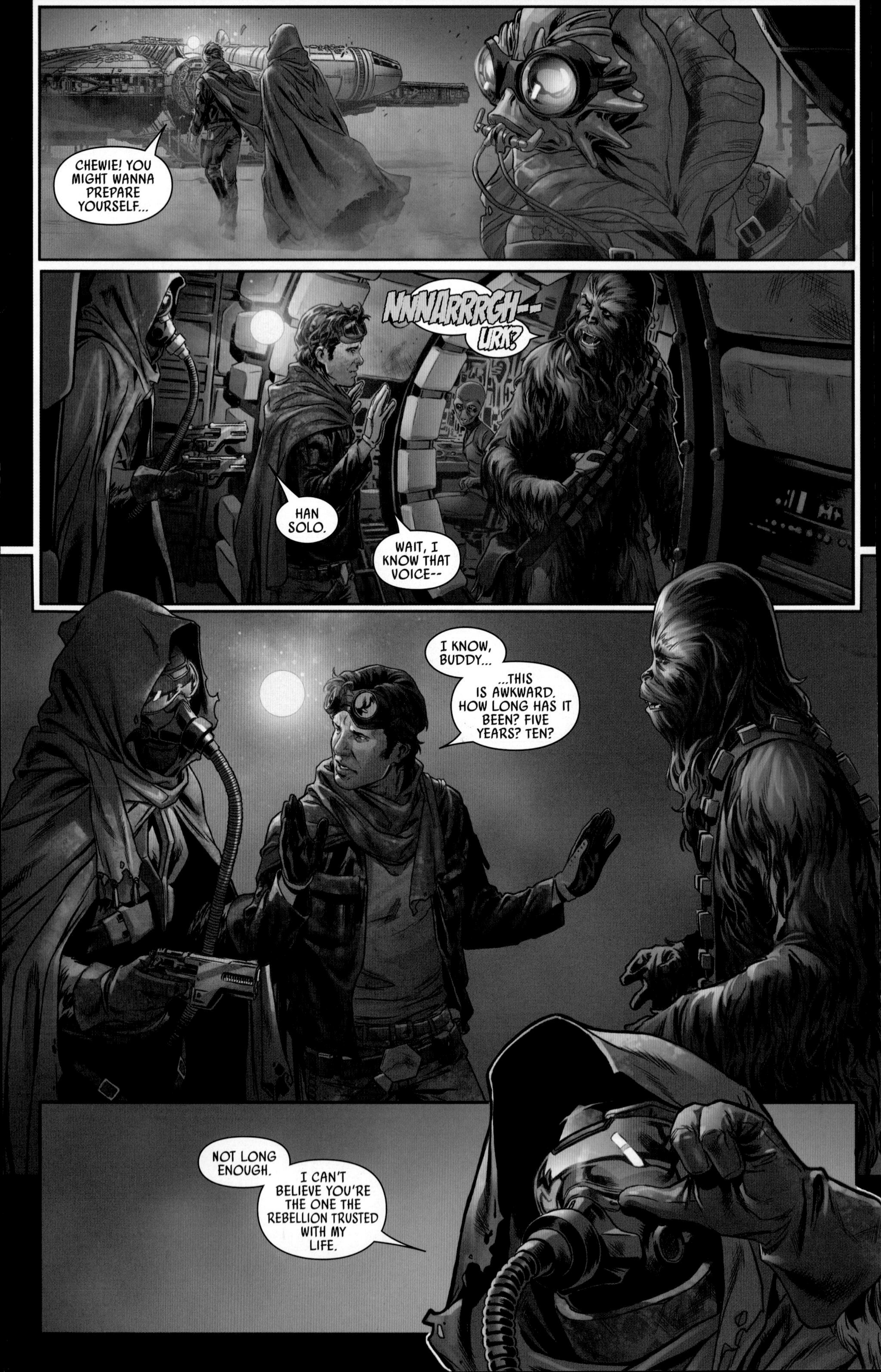

CHEWIE! YOU MIGHT WANNA PREPARE YOURSELF...
NNNARRRGH-- URK?
HAN SOLO.
WAIT, I KNOW THAT VOICE--
I KNOW, BUDDY...
...THIS IS AWKWARD. HOW LONG HAS IT BEEN? FIVE YEARS? TEN?
NOT LONG ENOUGH.
I CAN'T BELIEVE YOU'RE THE ONE THE REBELLION TRUSTED WITH MY LIFE.

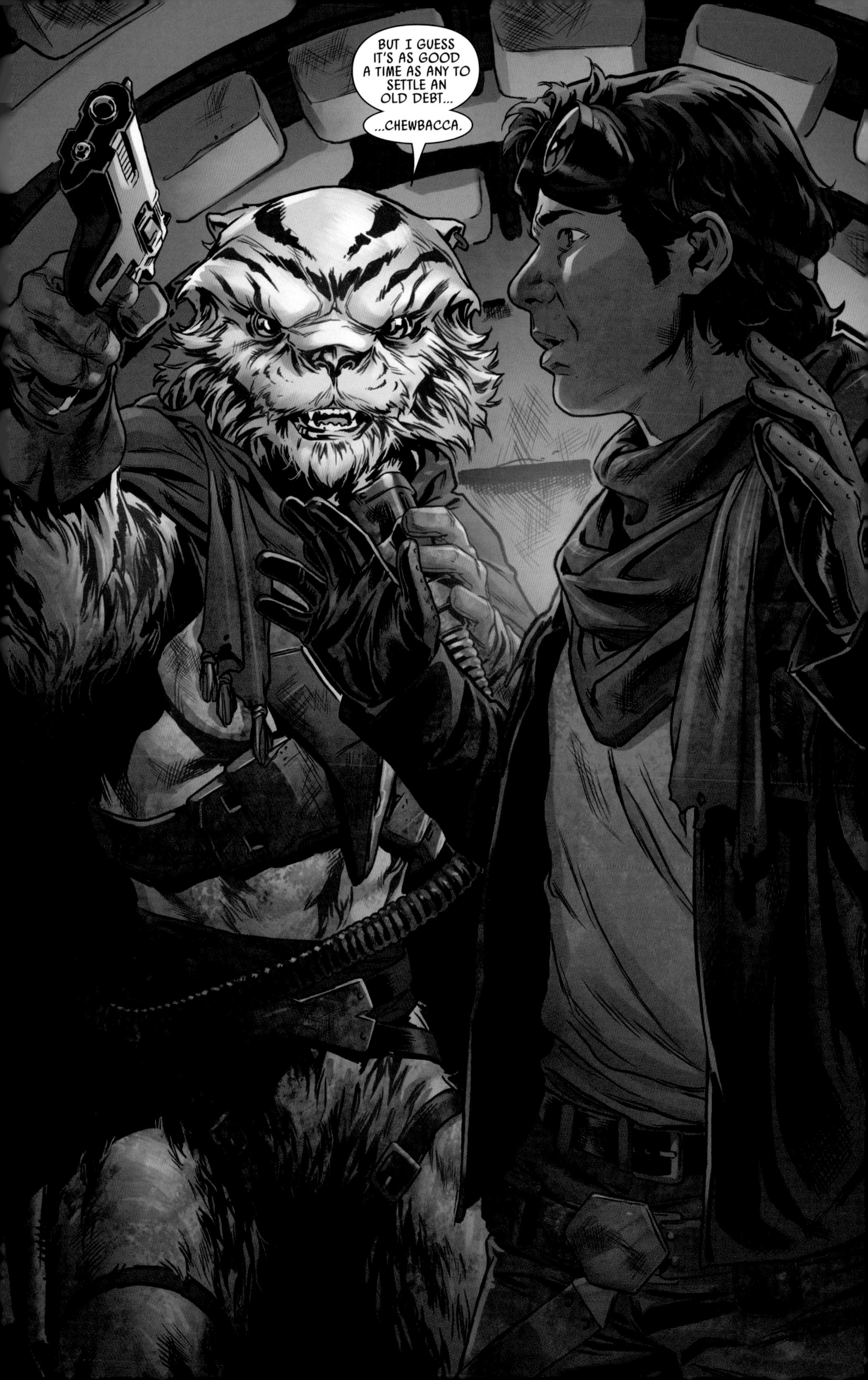
BUT I GUESS IT'S AS GOOD A TIME AS ANY TO SETTLE AN OLD DEBT...
...CHEWBACCA.

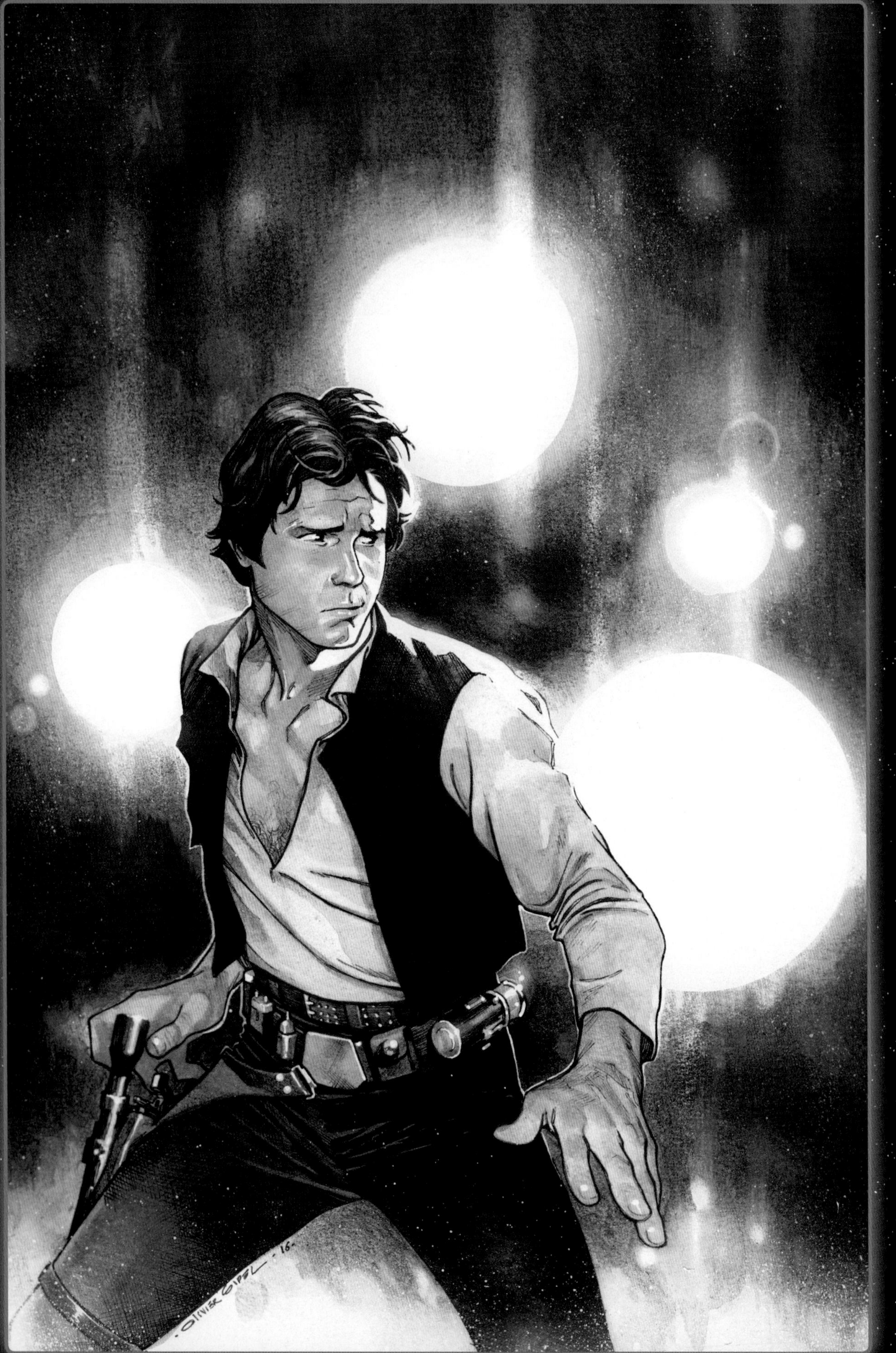

HAN SOLO 4

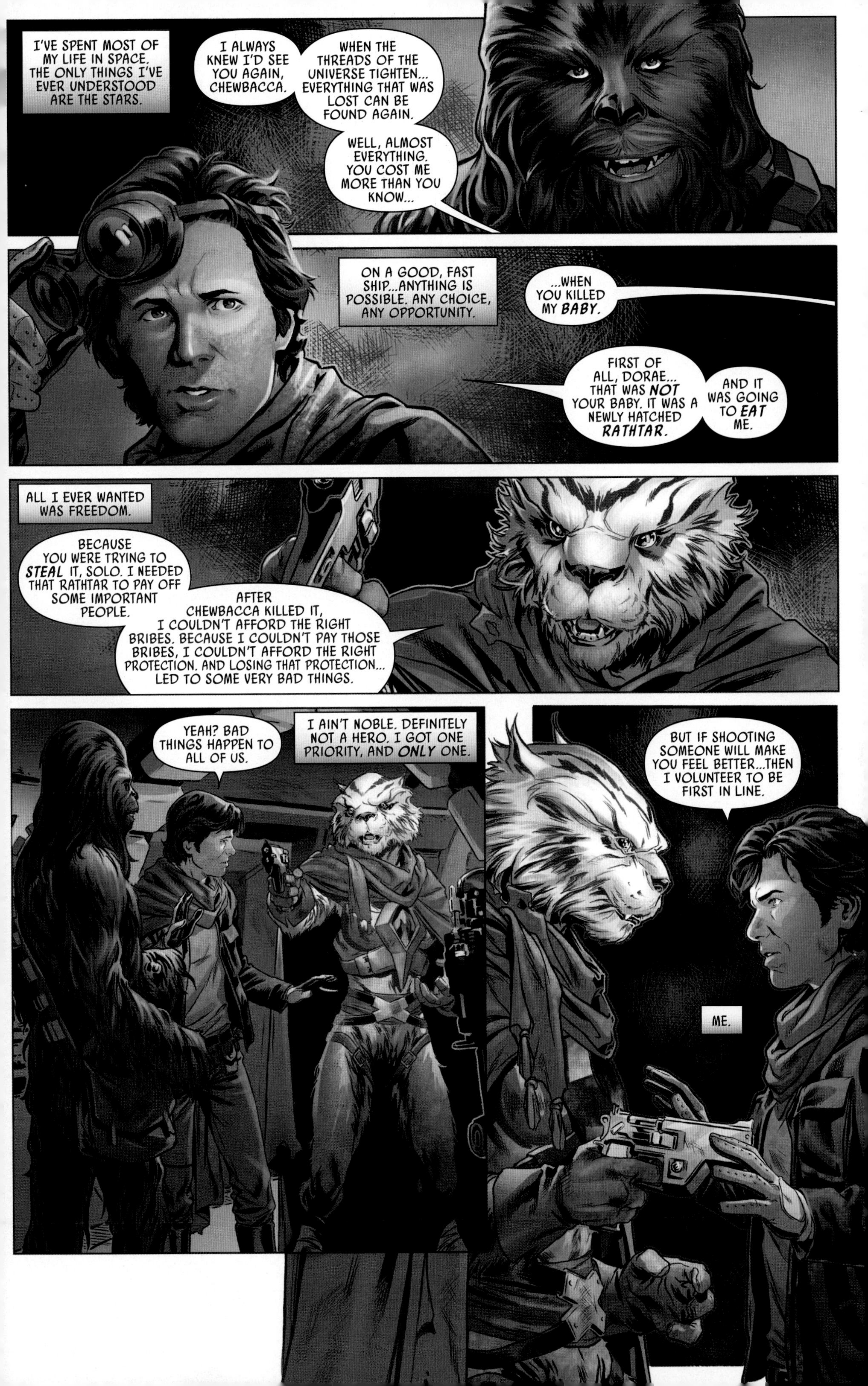
I'VE SPENT MOST OF MY LIFE IN SPACE. THE ONLY THINGS I'VE EVER UNDERSTOOD ARE THE STARS.
I ALWAYS KNEW I'D SEE YOU AGAIN, CHEWBACCA.
WHEN THE THREADS OF THE UNIVERSE TIGHTEN... EVERYTHING THAT WAS LOST CAN BE FOUND AGAIN.
WELL, ALMOST EVERYTHING. YOU COST ME MORE THAN YOU KNOW...
ON A GOOD, FAST SHIP...ANYTHING IS POSSIBLE. ANY CHOICE, ANY OPPORTUNITY.
...WHEN YOU KILLED MY BABY.
FIRST OF ALL, DORAE... THAT WAS NOT YOUR BABY. IT WAS A NEWLY HATCHED RATHTAR.
AND IT WAS GOING TO EAT ME.
ALL I EVER WANTED WAS FREEDOM.
BECAUSE YOU WERE TRYING TO STEAL IT, SOLO. I NEEDED THAT RATHTAR TO PAY OFF SOME IMPORTANT PEOPLE.
AFTER CHEWBACCA KILLED IT, I COULDN'T AFFORD THE RIGHT BRIBES. BECAUSE I COULDN'T PAY THOSE BRIBES, I COULDN'T AFFORD THE RIGHT PROTECTION. AND LOSING THAT PROTECTION... LED TO SOME VERY BAD THINGS.
YEAH? BAD THINGS HAPPEN TO ALL OF US.
I AIN'T NOBLE. DEFINITELY NOT A HERO. I GOT ONE PRIORITY, AND ONLY ONE.
BUT IF SHOOTING SOMEONE WILL MAKE YOU FEEL BETTER...THEN I VOLUNTEER TO BE FIRST IN LINE.
ME.

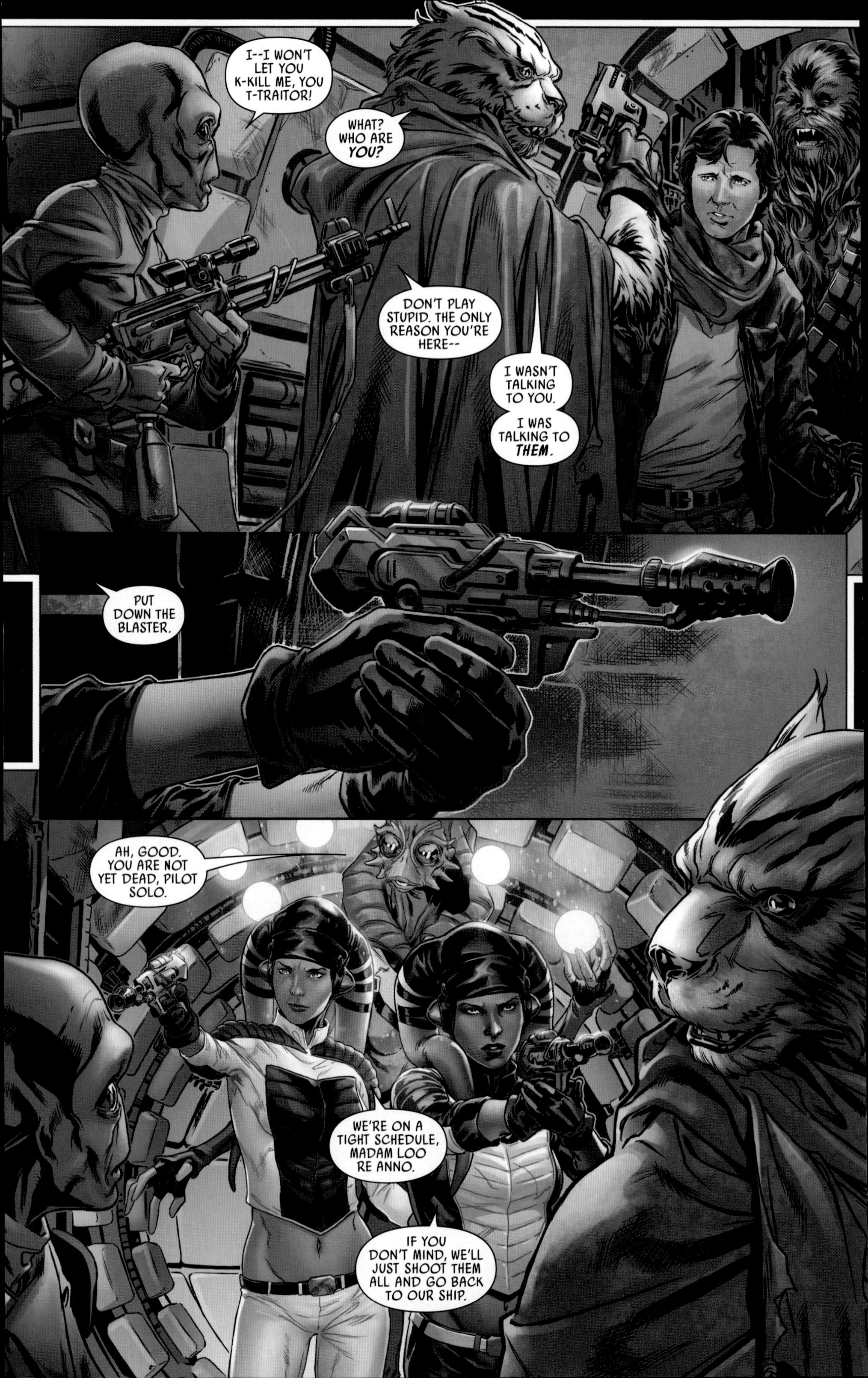
I--I WON'T LET YOU K-KILL ME, YOU T-TRAITOR!
WHAT? WHO ARE *YOU?*
DON'T PLAY STUPID. THE ONLY REASON YOU'RE HERE--
I WASN'T TALKING TO YOU.
I WAS TALKING TO ***THEM***.
PUT DOWN THE BLASTER.
AH, GOOD. YOU ARE NOT YET DEAD, PILOT SOLO.
WE'RE ON A TIGHT SCHEDULE, MADAM LOO RE ANNO.
IF YOU DON'T MIND, WE'LL JUST SHOOT THEM ALL AND GO BACK TO OUR SHIP.

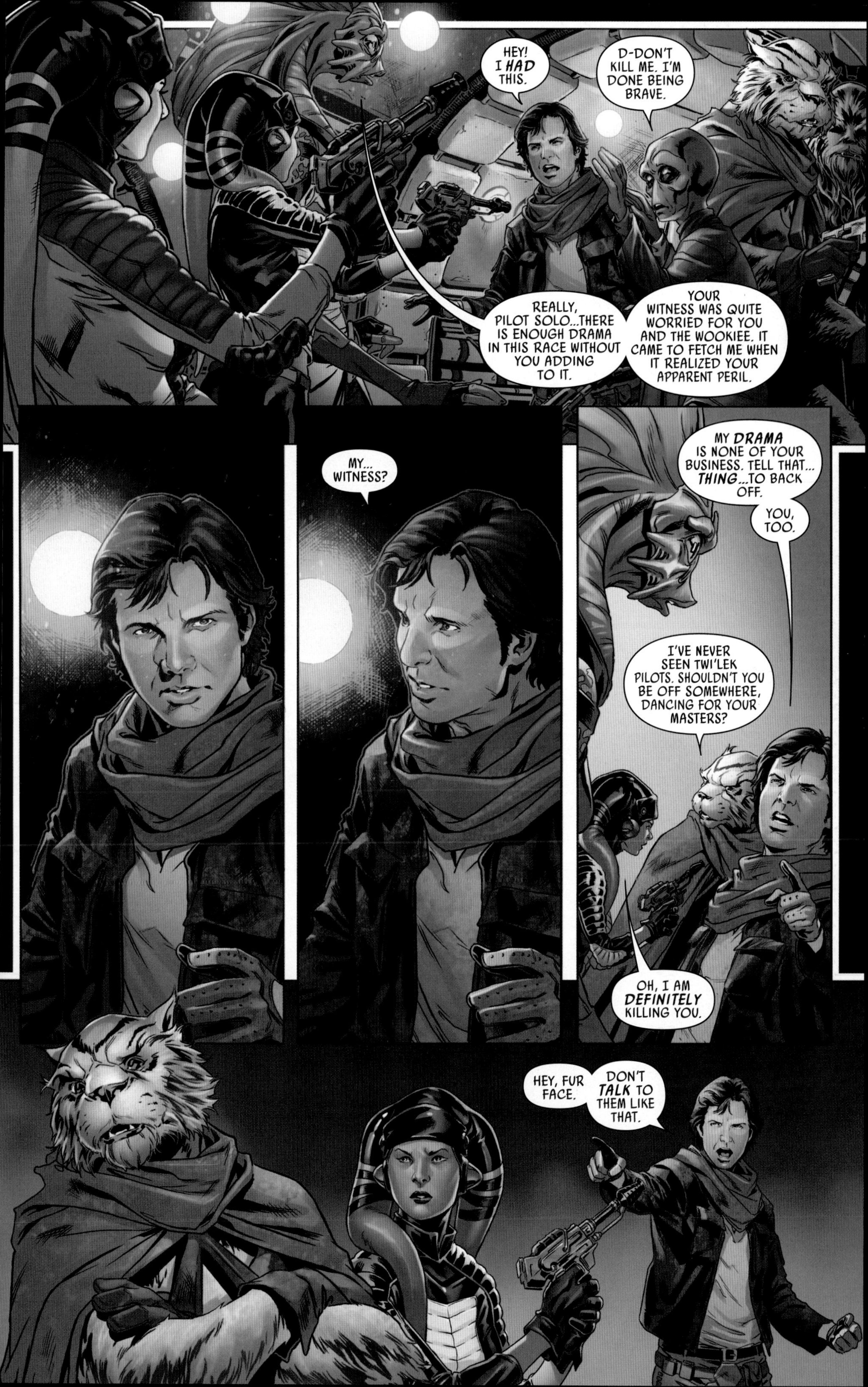
HEY! I HAD THIS.
D-DON'T KILL ME. I'M DONE BEING BRAVE.
REALLY, PILOT SOLO...THERE IS ENOUGH DRAMA IN THIS RACE WITHOUT YOU ADDING TO IT.
YOUR WITNESS WAS QUITE WORRIED FOR YOU AND THE WOOKIEE. IT CAME TO FETCH ME WHEN IT REALIZED YOUR APPARENT PERIL.
MY... WITNESS?
MY DRAMA IS NONE OF YOUR BUSINESS. TELL THAT... THING...TO BACK OFF.
YOU, TOO.
I'VE NEVER SEEN TWI'LEK PILOTS. SHOULDN'T YOU BE OFF SOMEWHERE, DANCING FOR YOUR MASTERS?
OH, I AM DEFINITELY KILLING YOU.
HEY, FUR FACE.
DON'T TALK TO THEM LIKE THAT.

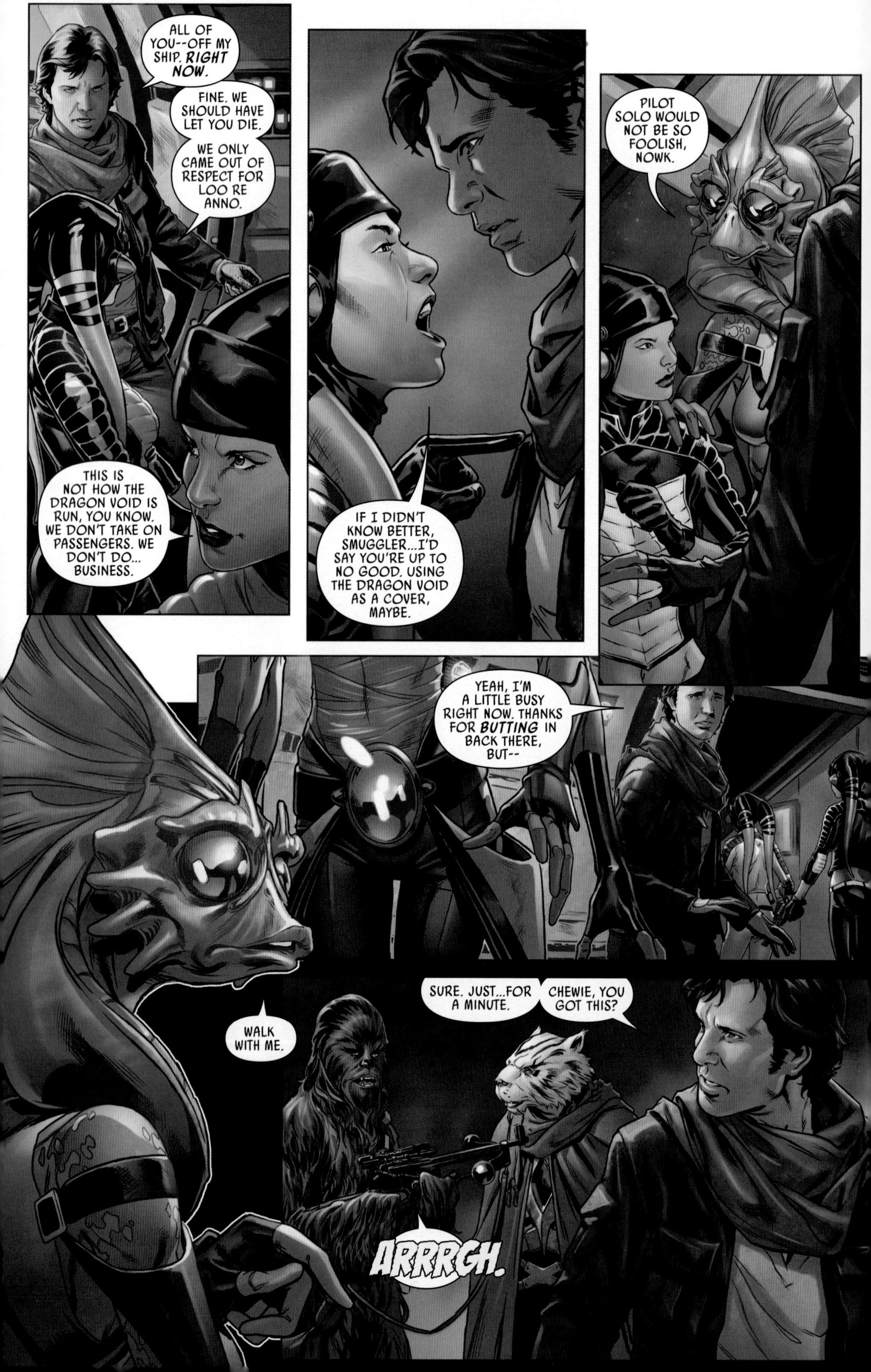
ALL OF YOU--OFF MY SHIP. **RIGHT NOW.**
FINE. WE SHOULD HAVE LET YOU DIE.
WE ONLY CAME OUT OF RESPECT FOR LOO RE ANNO.
THIS IS NOT HOW THE DRAGON VOID IS RUN, YOU KNOW. WE DON'T TAKE ON PASSENGERS. WE DON'T DO... BUSINESS.
IF I DIDN'T KNOW BETTER, SMUGGLER...I'D SAY YOU'RE UP TO NO GOOD. USING THE DRAGON VOID AS A COVER, MAYBE.
PILOT SOLO WOULD NOT BE SO FOOLISH, NOWK.
YEAH, I'M A LITTLE BUSY RIGHT NOW. THANKS FOR **BUTTING** IN BACK THERE, BUT--
WALK WITH ME.
SURE. JUST...FOR A MINUTE.
CHEWIE, YOU GOT THIS?
ARRRGH.

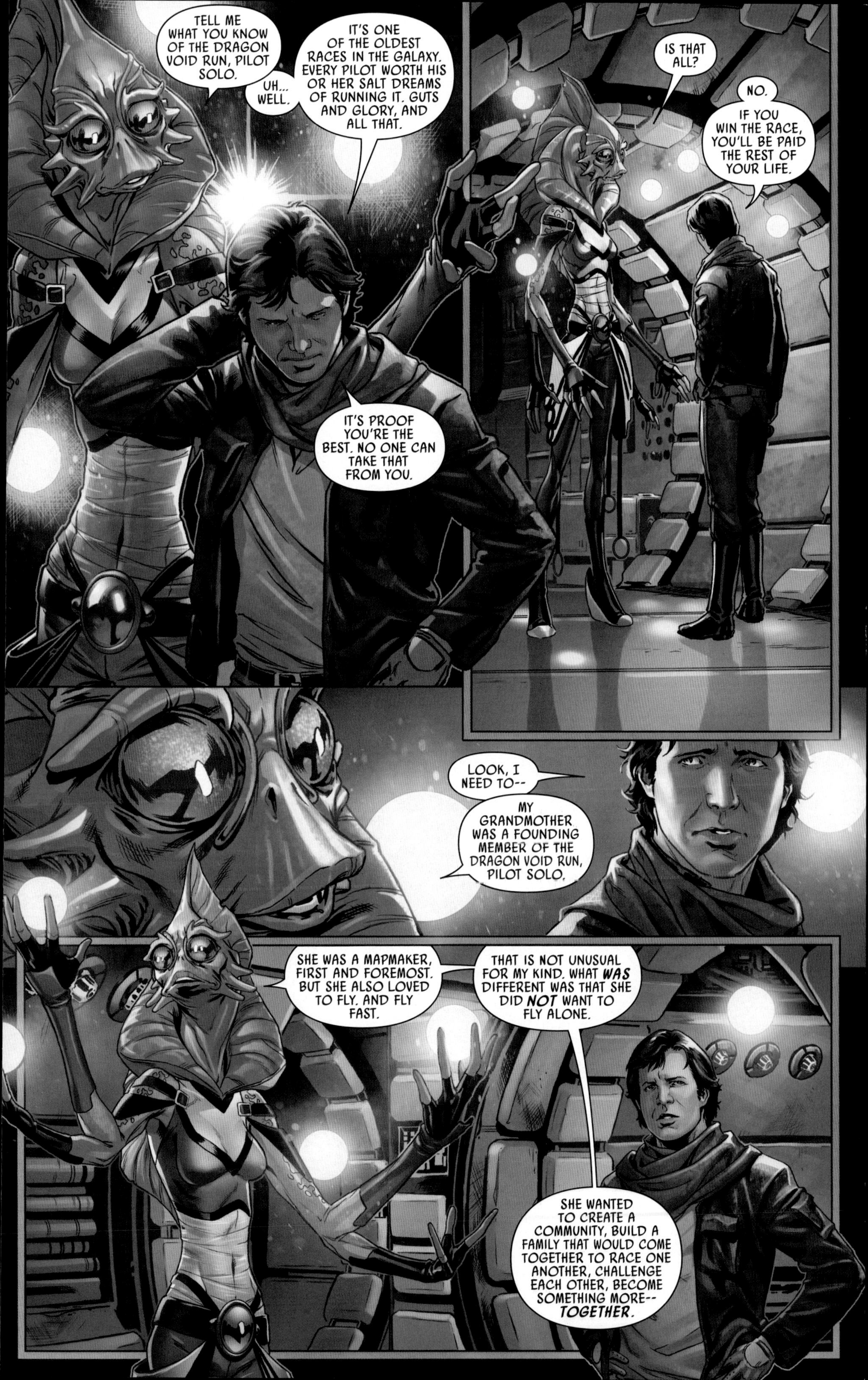

TELL ME WHAT YOU KNOW OF THE DRAGON VOID RUN, PILOT SOLO.
UH... WELL.
IT'S ONE OF THE OLDEST RACES IN THE GALAXY. EVERY PILOT WORTH HIS OR HER SALT DREAMS OF RUNNING IT. GUTS AND GLORY, AND ALL THAT.
IT'S PROOF YOU'RE THE BEST. NO ONE CAN TAKE THAT FROM YOU.
IS THAT ALL?
NO.
IF YOU WIN THE RACE, YOU'LL BE PAID THE REST OF YOUR LIFE.
LOOK, I NEED TO--
MY GRANDMOTHER WAS A FOUNDING MEMBER OF THE DRAGON VOID RUN, PILOT SOLO.
SHE WAS A MAPMAKER, FIRST AND FOREMOST. BUT SHE ALSO LOVED TO FLY. AND FLY FAST.
THAT IS NOT UNUSUAL FOR MY KIND. WHAT *WAS* DIFFERENT WAS THAT SHE DID *NOT* WANT TO FLY ALONE.
SHE WANTED TO CREATE A COMMUNITY, BUILD A FAMILY THAT WOULD COME TOGETHER TO RACE ONE ANOTHER, CHALLENGE EACH OTHER, BECOME SOMETHING MORE-- *TOGETHER*.

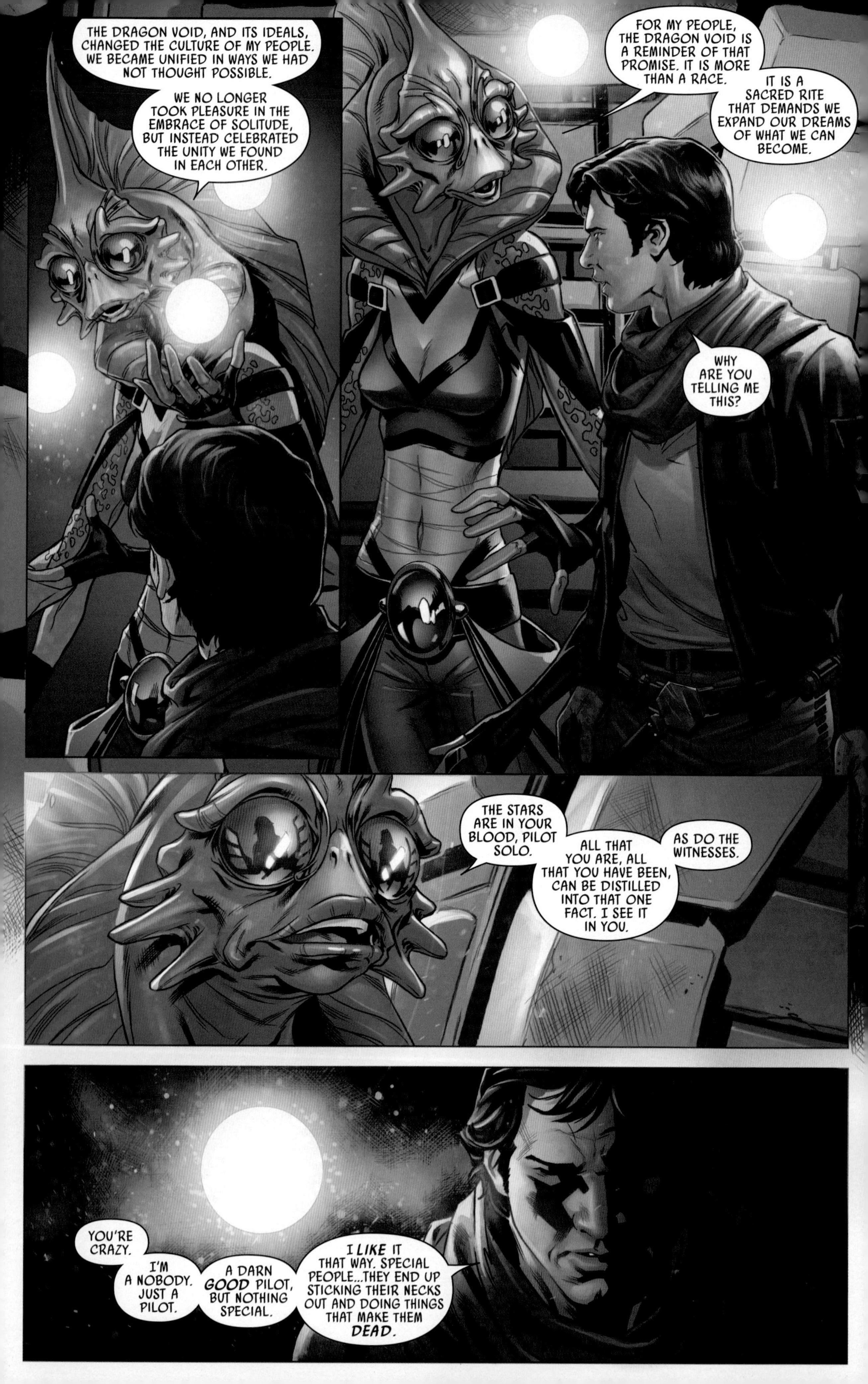
THE DRAGON VOID, AND ITS IDEALS, CHANGED THE CULTURE OF MY PEOPLE. WE BECAME UNIFIED IN WAYS WE HAD NOT THOUGHT POSSIBLE.
WE NO LONGER TOOK PLEASURE IN THE EMBRACE OF SOLITUDE, BUT INSTEAD CELEBRATED THE UNITY WE FOUND IN EACH OTHER.
FOR MY PEOPLE, THE DRAGON VOID IS A REMINDER OF THAT PROMISE. IT IS MORE THAN A RACE.
IT IS A SACRED RITE THAT DEMANDS WE EXPAND OUR DREAMS OF WHAT WE CAN BECOME.
WHY ARE YOU TELLING ME THIS?
THE STARS ARE IN YOUR BLOOD, PILOT SOLO.
ALL THAT YOU ARE, ALL THAT YOU HAVE BEEN, CAN BE DISTILLED INTO THAT ONE FACT. I SEE IT IN YOU.
AS DO THE WITNESSES.
YOU'RE CRAZY.
I'M A NOBODY. JUST A PILOT.
A DARN GOOD PILOT, BUT NOTHING SPECIAL.
I LIKE IT THAT WAY. SPECIAL PEOPLE...THEY END UP STICKING THEIR NECKS OUT AND DOING THINGS THAT MAKE THEM DEAD.

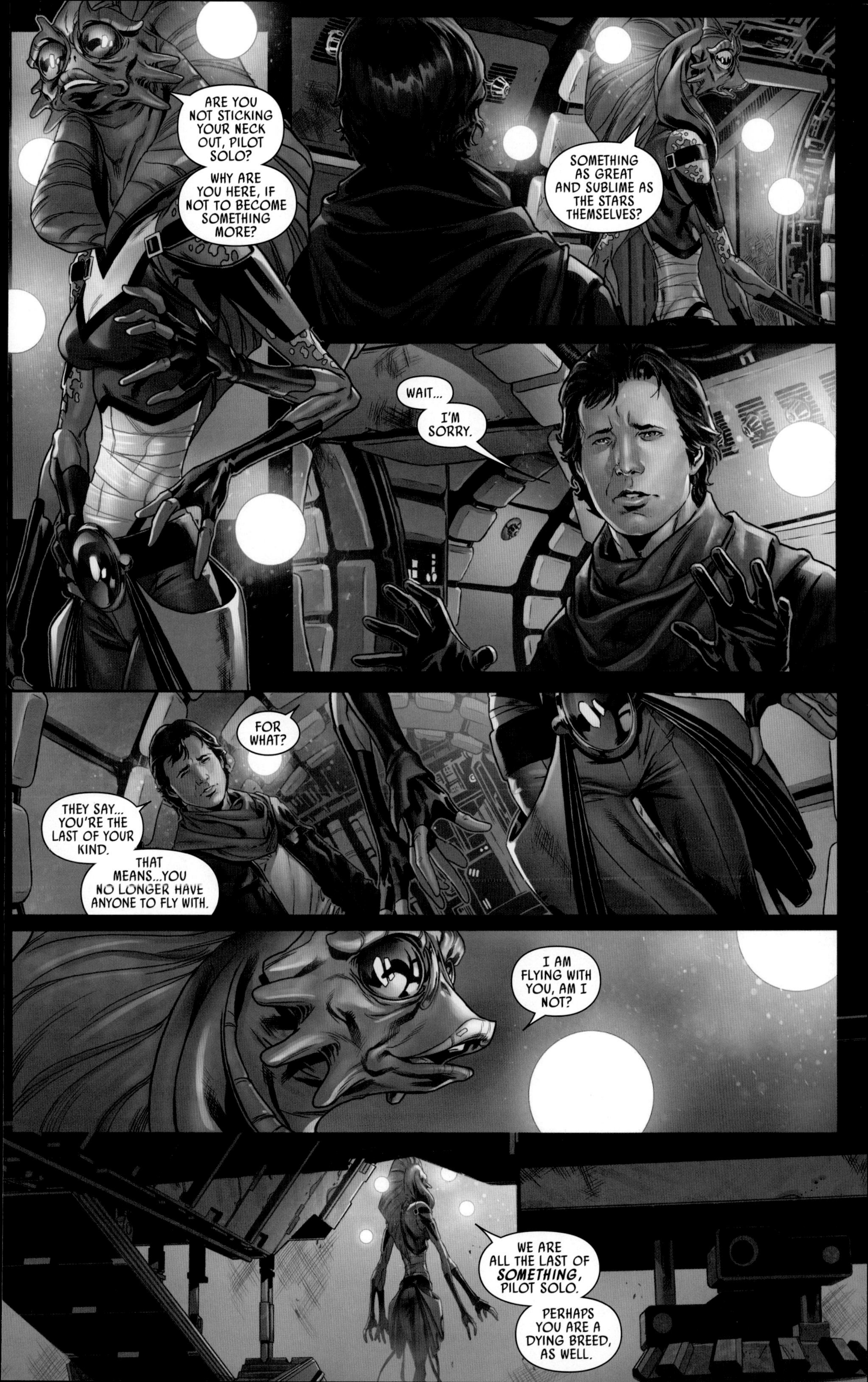
ARE YOU NOT STICKING YOUR NECK OUT, PILOT SOLO?
WHY ARE YOU HERE, IF NOT TO BECOME SOMETHING MORE?
SOMETHING AS GREAT AND SUBLIME AS THE STARS THEMSELVES?
WAIT...
I'M SORRY.
FOR WHAT?
THEY SAY... YOU'RE THE LAST OF YOUR KIND.
THAT MEANS...YOU NO LONGER HAVE ANYONE TO FLY WITH.
I AM FLYING WITH YOU, AM I NOT?
WE ARE ALL THE LAST OF *SOMETHING*, PILOT SOLO.
PERHAPS YOU ARE A DYING BREED, AS WELL.

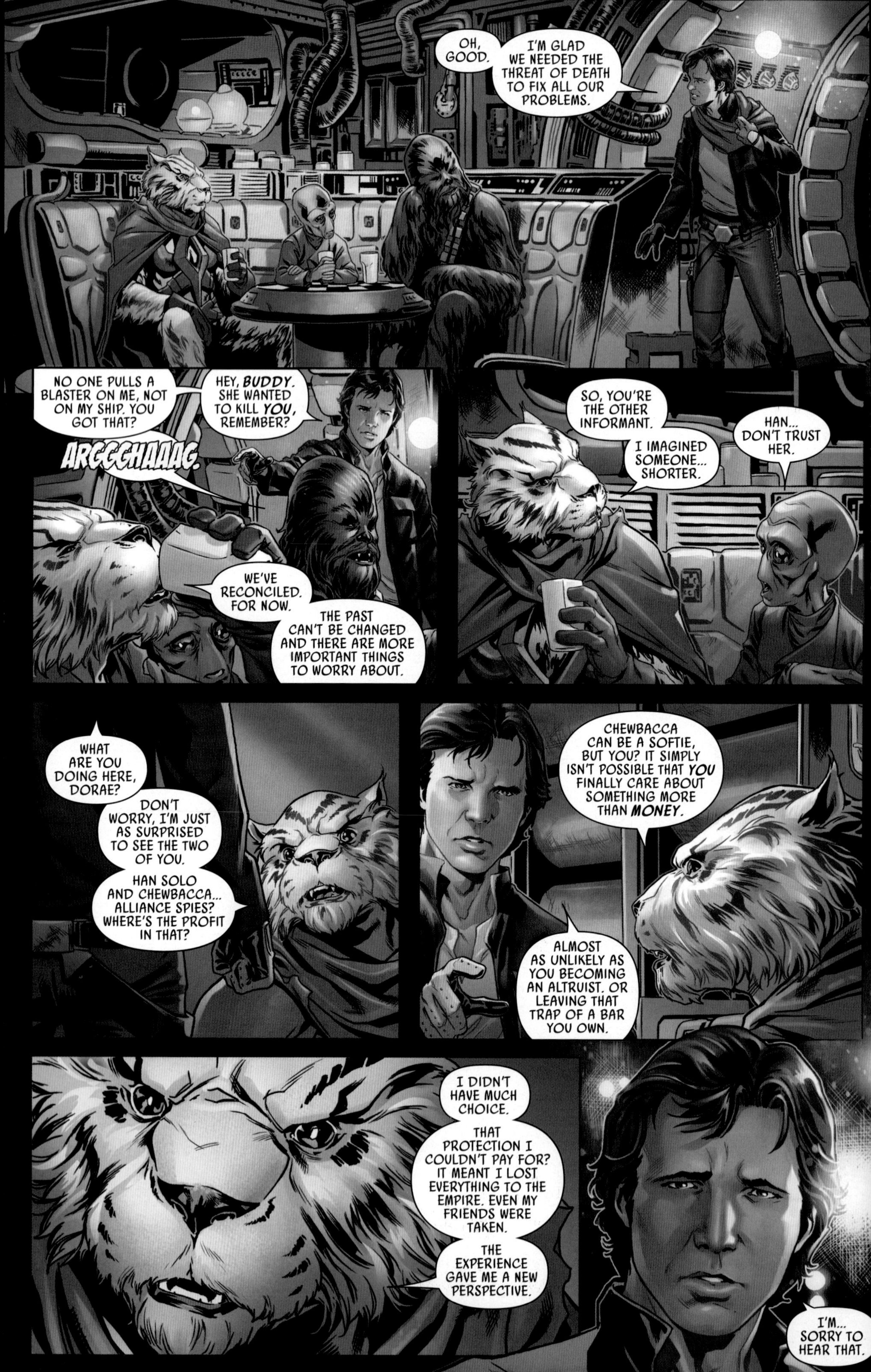
OH, GOOD.
I'M GLAD WE NEEDED THE THREAT OF DEATH TO FIX ALL OUR PROBLEMS.
NO ONE PULLS A BLASTER ON ME, NOT ON MY SHIP. YOU GOT THAT?
HEY, BUDDY. SHE WANTED TO KILL YOU, REMEMBER?
ARGGGHAAAG.
WE'VE RECONCILED. FOR NOW.
THE PAST CAN'T BE CHANGED AND THERE ARE MORE IMPORTANT THINGS TO WORRY ABOUT.
SO, YOU'RE THE OTHER INFORMANT.
I IMAGINED SOMEONE... SHORTER.
HAN... DON'T TRUST HER.
WHAT ARE YOU DOING HERE, DORAE?
DON'T WORRY, I'M JUST AS SURPRISED TO SEE THE TWO OF YOU.
HAN SOLO AND CHEWBACCA... ALLIANCE SPIES? WHERE'S THE PROFIT IN THAT?
CHEWBACCA CAN BE A SOFTIE, BUT YOU? IT SIMPLY ISN'T POSSIBLE THAT YOU FINALLY CARE ABOUT SOMETHING MORE THAN MONEY.
ALMOST AS UNLIKELY AS YOU BECOMING AN ALTRUIST. OR LEAVING THAT TRAP OF A BAR YOU OWN.
I DIDN'T HAVE MUCH CHOICE.
THAT PROTECTION I COULDN'T PAY FOR? IT MEANT I LOST EVERYTHING TO THE EMPIRE. EVEN MY FRIENDS WERE TAKEN.
THE EXPERIENCE GAVE ME A NEW PERSPECTIVE.
I'M... SORRY TO HEAR THAT.

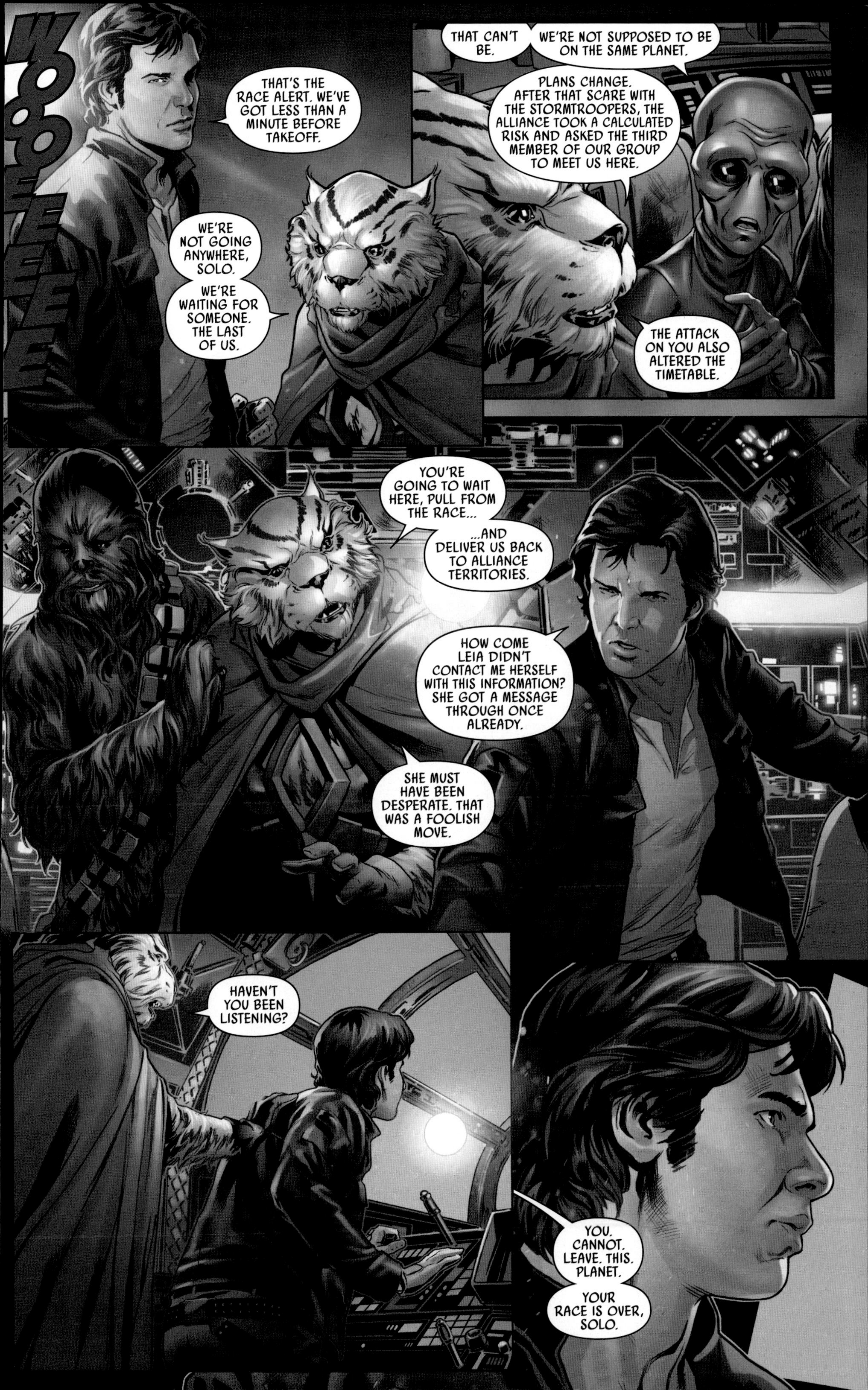
WOOOEEEEEE
THAT'S THE RACE ALERT. WE'VE GOT LESS THAN A MINUTE BEFORE TAKEOFF.
WE'RE NOT GOING ANYWHERE, SOLO.
WE'RE WAITING FOR SOMEONE. THE LAST OF US.
THAT CAN'T BE.
WE'RE NOT SUPPOSED TO BE ON THE SAME PLANET.
PLANS CHANGE. AFTER THAT SCARE WITH THE STORMTROOPERS, THE ALLIANCE TOOK A CALCULATED RISK AND ASKED THE THIRD MEMBER OF OUR GROUP TO MEET US HERE.
THE ATTACK ON YOU ALSO ALTERED THE TIMETABLE.
YOU'RE GOING TO WAIT HERE, PULL FROM THE RACE...
...AND DELIVER US BACK TO ALLIANCE TERRITORIES.
HOW COME LEIA DIDN'T CONTACT ME HERSELF WITH THIS INFORMATION? SHE GOT A MESSAGE THROUGH ONCE ALREADY.
SHE MUST HAVE BEEN DESPERATE. THAT WAS A FOOLISH MOVE.
HAVEN'T YOU BEEN LISTENING?
YOU. CANNOT. LEAVE. THIS. PLANET.
YOUR RACE IS OVER, SOLO.

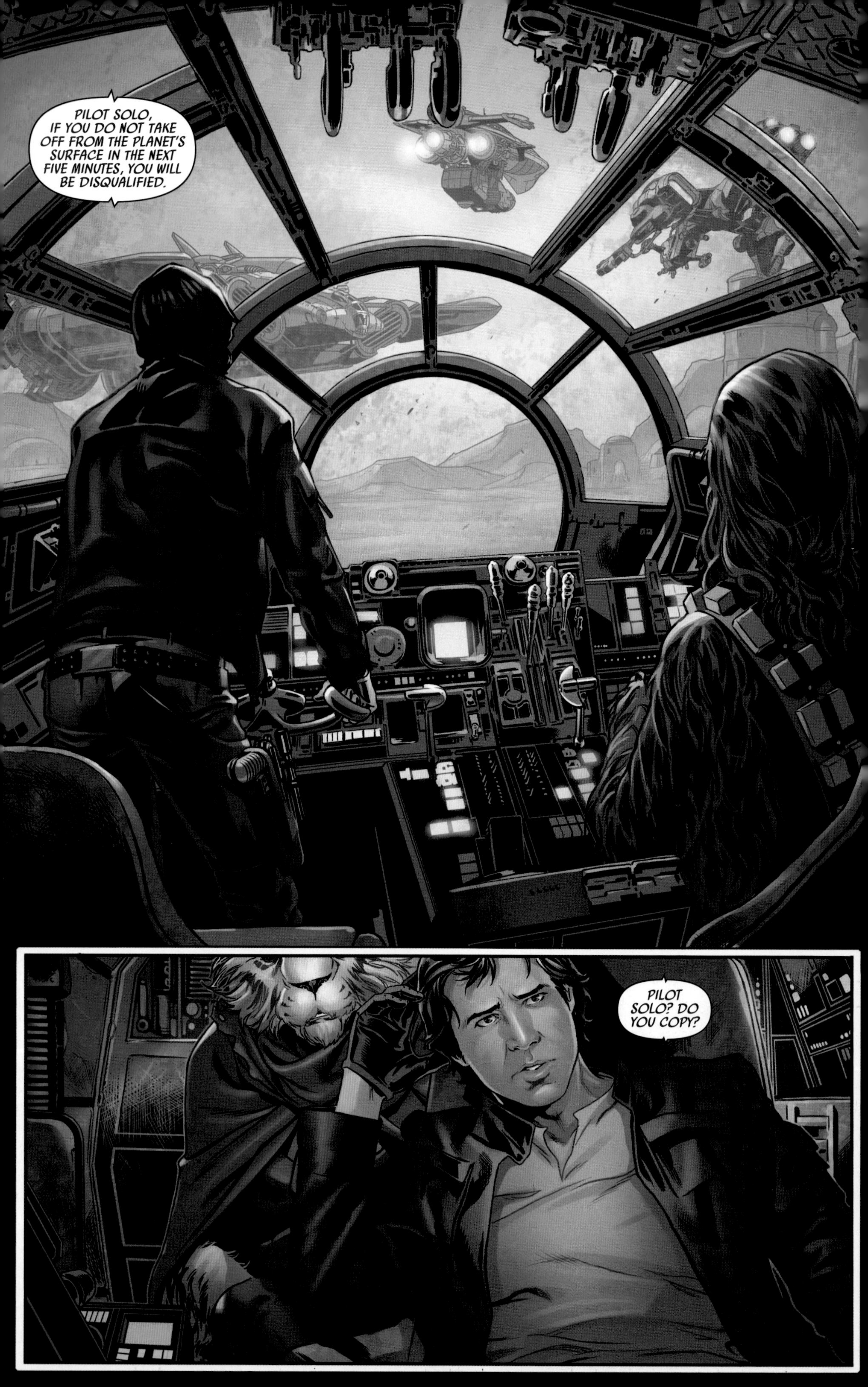
PILOT SOLO, IF YOU DO NOT TAKE OFF FROM THE PLANET'S SURFACE IN THE NEXT FIVE MINUTES, YOU WILL BE DISQUALIFIED.
PILOT SOLO? DO YOU COPY?

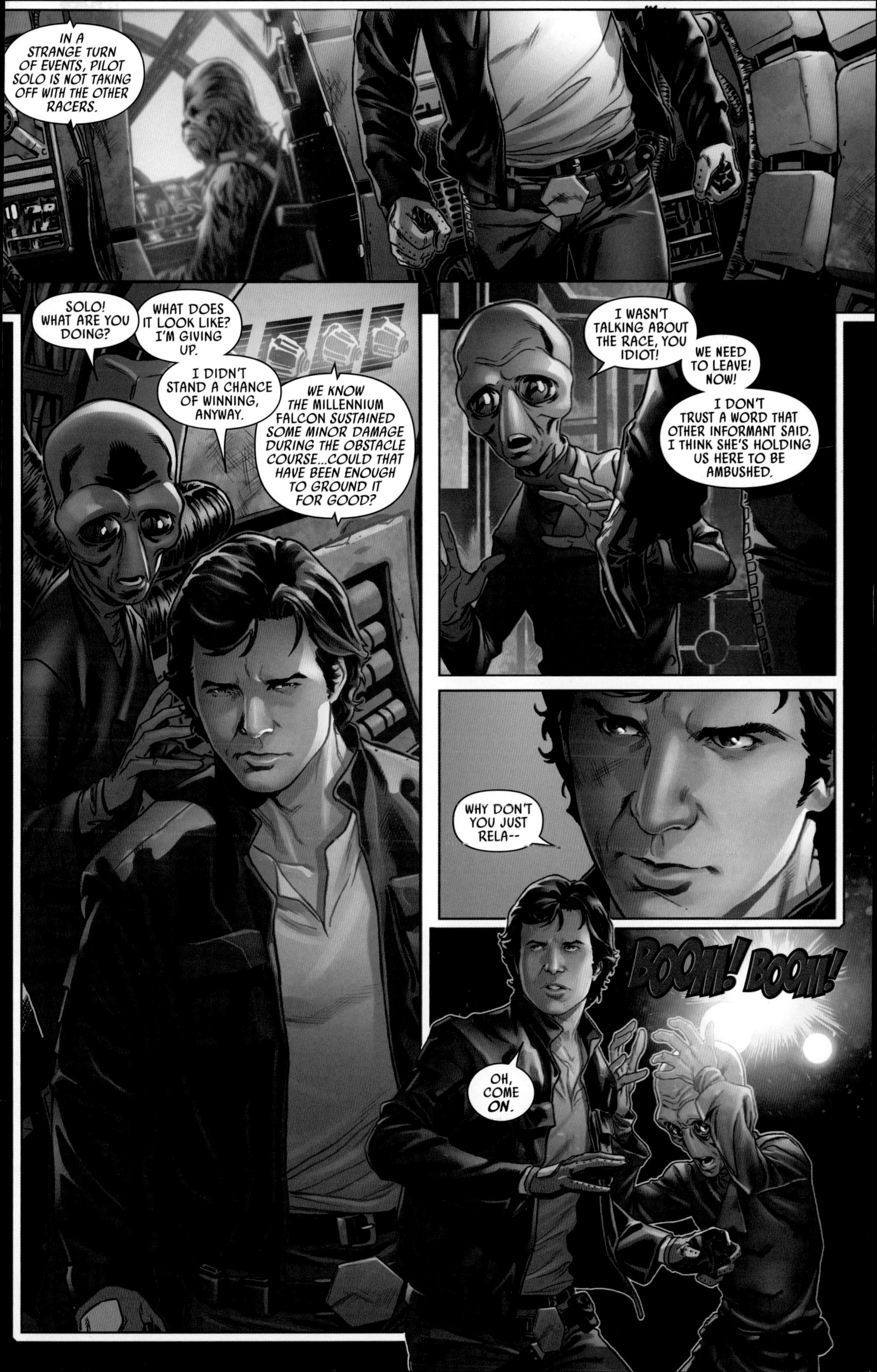
IN A STRANGE TURN OF EVENTS, PILOT SOLO IS NOT TAKING OFF WITH THE OTHER RACERS.
SOLO! WHAT ARE YOU DOING?
WHAT DOES IT LOOK LIKE? I'M GIVING UP.
I DIDN'T STAND A CHANCE OF WINNING, ANYWAY.
WE KNOW THE MILLENNIUM FALCON SUSTAINED SOME MINOR DAMAGE DURING THE OBSTACLE COURSE...COULD THAT HAVE BEEN ENOUGH TO GROUND IT FOR GOOD?
I WASN'T TALKING ABOUT THE RACE, YOU IDIOT!
WE NEED TO LEAVE! NOW!
I DON'T TRUST A WORD THAT OTHER INFORMANT SAID. I THINK SHE'S HOLDING US HERE TO BE AMBUSHED.
WHY DON'T YOU JUST RELA--
BOOM! BOOM!
OH, COME ON.

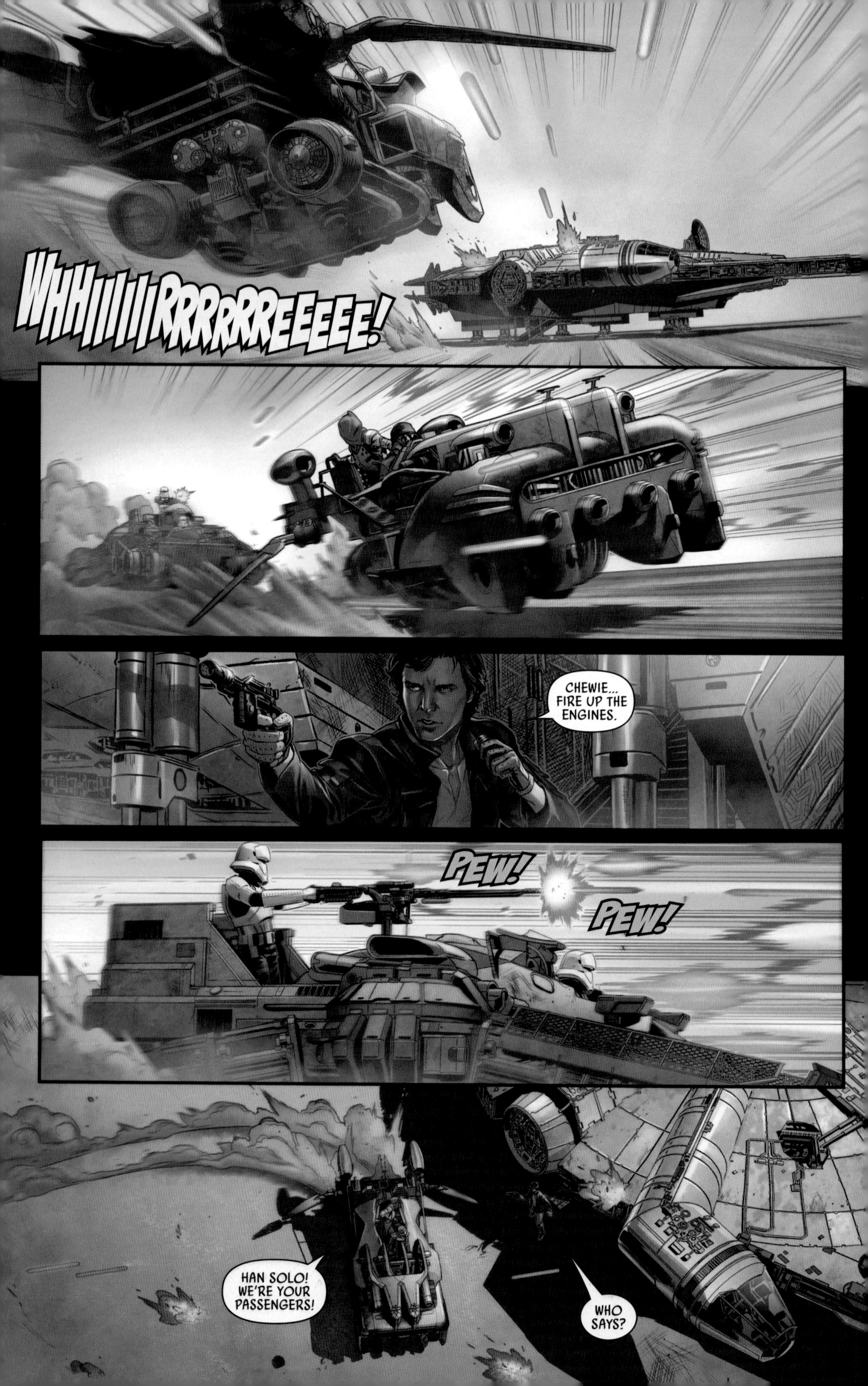
WHHIIIIIIIRRRRRREEEEEE!
CHEWIE... FIRE UP THE ENGINES.
PEW!
PEW!
HAN SOLO! WE'RE YOUR PASSENGERS!
WHO SAYS?

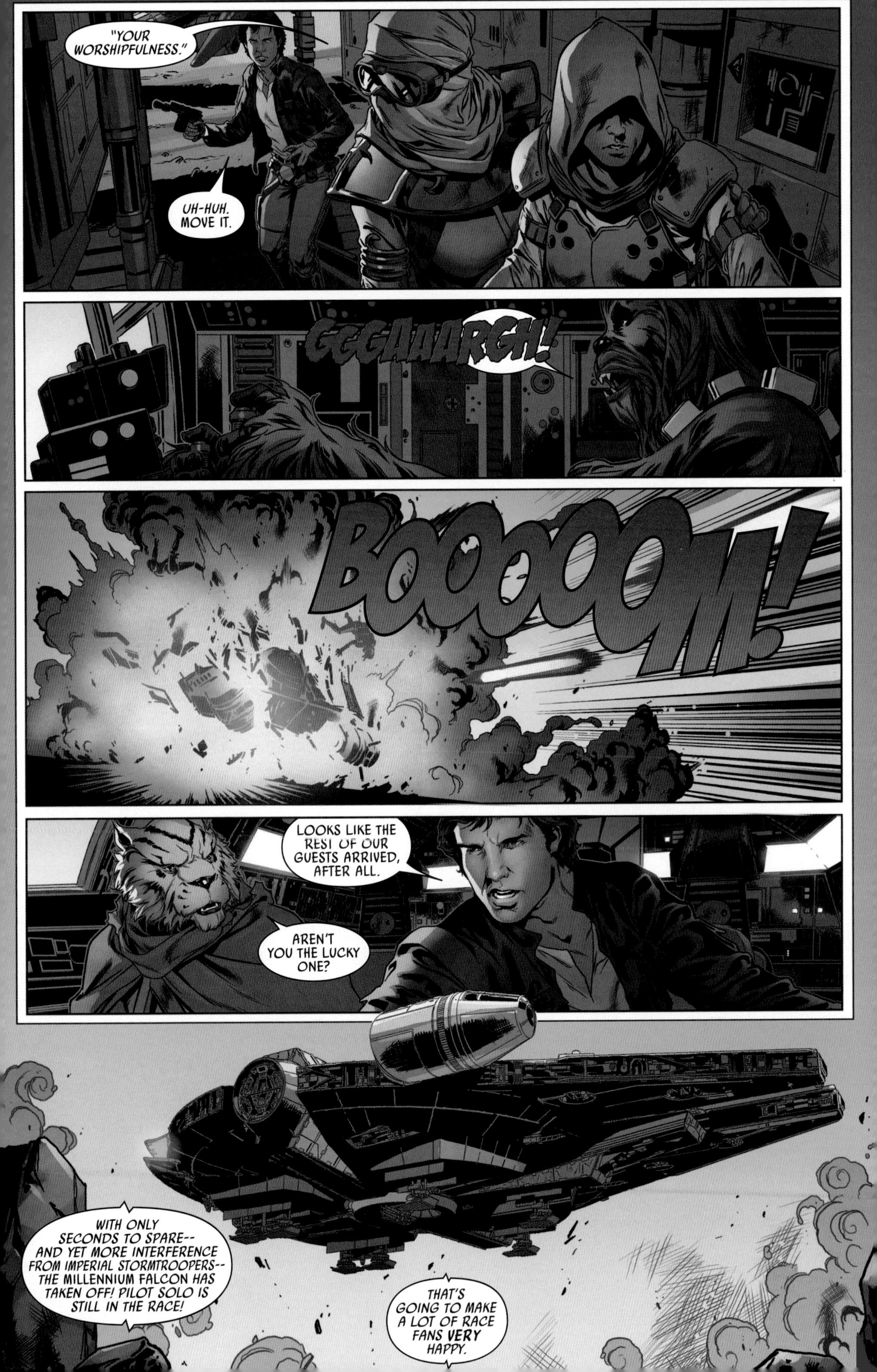
"YOUR WORSHIPFULNESS."
UH-HUH. MOVE IT.
GGGAAAARGH!
BOOOOOM!
LOOKS LIKE THE REST OF OUR GUESTS ARRIVED, AFTER ALL.
AREN'T YOU THE LUCKY ONE?
WITH ONLY SECONDS TO SPARE-- AND YET MORE INTERFERENCE FROM IMPERIAL STORMTROOPERS-- THE MILLENNIUM FALCON HAS TAKEN OFF! PILOT SOLO IS STILL IN THE RACE!
THAT'S GOING TO MAKE A LOT OF RACE FANS **VERY** HAPPY.

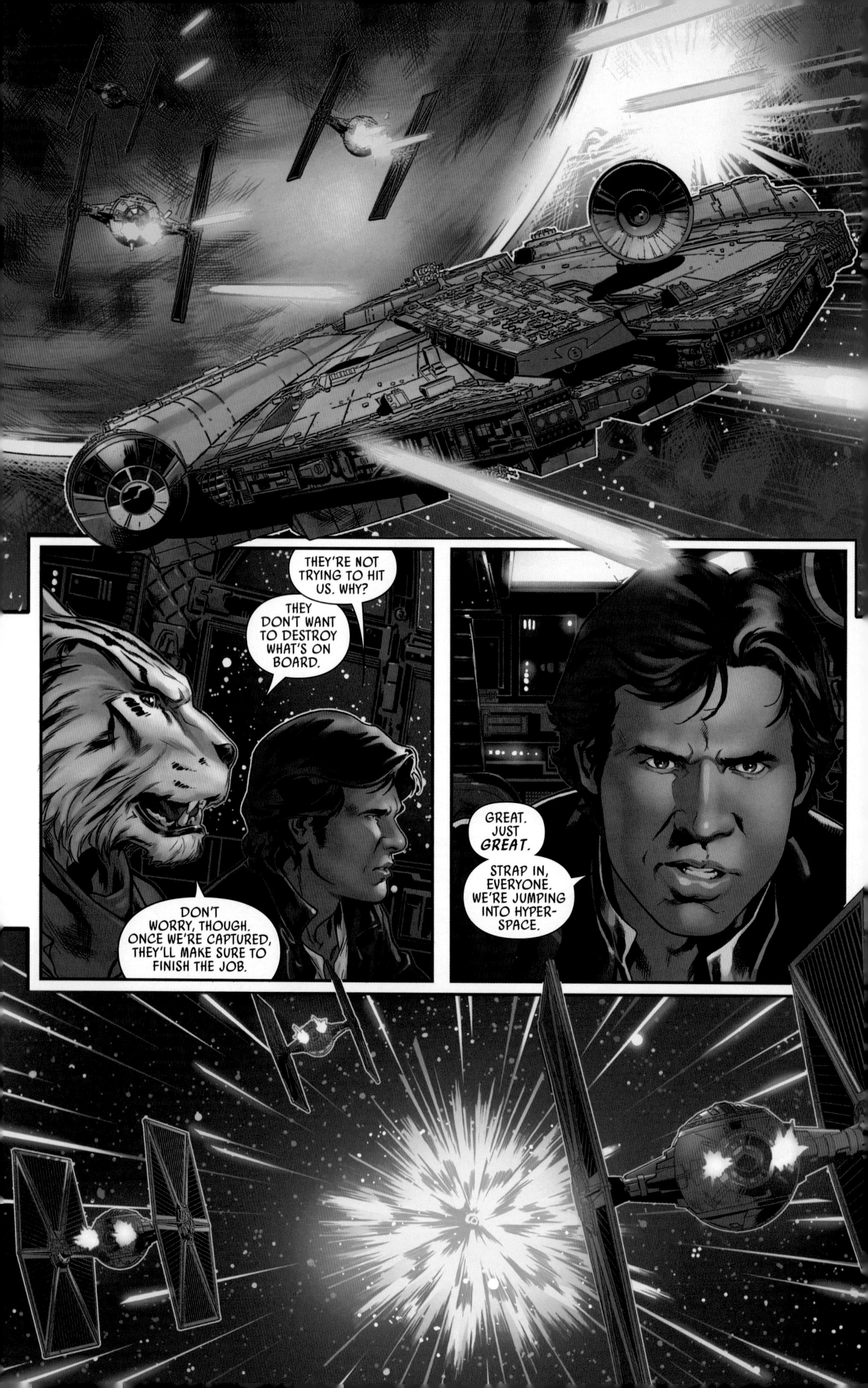
THEY'RE NOT TRYING TO HIT US. WHY?
THEY DON'T WANT TO DESTROY WHAT'S ON BOARD.
DON'T WORRY, THOUGH. ONCE WE'RE CAPTURED, THEY'LL MAKE SURE TO FINISH THE JOB.
GREAT. JUST GREAT.
STRAP IN, EVERYONE. WE'RE JUMPING INTO HYPER-SPACE.

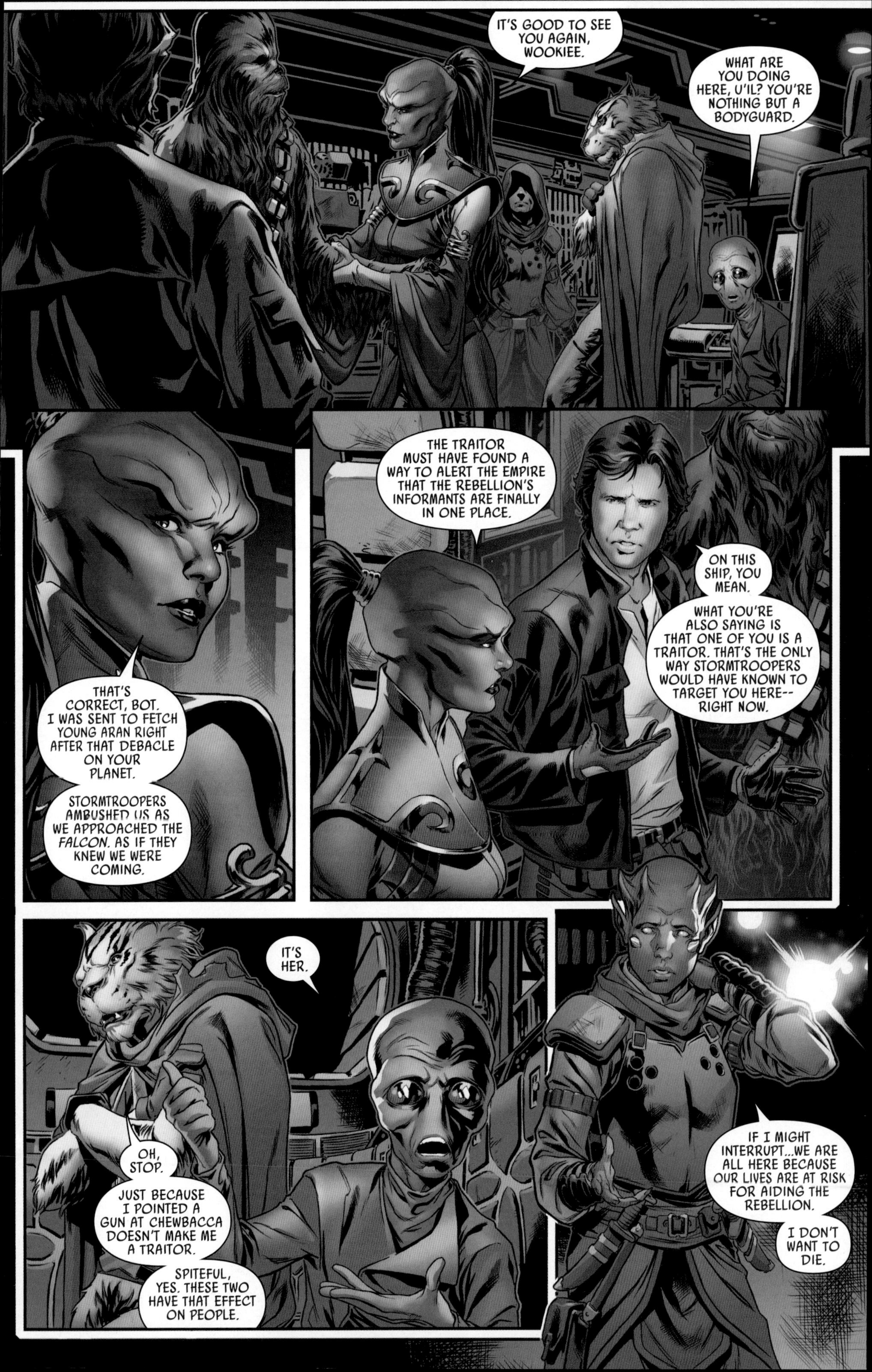
IT'S GOOD TO SEE YOU AGAIN, WOOKIEE.
WHAT ARE YOU DOING HERE, U'IL? YOU'RE NOTHING BUT A BODYGUARD.
THAT'S CORRECT, BOT. I WAS SENT TO FETCH YOUNG ARAN RIGHT AFTER THAT DEBACLE ON YOUR PLANET.
STORMTROOPERS AMBUSHED US AS WE APPROACHED THE *FALCON*. AS IF THEY KNEW WE WERE COMING.
THE TRAITOR MUST HAVE FOUND A WAY TO ALERT THE EMPIRE THAT THE REBELLION'S INFORMANTS ARE FINALLY IN ONE PLACE.
ON THIS SHIP, YOU MEAN.
WHAT YOU'RE ALSO SAYING IS THAT ONE OF YOU IS A TRAITOR. THAT'S THE ONLY WAY STORMTROOPERS WOULD HAVE KNOWN TO TARGET YOU HERE-- RIGHT NOW.
IT'S HER.
OH, STOP.
JUST BECAUSE I POINTED A GUN AT CHEWBACCA DOESN'T MAKE ME A TRAITOR.
SPITEFUL, YES. THESE TWO HAVE THAT EFFECT ON PEOPLE.
IF I MIGHT INTERRUPT...WE ARE ALL HERE BECAUSE OUR LIVES ARE AT RISK FOR AIDING THE REBELLION.
I DON'T WANT TO DIE.

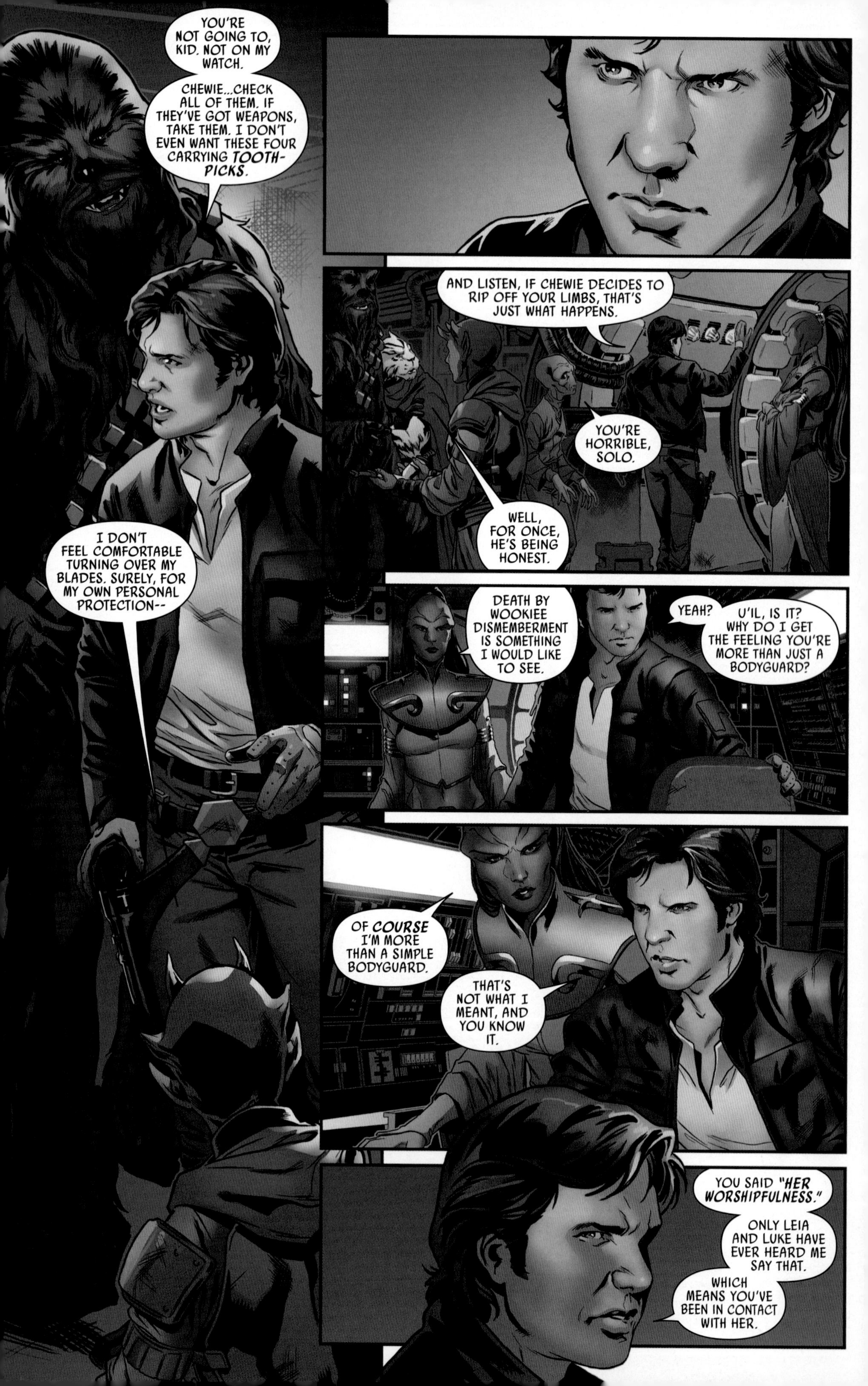
YOU'RE NOT GOING TO, KID. NOT ON MY WATCH.
CHEWIE...CHECK ALL OF THEM. IF THEY'VE GOT WEAPONS, TAKE THEM. I DON'T EVEN WANT THESE FOUR CARRYING *TOOTH-PICKS*.
I DON'T FEEL COMFORTABLE TURNING OVER MY BLADES. SURELY, FOR MY OWN PERSONAL PROTECTION--
AND LISTEN, IF CHEWIE DECIDES TO RIP OFF YOUR LIMBS, THAT'S JUST WHAT HAPPENS.
YOU'RE HORRIBLE, SOLO.
WELL, FOR ONCE, HE'S BEING HONEST.
DEATH BY WOOKIEE DISMEMBERMENT IS SOMETHING I WOULD LIKE TO SEE.
YEAH?
U'IL, IS IT? WHY DO I GET THE FEELING YOU'RE MORE THAN JUST A BODYGUARD?
OF *COURSE* I'M MORE THAN A SIMPLE BODYGUARD.
THAT'S NOT WHAT I MEANT, AND YOU KNOW IT.
YOU SAID "*HER WORSHIPFULNESS.*"
ONLY LEIA AND LUKE HAVE EVER HEARD ME SAY THAT.
WHICH MEANS YOU'VE BEEN IN CONTACT WITH HER.

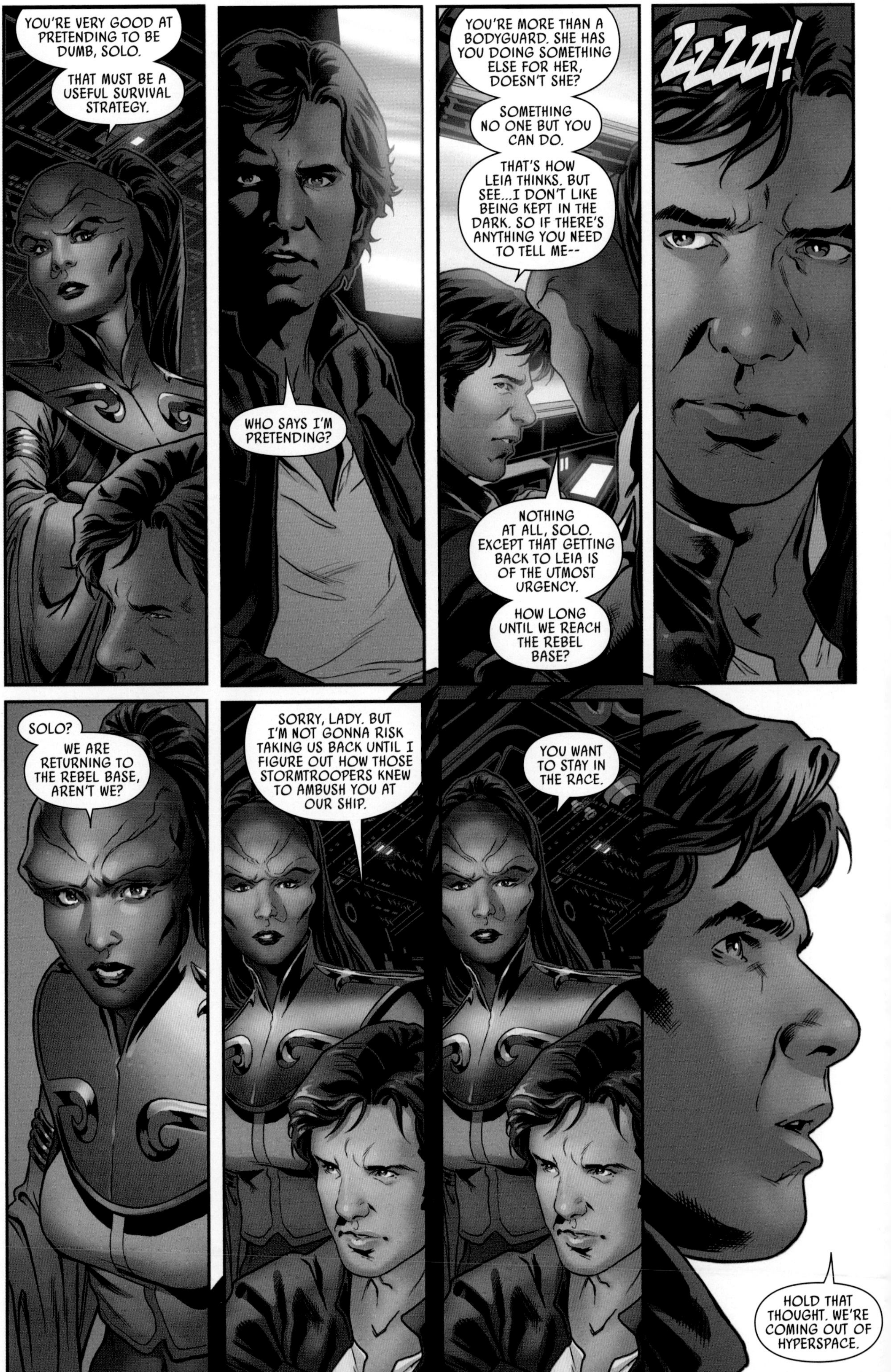

YOU'RE VERY GOOD AT PRETENDING TO BE DUMB, SOLO.
THAT MUST BE A USEFUL SURVIVAL STRATEGY.
WHO SAYS I'M PRETENDING?
YOU'RE MORE THAN A BODYGUARD. SHE HAS YOU DOING SOMETHING ELSE FOR HER, DOESN'T SHE?
SOMETHING NO ONE BUT YOU CAN DO.
THAT'S HOW LEIA THINKS. BUT SEE...I DON'T LIKE BEING KEPT IN THE DARK. SO IF THERE'S ANYTHING YOU NEED TO TELL ME--
NOTHING AT ALL, SOLO. EXCEPT THAT GETTING BACK TO LEIA IS OF THE UTMOST URGENCY.
HOW LONG UNTIL WE REACH THE REBEL BASE?
ZZZZT!
SOLO?
WE ARE RETURNING TO THE REBEL BASE, AREN'T WE?
SORRY, LADY. BUT I'M NOT GONNA RISK TAKING US BACK UNTIL I FIGURE OUT HOW THOSE STORMTROOPERS KNEW TO AMBUSH YOU AT OUR SHIP.
YOU WANT TO STAY IN THE RACE.
HOLD THAT THOUGHT. WE'RE COMING OUT OF HYPERSPACE.

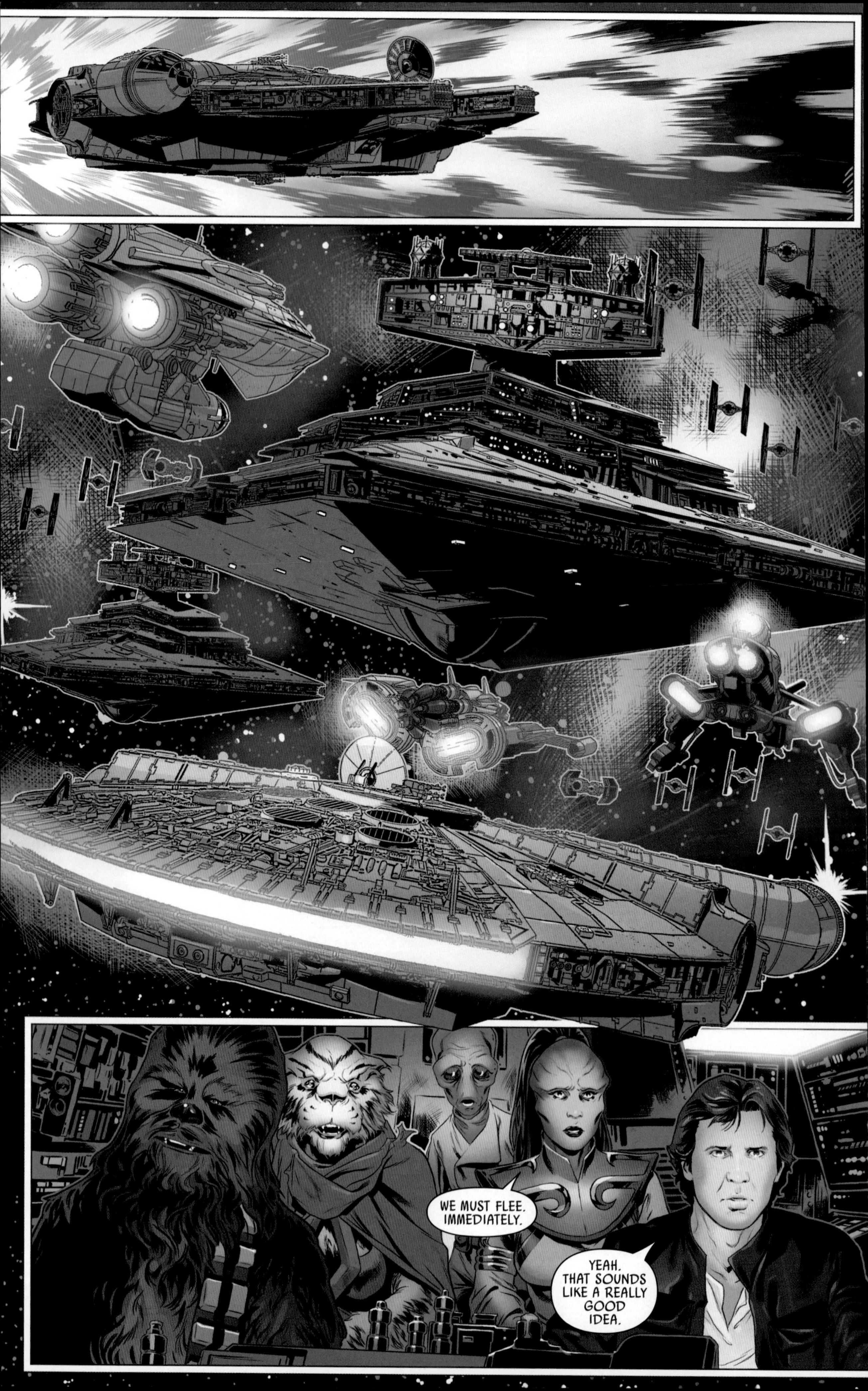
WE MUST FLEE. IMMEDIATELY.
YEAH. THAT SOUNDS LIKE A REALLY GOOD IDEA.

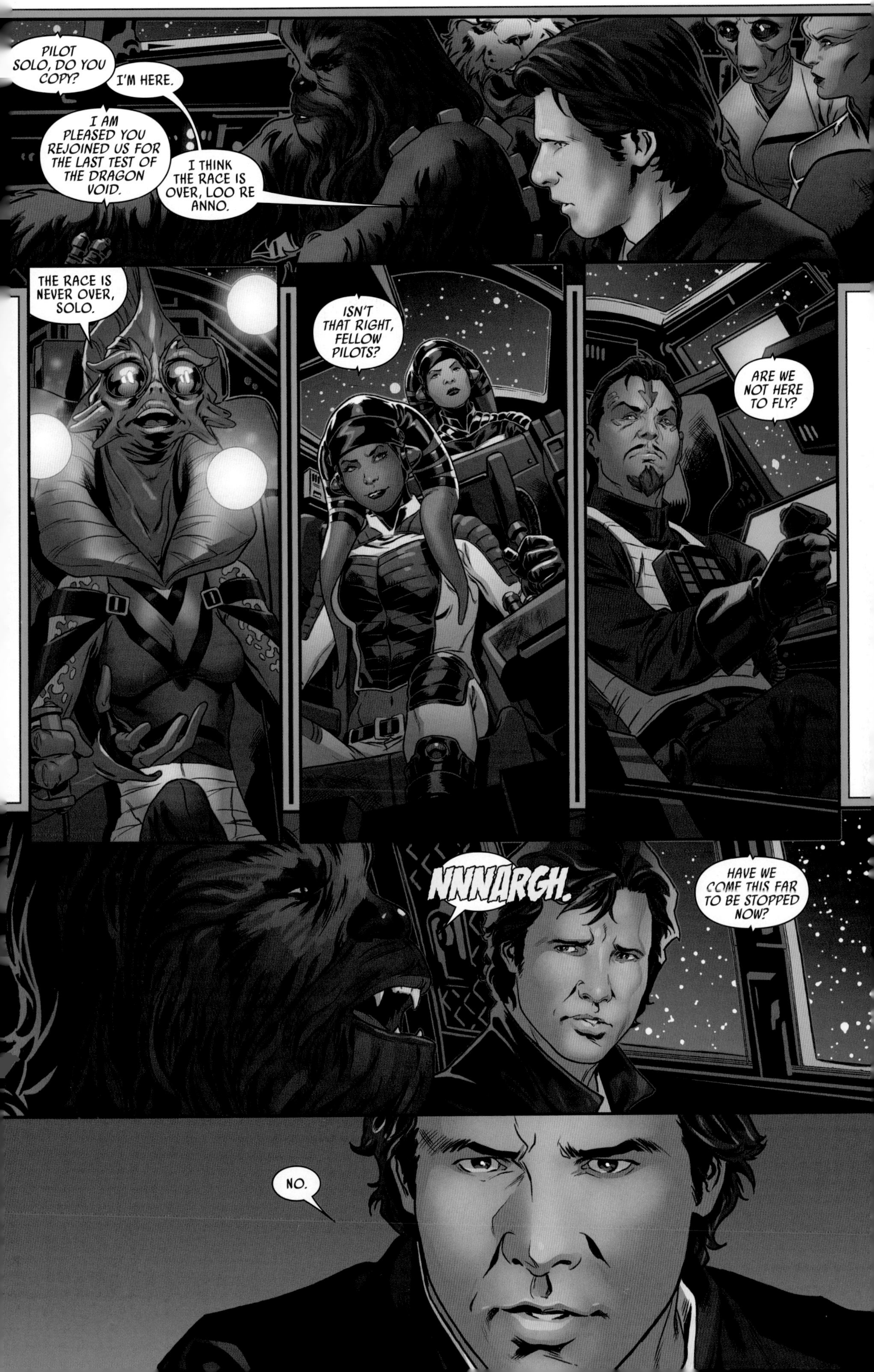
PILOT SOLO, DO YOU COPY?
I'M HERE.
I AM PLEASED YOU REJOINED US FOR THE LAST TEST OF THE DRAGON VOID.
I THINK THE RACE IS OVER, LOO RE ANNO.
THE RACE IS NEVER OVER, SOLO.
ISN'T THAT RIGHT, FELLOW PILOTS?
ARE WE NOT HERE TO FLY?
NNNARGH.
HAVE WE COME THIS FAR TO BE STOPPED NOW?
NO.

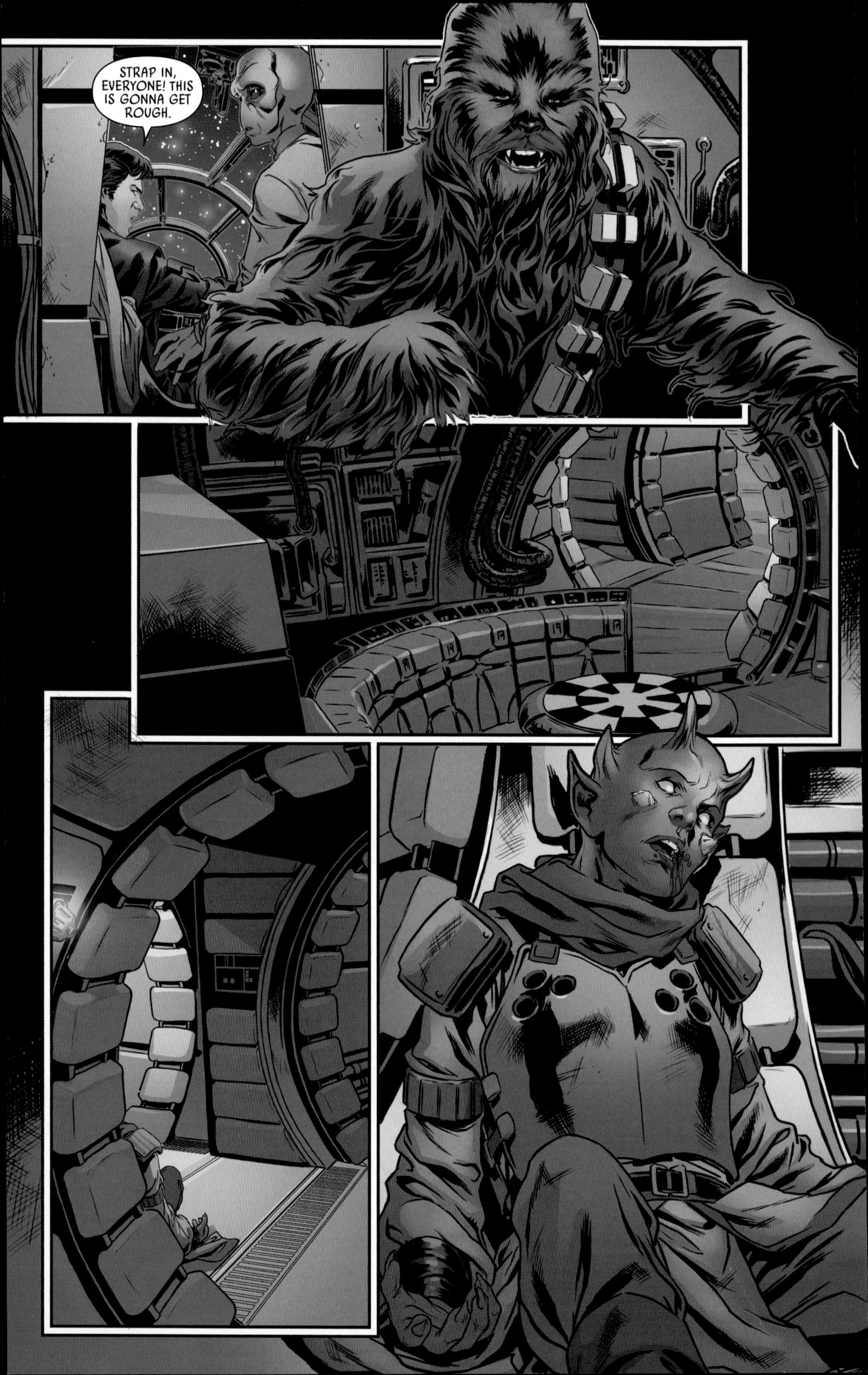
STRAP IN, EVERYONE! THIS IS GONNA GET ROUGH.

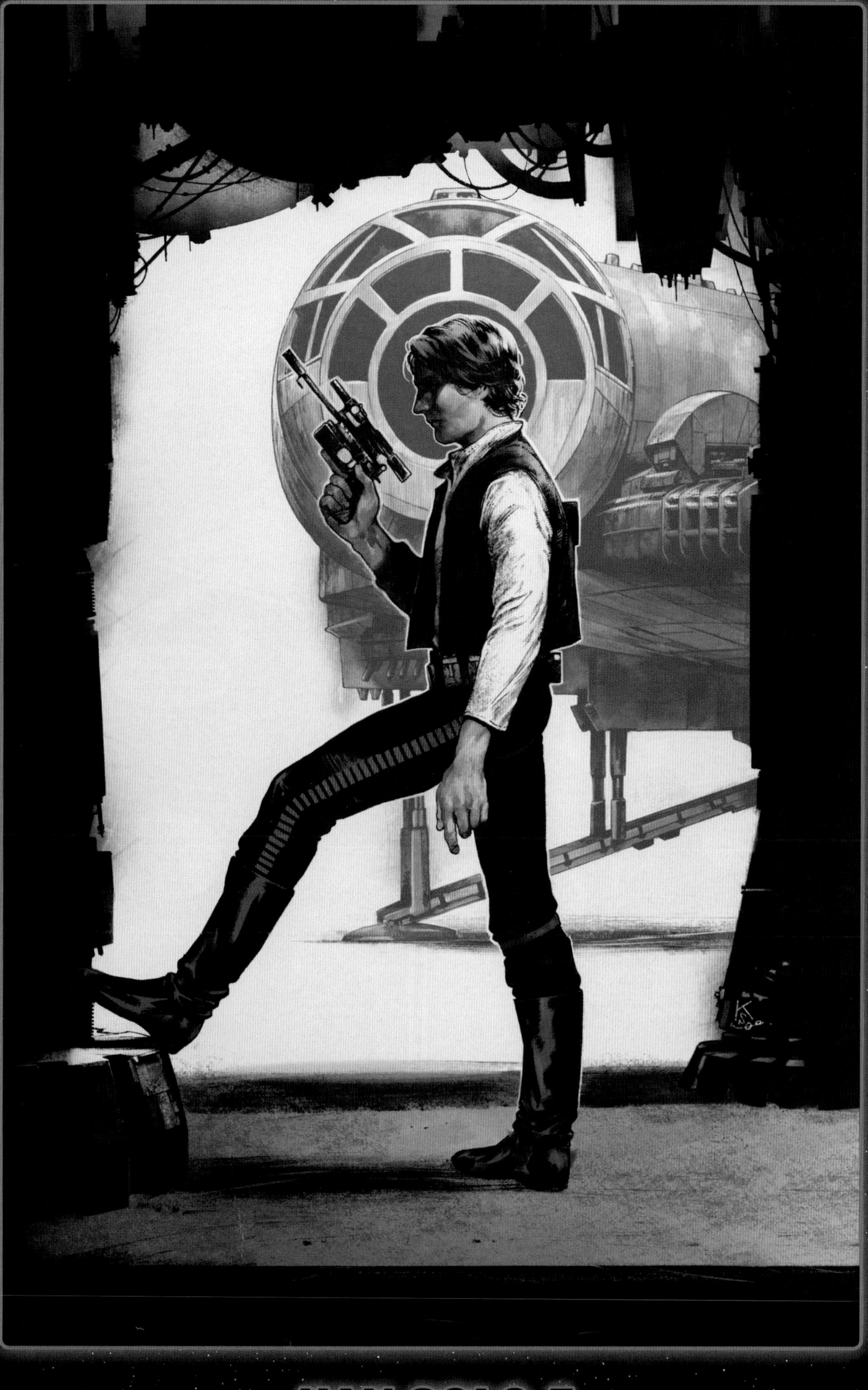

HAN SOLO 5

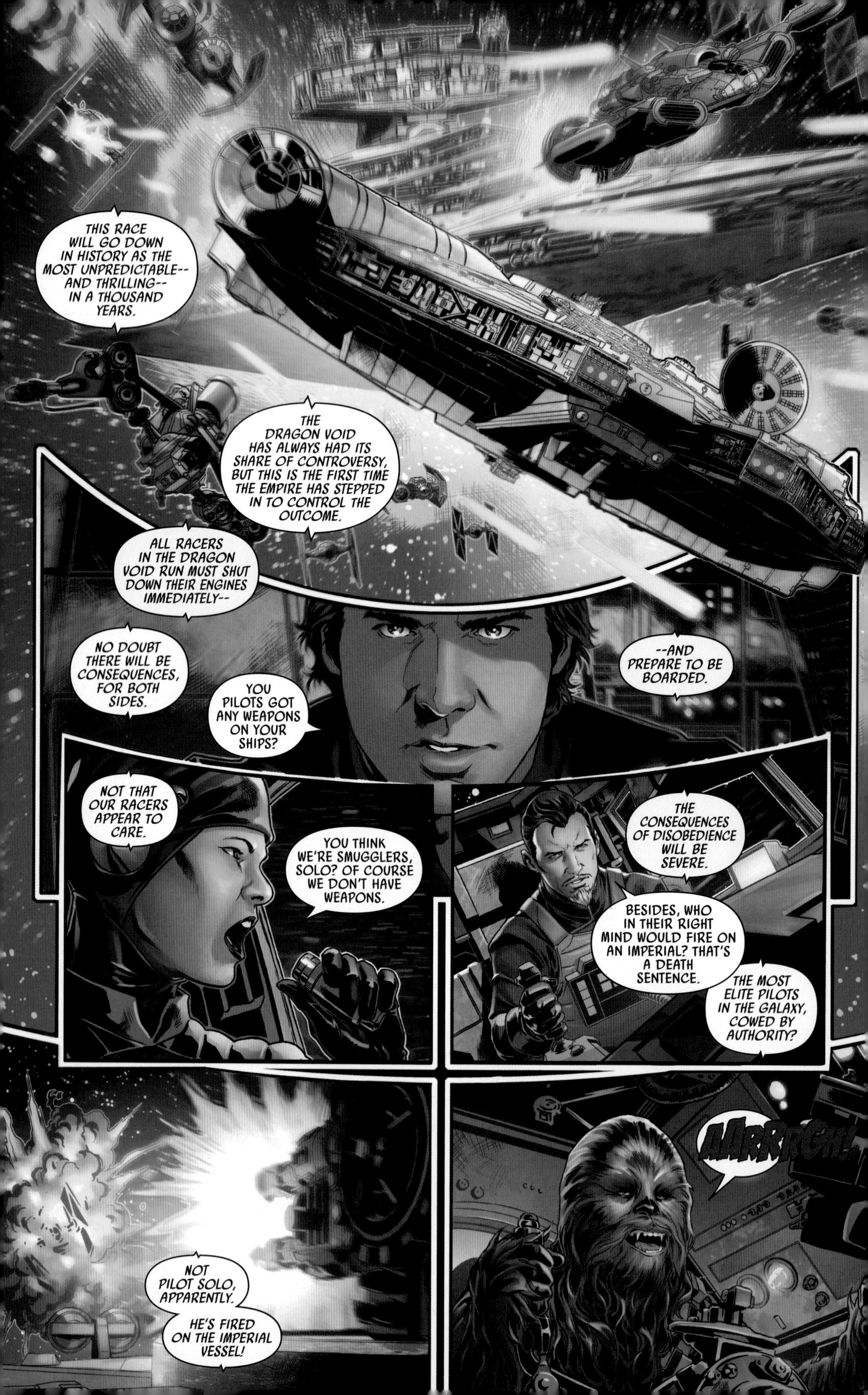
THIS RACE WILL GO DOWN IN HISTORY AS THE MOST UNPREDICTABLE-- AND THRILLING-- IN A THOUSAND YEARS.
THE DRAGON VOID HAS ALWAYS HAD ITS SHARE OF CONTROVERSY, BUT THIS IS THE FIRST TIME THE EMPIRE HAS STEPPED IN TO CONTROL THE OUTCOME.
ALL RACERS IN THE DRAGON VOID RUN MUST SHUT DOWN THEIR ENGINES IMMEDIATELY--
--AND PREPARE TO BE BOARDED.
NO DOUBT THERE WILL BE CONSEQUENCES, FOR BOTH SIDES.
YOU PILOTS GOT ANY WEAPONS ON YOUR SHIPS?
NOT THAT OUR RACERS APPEAR TO CARE.
YOU THINK WE'RE SMUGGLERS, SOLO? OF COURSE WE DON'T HAVE WEAPONS.
THE CONSEQUENCES OF DISOBEDIENCE WILL BE SEVERE.
BESIDES, WHO IN THEIR RIGHT MIND WOULD FIRE ON AN IMPERIAL? THAT'S A DEATH SENTENCE.
THE MOST ELITE PILOTS IN THE GALAXY, COWED BY AUTHORITY?
NOT PILOT SOLO, APPARENTLY.
HE'S FIRED ON THE IMPERIAL VESSEL!
AARRRGH!

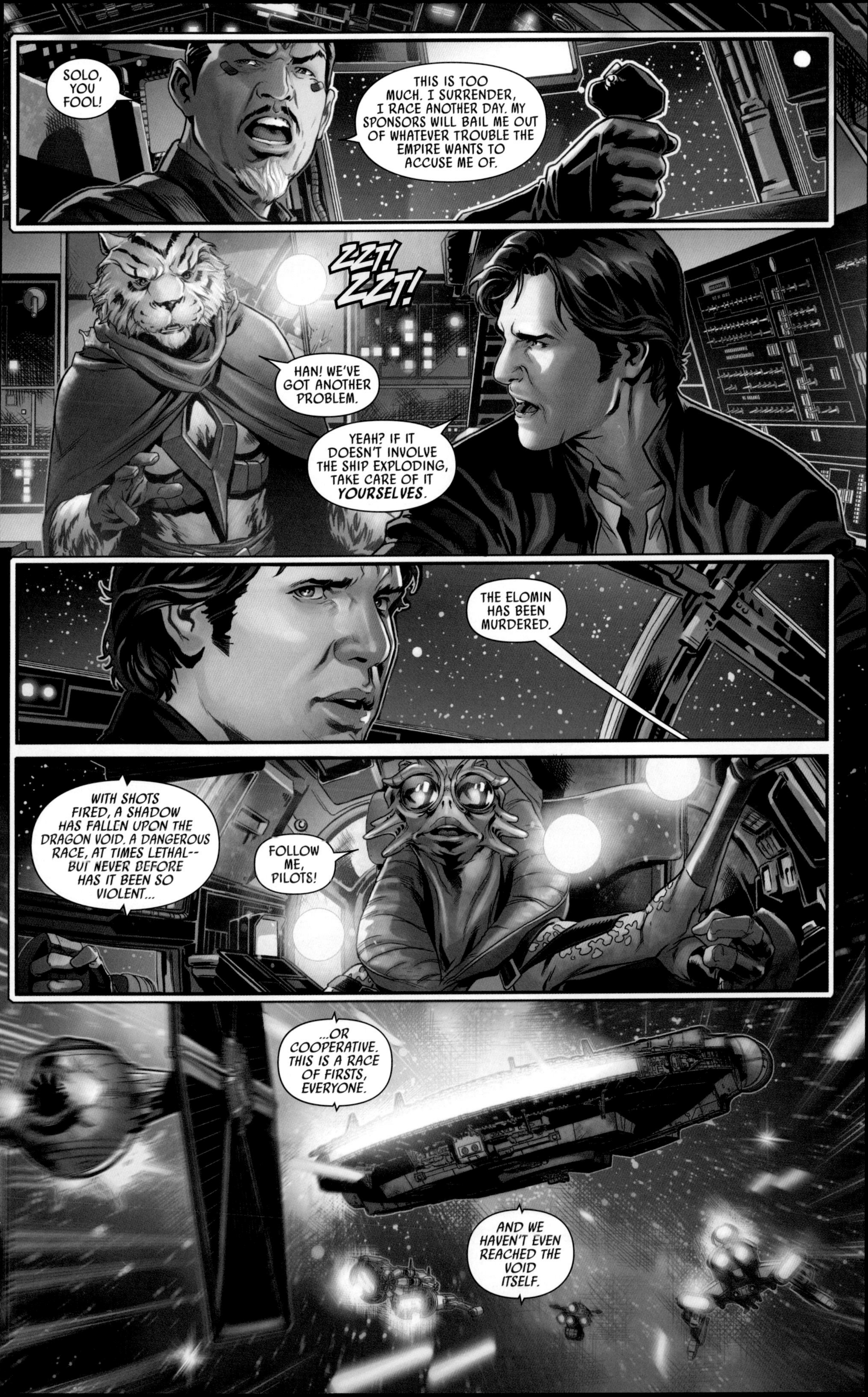

SOLO, YOU FOOL!
THIS IS TOO MUCH. I SURRENDER, I RACE ANOTHER DAY. MY SPONSORS WILL BAIL ME OUT OF WHATEVER TROUBLE THE EMPIRE WANTS TO ACCUSE ME OF.
ZZT! ZZT!
HAN! WE'VE GOT ANOTHER PROBLEM.
YEAH? IF IT DOESN'T INVOLVE THE SHIP EXPLODING, TAKE CARE OF IT YOURSELVES.
THE ELOMIN HAS BEEN MURDERED.
WITH SHOTS FIRED, A SHADOW HAS FALLEN UPON THE DRAGON VOID. A DANGEROUS RACE, AT TIMES LETHAL-- BUT NEVER BEFORE HAS IT BEEN SO VIOLENT...
FOLLOW ME, PILOTS!
...OR COOPERATIVE. THIS IS A RACE OF FIRSTS, EVERYONE.
AND WE HAVEN'T EVEN REACHED THE VOID ITSELF.

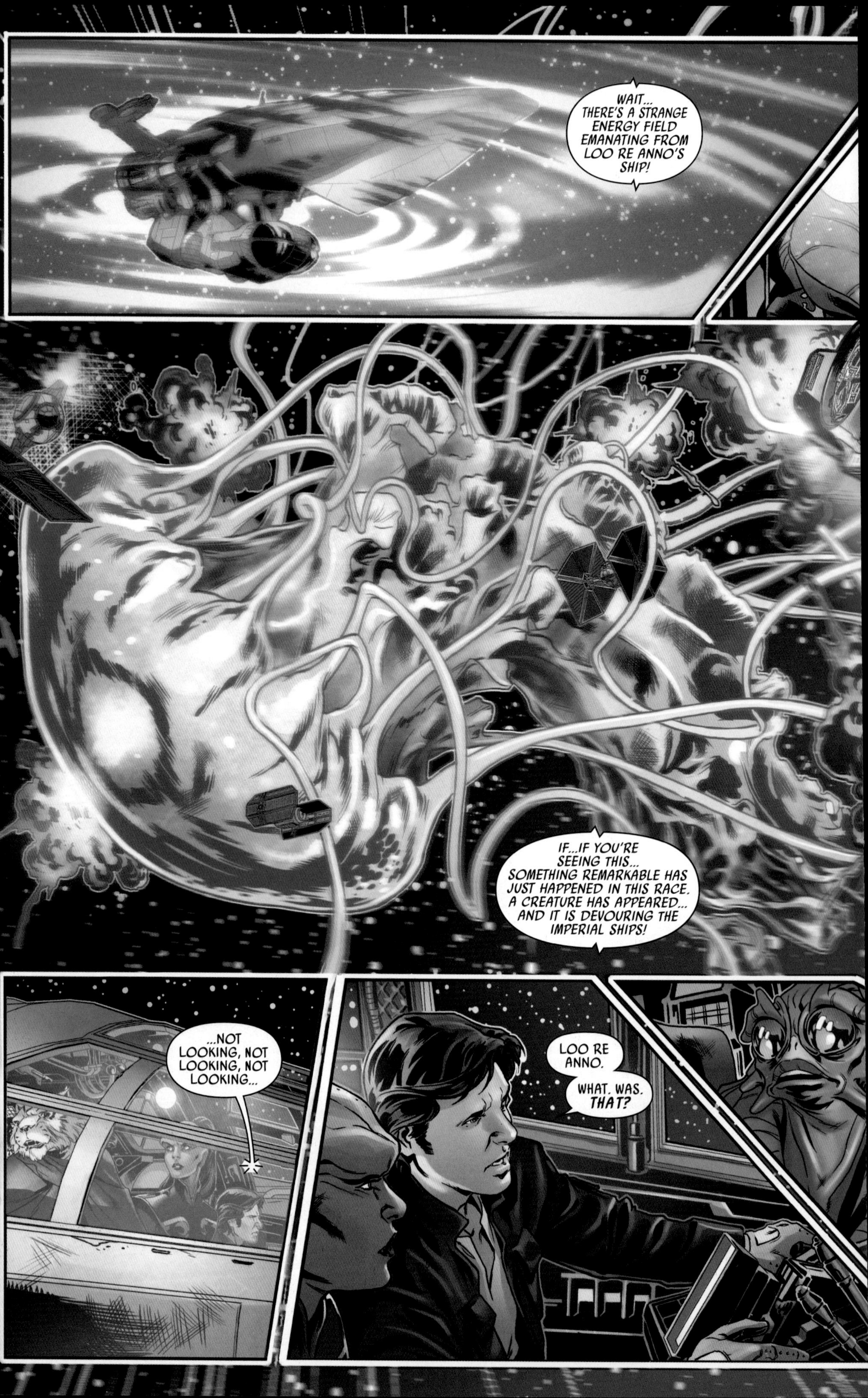
WAIT... THERE'S A STRANGE ENERGY FIELD EMANATING FROM LOO RE ANNO'S SHIP!
IF...IF YOU'RE SEEING THIS... SOMETHING REMARKABLE HAS JUST HAPPENED IN THIS RACE. A CREATURE HAS APPEARED... AND IT IS DEVOURING THE IMPERIAL SHIPS!
...NOT LOOKING, NOT LOOKING, NOT LOOKING...
LOO RE ANNO.
WHAT. WAS. THAT?

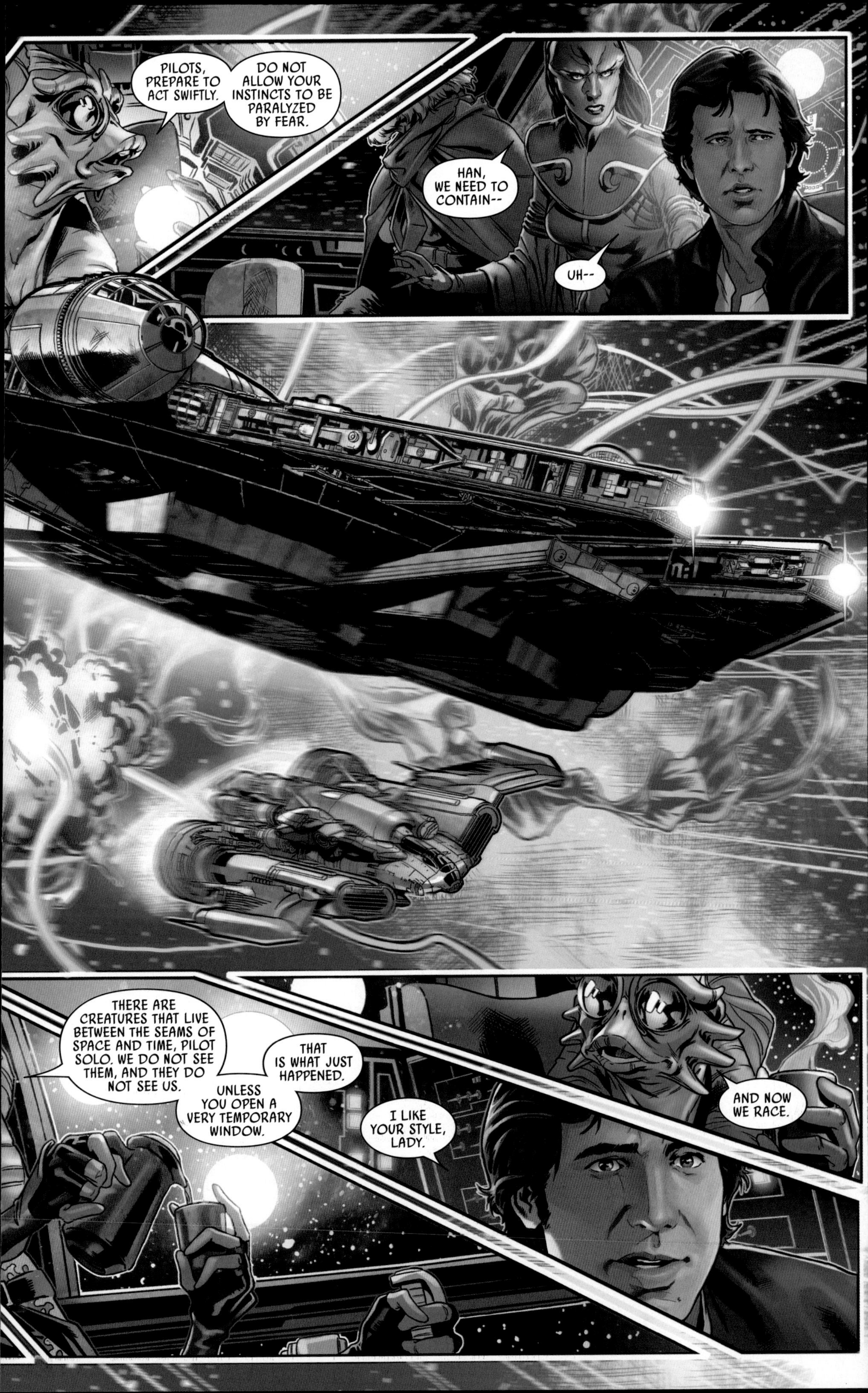
PILOTS, PREPARE TO ACT SWIFTLY.
DO NOT ALLOW YOUR INSTINCTS TO BE PARALYZED BY FEAR.
HAN, WE NEED TO CONTAIN--
UH--
THERE ARE CREATURES THAT LIVE BETWEEN THE SEAMS OF SPACE AND TIME, PILOT SOLO. WE DO NOT SEE THEM, AND THEY DO NOT SEE US.
UNLESS YOU OPEN A VERY TEMPORARY WINDOW.
THAT IS WHAT JUST HAPPENED.
I LIKE YOUR STYLE, LADY.
AND NOW WE RACE.

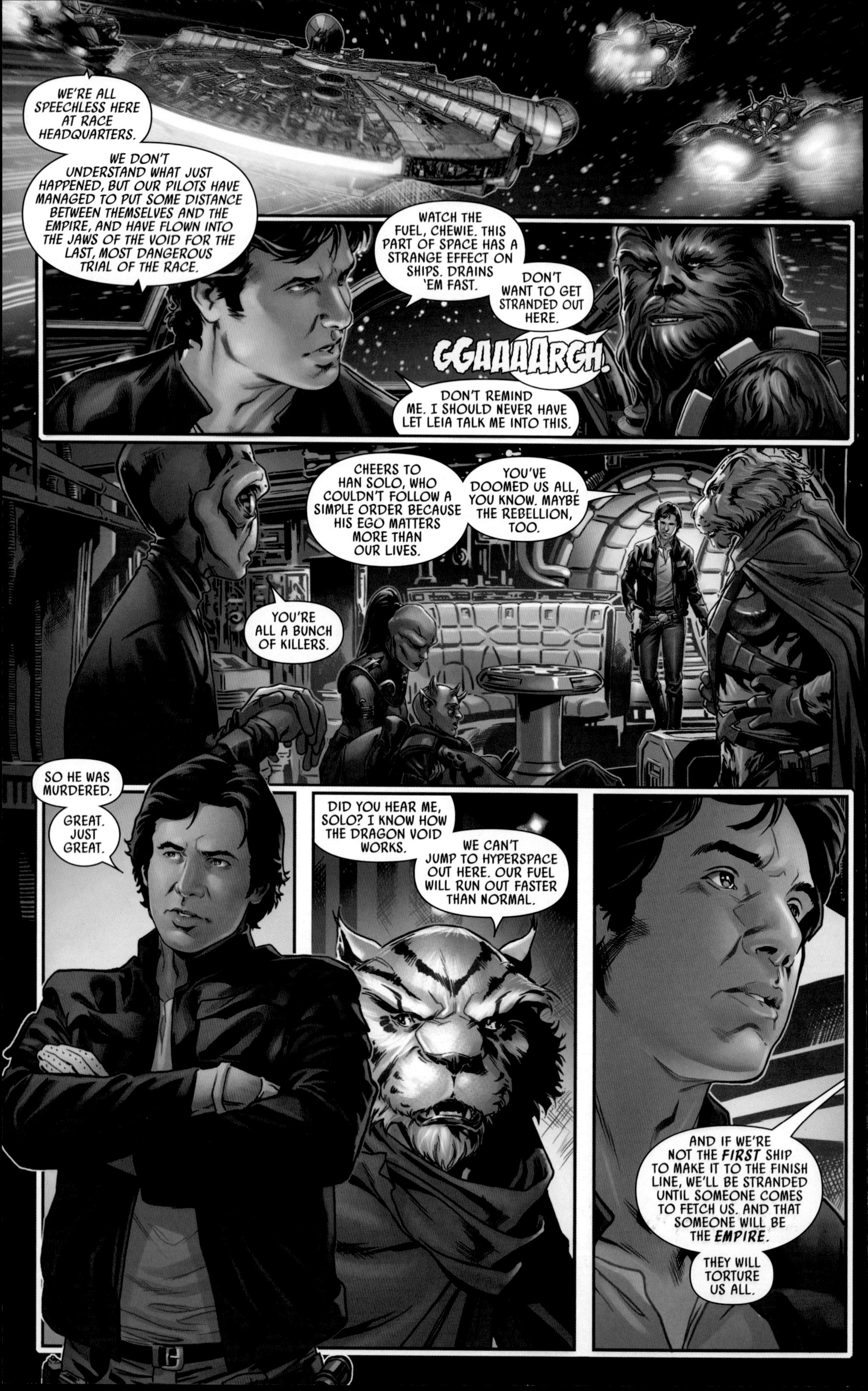

WE'RE ALL SPEECHLESS HERE AT RACE HEADQUARTERS.
WE DON'T UNDERSTAND WHAT JUST HAPPENED, BUT OUR PILOTS HAVE MANAGED TO PUT SOME DISTANCE BETWEEN THEMSELVES AND THE EMPIRE, AND HAVE FLOWN INTO THE JAWS OF THE VOID FOR THE LAST, MOST DANGEROUS TRIAL OF THE RACE.
WATCH THE FUEL, CHEWIE. THIS PART OF SPACE HAS A STRANGE EFFECT ON SHIPS. DRAINS 'EM FAST.
DON'T WANT TO GET STRANDED OUT HERE.
GGAAAARGH!
DON'T REMIND ME. I SHOULD NEVER HAVE LET LEIA TALK ME INTO THIS.
CHEERS TO HAN SOLO, WHO COULDN'T FOLLOW A SIMPLE ORDER BECAUSE HIS EGO MATTERS MORE THAN OUR LIVES.
YOU'VE DOOMED US ALL, YOU KNOW. MAYBE THE REBELLION, TOO.
YOU'RE ALL A BUNCH OF KILLERS.
SO HE WAS MURDERED.
GREAT. JUST GREAT.
DID YOU HEAR ME, SOLO? I KNOW HOW THE DRAGON VOID WORKS.
WE CAN'T JUMP TO HYPERSPACE OUT HERE. OUR FUEL WILL RUN OUT FASTER THAN NORMAL.
AND IF WE'RE NOT THE FIRST SHIP TO MAKE IT TO THE FINISH LINE, WE'LL BE STRANDED UNTIL SOMEONE COMES TO FETCH US. AND THAT SOMEONE WILL BE THE EMPIRE.
THEY WILL TORTURE US ALL.

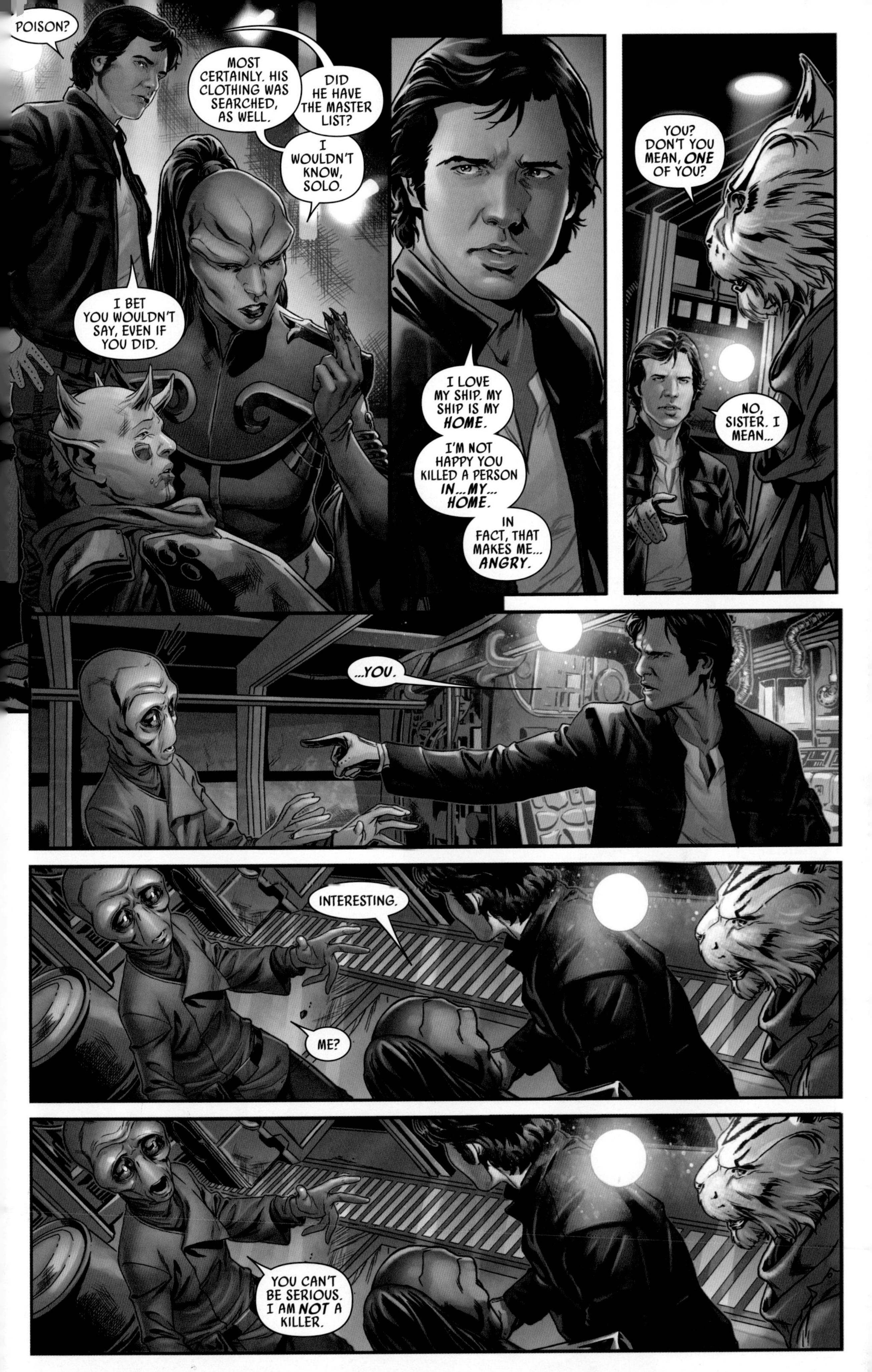
POISON?
MOST CERTAINLY. HIS CLOTHING WAS SEARCHED, AS WELL.
DID HE HAVE THE MASTER LIST?
I WOULDN'T KNOW, SOLO.
I BET YOU WOULDN'T SAY, EVEN IF YOU DID.
I LOVE MY SHIP. MY SHIP IS MY HOME.
I'M NOT HAPPY YOU KILLED A PERSON IN...MY... HOME.
IN FACT, THAT MAKES ME... ANGRY.
YOU? DON'T YOU MEAN, ONE OF YOU?
NO, SISTER. I MEAN...
...YOU.
INTERESTING.
ME?
YOU CAN'T BE SERIOUS. I AM NOT A KILLER.

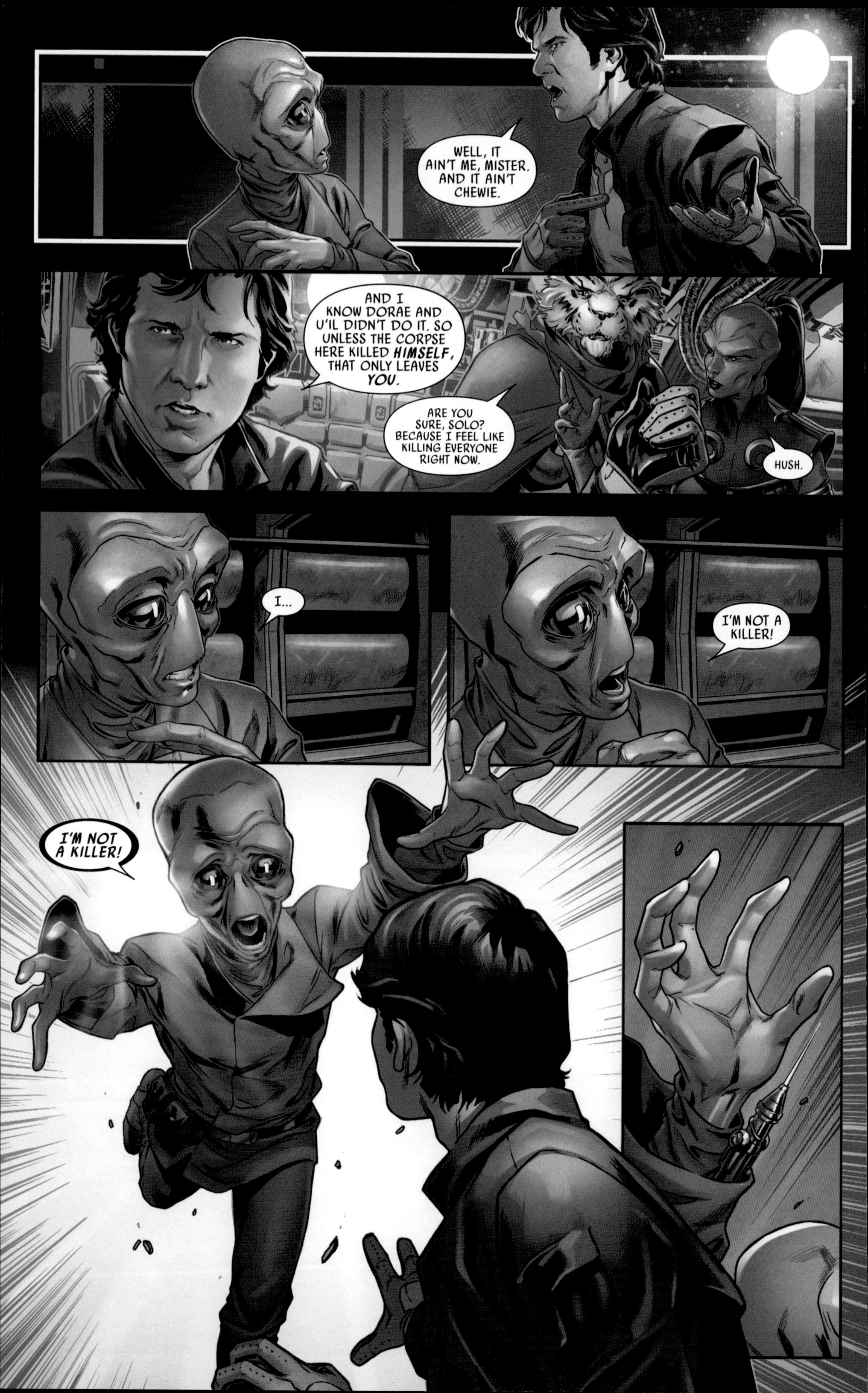
WELL, IT AIN'T ME, MISTER. AND IT AIN'T CHEWIE.
AND I KNOW DORAE AND U'IL DIDN'T DO IT. SO UNLESS THE CORPSE HERE KILLED **HIMSELF**, THAT ONLY LEAVES **YOU**.
ARE YOU SURE, SOLO? BECAUSE I FEEL LIKE KILLING EVERYONE RIGHT NOW.
HUSH.
I...
I'M NOT A KILLER!
I'M NOT A KILLER!

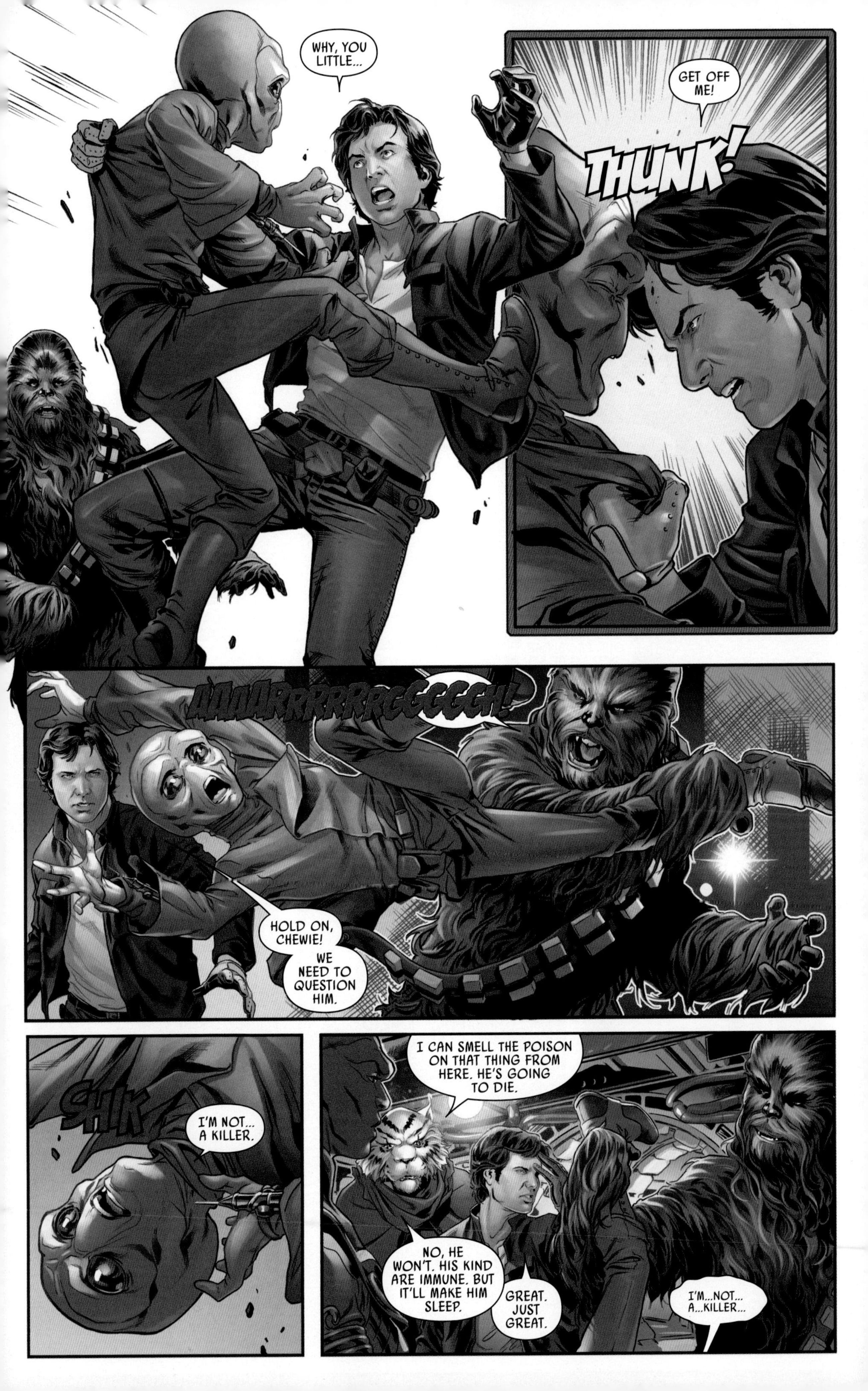
WHY, YOU LITTLE...
GET OFF ME!
THUNK!
AAAARRRRRRGGGGGH!
HOLD ON, CHEWIE!
WE NEED TO QUESTION HIM.
SHIK
I'M NOT... A KILLER.
I CAN SMELL THE POISON ON THAT THING FROM HERE. HE'S GOING TO DIE.
NO, HE WON'T. HIS KIND ARE IMMUNE. BUT IT'LL MAKE HIM SLEEP.
GREAT. JUST GREAT.
I'M...NOT... A...KILLER...

HARRGH?

YEAH, YEAH, I'M FINE.

THANKS, BUDDY.

I'M...NOT...A...KILLER...

WHY DOES HE KEEP SAYING THAT?

BOT DIDN'T BETRAY US BY CHOICE. HE WAS COMPELLED.

PROGRAMMED. BRAINWASHED.

BOT MUST HAVE BEEN COMPROMISED, AND THIS WAS THE PRICE HE PAID. HE'S THE ONE WHO LIKELY KILLED THE OTHER INFORMANTS.

YEAH? WELL, I'VE HAD ENOUGH. IF BOT WAKES UP, MAKE SURE HE CAN'T CAUSE ANY MORE TROUBLE.

KRRAAGH!

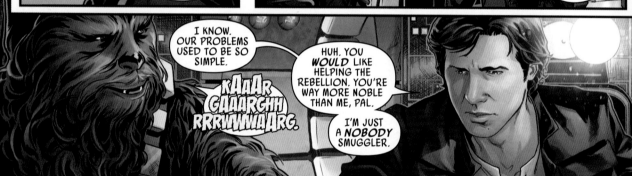

I KNOW. OUR PROBLEMS USED TO BE SO SIMPLE.

KAAAR GAAARGHH RRRWWWAARG.

HUH. YOU *WOULD* LIKE HELPING THE REBELLION. YOU'RE WAY MORE NOBLE THAN ME, PAL.

I'M JUST A *NOBODY* SMUGGLER.

AND I LIKE IT... THAT... WAY...

UH...PILOT LOO RE ANNO, DO YOU COPY?

I DO, PILOT SOLO. HOW CAN I HELP YOU?

WHAT ARE YOU GOING TO DO AFTER THIS RACE IS OVER? WHAT DO YOU... I DUNNO...GO HOME TO?

MY SHIP IS MY HOME. THE STARS, MY HOME.

BUT AS FOR THE RACE, PILOT SOLO...

...I WILL EITHER WIN...

...OR I WILL DIE.

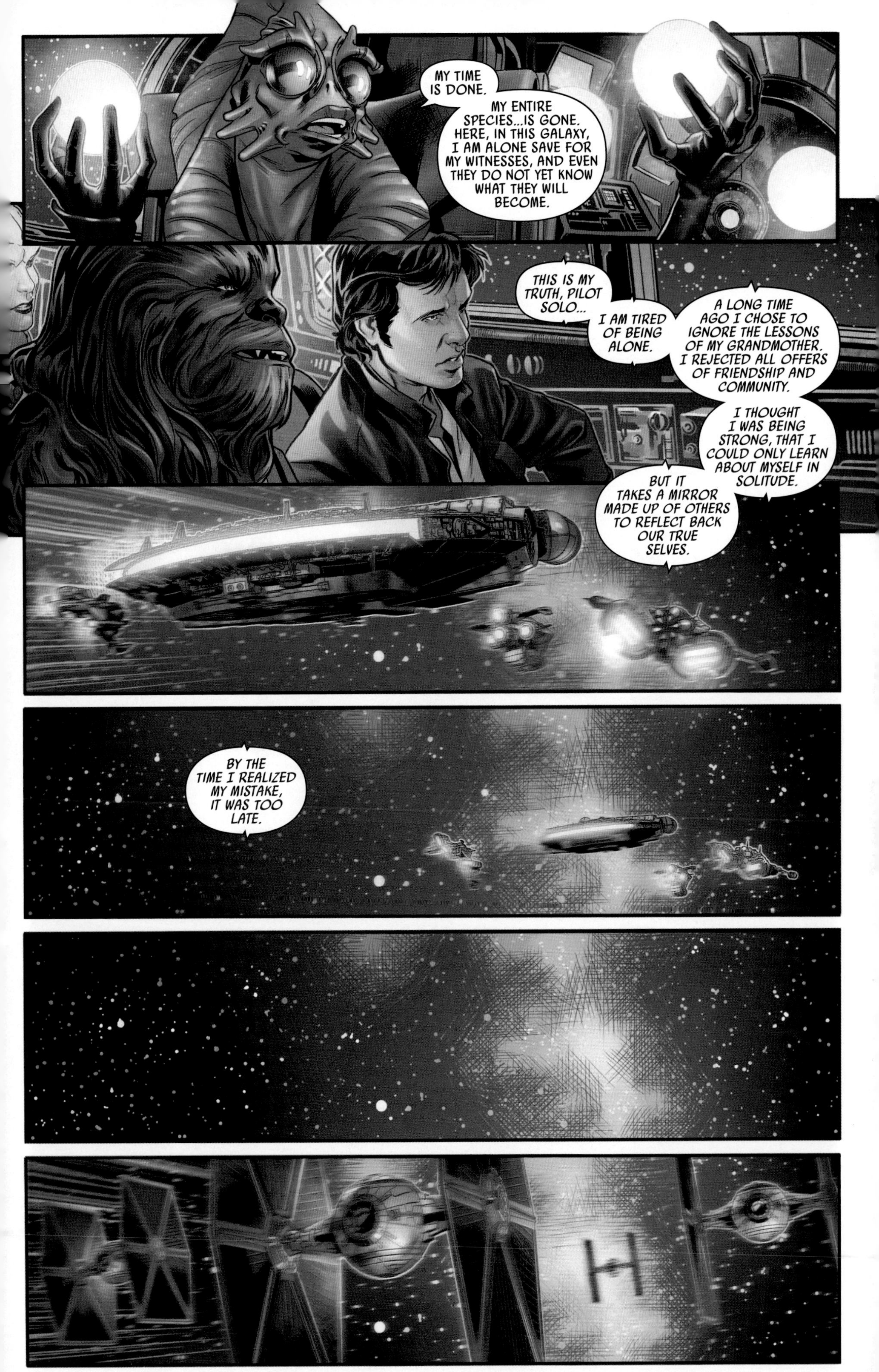
MY TIME IS DONE.
MY ENTIRE SPECIES...IS GONE. HERE, IN THIS GALAXY, I AM ALONE SAVE FOR MY WITNESSES, AND EVEN THEY DO NOT YET KNOW WHAT THEY WILL BECOME.
THIS IS MY TRUTH, PILOT SOLO...
I AM TIRED OF BEING ALONE.
A LONG TIME AGO I CHOSE TO IGNORE THE LESSONS OF MY GRANDMOTHER. I REJECTED ALL OFFERS OF FRIENDSHIP AND COMMUNITY.
I THOUGHT I WAS BEING STRONG, THAT I COULD ONLY LEARN ABOUT MYSELF IN SOLITUDE.
BUT IT TAKES A MIRROR MADE UP OF OTHERS TO REFLECT BACK OUR TRUE SELVES.
BY THE TIME I REALIZED MY MISTAKE, IT WAS TOO LATE.

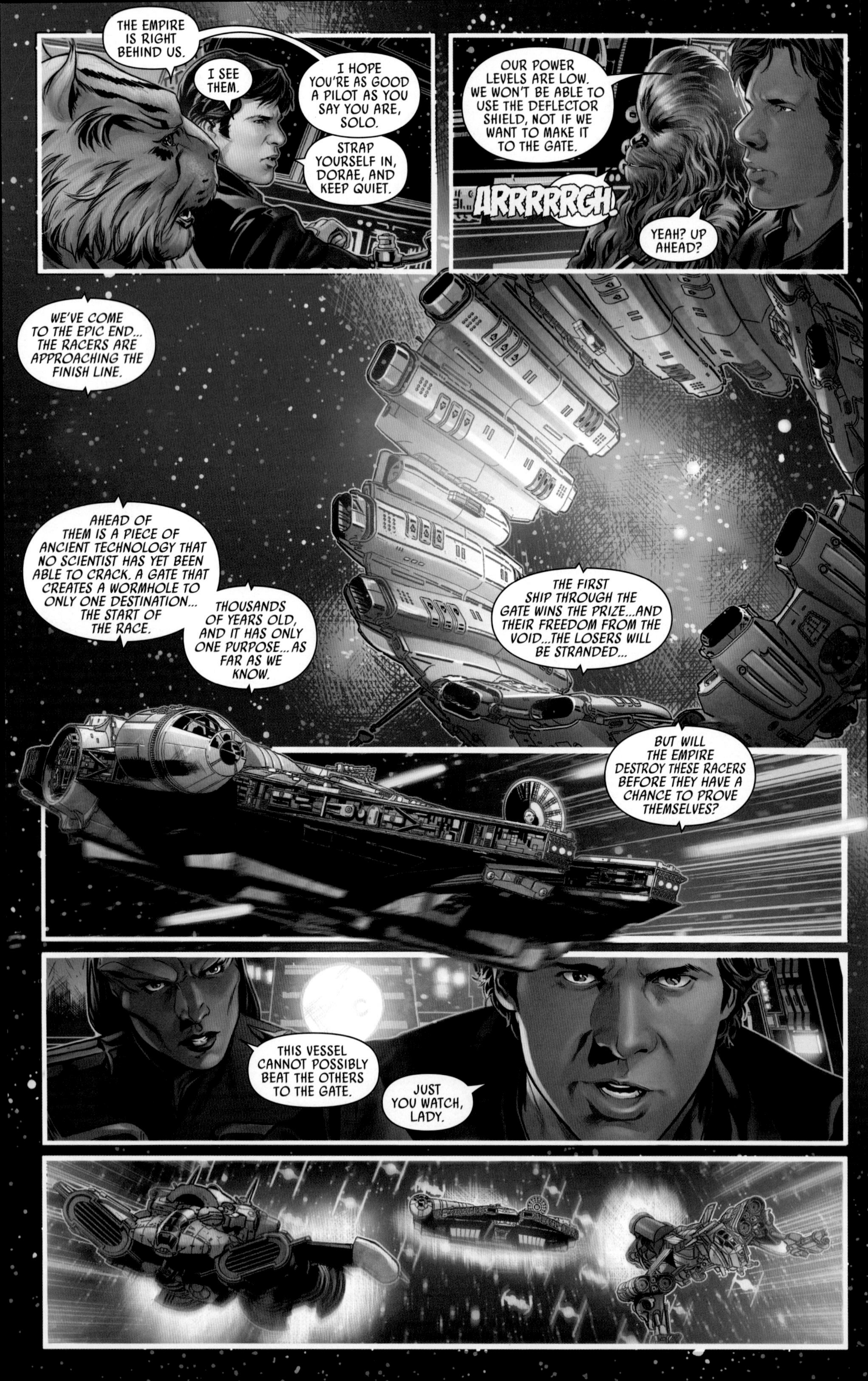
THE EMPIRE IS RIGHT BEHIND US.
I SEE THEM.
I HOPE YOU'RE AS GOOD A PILOT AS YOU SAY YOU ARE, SOLO.
STRAP YOURSELF IN, DORAE, AND KEEP QUIET.
OUR POWER LEVELS ARE LOW. WE WON'T BE ABLE TO USE THE DEFLECTOR SHIELD, NOT IF WE WANT TO MAKE IT TO THE GATE.
ARRRRRGH!
YEAH? UP AHEAD?
WE'VE COME TO THE EPIC END... THE RACERS ARE APPROACHING THE FINISH LINE.
AHEAD OF THEM IS A PIECE OF ANCIENT TECHNOLOGY THAT NO SCIENTIST HAS YET BEEN ABLE TO CRACK. A GATE THAT CREATES A WORMHOLE TO ONLY ONE DESTINATION... THE START OF THE RACE.
THOUSANDS OF YEARS OLD, AND IT HAS ONLY ONE PURPOSE...AS FAR AS WE KNOW.
THE FIRST SHIP THROUGH THE GATE WINS THE PRIZE...AND THEIR FREEDOM FROM THE VOID...THE LOSERS WILL BE STRANDED...
BUT WILL THE EMPIRE DESTROY THESE RACERS BEFORE THEY HAVE A CHANCE TO PROVE THEMSELVES?
THIS VESSEL CANNOT POSSIBLY BEAT THE OTHERS TO THE GATE.
JUST YOU WATCH, LADY.

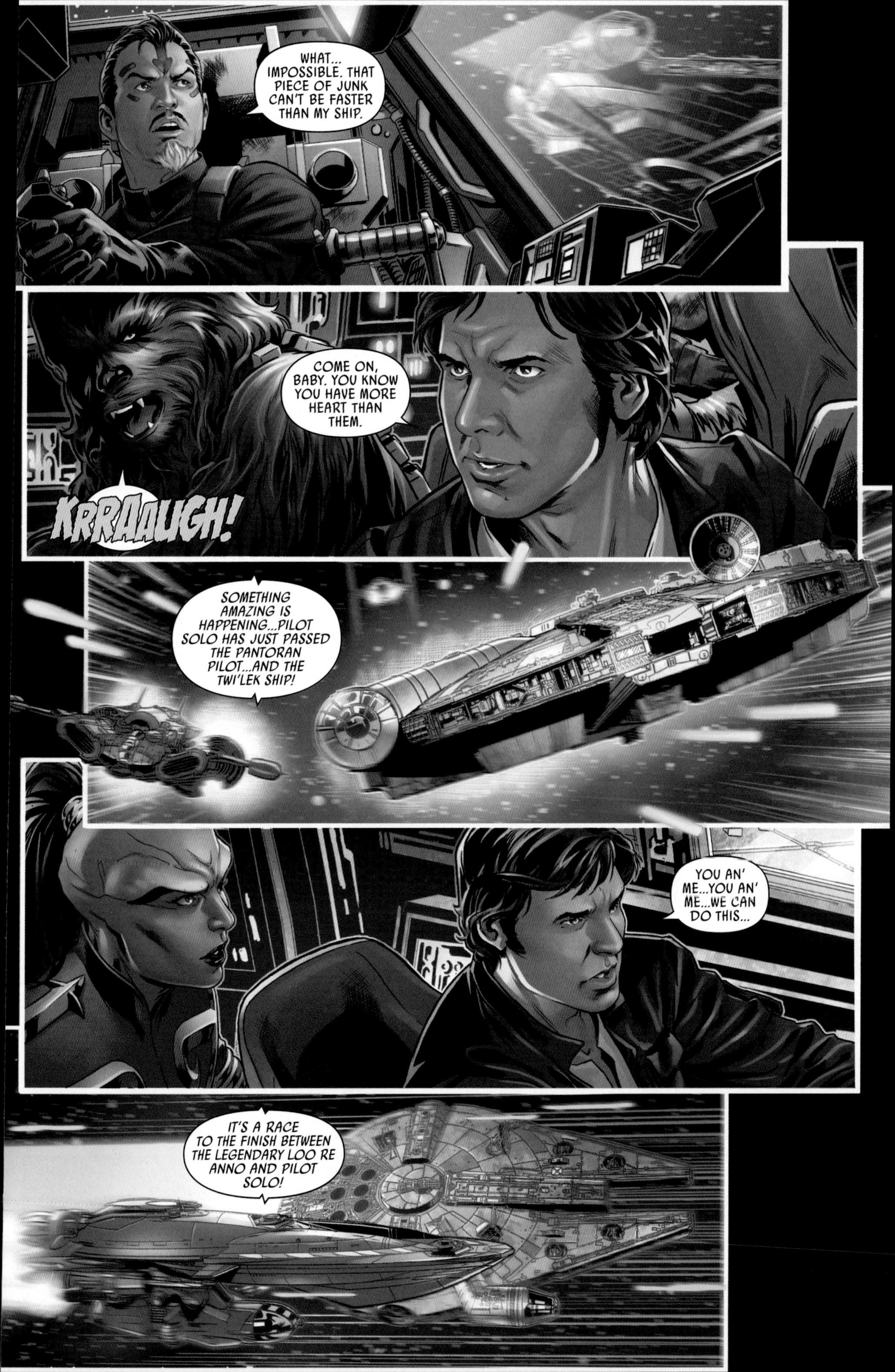
WHAT... IMPOSSIBLE. THAT PIECE OF JUNK CAN'T BE FASTER THAN MY SHIP.
COME ON, BABY. YOU KNOW YOU HAVE MORE HEART THAN THEM.
KRRAAUGH!
SOMETHING AMAZING IS HAPPENING...PILOT SOLO HAS JUST PASSED THE PANTORAN PILOT...AND THE TWI'LEK SHIP!
YOU AN' ME...YOU AN' ME...WE CAN DO THIS...
IT'S A RACE TO THE FINISH BETWEEN THE LEGENDARY LOO RE ANNO AND PILOT SOLO!

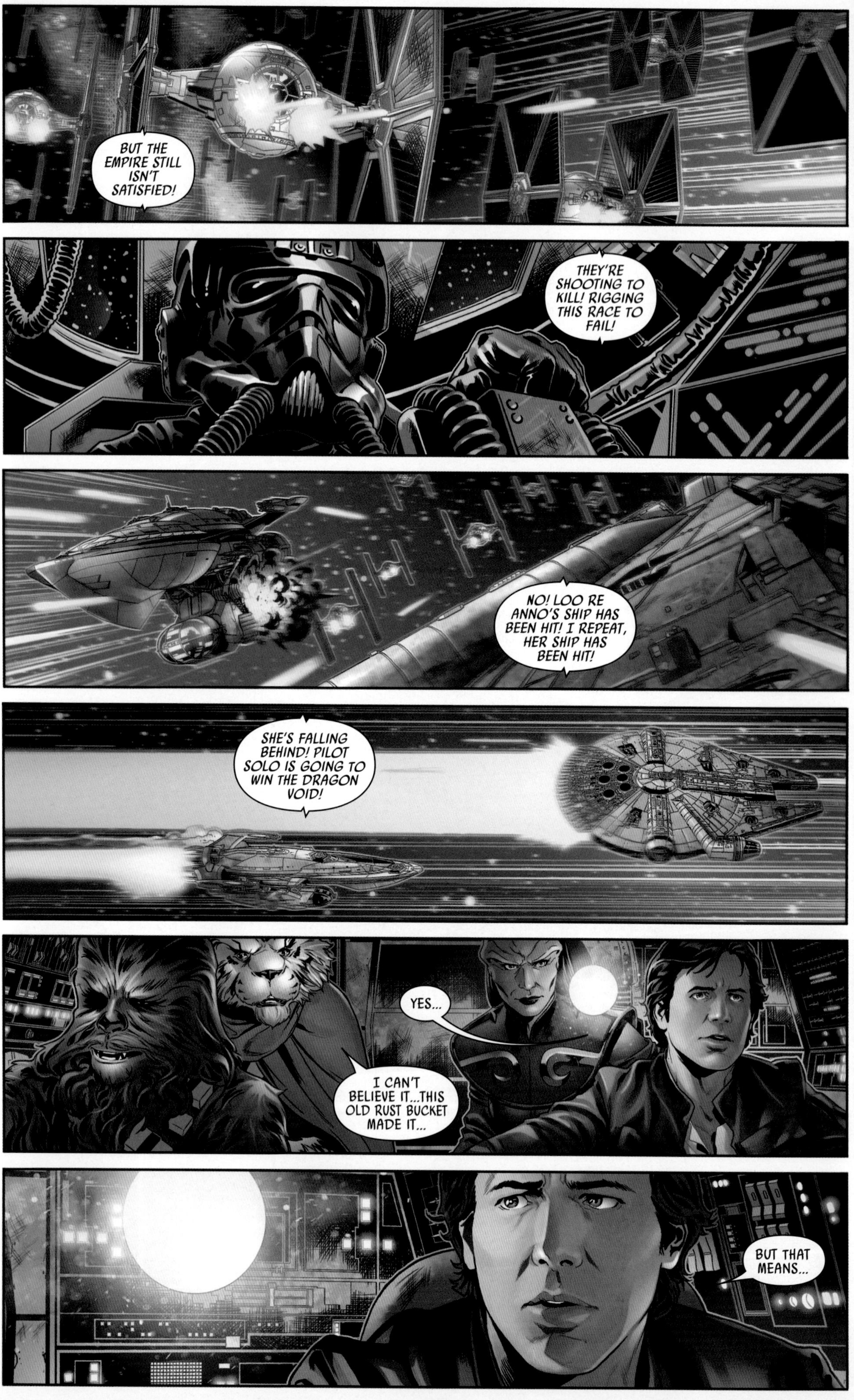
BUT THE EMPIRE STILL ISN'T SATISFIED!
THEY'RE SHOOTING TO KILL! RIGGING THIS RACE TO FAIL!
NO! LOO RE ANNO'S SHIP HAS BEEN HIT! I REPEAT, HER SHIP HAS BEEN HIT!
SHE'S FALLING BEHIND! PILOT SOLO IS GOING TO WIN THE DRAGON VOID!
YES...
I CAN'T BELIEVE IT...THIS OLD RUST BUCKET MADE IT...
BUT THAT MEANS...

WE'RE ALMOST THERE, SOLO!

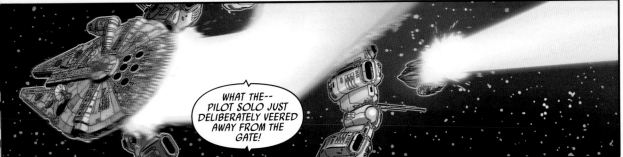

WHAT THE-- PILOT SOLO JUST DELIBERATELY VEERED AWAY FROM THE GATE!

HE'S FLYING BACK **TOWARD** THE IMPERIAL FIGHTERS!

WHAT IS HE THINKING?

YOU REALLY **DO** WANT TO DIE.

YOU **DON'T** KNOW WHAT I WANT, FUR FACE.

BUT I GUESS I KNOW WHAT MATTERS.

HOME.

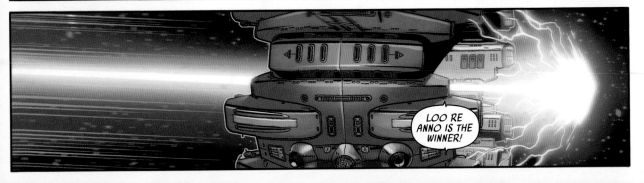

LOO RE ANNO IS THE WINNER!

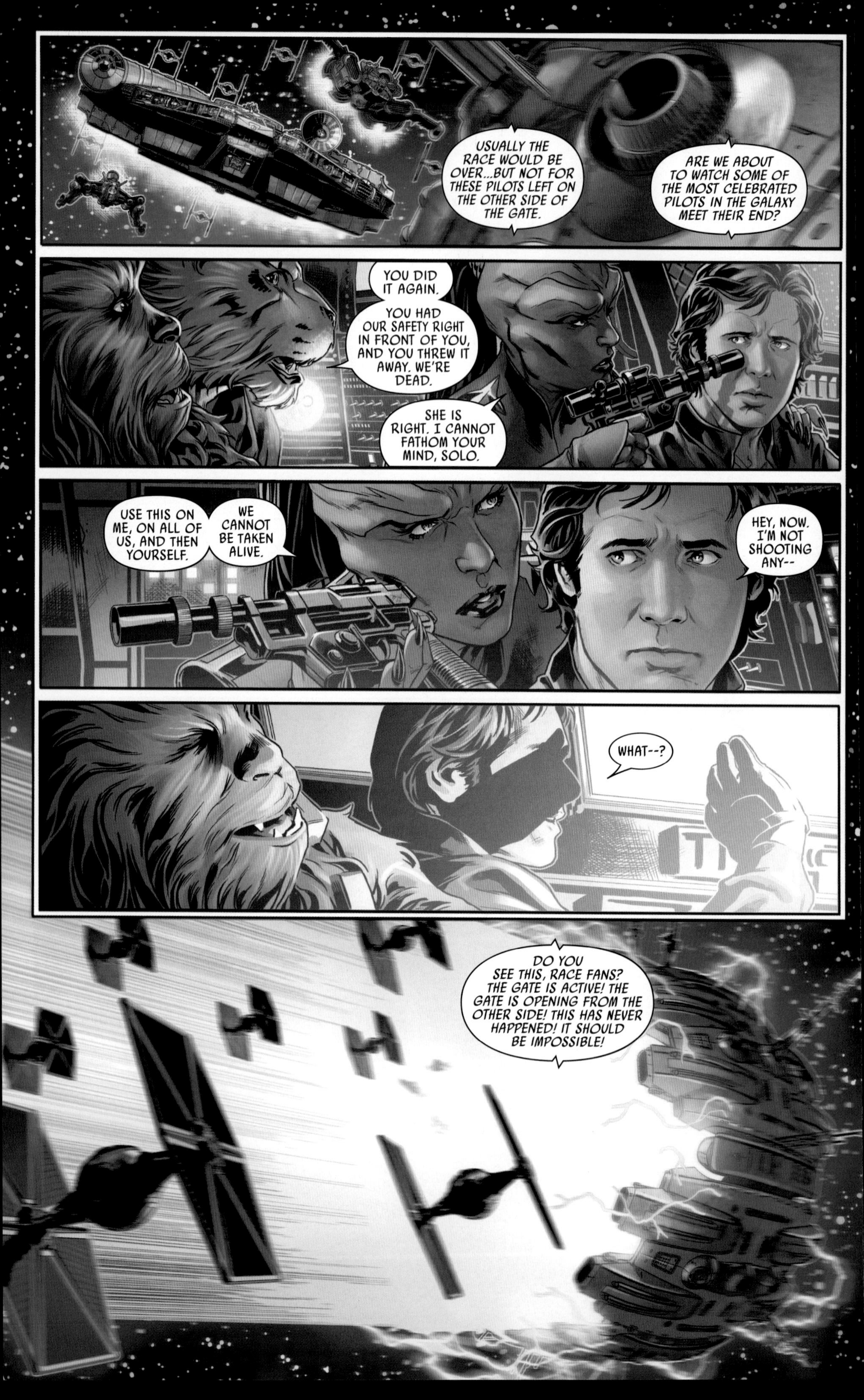
USUALLY THE RACE WOULD BE OVER...BUT NOT FOR THESE PILOTS LEFT ON THE OTHER SIDE OF THE GATE.
ARE WE ABOUT TO WATCH SOME OF THE MOST CELEBRATED PILOTS IN THE GALAXY MEET THEIR END?
YOU DID IT AGAIN.
YOU HAD OUR SAFETY RIGHT IN FRONT OF YOU, AND YOU THREW IT AWAY. WE'RE DEAD.
SHE IS RIGHT. I CANNOT FATHOM YOUR MIND, SOLO.
USE THIS ON ME, ON ALL OF US, AND THEN YOURSELF.
WE CANNOT BE TAKEN ALIVE.
HEY, NOW. I'M NOT SHOOTING ANY--
WHAT--?
DO YOU SEE THIS, RACE FANS? THE GATE IS ACTIVE! THE GATE IS OPENING FROM THE OTHER SIDE! THIS HAS NEVER HAPPENED! IT SHOULD BE IMPOSSIBLE!

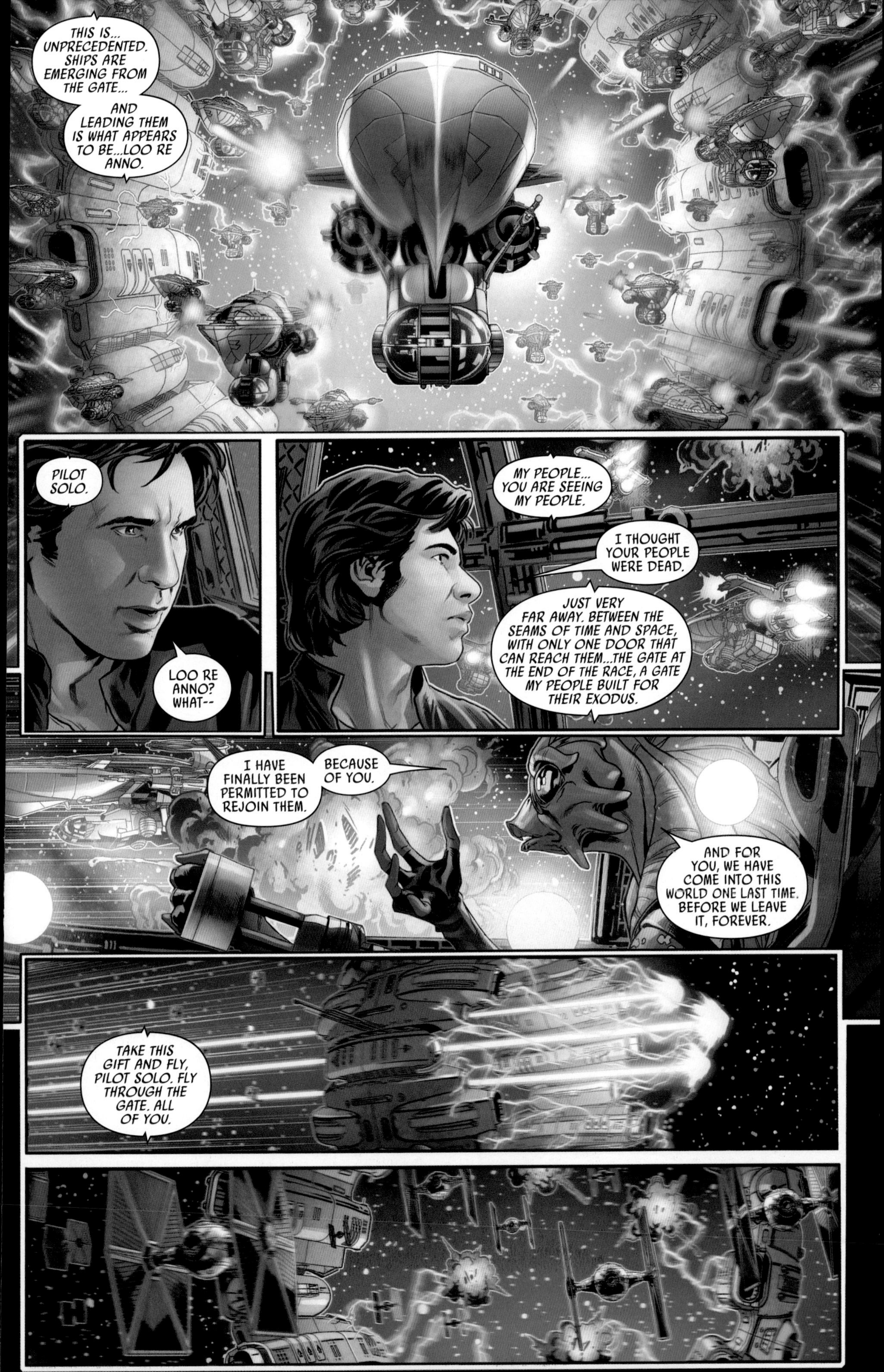
THIS IS... UNPRECEDENTED. SHIPS ARE EMERGING FROM THE GATE...
AND LEADING THEM IS WHAT APPEARS TO BE...LOO RE ANNO.
PILOT SOLO.
LOO RE ANNO? WHAT--
MY PEOPLE... YOU ARE SEEING MY PEOPLE.
I THOUGHT YOUR PEOPLE WERE DEAD.
JUST VERY FAR AWAY. BETWEEN THE SEAMS OF TIME AND SPACE, WITH ONLY ONE DOOR THAT CAN REACH THEM...THE GATE AT THE END OF THE RACE, A GATE MY PEOPLE BUILT FOR THEIR EXODUS.
I HAVE FINALLY BEEN PERMITTED TO REJOIN THEM.
BECAUSE OF YOU.
AND FOR YOU, WE HAVE COME INTO THIS WORLD ONE LAST TIME. BEFORE WE LEAVE IT, FOREVER.
TAKE THIS GIFT AND FLY, PILOT SOLO. FLY THROUGH THE GATE. ALL OF YOU.

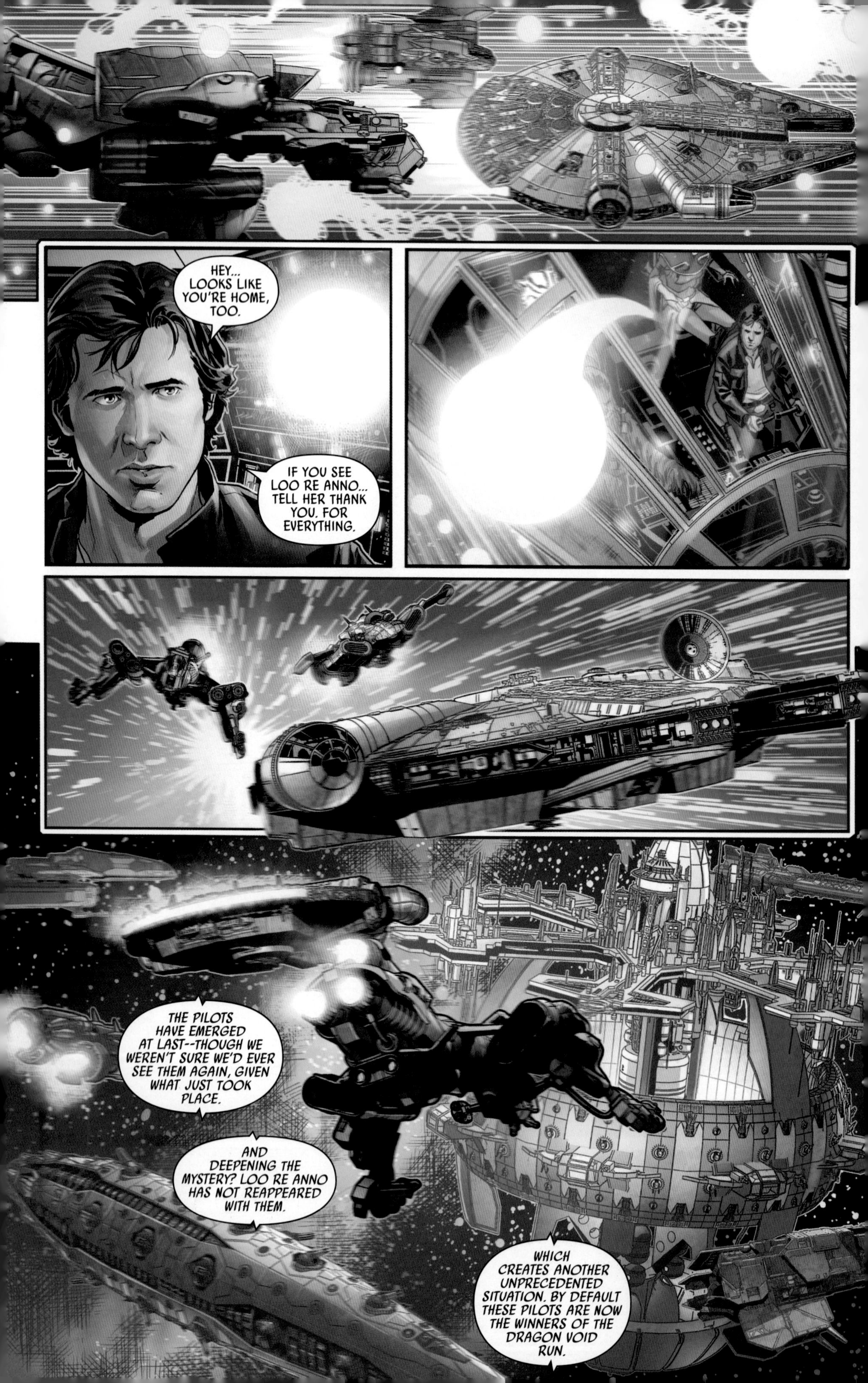
HEY... LOOKS LIKE YOU'RE HOME, TOO.
IF YOU SEE LOO RE ANNO... TELL HER THANK YOU. FOR EVERYTHING.
THE PILOTS HAVE EMERGED AT LAST--THOUGH WE WEREN'T SURE WE'D EVER SEE THEM AGAIN, GIVEN WHAT JUST TOOK PLACE.
AND DEEPENING THE MYSTERY? LOO RE ANNO HAS NOT REAPPEARED WITH THEM.
WHICH CREATES ANOTHER UNPRECEDENTED SITUATION. BY DEFAULT THESE PILOTS ARE NOW THE WINNERS OF THE DRAGON VOID RUN.

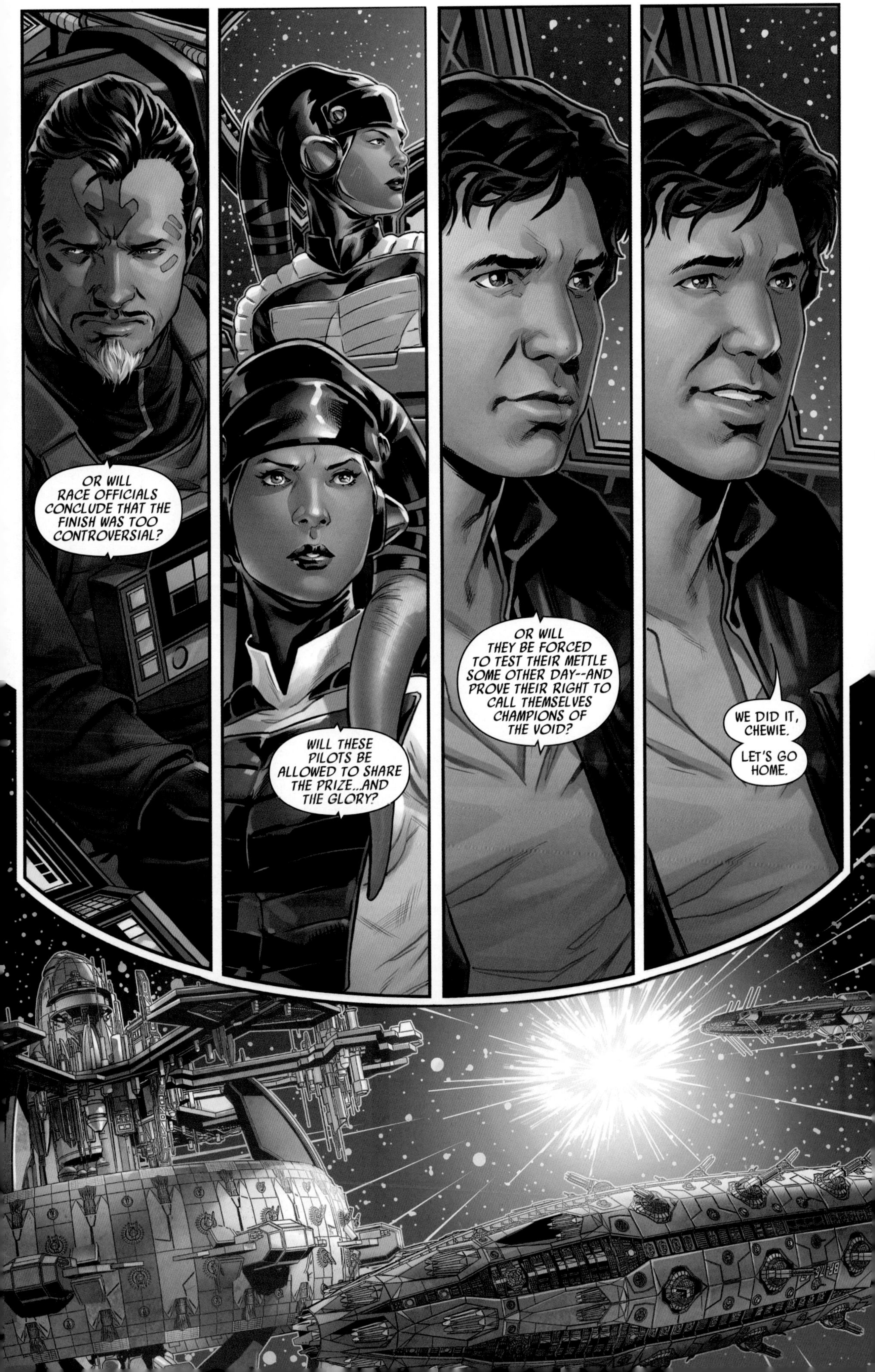

OR WILL RACE OFFICIALS CONCLUDE THAT THE FINISH WAS TOO CONTROVERSIAL?
WILL THESE PILOTS BE ALLOWED TO SHARE THE PRIZE...AND THE GLORY?
OR WILL THEY BE FORCED TO TEST THEIR METTLE SOME OTHER DAY--AND PROVE THEIR RIGHT TO CALL THEMSELVES CHAMPIONS OF THE VOID?
WE DID IT, CHEWIE.
LET'S GO HOME.

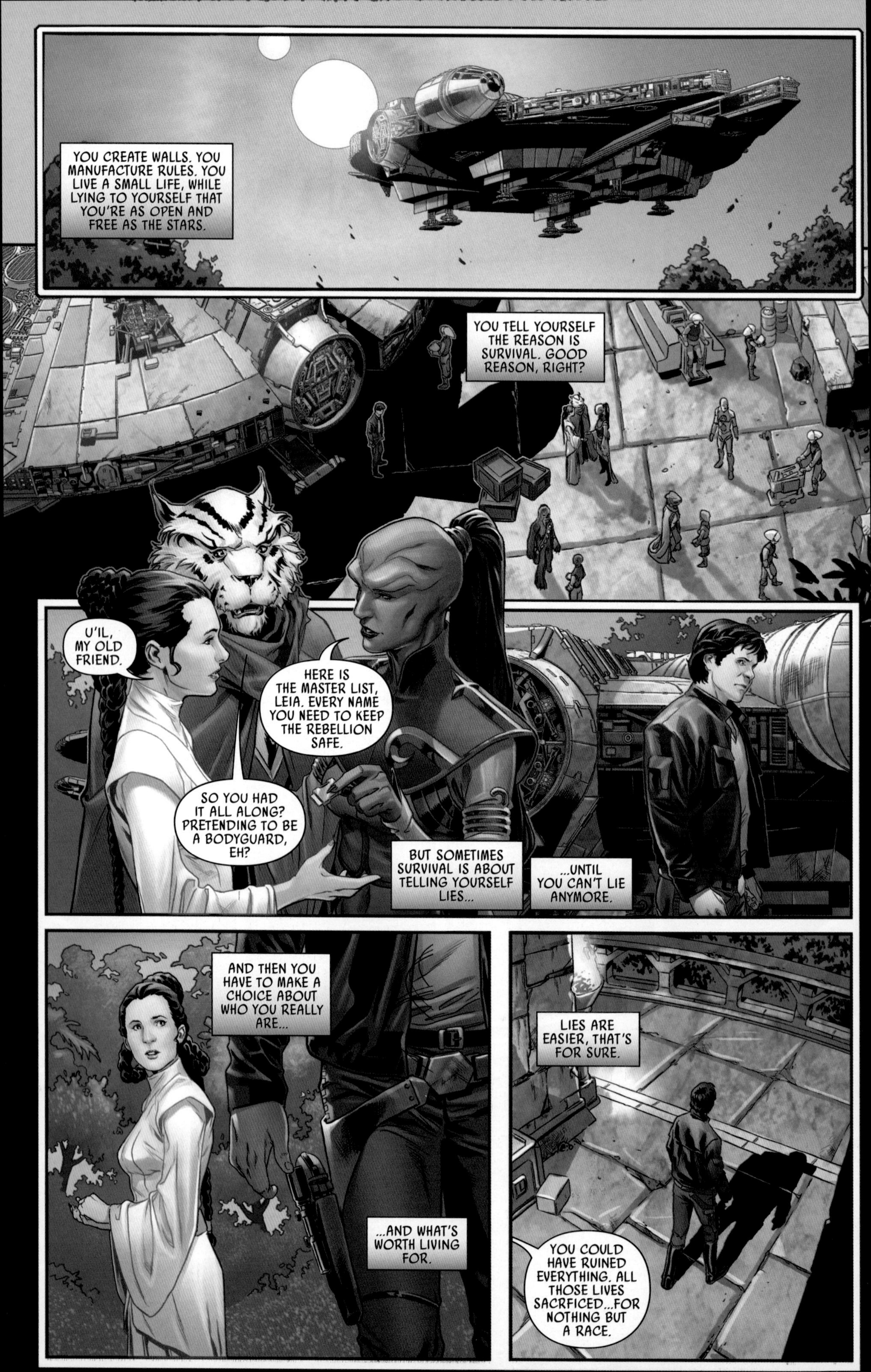
YOU CREATE WALLS. YOU MANUFACTURE RULES. YOU LIVE A SMALL LIFE, WHILE LYING TO YOURSELF THAT YOU'RE AS OPEN AND FREE AS THE STARS.
YOU TELL YOURSELF THE REASON IS SURVIVAL. GOOD REASON, RIGHT?
U'IL, MY OLD FRIEND.
HERE IS THE MASTER LIST, LEIA. EVERY NAME YOU NEED TO KEEP THE REBELLION SAFE.
SO YOU HAD IT ALL ALONG? PRETENDING TO BE A BODYGUARD, EH?
BUT SOMETIMES SURVIVAL IS ABOUT TELLING YOURSELF LIES...
...UNTIL YOU CAN'T LIE ANYMORE.
AND THEN YOU HAVE TO MAKE A CHOICE ABOUT WHO YOU REALLY ARE...
...AND WHAT'S WORTH LIVING FOR.
LIES ARE EASIER, THAT'S FOR SURE.
YOU COULD HAVE RUINED EVERYTHING. ALL THOSE LIVES SACRFICED...FOR NOTHING BUT A RACE.

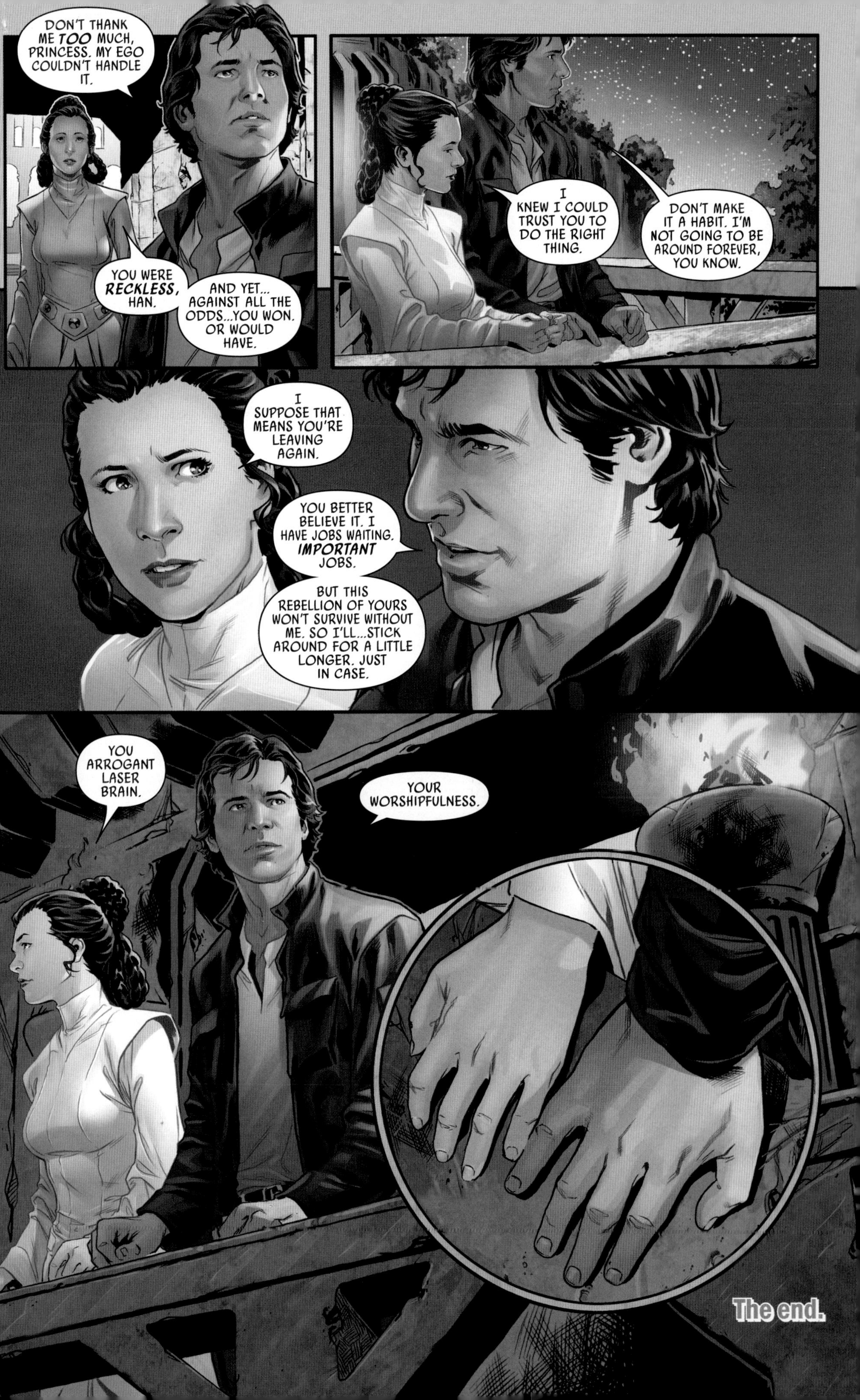
DON'T THANK ME TOO MUCH, PRINCESS. MY EGO COULDN'T HANDLE IT.
YOU WERE RECKLESS, HAN.
AND YET... AGAINST ALL THE ODDS...YOU WON. OR WOULD HAVE.
I KNEW I COULD TRUST YOU TO DO THE RIGHT THING.
DON'T MAKE IT A HABIT. I'M NOT GOING TO BE AROUND FOREVER, YOU KNOW.
I SUPPOSE THAT MEANS YOU'RE LEAVING AGAIN.
YOU BETTER BELIEVE IT. I HAVE JOBS WAITING. IMPORTANT JOBS.
BUT THIS REBELLION OF YOURS WON'T SURVIVE WITHOUT ME. SO I'LL...STICK AROUND FOR A LITTLE LONGER. JUST IN CASE.
YOU ARROGANT LASER BRAIN.
YOUR WORSHIPFULNESS.
The end.

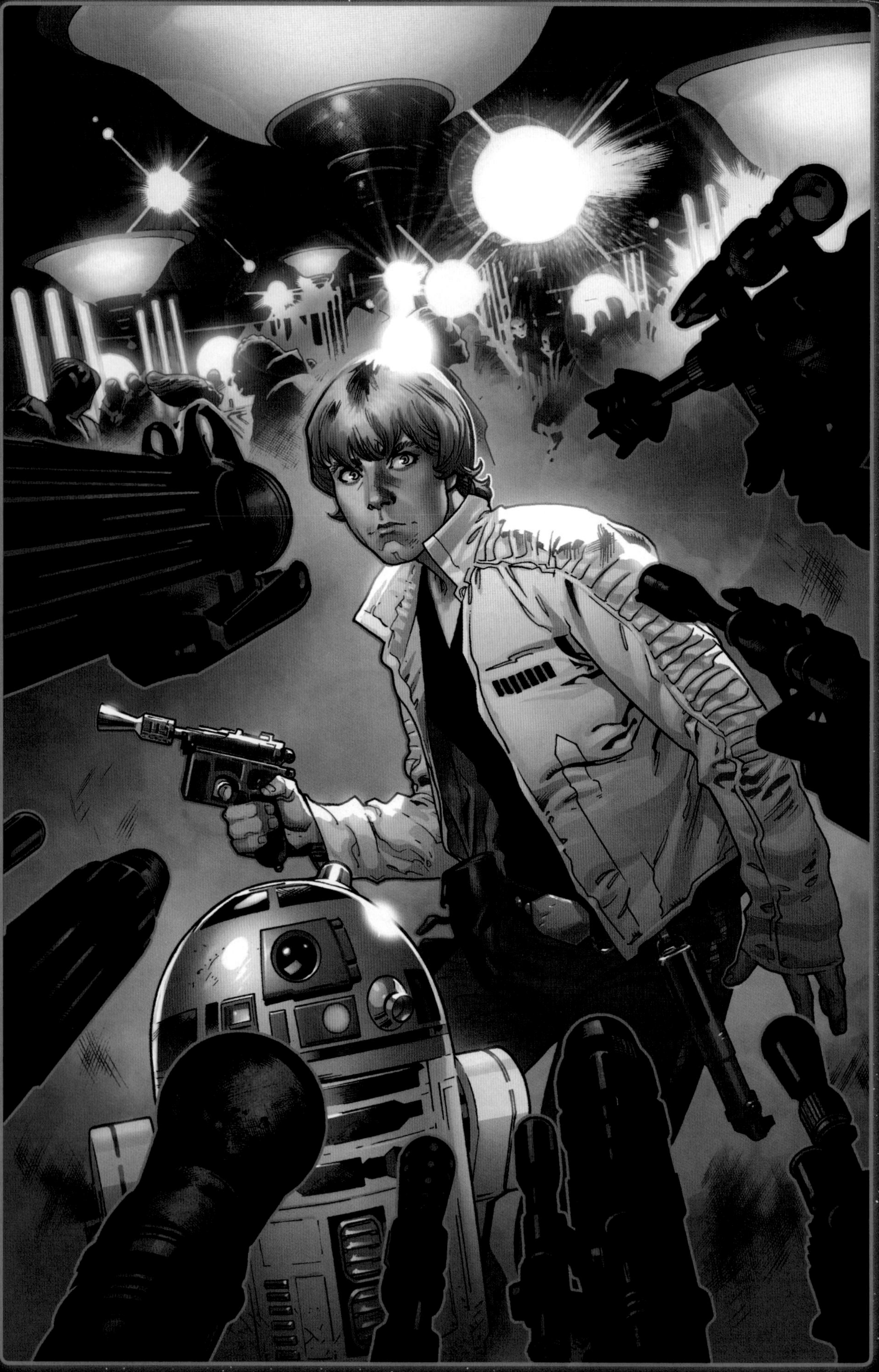

STAR WARS 8

Book II

SHOWDOWN ON THE SMUGGLER'S MOON

It is a period of renewed hope for the Rebellion. The evil Galactic Empire's greatest weapon, the Death Star, has been destroyed by the young rebel pilot Luke Skywalker.

But Skywalker knows he has a long way to go if he ever hopes to become a true Jedi. Seeking clues to his destiny, he recently returned to his home world of Tatooine, where he discovered a secret journal left for him by Jedi Master Obi-Wan Kenobi.

Meanwhile, Princess Leia and Han Solo have encountered some surprises of their own. While searching the galaxy for a suitable site for the new Rebel base, they ran afoul of Imperial patrol ships. Now hiding out on a remote planet, they find themselves facing a far more shocking encounter.

Her name is Sana Solo. And she claims to be Han Solo's wife....

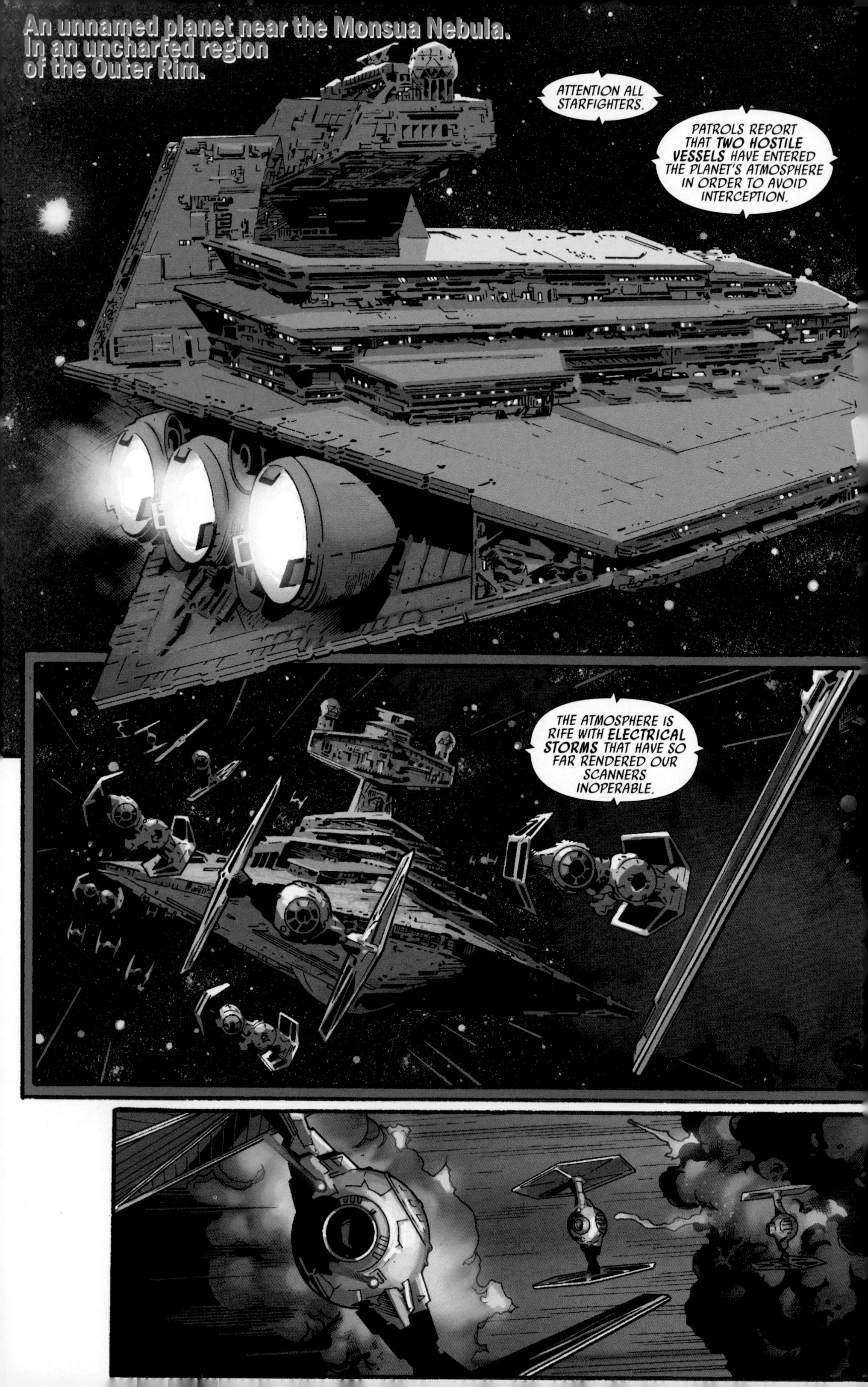
An unnamed planet near the Monsua Nebula. In an uncharted region of the Outer Rim.
ATTENTION ALL STARFIGHTERS.
PATROLS REPORT THAT **TWO HOSTILE VESSELS** HAVE ENTERED THE PLANET'S ATMOSPHERE IN ORDER TO AVOID INTERCEPTION.
THE ATMOSPHERE IS RIFE WITH **ELECTRICAL STORMS** THAT HAVE SO FAR RENDERED OUR SCANNERS INOPERABLE.

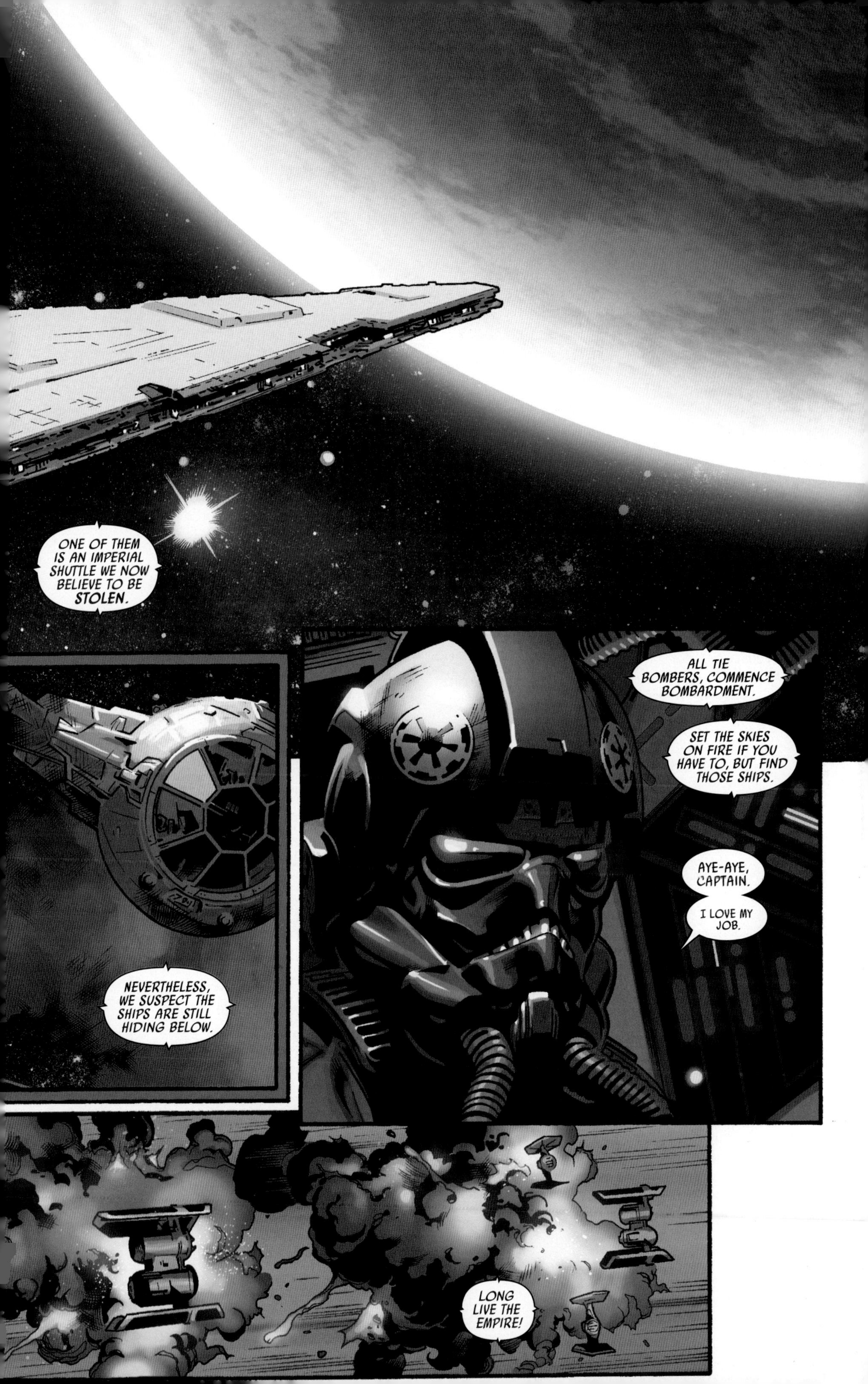

ONE OF THEM IS AN IMPERIAL SHUTTLE WE NOW BELIEVE TO BE STOLEN.
NEVERTHELESS, WE SUSPECT THE SHIPS ARE STILL HIDING BELOW.
ALL TIE BOMBERS, COMMENCE BOMBARDMENT.
SET THE SKIES ON FIRE IF YOU HAVE TO, BUT FIND THOSE SHIPS.
AYE-AYE, CAPTAIN.
I LOVE MY JOB.
LONG LIVE THE EMPIRE!

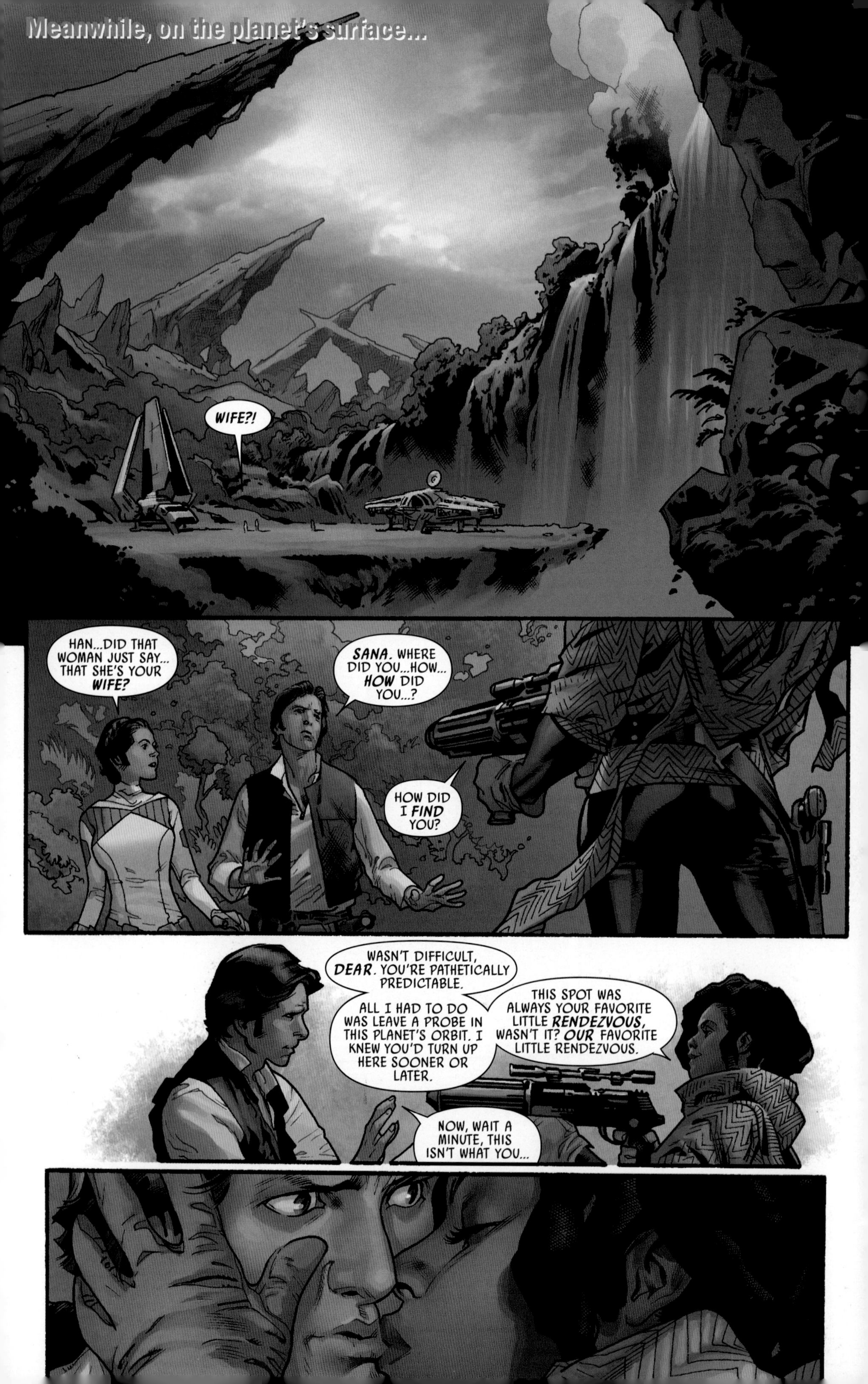
Meanwhile, on the planet's surface...
WIFE?!
HAN...DID THAT WOMAN JUST SAY... THAT SHE'S YOUR WIFE?
SANA. WHERE DID YOU...HOW... HOW DID YOU...?
HOW DID I FIND YOU?
WASN'T DIFFICULT, DEAR. YOU'RE PATHETICALLY PREDICTABLE.
ALL I HAD TO DO WAS LEAVE A PROBE IN THIS PLANET'S ORBIT. I KNEW YOU'D TURN UP HERE SOONER OR LATER.
THIS SPOT WAS ALWAYS YOUR FAVORITE LITTLE RENDEZVOUS, WASN'T IT? OUR FAVORITE LITTLE RENDEZVOUS.
NOW, WAIT A MINUTE, THIS ISN'T WHAT YOU...

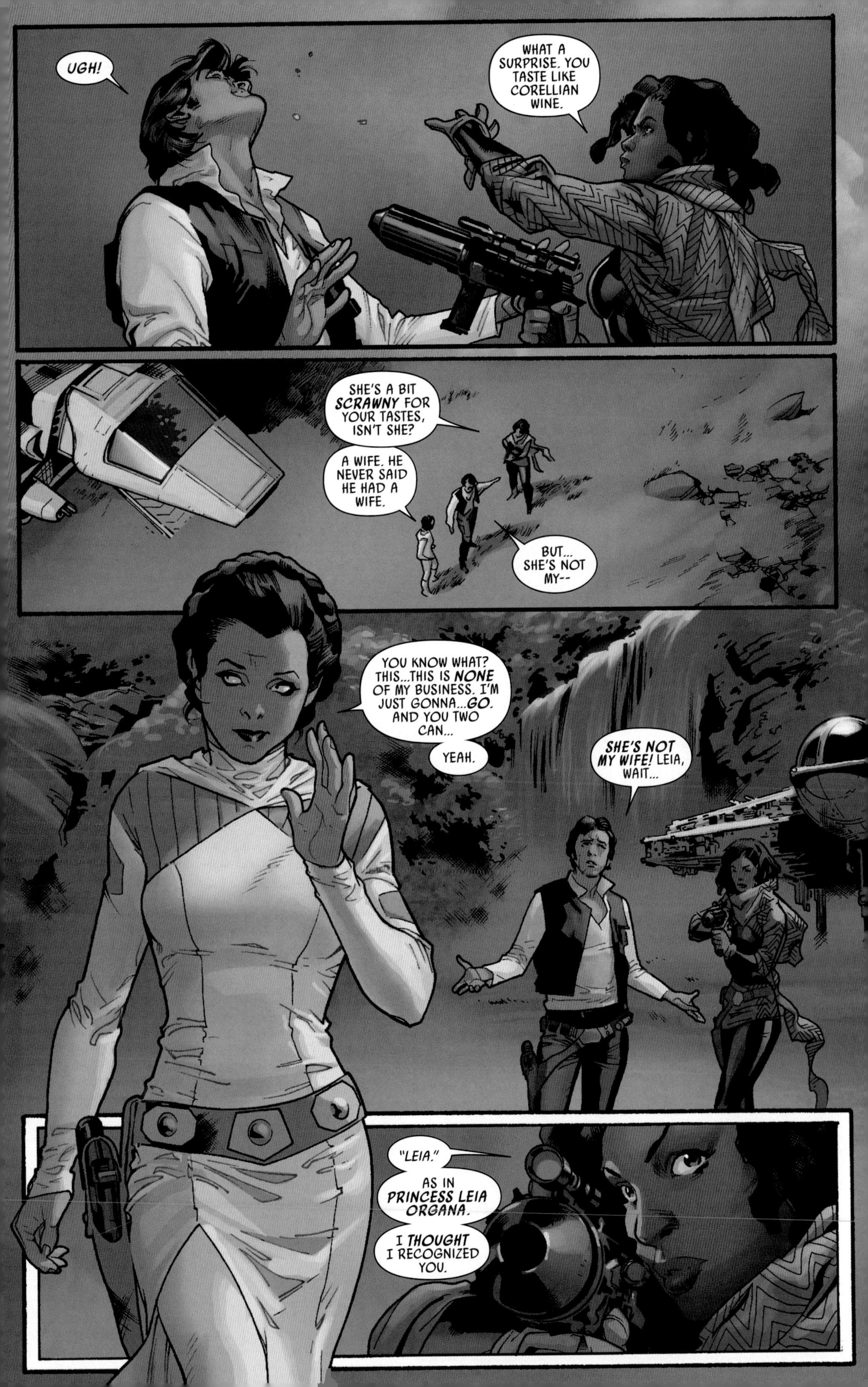
UGH!
WHAT A SURPRISE. YOU TASTE LIKE CORELLIAN WINE.
SHE'S A BIT **SCRAWNY** FOR YOUR TASTES, ISN'T SHE?
A WIFE. HE NEVER SAID HE HAD A WIFE.
BUT... SHE'S NOT MY--
YOU KNOW WHAT? THIS...THIS IS **NONE** OF MY BUSINESS. I'M JUST GONNA...**GO.** AND YOU TWO CAN...
YEAH.
SHE'S NOT MY WIFE! LEIA, WAIT...
"LEIA."
AS IN **PRINCESS LEIA ORGANA.**
I **THOUGHT** I RECOGNIZED YOU.

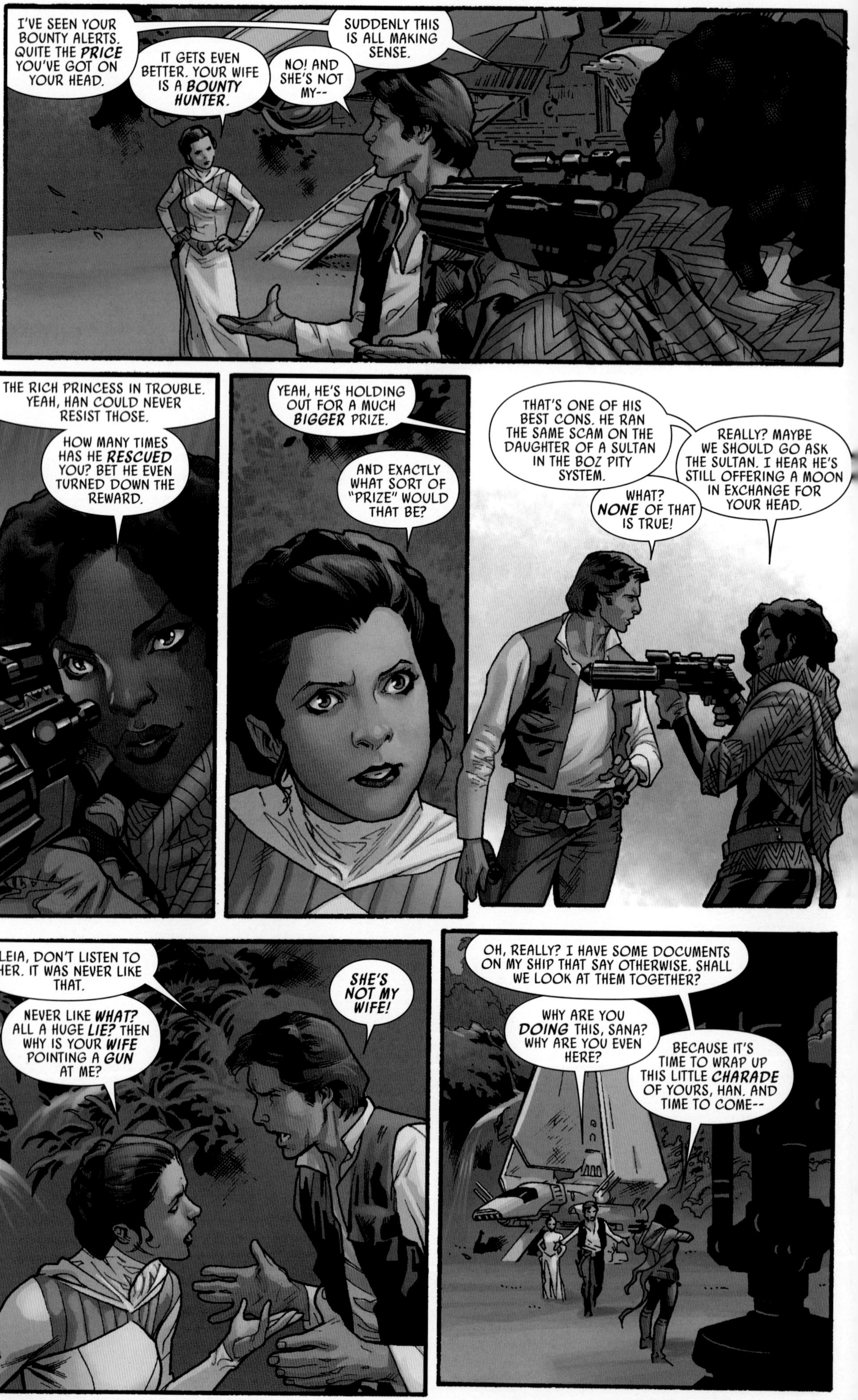
I'VE SEEN YOUR BOUNTY ALERTS. QUITE THE PRICE YOU'VE GOT ON YOUR HEAD.
SUDDENLY THIS IS ALL MAKING SENSE.
IT GETS EVEN BETTER. YOUR WIFE IS A BOUNTY HUNTER.
NO! AND SHE'S NOT MY--
THE RICH PRINCESS IN TROUBLE. YEAH, HAN COULD NEVER RESIST THOSE.
HOW MANY TIMES HAS HE RESCUED YOU? BET HE EVEN TURNED DOWN THE REWARD.
YEAH, HE'S HOLDING OUT FOR A MUCH BIGGER PRIZE.
AND EXACTLY WHAT SORT OF "PRIZE" WOULD THAT BE?
THAT'S ONE OF HIS BEST CONS. HE RAN THE SAME SCAM ON THE DAUGHTER OF A SULTAN IN THE BOZ PITY SYSTEM.
WHAT? NONE OF THAT IS TRUE!
REALLY? MAYBE WE SHOULD GO ASK THE SULTAN. I HEAR HE'S STILL OFFERING A MOON IN EXCHANGE FOR YOUR HEAD.
LEIA, DON'T LISTEN TO HER. IT WAS NEVER LIKE THAT.
NEVER LIKE WHAT? ALL A HUGE LIE? THEN WHY IS YOUR WIFE POINTING A GUN AT ME?
SHE'S NOT MY WIFE!
OH, REALLY? I HAVE SOME DOCUMENTS ON MY SHIP THAT SAY OTHERWISE. SHALL WE LOOK AT THEM TOGETHER?
WHY ARE YOU DOING THIS, SANA? WHY ARE YOU EVEN HERE?
BECAUSE IT'S TIME TO WRAP UP THIS LITTLE CHARADE OF YOURS, HAN. AND TIME TO COME--

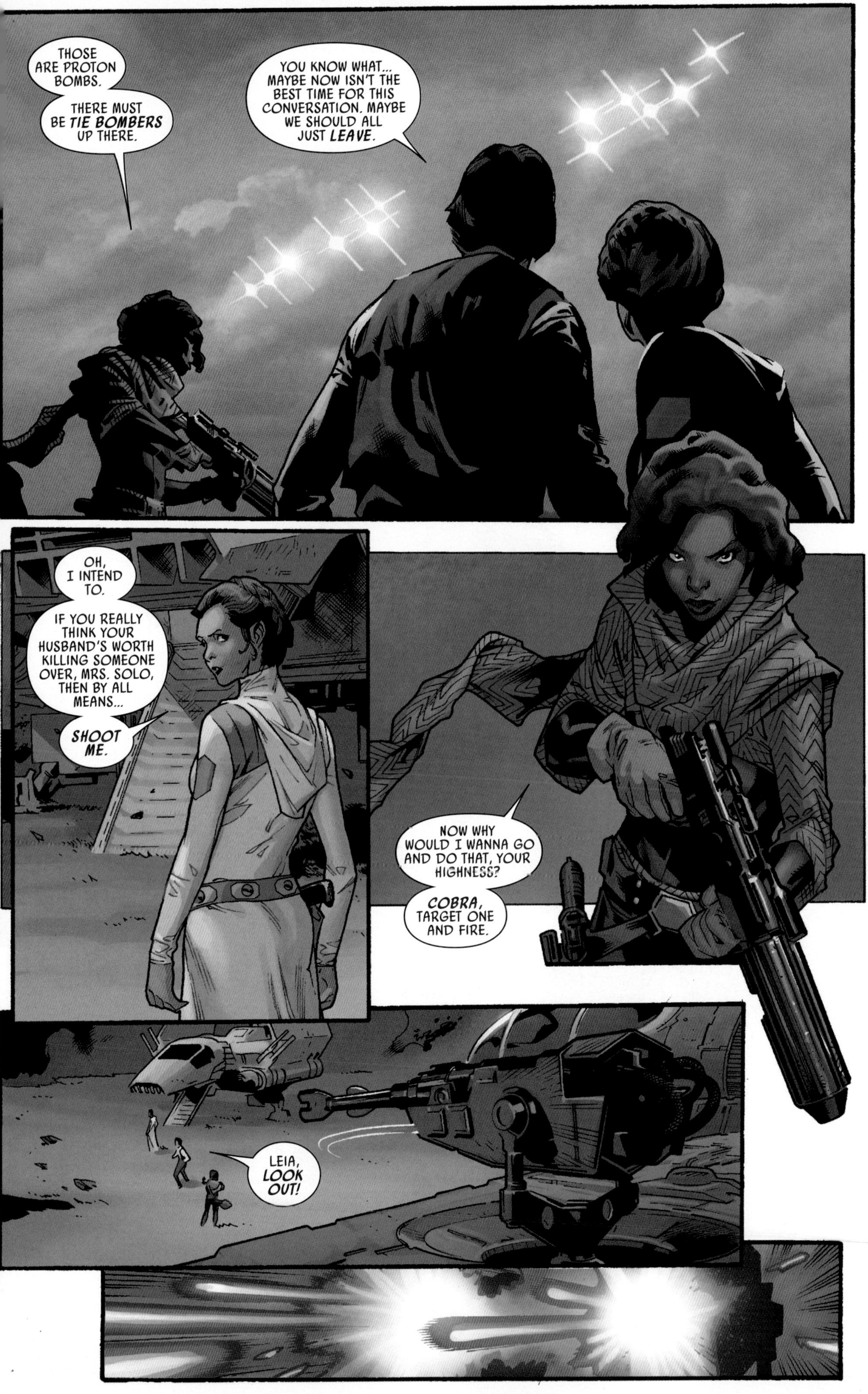
THOSE ARE PROTON BOMBS.
THERE MUST BE TIE BOMBERS UP THERE.
YOU KNOW WHAT... MAYBE NOW ISN'T THE BEST TIME FOR THIS CONVERSATION. MAYBE WE SHOULD ALL JUST LEAVE.
OH, I INTEND TO.
IF YOU REALLY THINK YOUR HUSBAND'S WORTH KILLING SOMEONE OVER, MRS. SOLO, THEN BY ALL MEANS...
SHOOT ME.
NOW WHY WOULD I WANNA GO AND DO THAT, YOUR HIGHNESS?
COBRA, TARGET ONE AND FIRE.
LEIA, LOOK OUT!

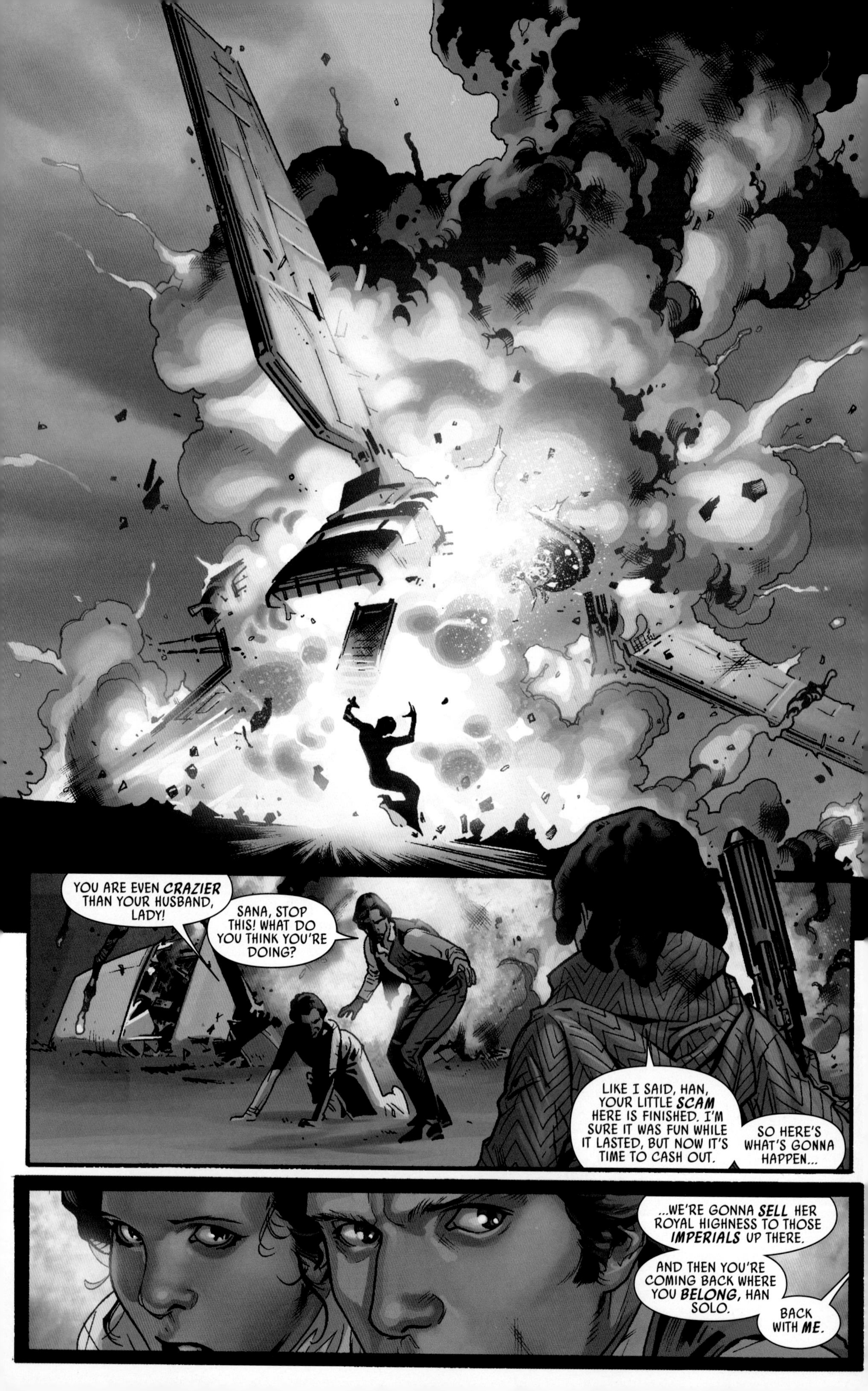
YOU ARE EVEN CRAZIER THAN YOUR HUSBAND, LADY!
SANA, STOP THIS! WHAT DO YOU THINK YOU'RE DOING?
LIKE I SAID, HAN, YOUR LITTLE SCAM HERE IS FINISHED. I'M SURE IT WAS FUN WHILE IT LASTED, BUT NOW IT'S TIME TO CASH OUT.
SO HERE'S WHAT'S GONNA HAPPEN...
...WE'RE GONNA SELL HER ROYAL HIGHNESS TO THOSE IMPERIALS UP THERE.
AND THEN YOU'RE COMING BACK WHERE YOU BELONG, HAN SOLO.
BACK WITH ME.

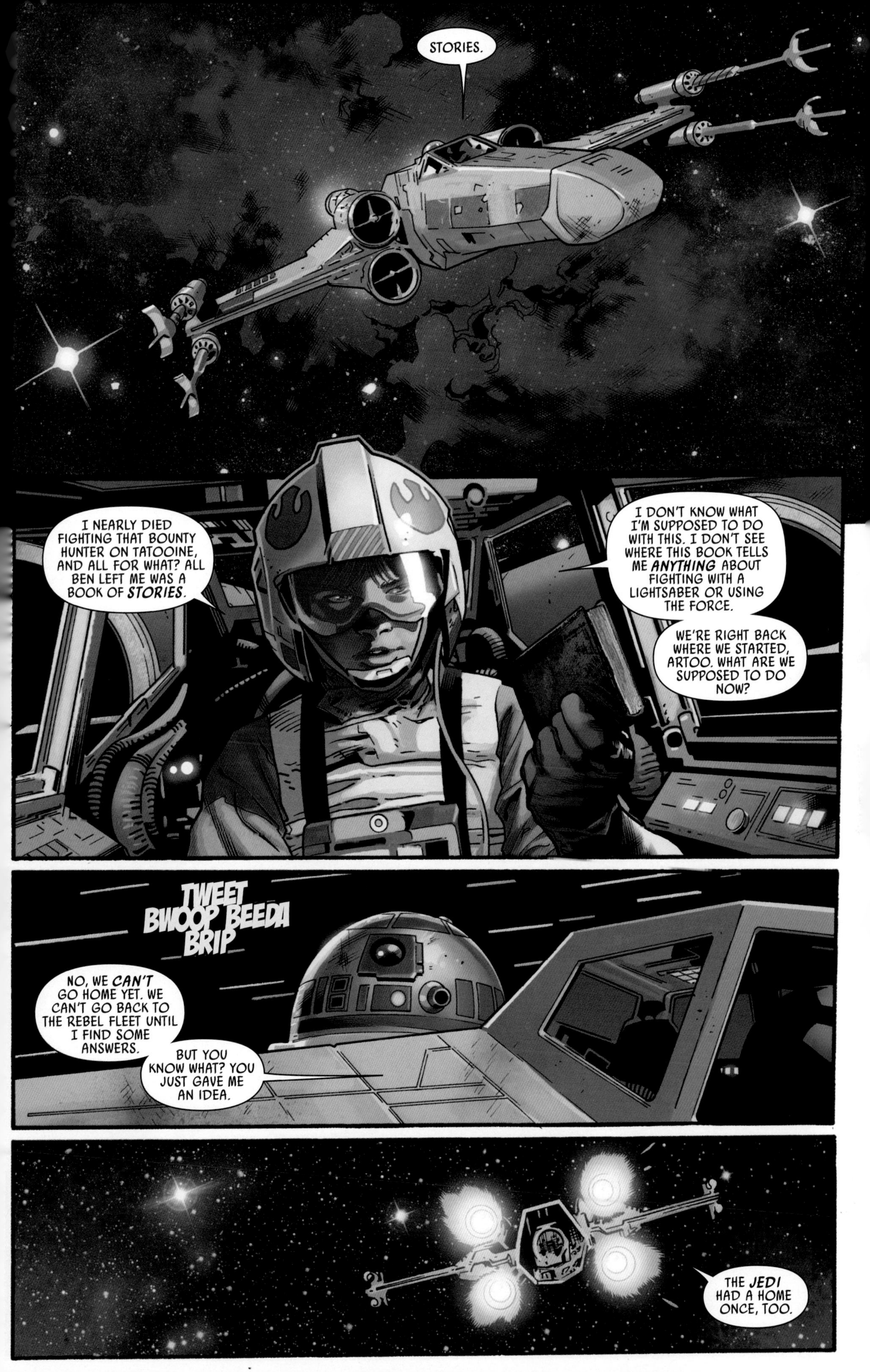
STORIES.
I NEARLY DIED FIGHTING THAT BOUNTY HUNTER ON TATOOINE, AND ALL FOR WHAT? ALL BEN LEFT ME WAS A BOOK OF STORIES.
I DON'T KNOW WHAT I'M SUPPOSED TO DO WITH THIS. I DON'T SEE WHERE THIS BOOK TELLS ME ANYTHING ABOUT FIGHTING WITH A LIGHTSABER OR USING THE FORCE.
WE'RE RIGHT BACK WHERE WE STARTED, ARTOO. WHAT ARE WE SUPPOSED TO DO NOW?
TWEET BWOOP BEEDA BRIP
NO, WE CAN'T GO HOME YET. WE CAN'T GO BACK TO THE REBEL FLEET UNTIL I FIND SOME ANSWERS.
BUT YOU KNOW WHAT? YOU JUST GAVE ME AN IDEA.
THE JEDI HAD A HOME ONCE, TOO.

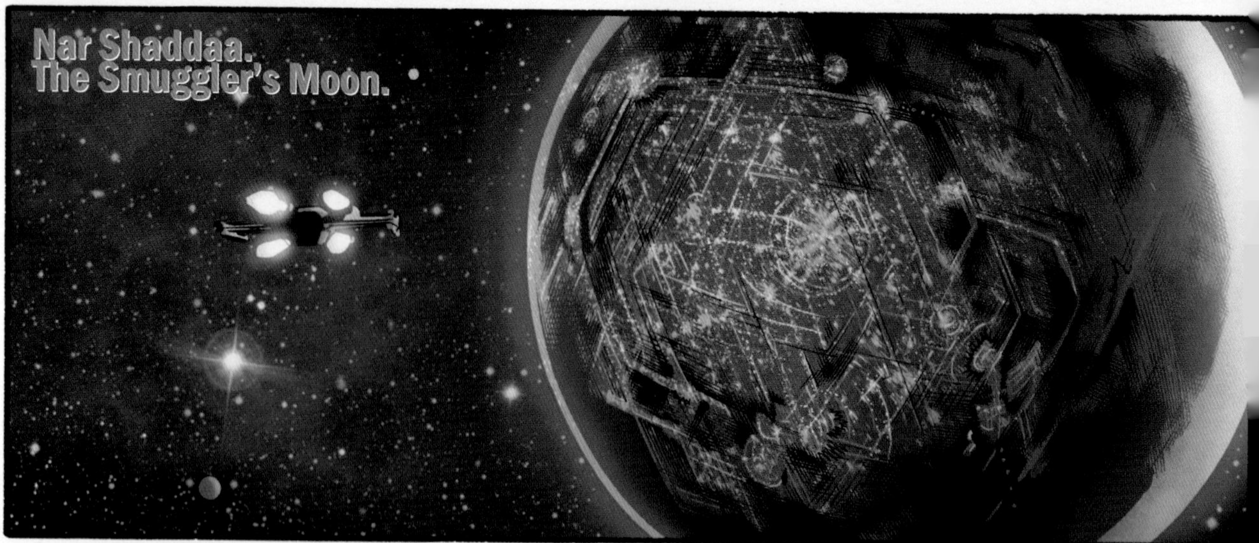
Nar Shaddaa.
The Smuggler's Moon.

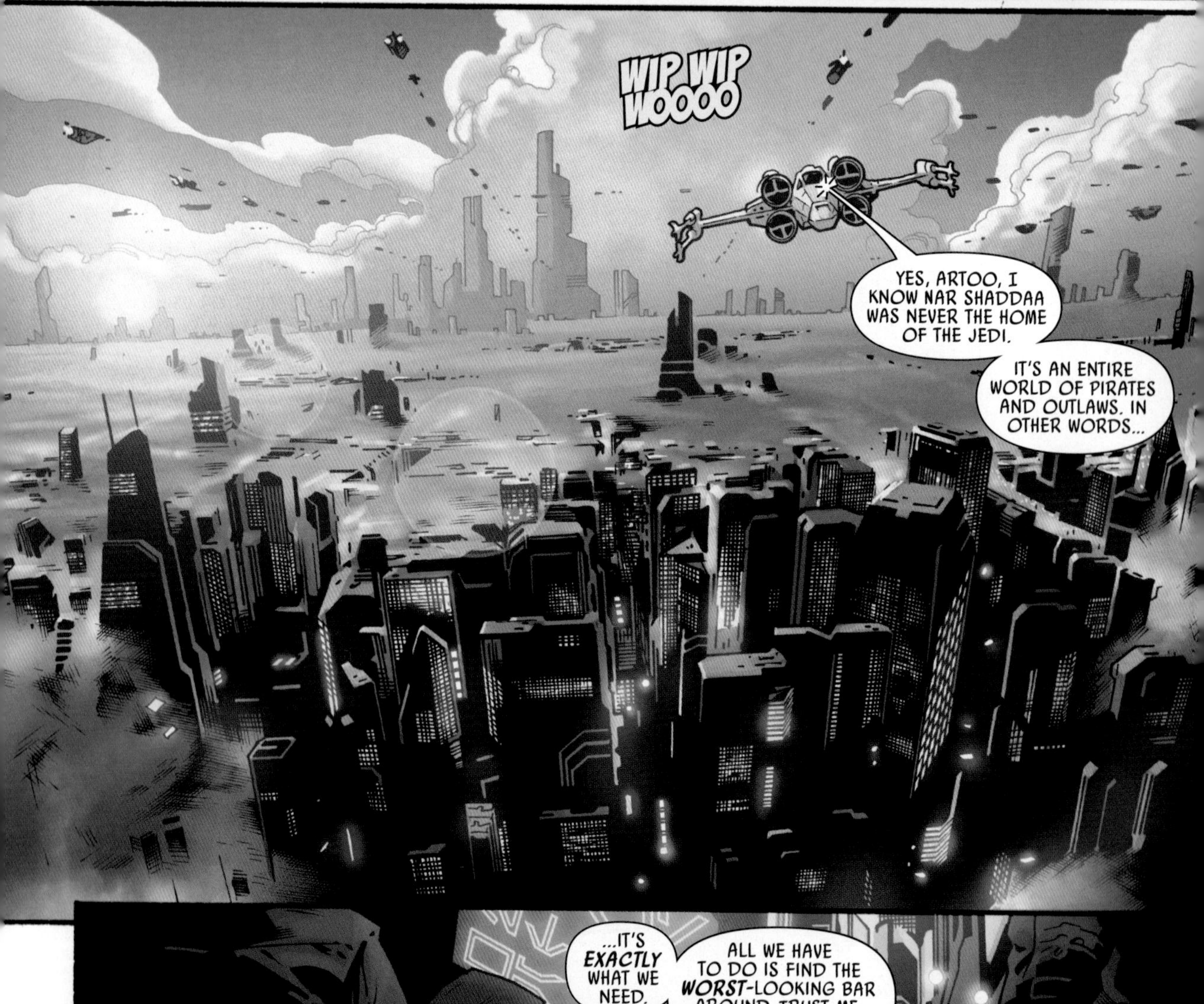
WIP WIP WOOOO
YES, ARTOO, I KNOW NAR SHADDAA WAS NEVER THE HOME OF THE JEDI.
IT'S AN ENTIRE WORLD OF PIRATES AND OUTLAWS. IN OTHER WORDS...

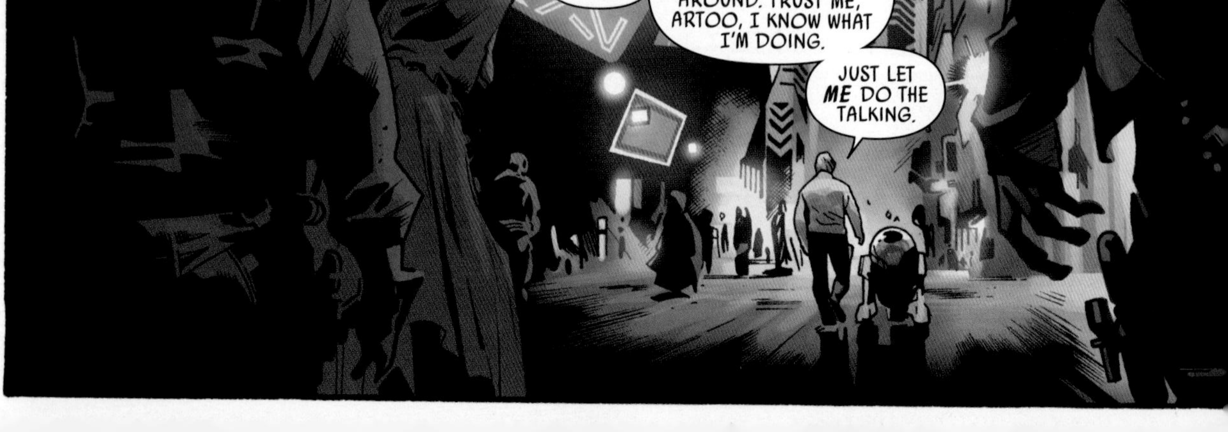
...IT'S EXACTLY WHAT WE NEED.
ALL WE HAVE TO DO IS FIND THE WORST-LOOKING BAR AROUND. TRUST ME, ARTOO, I KNOW WHAT I'M DOING.
JUST LET ME DO THE TALKING.

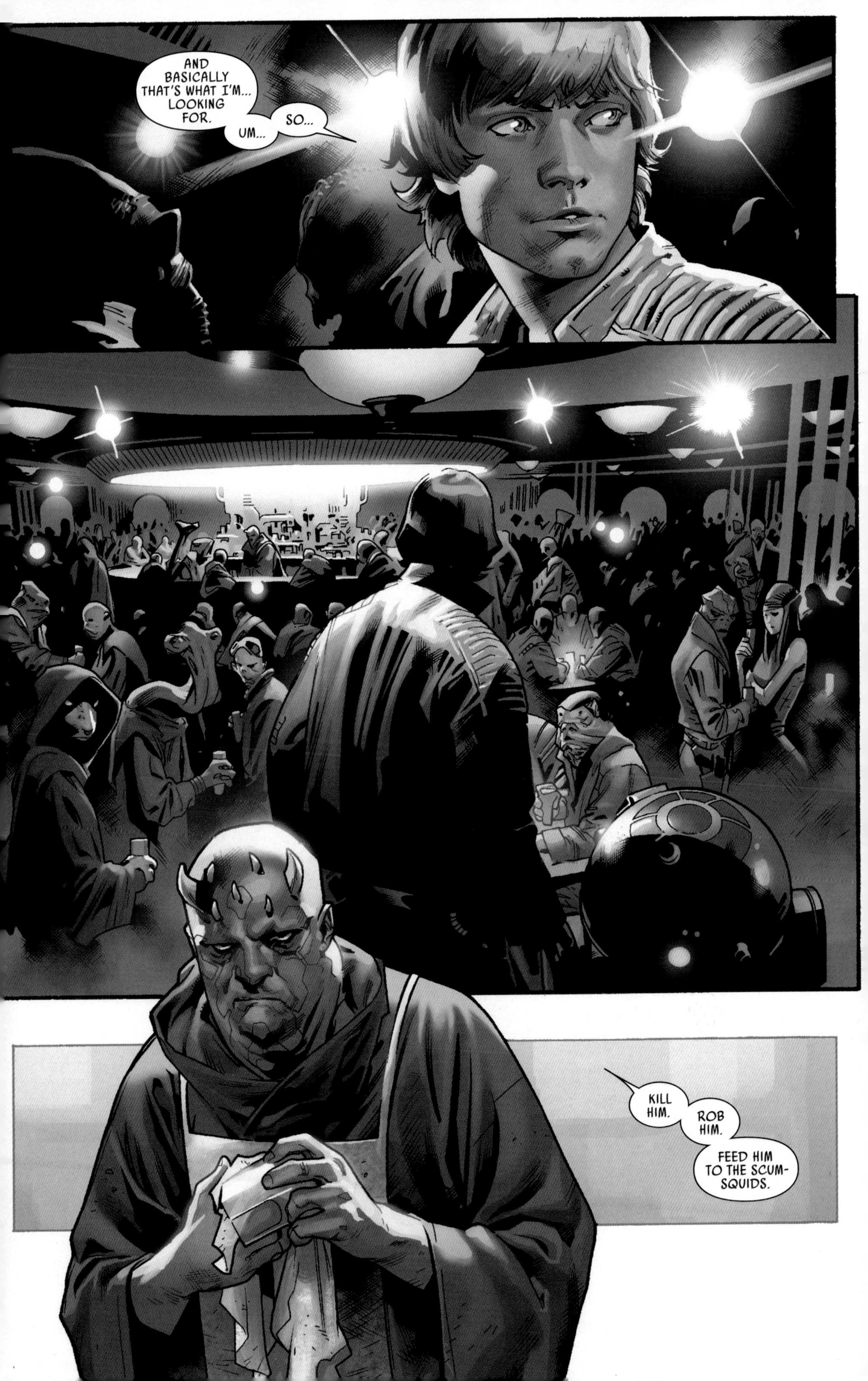
AND BASICALLY THAT'S WHAT I'M... LOOKING FOR.
UM...
SO...
KILL HIM.
ROB HIM.
FEED HIM TO THE SCUM-SQUIDS.

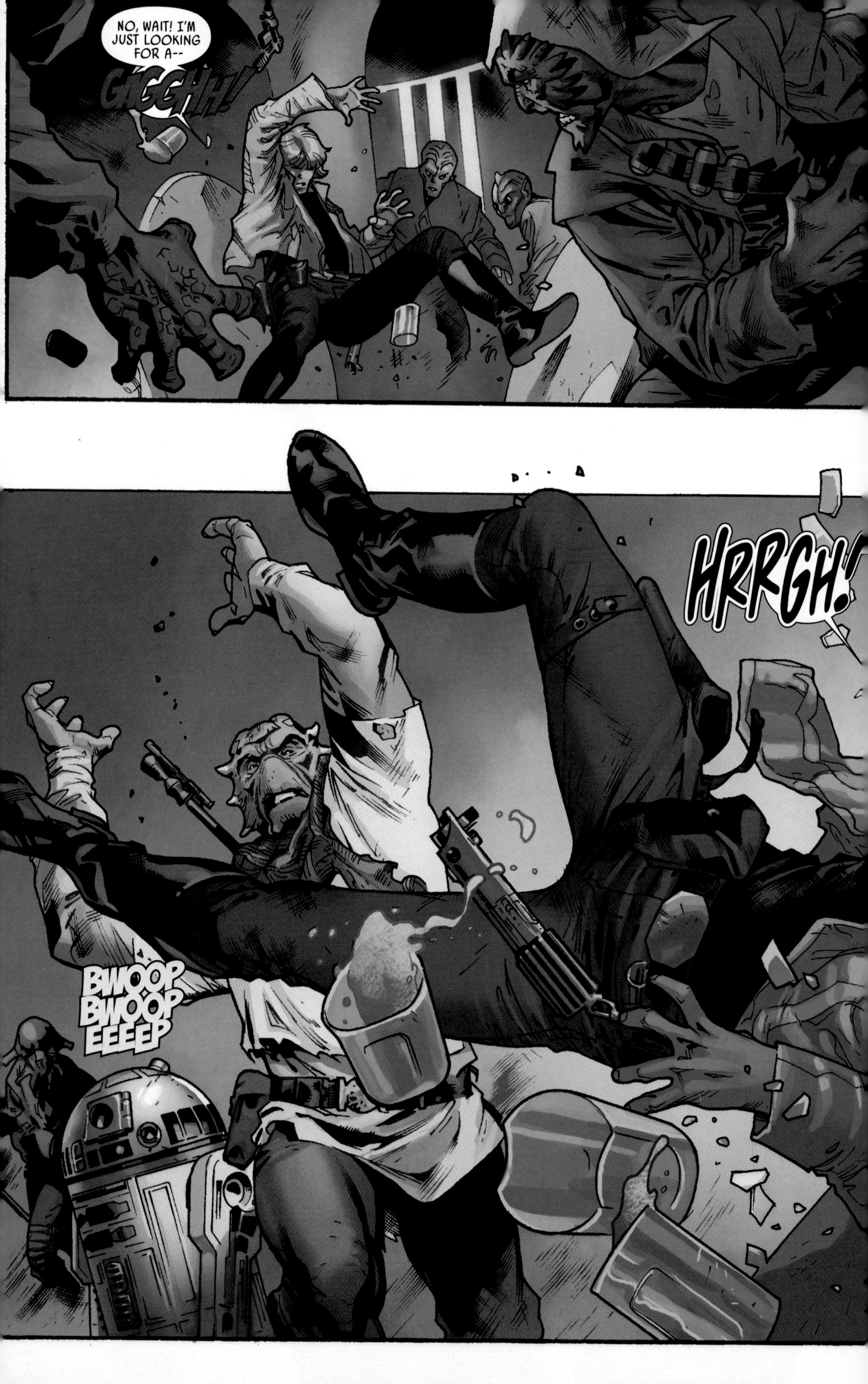
NO, WAIT! I'M JUST LOOKING FOR A--
GAGGHH!
HRRGH!
BWOOP BWOOP EEEEP

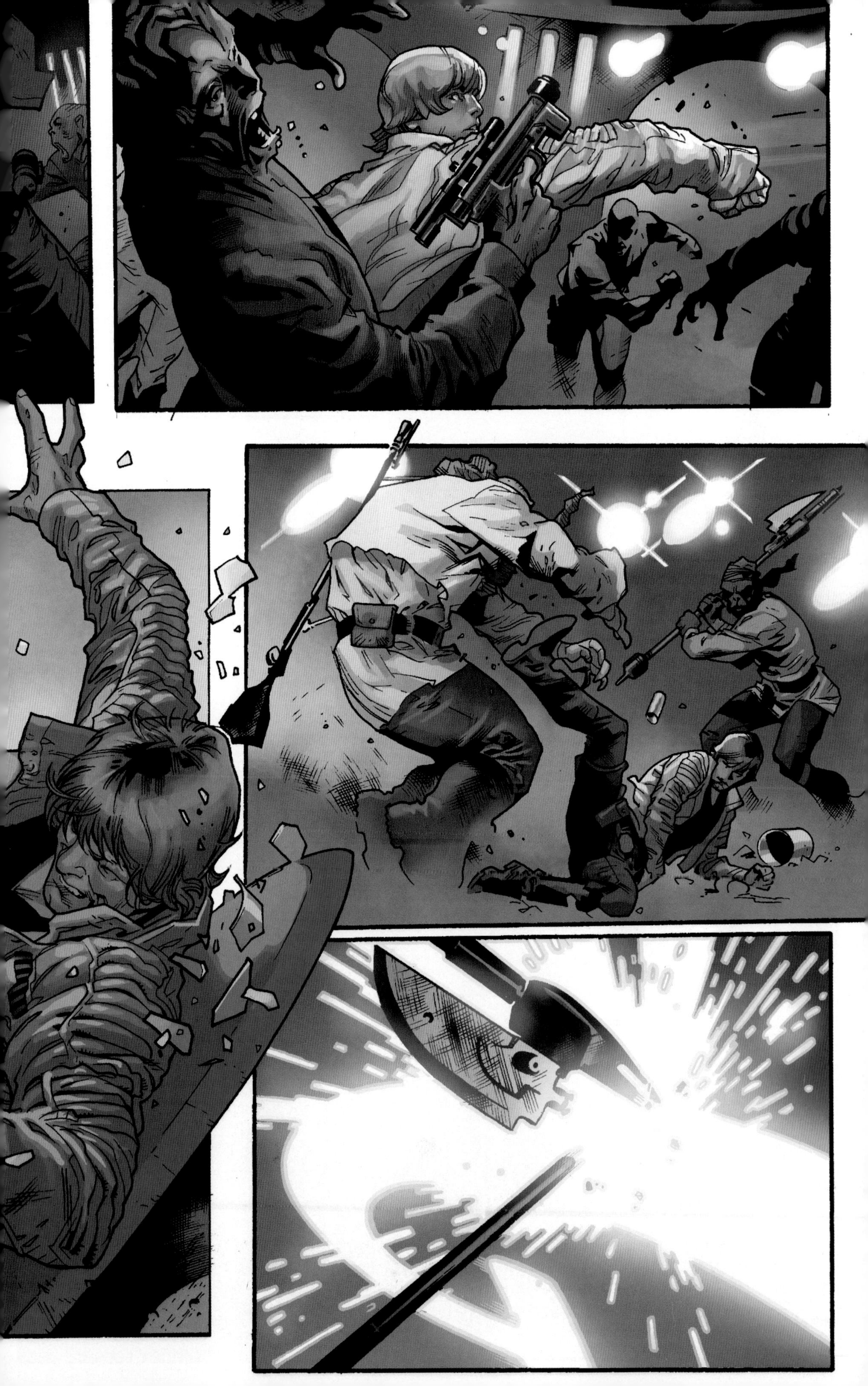

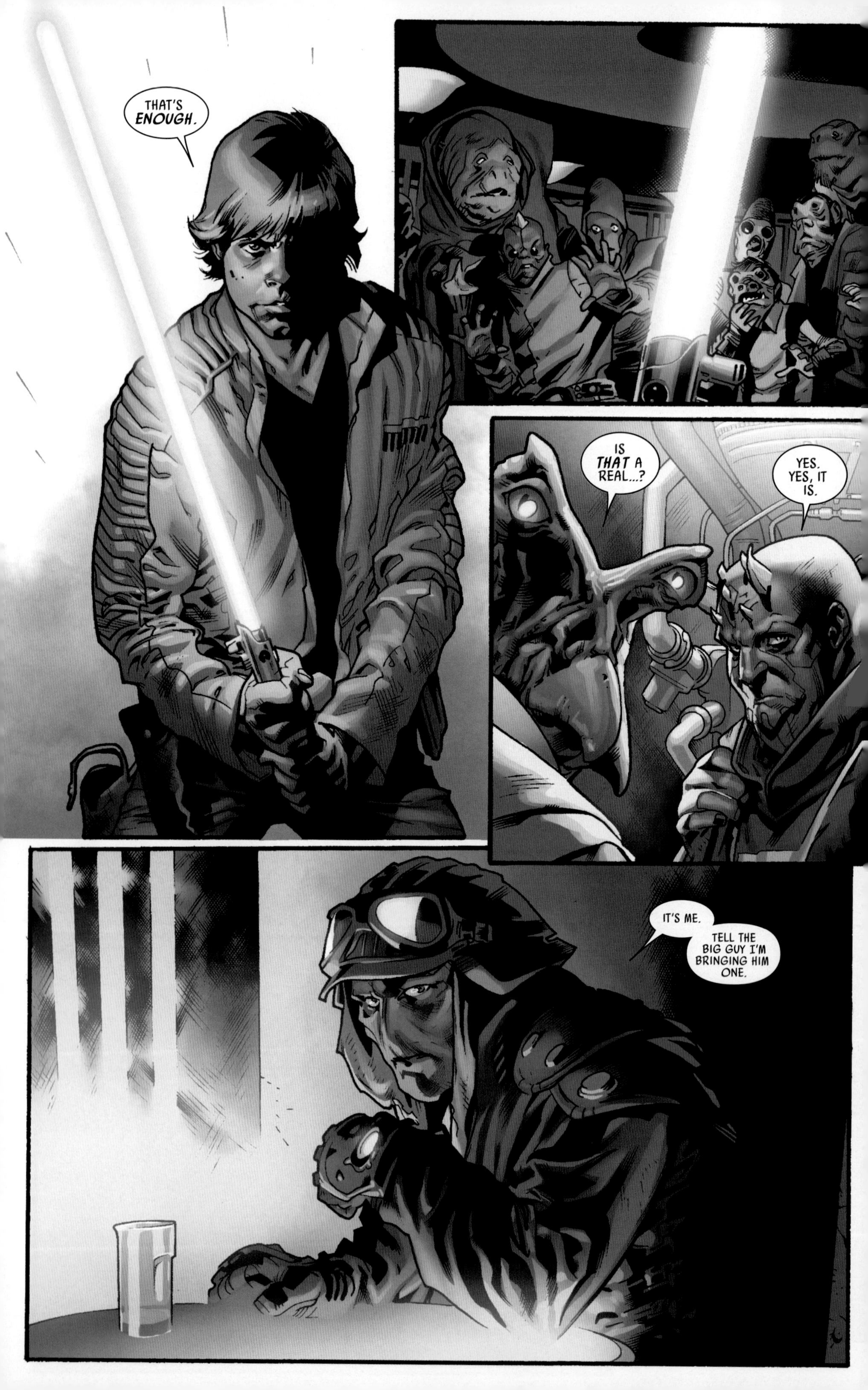
THAT'S ENOUGH.
IS THAT A REAL...?
YES. YES, IT IS.
IT'S ME.
TELL THE BIG GUY I'M BRINGING HIM ONE.

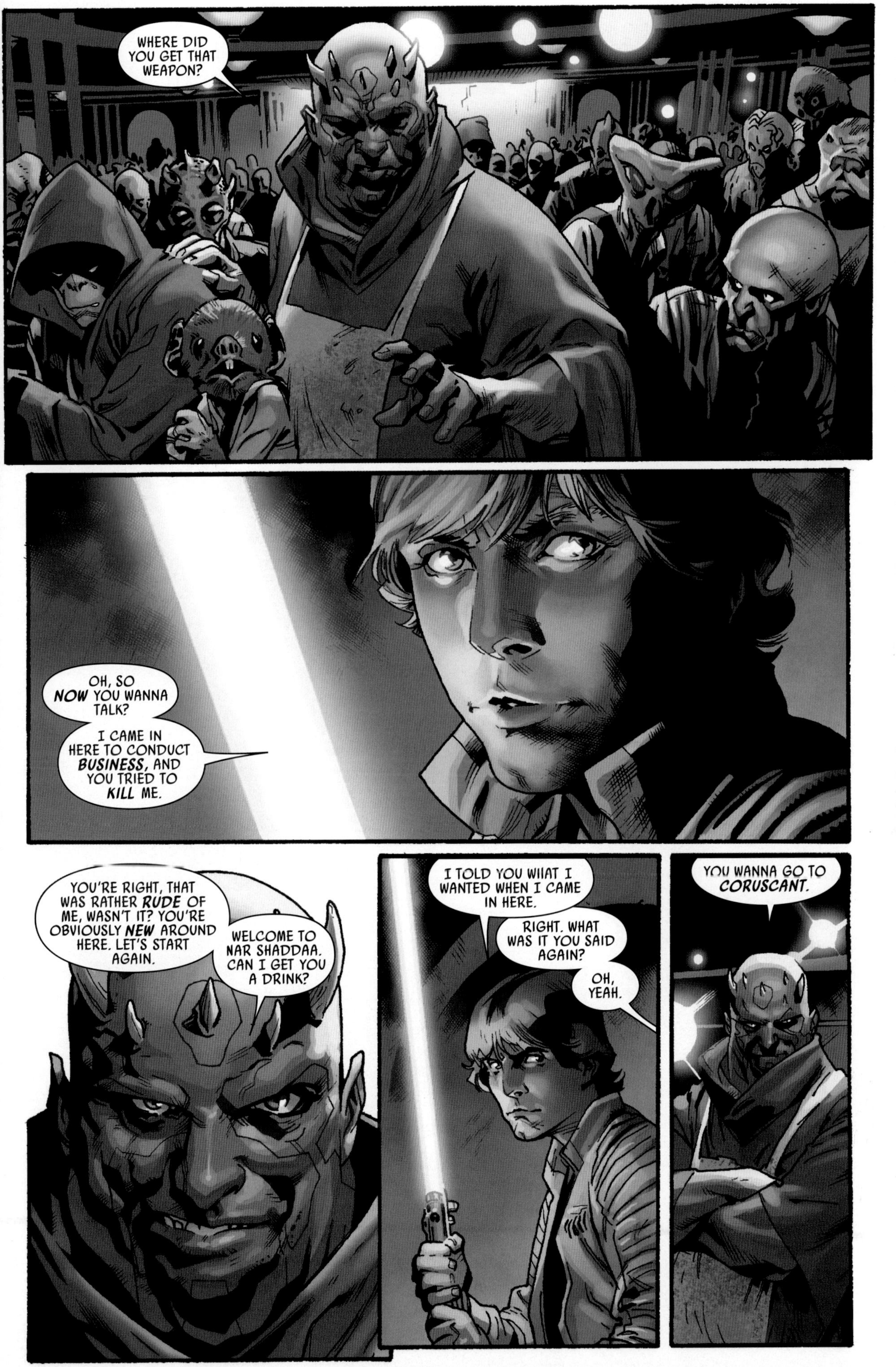
WHERE DID YOU GET THAT WEAPON?
OH, SO NOW YOU WANNA TALK?
I CAME IN HERE TO CONDUCT BUSINESS, AND YOU TRIED TO KILL ME.
YOU'RE RIGHT, THAT WAS RATHER RUDE OF ME, WASN'T IT? YOU'RE OBVIOUSLY NEW AROUND HERE. LET'S START AGAIN.
WELCOME TO NAR SHADDAA. CAN I GET YOU A DRINK?
I TOLD YOU WHAT I WANTED WHEN I CAME IN HERE.
RIGHT. WHAT WAS IT YOU SAID AGAIN?
OH, YEAH.
YOU WANNA GO TO CORUSCANT.

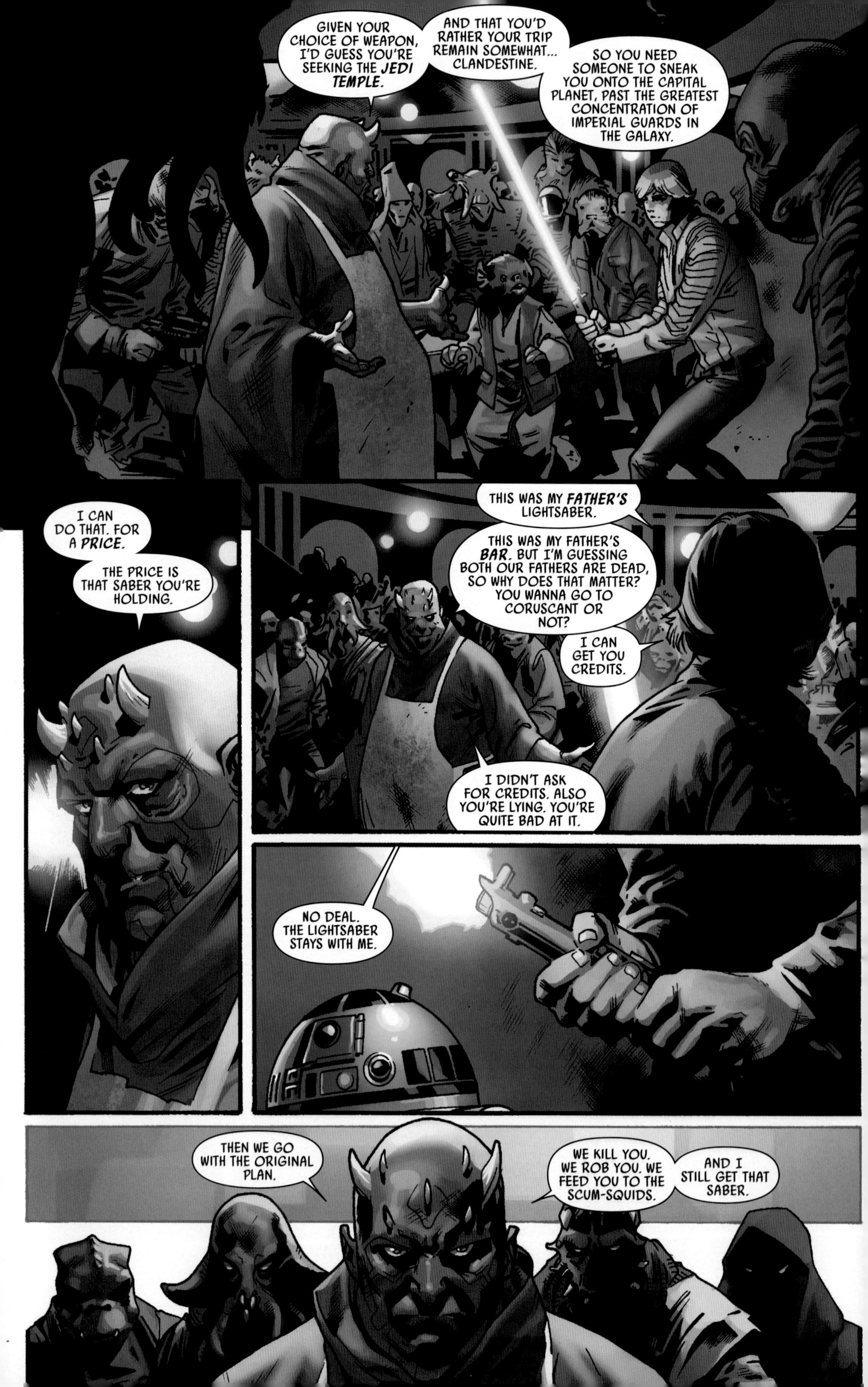
GIVEN YOUR CHOICE OF WEAPON, I'D GUESS YOU'RE SEEKING THE JEDI TEMPLE.
AND THAT YOU'D RATHER YOUR TRIP REMAIN SOMEWHAT... CLANDESTINE.
SO YOU NEED SOMEONE TO SNEAK YOU ONTO THE CAPITAL PLANET, PAST THE GREATEST CONCENTRATION OF IMPERIAL GUARDS IN THE GALAXY.
I CAN DO THAT. FOR A PRICE.
THE PRICE IS THAT SABER YOU'RE HOLDING.
THIS WAS MY FATHER'S LIGHTSABER.
THIS WAS MY FATHER'S BAR. BUT I'M GUESSING BOTH OUR FATHERS ARE DEAD, SO WHY DOES THAT MATTER? YOU WANNA GO TO CORUSCANT OR NOT?
I CAN GET YOU CREDITS.
I DIDN'T ASK FOR CREDITS. ALSO YOU'RE LYING. YOU'RE QUITE BAD AT IT.
NO DEAL. THE LIGHTSABER STAYS WITH ME.
THEN WE GO WITH THE ORIGINAL PLAN.
WE KILL YOU. WE ROB YOU. WE FEED YOU TO THE SCUM-SQUIDS.
AND I STILL GET THAT SABER.

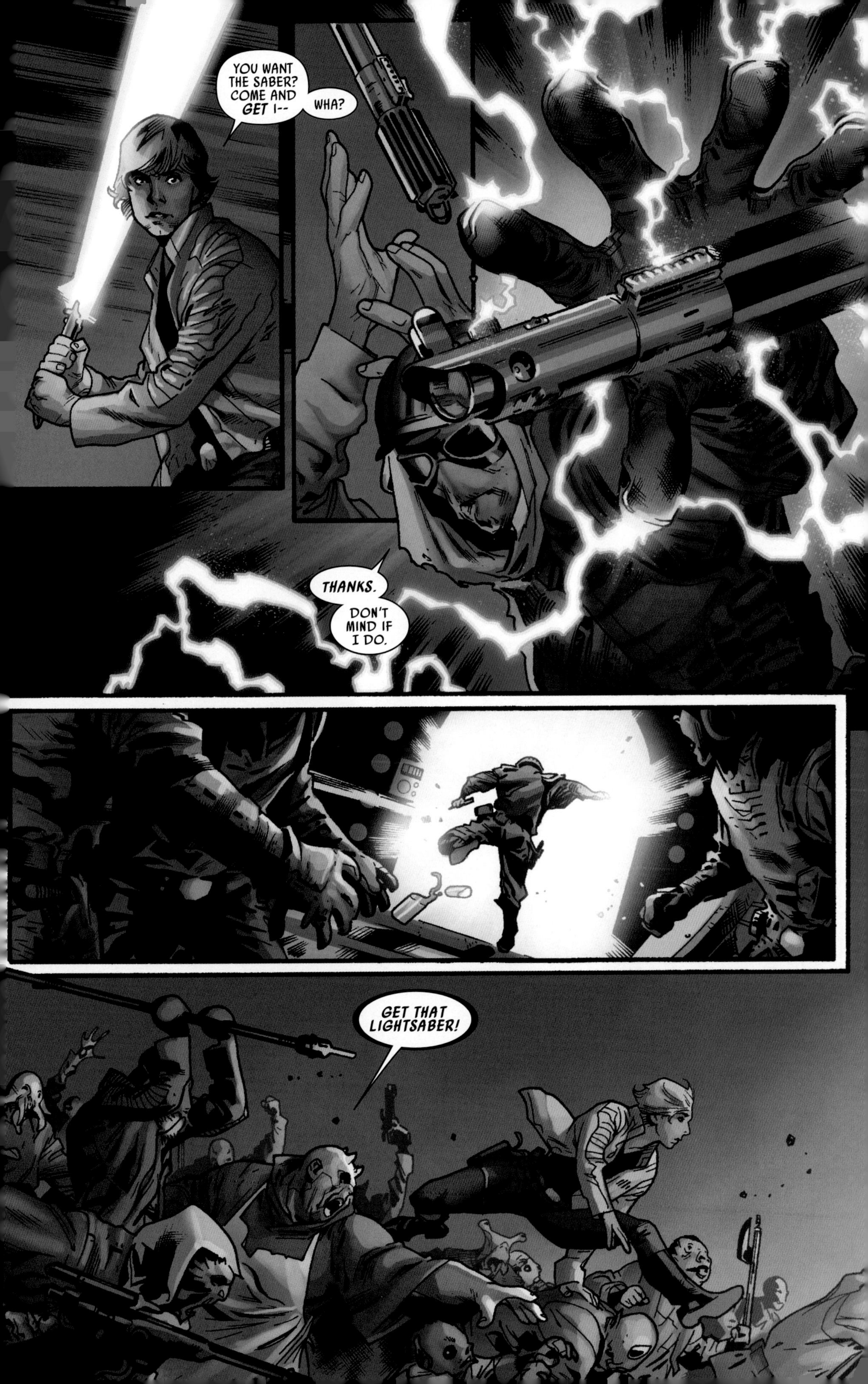
YOU WANT THE SABER? COME AND GET I--
WHA?
THANKS.
DON'T MIND IF I DO.
GET THAT LIGHTSABER!

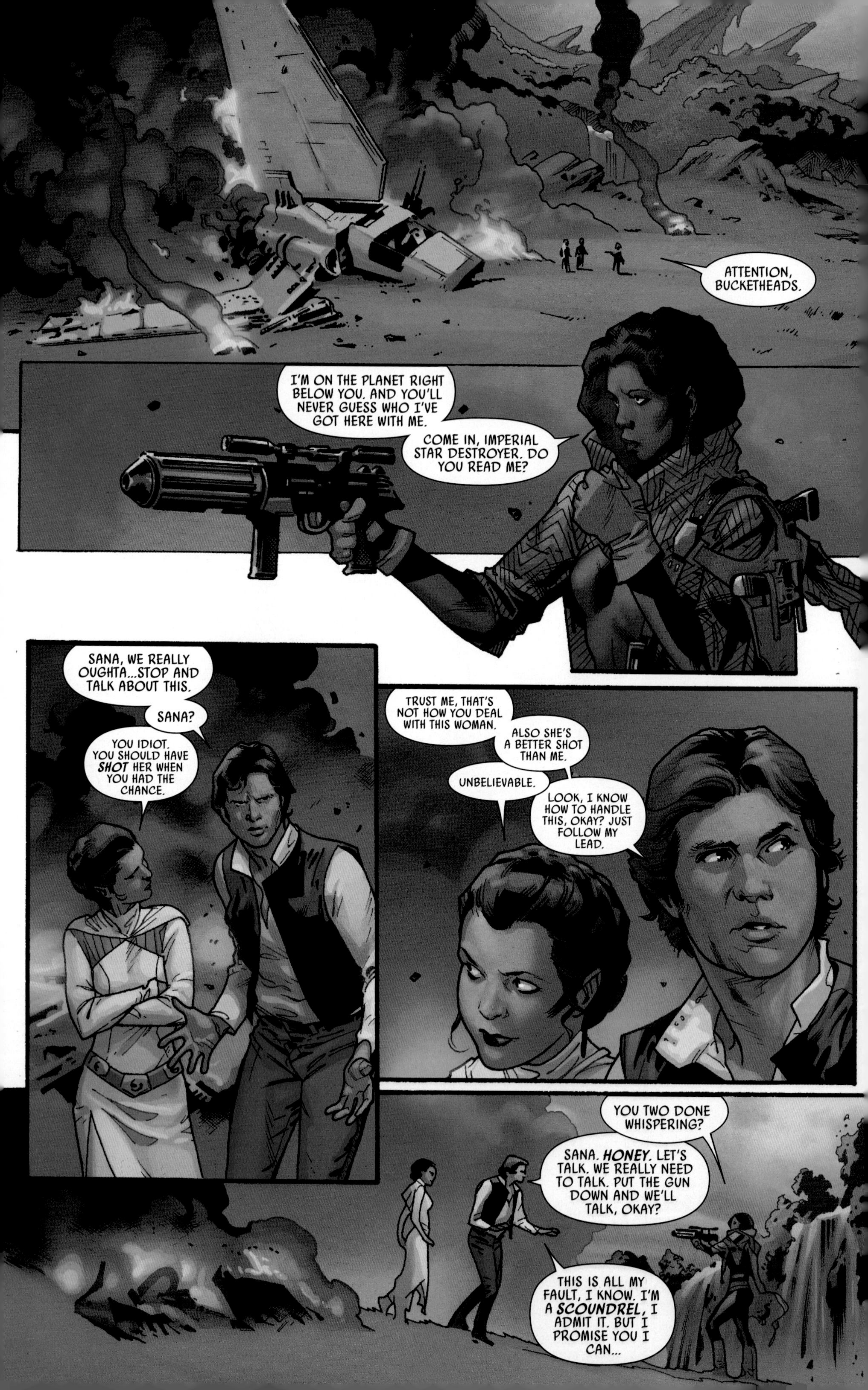
ATTENTION, BUCKETHEADS.
I'M ON THE PLANET RIGHT BELOW YOU. AND YOU'LL NEVER GUESS WHO I'VE GOT HERE WITH ME.
COME IN, IMPERIAL STAR DESTROYER. DO YOU READ ME?
SANA, WE REALLY OUGHTA...STOP AND TALK ABOUT THIS.
SANA?
YOU IDIOT. YOU SHOULD HAVE SHOT HER WHEN YOU HAD THE CHANCE.
TRUST ME, THAT'S NOT HOW YOU DEAL WITH THIS WOMAN.
ALSO SHE'S A BETTER SHOT THAN ME.
UNBELIEVABLE.
LOOK, I KNOW HOW TO HANDLE THIS, OKAY? JUST FOLLOW MY LEAD.
YOU TWO DONE WHISPERING?
SANA. HONEY. LET'S TALK. WE REALLY NEED TO TALK. PUT THE GUN DOWN AND WE'LL TALK, OKAY?
THIS IS ALL MY FAULT, I KNOW. I'M A SCOUNDREL, I ADMIT IT. BUT I PROMISE YOU I CAN...

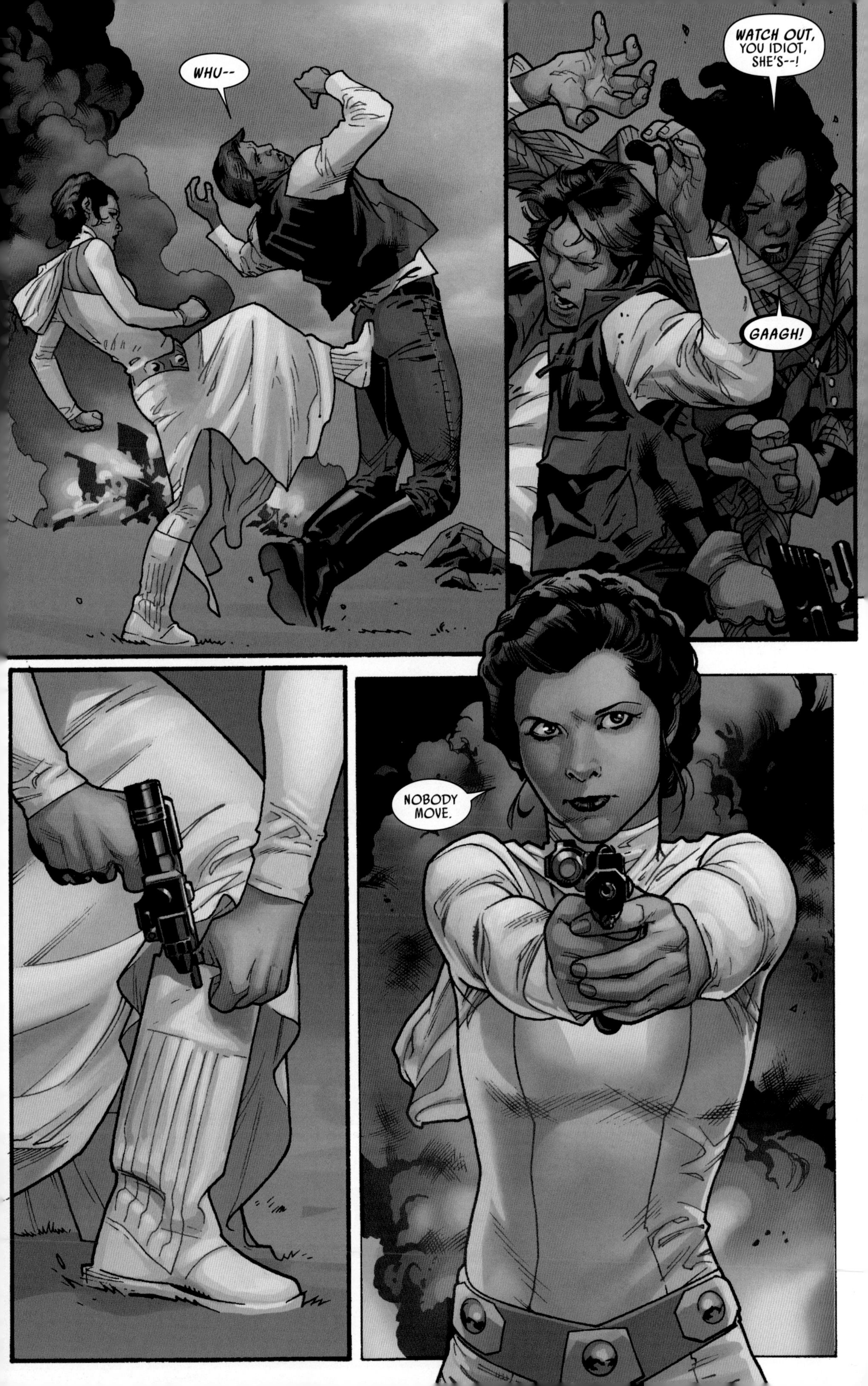
WHU--
WATCH OUT, YOU IDIOT, SHE'S--!
GAAGH!
NOBODY MOVE.

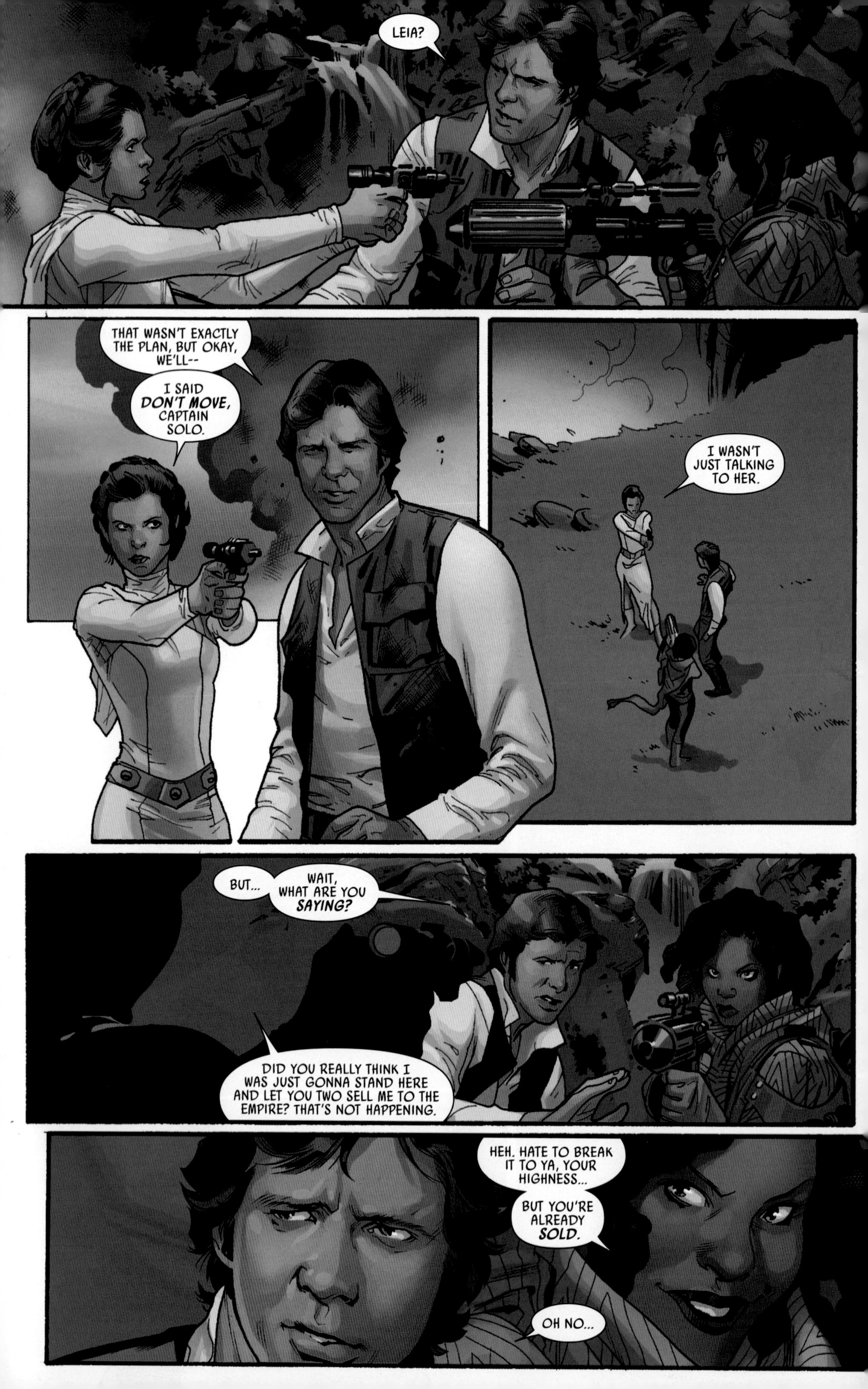
LEIA?
THAT WASN'T EXACTLY THE PLAN, BUT OKAY, WE'LL--
I SAID DON'T MOVE, CAPTAIN SOLO.
I WASN'T JUST TALKING TO HER.
BUT...
WAIT, WHAT ARE YOU SAYING?
DID YOU REALLY THINK I WAS JUST GONNA STAND HERE AND LET YOU TWO SELL ME TO THE EMPIRE? THAT'S NOT HAPPENING.
HEH. HATE TO BREAK IT TO YA, YOUR HIGHNESS...
BUT YOU'RE ALREADY SOLD.
OH NO...

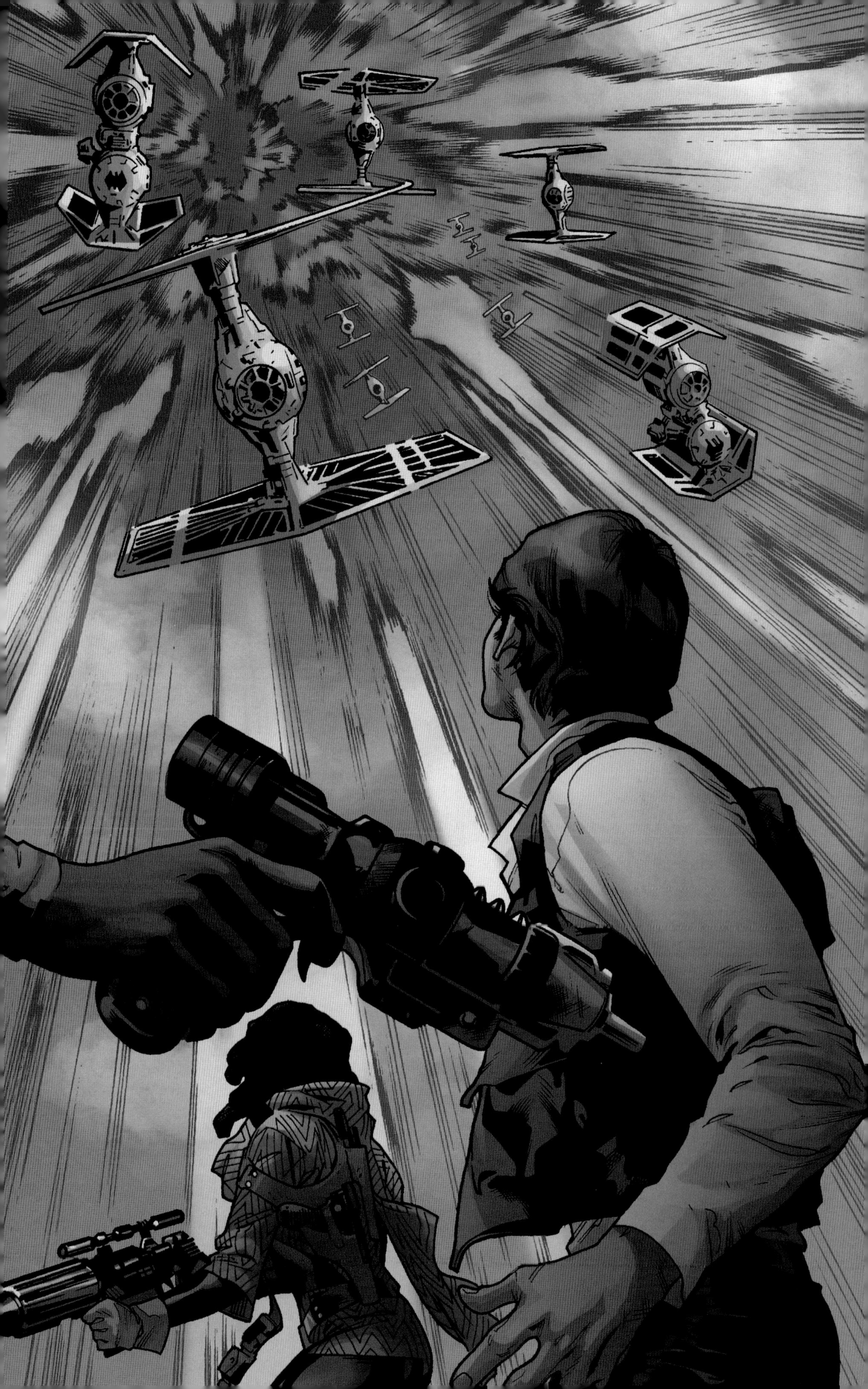

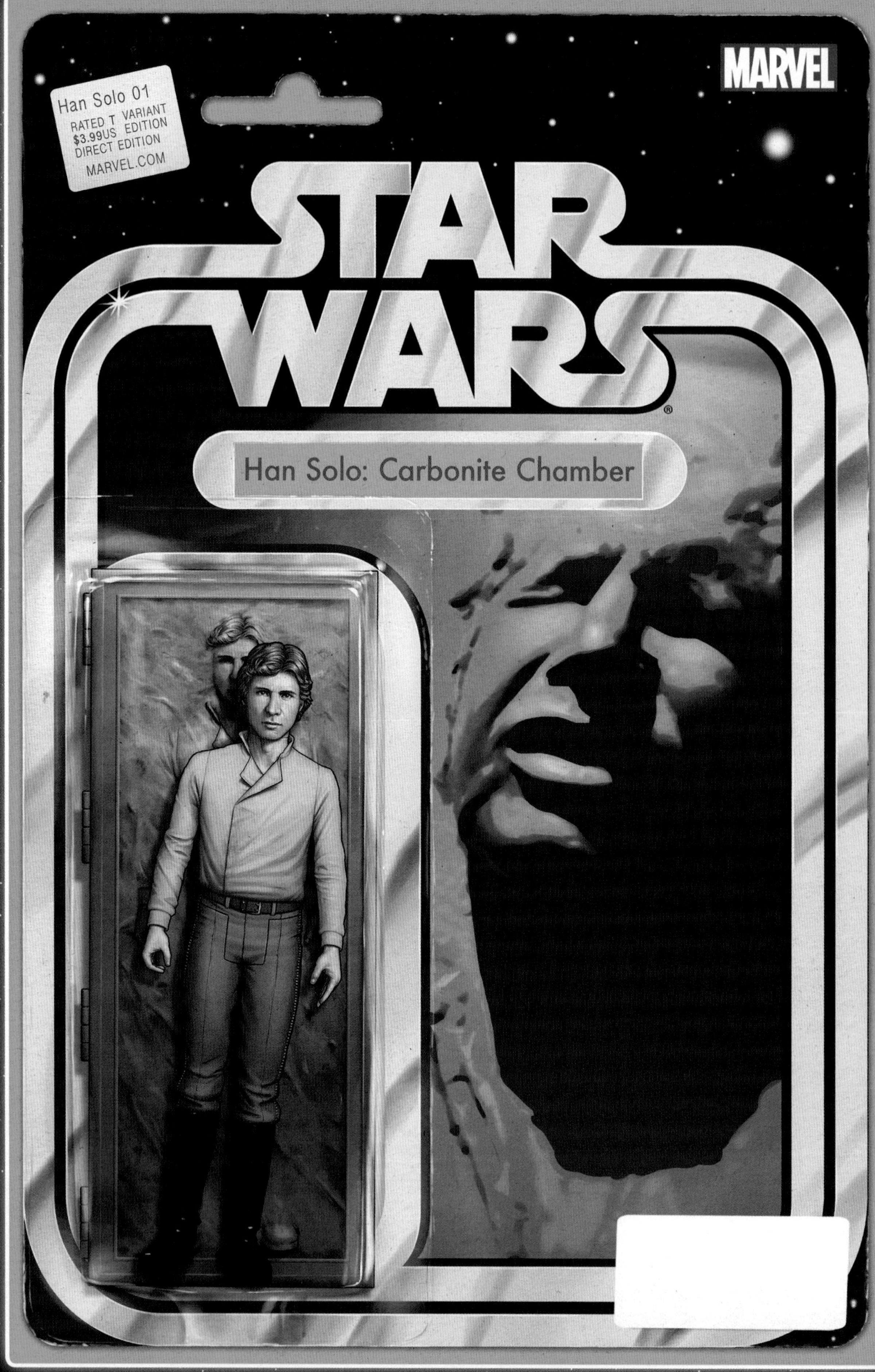
MARVEL
Han Solo 01
RATED T VARIANT
$3.99US EDITION
DIRECT EDITION
MARVEL.COM
STAR WARS
Han Solo: Carbonite Chamber

HAN SOLO 1 **Action Figure Variant**
by JOHN TYLER CHRISTOPHER

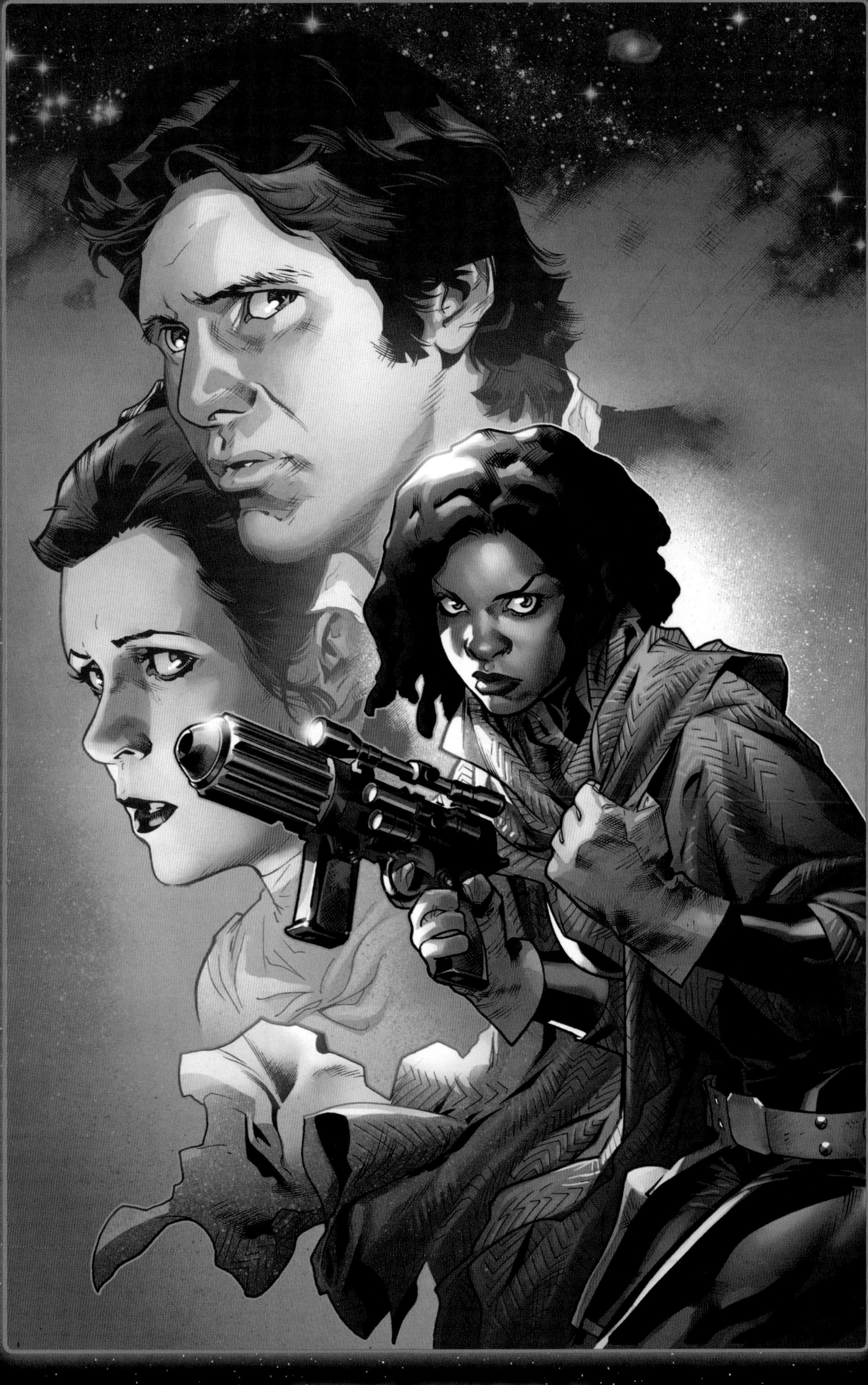

STAR WARS 9

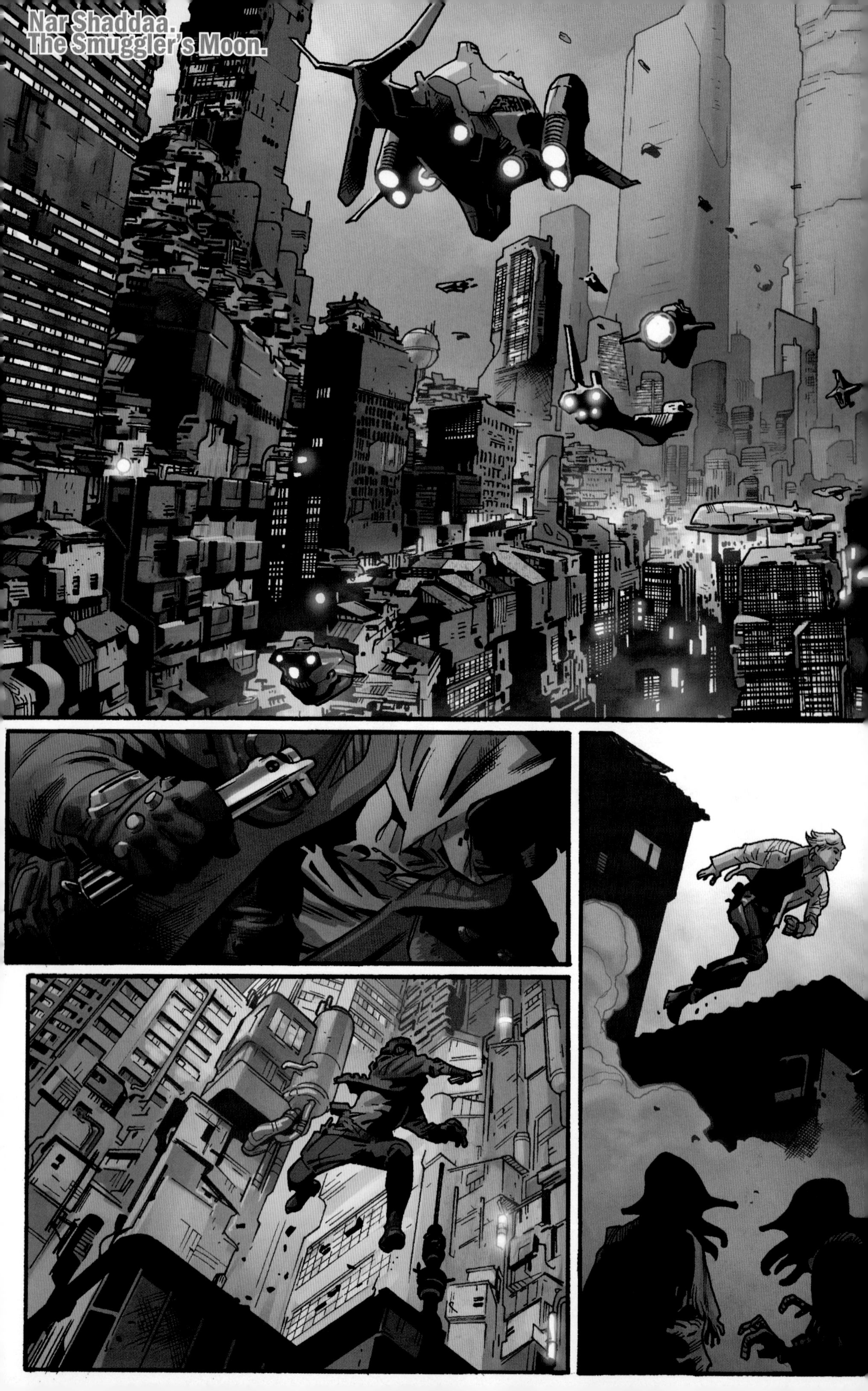
Nar Shaddaa.
The Smuggler's Moon.

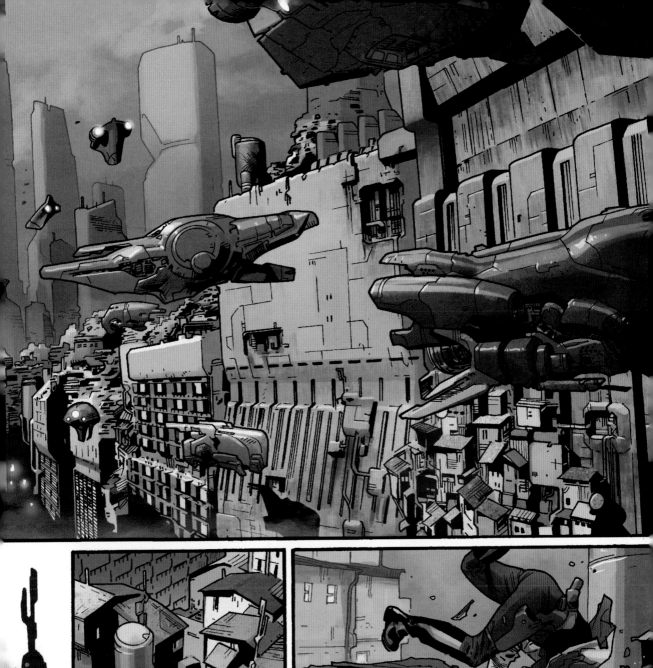

ARTOO! WHERE ARE YOU?!

WE CAN'T LET HIM GET AWAY! THAT *LIGHTSABER* IS ALL I HAVE!

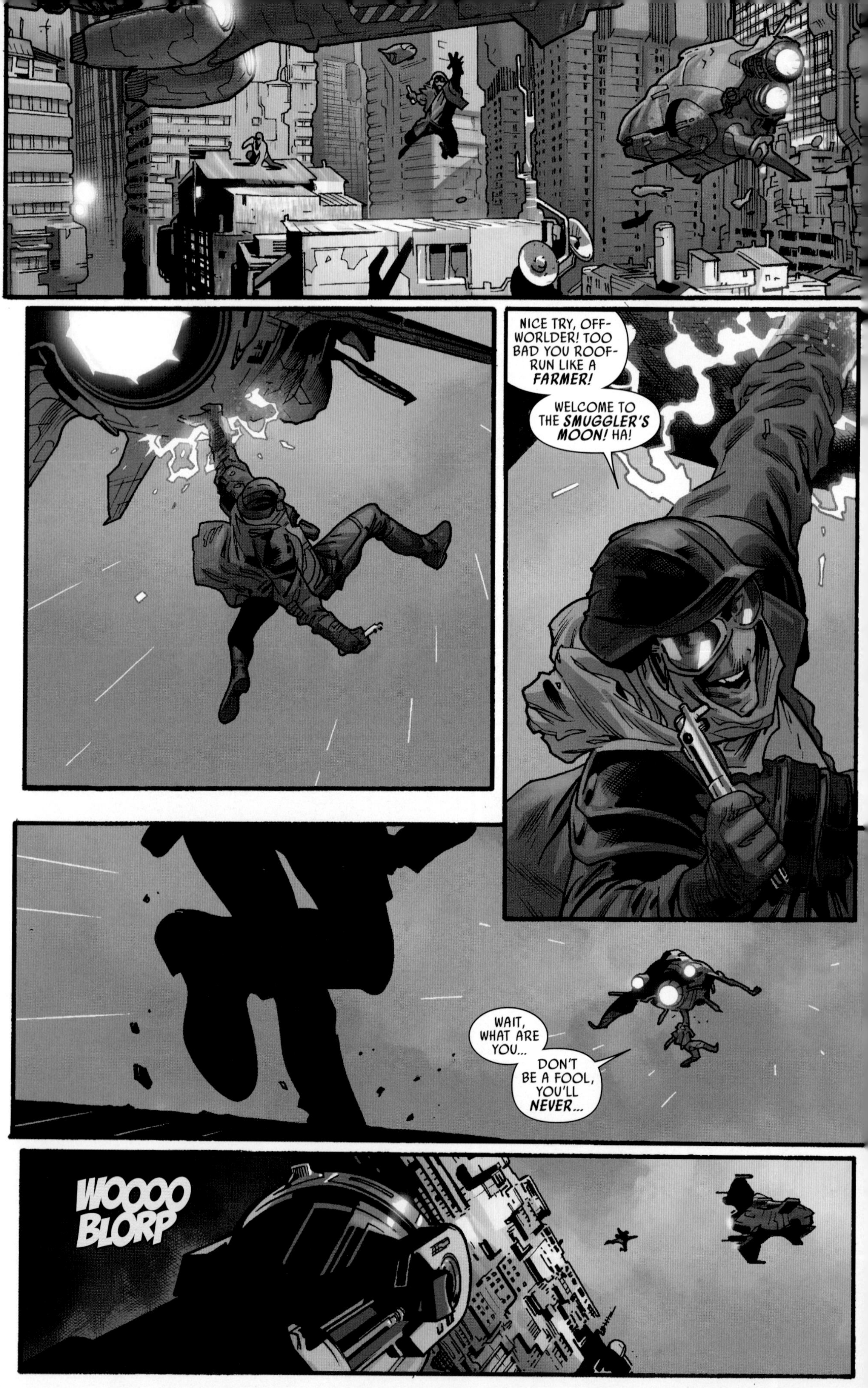
NICE TRY, OFF-WORLDER! TOO BAD YOU ROOF-RUN LIKE A FARMER!
WELCOME TO THE SMUGGLER'S MOON! HA!
WAIT, WHAT ARE YOU...
DON'T BE A FOOL, YOU'LL NEVER...
WOOOO BLORP

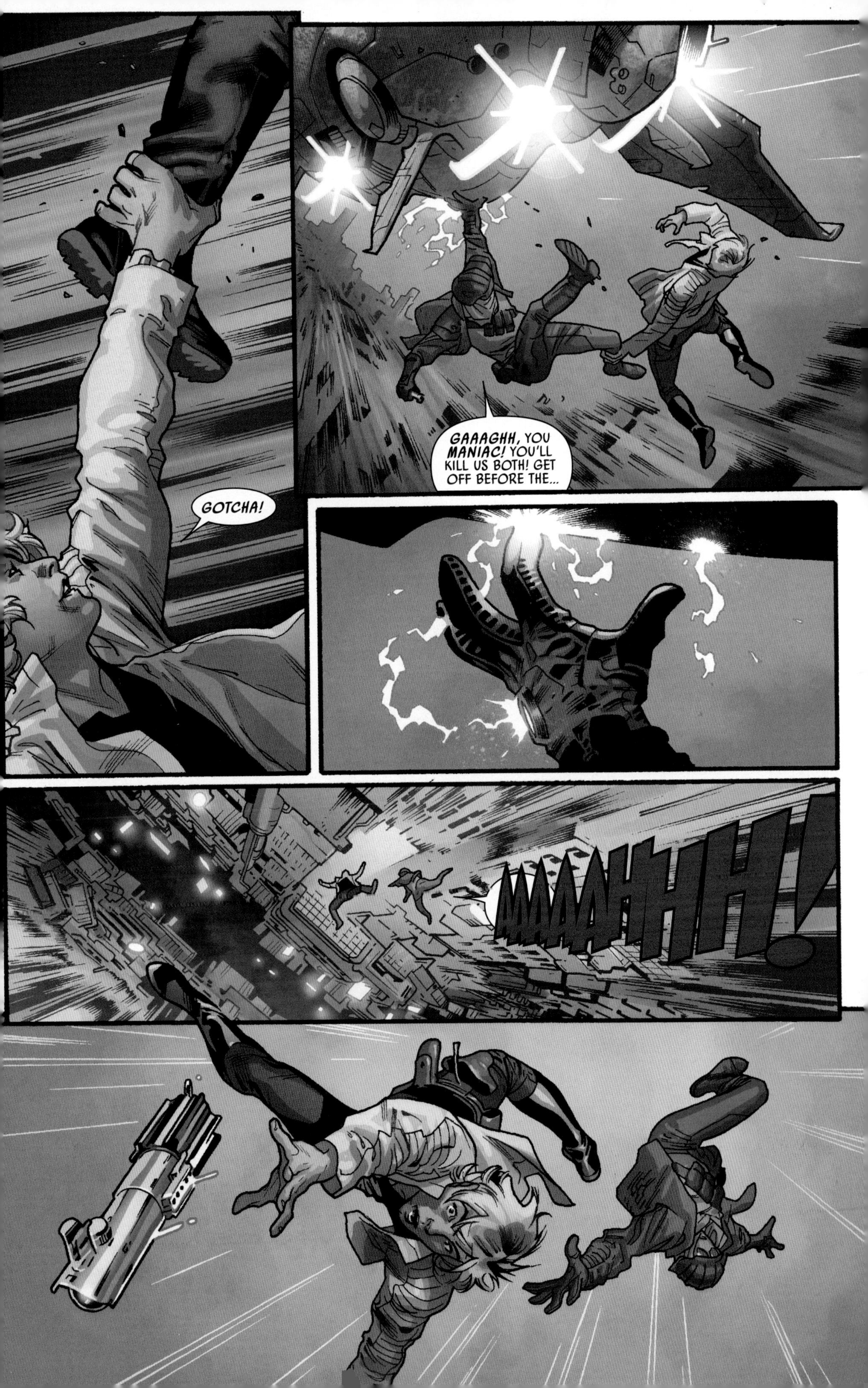
GAAAGHH, YOU MANIAC! YOU'LL KILL US BOTH! GET OFF BEFORE THE...
GOTCHA!
AAAAAHHHH!

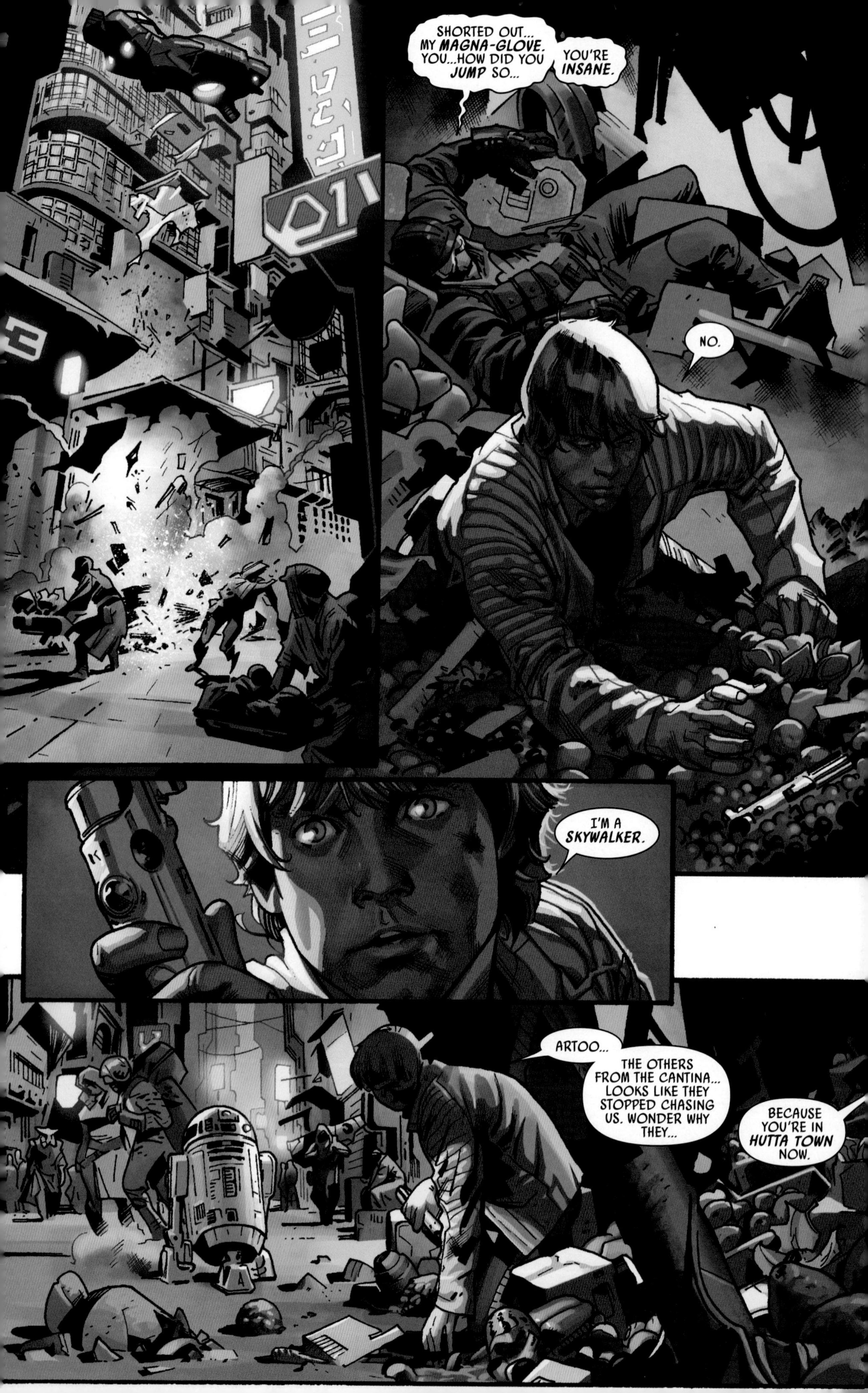
SHORTED OUT... MY MAGNA-GLOVE. YOU...HOW DID YOU JUMP SO...
YOU'RE INSANE.
NO.
I'M A SKYWALKER.
ARTOO...
THE OTHERS FROM THE CANTINA... LOOKS LIKE THEY STOPPED CHASING US. WONDER WHY THEY...
BECAUSE YOU'RE IN HUTTA TOWN NOW.

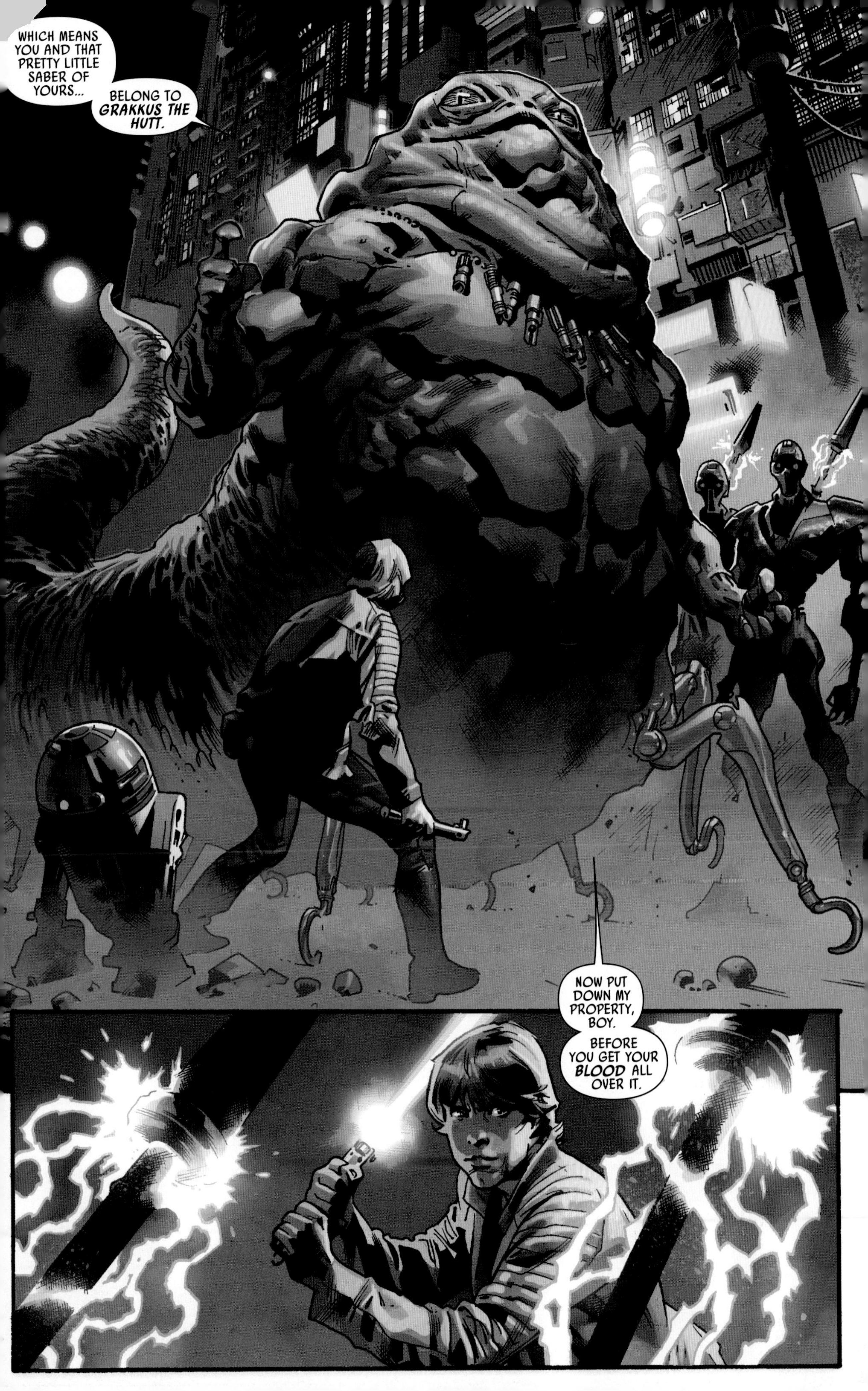

WHICH MEANS YOU AND THAT PRETTY LITTLE SABER OF YOURS...
BELONG TO GRAKKUS THE HUTT.
NOW PUT DOWN MY PROPERTY, BOY.
BEFORE YOU GET YOUR BLOOD ALL OVER IT.

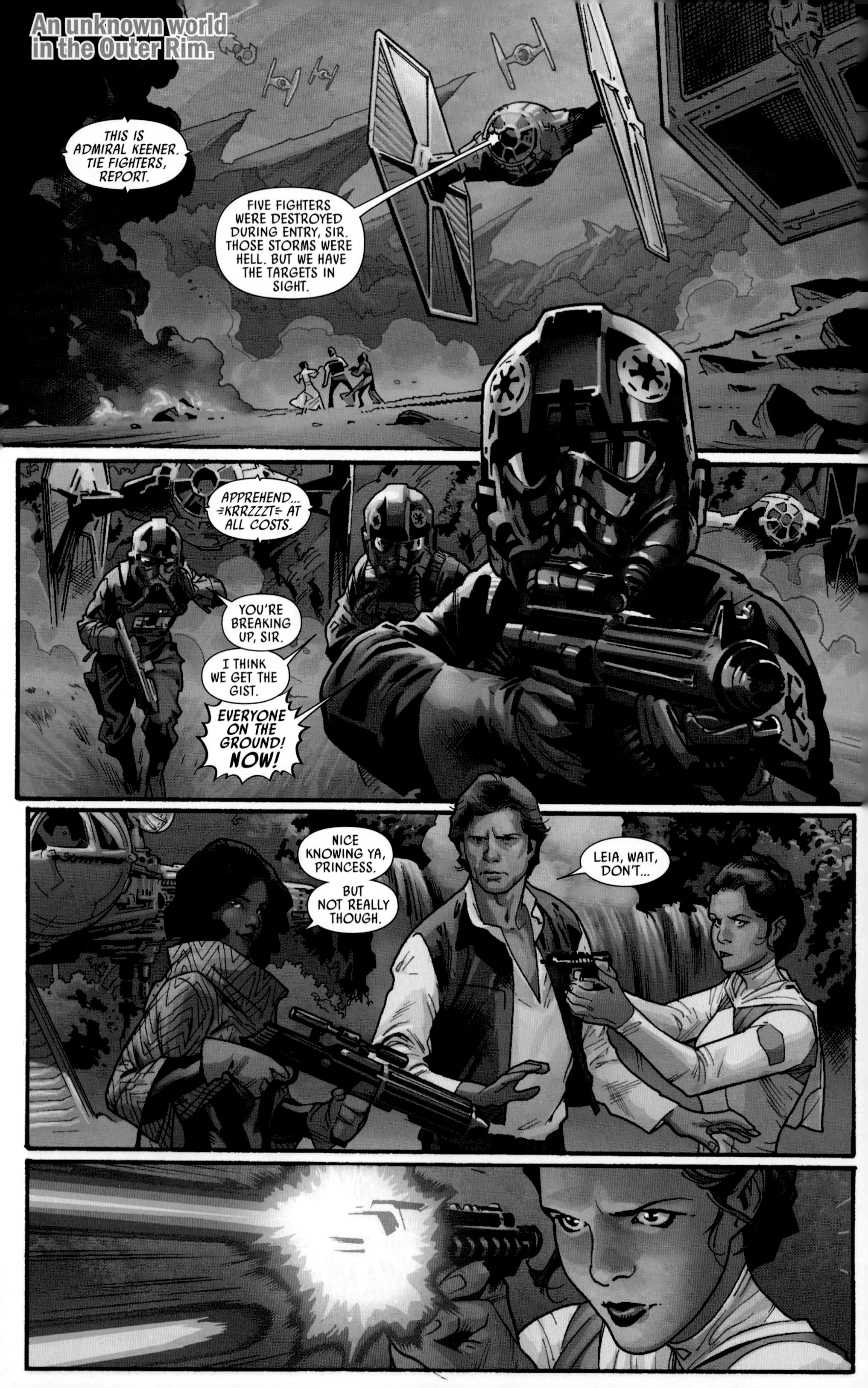
An unknown world in the Outer Rim.
THIS IS ADMIRAL KEENER. TIE FIGHTERS, REPORT.
FIVE FIGHTERS WERE DESTROYED DURING ENTRY, SIR. THOSE STORMS WERE HELL. BUT WE HAVE THE TARGETS IN SIGHT.
APPREHEND... =KRRZZZT= AT ALL COSTS.
YOU'RE BREAKING UP, SIR.
I THINK WE GET THE GIST.
EVERYONE ON THE GROUND! NOW!
NICE KNOWING YA, PRINCESS.
BUT NOT REALLY THOUGH.
LEIA, WAIT, DON'T...

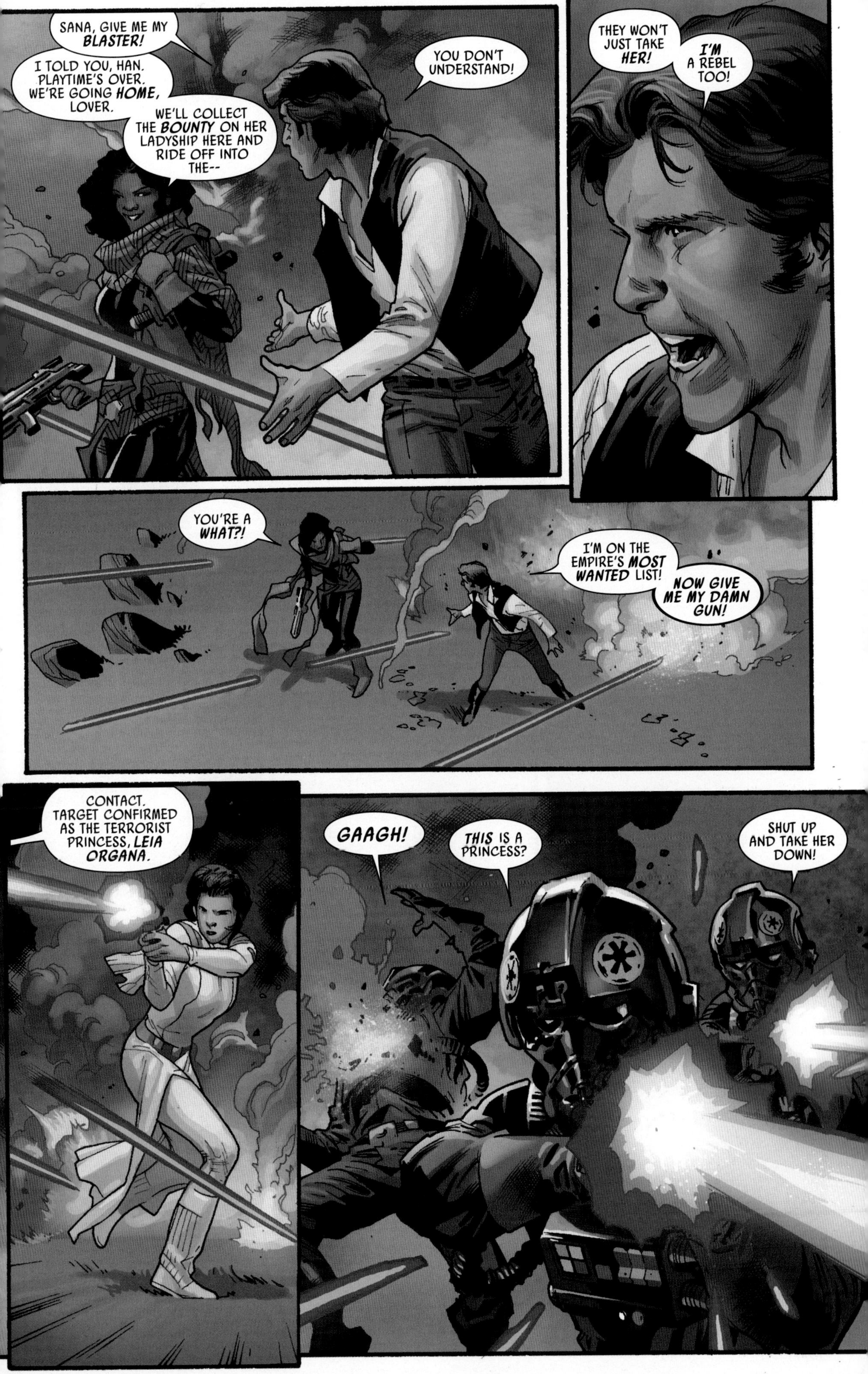
SANA, GIVE ME MY BLASTER!
I TOLD YOU, HAN. PLAYTIME'S OVER. WE'RE GOING HOME, LOVER.
WE'LL COLLECT THE BOUNTY ON HER LADYSHIP HERE AND RIDE OFF INTO THE--
YOU DON'T UNDERSTAND!
THEY WON'T JUST TAKE HER!
I'M A REBEL TOO!
YOU'RE A WHAT?!
I'M ON THE EMPIRE'S MOST WANTED LIST!
NOW GIVE ME MY DAMN GUN!
CONTACT. TARGET CONFIRMED AS THE TERRORIST PRINCESS, LEIA ORGANA.
GAAGH!
THIS IS A PRINCESS?
SHUT UP AND TAKE HER DOWN!

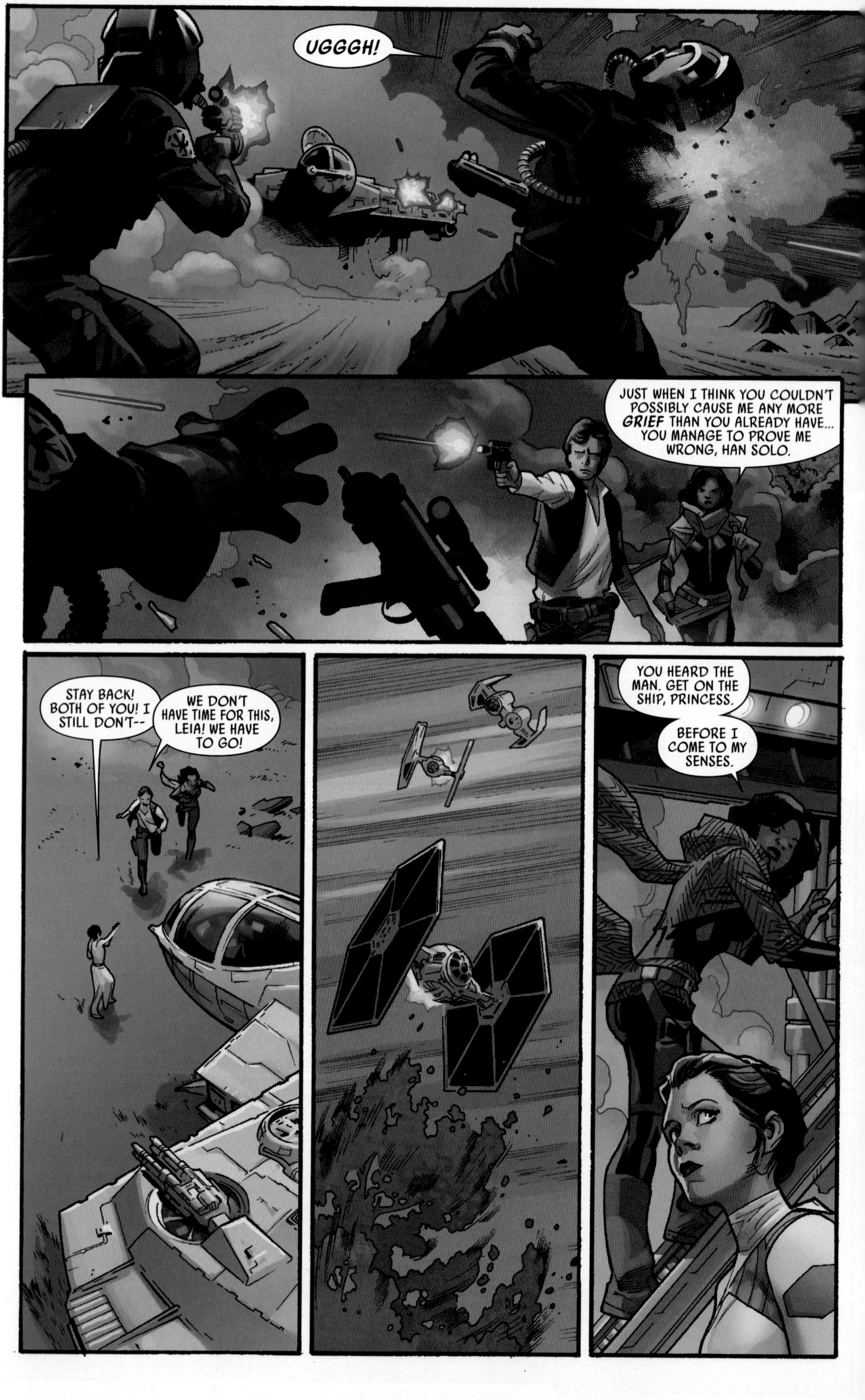
UGGGH!
JUST WHEN I THINK YOU COULDN'T POSSIBLY CAUSE ME ANY MORE GRIEF THAN YOU ALREADY HAVE... YOU MANAGE TO PROVE ME WRONG, HAN SOLO.
STAY BACK! BOTH OF YOU! I STILL DON'T--
WE DON'T HAVE TIME FOR THIS, LEIA! WE HAVE TO GO!
YOU HEARD THE MAN. GET ON THE SHIP, PRINCESS.
BEFORE I COME TO MY SENSES.

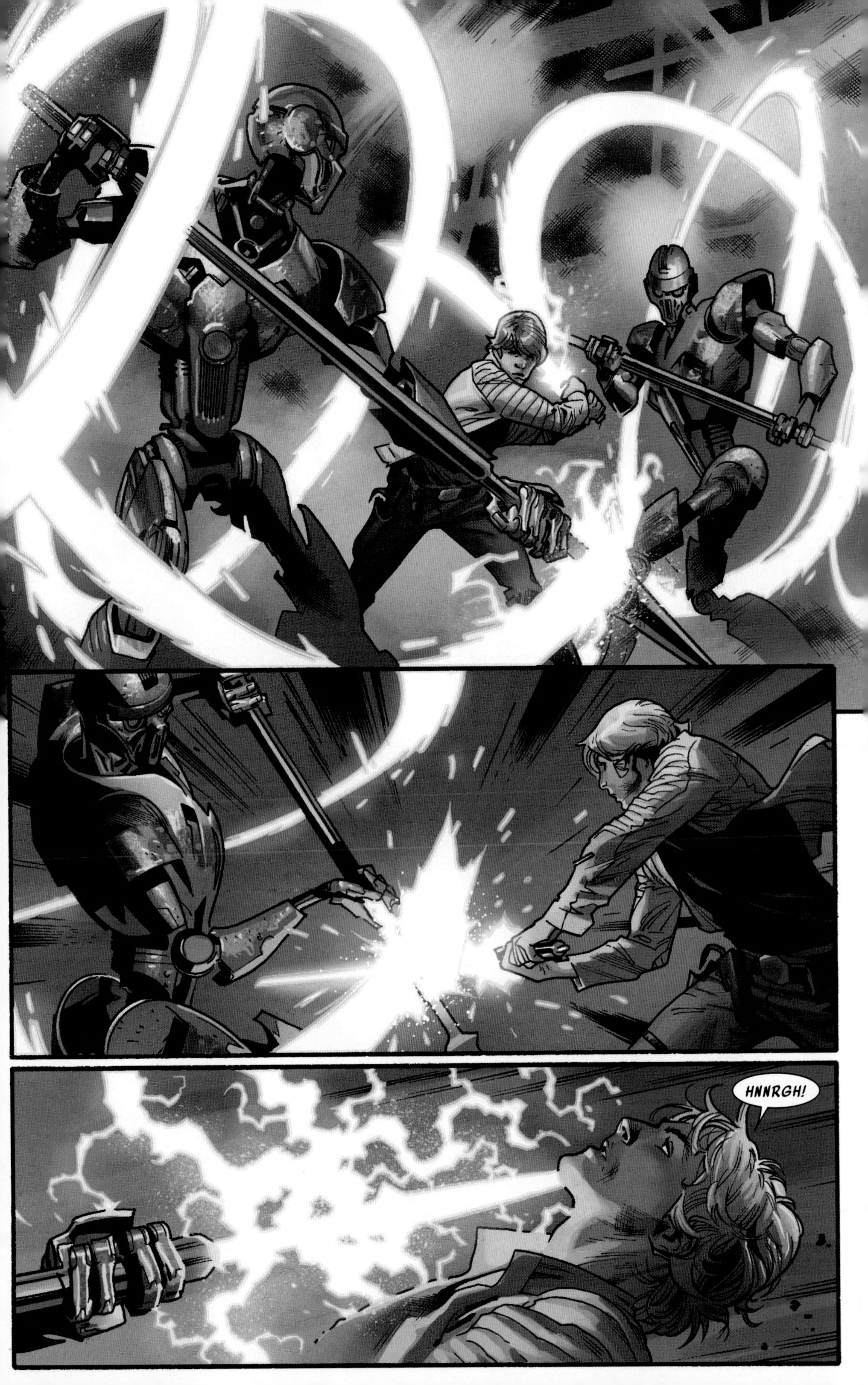
HNNRGH!

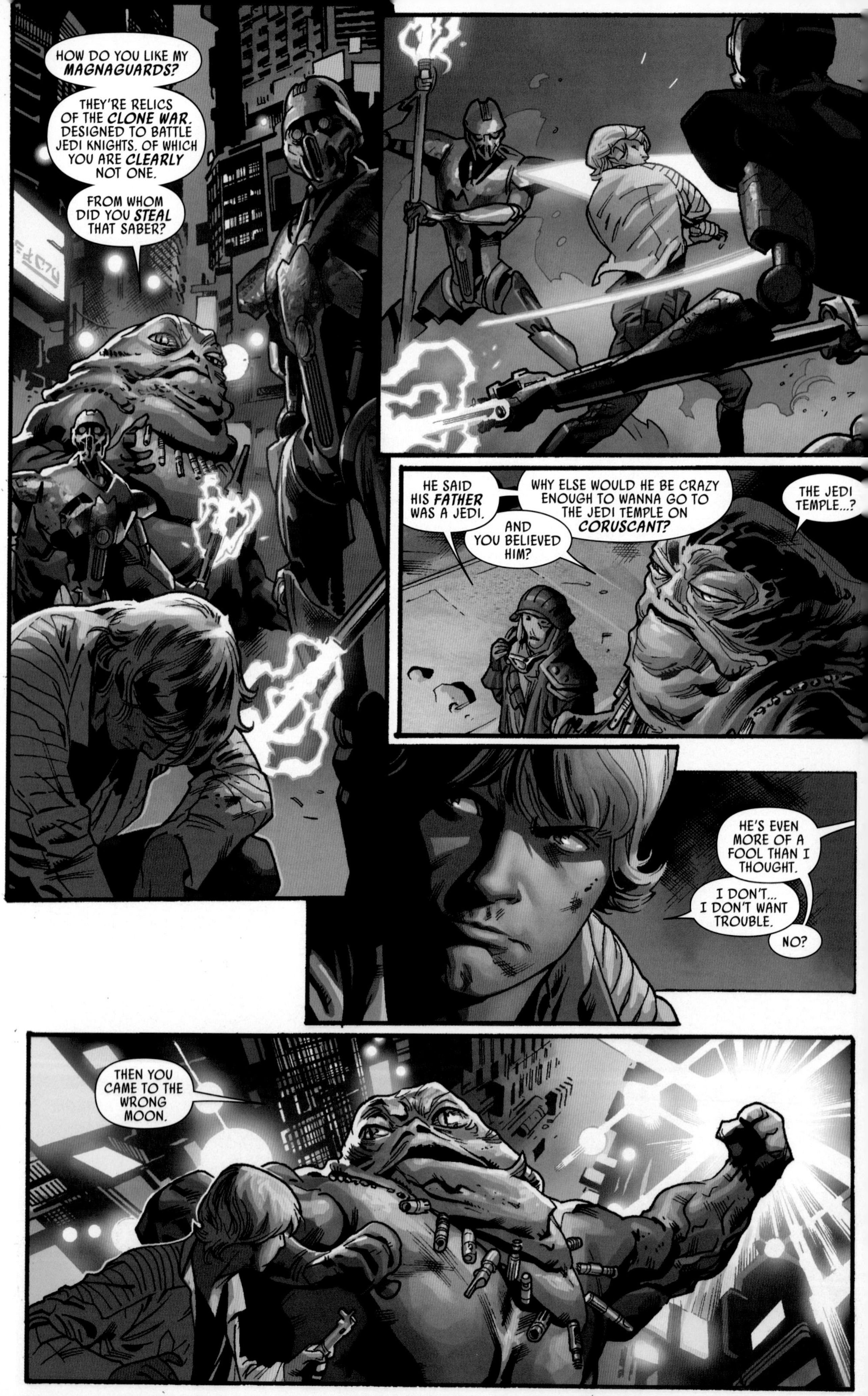
HOW DO YOU LIKE MY MAGNAGUARDS?
THEY'RE RELICS OF THE CLONE WAR. DESIGNED TO BATTLE JEDI KNIGHTS. OF WHICH YOU ARE CLEARLY NOT ONE.
FROM WHOM DID YOU STEAL THAT SABER?
HE SAID HIS FATHER WAS A JEDI.
WHY ELSE WOULD HE BE CRAZY ENOUGH TO WANNA GO TO THE JEDI TEMPLE ON CORUSCANT?
AND YOU BELIEVED HIM?
THE JEDI TEMPLE...?
HE'S EVEN MORE OF A FOOL THAN I THOUGHT.
I DON'T... I DON'T WANT TROUBLE.
NO?
THEN YOU CAME TO THE WRONG MOON.

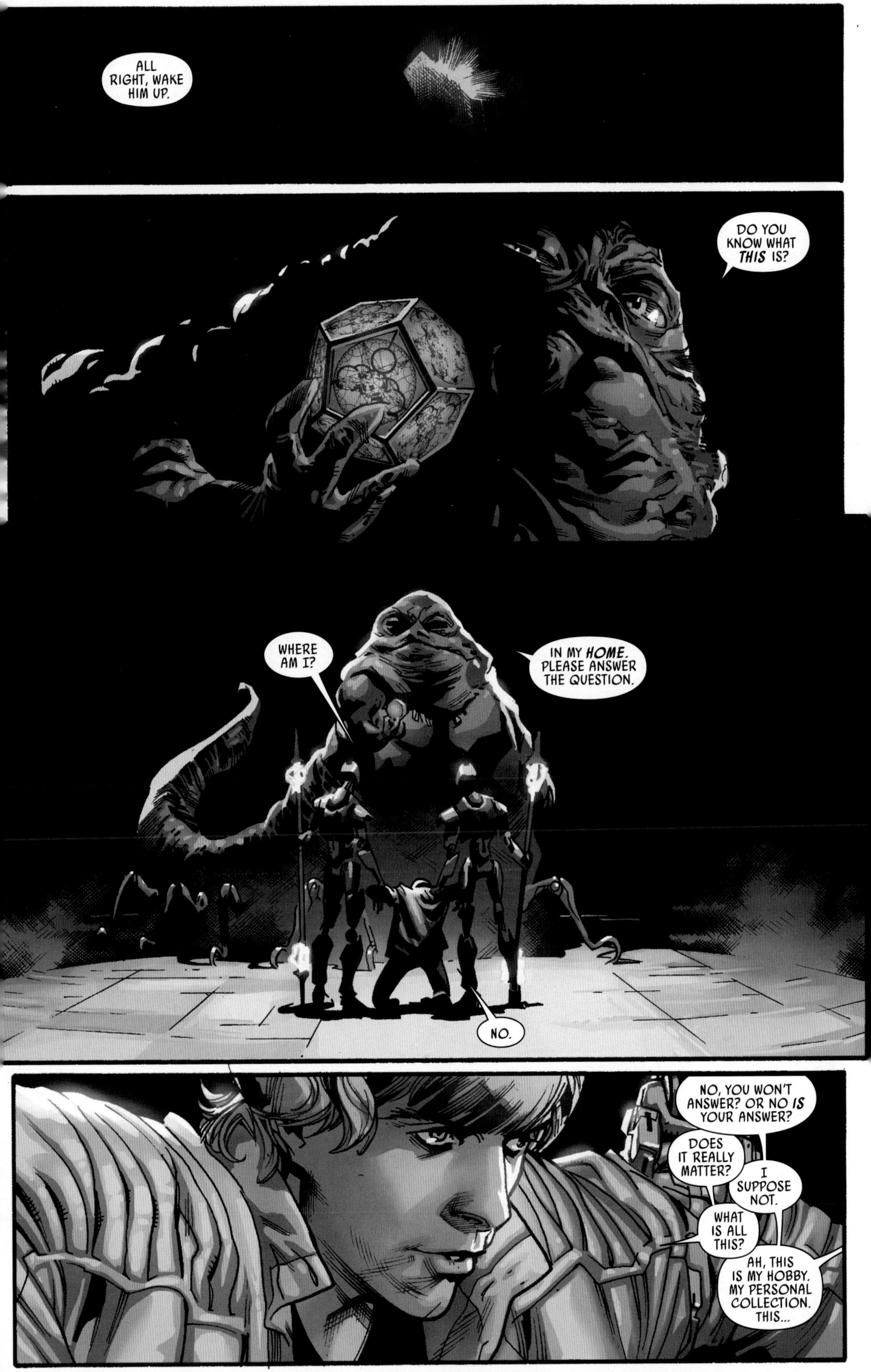
ALL RIGHT, WAKE HIM UP.
DO YOU KNOW WHAT *THIS* IS?
WHERE AM I?
IN MY *HOME*. PLEASE ANSWER THE QUESTION.
NO.
NO, YOU WON'T ANSWER? OR NO *IS* YOUR ANSWER?
DOES IT REALLY MATTER?
I SUPPOSE NOT.
WHAT IS ALL THIS?
AH, THIS IS MY HOBBY. MY PERSONAL COLLECTION. THIS...

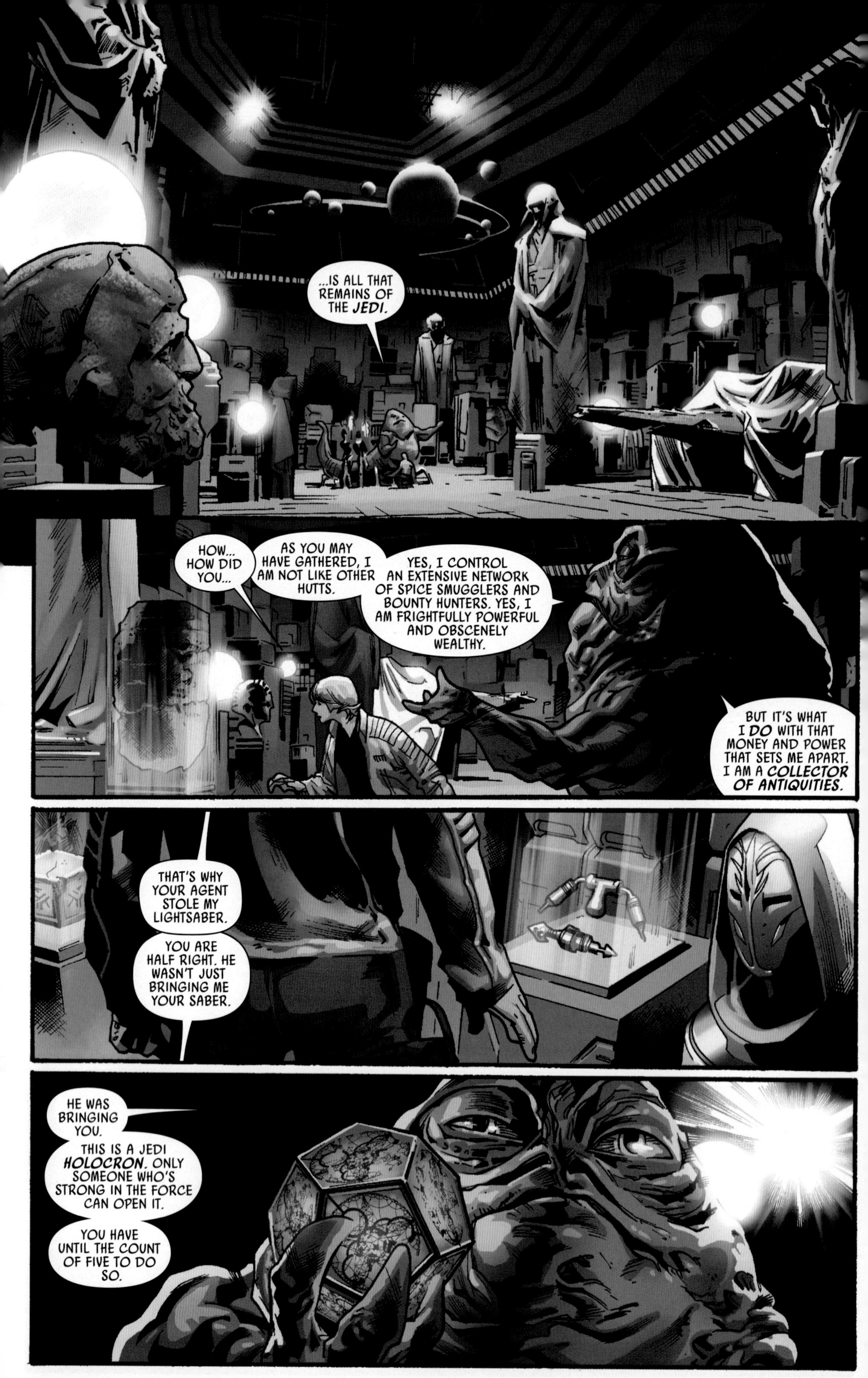
...IS ALL THAT REMAINS OF THE *JEDI.*
HOW... HOW DID YOU...
AS YOU MAY HAVE GATHERED, I AM NOT LIKE OTHER HUTTS.
YES, I CONTROL AN EXTENSIVE NETWORK OF SPICE SMUGGLERS AND BOUNTY HUNTERS. YES, I AM FRIGHTFULLY POWERFUL AND OBSCENELY WEALTHY.
BUT IT'S WHAT I *DO* WITH THAT MONEY AND POWER THAT SETS ME APART. I AM A *COLLECTOR OF ANTIQUITIES.*
THAT'S WHY YOUR AGENT STOLE MY LIGHTSABER.
YOU ARE HALF RIGHT. HE WASN'T JUST BRINGING ME YOUR SABER.
HE WAS BRINGING YOU.
THIS IS A JEDI *HOLOCRON.* ONLY SOMEONE WHO'S STRONG IN THE FORCE CAN OPEN IT.
YOU HAVE UNTIL THE COUNT OF FIVE TO DO SO.

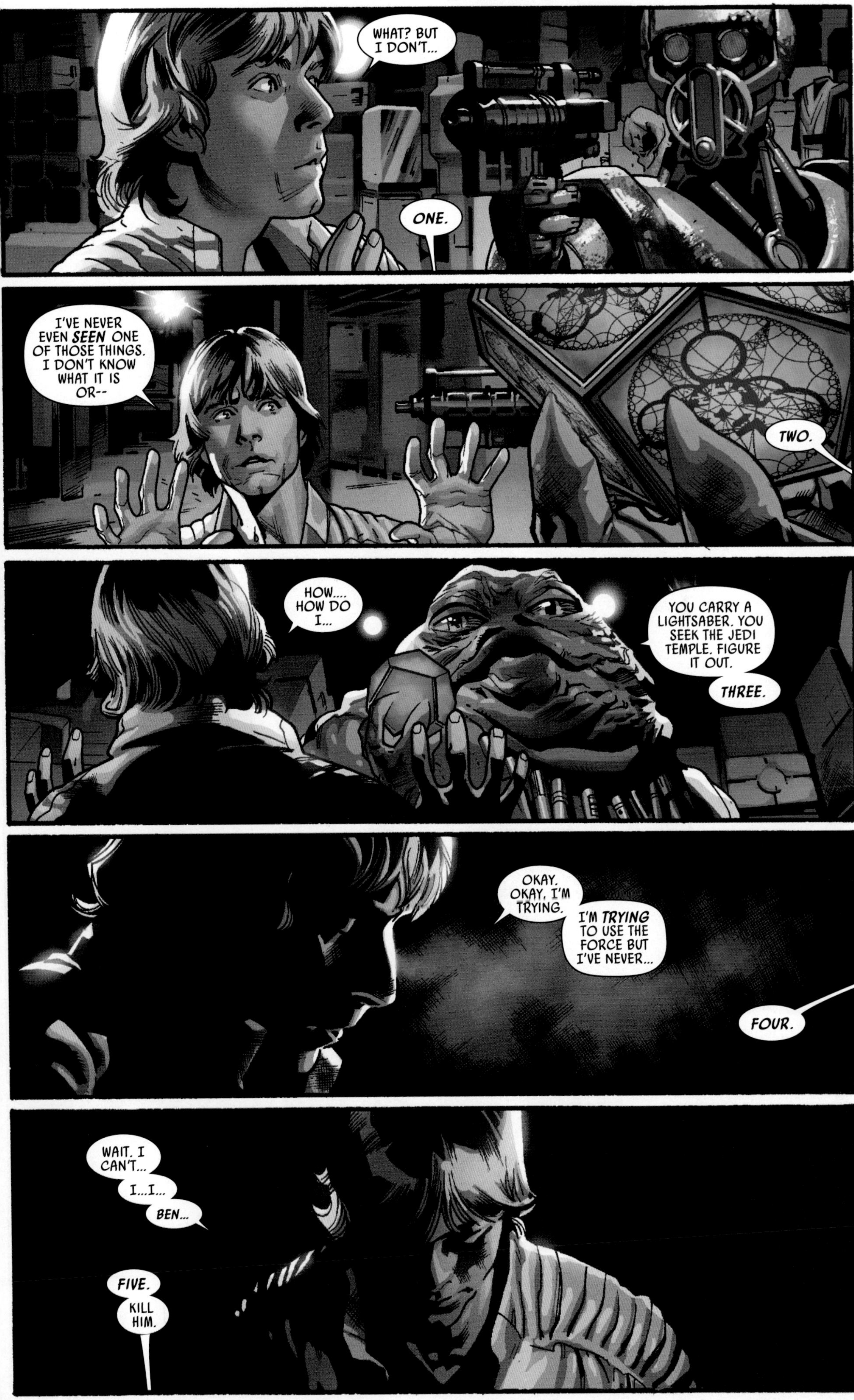
WHAT? BUT I DON'T...
ONE.
I'VE NEVER EVEN SEEN ONE OF THOSE THINGS. I DON'T KNOW WHAT IT IS OR--
TWO.
HOW.... HOW DO I...
YOU CARRY A LIGHTSABER. YOU SEEK THE JEDI TEMPLE. FIGURE IT OUT.
THREE.
OKAY. OKAY, I'M TRYING.
I'M TRYING TO USE THE FORCE BUT I'VE NEVER...
FOUR.
WAIT. I CAN'T...
I...I...
BEN...
FIVE.
KILL HIM.

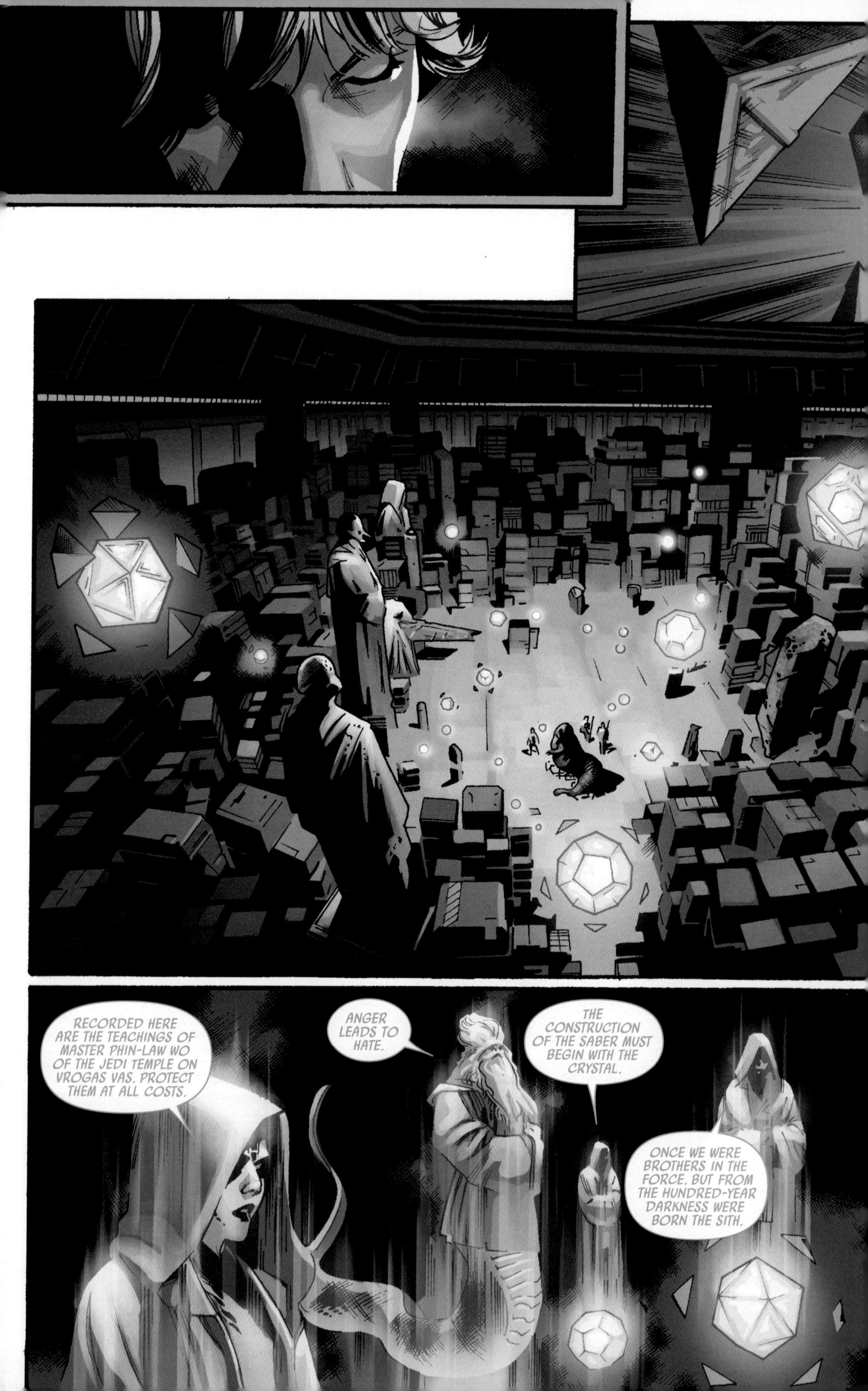
RECORDED HERE ARE THE TEACHINGS OF MASTER PHIN-LAW WO OF THE JEDI TEMPLE ON VROGAS VAS. PROTECT THEM AT ALL COSTS.
ANGER LEADS TO HATE.
THE CONSTRUCTION OF THE SABER MUST BEGIN WITH THE CRYSTAL.
ONCE WE WERE BROTHERS IN THE FORCE. BUT FROM THE HUNDRED-YEAR DARKNESS WERE BORN THE SITH.

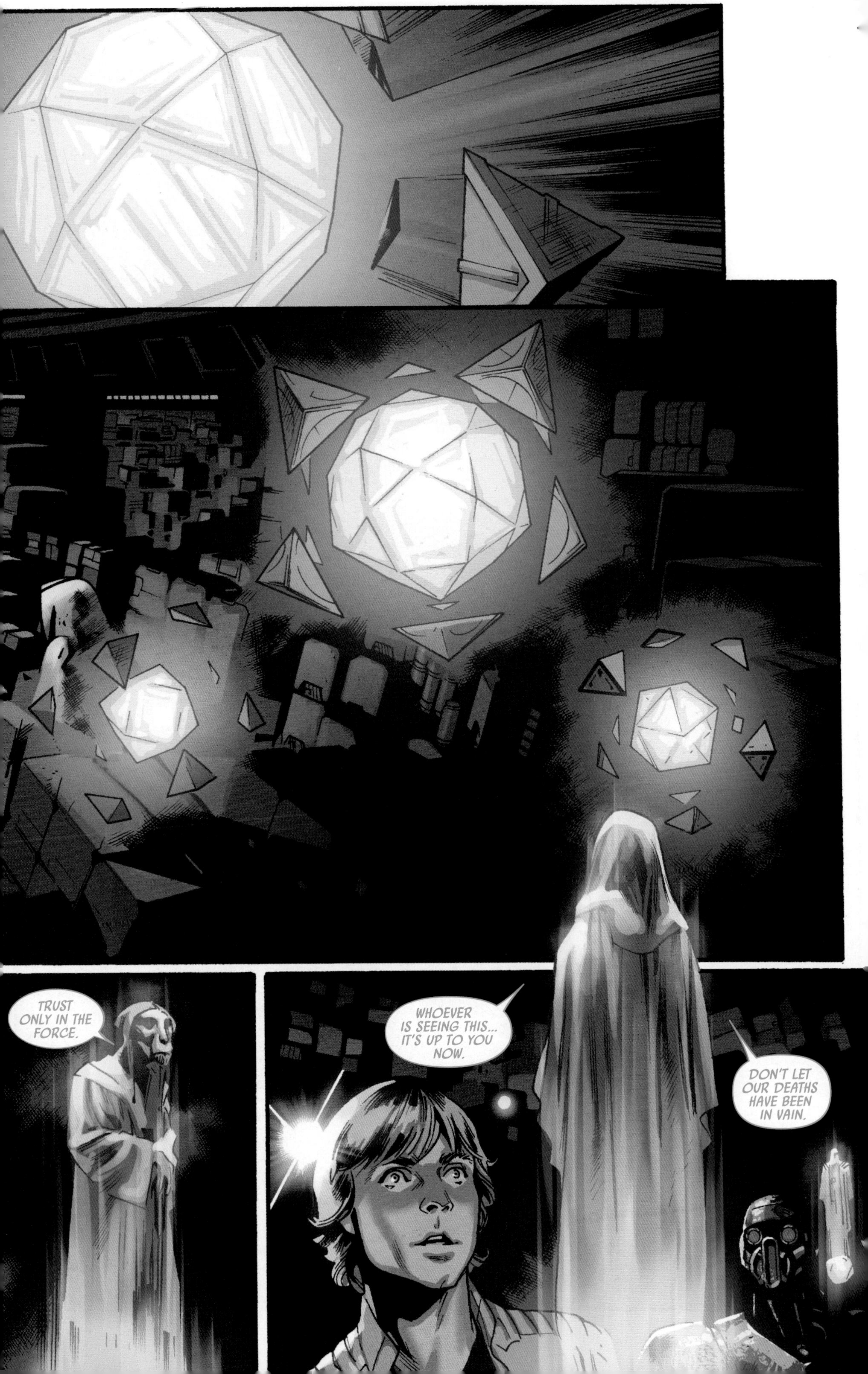
TRUST ONLY IN THE FORCE.
WHOEVER IS SEEING THIS... IT'S UP TO YOU NOW.
DON'T LET OUR DEATHS HAVE BEEN IN VAIN.

DON'T LET THIS BE THE END OF THE JEDI.

WELL, WHAT DO YOU KNOW...IT APPEARS YOU WILL MAKE A FINE ADDITION TO MY COLLECTION AFTER ALL.

BUT...I'M NOT...

WHAT YOU *ARE*, DEAR BOY...IS THE *LAST JEDI.*

AND NOW YOU BELONG TO *ME.*

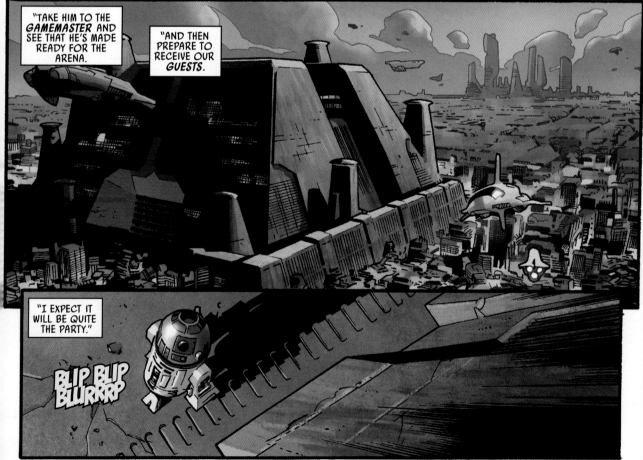

"TAKE HIM TO THE *GAMEMASTER* AND SEE THAT HE'S MADE READY FOR THE ARENA.

"AND THEN PREPARE TO RECEIVE OUR *GUESTS.*

"I EXPECT IT WILL BE QUITE THE PARTY."

BLIP BLIP BLURRRP

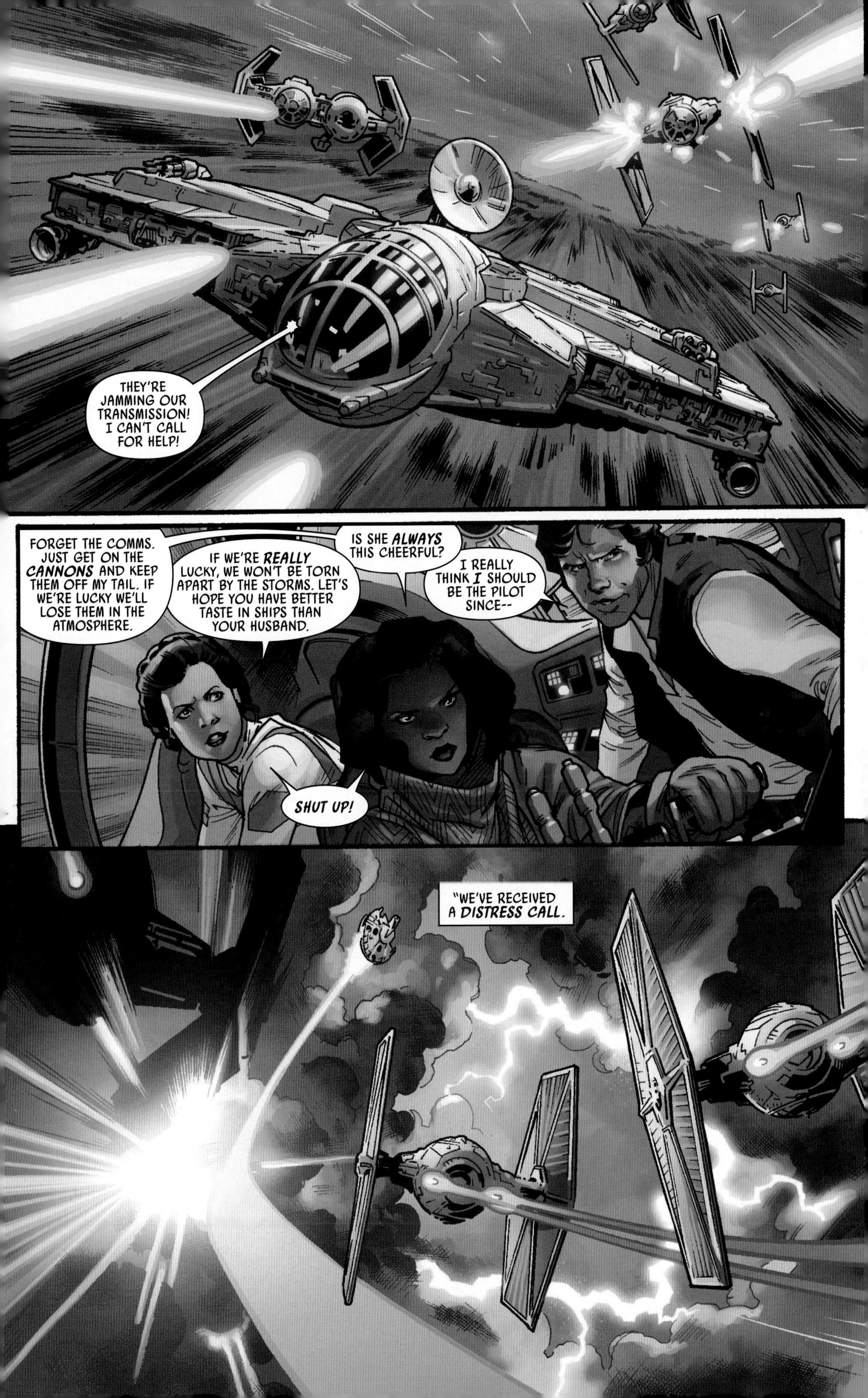
THEY'RE JAMMING OUR TRANSMISSION! I CAN'T CALL FOR HELP!
FORGET THE COMMS. JUST GET ON THE CANNONS AND KEEP THEM OFF MY TAIL. IF WE'RE LUCKY WE'LL LOSE THEM IN THE ATMOSPHERE.
IF WE'RE REALLY LUCKY, WE WON'T BE TORN APART BY THE STORMS. LET'S HOPE YOU HAVE BETTER TASTE IN SHIPS THAN YOUR HUSBAND.
IS SHE ALWAYS THIS CHEERFUL?
I REALLY THINK I SHOULD BE THE PILOT SINCE--
SHUT UP!
"WE'VE RECEIVED A DISTRESS CALL.

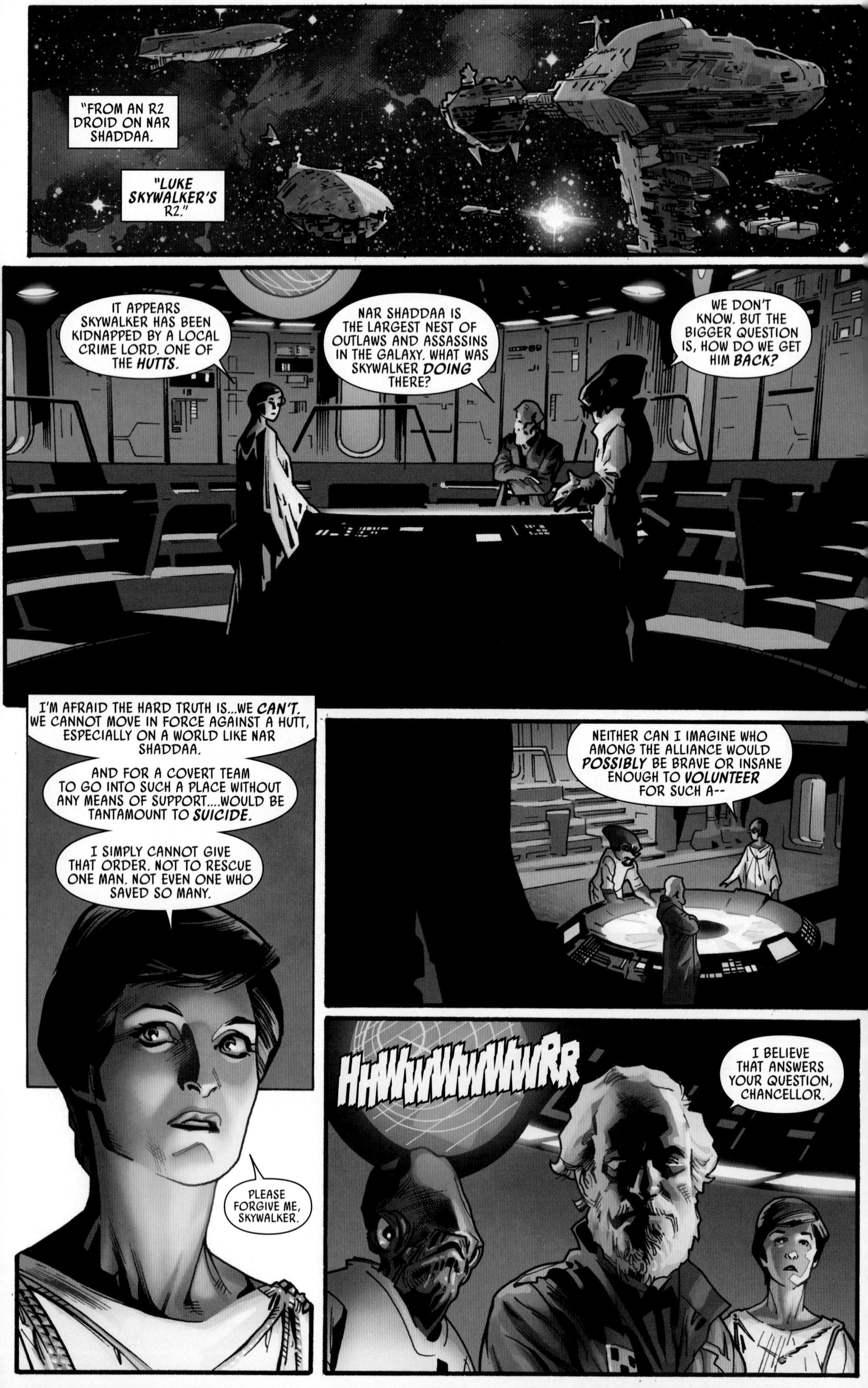
"FROM AN R2 DROID ON NAR SHADDAA.
"LUKE SKYWALKER'S R2."
IT APPEARS SKYWALKER HAS BEEN KIDNAPPED BY A LOCAL CRIME LORD. ONE OF THE HUTTS.
NAR SHADDAA IS THE LARGEST NEST OF OUTLAWS AND ASSASSINS IN THE GALAXY. WHAT WAS SKYWALKER DOING THERE?
WE DON'T KNOW. BUT THE BIGGER QUESTION IS, HOW DO WE GET HIM BACK?
I'M AFRAID THE HARD TRUTH IS...WE CAN'T. WE CANNOT MOVE IN FORCE AGAINST A HUTT, ESPECIALLY ON A WORLD LIKE NAR SHADDAA.
AND FOR A COVERT TEAM TO GO INTO SUCH A PLACE WITHOUT ANY MEANS OF SUPPORT....WOULD BE TANTAMOUNT TO SUICIDE.
I SIMPLY CANNOT GIVE THAT ORDER. NOT TO RESCUE ONE MAN. NOT EVEN ONE WHO SAVED SO MANY.
PLEASE FORGIVE ME, SKYWALKER.
NEITHER CAN I IMAGINE WHO AMONG THE ALLIANCE WOULD POSSIBLY BE BRAVE OR INSANE ENOUGH TO VOLUNTEER FOR SUCH A--
HHWWWWWWWRR
I BELIEVE THAT ANSWERS YOUR QUESTION, CHANCELLOR.

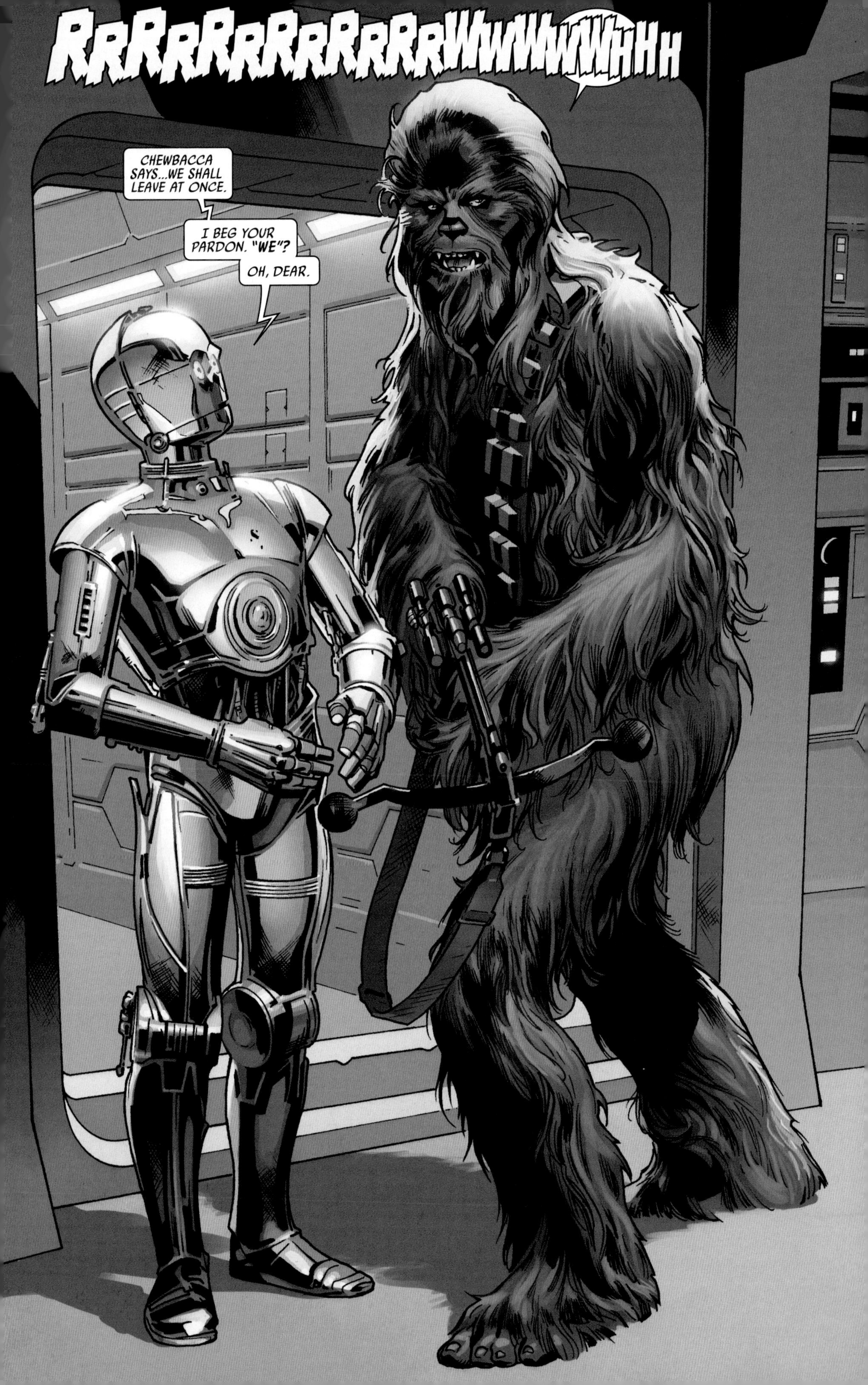
RRRRRRRRRRRRRRRWWWWWWWHHH
CHEWBACCA SAYS...WE SHALL LEAVE AT ONCE.
I BEG YOUR PARDON. "WE"?
OH, DEAR.

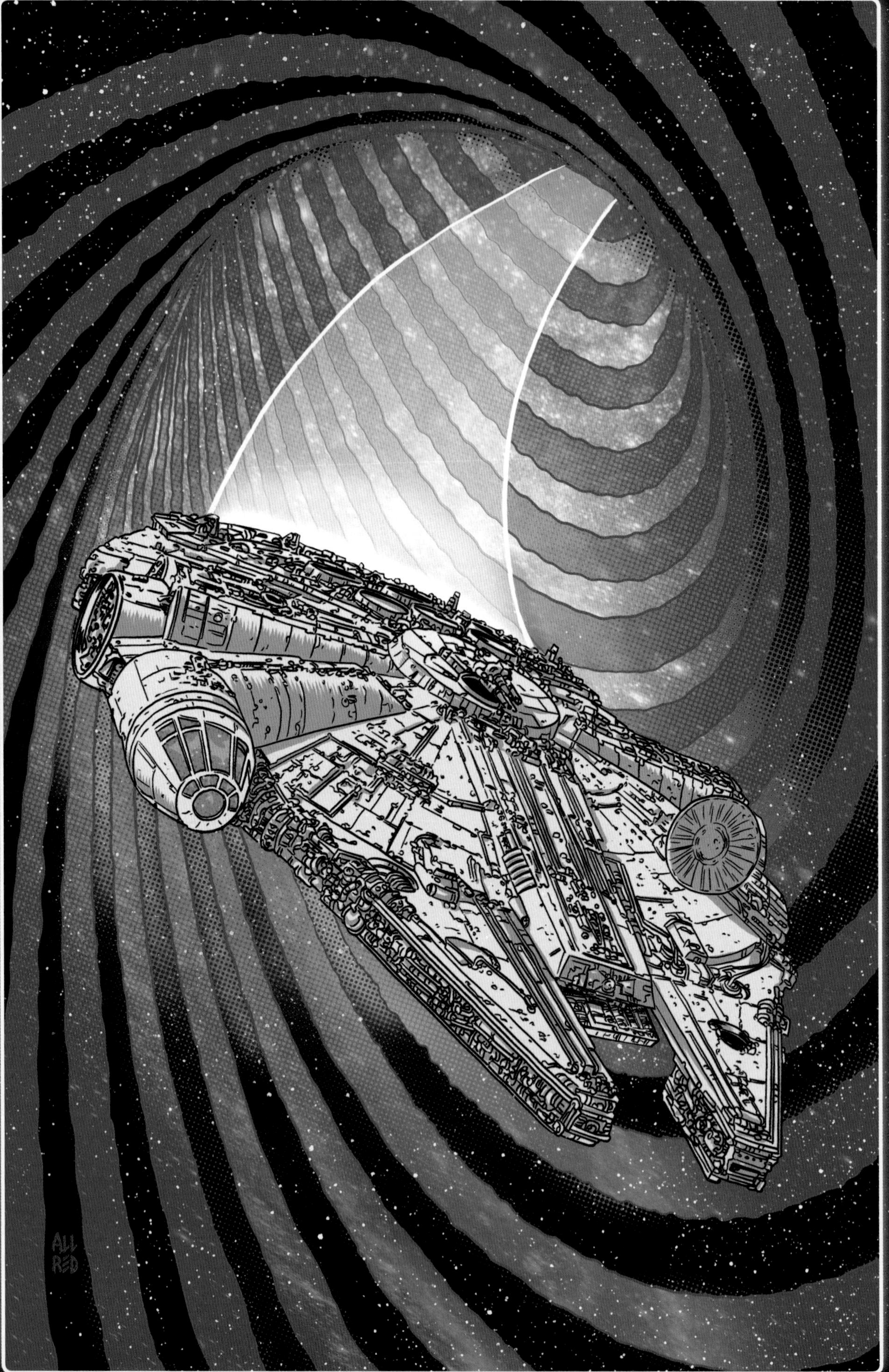
ALL
RED

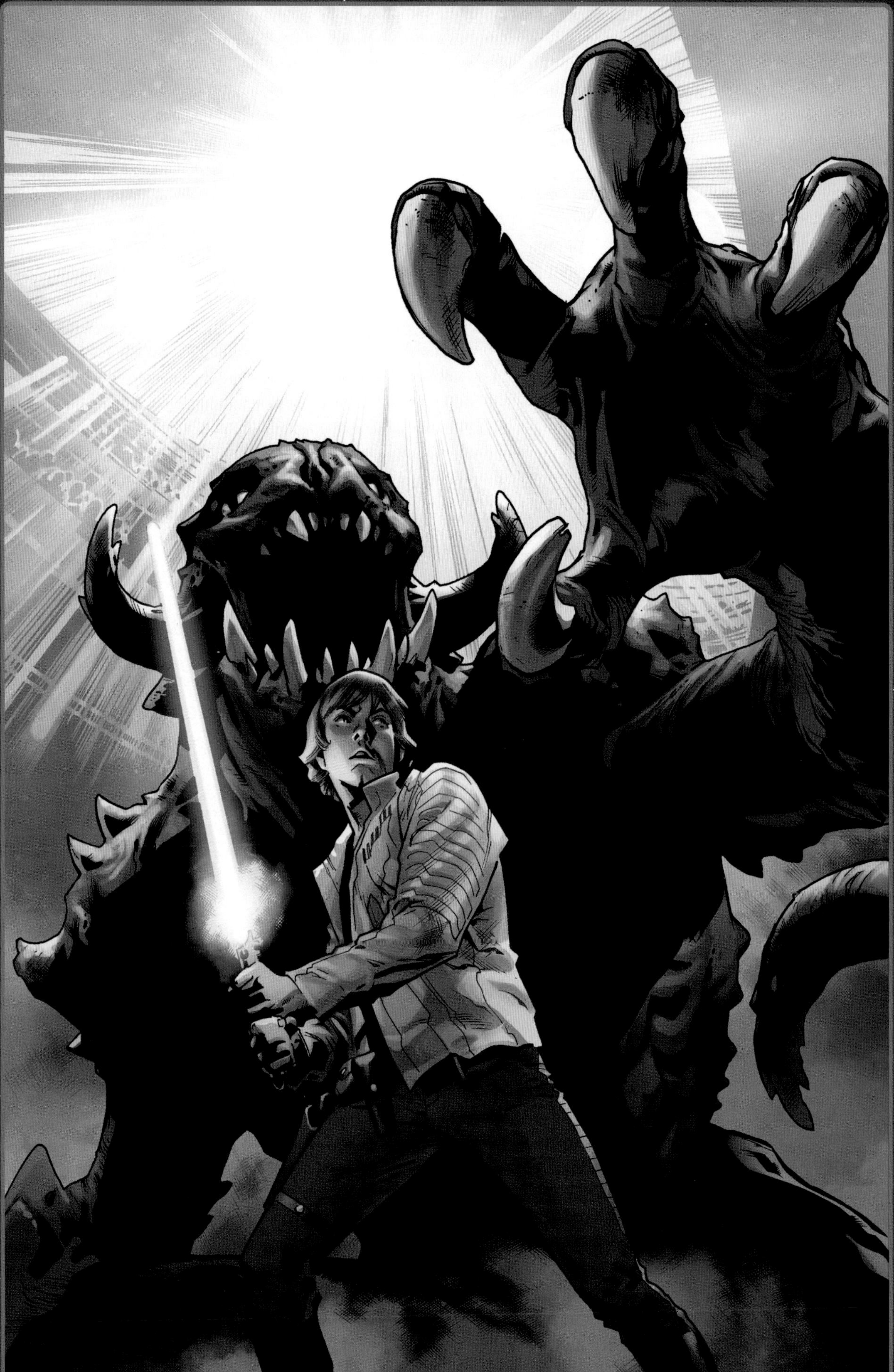

STAR WARS 10

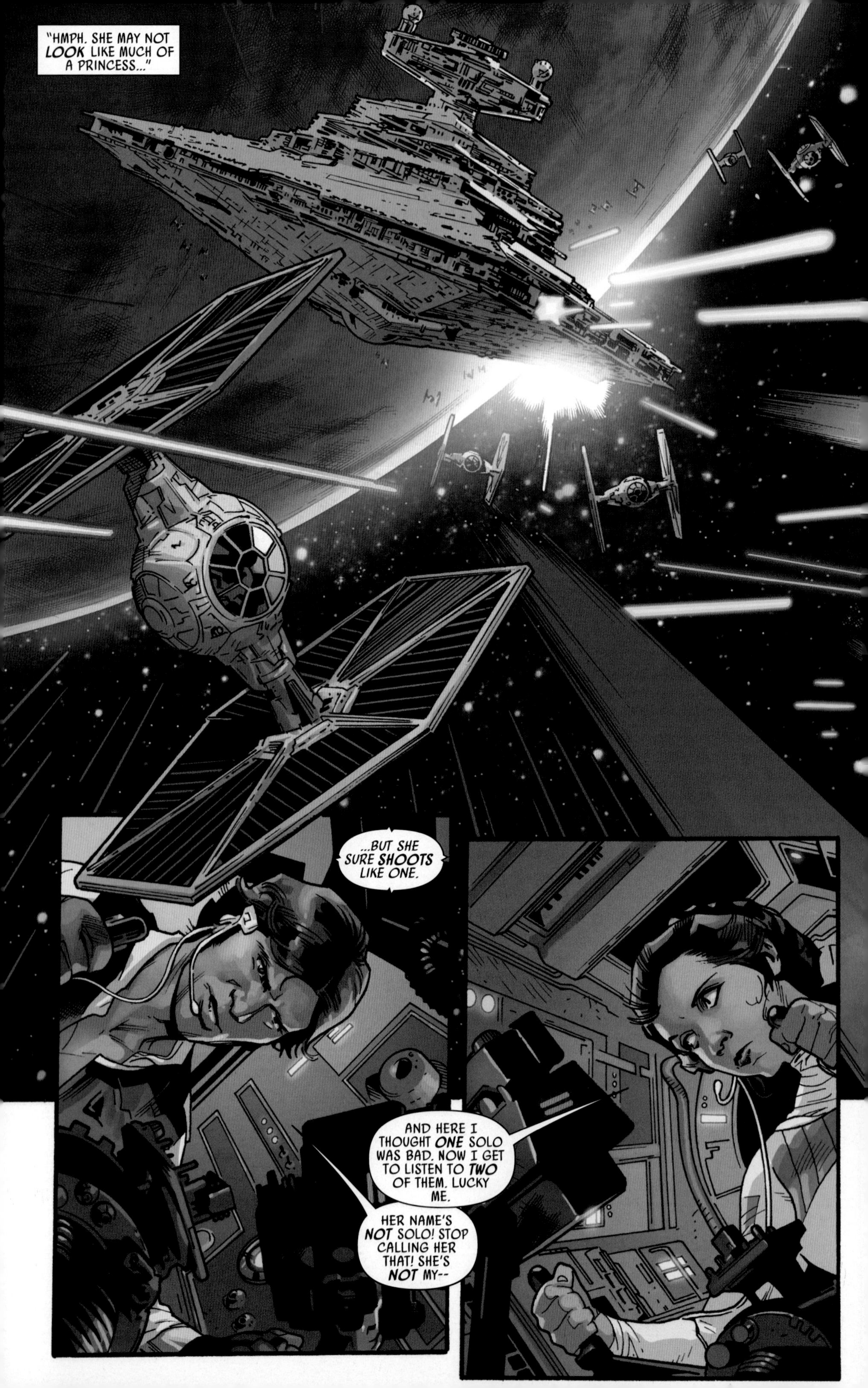

"HMPH. SHE MAY NOT LOOK LIKE MUCH OF A PRINCESS..."
...BUT SHE SURE SHOOTS LIKE ONE.
AND HERE I THOUGHT ONE SOLO WAS BAD. NOW I GET TO LISTEN TO TWO OF THEM. LUCKY ME.
HER NAME'S NOT SOLO! STOP CALLING HER THAT! SHE'S NOT MY--

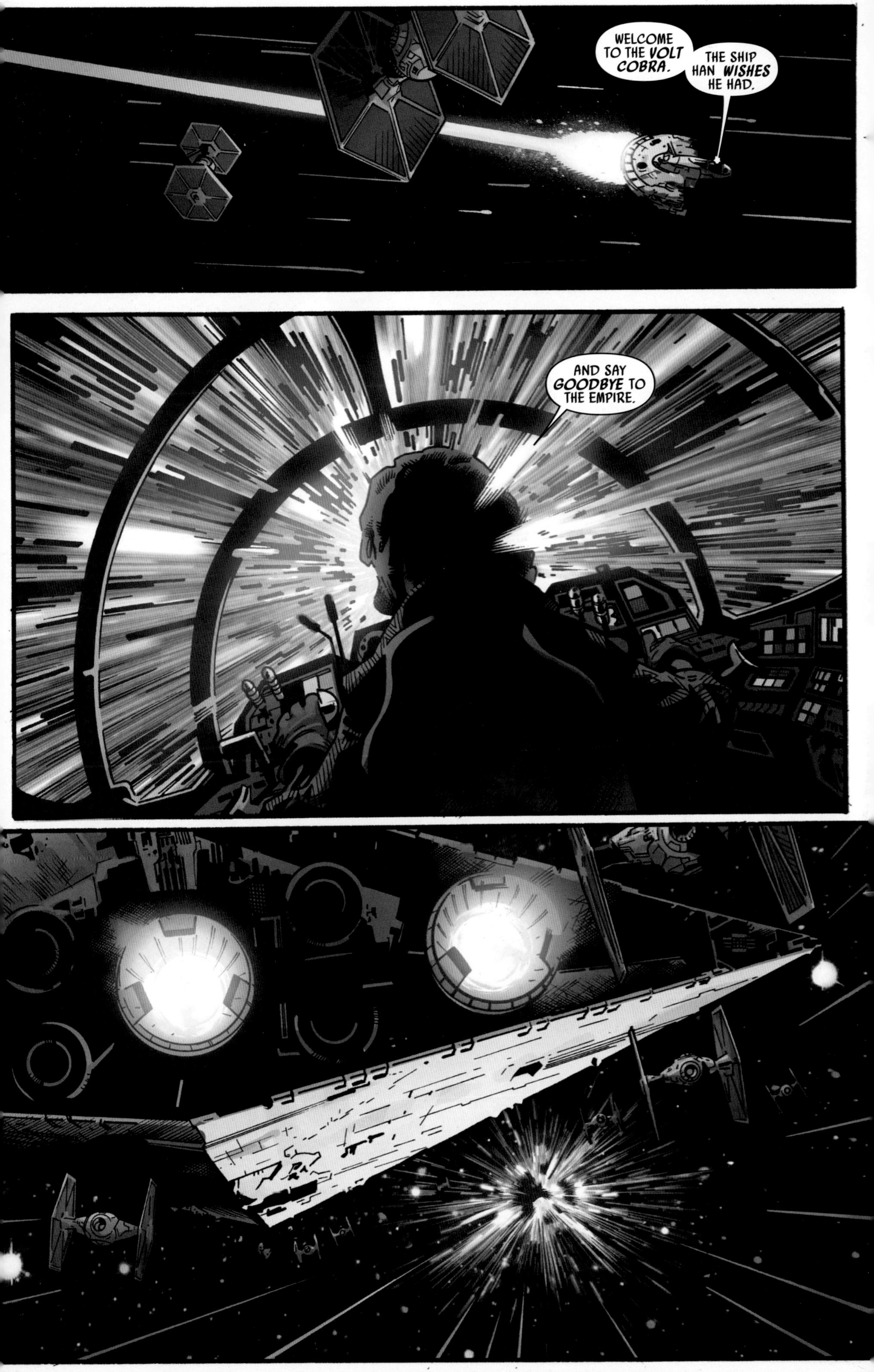
WELCOME TO THE VOLT COBRA.
THE SHIP HAN WISHES HE HAD.
AND SAY GOODBYE TO THE EMPIRE.

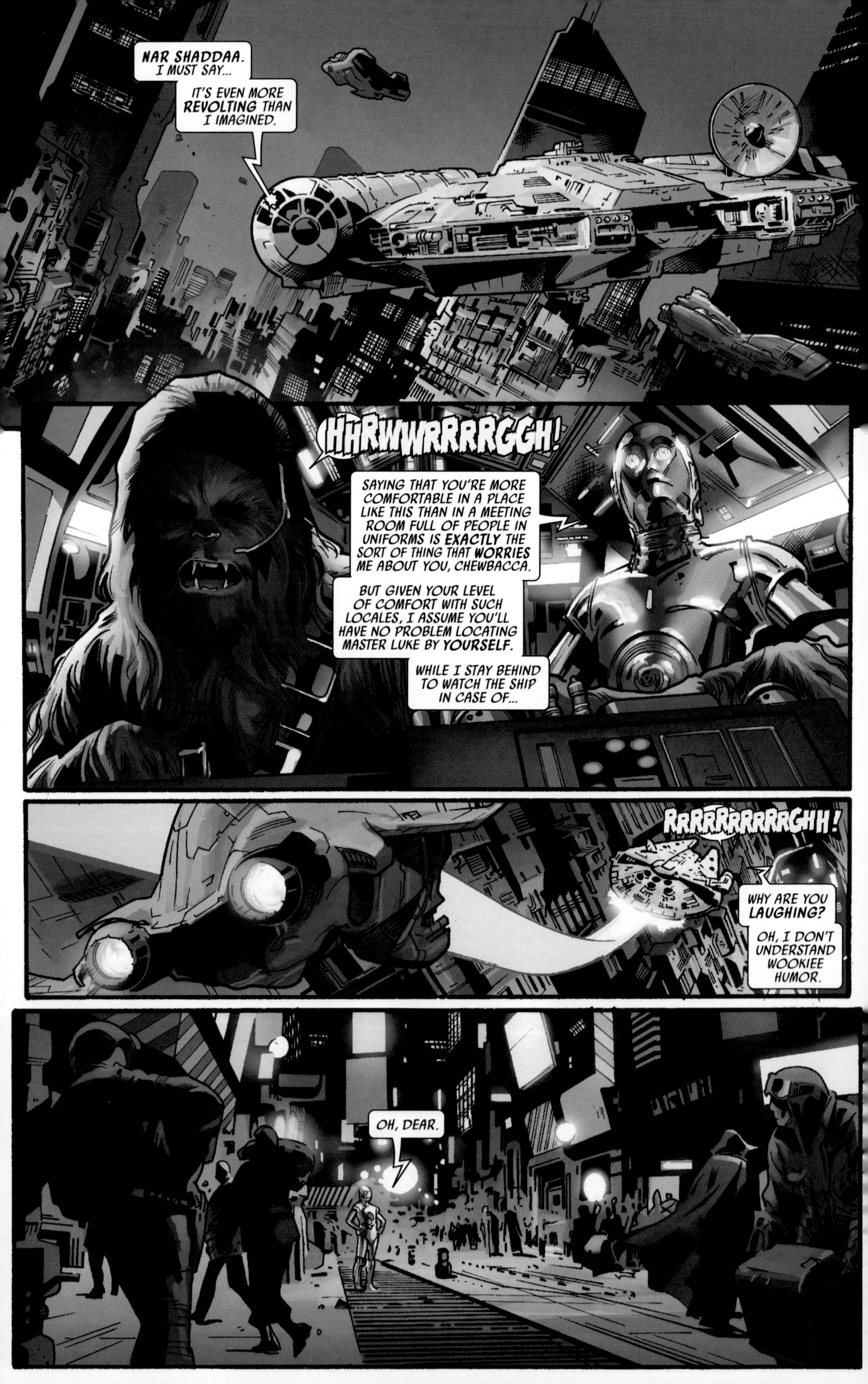
NAR SHADDAA. I MUST SAY...
IT'S EVEN MORE REVOLTING THAN I IMAGINED.
HHRWWRRRRRGGH!
SAYING THAT YOU'RE MORE COMFORTABLE IN A PLACE LIKE THIS THAN IN A MEETING ROOM FULL OF PEOPLE IN UNIFORMS IS EXACTLY THE SORT OF THING THAT WORRIES ME ABOUT YOU, CHEWBACCA.
BUT GIVEN YOUR LEVEL OF COMFORT WITH SUCH LOCALES, I ASSUME YOU'LL HAVE NO PROBLEM LOCATING MASTER LUKE BY YOURSELF.
WHILE I STAY BEHIND TO WATCH THE SHIP IN CASE OF...
RRRRRRRRRRGHH!
WHY ARE YOU LAUGHING?
OH, I DON'T UNDERSTAND WOOKIEE HUMOR.
OH, DEAR.

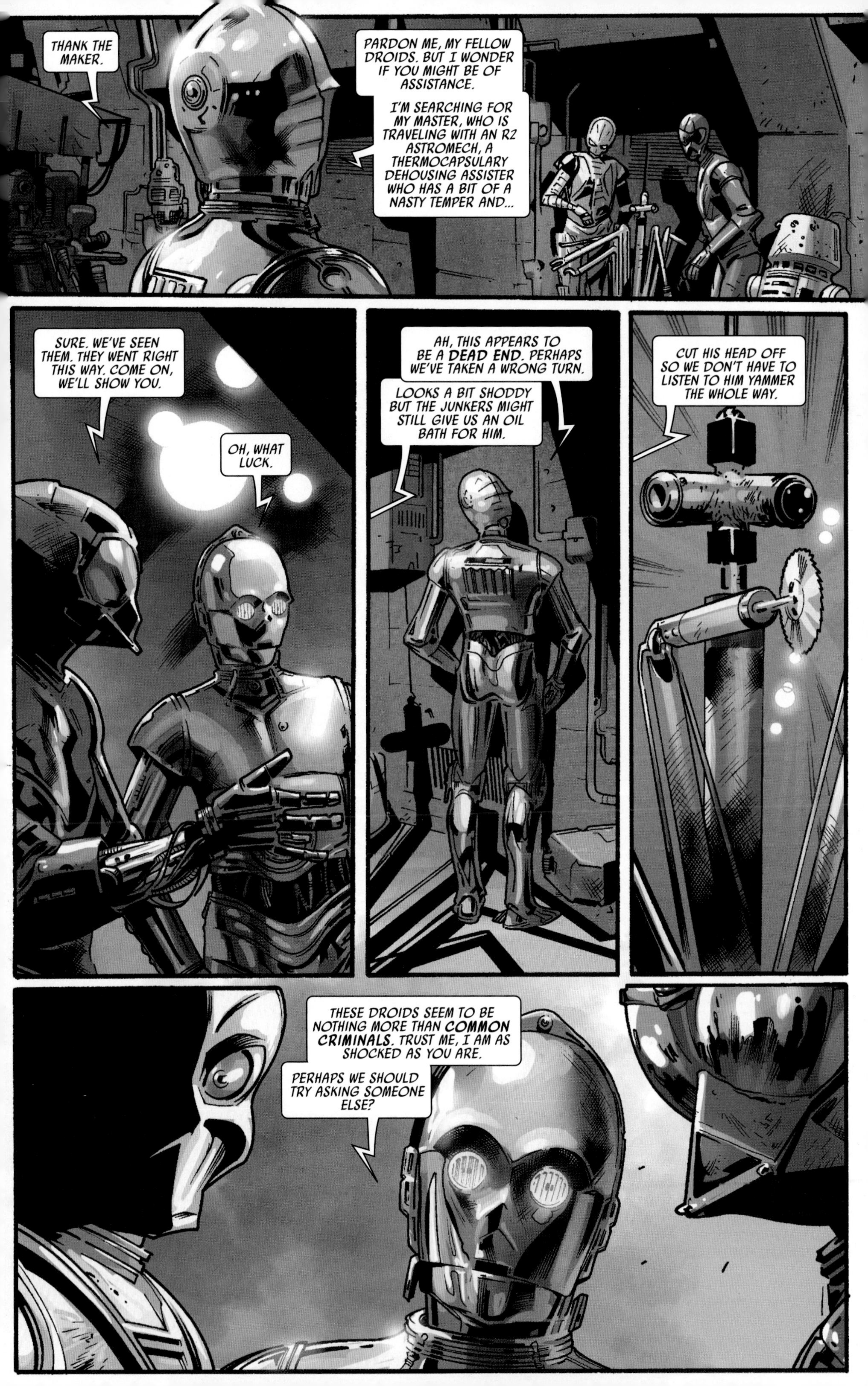
THANK THE MAKER.
PARDON ME, MY FELLOW DROIDS. BUT I WONDER IF YOU MIGHT BE OF ASSISTANCE.
I'M SEARCHING FOR MY MASTER, WHO IS TRAVELING WITH AN R2 ASTROMECH, A THERMOCAPSULARY DEHOUSING ASSISTER WHO HAS A BIT OF A NASTY TEMPER AND...
SURE. WE'VE SEEN THEM. THEY WENT RIGHT THIS WAY. COME ON, WE'LL SHOW YOU.
OH, WHAT LUCK.
AH, THIS APPEARS TO BE A DEAD END. PERHAPS WE'VE TAKEN A WRONG TURN.
LOOKS A BIT SHODDY BUT THE JUNKERS MIGHT STILL GIVE US AN OIL BATH FOR HIM.
CUT HIS HEAD OFF SO WE DON'T HAVE TO LISTEN TO HIM YAMMER THE WHOLE WAY.
THESE DROIDS SEEM TO BE NOTHING MORE THAN COMMON CRIMINALS. TRUST ME, I AM AS SHOCKED AS YOU ARE.
PERHAPS WE SHOULD TRY ASKING SOMEONE ELSE?

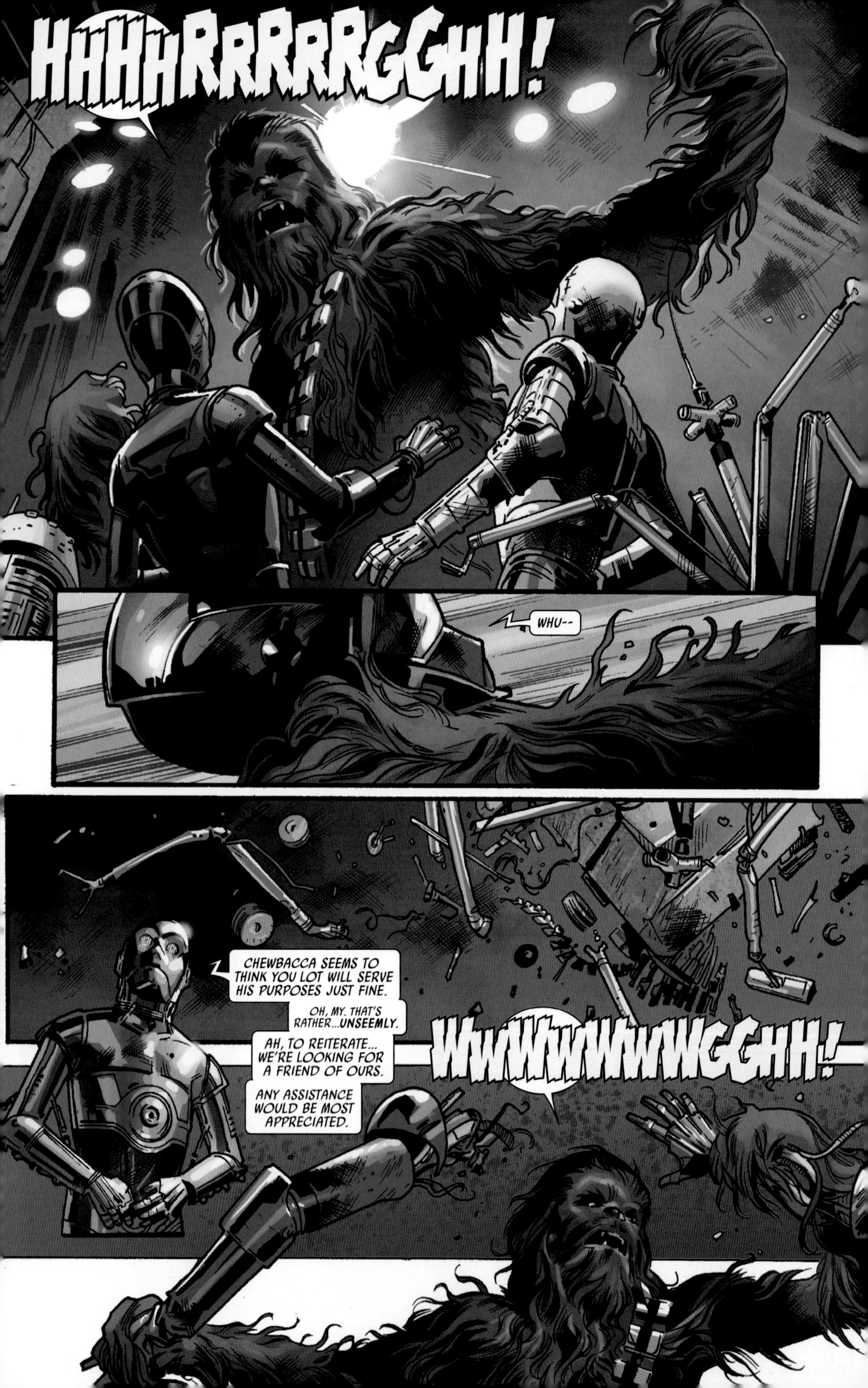
HHHHRRRRRRGGHH!
WHU--
CHEWBACCA SEEMS TO THINK YOU LOT WILL SERVE HIS PURPOSES JUST FINE.
OH, MY. THAT'S RATHER...UNSEEMLY.
AH, TO REITERATE... WE'RE LOOKING FOR A FRIEND OF OURS.
ANY ASSISTANCE WOULD BE MOST APPRECIATED.
WWWWWWWWGGHH!

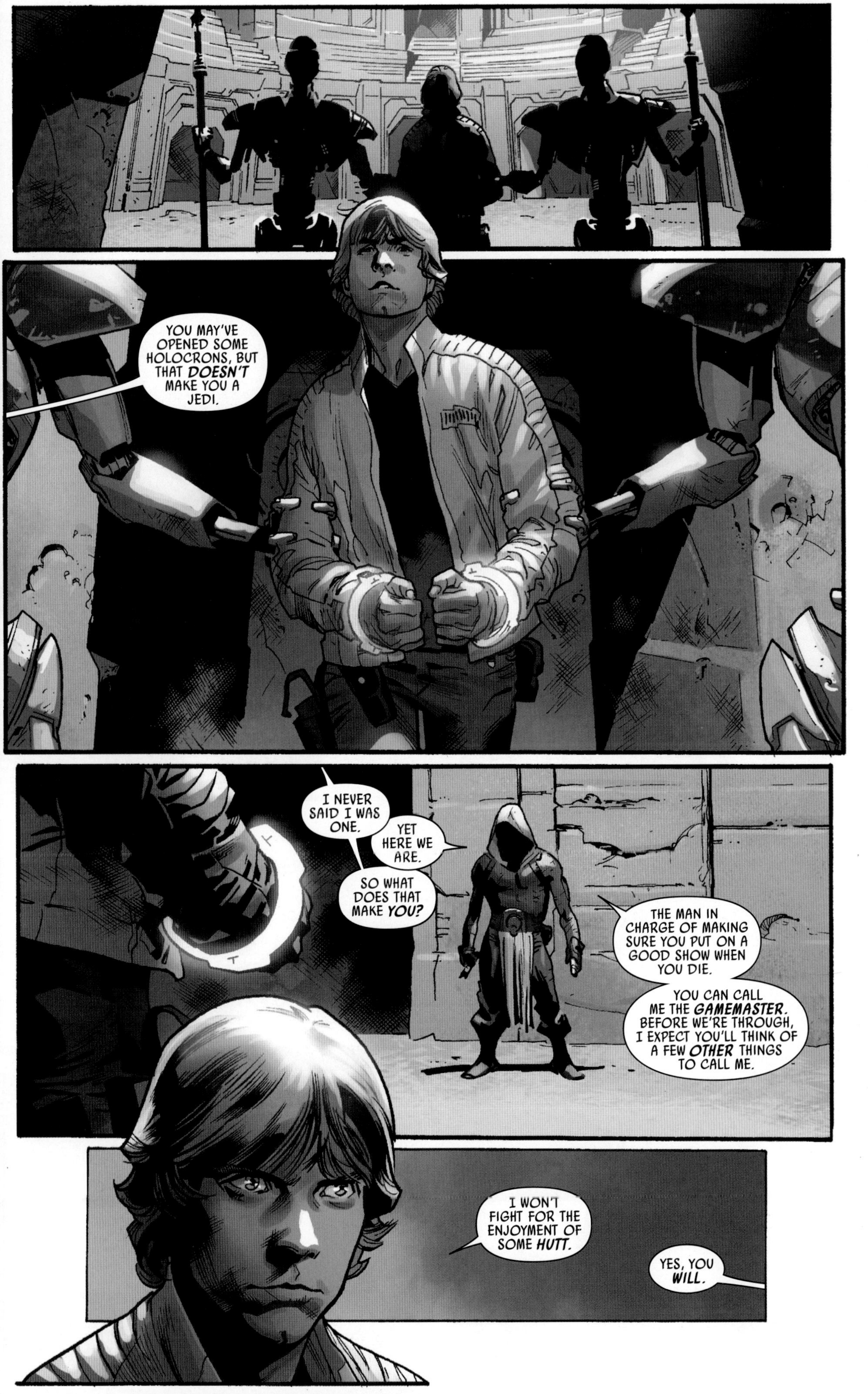
YOU MAY'VE OPENED SOME HOLOCRONS, BUT THAT DOESN'T MAKE YOU A JEDI.
I NEVER SAID I WAS ONE.
YET HERE WE ARE.
SO WHAT DOES THAT MAKE YOU?
THE MAN IN CHARGE OF MAKING SURE YOU PUT ON A GOOD SHOW WHEN YOU DIE.
YOU CAN CALL ME THE GAMEMASTER. BEFORE WE'RE THROUGH, I EXPECT YOU'LL THINK OF A FEW OTHER THINGS TO CALL ME.
I WON'T FIGHT FOR THE ENJOYMENT OF SOME HUTT.
YES, YOU WILL.

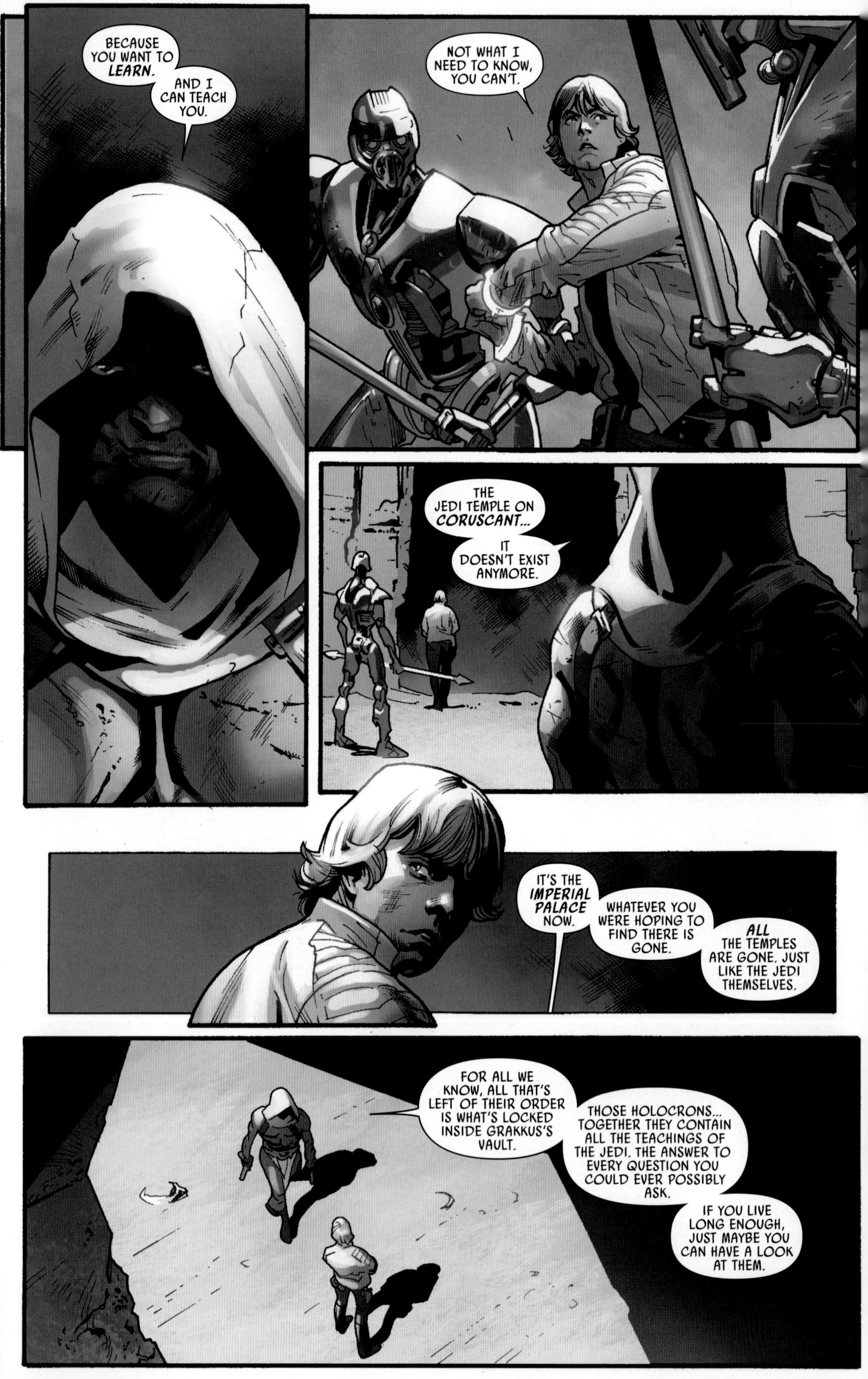
BECAUSE YOU WANT TO LEARN.
AND I CAN TEACH YOU.
NOT WHAT I NEED TO KNOW, YOU CAN'T.
THE JEDI TEMPLE ON CORUSCANT...
IT DOESN'T EXIST ANYMORE.
IT'S THE IMPERIAL PALACE NOW.
WHATEVER YOU WERE HOPING TO FIND THERE IS GONE.
ALL THE TEMPLES ARE GONE. JUST LIKE THE JEDI THEMSELVES.
FOR ALL WE KNOW, ALL THAT'S LEFT OF THEIR ORDER IS WHAT'S LOCKED INSIDE GRAKKUS'S VAULT.
THOSE HOLOCRONS... TOGETHER THEY CONTAIN ALL THE TEACHINGS OF THE JEDI. THE ANSWER TO EVERY QUESTION YOU COULD EVER POSSIBLY ASK.
IF YOU LIVE LONG ENOUGH, JUST MAYBE YOU CAN HAVE A LOOK AT THEM.

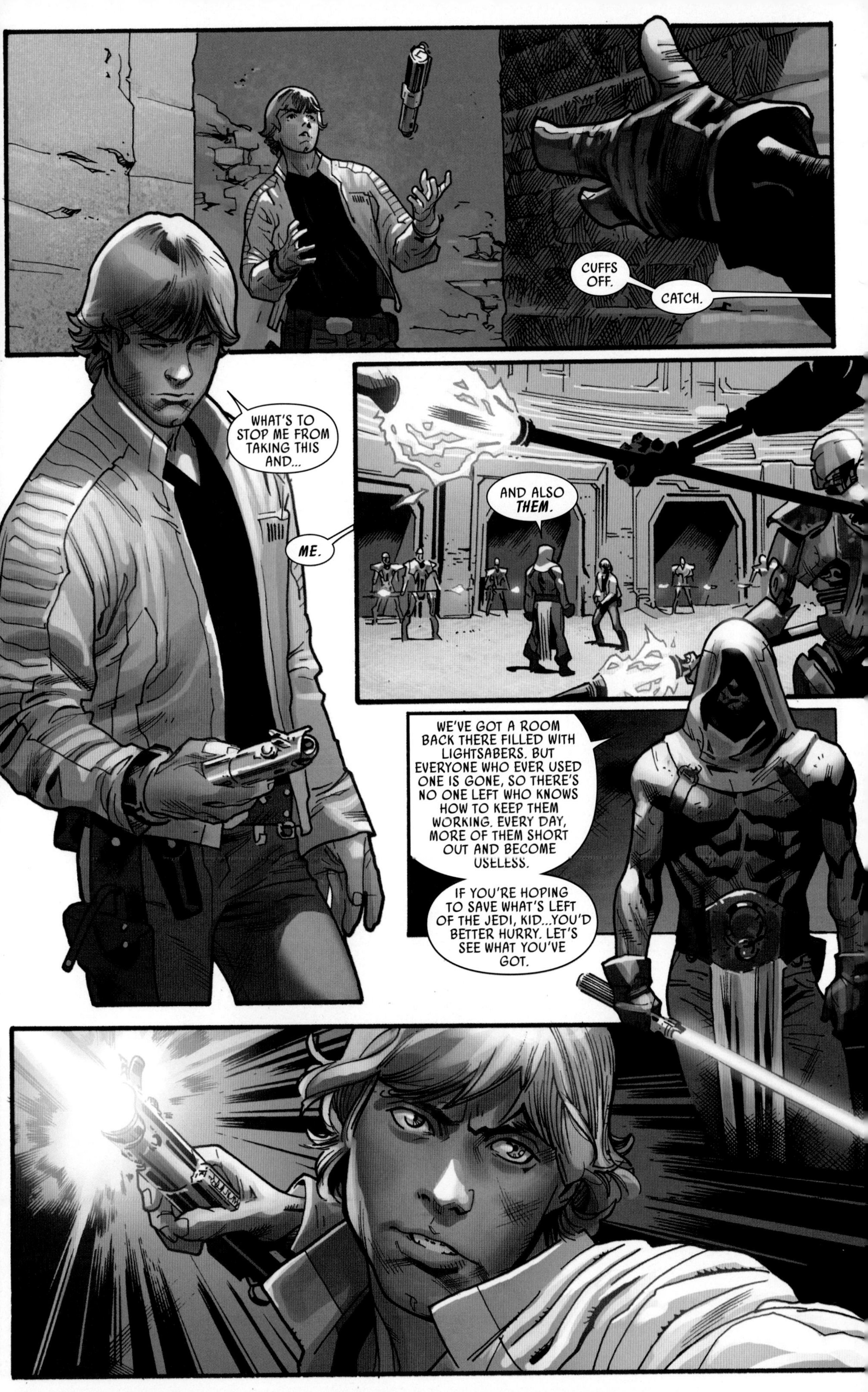
CUFFS OFF.
CATCH.
WHAT'S TO STOP ME FROM TAKING THIS AND...
ME.
AND ALSO *THEM*.
WE'VE GOT A ROOM BACK THERE FILLED WITH LIGHTSABERS. BUT EVERYONE WHO EVER USED ONE IS GONE, SO THERE'S NO ONE LEFT WHO KNOWS HOW TO KEEP THEM WORKING. EVERY DAY, MORE OF THEM SHORT OUT AND BECOME USELESS.
IF YOU'RE HOPING TO SAVE WHAT'S LEFT OF THE JEDI, KID...YOU'D BETTER HURRY. LET'S SEE WHAT YOU'VE GOT.

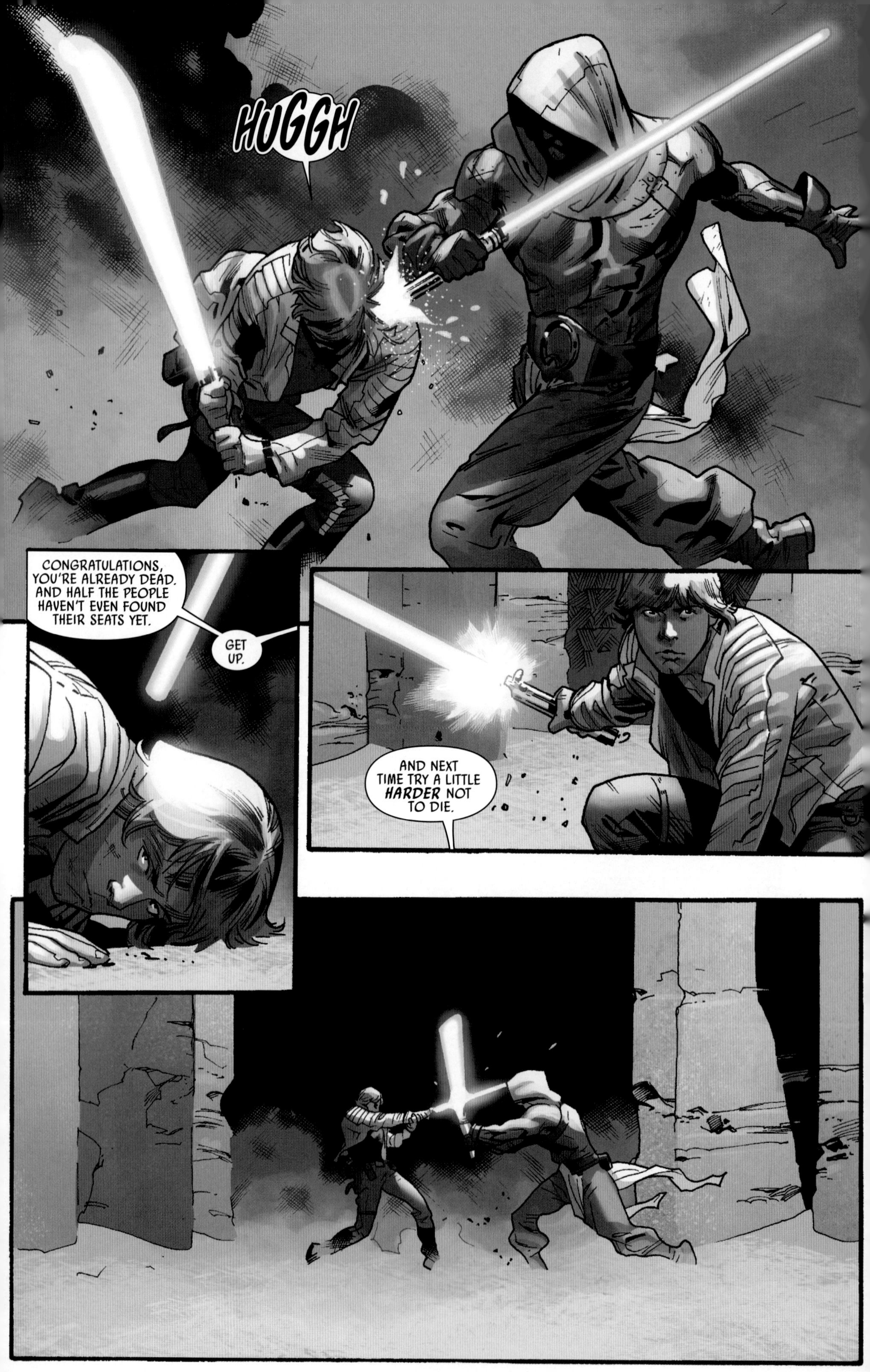
HUGGH
CONGRATULATIONS, YOU'RE ALREADY DEAD. AND HALF THE PEOPLE HAVEN'T EVEN FOUND THEIR SEATS YET.
GET UP.
AND NEXT TIME TRY A LITTLE HARDER NOT TO DIE.

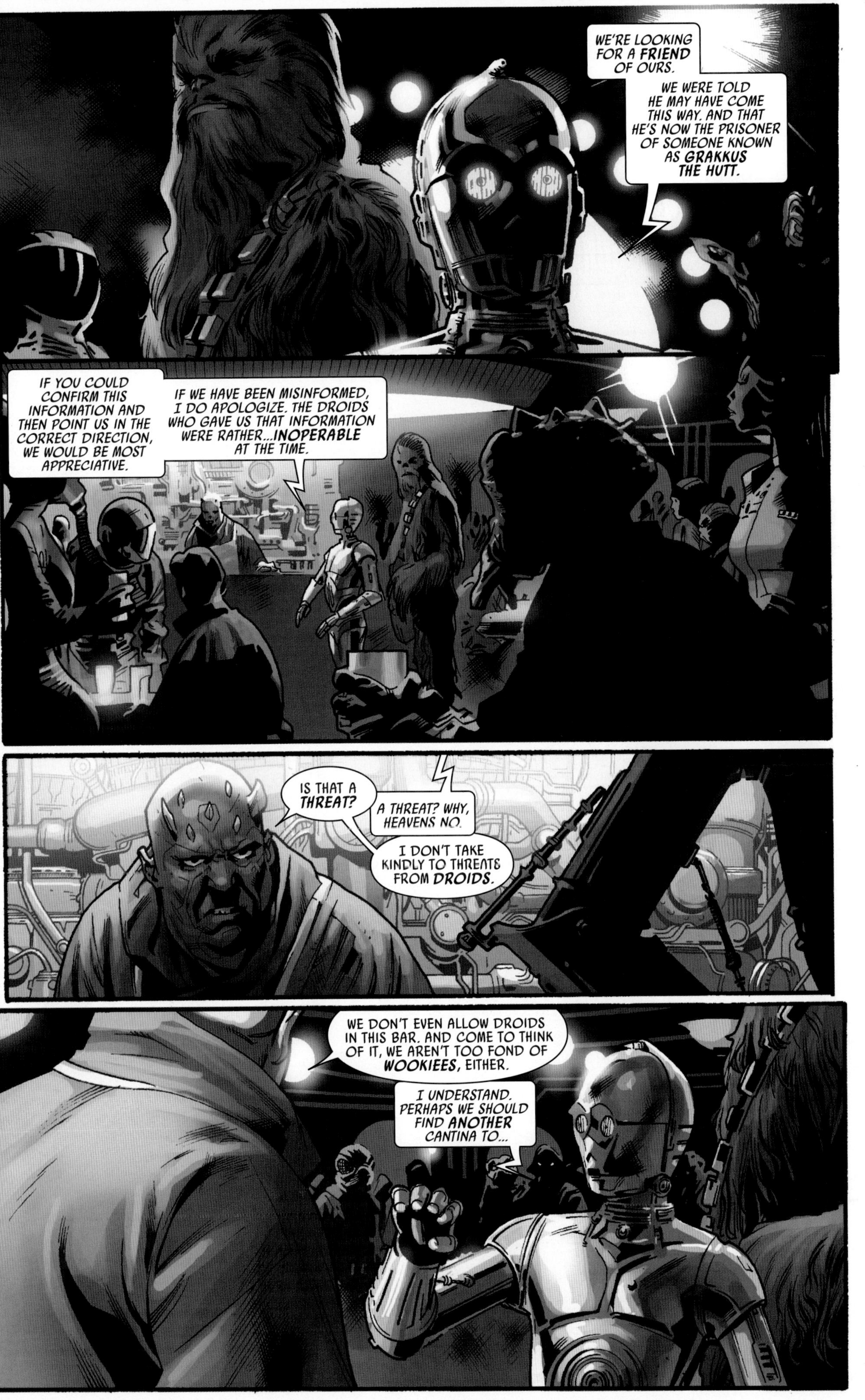
WE'RE LOOKING FOR A FRIEND OF OURS.
WE WERE TOLD HE MAY HAVE COME THIS WAY. AND THAT HE'S NOW THE PRISONER OF SOMEONE KNOWN AS GRAKKUS THE HUTT.
IF YOU COULD CONFIRM THIS INFORMATION AND THEN POINT US IN THE CORRECT DIRECTION, WE WOULD BE MOST APPRECIATIVE.
IF WE HAVE BEEN MISINFORMED, I DO APOLOGIZE. THE DROIDS WHO GAVE US THAT INFORMATION WERE RATHER...INOPERABLE AT THE TIME.
IS THAT A THREAT?
A THREAT? WHY, HEAVENS NO.
I DON'T TAKE KINDLY TO THREATS FROM DROIDS.
WE DON'T EVEN ALLOW DROIDS IN THIS BAR. AND COME TO THINK OF IT, WE AREN'T TOO FOND OF WOOKIEES, EITHER.
I UNDERSTAND. PERHAPS WE SHOULD FIND ANOTHER CANTINA TO...

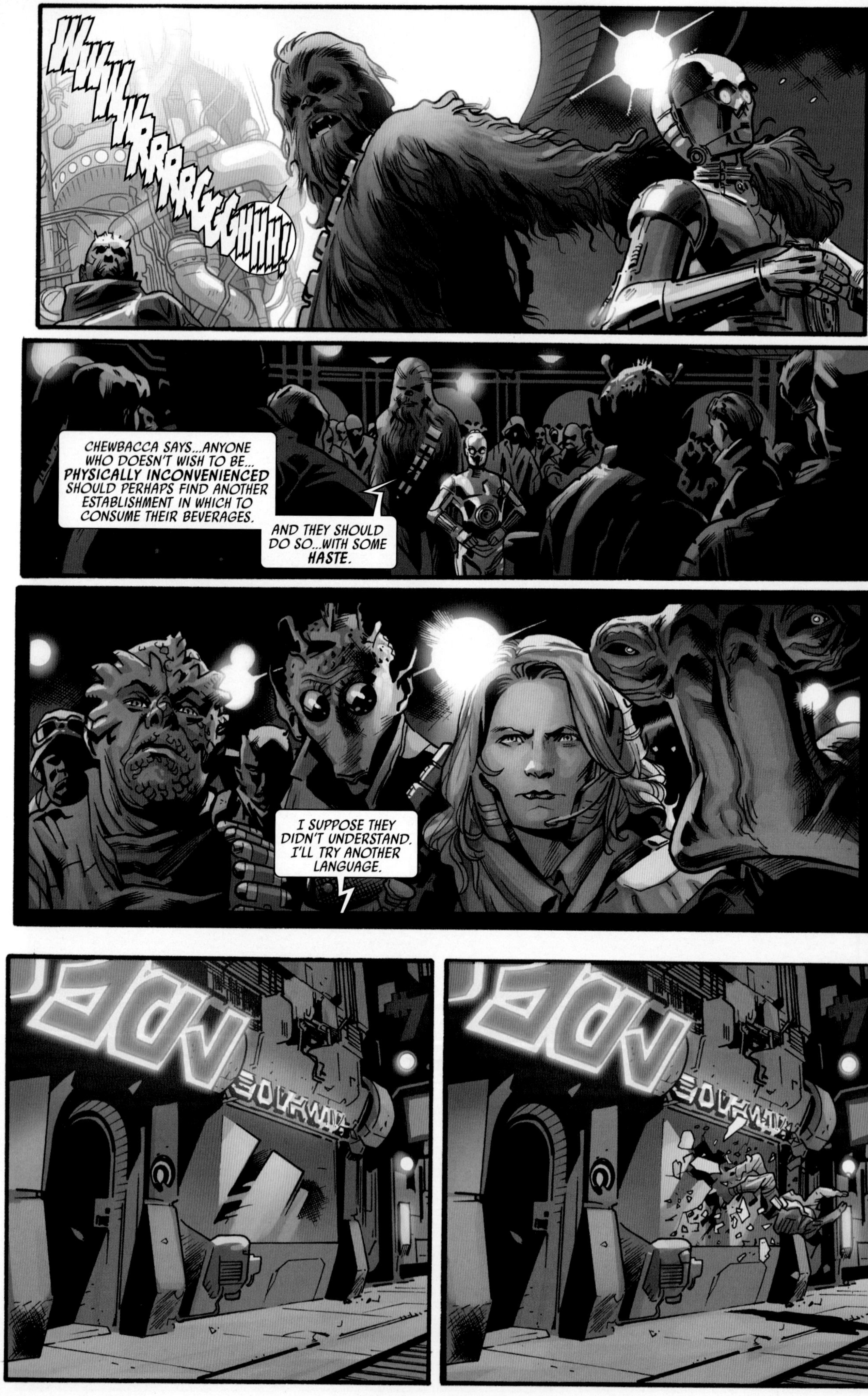
WWWWRRRRRGGHHH!!
CHEWBACCA SAYS...ANYONE WHO DOESN'T WISH TO BE... PHYSICALLY INCONVENIENCED SHOULD PERHAPS FIND ANOTHER ESTABLISHMENT IN WHICH TO CONSUME THEIR BEVERAGES.
AND THEY SHOULD DO SO...WITH SOME HASTE.
I SUPPOSE THEY DIDN'T UNDERSTAND. I'LL TRY ANOTHER LANGUAGE.

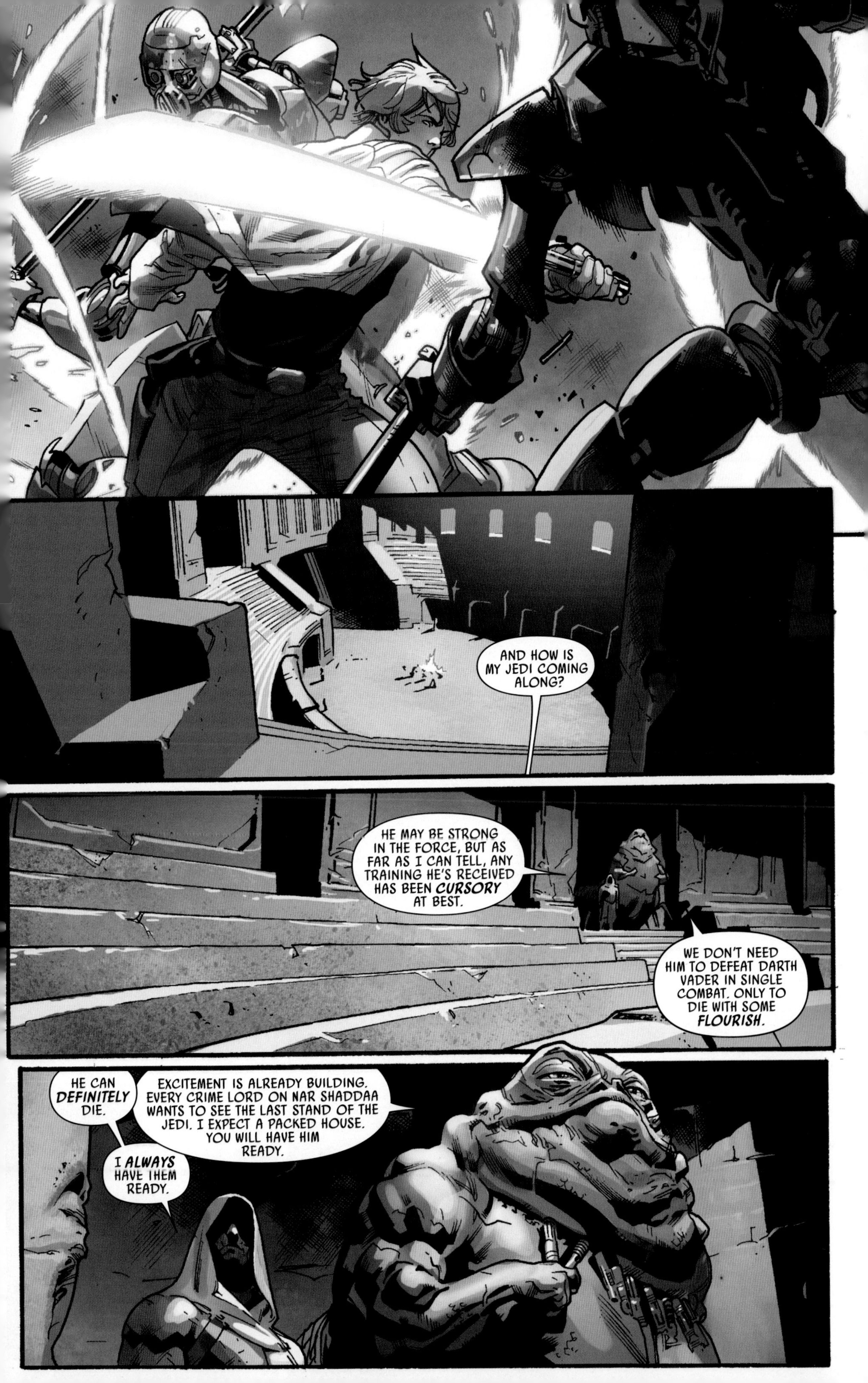
AND HOW IS MY JEDI COMING ALONG?
HE MAY BE STRONG IN THE FORCE, BUT AS FAR AS I CAN TELL, ANY TRAINING HE'S RECEIVED HAS BEEN CURSORY AT BEST.
WE DON'T NEED HIM TO DEFEAT DARTH VADER IN SINGLE COMBAT. ONLY TO DIE WITH SOME FLOURISH.
HE CAN DEFINITELY DIE.
EXCITEMENT IS ALREADY BUILDING. EVERY CRIME LORD ON NAR SHADDAA WANTS TO SEE THE LAST STAND OF THE JEDI. I EXPECT A PACKED HOUSE. YOU WILL HAVE HIM READY.
I ALWAYS HAVE THEM READY.

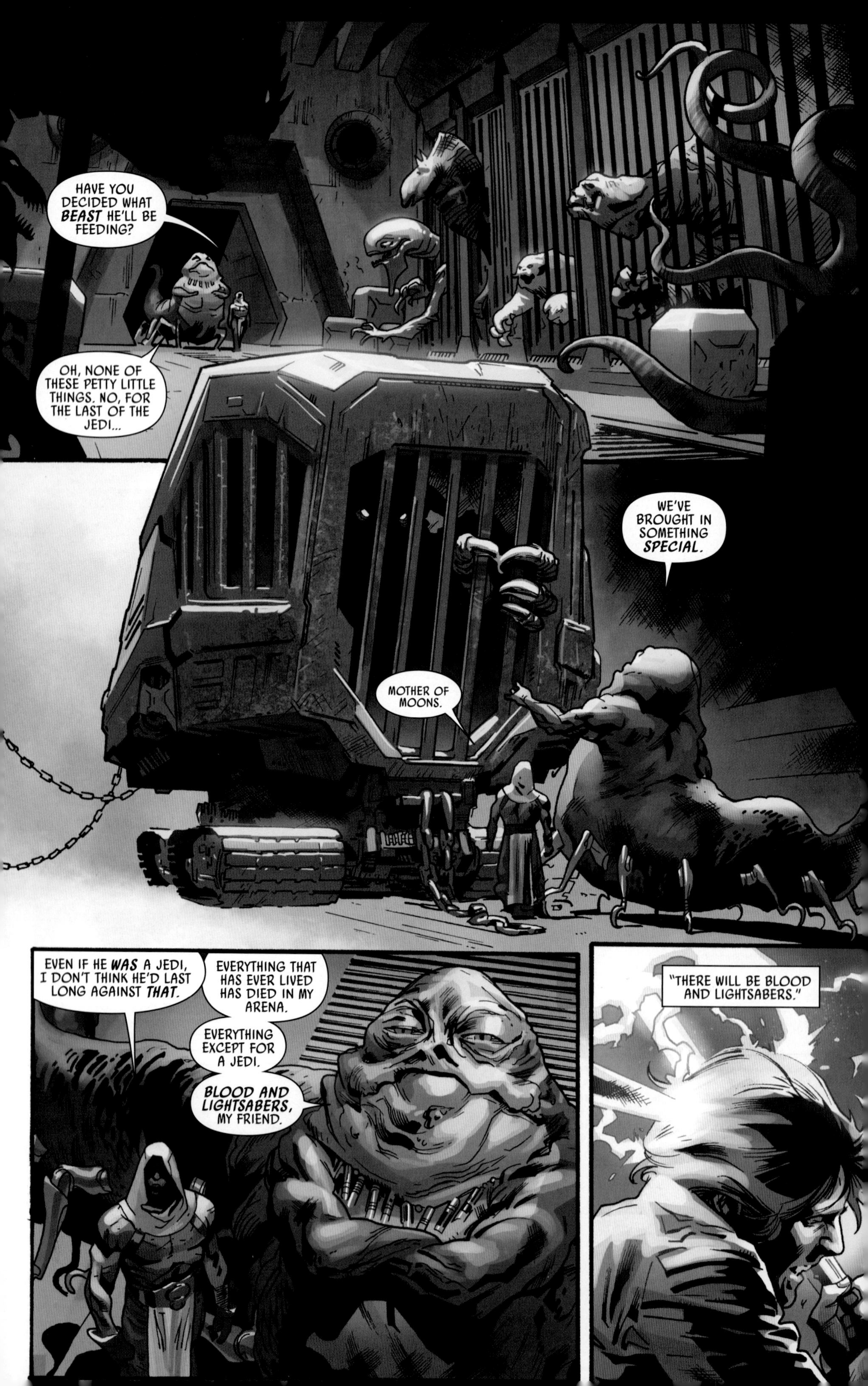
HAVE YOU DECIDED WHAT BEAST HE'LL BE FEEDING?
OH, NONE OF THESE PETTY LITTLE THINGS. NO, FOR THE LAST OF THE JEDI...
WE'VE BROUGHT IN SOMETHING SPECIAL.
MOTHER OF MOONS.
EVEN IF HE WAS A JEDI, I DON'T THINK HE'D LAST LONG AGAINST THAT.
EVERYTHING THAT HAS EVER LIVED HAS DIED IN MY ARENA.
EVERYTHING EXCEPT FOR A JEDI.
BLOOD AND LIGHTSABERS, MY FRIEND.
"THERE WILL BE BLOOD AND LIGHTSABERS."

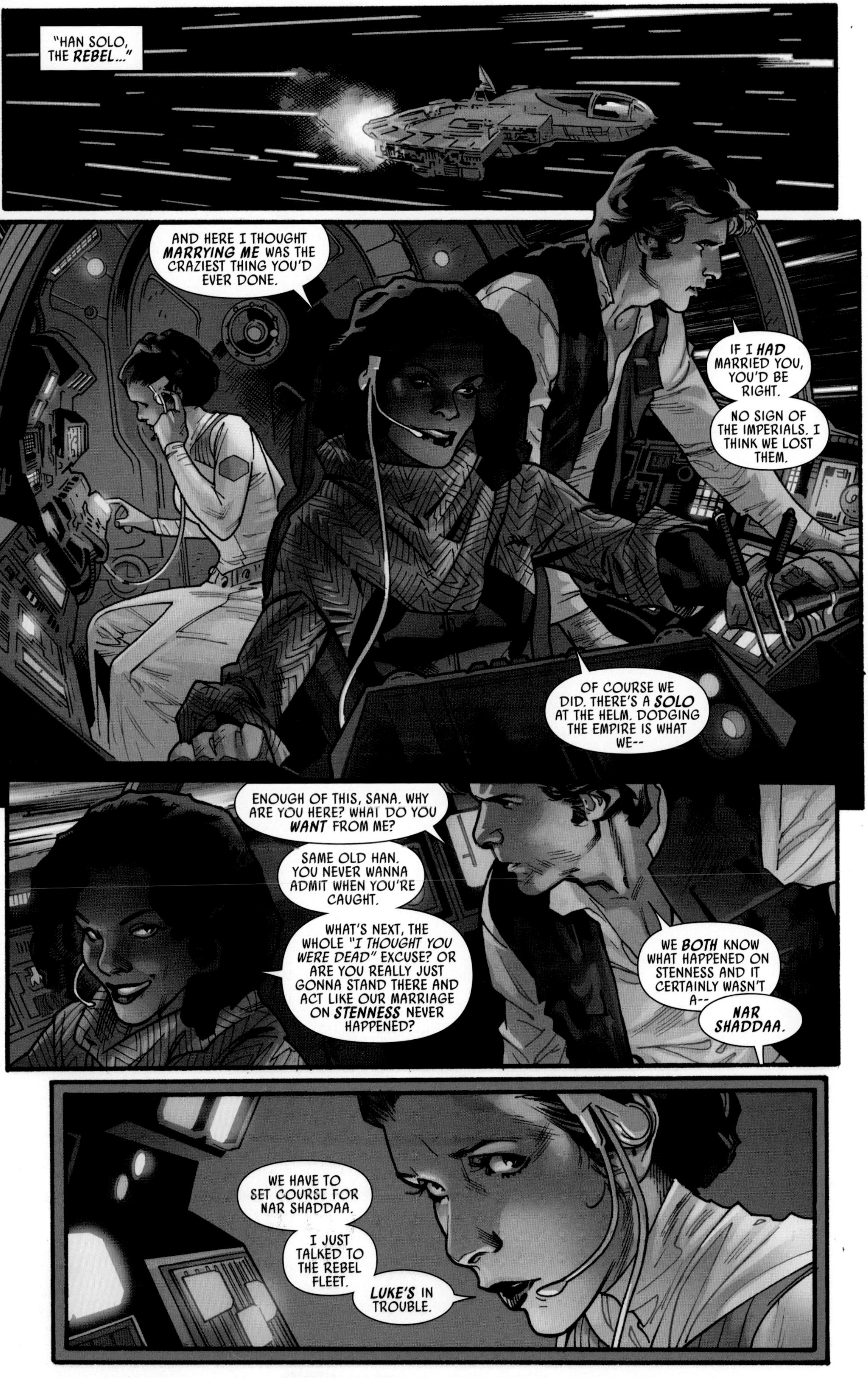
"HAN SOLO, THE REBEL..."
AND HERE I THOUGHT MARRYING ME WAS THE CRAZIEST THING YOU'D EVER DONE.
IF I HAD MARRIED YOU, YOU'D BE RIGHT.
NO SIGN OF THE IMPERIALS. I THINK WE LOST THEM.
OF COURSE WE DID. THERE'S A SOLO AT THE HELM. DODGING THE EMPIRE IS WHAT WE--
ENOUGH OF THIS, SANA. WHY ARE YOU HERE? WHAT DO YOU WANT FROM ME?
SAME OLD HAN. YOU NEVER WANNA ADMIT WHEN YOU'RE CAUGHT.
WHAT'S NEXT, THE WHOLE "I THOUGHT YOU WERE DEAD" EXCUSE? OR ARE YOU REALLY JUST GONNA STAND THERE AND ACT LIKE OUR MARRIAGE ON STENNESS NEVER HAPPENED?
WE BOTH KNOW WHAT HAPPENED ON STENNESS AND IT CERTAINLY WASN'T A--
NAR SHADDAA.
WE HAVE TO SET COURSE FOR NAR SHADDAA.
I JUST TALKED TO THE REBEL FLEET.
LUKE'S IN TROUBLE.

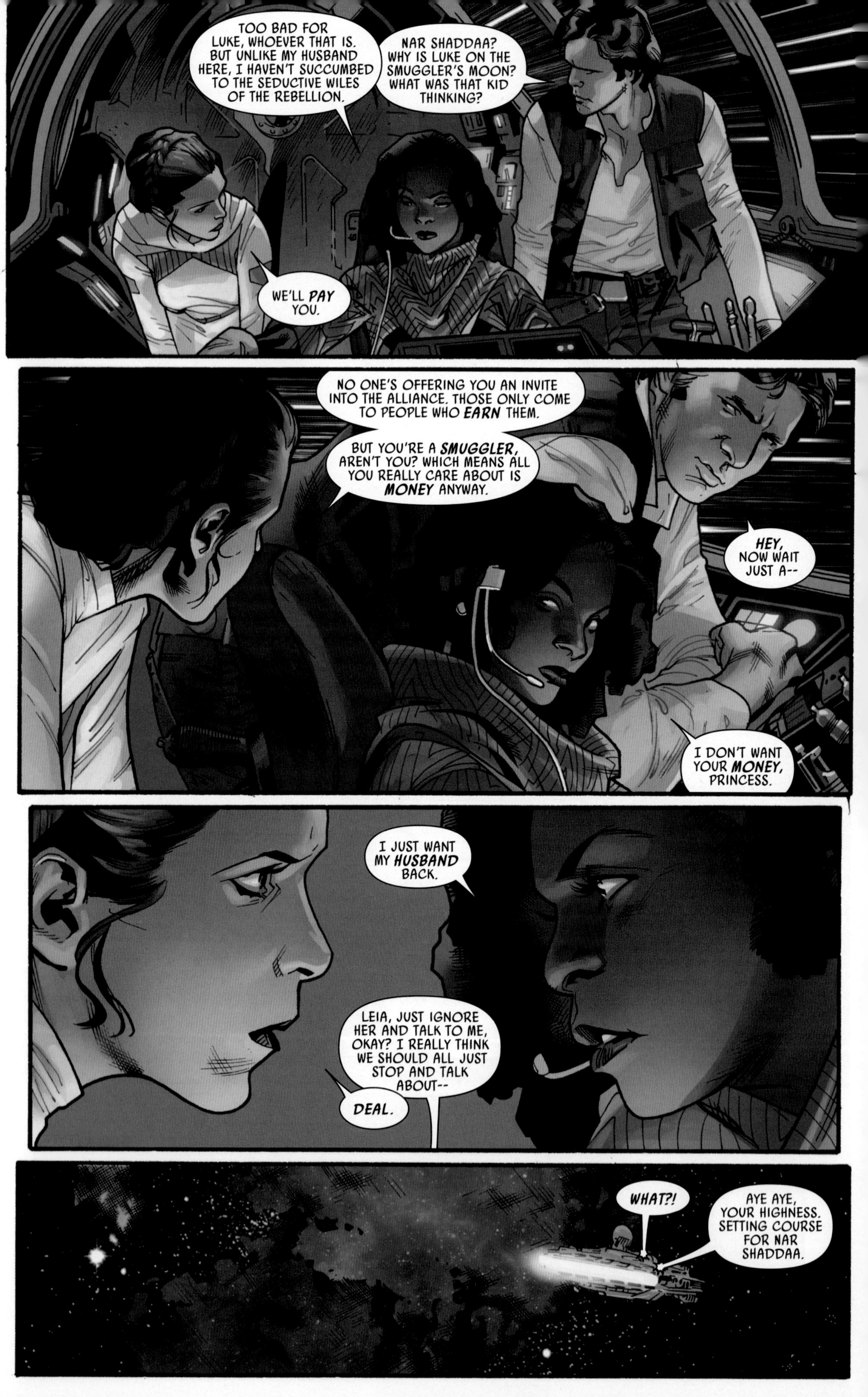
TOO BAD FOR LUKE, WHOEVER THAT IS. BUT UNLIKE MY HUSBAND HERE, I HAVEN'T SUCCUMBED TO THE SEDUCTIVE WILES OF THE REBELLION.
NAR SHADDAA? WHY IS LUKE ON THE SMUGGLER'S MOON? WHAT WAS THAT KID THINKING?
WE'LL PAY YOU.
NO ONE'S OFFERING YOU AN INVITE INTO THE ALLIANCE. THOSE ONLY COME TO PEOPLE WHO EARN THEM.
BUT YOU'RE A SMUGGLER, AREN'T YOU? WHICH MEANS ALL YOU REALLY CARE ABOUT IS MONEY ANYWAY.
HEY, NOW WAIT JUST A--
I DON'T WANT YOUR MONEY, PRINCESS.
I JUST WANT MY HUSBAND BACK.
LEIA, JUST IGNORE HER AND TALK TO ME, OKAY? I REALLY THINK WE SHOULD ALL JUST STOP AND TALK ABOUT--
DEAL.
WHAT?!
AYE AYE, YOUR HIGHNESS. SETTING COURSE FOR NAR SHADDAA.

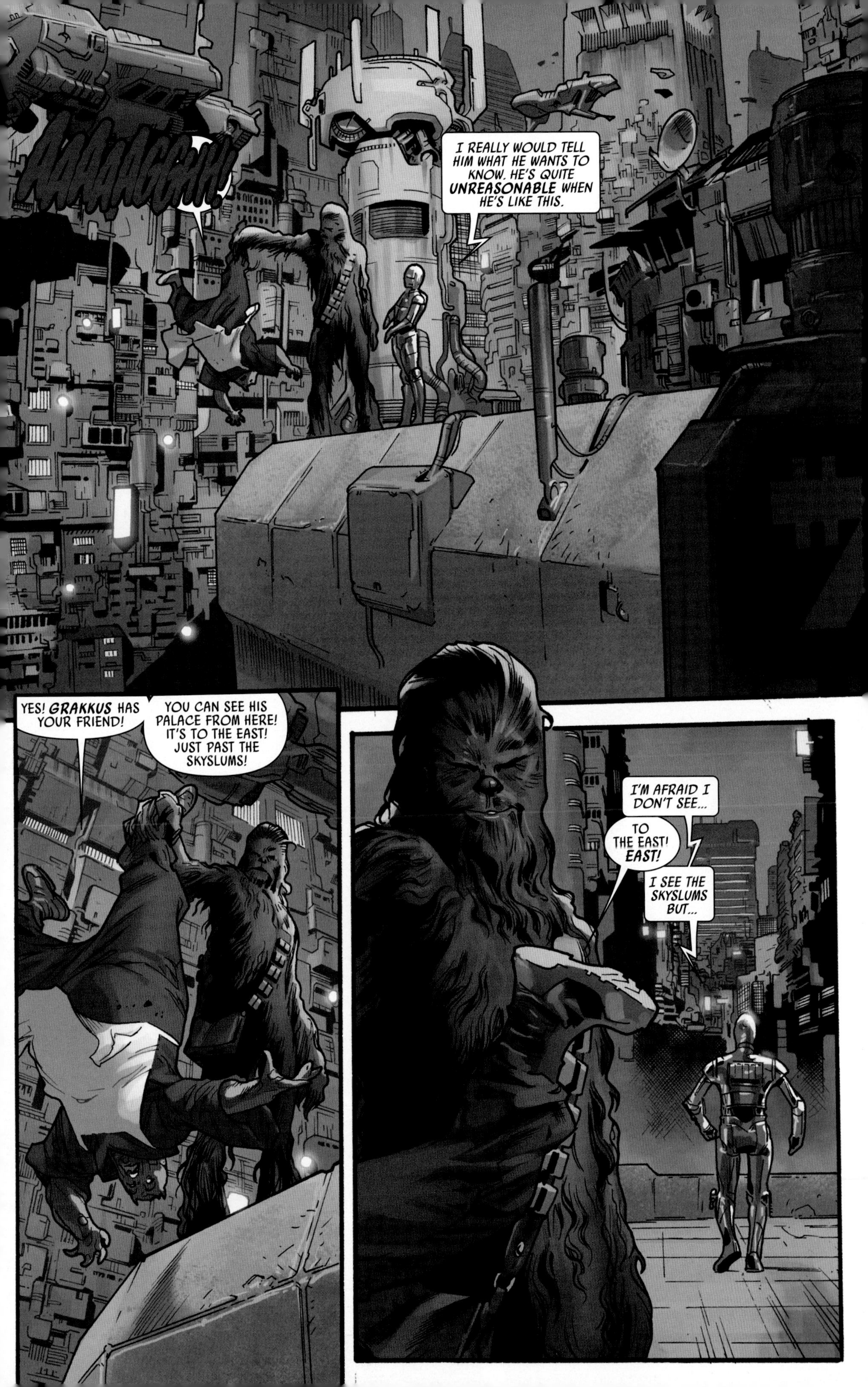
AAAAAGGHH!
I REALLY WOULD TELL HIM WHAT HE WANTS TO KNOW. HE'S QUITE UNREASONABLE WHEN HE'S LIKE THIS.
YES! GRAKKUS HAS YOUR FRIEND!
YOU CAN SEE HIS PALACE FROM HERE! IT'S TO THE EAST! JUST PAST THE SKYSLUMS!
I'M AFRAID I DON'T SEE...
TO THE EAST! EAST!
I SEE THE SKYSLUMS BUT...

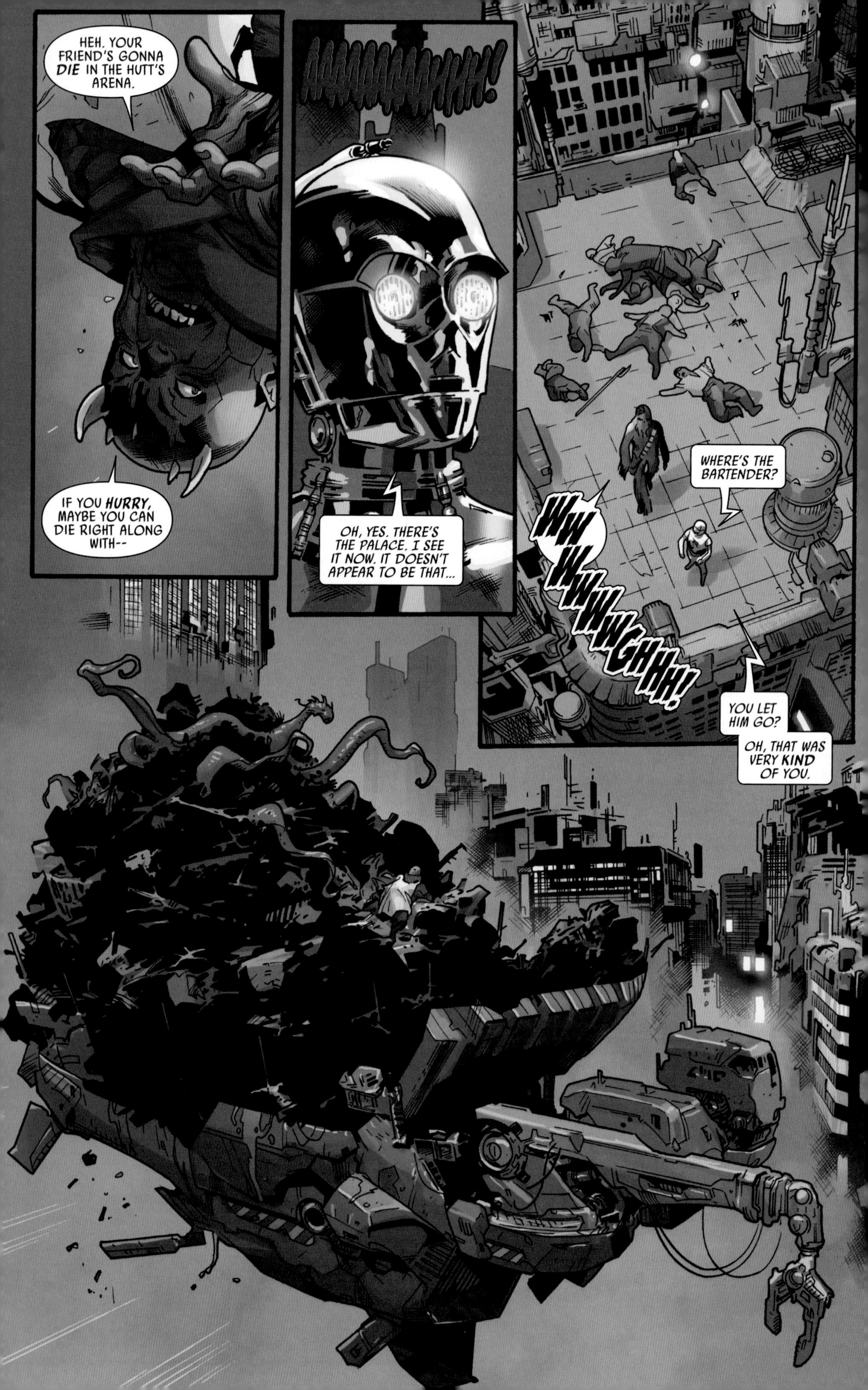
HEH. YOUR FRIEND'S GONNA *DIE* IN THE HUTT'S ARENA.
IF YOU *HURRY,* MAYBE YOU CAN DIE RIGHT ALONG WITH--
AAAAAAAAAAHHH!
OH, YES. THERE'S THE PALACE. I SEE IT NOW. IT DOESN'T APPEAR TO BE THAT...
WHERE'S THE BARTENDER?
WWWWWWGHHH!
YOU LET HIM GO?
OH, THAT WAS VERY **KIND** OF YOU.

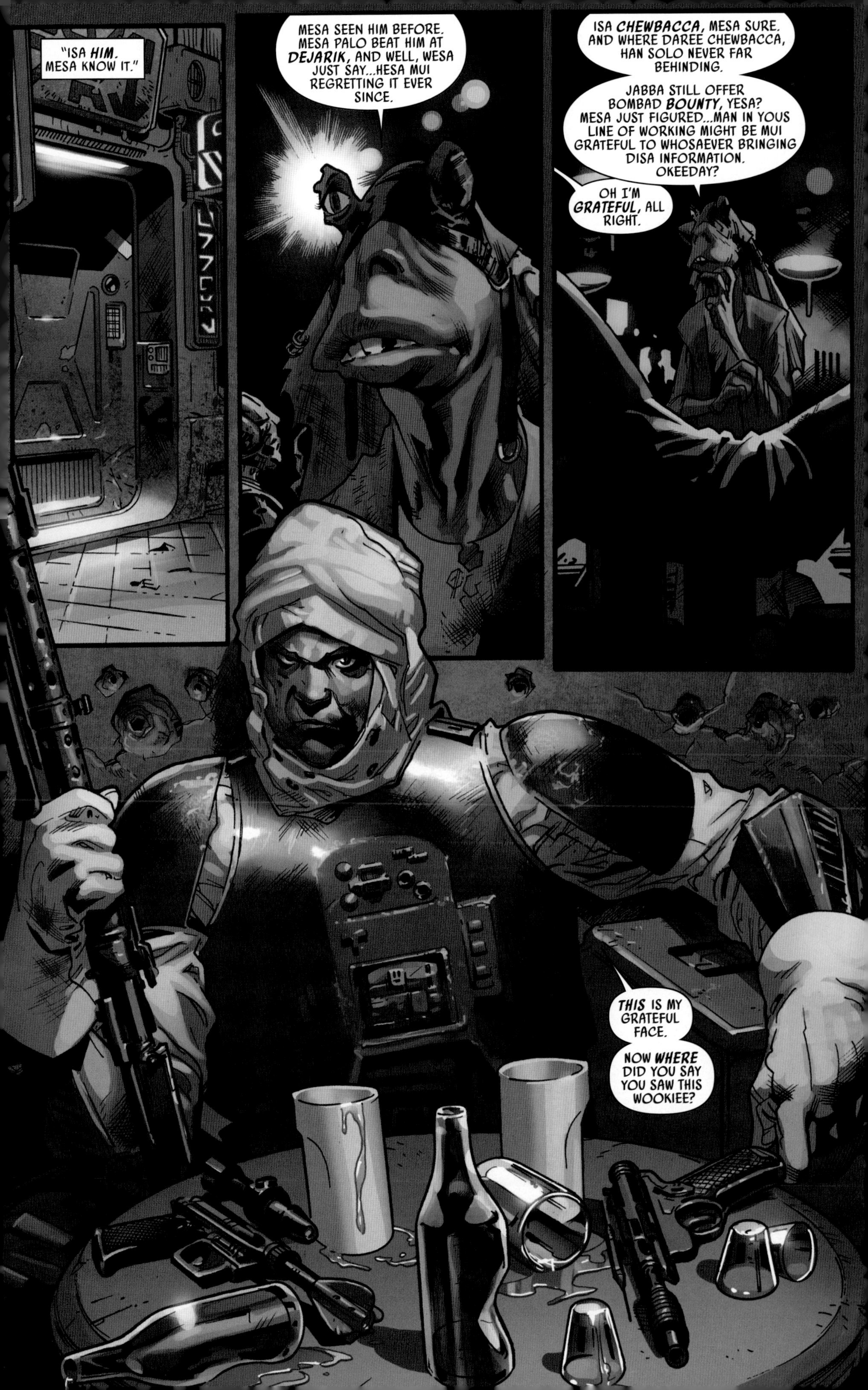
"ISA HIM. MESA KNOW IT."
MESA SEEN HIM BEFORE. MESA PALO BEAT HIM AT DEJARIK, AND WELL, WESA JUST SAY...HESA MUI REGRETTING IT EVER SINCE.
ISA CHEWBACCA, MESA SURE. AND WHERE DAREE CHEWBACCA, HAN SOLO NEVER FAR BEHINDING.
JABBA STILL OFFER BOMBAD BOUNTY, YESA? MESA JUST FIGURED...MAN IN YOUS LINE OF WORKING MIGHT BE MUI GRATEFUL TO WHOSAEVER BRINGING DISA INFORMATION. OKEEDAY?
OH I'M GRATEFUL, ALL RIGHT.
THIS IS MY GRATEFUL FACE.
NOW WHERE DID YOU SAY YOU SAW THIS WOOKIEE?

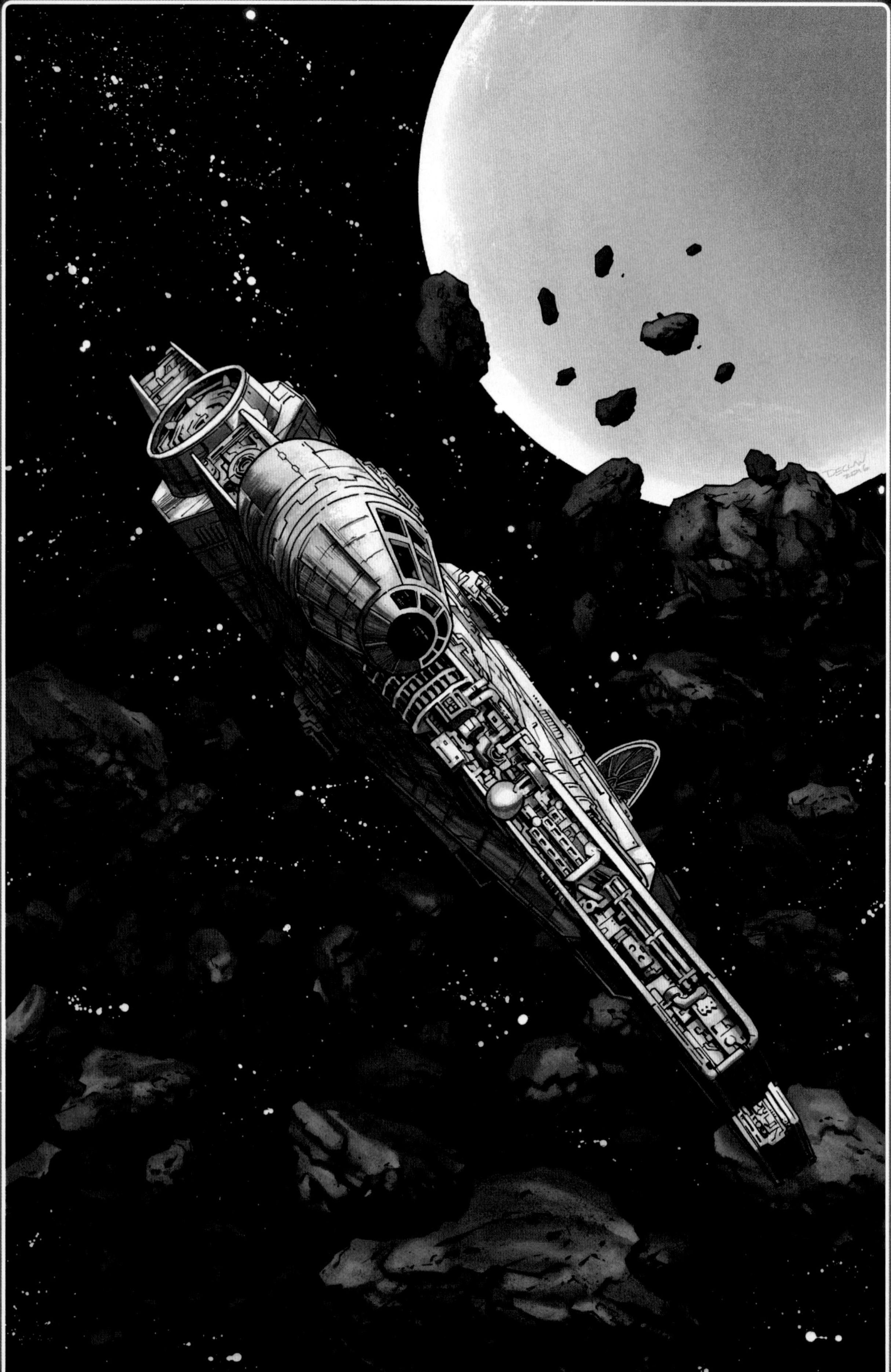
DECLAN 2016

HAN SOLO 3 Variant
by **DECLAN SHALVEY & JORDIE BELLAIRE**

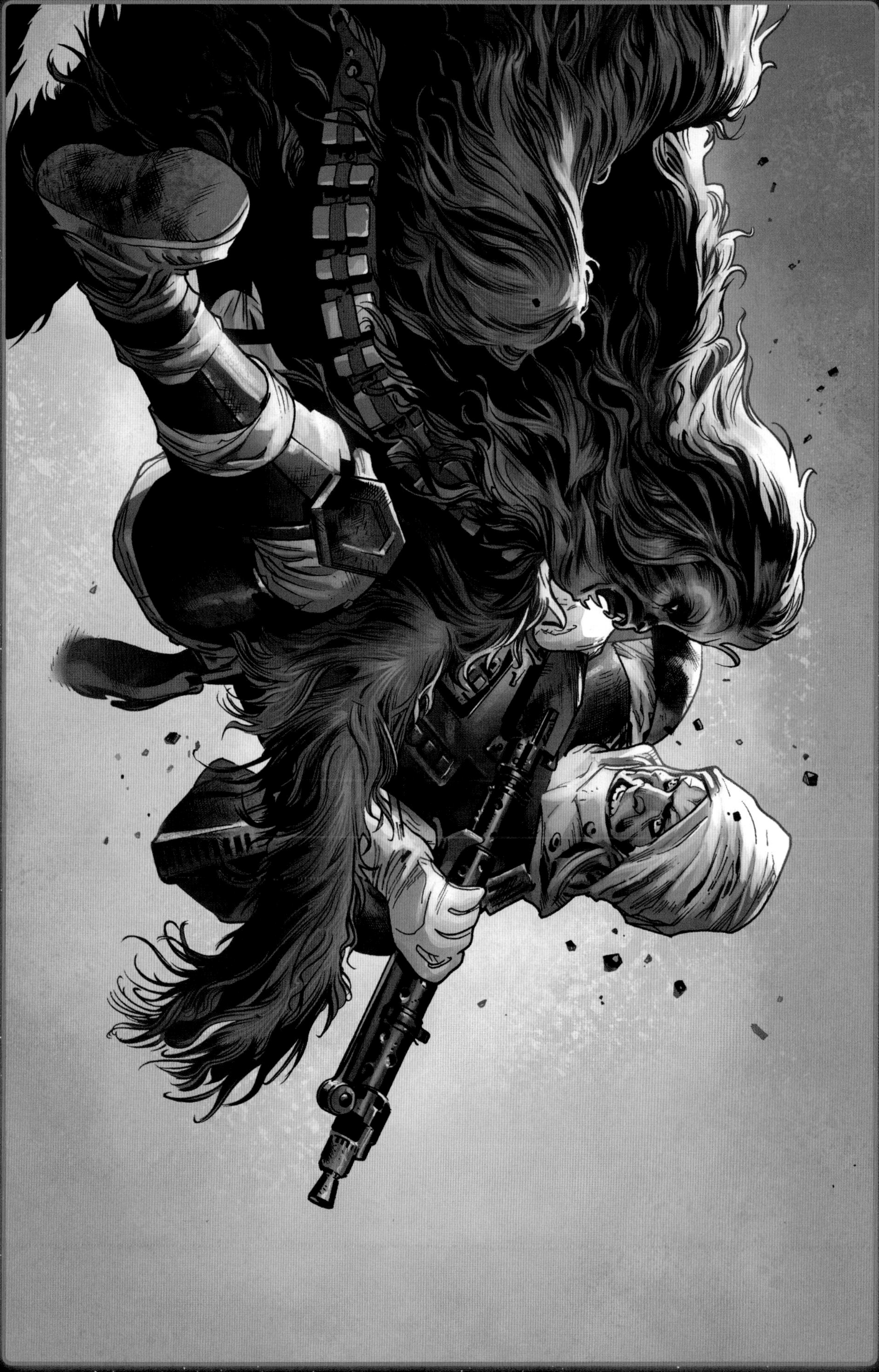

STAR WARS 11

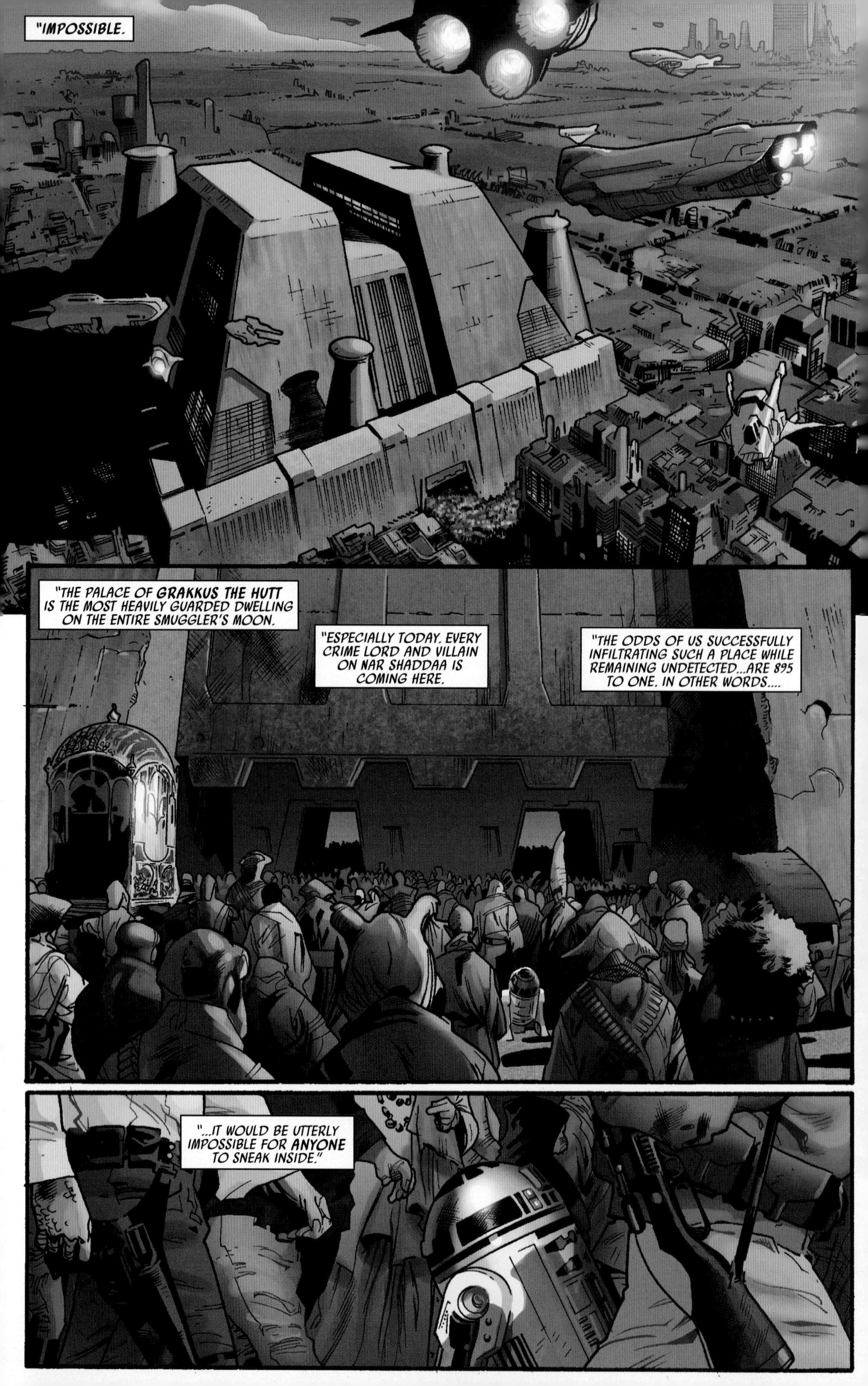
"IMPOSSIBLE.
"THE PALACE OF GRAKKUS THE HUTT IS THE MOST HEAVILY GUARDED DWELLING ON THE ENTIRE SMUGGLER'S MOON.
"ESPECIALLY TODAY. EVERY CRIME LORD AND VILLAIN ON NAR SHADDAA IS COMING HERE.
"THE ODDS OF US SUCCESSFULLY INFILTRATING SUCH A PLACE WHILE REMAINING UNDETECTED...ARE 895 TO ONE. IN OTHER WORDS....
"...IT WOULD BE UTTERLY IMPOSSIBLE FOR ANYONE TO SNEAK INSIDE."

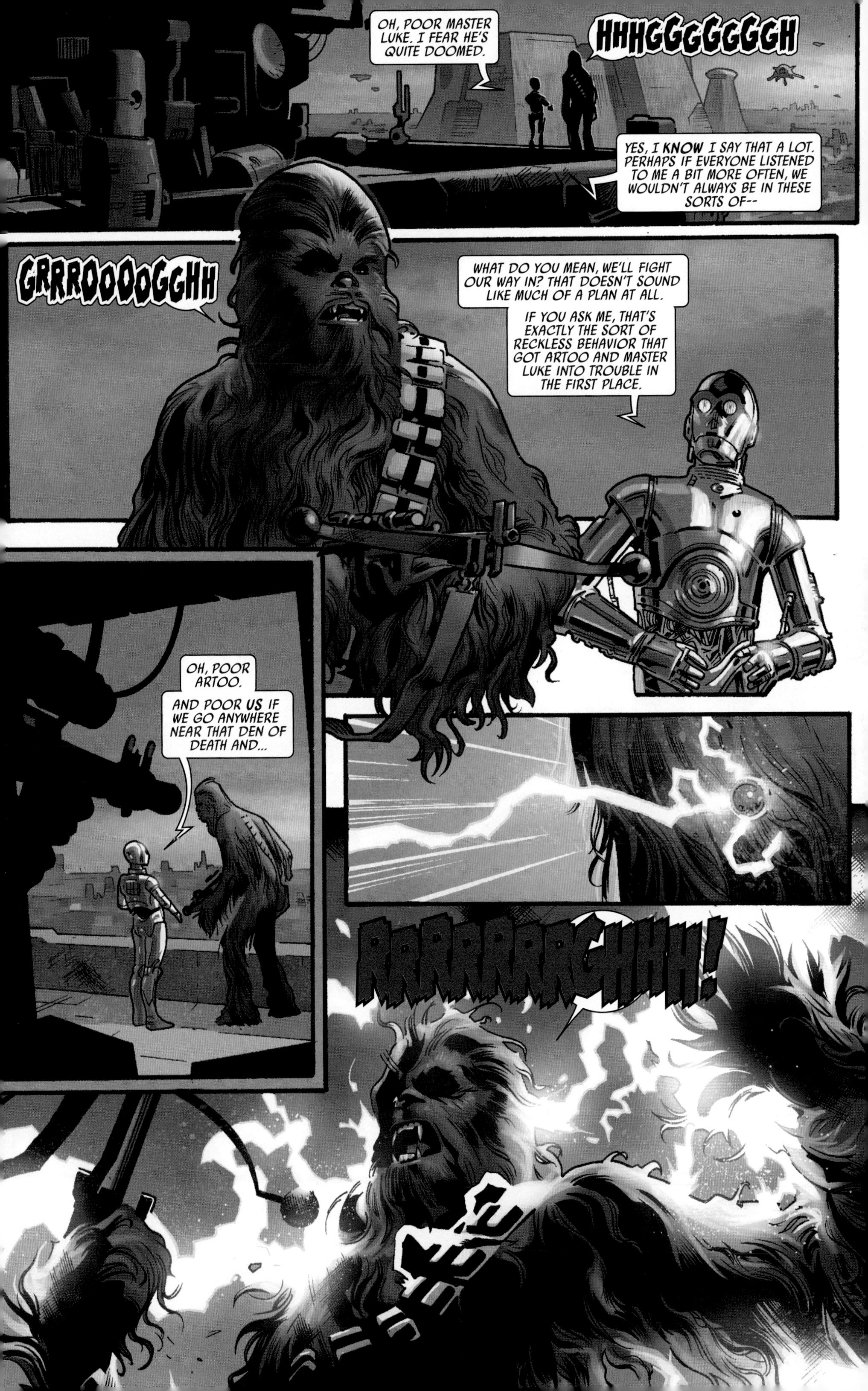
OH, POOR MASTER LUKE. I FEAR HE'S QUITE DOOMED.
HHHGGGGGGGH
YES, I KNOW I SAY THAT A LOT. PERHAPS IF EVERYONE LISTENED TO ME A BIT MORE OFTEN, WE WOULDN'T ALWAYS BE IN THESE SORTS OF--
GRRROOOOOGGHH
WHAT DO YOU MEAN, WE'LL FIGHT OUR WAY IN? THAT DOESN'T SOUND LIKE MUCH OF A PLAN AT ALL.
IF YOU ASK ME, THAT'S EXACTLY THE SORT OF RECKLESS BEHAVIOR THAT GOT ARTOO AND MASTER LUKE INTO TROUBLE IN THE FIRST PLACE.
OH, POOR ARTOO.
AND POOR US IF WE GO ANYWHERE NEAR THAT DEN OF DEATH AND...
RRRRRRRRGHHH!

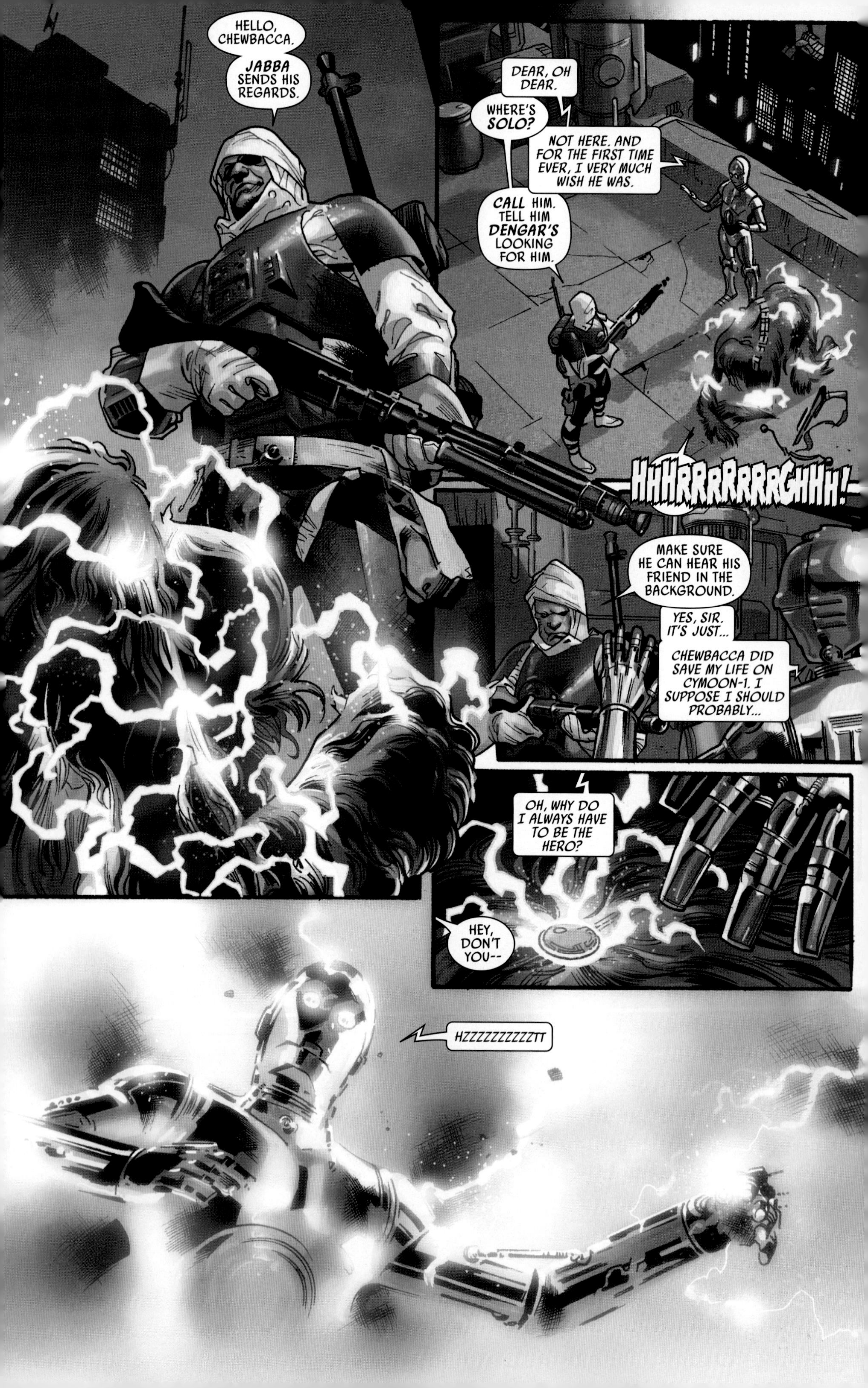
HELLO, CHEWBACCA.
JABBA SENDS HIS REGARDS.
DEAR, OH DEAR.
WHERE'S SOLO?
NOT HERE. AND FOR THE FIRST TIME EVER, I VERY MUCH WISH HE WAS.
CALL HIM. TELL HIM DENGAR'S LOOKING FOR HIM.
HHHRRRRRRRGHHH!
MAKE SURE HE CAN HEAR HIS FRIEND IN THE BACKGROUND.
YES, SIR. IT'S JUST...
CHEWBACCA DID SAVE MY LIFE ON CYMOON-1. I SUPPOSE I SHOULD PROBABLY...
OH, WHY DO I ALWAYS HAVE TO BE THE HERO?
HEY, DON'T YOU--
HZZZZZZZZZZZTT

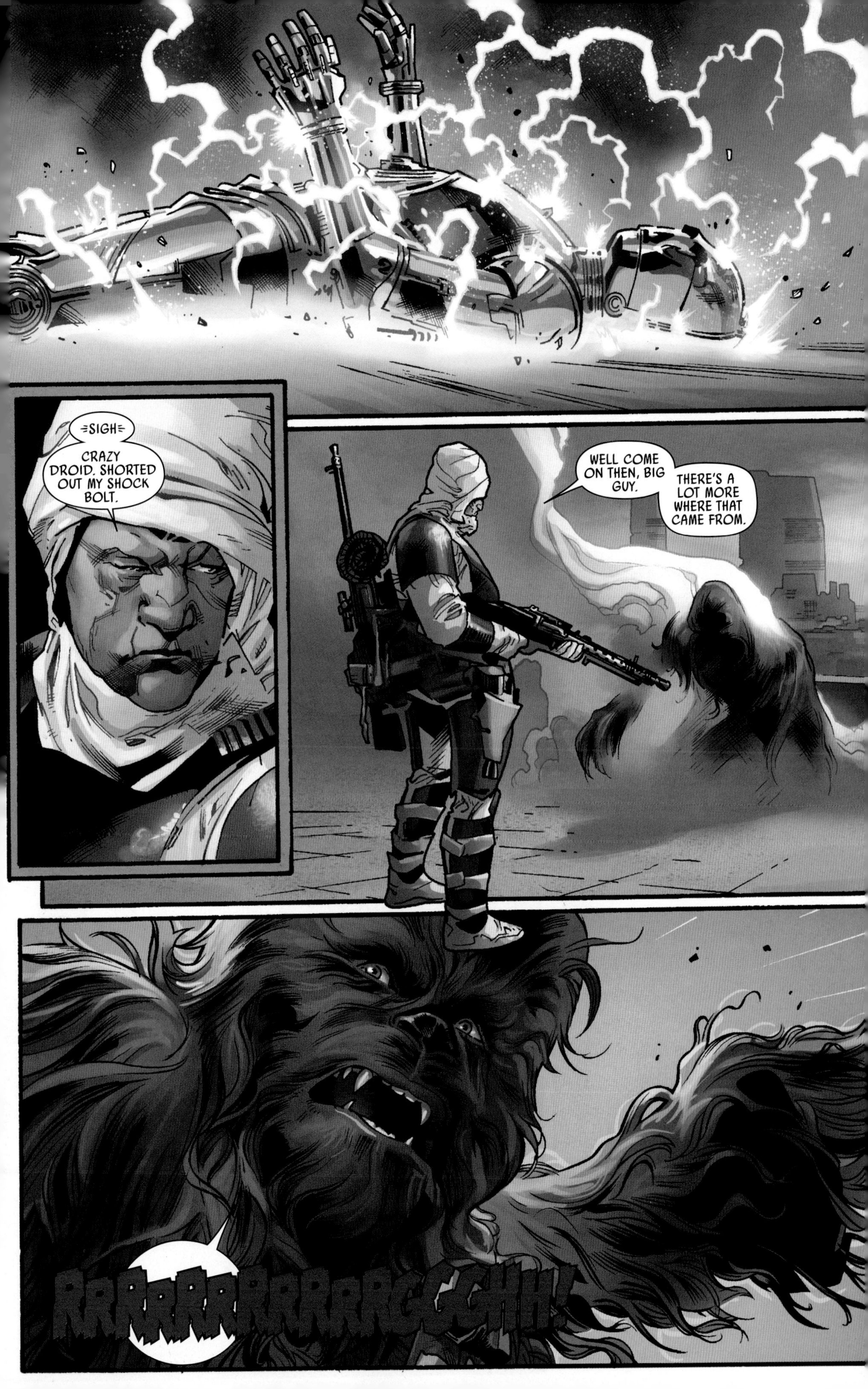

=SIGH=
CRAZY DROID. SHORTED OUT MY SHOCK BOLT.
WELL COME ON THEN, BIG GUY.
THERE'S A LOT MORE WHERE THAT CAME FROM.
RRRRRRRRRRRGGHH!

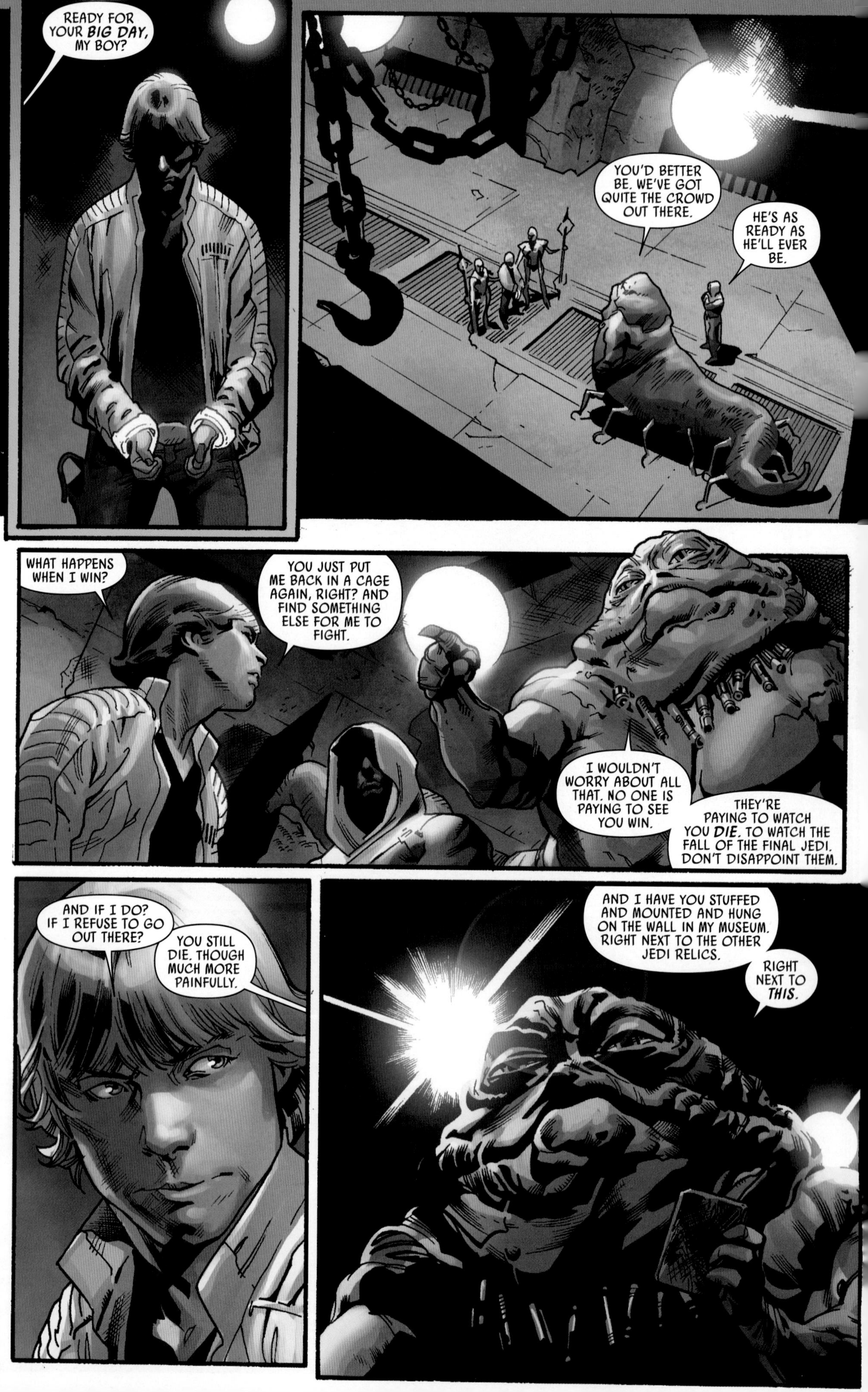
READY FOR YOUR BIG DAY, MY BOY?
YOU'D BETTER BE. WE'VE GOT QUITE THE CROWD OUT THERE.
HE'S AS READY AS HE'LL EVER BE.
WHAT HAPPENS WHEN I WIN?
YOU JUST PUT ME BACK IN A CAGE AGAIN, RIGHT? AND FIND SOMETHING ELSE FOR ME TO FIGHT.
I WOULDN'T WORRY ABOUT ALL THAT. NO ONE IS PAYING TO SEE YOU WIN.
THEY'RE PAYING TO WATCH YOU DIE. TO WATCH THE FALL OF THE FINAL JEDI. DON'T DISAPPOINT THEM.
AND IF I DO? IF I REFUSE TO GO OUT THERE?
YOU STILL DIE. THOUGH MUCH MORE PAINFULLY.
AND I HAVE YOU STUFFED AND MOUNTED AND HUNG ON THE WALL IN MY MUSEUM. RIGHT NEXT TO THE OTHER JEDI RELICS.
RIGHT NEXT TO THIS.

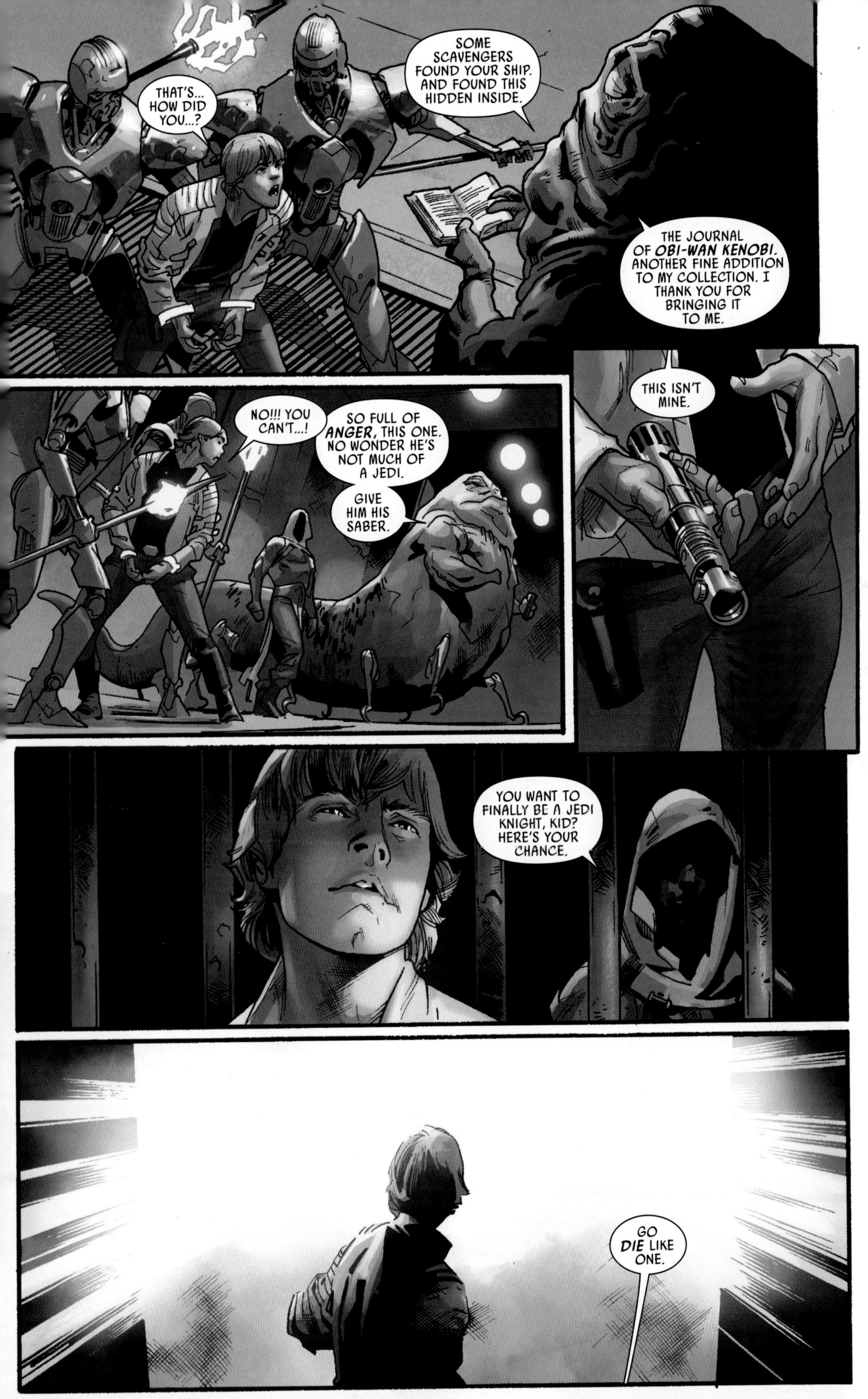
THAT'S... HOW DID YOU...?
SOME SCAVENGERS FOUND YOUR SHIP. AND FOUND THIS HIDDEN INSIDE.
THE JOURNAL OF OBI-WAN KENOBI. ANOTHER FINE ADDITION TO MY COLLECTION. I THANK YOU FOR BRINGING IT TO ME.
NO!!! YOU CAN'T...!
SO FULL OF ANGER, THIS ONE. NO WONDER HE'S NOT MUCH OF A JEDI.
GIVE HIM HIS SABER.
THIS ISN'T MINE.
YOU WANT TO FINALLY BE A JEDI KNIGHT, KID? HERE'S YOUR CHANCE.
GO DIE LIKE ONE.

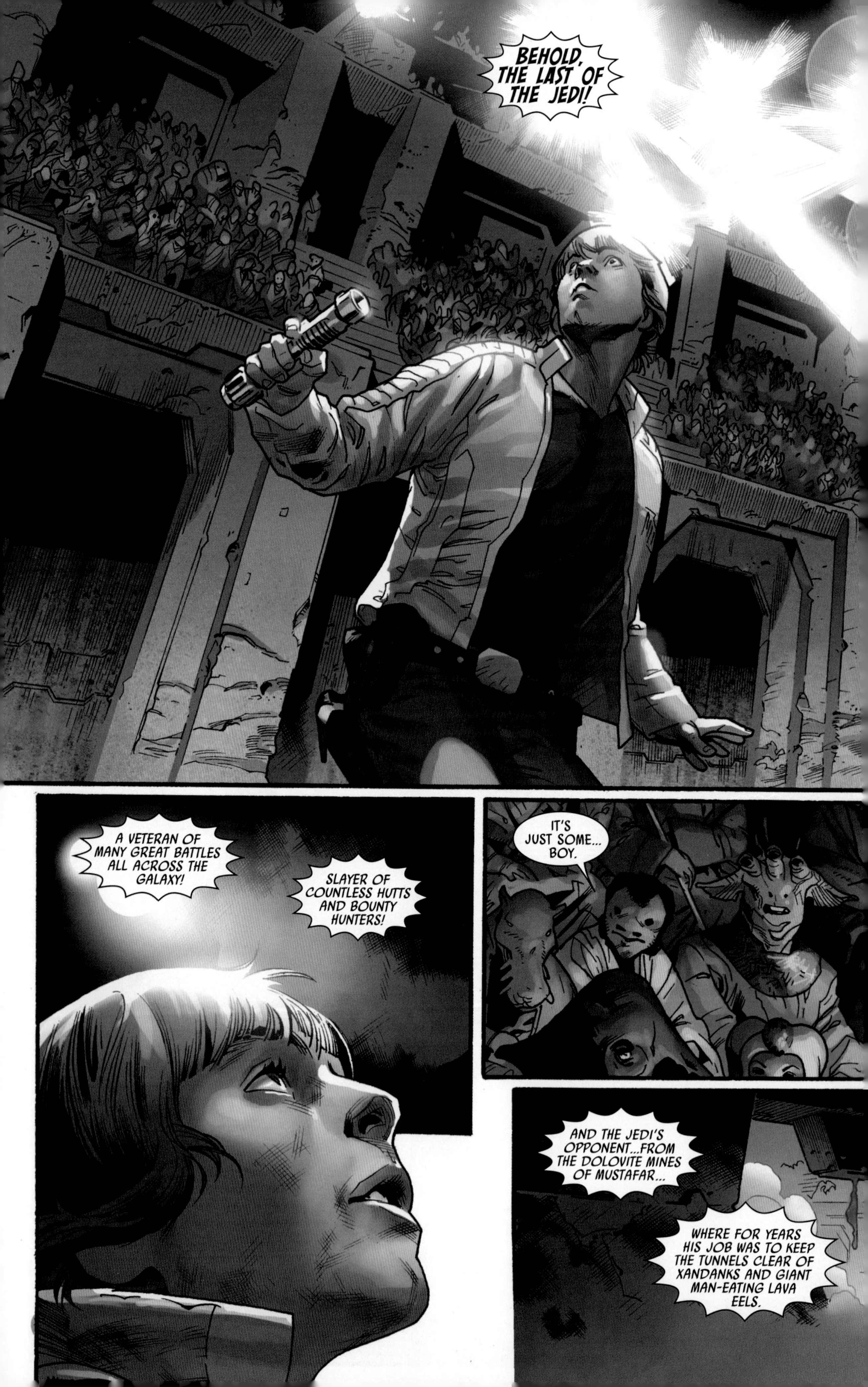
BEHOLD, THE LAST OF THE JEDI!
A VETERAN OF MANY GREAT BATTLES ALL ACROSS THE GALAXY!
SLAYER OF COUNTLESS HUTTS AND BOUNTY HUNTERS!
IT'S JUST SOME... BOY.
AND THE JEDI'S OPPONENT...FROM THE DOLOVITE MINES OF MUSTAFAR...
WHERE FOR YEARS HIS JOB WAS TO KEEP THE TUNNELS CLEAR OF XANDANKS AND GIANT MAN-EATING LAVA EELS.

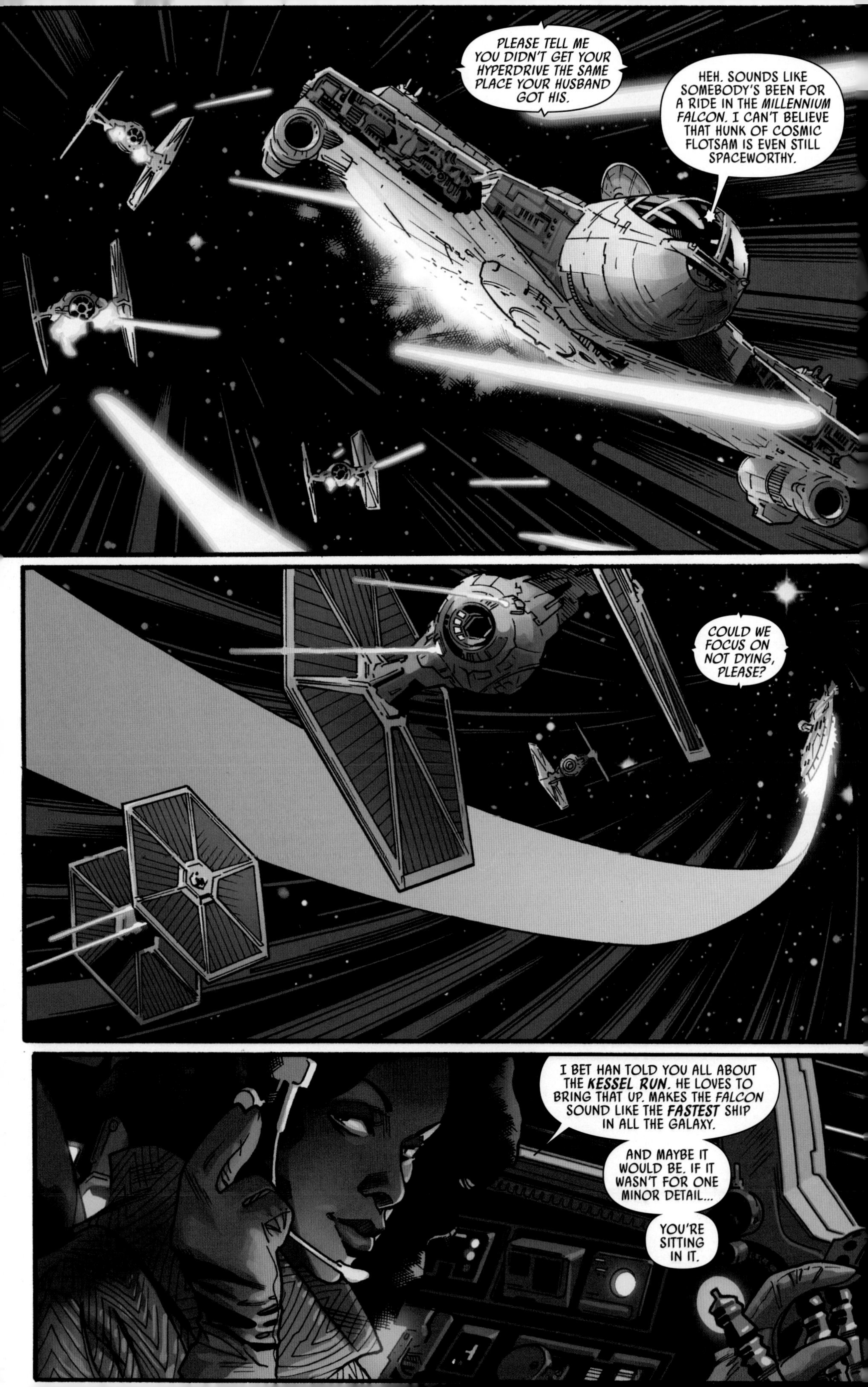
PLEASE TELL ME YOU DIDN'T GET YOUR HYPERDRIVE THE SAME PLACE YOUR HUSBAND GOT HIS.
HEH. SOUNDS LIKE SOMEBODY'S BEEN FOR A RIDE IN THE *MILLENNIUM FALCON*. I CAN'T BELIEVE THAT HUNK OF COSMIC FLOTSAM IS EVEN STILL SPACEWORTHY.
COULD WE FOCUS ON NOT DYING, PLEASE?
I BET HAN TOLD YOU ALL ABOUT THE ***KESSEL RUN.*** HE LOVES TO BRING THAT UP. MAKES THE *FALCON* SOUND LIKE THE ***FASTEST*** SHIP IN ALL THE GALAXY.
AND MAYBE IT WOULD BE. IF IT WASN'T FOR ONE MINOR DETAIL...
YOU'RE SITTING IN IT.

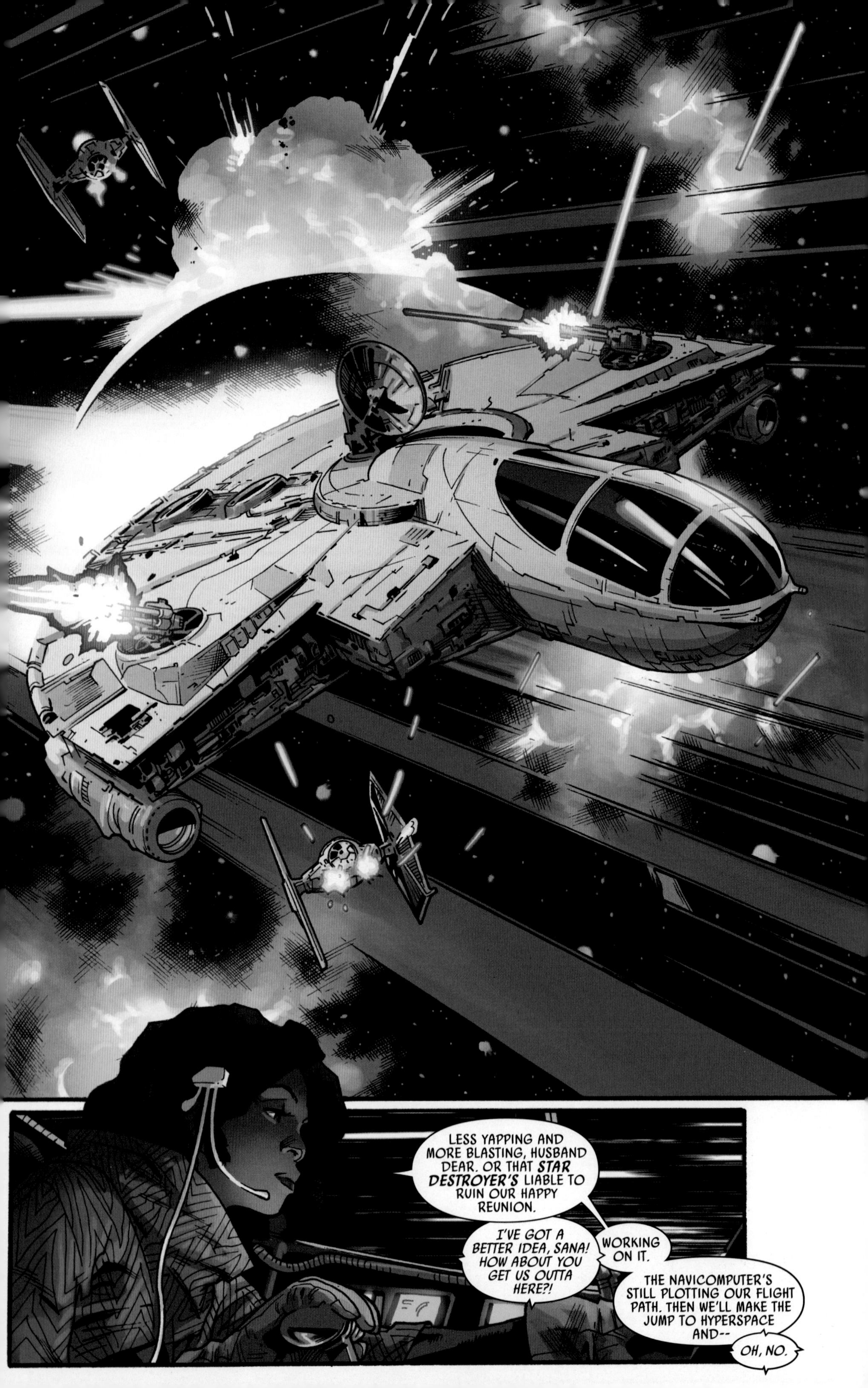
LESS YAPPING AND MORE BLASTING, HUSBAND DEAR. OR THAT STAR DESTROYER'S LIABLE TO RUIN OUR HAPPY REUNION.
I'VE GOT A BETTER IDEA, SANA! HOW ABOUT YOU GET US OUTTA HERE?!
WORKING ON IT.
THE NAVICOMPUTER'S STILL PLOTTING OUR FLIGHT PATH. THEN WE'LL MAKE THE JUMP TO HYPERSPACE AND--
OH, NO.

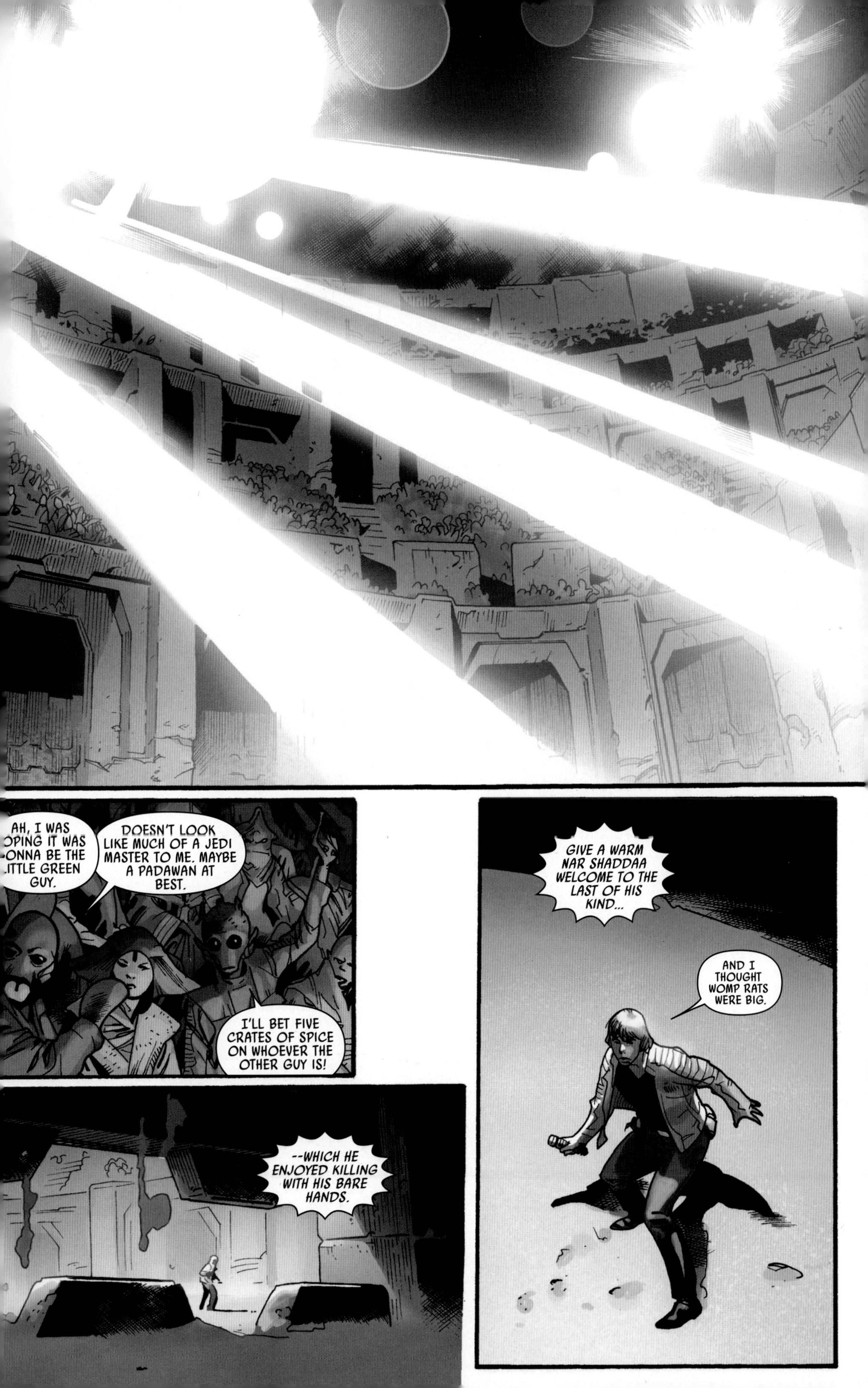
AH, I WAS
OPING IT WAS
ONNA BE THE
ITTLE GREEN
GUY.
DOESN'T LOOK LIKE MUCH OF A JEDI MASTER TO ME. MAYBE A PADAWAN AT BEST.
I'LL BET FIVE CRATES OF SPICE ON WHOEVER THE OTHER GUY IS!
GIVE A WARM NAR SHADDAA WELCOME TO THE LAST OF HIS KIND...
--WHICH HE ENJOYED KILLING WITH HIS BARE HANDS.
AND I THOUGHT WOMP RATS WERE BIG.

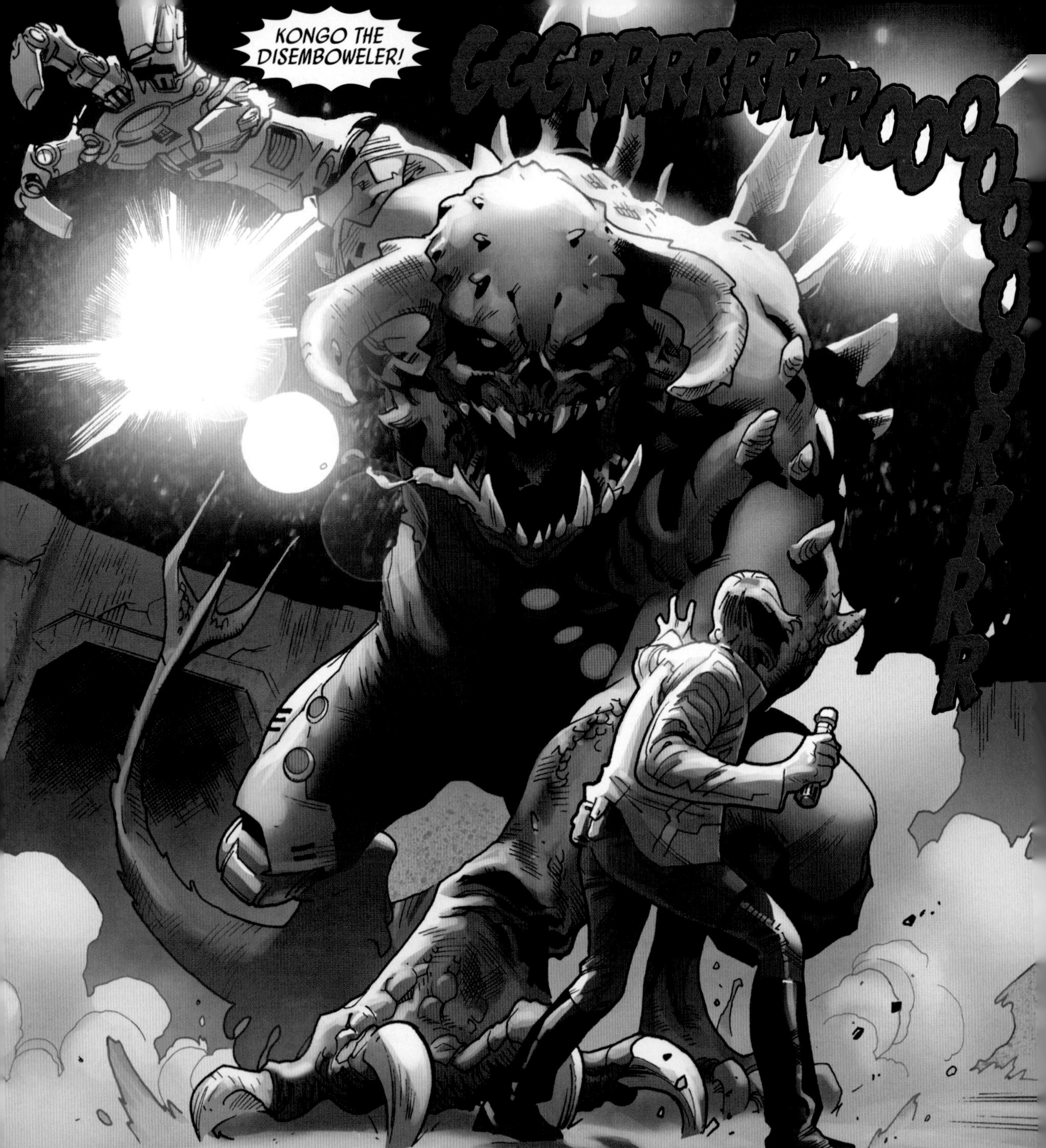
KONGO THE DISEMBOWELER!
GGGRRRRRRRRRROOOOOOOOORRRRR

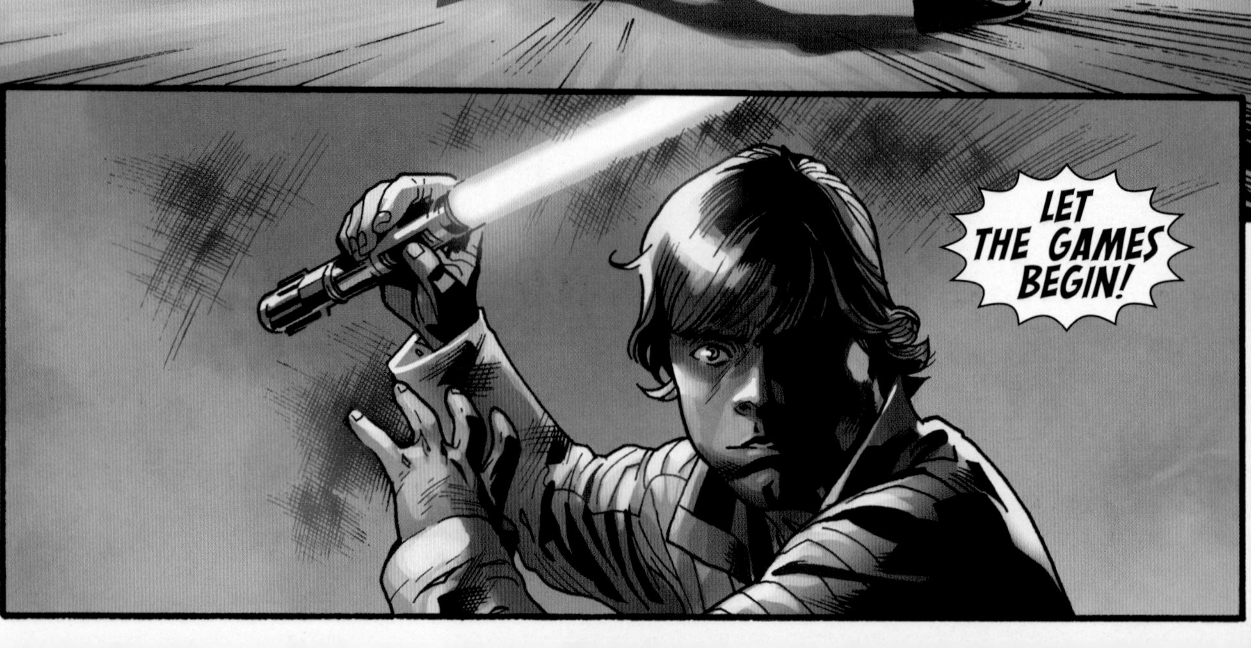
LET THE GAMES BEGIN!

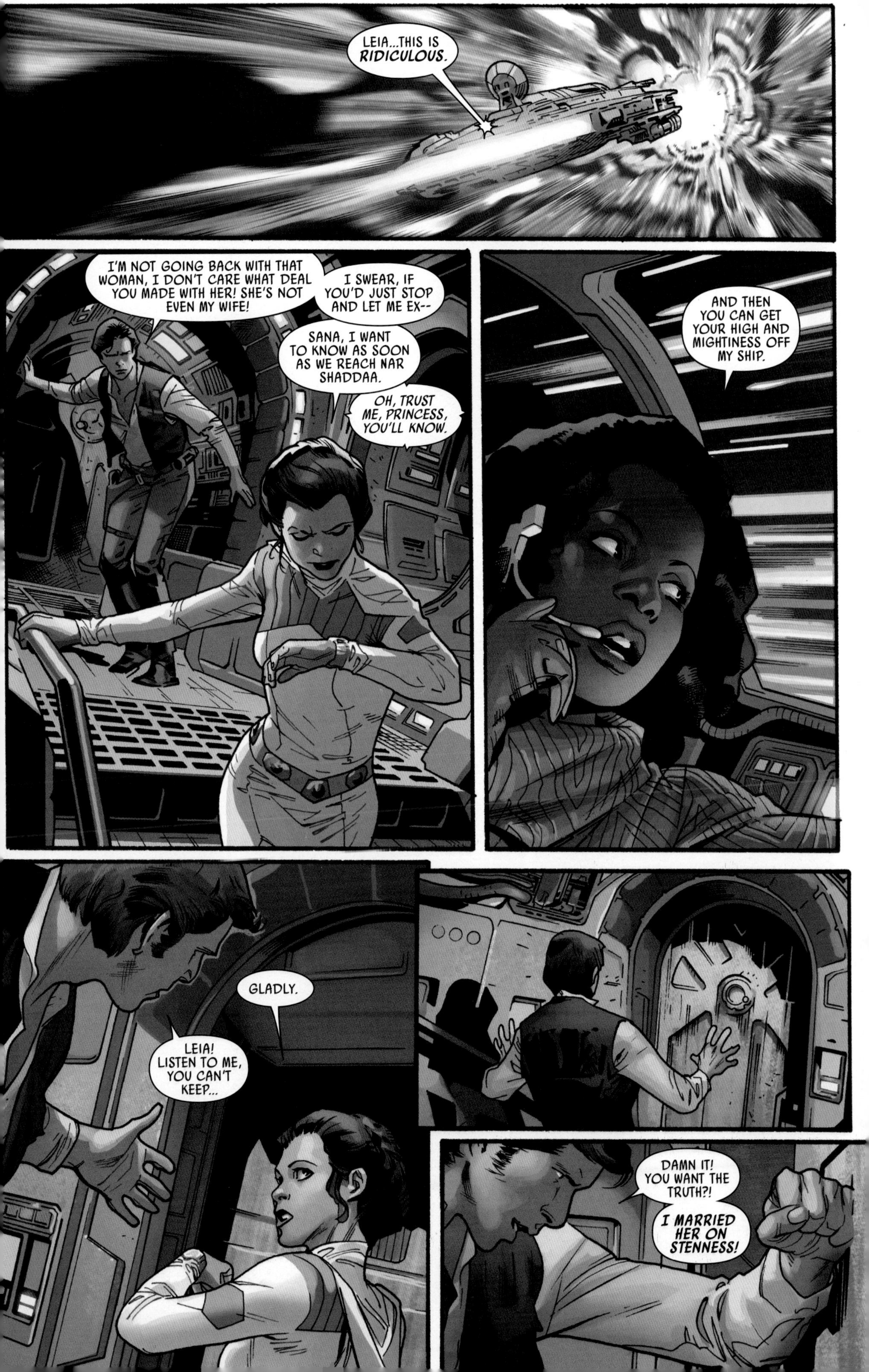
LEIA...THIS IS RIDICULOUS.
I'M NOT GOING BACK WITH THAT WOMAN, I DON'T CARE WHAT DEAL YOU MADE WITH HER! SHE'S NOT EVEN MY WIFE!
I SWEAR, IF YOU'D JUST STOP AND LET ME EX--
SANA, I WANT TO KNOW AS SOON AS WE REACH NAR SHADDAA.
OH, TRUST ME, PRINCESS, YOU'LL KNOW.
AND THEN YOU CAN GET YOUR HIGH AND MIGHTINESS OFF MY SHIP.
GLADLY.
LEIA! LISTEN TO ME, YOU CAN'T KEEP...
DAMN IT! YOU WANT THE TRUTH?!
I MARRIED HER ON STENNESS!

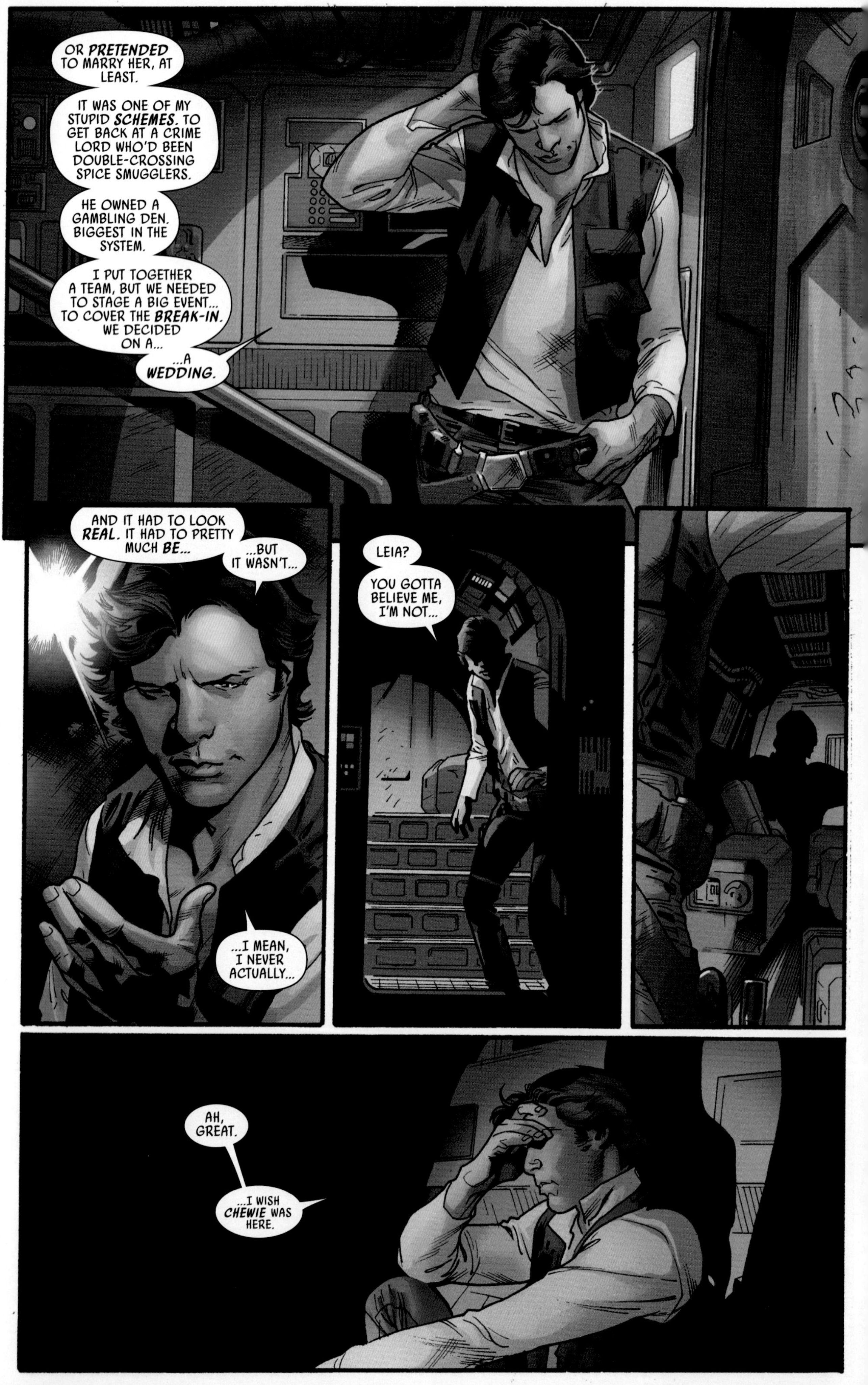
OR PRETENDED TO MARRY HER, AT LEAST.
IT WAS ONE OF MY STUPID SCHEMES. TO GET BACK AT A CRIME LORD WHO'D BEEN DOUBLE-CROSSING SPICE SMUGGLERS.
HE OWNED A GAMBLING DEN. BIGGEST IN THE SYSTEM.
I PUT TOGETHER A TEAM, BUT WE NEEDED TO STAGE A BIG EVENT... TO COVER THE BREAK-IN. WE DECIDED ON A...
...A WEDDING.
AND IT HAD TO LOOK REAL. IT HAD TO PRETTY MUCH BE...
...BUT IT WASN'T...
...I MEAN, I NEVER ACTUALLY...
LEIA?
YOU GOTTA BELIEVE ME, I'M NOT...
AH, GREAT.
...I WISH CHEWIE WAS HERE.

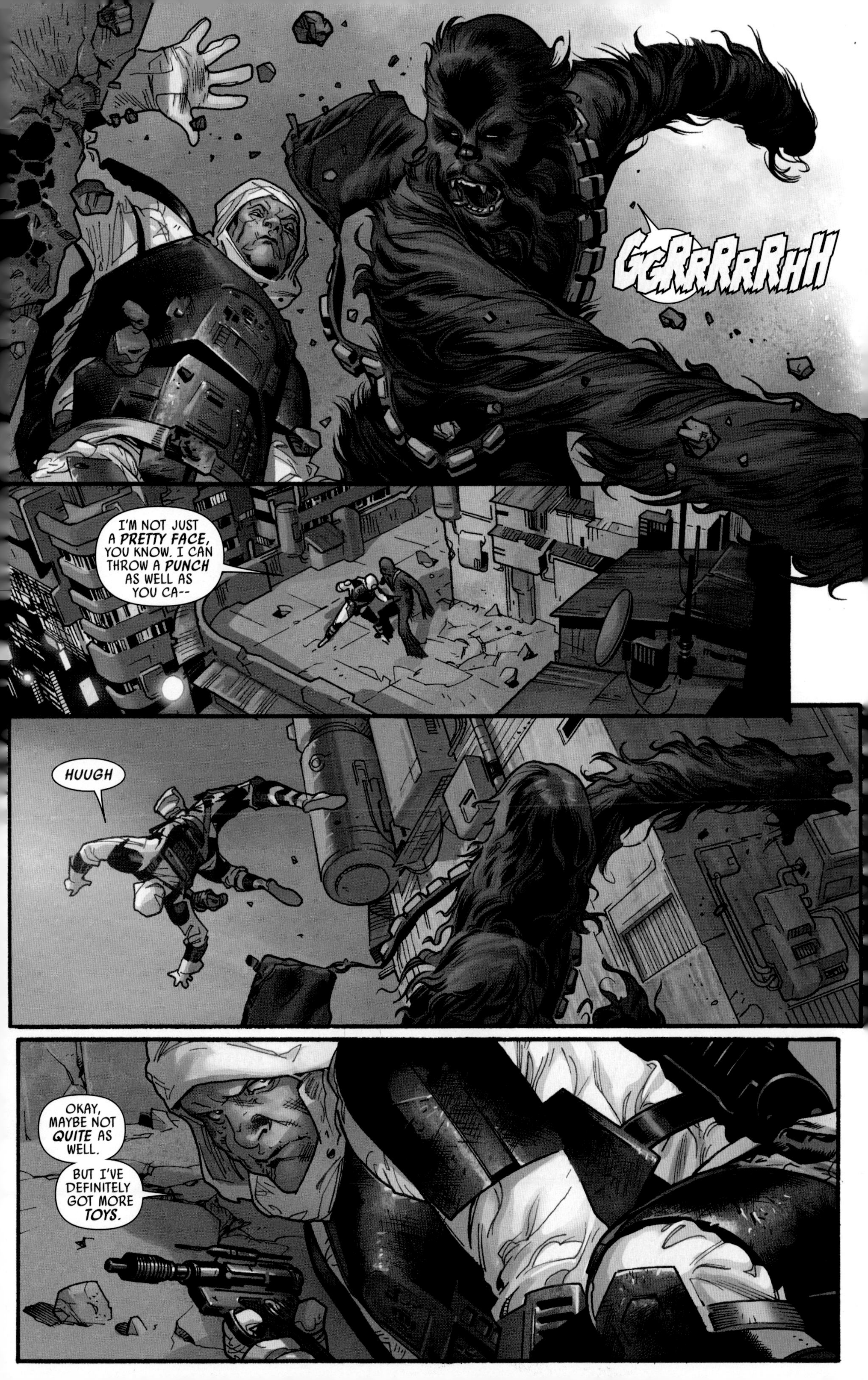
GGRRRRRHH
I'M NOT JUST A PRETTY FACE, YOU KNOW. I CAN THROW A PUNCH AS WELL AS YOU CA--
HUUGH
OKAY, MAYBE NOT QUITE AS WELL.
BUT I'VE DEFINITELY GOT MORE TOYS.

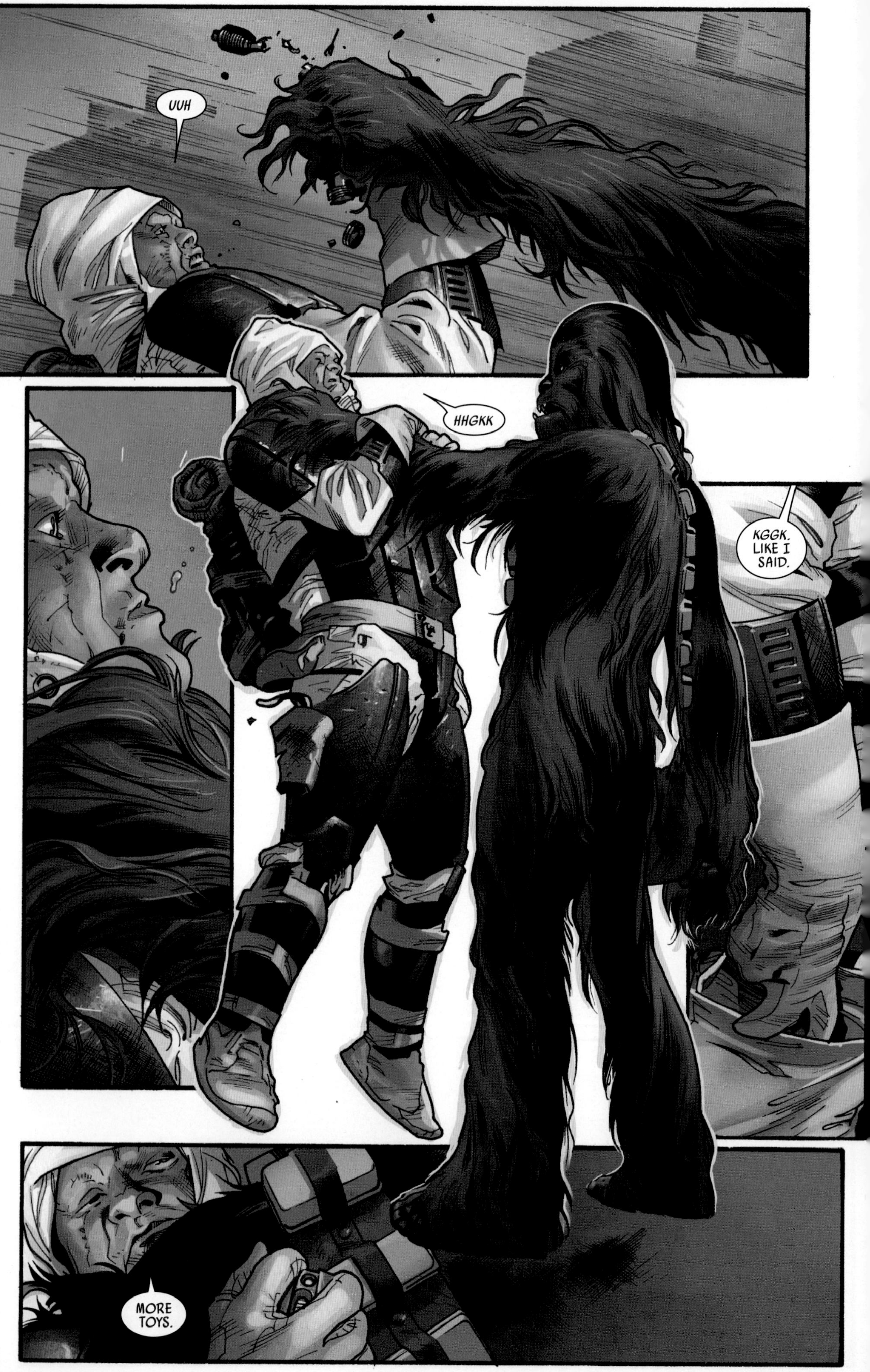
UUH
HHGKK
KGGK. LIKE I SAID.
MORE TOYS.

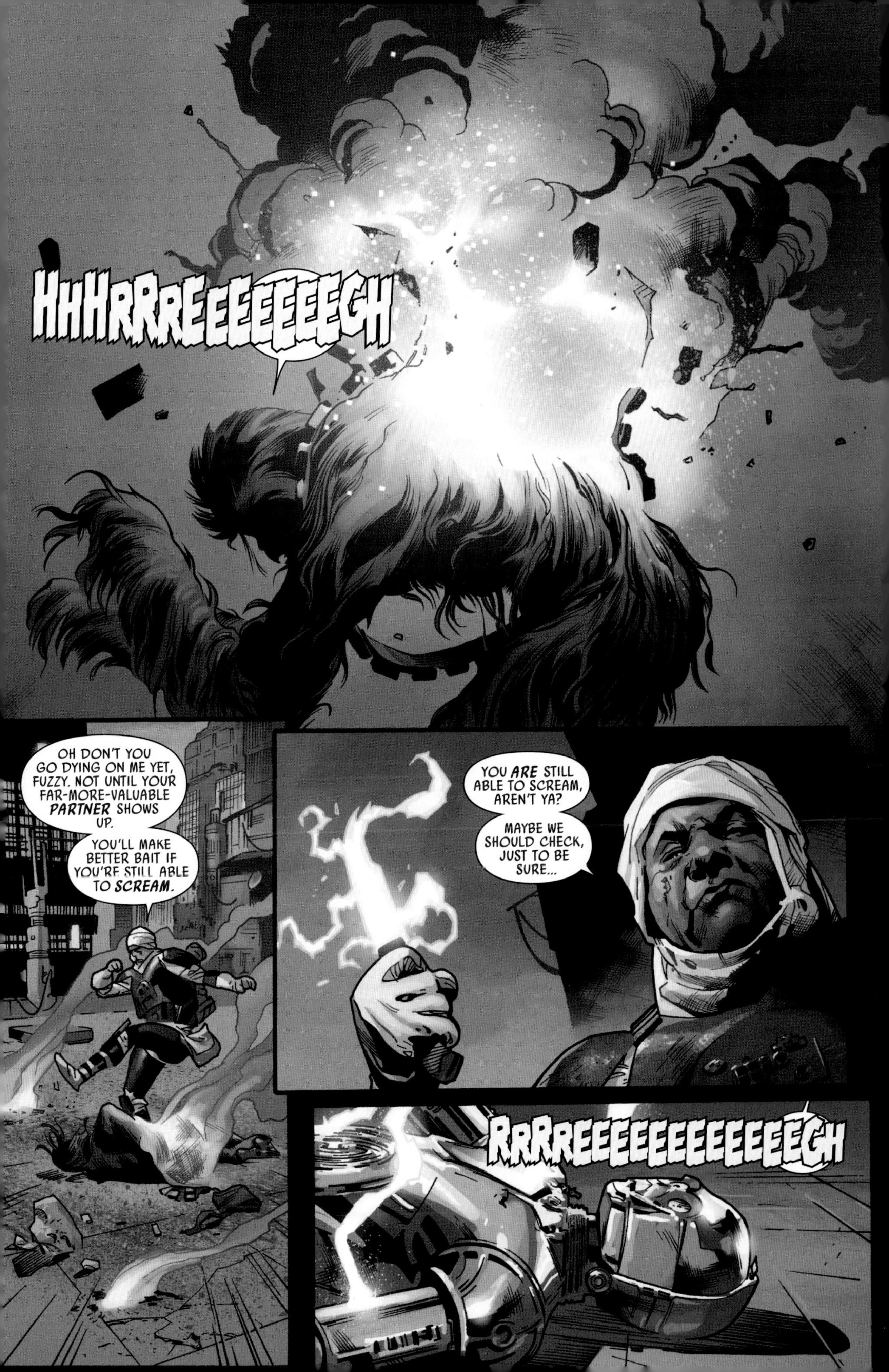
HHHRRREEEEEEEEEGH
OH DON'T YOU GO DYING ON ME YET, FUZZY. NOT UNTIL YOUR FAR-MORE-VALUABLE PARTNER SHOWS UP.
YOU'LL MAKE BETTER BAIT IF YOU'RE STILL ABLE TO SCREAM.
YOU ARE STILL ABLE TO SCREAM, AREN'T YA?
MAYBE WE SHOULD CHECK, JUST TO BE SURE...
RRRREEEEEEEEEEEEEGH

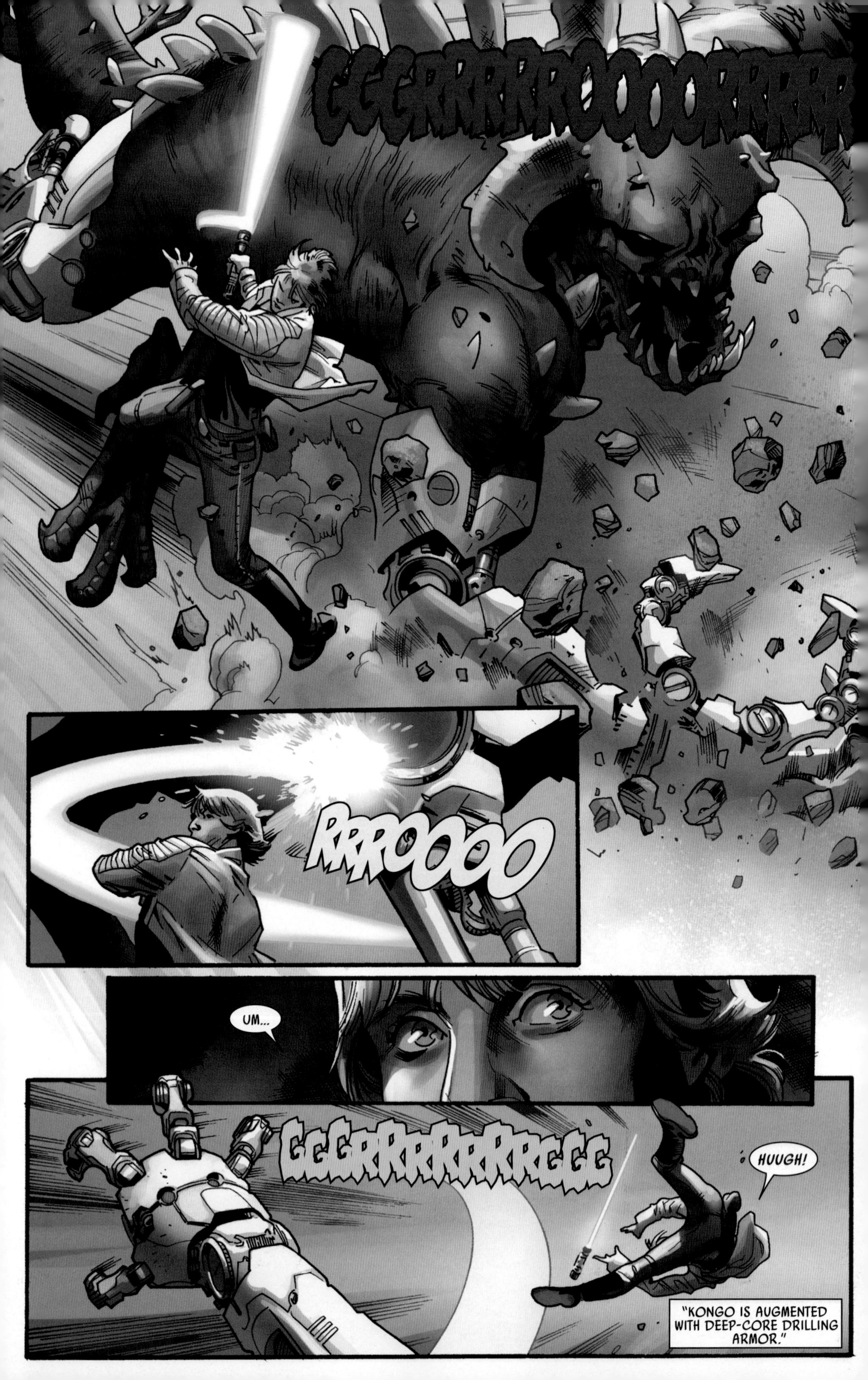
GGGRRRRRROOOORRRRR
RRROOOO
UM...
GGGRRRRRRRRGGG
HUUGH!
"KONGO IS AUGMENTED WITH DEEP-CORE DRILLING ARMOR."

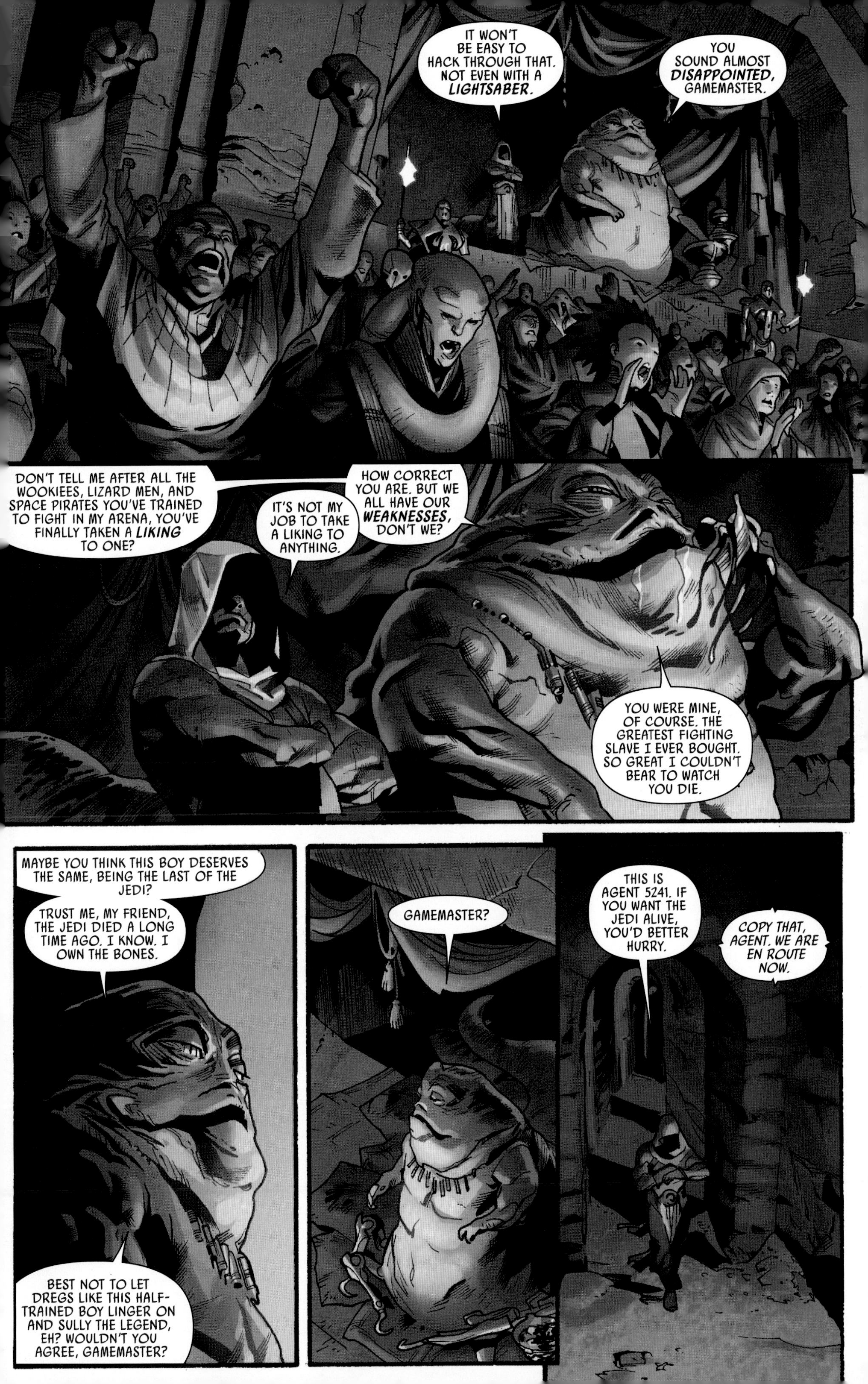
IT WON'T BE EASY TO HACK THROUGH THAT. NOT EVEN WITH A LIGHTSABER.
YOU SOUND ALMOST DISAPPOINTED, GAMEMASTER.
DON'T TELL ME AFTER ALL THE WOOKIEES, LIZARD MEN, AND SPACE PIRATES YOU'VE TRAINED TO FIGHT IN MY ARENA, YOU'VE FINALLY TAKEN A LIKING TO ONE?
IT'S NOT MY JOB TO TAKE A LIKING TO ANYTHING.
HOW CORRECT YOU ARE. BUT WE ALL HAVE OUR WEAKNESSES, DON'T WE?
YOU WERE MINE, OF COURSE. THE GREATEST FIGHTING SLAVE I EVER BOUGHT. SO GREAT I COULDN'T BEAR TO WATCH YOU DIE.
MAYBE YOU THINK THIS BOY DESERVES THE SAME, BEING THE LAST OF THE JEDI?
TRUST ME, MY FRIEND, THE JEDI DIED A LONG TIME AGO. I KNOW. I OWN THE BONES.
BEST NOT TO LET DREGS LIKE THIS HALF-TRAINED BOY LINGER ON AND SULLY THE LEGEND, EH? WOULDN'T YOU AGREE, GAMEMASTER?
GAMEMASTER?
THIS IS AGENT 5241. IF YOU WANT THE JEDI ALIVE, YOU'D BETTER HURRY.
COPY THAT, AGENT. WE ARE EN ROUTE NOW.

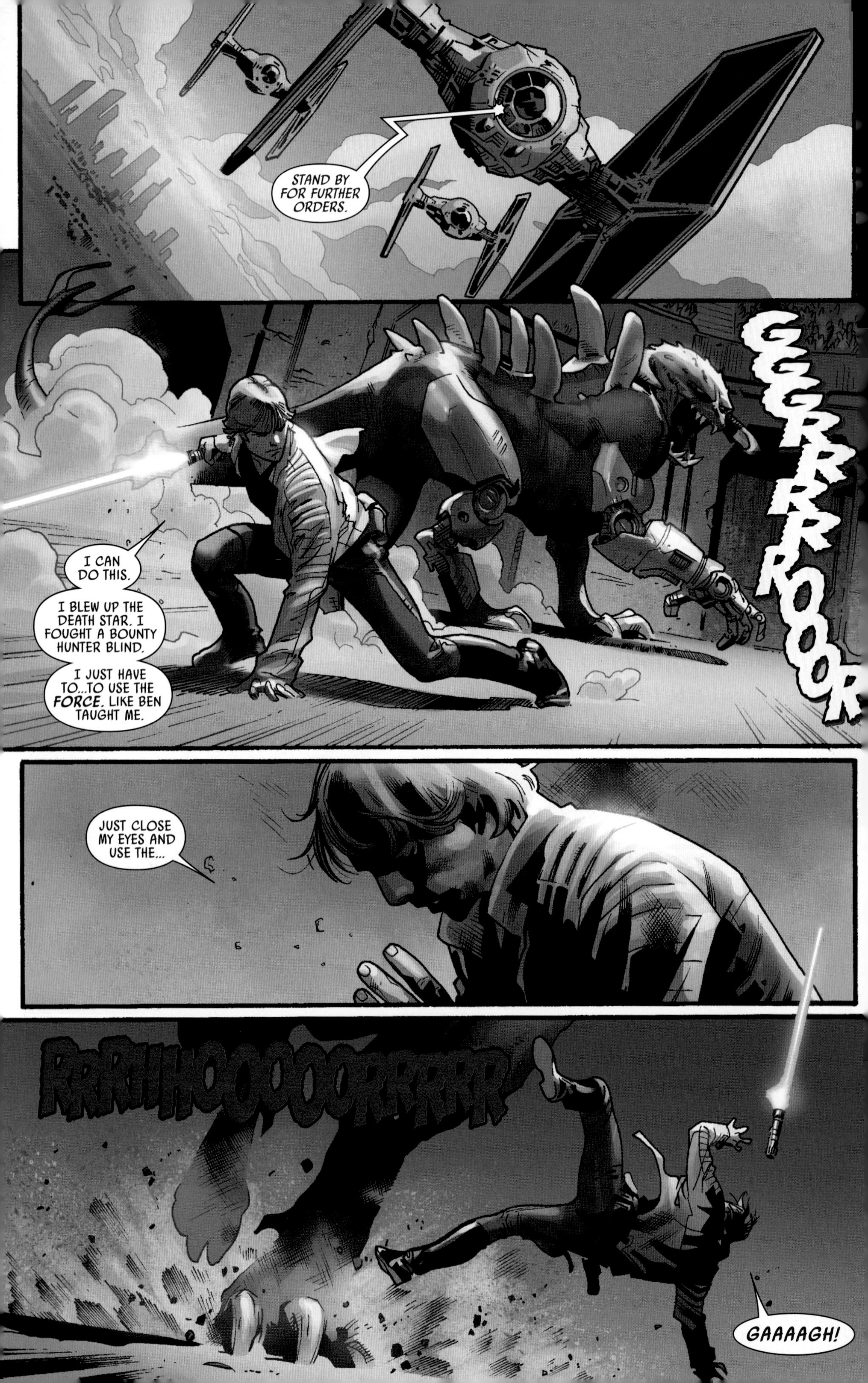

STAND BY FOR FURTHER ORDERS.
GGGRRRRROOOR
I CAN DO THIS.
I BLEW UP THE DEATH STAR. I FOUGHT A BOUNTY HUNTER BLIND.
I JUST HAVE TO...TO USE THE FORCE. LIKE BEN TAUGHT ME.
JUST CLOSE MY EYES AND USE THE...
RRRHHOOOOORRRRR
GAAAAGH!

OKAY, SO...

CLOSING MY EYES... DOESN'T ALWAYS WORK.

RRRRRRRROOOOORRRRR

WWOOOOWOOO WHEE

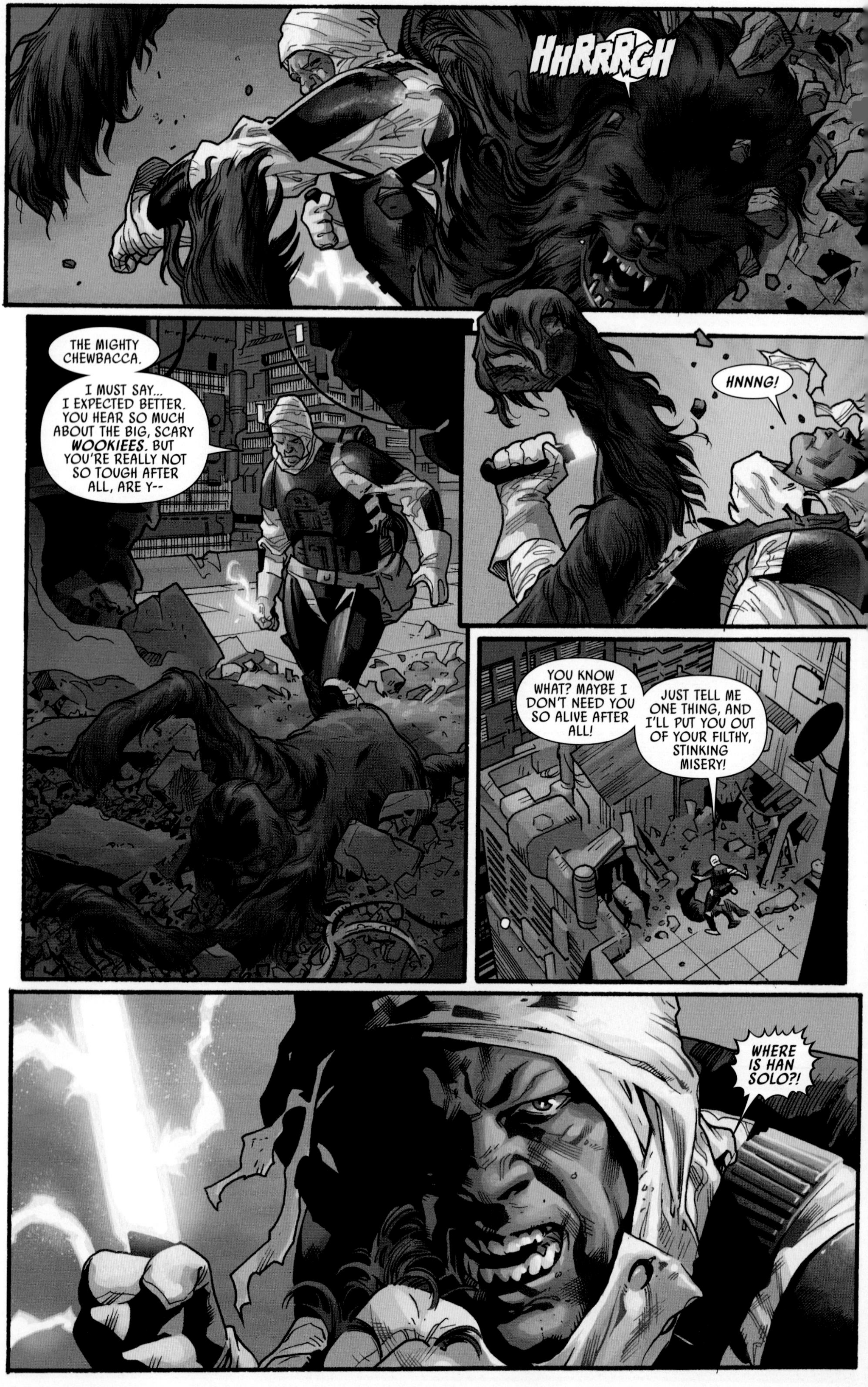
HHRRRGH
THE MIGHTY CHEWBACCA.
I MUST SAY... I EXPECTED BETTER. YOU HEAR SO MUCH ABOUT THE BIG, SCARY WOOKIEES. BUT YOU'RE REALLY NOT SO TOUGH AFTER ALL, ARE Y--
HNNNG!
YOU KNOW WHAT? MAYBE I DON'T NEED YOU SO ALIVE AFTER ALL!
JUST TELL ME ONE THING, AND I'LL PUT YOU OUT OF YOUR FILTHY, STINKING MISERY!
WHERE IS HAN SOLO?!

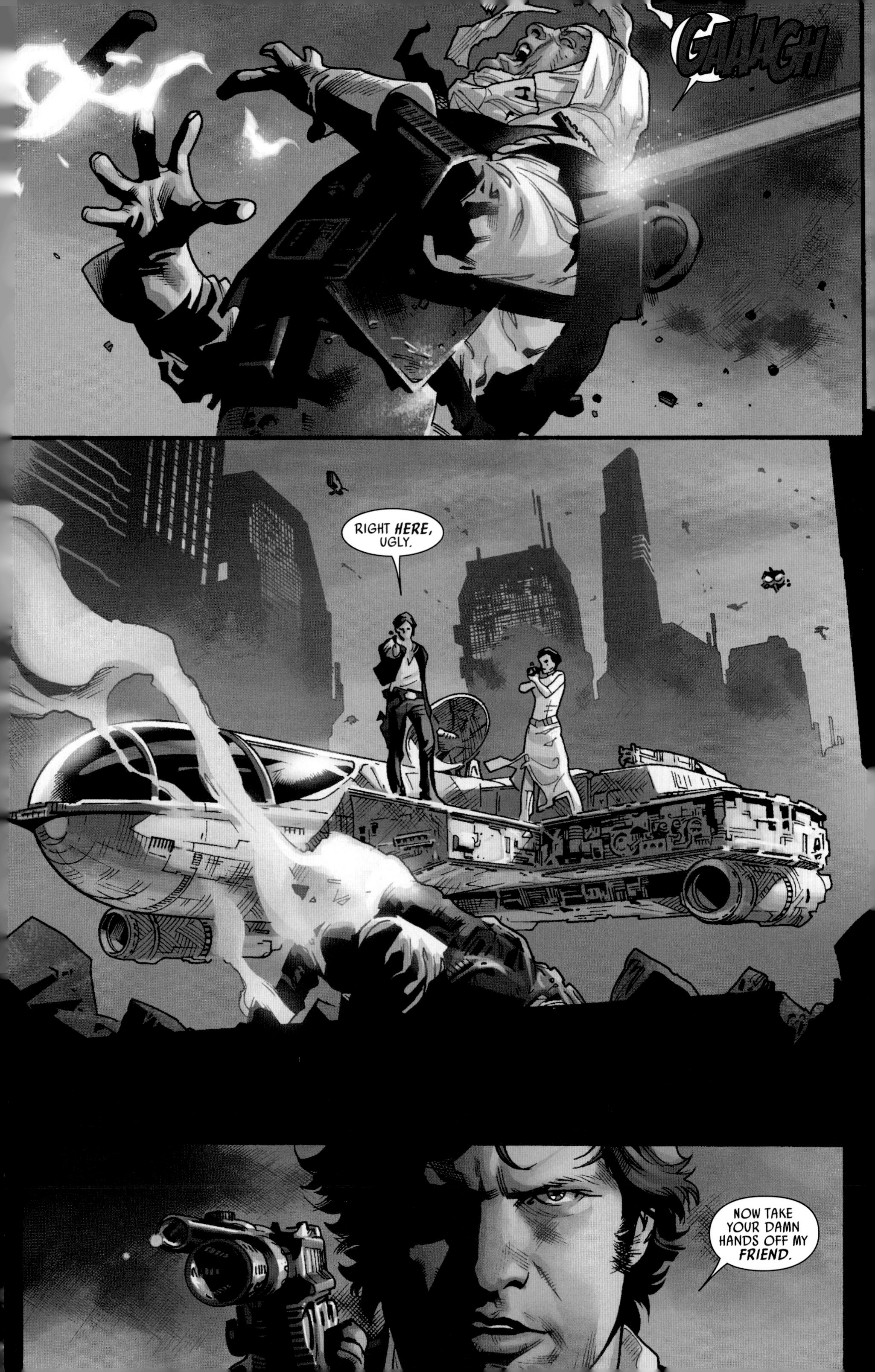
GAAAGH
RIGHT HERE, UGLY.
NOW TAKE YOUR DAMN HANDS OFF MY FRIEND.

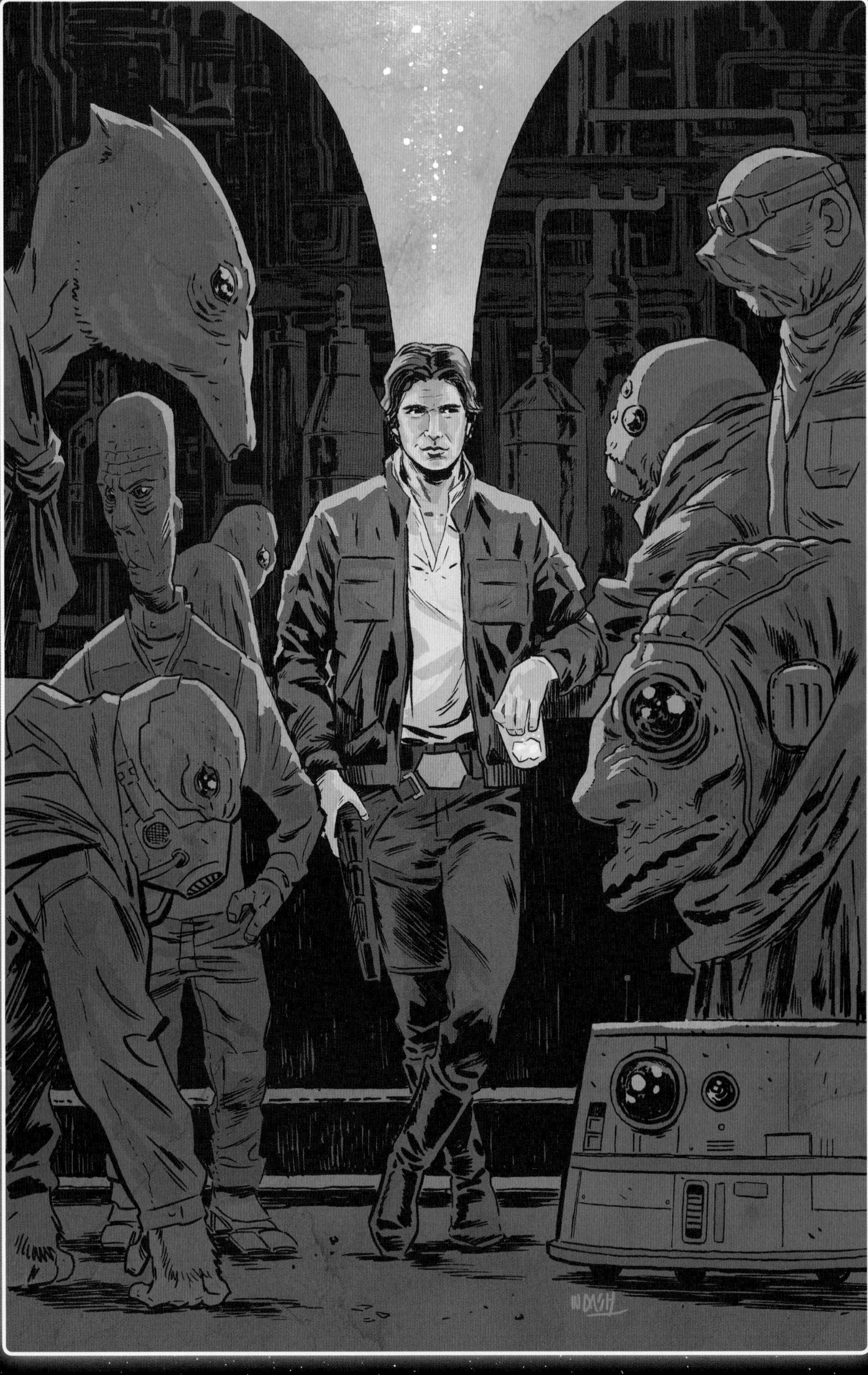

***HAN SOLO* 3 Variant**
by **MICHAEL WALSH**

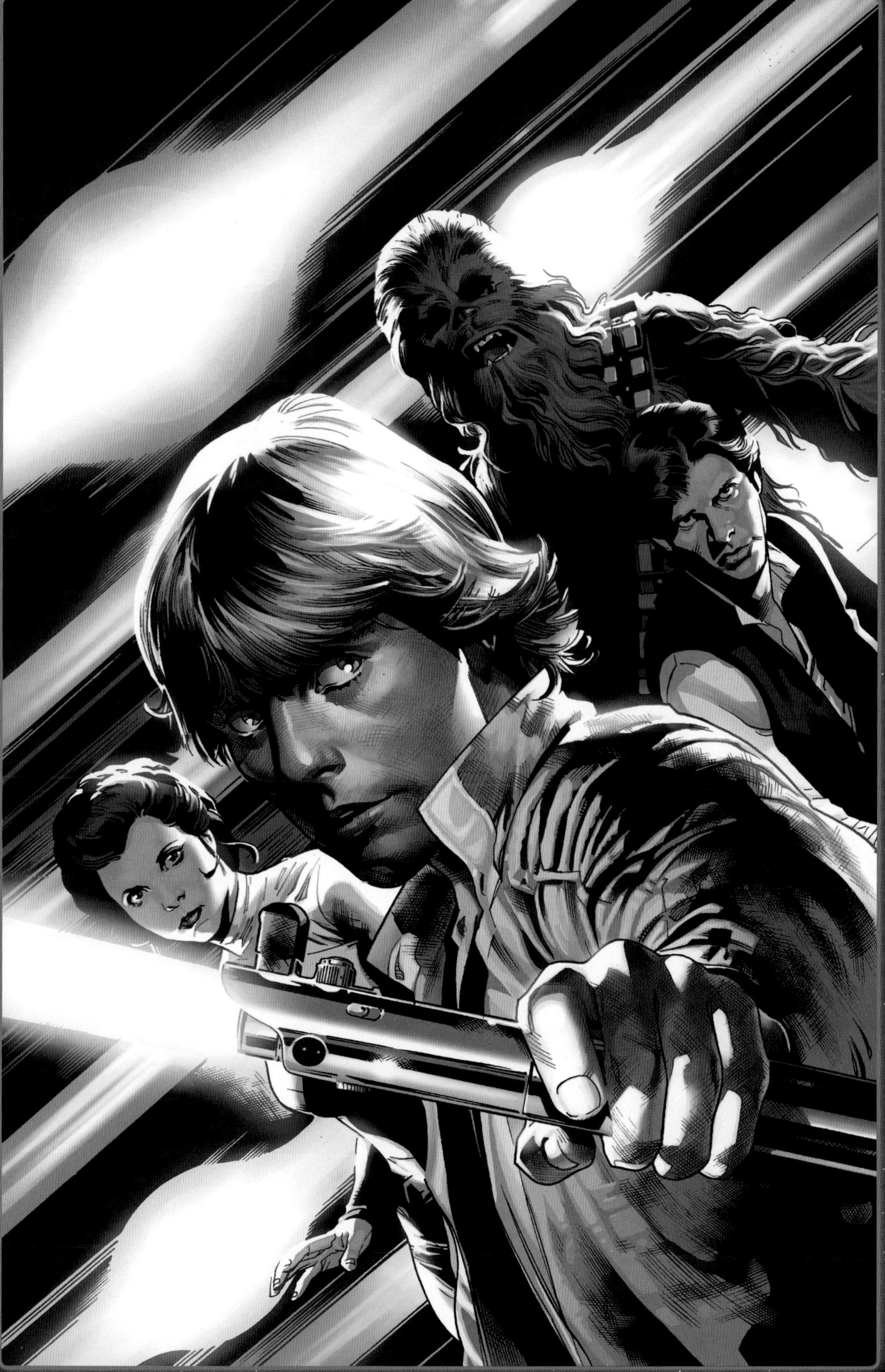

STAR WARS 12

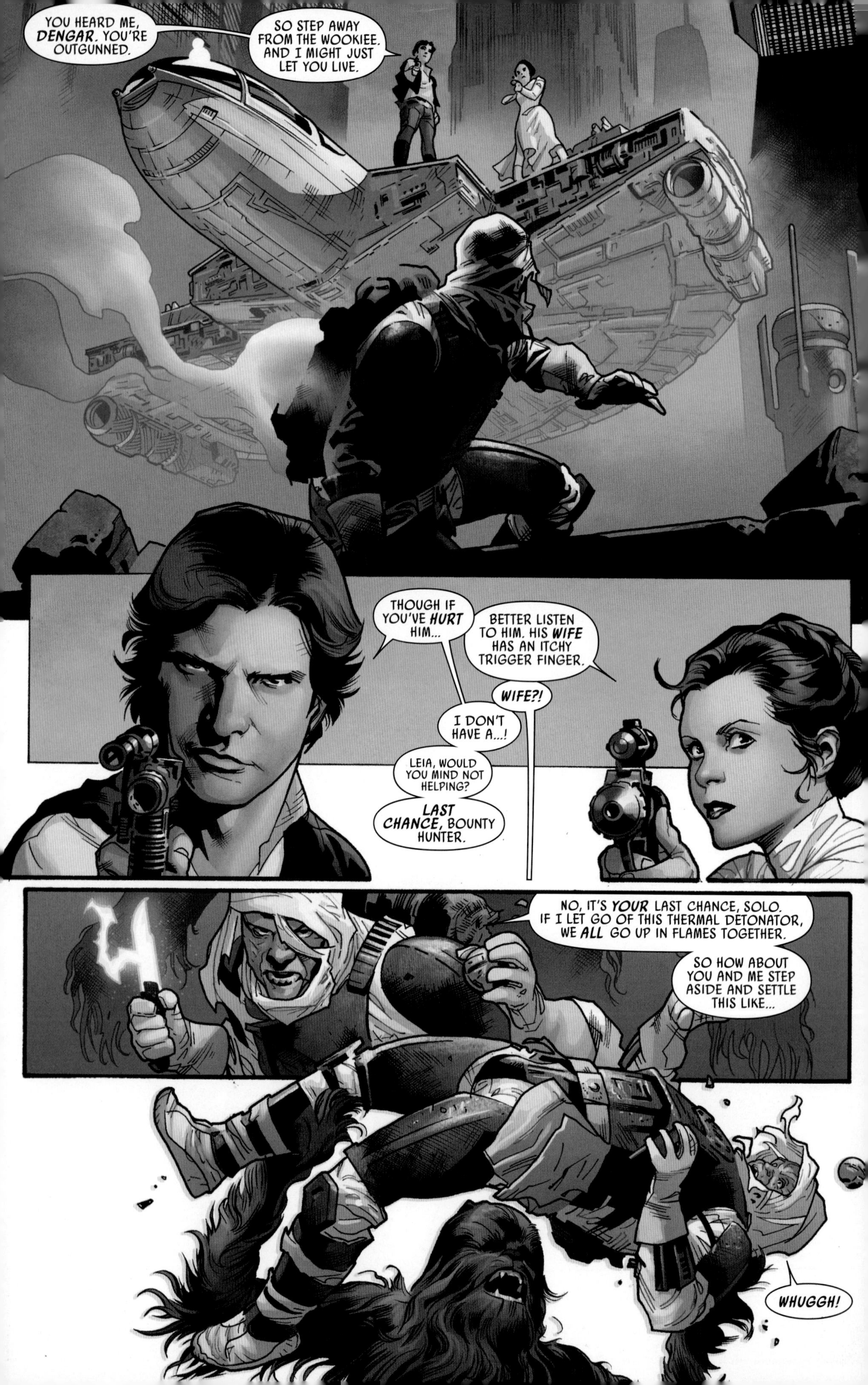
YOU HEARD ME, DENGAR. YOU'RE OUTGUNNED.
SO STEP AWAY FROM THE WOOKIEE. AND I MIGHT JUST LET YOU LIVE.
THOUGH IF YOU'VE HURT HIM...
BETTER LISTEN TO HIM. HIS WIFE HAS AN ITCHY TRIGGER FINGER.
WIFE?!
I DON'T HAVE A...!
LEIA, WOULD YOU MIND NOT HELPING?
LAST CHANCE, BOUNTY HUNTER.
NO, IT'S YOUR LAST CHANCE, SOLO. IF I LET GO OF THIS THERMAL DETONATOR, WE ALL GO UP IN FLAMES TOGETHER.
SO HOW ABOUT YOU AND ME STEP ASIDE AND SETTLE THIS LIKE...
WHUGGH!

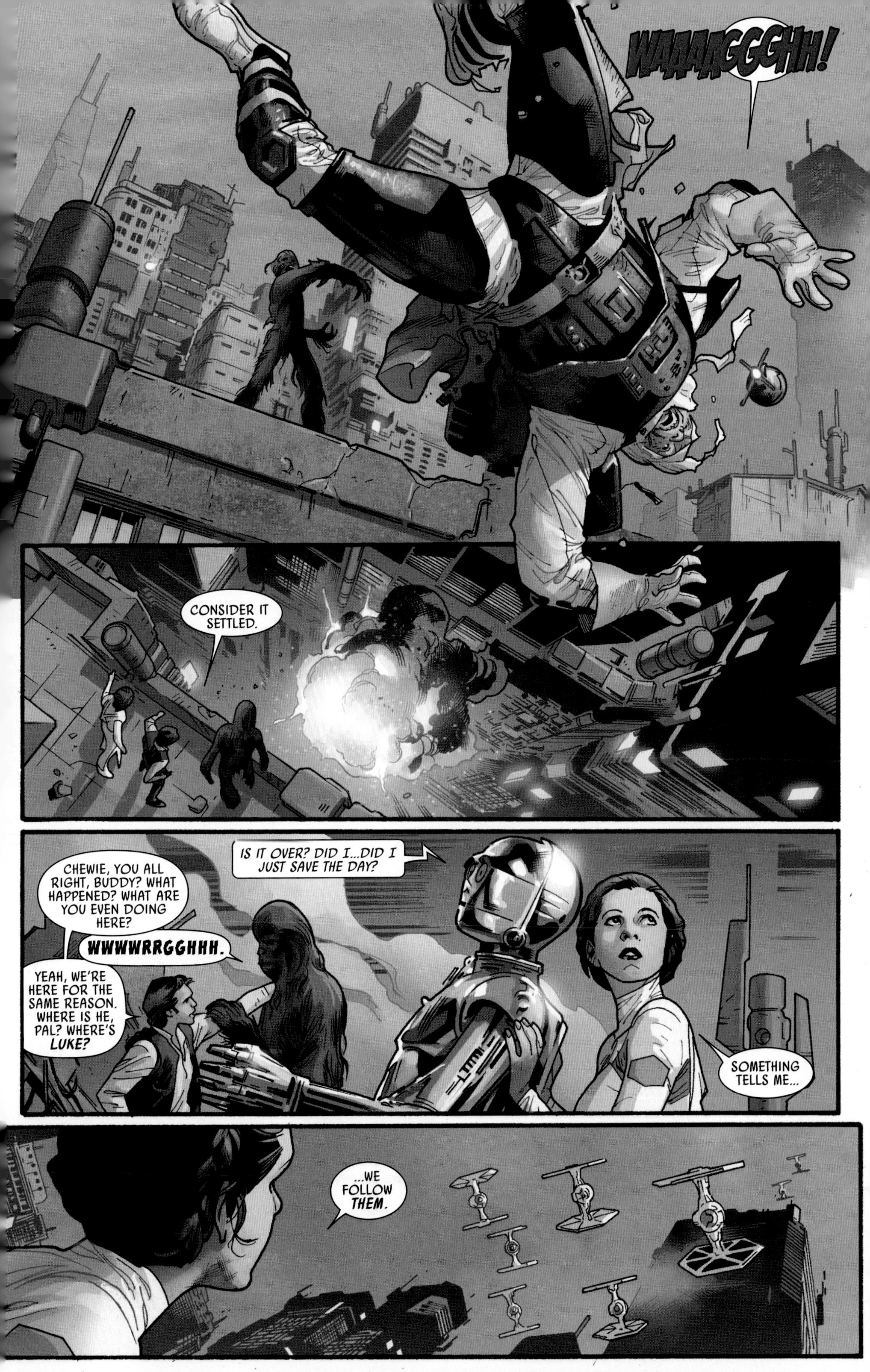
WAAAAGGGHH!
CONSIDER IT SETTLED.
IS IT OVER? DID I...DID I JUST SAVE THE DAY?
CHEWIE, YOU ALL RIGHT, BUDDY? WHAT HAPPENED? WHAT ARE YOU EVEN DOING HERE?
WWWWRRGGHHH.
YEAH, WE'RE HERE FOR THE SAME REASON. WHERE IS HE, PAL? WHERE'S LUKE?
SOMETHING TELLS ME...
...WE FOLLOW THEM.

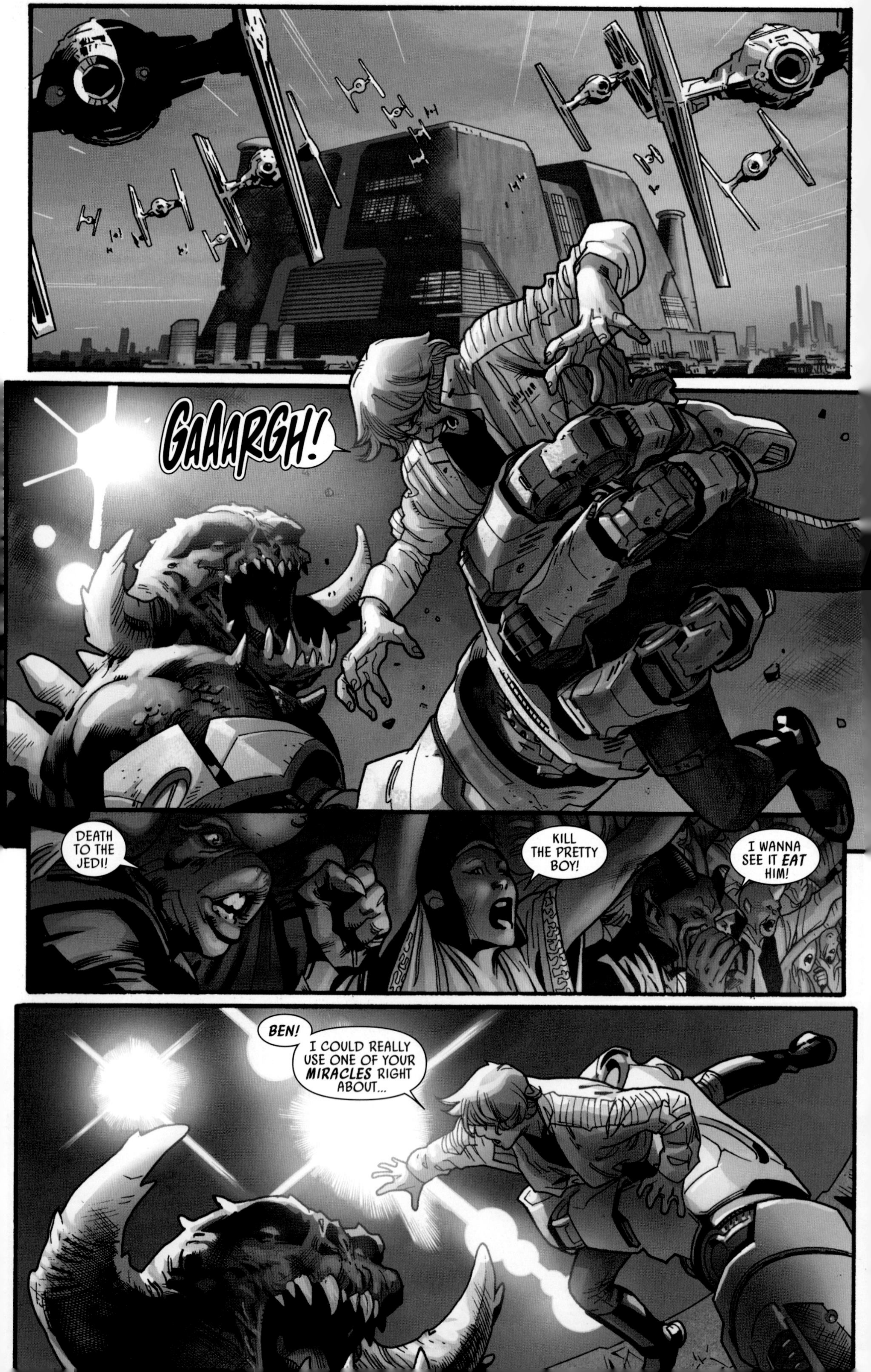
GAAARGH!
DEATH TO THE JEDI!
KILL THE PRETTY BOY!
I WANNA SEE IT EAT HIM!
BEN!
I COULD REALLY USE ONE OF YOUR MIRACLES RIGHT ABOUT...

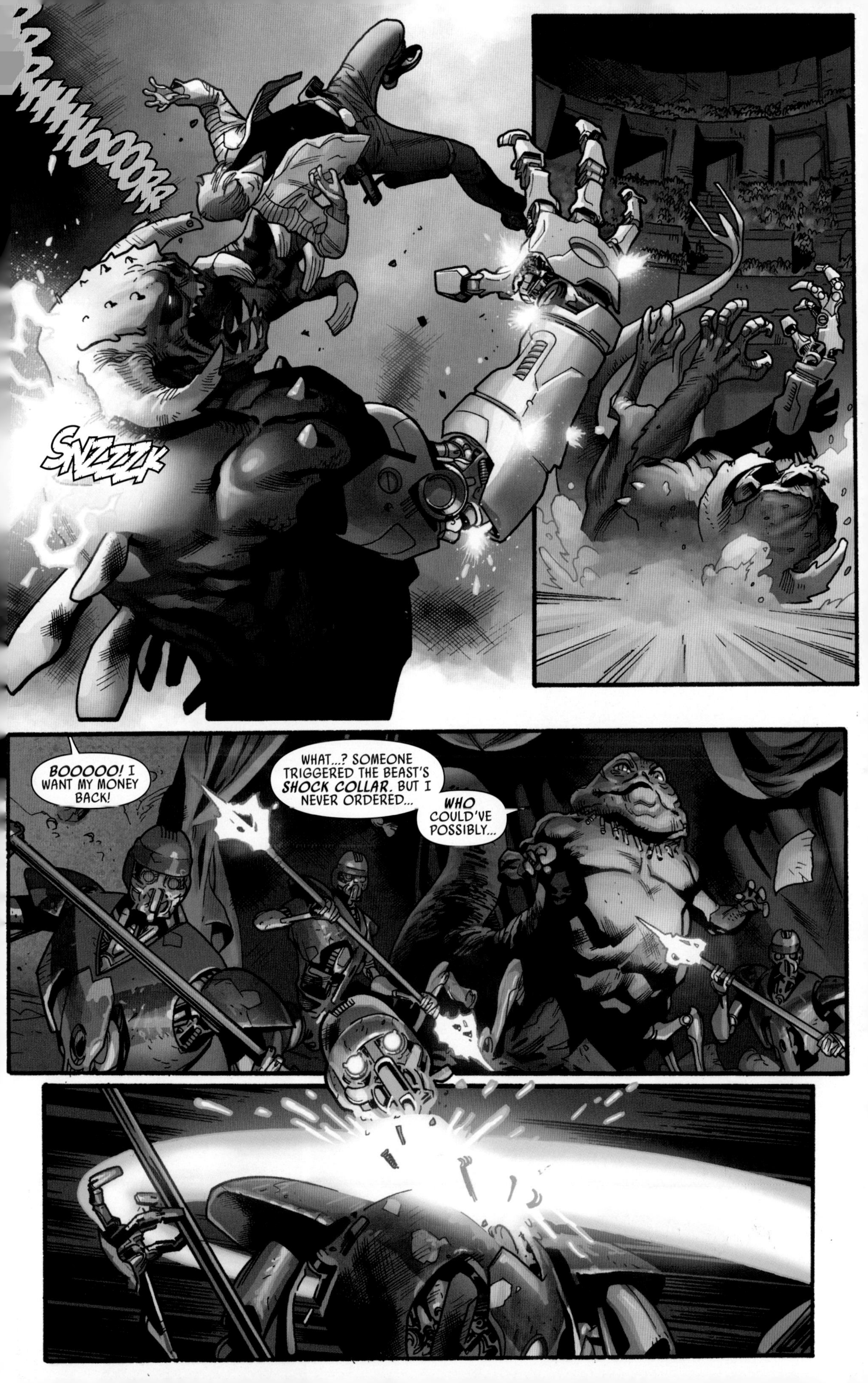
RRRHHHOOOORR
SNZZZK
BOOOOO! I WANT MY MONEY BACK!
WHAT...? SOMEONE TRIGGERED THE BEAST'S SHOCK COLLAR. BUT I NEVER ORDERED...
WHO COULD'VE POSSIBLY...

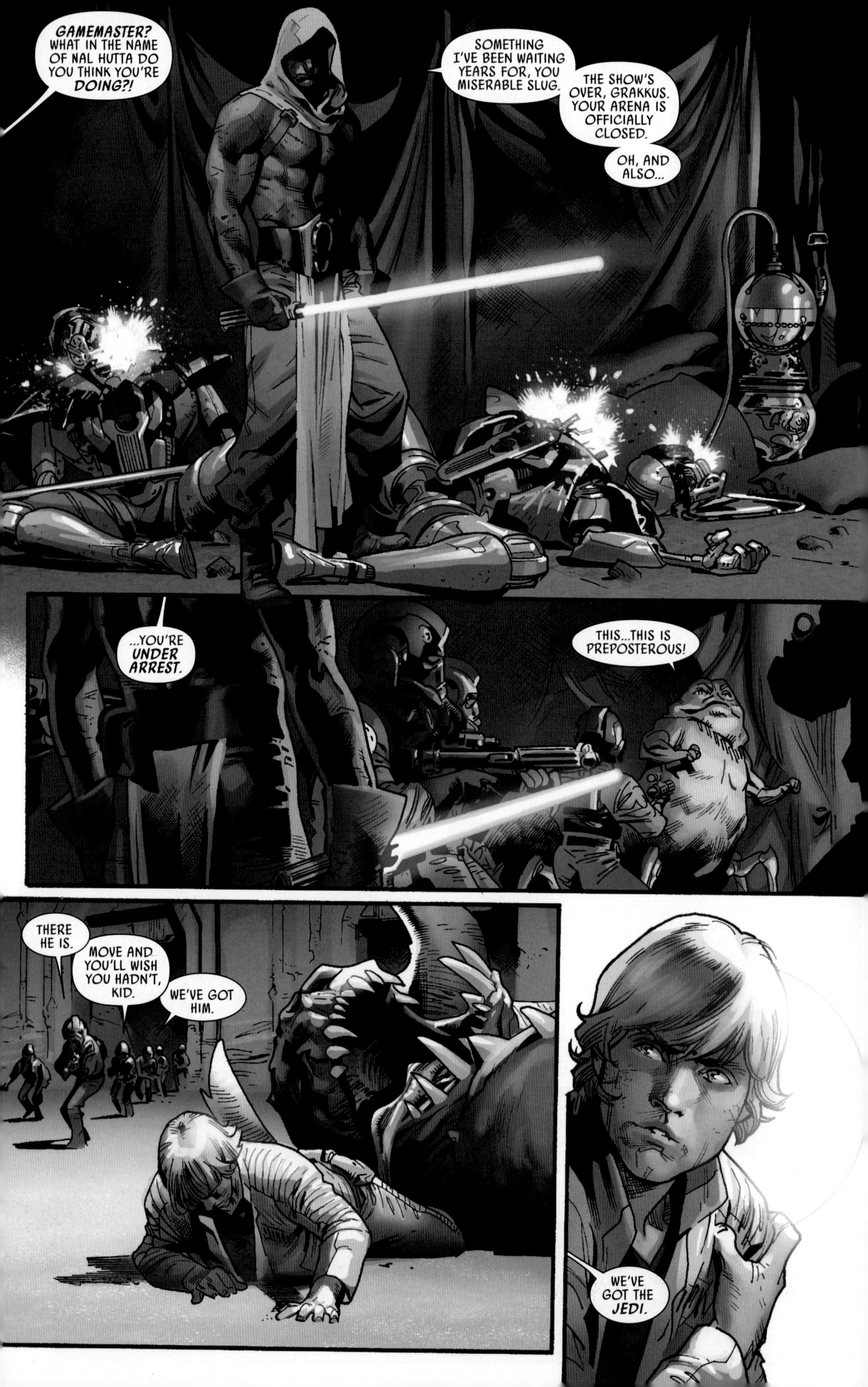
GAMEMASTER? WHAT IN THE NAME OF NAL HUTTA DO YOU THINK YOU'RE DOING?!
SOMETHING I'VE BEEN WAITING YEARS FOR, YOU MISERABLE SLUG.
THE SHOW'S OVER, GRAKKUS. YOUR ARENA IS OFFICIALLY CLOSED.
OH, AND ALSO...
...YOU'RE UNDER ARREST.
THIS...THIS IS PREPOSTEROUS!
THERE HE IS.
MOVE AND YOU'LL WISH YOU HADN'T, KID.
WE'VE GOT HIM.
WE'VE GOT THE JEDI.

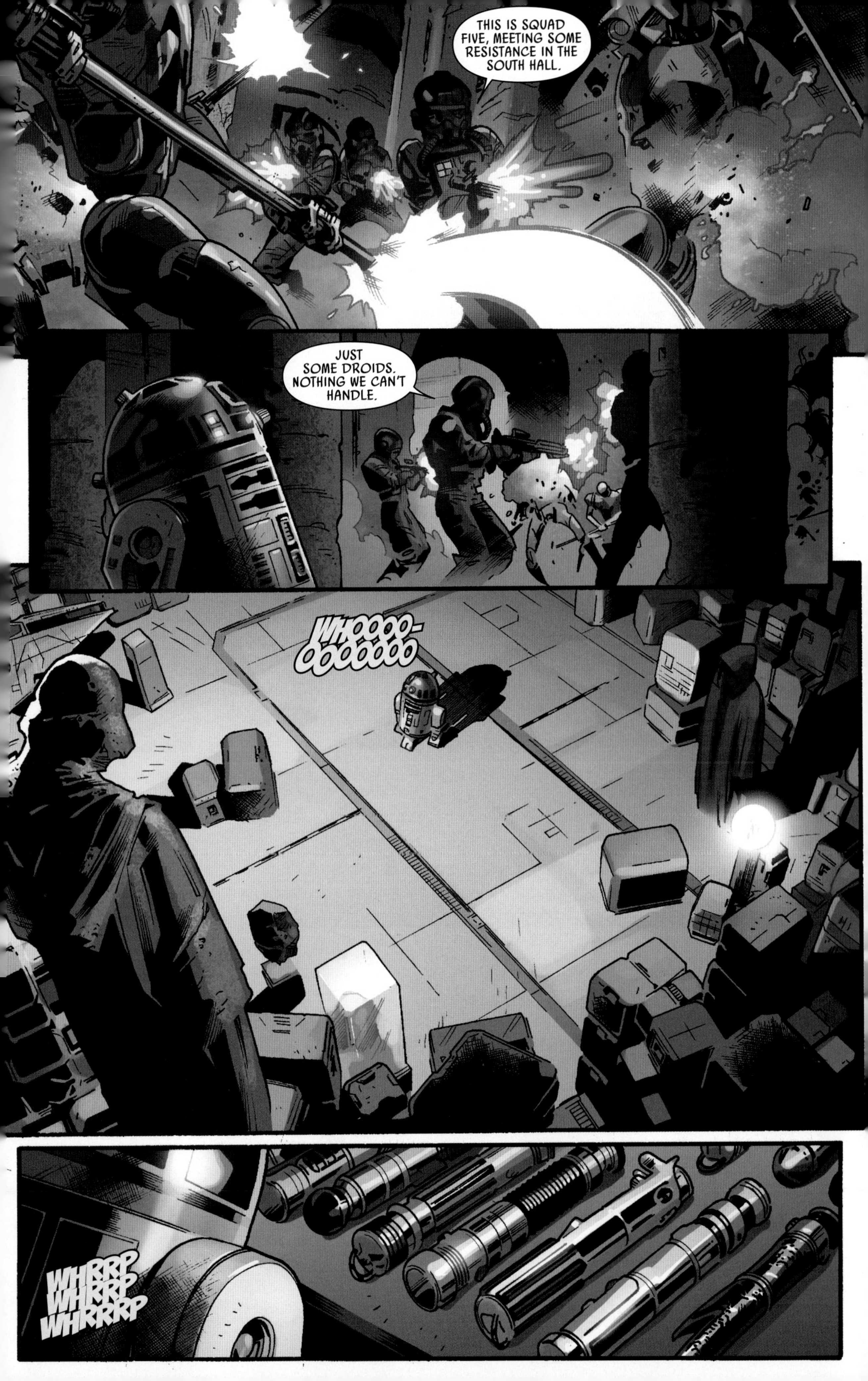
THIS IS SQUAD FIVE, MEETING SOME RESISTANCE IN THE SOUTH HALL.
JUST SOME DROIDS. NOTHING WE CAN'T HANDLE.
WHOOOO-OOOOOOO
WHRRP WHRRP WHRRRP

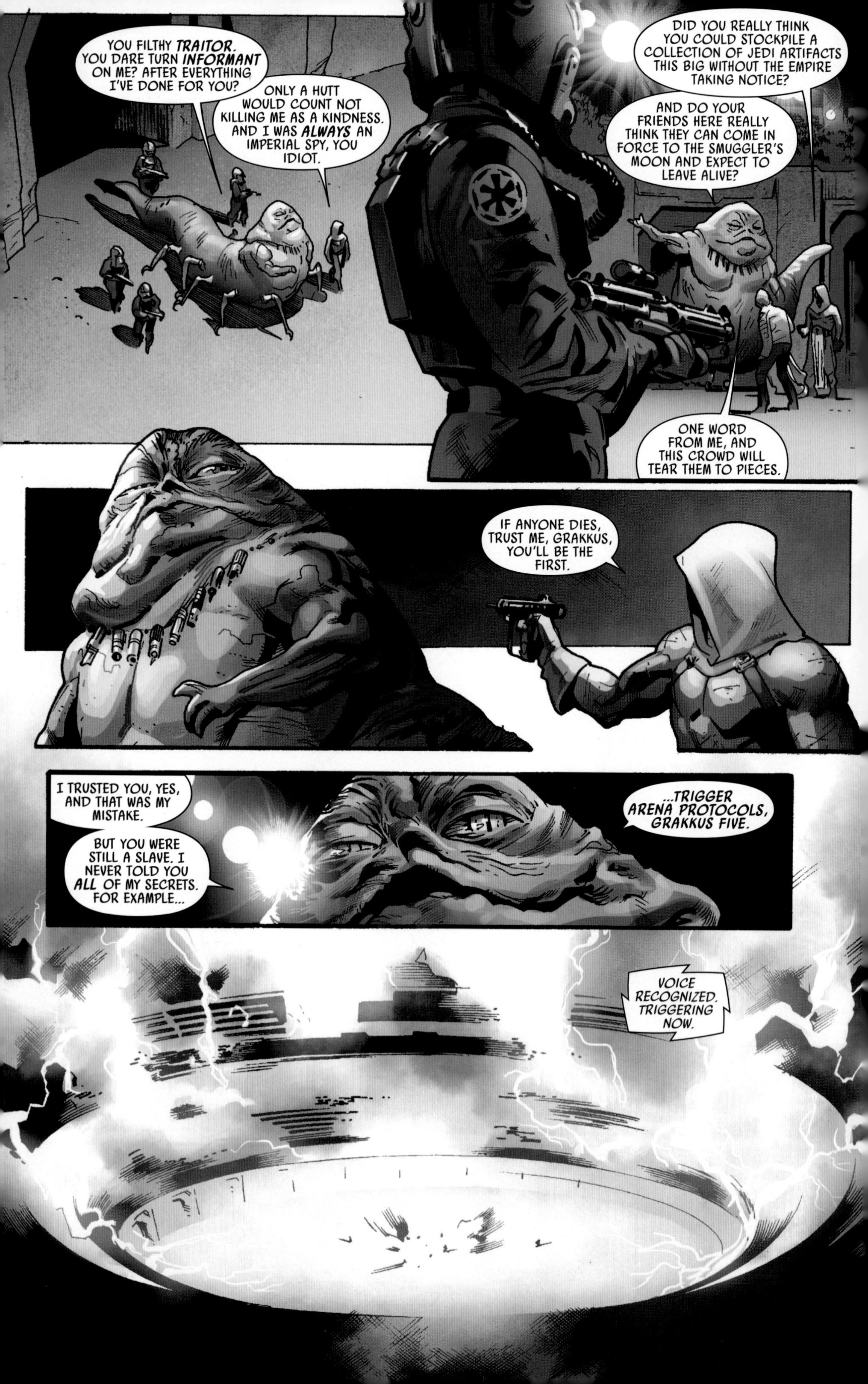

YOU FILTHY TRAITOR. YOU DARE TURN INFORMANT ON ME? AFTER EVERYTHING I'VE DONE FOR YOU?
ONLY A HUTT WOULD COUNT NOT KILLING ME AS A KINDNESS. AND I WAS ALWAYS AN IMPERIAL SPY, YOU IDIOT.
DID YOU REALLY THINK YOU COULD STOCKPILE A COLLECTION OF JEDI ARTIFACTS THIS BIG WITHOUT THE EMPIRE TAKING NOTICE?
AND DO YOUR FRIENDS HERE REALLY THINK THEY CAN COME IN FORCE TO THE SMUGGLER'S MOON AND EXPECT TO LEAVE ALIVE?
ONE WORD FROM ME, AND THIS CROWD WILL TEAR THEM TO PIECES.
IF ANYONE DIES, TRUST ME, GRAKKUS, YOU'LL BE THE FIRST.
I TRUSTED YOU, YES, AND THAT WAS MY MISTAKE.
BUT YOU WERE STILL A SLAVE. I NEVER TOLD YOU ALL OF MY SECRETS. FOR EXAMPLE...
...TRIGGER ARENA PROTOCOLS, GRAKKUS FIVE.
VOICE RECOGNIZED. TRIGGERING NOW.

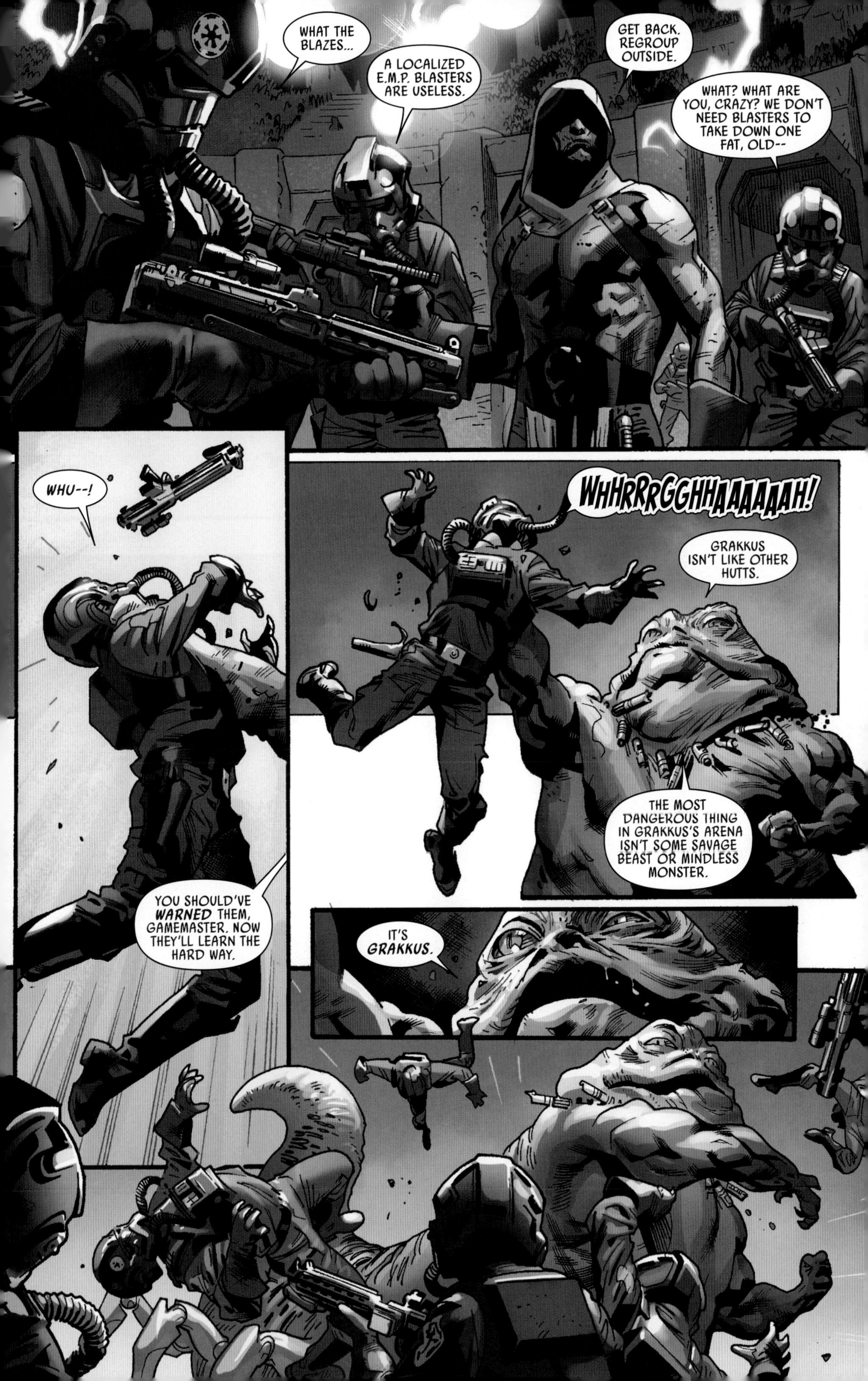
WHAT THE BLAZES...
A LOCALIZED E.M.P. BLASTERS ARE USELESS.
GET BACK. REGROUP OUTSIDE.
WHAT? WHAT ARE YOU, CRAZY? WE DON'T NEED BLASTERS TO TAKE DOWN ONE FAT, OLD--
WHU--!
WHHRRRGGHHAAAAAAH!
GRAKKUS ISN'T LIKE OTHER HUTTS.
THE MOST DANGEROUS THING IN GRAKKUS'S ARENA ISN'T SOME SAVAGE BEAST OR MINDLESS MONSTER.
YOU SHOULD'VE WARNED THEM, GAMEMASTER. NOW THEY'LL LEARN THE HARD WAY.
IT'S GRAKKUS.

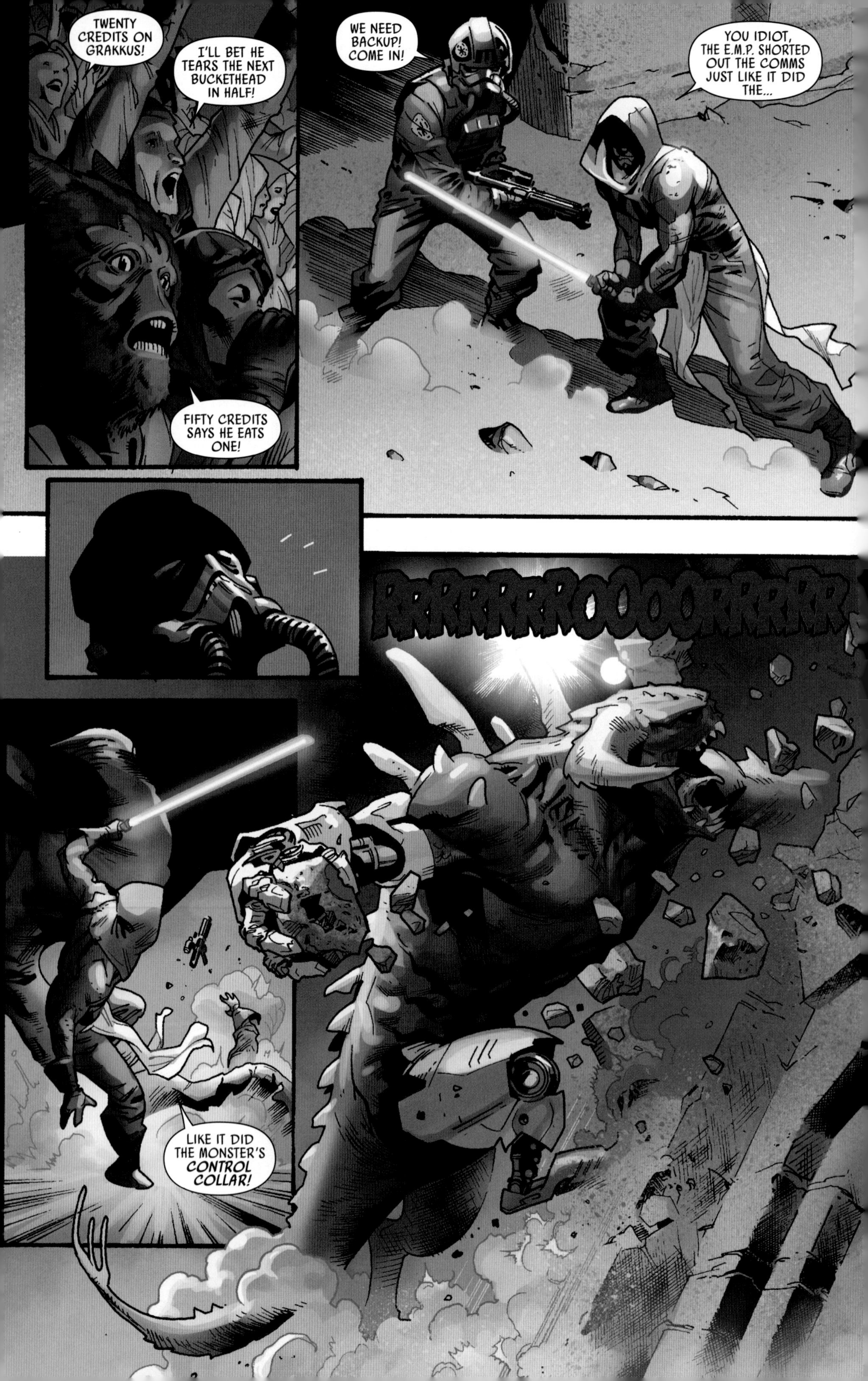
TWENTY CREDITS ON GRAKKUS!
I'LL BET HE TEARS THE NEXT BUCKETHEAD IN HALF!
FIFTY CREDITS SAYS HE EATS ONE!
WE NEED BACKUP! COME IN!
YOU IDIOT, THE E.M.P. SHORTED OUT THE COMMS JUST LIKE IT DID THE...
RRRRRRROOOORRRRR
LIKE IT DID THE MONSTER'S *CONTROL COLLAR!*

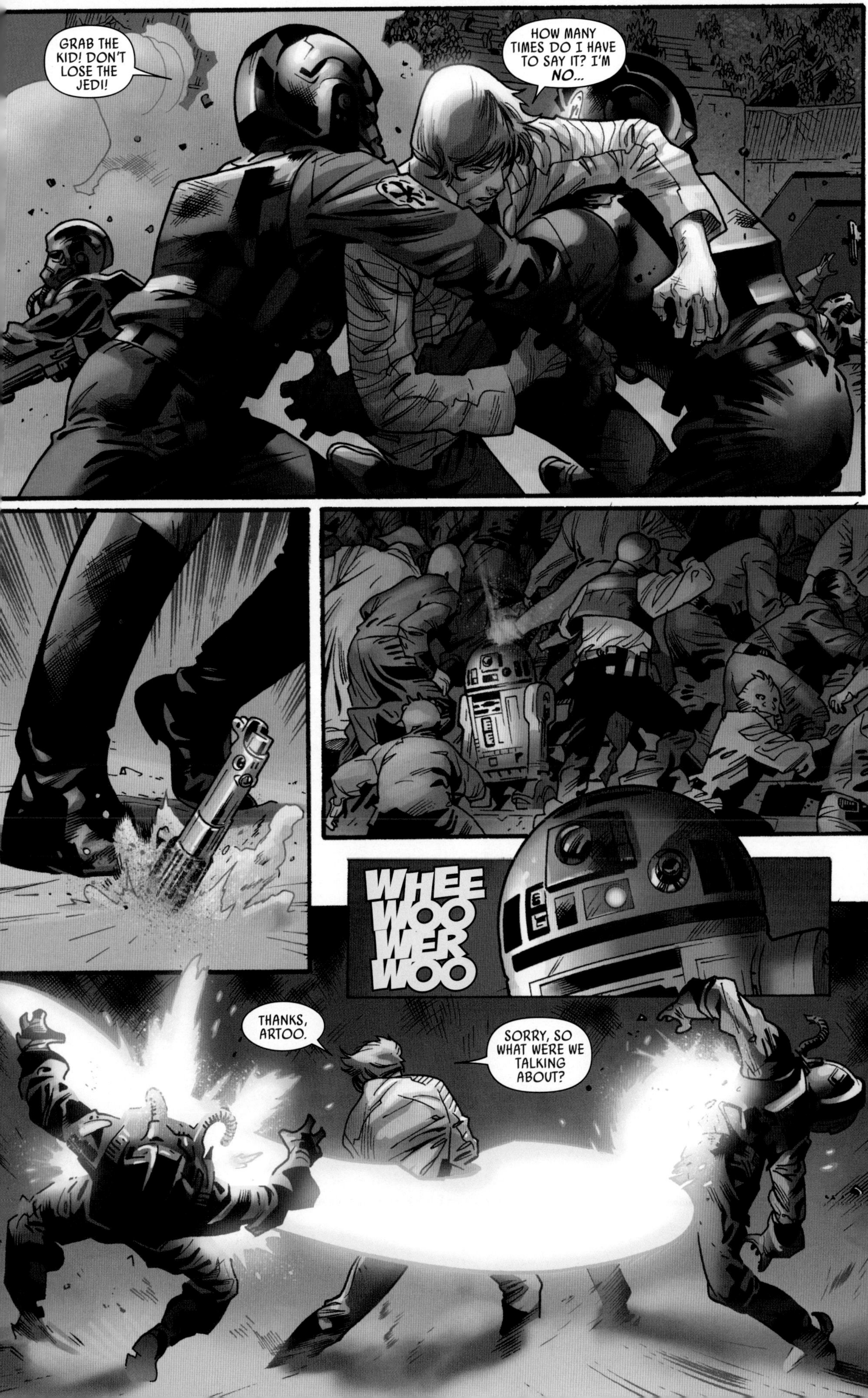
GRAB THE KID! DON'T LOSE THE JEDI!
HOW MANY TIMES DO I HAVE TO SAY IT? I'M NO...
WHEE WOO WER WOO
THANKS, ARTOO.
SORRY, SO WHAT WERE WE TALKING ABOUT?

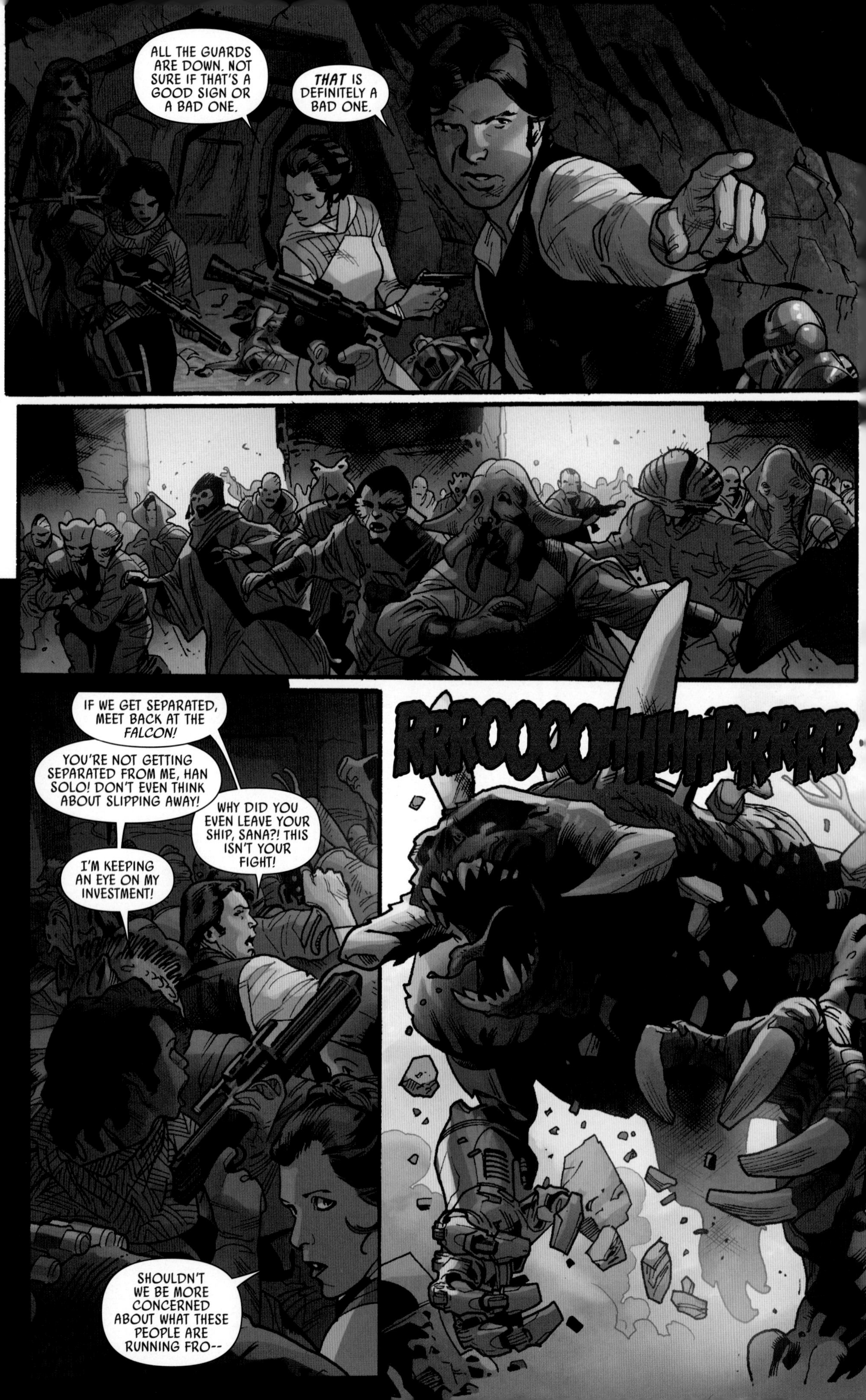

ALL THE GUARDS ARE DOWN. NOT SURE IF THAT'S A GOOD SIGN OR A BAD ONE.
THAT IS DEFINITELY A BAD ONE.
IF WE GET SEPARATED, MEET BACK AT THE FALCON!
YOU'RE NOT GETTING SEPARATED FROM ME, HAN SOLO! DON'T EVEN THINK ABOUT SLIPPING AWAY!
WHY DID YOU EVEN LEAVE YOUR SHIP, SANA?! THIS ISN'T YOUR FIGHT!
I'M KEEPING AN EYE ON MY INVESTMENT!
SHOULDN'T WE BE MORE CONCERNED ABOUT WHAT THESE PEOPLE ARE RUNNING FRO--
RRROOOOOHHHHHRRRRRR

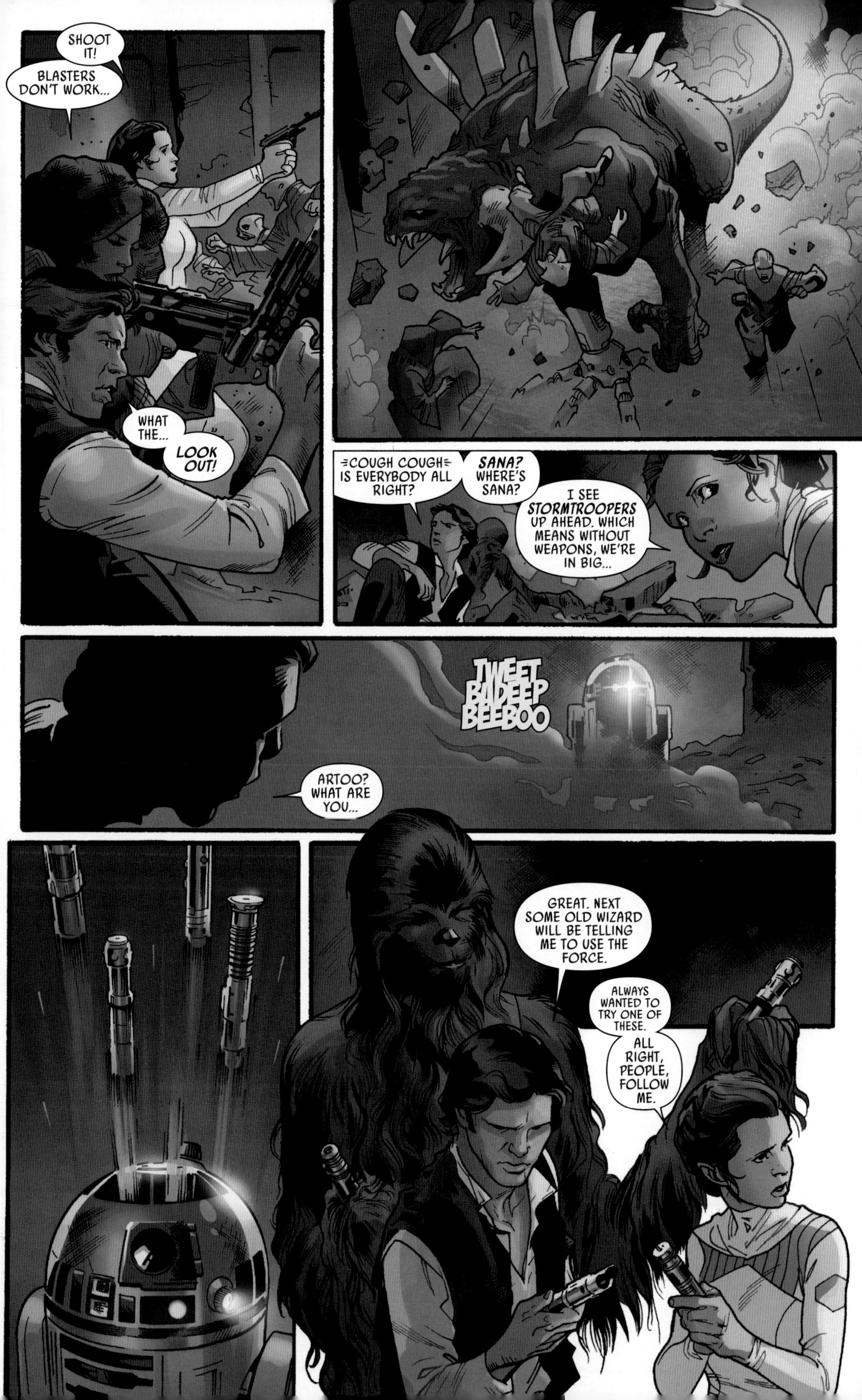
SHOOT IT!
BLASTERS DON'T WORK...
WHAT THE...
LOOK OUT!
=COUGH COUGH= IS EVERYBODY ALL RIGHT?
SANA? WHERE'S SANA?
I SEE STORMTROOPERS UP AHEAD. WHICH MEANS WITHOUT WEAPONS, WE'RE IN BIG...
TWEET BADEEP BEEBOO
ARTOO? WHAT ARE YOU...
GREAT. NEXT SOME OLD WIZARD WILL BE TELLING ME TO USE THE FORCE.
ALWAYS WANTED TO TRY ONE OF THESE.
ALL RIGHT, PEOPLE, FOLLOW ME.

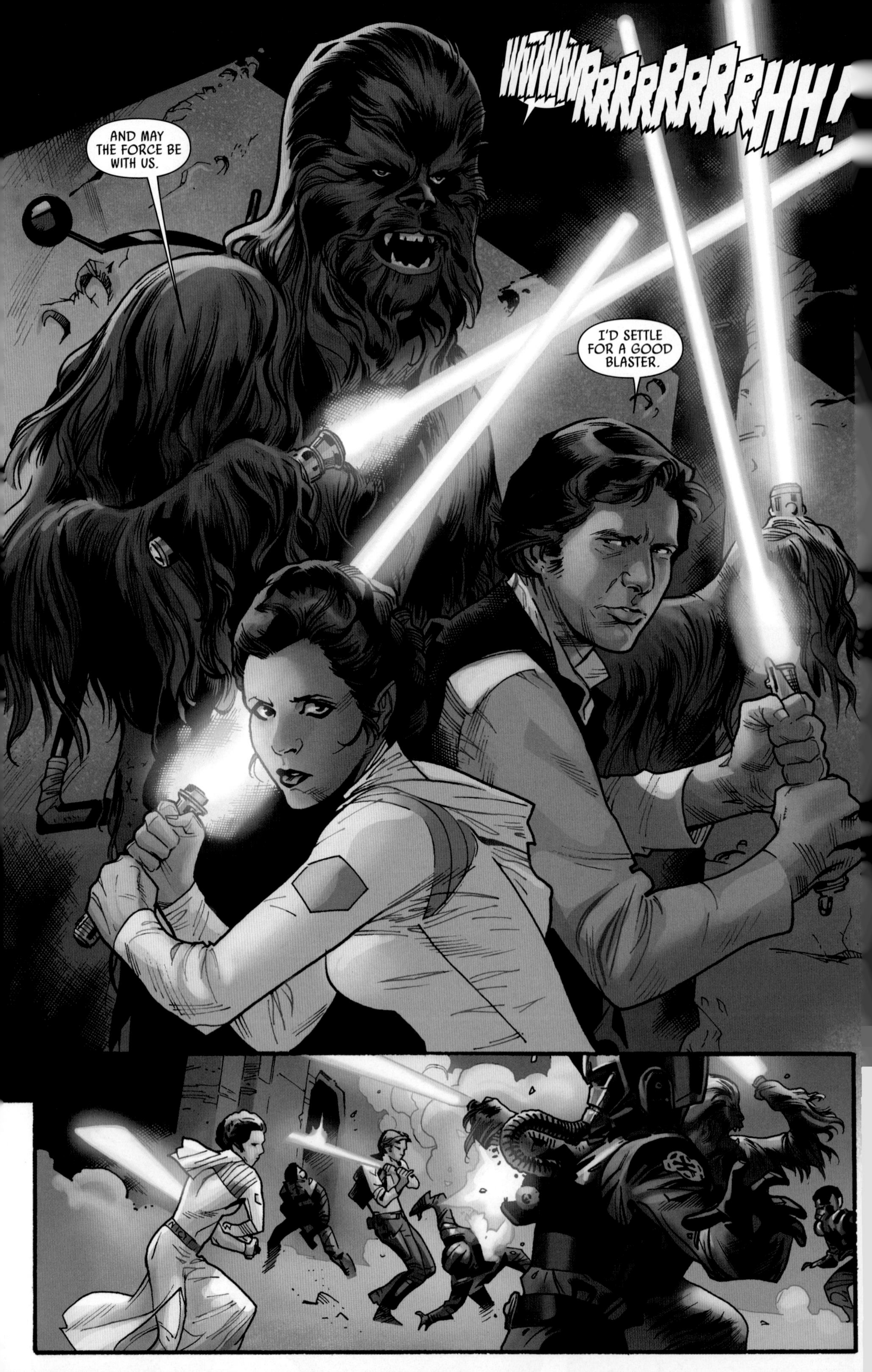
AND MAY THE FORCE BE WITH US.
WWWWRRRRRRRRHH!
I'D SETTLE FOR A GOOD BLASTER.

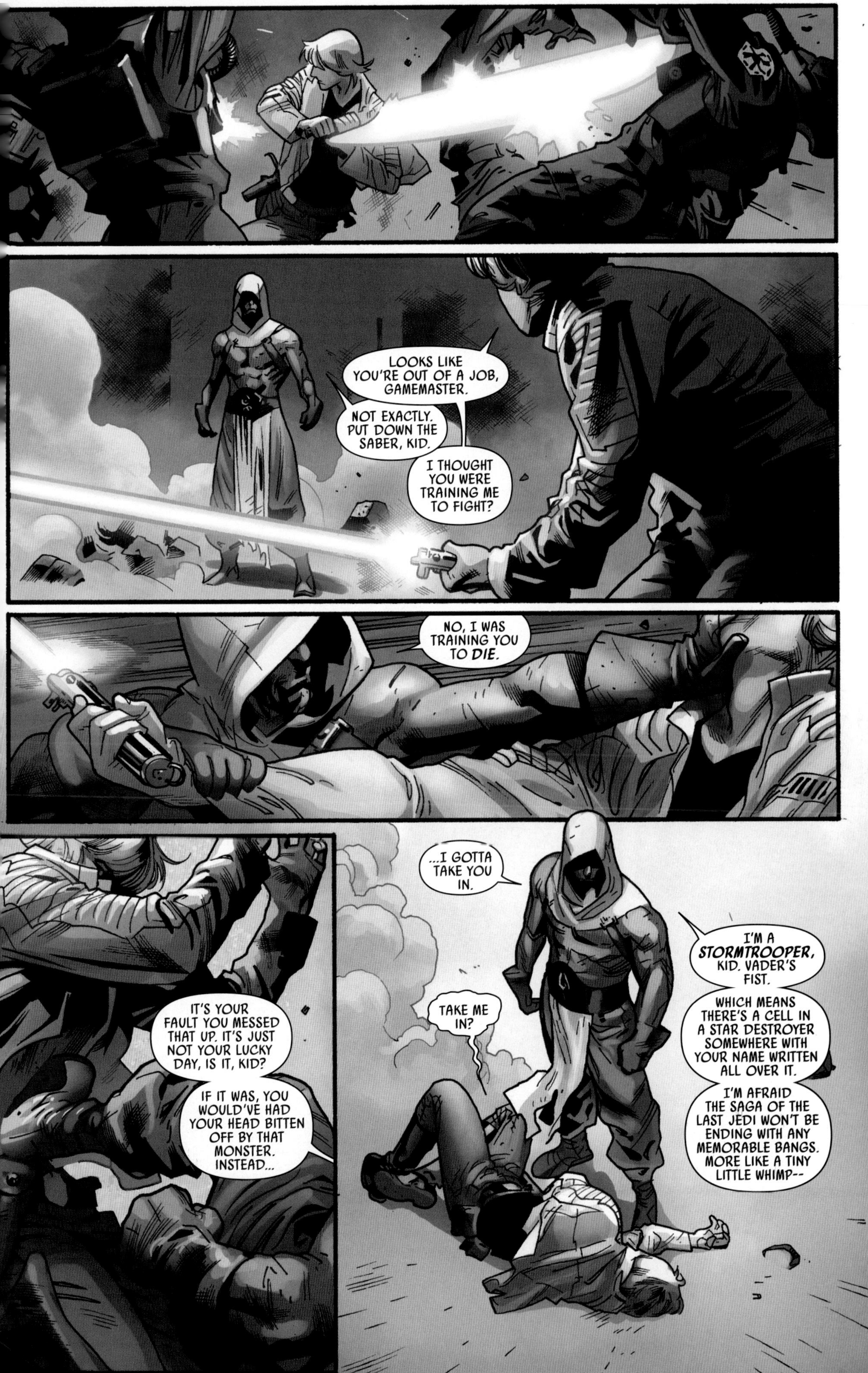
LOOKS LIKE YOU'RE OUT OF A JOB, GAMEMASTER.
NOT EXACTLY. PUT DOWN THE SABER, KID.
I THOUGHT YOU WERE TRAINING ME TO FIGHT?
NO, I WAS TRAINING YOU TO *DIE.*
IT'S YOUR FAULT YOU MESSED THAT UP. IT'S JUST NOT YOUR LUCKY DAY, IS IT, KID?
IF IT WAS, YOU WOULD'VE HAD YOUR HEAD BITTEN OFF BY THAT MONSTER. INSTEAD...
...I GOTTA TAKE YOU IN.
TAKE ME IN?
I'M A *STORMTROOPER,* KID. VADER'S FIST.
WHICH MEANS THERE'S A CELL IN A STAR DESTROYER SOMEWHERE WITH YOUR NAME WRITTEN ALL OVER IT.
I'M AFRAID THE SAGA OF THE LAST JEDI WON'T BE ENDING WITH ANY MEMORABLE BANGS. MORE LIKE A TINY LITTLE WHIMP--

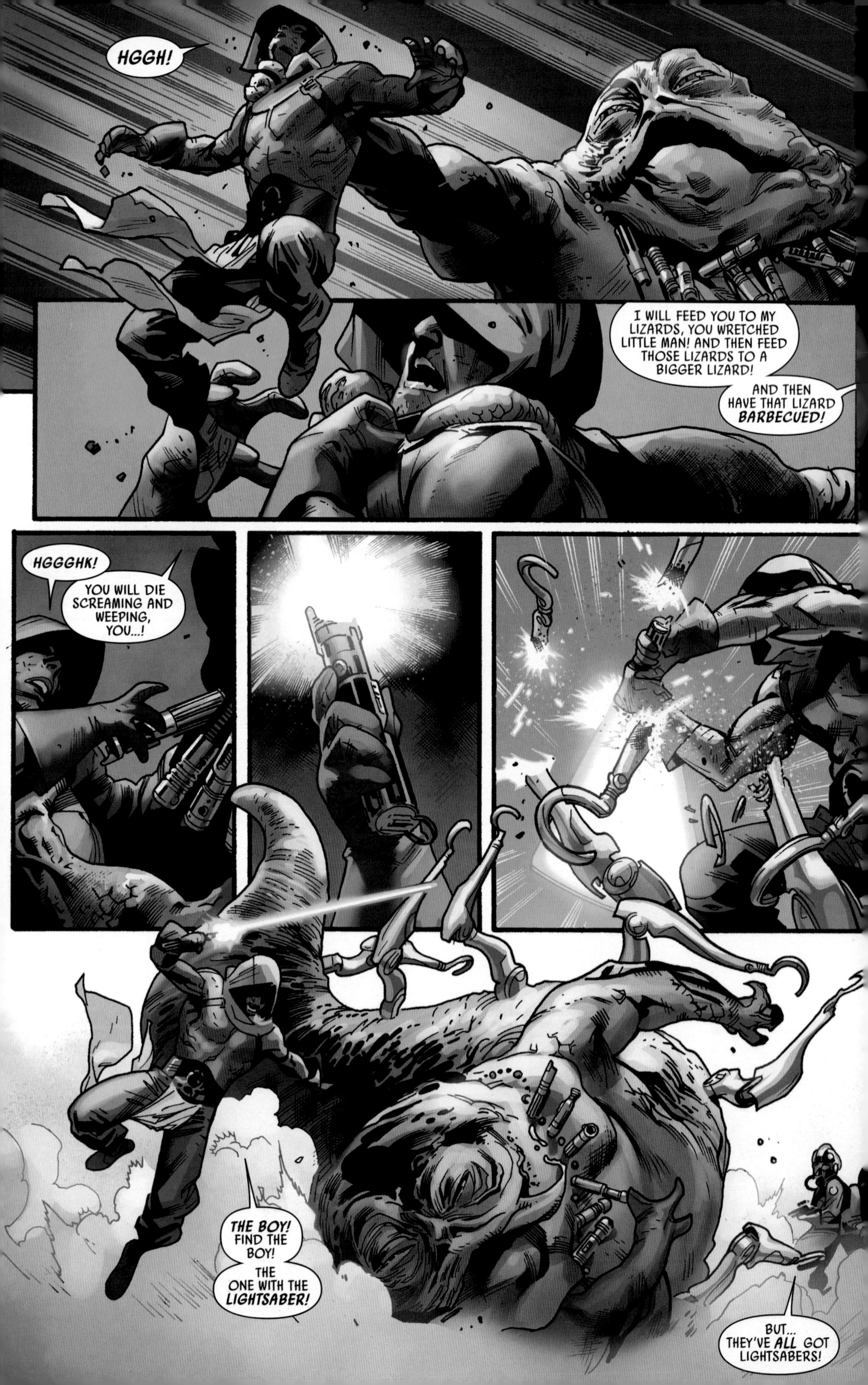
HGGH!
I WILL FEED YOU TO MY LIZARDS, YOU WRETCHED LITTLE MAN! AND THEN FEED THOSE LIZARDS TO A BIGGER LIZARD!
AND THEN HAVE THAT LIZARD BARBECUED!
HGGGHK!
YOU WILL DIE SCREAMING AND WEEPING, YOU...!
THE BOY! FIND THE BOY!
THE ONE WITH THE LIGHTSABER!
BUT... THEY'VE ALL GOT LIGHTSABERS!

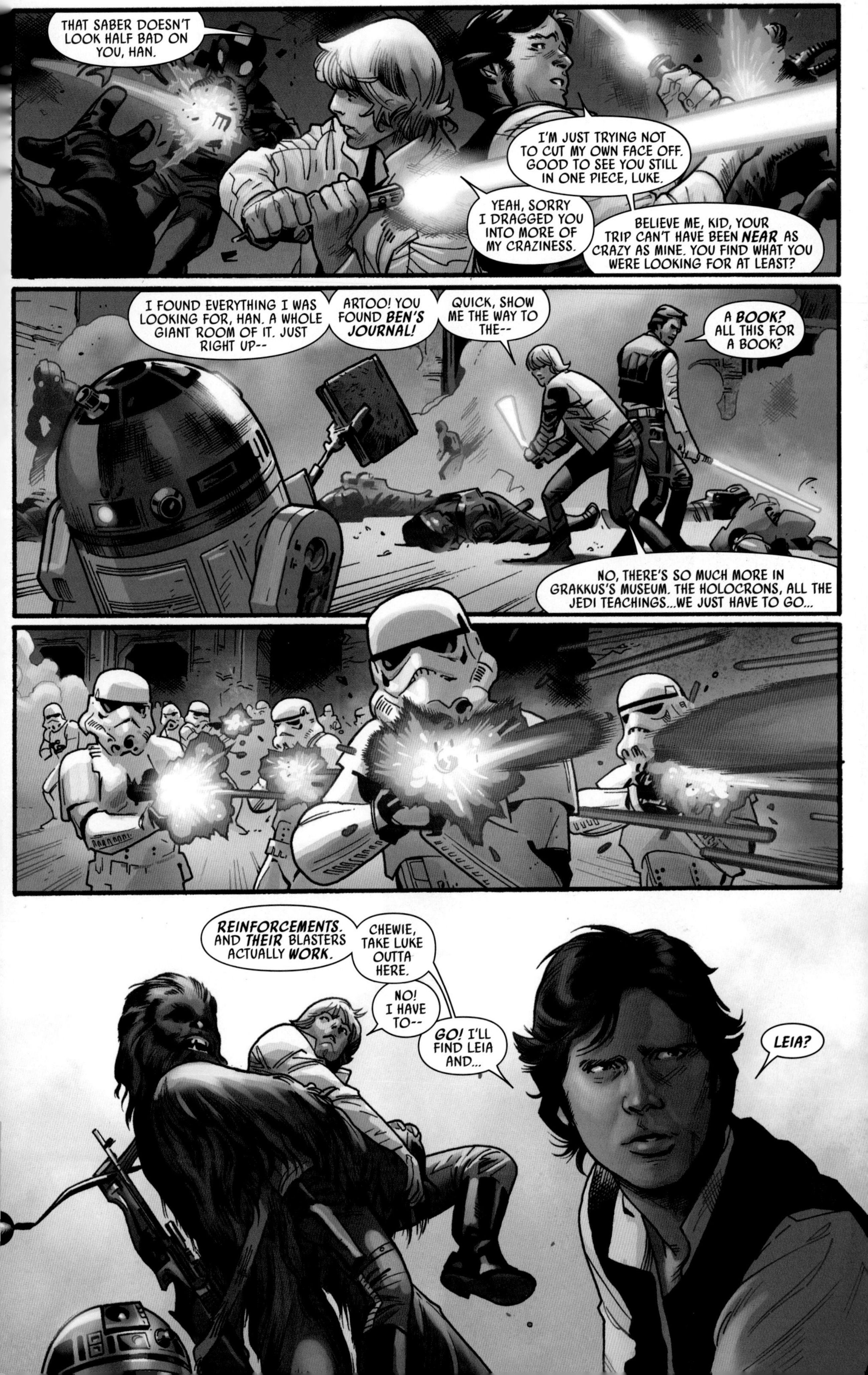
THAT SABER DOESN'T LOOK HALF BAD ON YOU, HAN.
I'M JUST TRYING NOT TO CUT MY OWN FACE OFF. GOOD TO SEE YOU STILL IN ONE PIECE, LUKE.
YEAH, SORRY I DRAGGED YOU INTO MORE OF MY CRAZINESS.
BELIEVE ME, KID, YOUR TRIP CAN'T HAVE BEEN NEAR AS CRAZY AS MINE. YOU FIND WHAT YOU WERE LOOKING FOR AT LEAST?
I FOUND EVERYTHING I WAS LOOKING FOR, HAN. A WHOLE GIANT ROOM OF IT. JUST RIGHT UP--
ARTOO! YOU FOUND BEN'S JOURNAL!
QUICK, SHOW ME THE WAY TO THE--
A BOOK? ALL THIS FOR A BOOK?
NO, THERE'S SO MUCH MORE IN GRAKKUS'S MUSEUM. THE HOLOCRONS, ALL THE JEDI TEACHINGS...WE JUST HAVE TO GO...
REINFORCEMENTS. AND THEIR BLASTERS ACTUALLY WORK.
CHEWIE, TAKE LUKE OUTTA HERE.
NO! I HAVE TO--
GO! I'LL FIND LEIA AND...
LEIA?

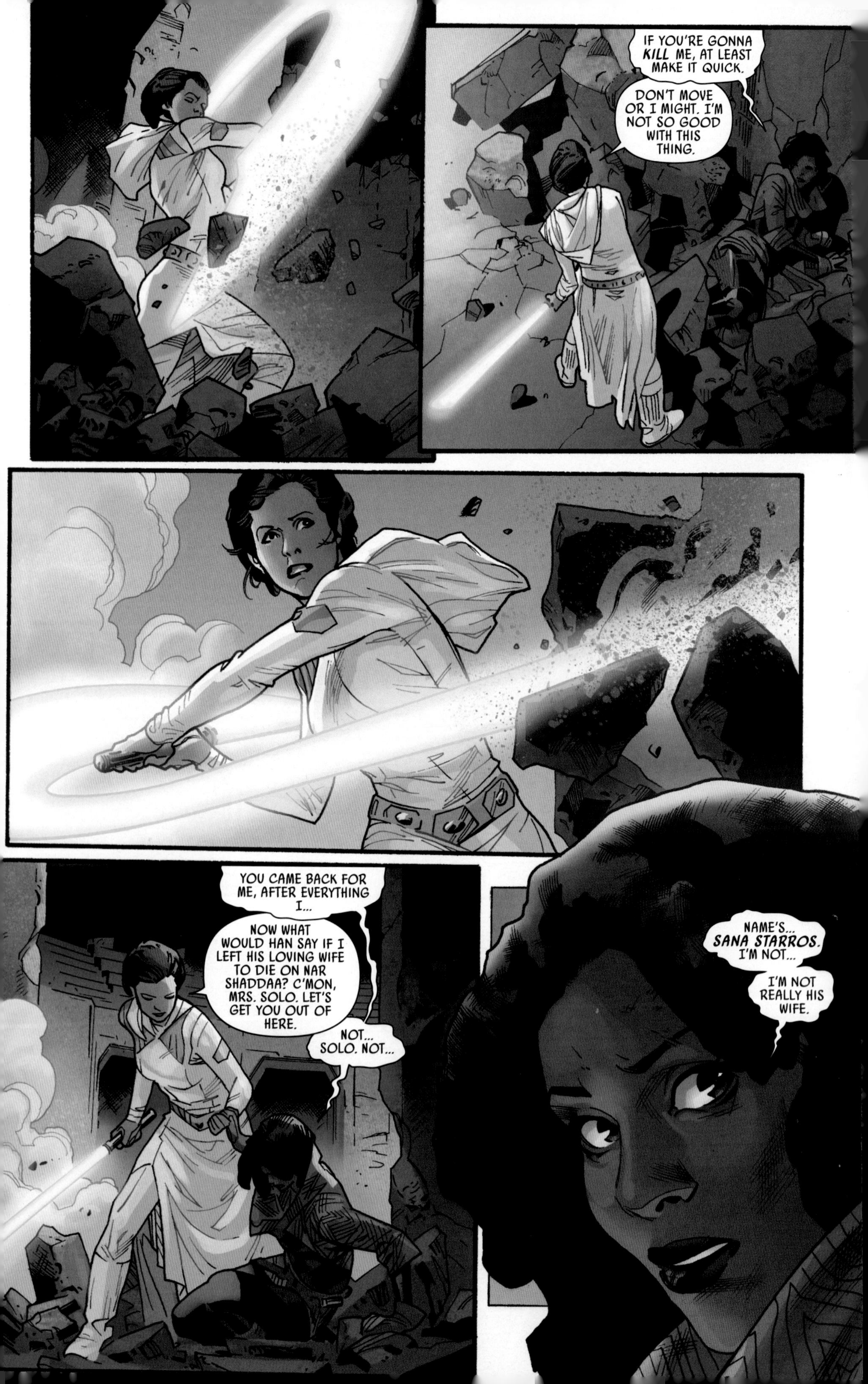
IF YOU'RE GONNA KILL ME, AT LEAST MAKE IT QUICK.
DON'T MOVE OR I MIGHT. I'M NOT SO GOOD WITH THIS THING.
YOU CAME BACK FOR ME, AFTER EVERYTHING I...
NOW WHAT WOULD HAN SAY IF I LEFT HIS LOVING WIFE TO DIE ON NAR SHADDAA? C'MON, MRS. SOLO. LET'S GET YOU OUT OF HERE.
NOT... SOLO. NOT...
NAME'S... SANA STARROS. I'M NOT...
I'M NOT REALLY HIS WIFE.

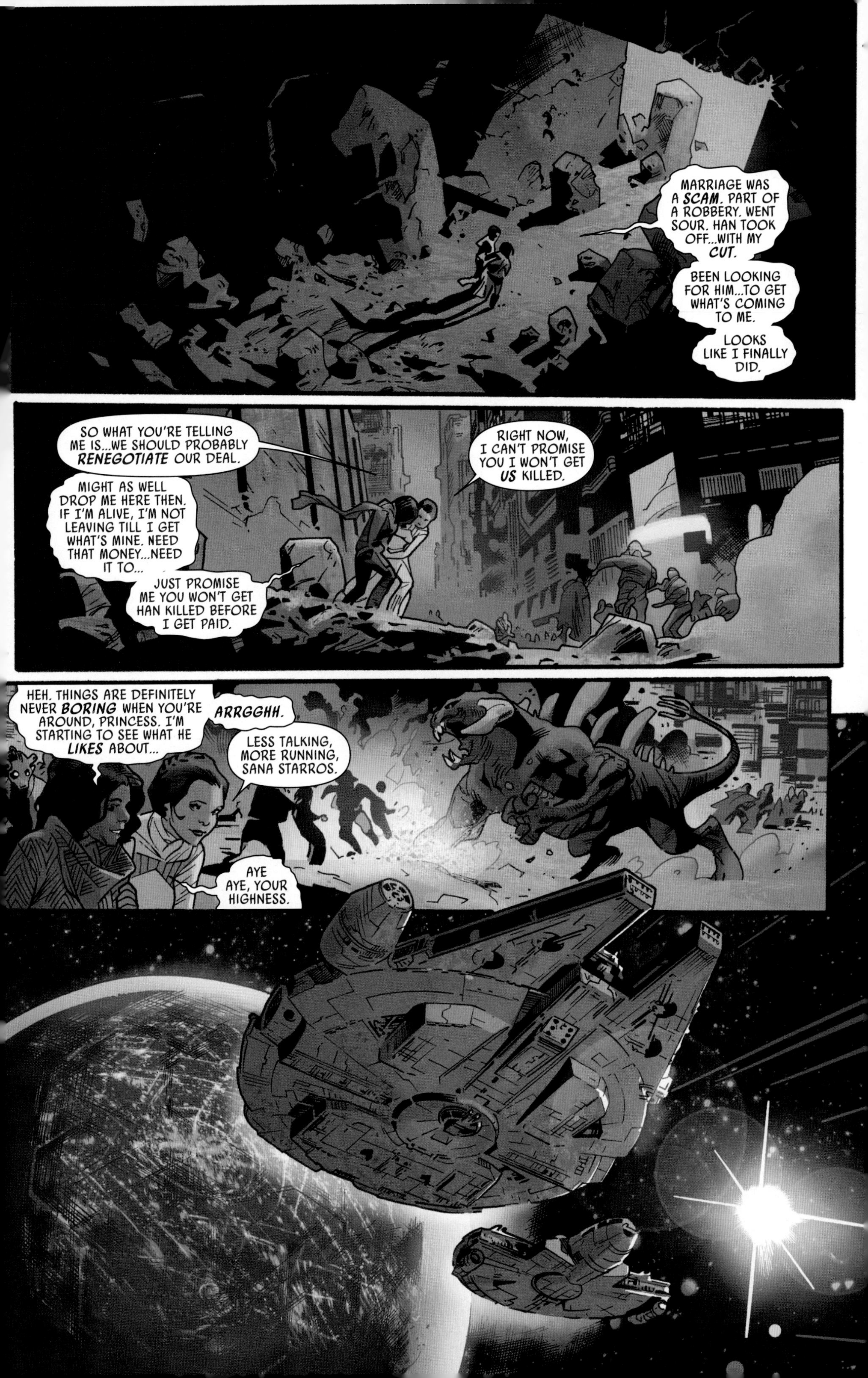

MARRIAGE WAS A SCAM. PART OF A ROBBERY. WENT SOUR. HAN TOOK OFF...WITH MY CUT.
BEEN LOOKING FOR HIM...TO GET WHAT'S COMING TO ME.
LOOKS LIKE I FINALLY DID.
SO WHAT YOU'RE TELLING ME IS...WE SHOULD PROBABLY RENEGOTIATE OUR DEAL.
RIGHT NOW, I CAN'T PROMISE YOU I WON'T GET US KILLED.
MIGHT AS WELL DROP ME HERE THEN. IF I'M ALIVE, I'M NOT LEAVING TILL I GET WHAT'S MINE. NEED THAT MONEY...NEED IT TO...
JUST PROMISE ME YOU WON'T GET HAN KILLED BEFORE I GET PAID.
HEH. THINGS ARE DEFINITELY NEVER BORING WHEN YOU'RE AROUND, PRINCESS. I'M STARTING TO SEE WHAT HE LIKES ABOUT...
ARRGGHH.
LESS TALKING, MORE RUNNING, SANA STARROS.
AYE AYE, YOUR HIGHNESS.

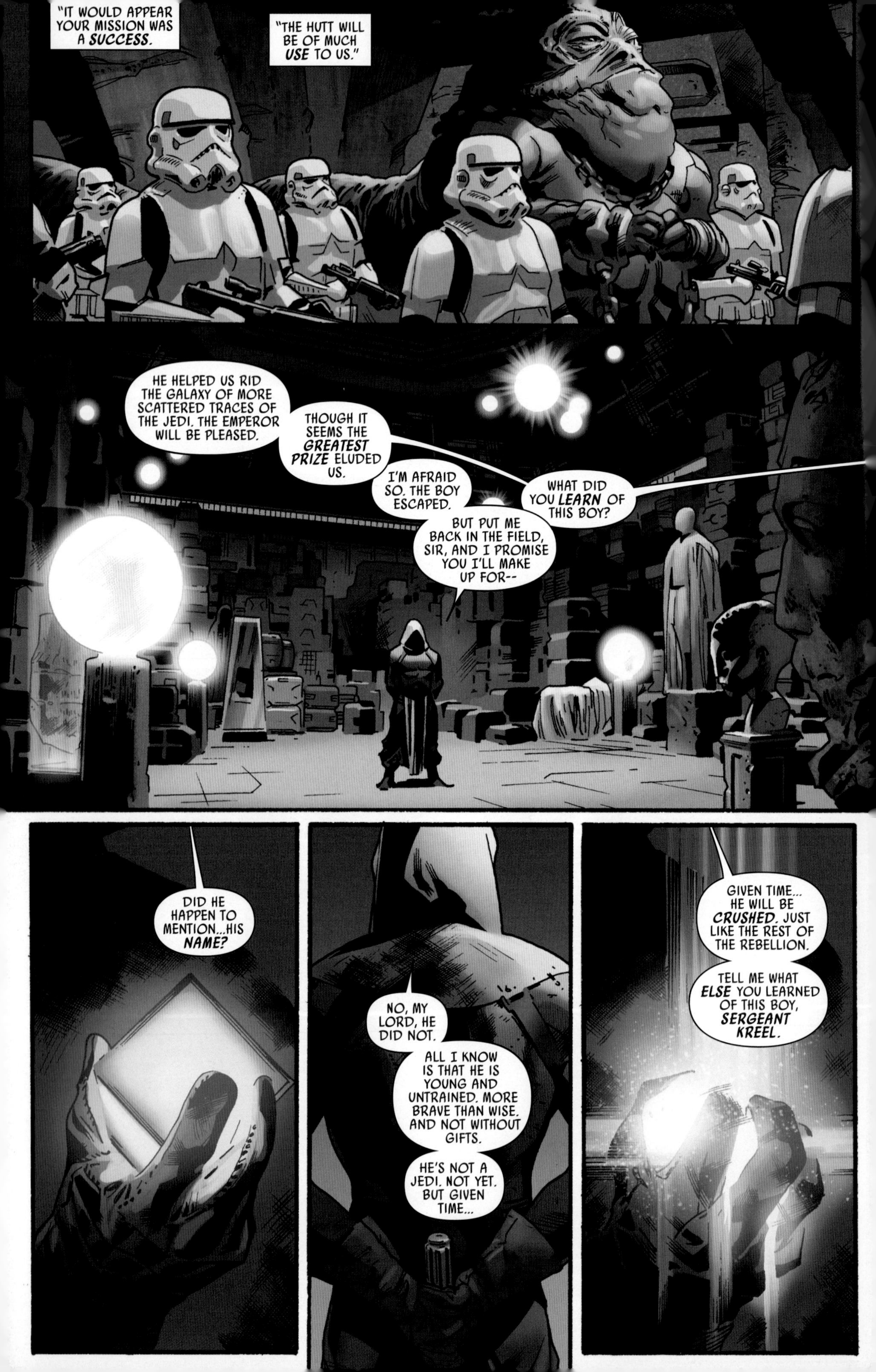
"IT WOULD APPEAR YOUR MISSION WAS A SUCCESS.
"THE HUTT WILL BE OF MUCH USE TO US."
HE HELPED US RID THE GALAXY OF MORE SCATTERED TRACES OF THE JEDI. THE EMPEROR WILL BE PLEASED.
THOUGH IT SEEMS THE GREATEST PRIZE ELUDED US.
I'M AFRAID SO. THE BOY ESCAPED.
BUT PUT ME BACK IN THE FIELD, SIR, AND I PROMISE YOU I'LL MAKE UP FOR--
WHAT DID YOU LEARN OF THIS BOY?
DID HE HAPPEN TO MENTION...HIS NAME?
NO, MY LORD, HE DID NOT.
ALL I KNOW IS THAT HE IS YOUNG AND UNTRAINED. MORE BRAVE THAN WISE. AND NOT WITHOUT GIFTS.
HE'S NOT A JEDI. NOT YET. BUT GIVEN TIME...
GIVEN TIME... HE WILL BE CRUSHED. JUST LIKE THE REST OF THE REBELLION.
TELL ME WHAT ELSE YOU LEARNED OF THIS BOY, SERGEANT KREEL.

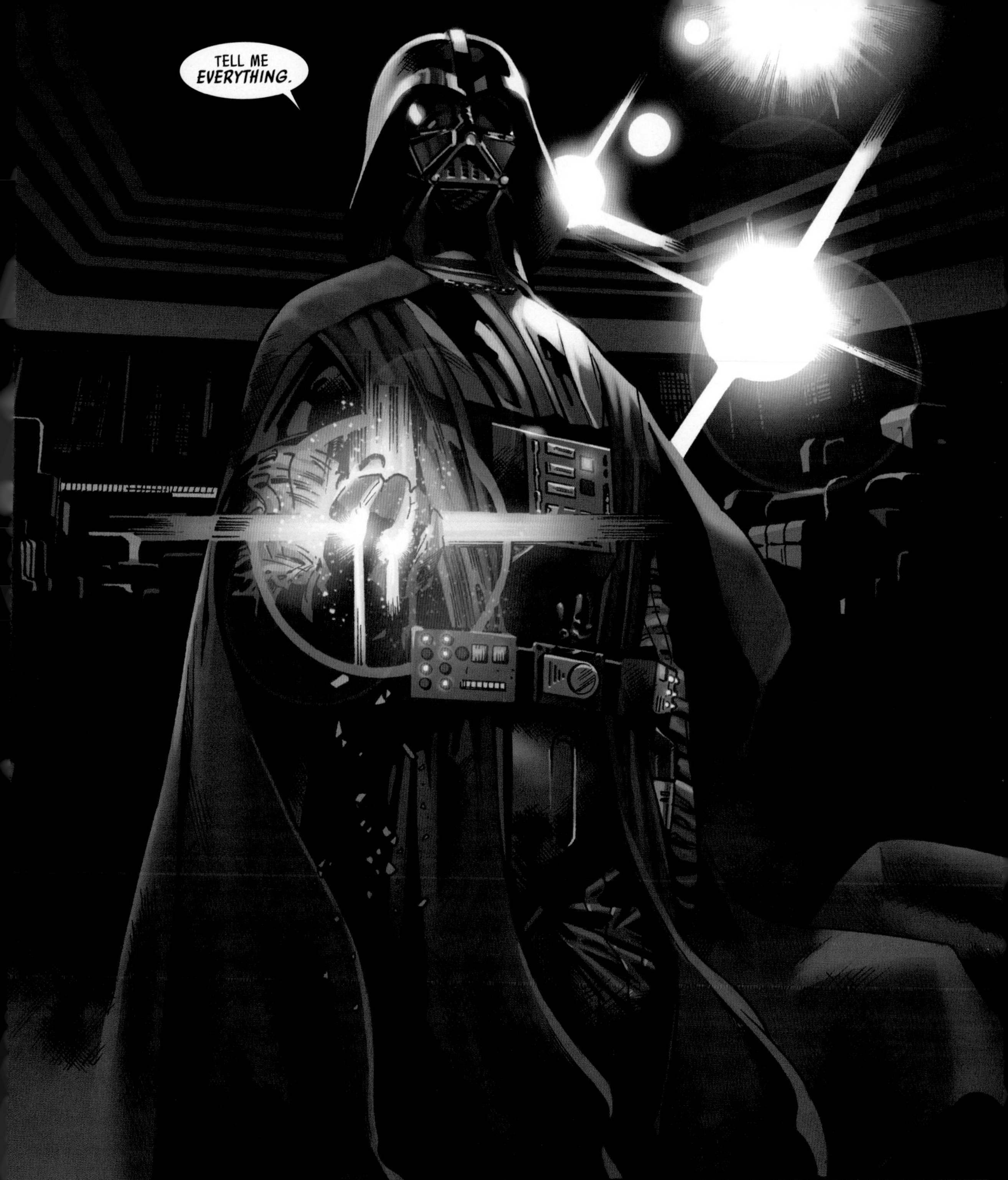
TELL ME
EVERYTHING.

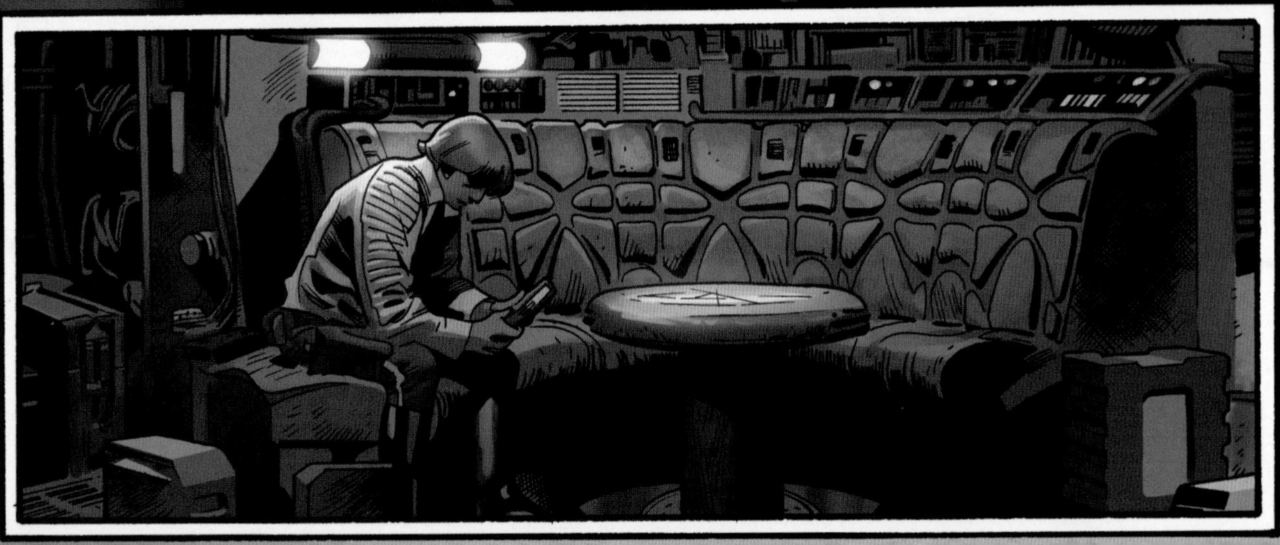

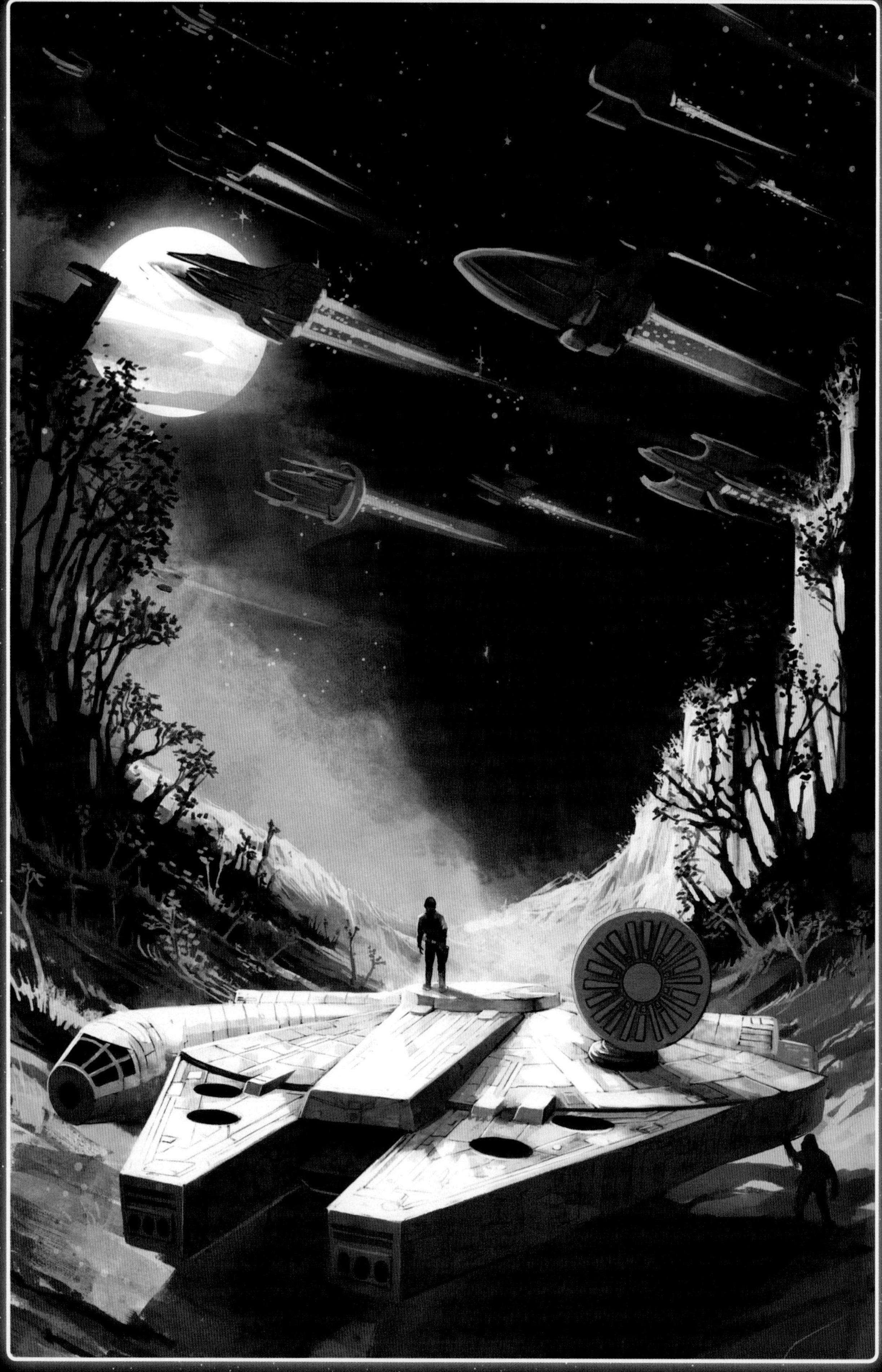

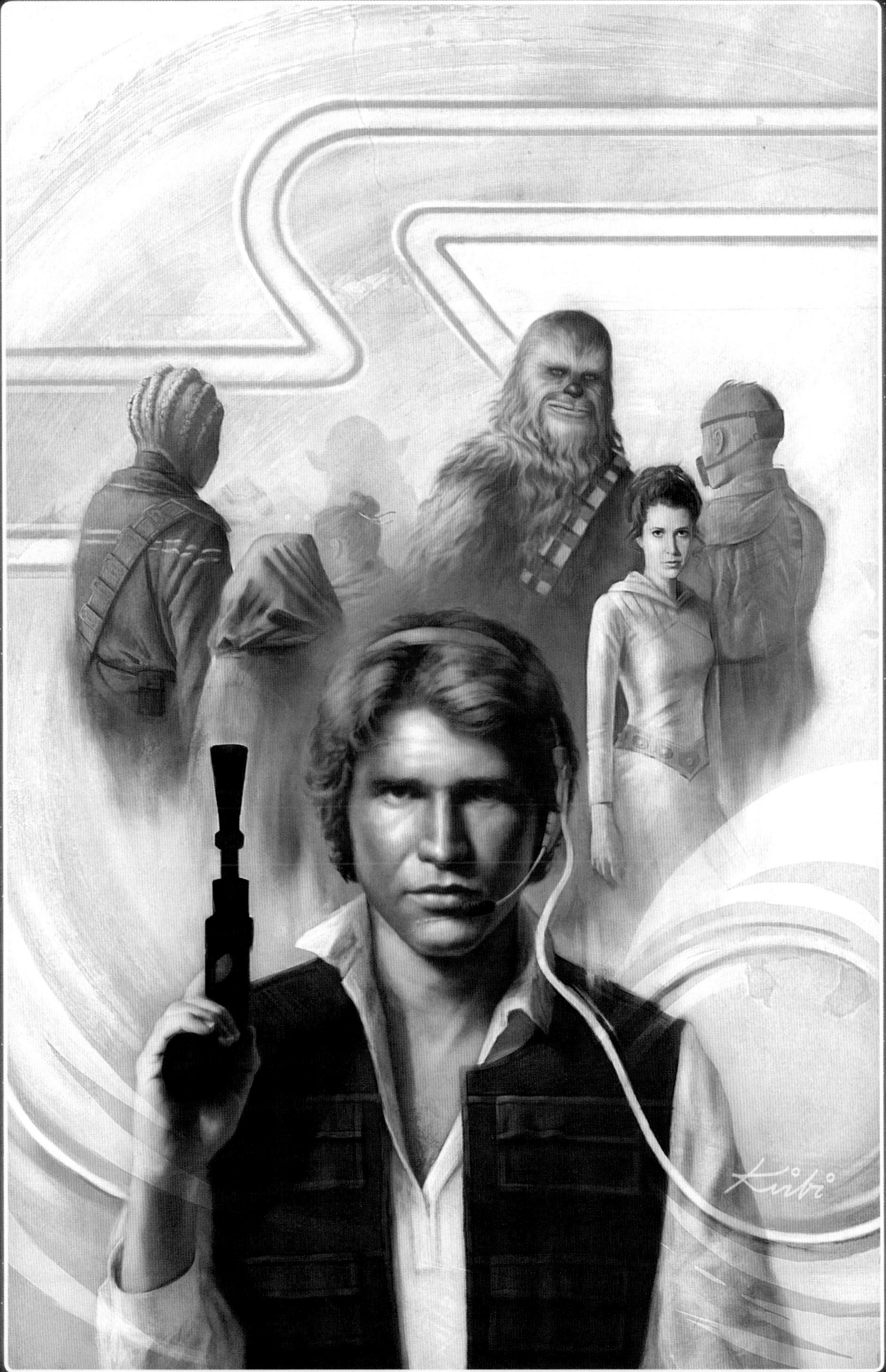

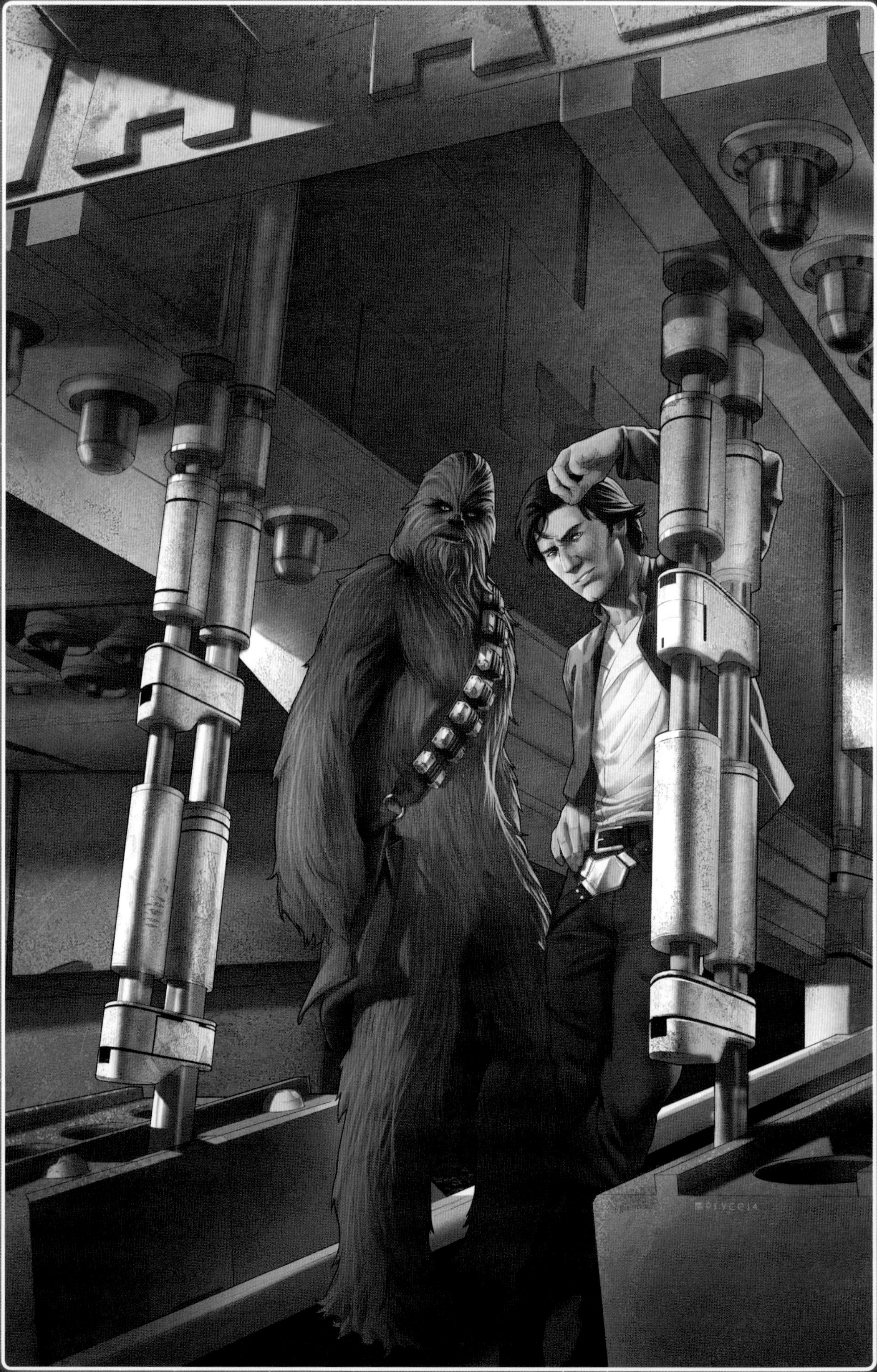
pryce14

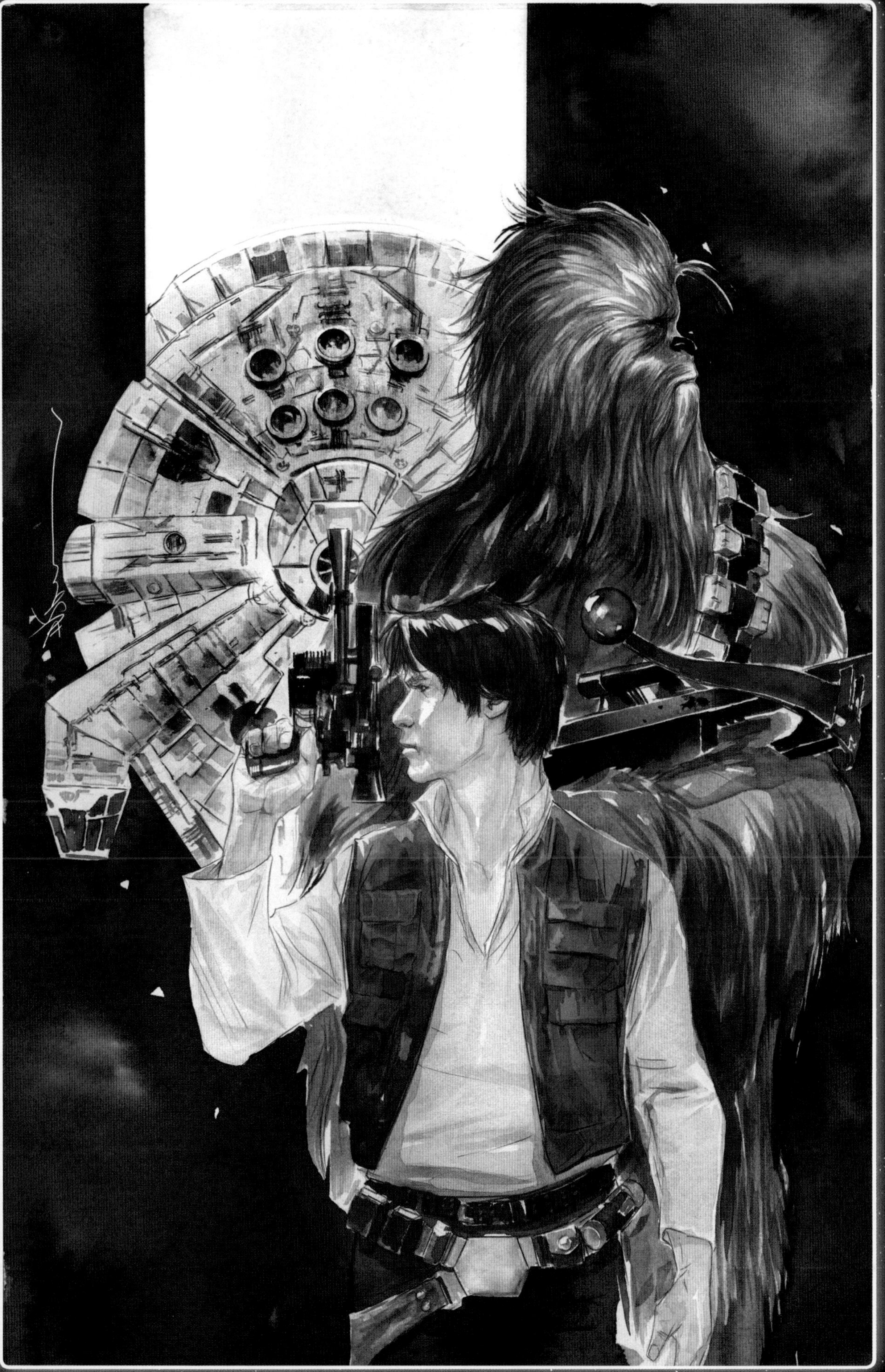

HAN SOLO 4 Variant
by **DUSTIN NGUYEN**

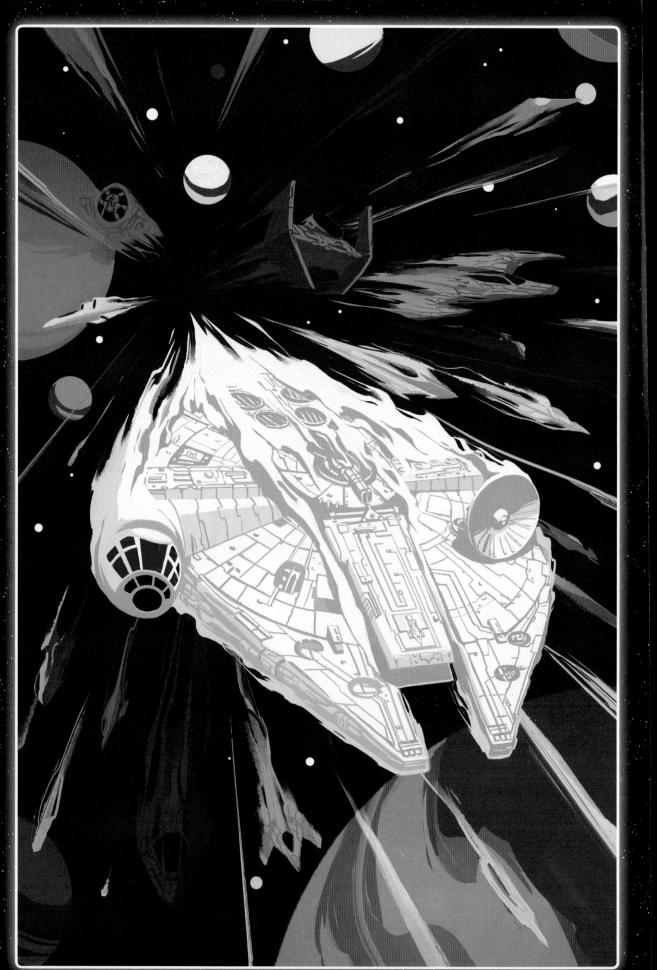

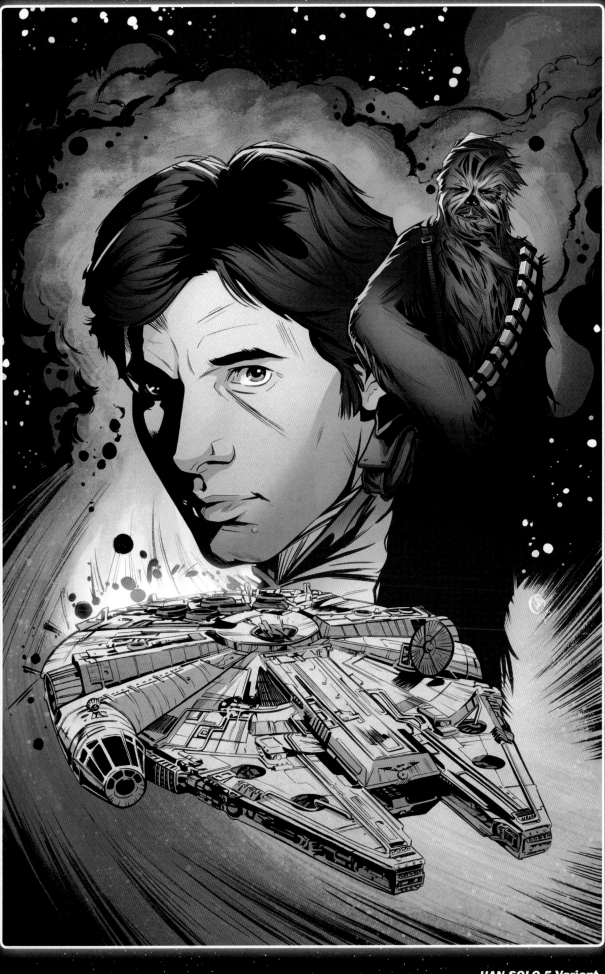

HAN SOLO 5 Variant
by JOËLLE JONES

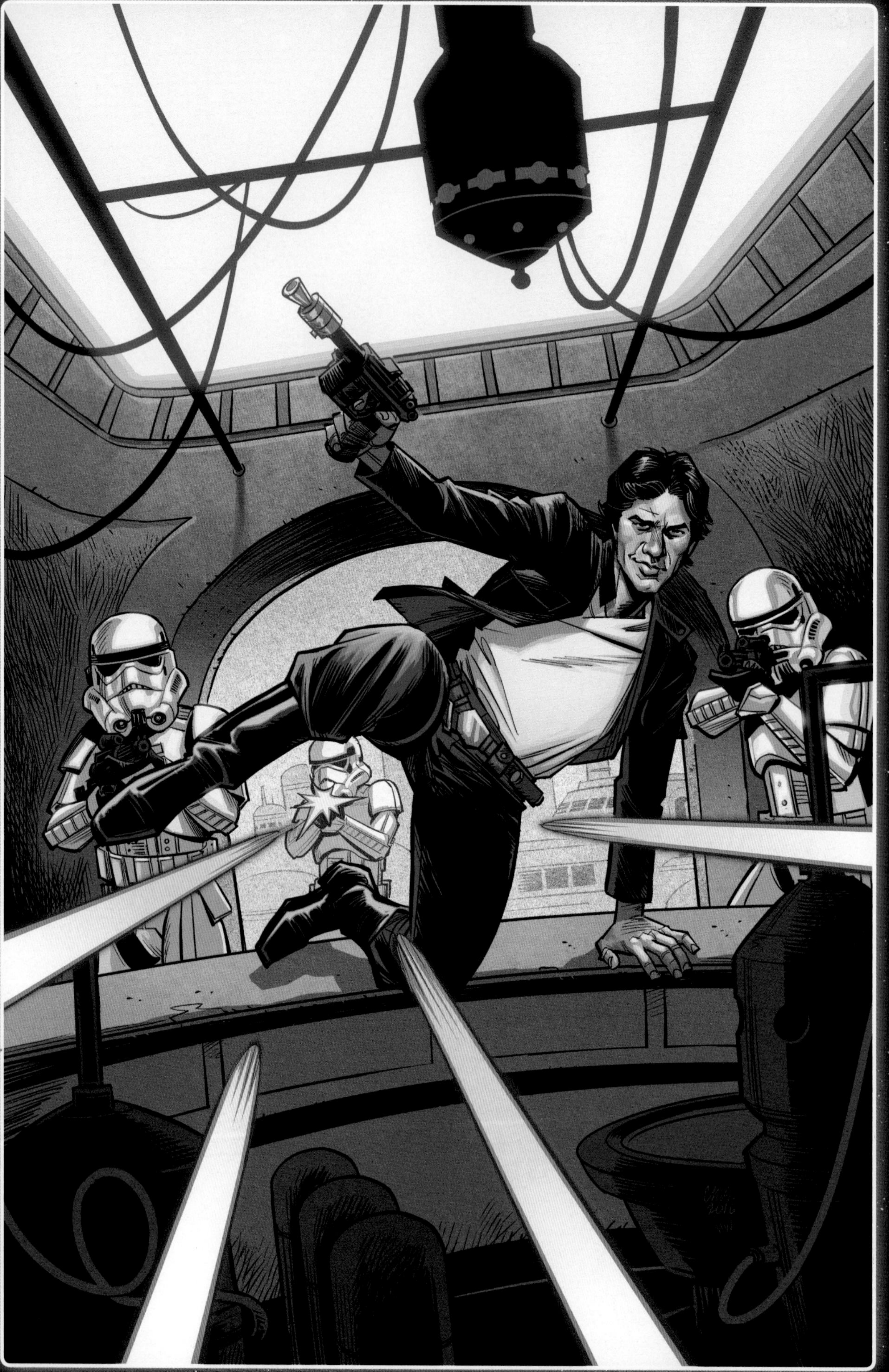

HAN SOLO 5 Variant
by **CAMERON STEWART & MATTHEW WILSON**